Communications in Computer and Information Science   681

Commenced Publication in 2007
Founding and Former Series Editors:
Alfredo Cuzzocrea, Dominik Ślęzak, and Xiaokang Yang

More information about this series at http://www.springer.com/series/7899

Maoguo Gong · Linqiang Pan
Tao Song · Gexiang Zhang (Eds.)

Bio-inspired Computing – Theories and Applications

11th International Conference, BIC-TA 2016
Xi'an, China, October 28–30, 2016
Revised Selected Papers, Part I

 Springer

Editors

Maoguo Gong
Xidian University
Xi'an
China

Linqiang Pan
Huazhong University of Science
   and Technology
Wuhan
China

Tao Song
China University of Petroleum
Qingdao
China

and

Faculty of Engineering, Computing
   and Science
Swinburne University of Technology
   Sarawak Campus
Kuching
Malaysia

Gexiang Zhang
Southwest Jiaotong University
Chengdu
China

ISSN 1865-0929   ISSN 1865-0937 (electronic)
Communications in Computer and Information Science
ISBN 978-981-10-3610-1   ISBN 978-981-10-3611-8 (eBook)
DOI 10.1007/978-981-10-3611-8

Library of Congress Control Number: 2016962020

Printed on acid-free paper

This Springer imprint is published by Springer Nature
The registered company is Springer Nature Singapore Pte Ltd.
The registered company address is: 152 Beach Road, #21-01/04 Gateway East, Singapore 189721, Singapore

Preface

Bio-inspired computing is a field of study that abstracts computing ideas (data structures, operations with data, ways to control operations, computing models, etc.) from living phenomena or biological systems such as evolution, cells, tissues, neural networks, immune system, and ant colonies. Bio-Inspired Computing: Theories and Applications (BIC-TA) is a series of conferences that aims to bring together researchers working in the main areas of natural computing inspired from biology, for presenting their recent results, exchanging ideas, and cooperating in a friendly framework. The conference has four main topics: evolutionary computing, neural computing, DNA computing, and membrane computing.

Since 2006, the conference has taken place at Wuhan (2006), Zhengzhou (2007), Adelaide (2008), Beijing (2009), Liverpool and Changsha (2010), Penang (2011), Gwalior (2012), Anhui (2013), Wuhan (2014), and Anhui (2015). Following the success of previous editions, the 11th International Conference on Bio-Inspired Computing: Theories and Applications (BIC-TA 2016) was organized by Xidian University, during October 28–30, 2016.

BIC-TA 2016 attracted a wide spectrum of interesting research papers on various aspects of bio-inspired computing with a diverse range of theories and applications. We received 343 submissions, of which 115 papers were selected for two volumes of *Communications in Computer and Information Science*.

We gratefully thank Xidian University, Huazhong University of Science and Technology, and Northwestern Polytechnical University for extensive assistance in organizing the conference. We also thank Dr. Jiao Shi and all other volunteers, whose efforts ensured the smooth running of the conference.

The editors warmly thank the Program Committee members for their prompt and efficient support in reviewing the papers, and the authors of the submitted papers for their interesting papers.

Special thanks are due to Springer for their skilled cooperation in the timely production of these volumes.

October 2016

Maoguo Gong
Linqiang Pan
Tao Song
Gexiang Zhang

Organization

Steering Committee

Guangzhao Cui	Zhengzhou University of Light Industry, China
Kalyanmoy Deb	Indian Institute of Technology Kanpur, India
Miki Hirabayashi	National Institute of Information and Communications Technology (NICT), Japan
Joshua Knowles	University of Manchester, UK
Thom LaBean	North Carolina State University, USA
Jiuyong Li	University of South Australia, Australia
Kenli Li	University of Hunan, China
Giancarlo Mauri	Università di Milano-Bicocca, Italy
Yongli Mi	Hong Kong University of Science and Technology, Hong Kong, SAR China
Atulya K. Nagar	Liverpool Hope University, UK
Linqiang Pan	Huazhong University of Science and Technology, China
Gheorghe Păun	Romanian Academy, Bucharest, Romania
Mario J. Pérez-Jiménez	University of Seville, Spain
K.G. Subramanian	Universiti Sains Malaysia, Malaysia
Robinson Thamburaj	Madras Christian College, India
Jin Xu	Peking University, China
Hao Yan	Arizona State University, USA

Program Committee

Rosni Abdullah, Malaysia
Muhammad Abulaish, Saudi Arabia
Chang Wook Ahn, South Korea
Adel Al-Jumaily, Australia
Bahareh Asadi, Iran
Li He, USA
Eduard Babulak, European Commission, Community Research and Development Information
Mehdi Bahrami, Iran
Soumya Banerjee, India
Jagdish Chand Bansal, India
Debnath Bhattacharyya, India
Monowar H. Bhuyan, India
Kavita Burse, India

Michael Chen, China
Tsung-Che Chiang, Taiwan, China
Sung-Bae Cho, South Korea
Kadian Davis, Jamaica
Sumithra Devi K.A., India
Ciprian Dobre, Romania
Amit Dutta, India
Carlos Fernandez-Llatas, Spain
Pierluigi Frisco, UK
Maoguo Gong, China (Chair)
Shan He, UK
Jer Lang Hong, Malaysia
Tzung-Pei Hong, Taiwan, China
Wei-Chiang Hong, Taiwan, China
Mo Hongwei, China

Sriman Narayana Iyengar, India
Antonio J. Jara, Spain
Sunil Kumar Jha, India
Guoli Ji, China
Mohamed Rawidean Mohd Kassim,
  Malaysia
M. Ayoub Khan, India
Razib Hayat Khan, Norway
Joanna Kolodziej, Poland
Ashwani Kush, India
Shyam Lal, India
Kenli Li, China
Chun-Wei Lin, China
Wenjian Luo, China
Mario J. Pérez-Jiménez, Spain
Vittorio Maniezzo, Italy
Francesco Marcelloni, Italy
Hasimah Mohamed, Malaysia
Chilukuri K. Mohan, USA
Abdulqader Mohsen, Malaysia
Holger Morgenstern, Germany
Andres Muñoz, Spain
G.R.S. Murthy, India
Akila Muthuramalingam, India
Atulya Nagar, UK
Asoke Nath, India
Linqiang Pan, China (Chair)
Mrutyunjaya Panda, India
Manjaree Pandit, India
Gheorghe Păun, Romania
Andrei Păun, USA
Yoseba Penya, Spain
Ninan Sajeeth Philip, India
Hugo Proença, Portugal

Balwinder Raj, India
Balasubramanian Raman, India
Nur' Aini Abdul Rashid, Malaysia
Mehul Raval, India
Rawya Rizk, Egypt
Thamburaj Robinson, India
Samrat Sabat, India
S.M. Sameer, India
Rajesh Sanghvi, India
Aradhana Saxena, India
Sonia Schulenburg, UK
G. Shivaprasad, India
K.K. Shukla, India
Madhusudan Singh, South Korea
Pramod Kumar Singh, India
Ravindra Singh, India
Sanjeev Singh, India
Satvir Singh, India
Don Sofge, USA
Tao Song, China
Kumbakonam Govindarajan
  Subramanian, Malaysia
Ponnuthurai Suganthan, Singapore
S.R. Thangiah, USA
Nikolaos Thomaidis, India
D.G. Thomas, India
Ravi Sankar Vadali, India
Ibrahim Venkat, Malaysia
Sudhir Warier, India
Ram Yadav, USA
Umi Kalsom Yusof, Malaysia
Sotirios Ziavras, USA
Pan Zheng, Malaysia

Sponsors

Xidian University
Huazhong University of Science and Technology
Northwestern Polytechnical University

Contents – Part I

Neural Computing

Machine Learning

Contents – Part II

Evolutionary Computing

Multi-objective Optimization

Pattern Recognition

Others

DNA Computing

DNA Self-assembly Model to Solve Compound Logic Operators Problem

Shihua Zhou$^{(\boxtimes)}$, Bin Wang, Xuedong Zheng, and Changjun Zhou

Key Laboratory of Advanced Design and Intelligent Computing, Dalian University,
Ministry of Education, Dalian 116622, China
shihuajo@gmail.com

Abstract. Self-assembly is the process that the component form an ordered form or structure. Because of the biochemical characteristics of DNA molecules, they become a research emphasis in the field of self-assembly. DNA-based self-assembly technology has been widely used in the fields of nanometer machining, molecular circuit, polymer materials, and so on. DNA self-assembly is an effective mechanism that nanometer structure is built bottom-up. In order to overcome the problem that any kind of self-assembled model can only solve the single algorithm, in this paper, a new DNA self-assembly algorithmic model is designed to solve compound logic operators problem. Five types of DNA tiles are designed according to the characteristic of compound operation problem, namely Initial Tile, Process Tile, Operation Tile, End Tile and Boundary Tile. At last, the process of self-assembly are demonstrated by an instance.

Keywords: DNA self-assembly · Compound logic operators · Algorithmic model

1 Introduction

DNA computing [1–3] is an important research content in the crossing field of computer science and biological science. It is a new and fast-developing direction along with the successful completion of human genome project. In 1994, Adleman implemented to solve Hamiltonian Path Problem that there are seven vertices by the biological method according to the complementarity principle of DNA molecular bases [4]. The birth of DNA computing marks the appearance of a new computing mode and breaks the original calculation model. It opens up a new path for solving various complicated problem.

The basic principle of DNA computing [5] is that DNA sequences are used as a carrier of information coding, and the specific DNA sequences are used to map the problem by the double helix of DNA molecules and the properties of the complementary base pairing. Using enzymes as operator, the solution space is generated by controllable biochemical reactions. Then, the solution results are extracted by polymerase chain reaction PCR, aggregation, overlapping amplification technology POA, ultrasonic degradation, affinity chromatography, electrophoresis, molecular and purification, separation of magnetic beads and other modern molecular biological technology.

© Springer Nature Singapore Pte Ltd. 2016
M. Gong et al. (Eds.): BIC-TA 2016, Part I, CCIS 681, pp. 3–11, 2016.
DOI: 10.1007/978-981-10-3611-8_1

Self-assembly is an extremely common phenomenon in the nature. The biochemical process of synthesis of DNA, transcription and regulation of RNA, synthesis and folding of protein synthesis or the generation of living organisms is the product of self-assembly. In the process of self-assembly, human only can design product and open the process of self-assembly. When self-assembly process begins automatically, no longer need any external forces. Winfree et al. [6] firstly came up with the idea of computing by self-assembly tiles. In 2000, Mao et al. first put forward three cross Tile based-DNA self-assembly model, then the model was verified that it can implement accumulation of exclusive or operation by biological experiment [7]. In 2006, He et al. presented a kind of self-assembly model that can realize two nonnegative binary integer addition by coding DNA single sequence [8]. In 2009, on the basis of Brun work, Zhang et al. formed the division operation system by DNA self-assembly [9]. In 2010, Lai et al. used linear self-assembly to implement two nonnegative binary integer subtraction [10]. In 2011, Zhang et al. combined AuNP self-assembled polymerization with DNA computing, and constructed DNA self-assembly logic calculation model [11]. In 2013, Fan et al. built logic gates to implement the single logic operator by DNA self-assembly [12]. In 2016, Bi et al. used self-assembly of duplex-looped DNA hairpin motif based on strand displacement reaction to solve logic operations [13].

At present, using self-assembly model to solve simple operation has gained some achievement, including mathematics, logic, and other operations. However, any kind of self-assembled model can only solve the single algorithm. For compound operation, even the most basic operations, the existing models are unable to realize. Only through the way of dismantling, compound operations was dismantled into several simple operations, then they are solved one by one. This paper proposes a new DNA self-assembly system, in which both additive operation and subtraction operation can been realized simultaneously.

2   The Principle of DNA Self-assembly

DNA self-assembly [6] is a Tile-based calculation mode. Problem is mapped to the initial framework. Under the condition of certain biochemical reaction, the assembly process between Tile and assembly is implemented through the complementary matching. Final assembly is the output of problem. DNA self-assembly models are divided into three types, namely linear model, 2D self-assembly model and 3D self-assembly, in which, 2D self-assembly model is currently the most widely used model. 2D self-assembly model is made up of four parts, namely basic Tile, bonding strength function, seed Tile and strength parameters. Basic Tile is used to build the various calculation operator, store data that is produced in the operation process and perform various calculations. Each side of Tile has some identification in order to indicate different numerical or operator. Bonding strength function is used to define the combination intensity between two stick ends of two adjacent tiles. Seed Tile is used to define start and end of the self-assembly. Strength parameters are used to represent thermal and kinetic parameters. Only when the summation of bonding strength parameters between every two tiles is greater than the given parameter, the assembly reaches the steady state.

In the process of solving practical problems, we usually abstract and simplify the molecule so as to improve the efficiency of modeling. Every abstract DNA Tile owns four coupling ends, and every coupling end expresses a special sticky end. Two sticky ends with complementary characteristics can be connected together. σ_{LU}, σ_{LD}, σ_{RU} and σ_{RD} represent four sticky ends respectively. According to the needs of the problem, a variety of different DNA structures can been constructed through the design of their operational function so as to realize a variety of different operations (Fig. 1).

Fig. 1. The abstract diagram of DNA Tile

3   Compound Logic Operators

Logic operation [11–13] is also called Boolean operation. Boolean used mathematical method to study on logic problems, and created succeeded the logical calculus. He uses equation to express verdict, and the ratiocination is regarded as the transformation of the equation. The effectiveness of this transformation is not depend on the explanation of symbols, and only depends on the combination of the symbols. This logic theory is referred to as Boolean algebra. In the 1930s, logic algebra was applied to the circuit system. And then, due to the development of electronic technology and computer, the transformation rules of all sorts of complex large systems compliance with laws that Boolean reveals. Logical operators are usually used to test the true and false value. One of the most common logic operator is used to determine whether leave cycle or continue to execute the instruction in the cycle. There are only two logic constants, namely 0 and 1, and they are used to represent two contrary logic states. As with ordinary algebra, logic variables can also been expressed by letters, symbols, Numbers and their combination. But they have the essential difference. The values of logic constant only have two possibilities, namely 0 and 1, and no have intermediate value. Table 1 shows the rules of three common logic operators. They are XOR, NOR and NAND respectively.

Table 1. The rules of three common logic operators

x_1	x_2	XOR	NOR	NAND
0	0	0	1	1
0	1	1	0	1
1	0	1	0	1
1	1	0	0	0

4   Theoretical Model of Compound Logic Operators

Theoretical model of compound logic operators is designed contains five types of Tile, namely Initial Tile, Process Tile, Operation Tile, End Tile and Boundary Tile. Initial Tile express the start of the self-assembly process and record the first parameter of compound logic operators. Process Tile is the passing tile, and it is used to pass the calculation parameter and intermediate result. Operation Tile is the operational rule tile, and End Tile is the final result tile. Boundary Tile is used to control the growth direction and array orientation of self-assembly.

4.1   Initial Tile

Initial Tile is used to express the start of the self-assembly process and record the first parameter of compound logic operators. This type of Tile owns three stick ends, namely σ_{LU}, σ_{RU} and σ_{RD}. σ_{LU} and σ_{RD} are responsible for the connection. When bonding strength is greater than the given parameter, Initial Tiles are connected by σ_{LU} and σ_{RD}. σ_{RU} is used to transmit the first parameter and connect Operation Tile. Initial Tile only owns two types. One type expresses '0', and the other expresses '1' (Fig. 2).

Fig. 2. Initial Tile

4.2   Process Tile

The role of Process Tile is the other parameter of compound logic operators or the store of intermediate result. Process Tile also owns two types. One type expresses '0', and the other expresses '1'. Process Tile owns four stick ends, namely σ_{LU}, σ_{LD}, σ_{RU} and σ_{RD}. When bonding strength is greater than the given parameter, Process Tiles are connected by σ_{LU} and σ_{RD}. σ_{LD} is used to receive the intermediate result and the front logic operator and connected with Operation Tile, and owns six states. The intermediate result is transmitted by σ_{RU} (Fig. 3).

Fig. 3. Process Tile

4.3 Operation Tile

Two calculation parameters are connected by Operation Tile. In this paper, compound logic operators contain XOR, NOR and NAND, therefore, Operation Tile owns three types. Operation Tile also owns four stick ends, namely σ_{LU}, σ_{LD}, σ_{RU} and σ_{RD}. When bonding strength is greater than the given parameter, σ_{LU} and σ_{RD} are used to connect two adjacent Operation Tiles. The front parameter is transmitted by σ_{LD}, and the arithmetic is transmitted by σ_{RU} (Fig. 4).

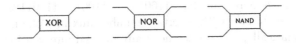

Fig. 4. Operation Tile

4.4 End Tile

End Tile marks the end of the operation and outputs the final result. End Tile only owns two types. End Tile owns three stick ends, namely σ_{LU}, σ_{LD} and σ_{RD}. σ_{LU} and σ_{RD} play an role in connecting End Tiles. σ_{LD} is used to receive the final result of compound logic operators (Fig. 5).

Fig. 5. End Tile

4.5 Boundary Tile

Boundary Tile is used to control the growth direction and array orientation of self-assembly, and is divided into two types. One is Start Boundary Tile which marks the beginning of a line of tile assembly. The other is End Boundary Tile which marks the end of a line of tile assembly. The role of all of their stick ends is the connection (Figs. 6 and 7).

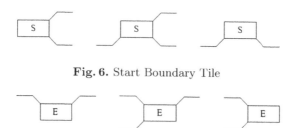

Fig. 6. Start Boundary Tile

Fig. 7. End Boundary Tile

5   The Model Instance of Compound Logic Operators

In this paper, a model instance of compound logic operators is given as so to illustrate the correctness of the self-assembly model. The model of compound logic operators is used to calculate $110010 \oplus 011001 \wedge 110011 \vee 001010$. Five kinds of tile in accordance with a certain number mix into the mix pool. They can react automatically, and do not need any manual intervention. Figures 8, 9 and 10 show the bottom-up process. Figure 8 shows the self-assembly process of XOR operation, and Fig. 9 shows the self-assembly process of NAND operation. Figure 10 shows the self-assembly process of NOR operation.

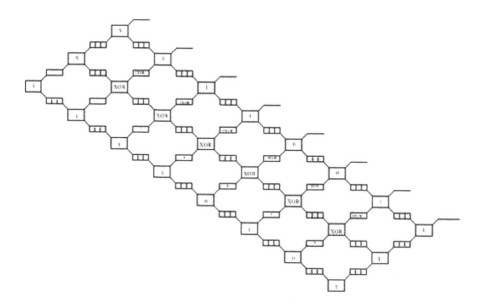

Fig. 8. Self-assembly of XOR operation

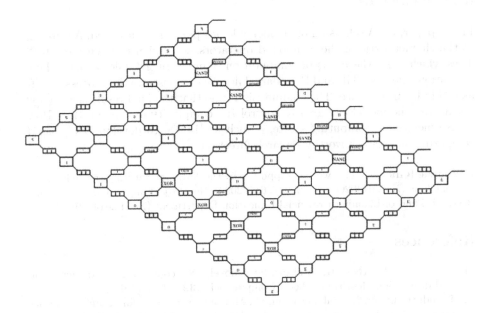

Fig. 9. Self-assembly of NAND operation

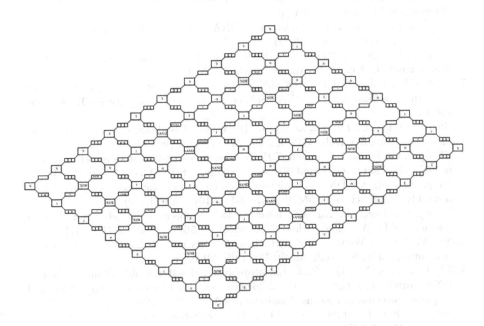

Fig. 10. Self-assembly of NOR operation

6 Conclusions

In this paper, DNA self-assembly model of logic operators is designed. According to the characteristic of the compound operators, we design five types of DNA Tiles which meet the needs of computation, namely Initial Tile, Process Tile, Operation Tile, End Tile and Boundary Tile. We demonstrate the process of self-assembly by an instance. The computation time that the final result is gotten is linear, and the model can greatly control the complexity of computation. How to use membrane computing strategy, such as [14–18] to develop DNA based computing models is a worthy research direction.

Acknowledgments. This work is supported by the National Natural Science Foundation of China (Nos. 61402066, 61402067, 61572093), the Project Supported by Scientific Research Fund of Liaoning Provincial Education Department (No. L2014499).

References

1. Rasmus, L., Matthew, R., Andrew, P.: A novel DNA computing based encryption and decryption algorithm. Theor. Comput. Sci. **632**, 43–73 (2016)
2. UbaidurRahman, N., Balamurugan, C., Mariappan, R.: A strand graph semantics for DNA-based computation. Procedia Comput. Sci. **46**, 463–475 (2015)
3. Ullah, A., D'Addona, D., Arai, N.: DNA based computing for understanding complex shapes. Biosystems **117**, 40–53 (2014)
4. Adleman, L.M.: Molecular computation of solutions to combinatorial problems. Science **266**(5187), 1021–1024 (1994)
5. Hossein, E., Majid, D.: Application of DNA computing in graph theory. Artif. Intell. Rev. **38**(3), 223–235 (2012)
6. Winfree, E., Liu, F., Wenzler, L., Seeman, N.: Design and self-assembly of two-dimensional DNA crystals. Nature **394**(6693), 539–544 (1998)
7. Mao, C.D., LaBean, T.H., Reif, J.H., Seeman, N.C.: Logical computation using algorithmic self-assembly of DNA triple-crossover molecules. Nature **407**, 493–496 (2000)
8. Zhao, J., Qian, L., Liu, Q., Zhang, Z., He, L.: DNA addition based on linear self-assembly. Chin. Sci. Bull. **51**(21), 2485–2489 (2006). (in Chinese)
9. Zhang, X.C., Wang, Y.F., Chen, Z.H.: Arithmetic computation using self-assembly of DNA tiles: subtraction and division. Prog. Nat. Sci. **19**(3), 377–388 (2009)
10. Fang, X., Lai, X.: DNA subtraction modular arithmetic based on linear self-assembly. Chin. Sci. Bull. **55**(10), 957–963 (2010). (in Chinese)
11. Zhang, C., Yang, J., Xu, J.: Molecular logic computing model based on self-assembly of DNA nanoparticles. Chin. Sci. Bull. **56**(33), 3566–3571 (2011)
12. Yu, Y., Lu, J., Wang, D., Pei, H., Fan, C.: DNA/RNA based logic gates and computing. Chin. Sci. Bull. **58**(2), 131–140 (2013). (in Chinese)
13. Bi, S., Yue, S., Wu, Q., Ye, J.: Initiator-catalyzed self-assembly of duplex-looped DNA hairpin motif based on strand displacement reaction for logic operations and amplified biosensing. Biosens. Bioelectron. **83**, 281–286 (2016)
14. Song, T., Pan, L.: Spiking neural P systems with request rules. Neurocomputing **193**(12), 193–200 (2016)
15. Song, T., Liu, X., Zhao, Y., Zhang, X.: Spiking neural P systems with white hole neurons. IEEE Trans. Nanobiosci. (2016). doi:10.1109/TNB.2016.2598879

16. Song, T., Pan, Z., Wong, D.M., Wang, X.: Design of logic gates using spiking neural P systems with homogeneous neurons and astrocytes-like control. Inf. Sci. **372**, 380–391 (2016)
17. Wang, X., Song, T., Gong, F., Pan, Z.: On the computational power of spiking neural P systems with self-organization. Scientific Reports. doi:10.1038/srep27624
18. Shi, X., Wu, X., Song, T., Li, X.: Construction of DNA nanotubes with controllable diameters and patterns by using hierarchical DNA sub-tiles. Nanoscale. doi:10.1039/C6NR02695H

Model Checking Computational Tree Logic Using Sticker Automata

Weijun Zhu[1]([✉]), Yanfeng Wang[2], Qinglei Zhou[1], and Kai Nie[1]

[1] School of Information Engineering, Zhengzhou University,
Zhengzhou 450001, Henan, China
`zhuweijun@zzu.edu.cn`
[2] College of Electric Information Engineering,
Zhengzhou University of Light Industry, Zhengzhou 450002, China

Abstract. The molecular computing has been successfully employed to solve more and more complex computation problems. However, as an important complex problem, the Computational Tree Logic (CTL) model checking is still far from resolved under the circumstance of molecular computing, since it is still a lack of method. To address this issue, an autonomous model checking method is presented for checking all the basic constructs of CTL using DNA computing and sticker automata. As a result, the CTL model checking problem under the circumstance of molecular computing is solved preliminary. The simulated experimental results demonstrate the effectiveness of the new method in molecular biology.

Keywords: Model checking · Computational tree logic · DNA computing · Sticker automata

1 Introduction

Differ from an electronic computer, a DNA computer use DNA molecules as the carrier of computation. In 1994, a Turing Award winner professor Adleman solved a small scale Hamilton path problem with a DNA experiment [5], and it is considered the pioneer work in the field of DNA computing. Since the DNA computing has a huge advantage of parallel computing, this technique was subsequently developed rapidly. After this famous experiment, many models and methods based on DNA computing were presented for solving some complex computational problems, especially the famous NP-hard problems and PSPACE-hard ones. For examples, Lipton reported that promoted Adlemans idea and tried to solve the SAT problem [6], Ouyang presented a DNA-computing-based model for solving the maximal clique problem [7], Shapiro solved an automata problem of two states and two characters using the autonomous DNA computing technique [8].

One of the key differences between computer and other computing tools is the universality. Xu constructed a mathematical model called "probe machine" for the general DNA computer [10]. By integrating the storage system, operation system, detection system and control system into a whole, he gradually obtains

M. Gong et al. (Eds.): BIC-TA 2016, Part I, CCIS 681, pp. 12–20, 2016.
DOI: 10.1007/978-981-10-3611-8_2

a real general DNA computer—"Zhongzhou DNA computer" [10]. According to result from [9], a probe machine is a nine-tuples consisting of data library, probe library, data controller, probe controller, probe operation, computing platform, detector, true solution storage and residue collector. It is an universal DNA computing model which can be realized in biology, and a Turing machine is just a "special case" of a probe machine [9]. This significant progress has raised the practical importance of the researches on DNA computing.

Beside the satisfiablity problem, the Model Checking (MC) one is another important computational problem. And the two problems are correlative. The MC was proposed by the Turing Award winner Clarke et al. [1]. In order to describe the different temporal properties, the researchers have presented some different temporal logics. The Turing Award winner Pnueli introduced Linear Temporal Logic (LTL for short) into computer science in [2], and this logic can express the linear properties. The Turing Award winner Clarke proposed Computation Tree Logic (CTL for short) in [3,4], and this logic can express the branch properties.

As a complex computational problem, the model checking under the circumstance of DNA computing is always the goal of researchers. In 2006, the Turing Award winner Prof. Emerson employed some DNA molecules to conduct CTL model checking for the first time [11]. As for LTL, the model checking is a PSPACE problem in the classical computing, and we have found a DNA-computing-based method, see Reference [12,13], which can be used for checking all four basic constructs and some popular formulas. The basic constructs in CTL are: EpUq, ApUq, EFp, AFp, EGp, AGp, EXp, AXp. We can obtain arbitrary CTL formula by combining these basic constructs recursively. Up to now, many basic constructs in CTL cannot be conducted model checking within the framework of DNA computing. This is the problem to be solved in this paper.

2 Preliminary

2.1 The Basic Constructs in CTL [1]

Definition 1. Let p and q be atomic propositions, EpUq, ApUq, EFp, AFp, EGp, AGp, EXp and AXp be the basic CTL construct. An arbitrary CTL formula can be obtained by combining recursively some basic CTL constructs. An atomic proposition and a basic CTL construct are interpreted on a system model M, and their intuitive meanings are given as follows.

- p or q is satisfied in a state s, or not.
- EpUq describes the following property: There exists at least one path in M, such that p is always satisfied until q is satisfied.
- ApUq describes the following property: For each path in M, p is always satisfied until q is satisfied.
- EFp describes the following property: There exists at least one path in M, such that p is eventually satisfied.

- AFp describes the following property: For each path in M, p is eventually satisfied.
- EGp describes the following property: There exists at least one path in M, such that p is always satisfied.
- AGp describes the following property: For each path in M, p is always satisfied.
- EXp describes the following property: There exists at least one path in M, such that p is satisfied in the next state.
- AXp describes the following property: For each path in M, p is satisfied in the next state.

Given an arbitrary model M, how to use the DNA-computing-based method to determine whether the basic CTL constructs be satisfied by M or not? To this end, Sect. 3 will give such an approach (Fig. 1).

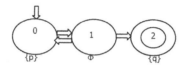

Fig. 1. An example on LFSA: systematic FSA model M_1 which is used in experiments

2.2   Finite State Automata and Model Checking

Definition 2. A Finite State Automaton (FSA) is a five-tuples (Σ, Q, T, q_0, F), where

- Σ is a finite alphabet
- Q is a finite set of states
- T is a finite set of transitions: $T : Q \times \Sigma \to R(Q)$
- $q_0 \in Q$ is an initial state
- $F \subseteq Q$ is a set of acceptance states

2.3   Sticker Automata and DNA Model Checking

2.3.1   Sticker Automata

As a model of DNA computing, a sticker automaton can realize a FSA. Given a DNA strand charactering an input string and a FSA, the sticker automaton can determine whether or not the string is accepted by the FSA.

2.3.1.1 The Encoding Way of FSA and Input String

Reference [14] gives the following way of DNA encoding

Supposing $M = (\Sigma, S, T, s_0, F)$ is a FSA, and every character a in the alphabet Σ can be encoded as C(a), we have:

(1) An input string $a_1, \ldots, a_n$ in Σ can be encoded with the following single-stranded DNA molecule: $5'$ I_1 $X_0 \ldots X_m$ $C(a_1) \ldots X_0 \ldots X_m$ $C(a_n)$ $X_0 \ldots X_m$ I_2 $3'$, where I_1 is an initiator sequence, $X_0 \ldots X_m$ is a spacer sequence separating $C(a_i)$, and I_1 is a terminator sequence.

(2) A transition $T(s_i, a) = s_j$ is encoded as $3' \overline{X_{i+1}} \ldots \overline{X_m}$ $\overline{C(a)}$ $\overline{X_0} \ldots \overline{X_j} 5'$, where $\overline{X}$ means the Watson-Crick complement (WC for short) of a nucleotide X, $\overline{C(a)}$ means the WC of the DNA strand charactering a.

(3) An initial state s_i is encoded as $3' \overline{I_1} \overline{X_0} \ldots \overline{X_i} 5'$.

(4) An acceptance state s_j is encoded as $3' \overline{X_{j+1}} \ldots \overline{X_m} \overline{I_2} 5'$.

2.3.1.2 The Process of DNA Computing Based on Sticker Automata

The computational process of sticker automata can be concluded as follows [14].

Step 1: Data preprocessing

(1) Synthesize some DNA strands charactering an automaton and its input strings.

(2) Put all the DNA strands into the test tube T, and anneal to make sure that the strands and their WC complements can be hybridized completely. The process of base pairing and the placement of ligase can form complete or partial double stranded DNA molecules.

Step 2: Computation

After the first step, we will see the following phenomena. If the input string is accepted by the automaton, the tube T contains only the complete double stranded DNA molecules which begin with an initiator sequence and terminate at a terminator sequence. Otherwise, there are partial double stranded DNA molecules or single stranded DNA molecules in T. Therefore, we add some ribozymes called Mung Bean into the test tube T, in order to degrade the single stranded DNA fragment, and retain the complete double stranded DNA molecules.

Step 3: Output of results

We can separate the different DNA molecules with different lengths using electrophoretic technique. If there exists a variety of length of DNA molecules, it indicates that there are some partial double stranded DNA molecules in T before we add the ribozymes, and the input string cannot be accepted by the automaton. Otherwise, T contains only complete double stranded DNA molecules before we add the ribozymes, and the input string can be accepted by the automaton.

2.3.2   DNA Model Checking

On the basis of sticker automata, Reference [13] presented a DNA-computing-based LTL model checking method, which can be denoted as the algorithm TL-MC-DNA(DNACODE(A),x), where DNACODE(A) and x are two input of the algorithm, A is a FSA expressing a run of a system, DNACODE(A) is an encoding with a sticker automaton for charactering A, x = DNACODE(A(f)) is an encoding with a sticker automaton for charactering A(f), and A(f) is a FSA model of a formula f. In Reference [13], the scope of f includes the all the basic LTL formulas and some popular LTL formulas, f formula for short. The output of the algorithm is yes or no, representing the result of the model checking.

3 The DNA Model Checking Method for the Basic CTL Constructs

If the encoding of sticker automaton which realizes a FSA of a system and the encoding of sticker automaton which realizes a FSA of a formula are inputted, the algorithm TL-MC-DNA(DNACODE(A), DNACODE(A(f))) in [13] can compute and return a result of model checking. This paper expands range of f, and a series of new encoding of sticker automata. By computing TL-MC-DNA(DNACODE(A), DNACODE(A(f''))), where f'' = $\{\varphi_1\}$, (f'' formula for short), we can perform DNA model checking for the one temporal logic formula. Ref. [13] has confirmed the effectiveness of the algorithm TL-MC-DNA for the f formulas by simulated biological experiments.

3.1 The DNA Model Checking for the Four Universal Formulas

Comparing the CTL formula ApUq and the LTL formula pUq, we can clearly see that these two formulas have the same semantics. Therefore, we can use the algorithm TL-MC-DNA(DNACODE(A), x) to check the CTL formula ApUq. Similarly, the algorithm TL-MC-DNA(DNACODE(A), x) can also be employed to check the CTL constructs AFp, AGp and AXp. The obtained algorithm is formulated as follows.

Algorithm 1. The DNA model checking algorithm for the universal CTL formulas
CTLQ-MC-DNA(DNACODE(A), DNACODE(A(f_q))
INPUT: the encoding of sticker automaton which realizes a systematic FSA A, the encoding of sticker automaton which realizes a FSA of an universal CTL formula f_q, where f_q=ApUq, AFp, AGp or AXp
OUTPUT: whether A satisfies f_q, or not

BEGIN
Step 1:
SELECT CASE f_q
   CASE ApUq
     g:=pUq   // where g is a f formula
   CASE AFp
     g:=Fp   // where g is a f formula
   CASE AGp
     g:=Gp // where g is a f formula
   CASE AXp
     g:=Xp // where g is a f formula
ENDSELECT
Step 2: y:=TL-MC-DNA(DNACODE(A), DNACODE (A(g))
Step 3: IF y="yes",THEN return "yes", ELSE return "no"
END

3.2   The DNA Model Checking for the Four Existence Formulas

The formula EpUq and the formula ApUq have the following relationship: $\neg$EpUq $=$ A$\neg$p $\overline{\overline{U}}$ $\neg$q. That is to say, EpUq $= \neg$A$\neg$p $\overline{\overline{U}}$ $\neg$q. The formula EGp and the formula AFp have the following relationship:$\neg$EGp $=$ AF$\neg$p, that is to say, EGp $= \neg$AF$\neg$p. The formula EFp and the formula AGp have the following relationship:$\neg$EFp $=$ AG$\neg$p, that is to say, EFp $= \neg$AG$\neg$p. The formula EXp and the formula AXp have the following relationship: $\neg$EXp $=$ AX$\neg$p, that is to say, EXp $= \neg$AX$\neg$p. Comparing A$\neg$p $\overline{\overline{U}}$ $\neg$q and $\varphi_1 = \neg$p $\overline{\overline{U}}$ $\neg$q, we can clearly see that these two formulas have the same semantics. Thus, $\neg\varphi_1 =$ EpUq. Therefore, we can use the algorithm TL-MC-DNA (DNA-CODE(A), DNACODE(A($f'' = \varphi_1$)) to check the CTL formula EpUq. Similarly, the algorithm TL-MC-DNA(DNACODE(A), x) can also be employed to check the CTL formulas EFp, EGp and EXp. The obtained algorithm is formulated as follows.

Algorithm 2. The DNA model checking algorithm for the existence CTL formulas
CTLC-MC-DNA(DNACODE(A), DNACODE(A(f_c)))
INPUT: the encoding of sticker automaton which realizes a systematic FSA A, the encoding of sticker automaton which realizes a FSA of an existence CTL formula f_c, where f_c=EpUq, EFp, EGp or EXp
OUTPUT: whether A satisfies f_c, or not

BEGIN
Step 1:
SELECT CASE f_c
  CASE EpUq
    Step 1: g:= φ_1
    Step 2: y:=TL-MC-DNA(DNACODE(A), DNACODE(A(g))) //where g is a f'' formula
    Step 3: IF y="yes",THEN return "no", ELSE return "yes" //$\varphi_1 = \neg$(EpUq)
  CASE EFp
    Step 1: g:=G$\neg$p
    Step 2: y:=TL-MC-DNA(DNACODE(A), DNACODE(A(g))) //where g is a f'' formula
    Step 3: IF y="yes",THEN return "no", ELSE return "yes" // G$\neg$p$=\neg$(EFp)
  CASE EGp
    Step 1: g:=F$\neg$p
    Step 2: y:=TL-MC-DNA(DNACODE(A), DNACODE(A(g))) //where g is a f'' formula
    Step 3: IF y="yes",THEN return "no", ELSE return "yes" // F$\neg$p$=\neg$(EGp)
  CASE EXp
    Step 1: g:=X$\neg$p
    Step 2: y:=TL-MC-DNA(DNACODE(A), DNACODE(A(g))) //where g is a f'' formula
    Step 3: IF y="yes",THEN return "no", ELSE return "yes" // X$\neg$p$=\neg$(EXp)
ENDSELECT
END

3.3   The DNA Model Checking for the Basic CTL Constructs

The principle of this algorithm is: (1) If a basic CTL construct is an universal formula, the Algorithm 1 will be called. (2) And if a basic CTL construct is an existence formula, the Algorithm 2 will be called. In this way, the model checking of the basic CTL constructs can be conducted. The algorithm is formulated as follows.

Algorithm 3. The DNA model checking algorithm for the basic CTL constructs CTL-MC-DNA(DNACODE(A), DNACODE(A(f_{CTL})))
INPUT: the encoding of sticker automaton which realizes a systematic FSA A, the encoding of sticker automaton which realizes a FSA of a basic CTL construct f_{CTL}
OUTPUT: whether A satisfies f_{CTL}, or not

BEGIN
Step 1: IF there exists f_c, such that $f_{CTL}=f_c$,
THEN call CTLC-MC-DNA(DNACODE(A), DNACODE(A(f_c)))
ELSEIF there exists f_q, such that $f_{CTL}=f_q$,
THEN call CTLQ-MC-DNA(DNACODE(A), DNACODE(A(f_q)))
ENDSELECT
END

---

4   Simulated Experiments

Experimental platform: NUPACK [15]

Experimental procedure: (1) one can design the encoding of the sticker automata for the systematic FSA, as well as the encoding of the sticker automata for the FSA of formula, respectively; (2) for these FSAs mentioned above, one can simulate the process of hybridization between some single stranded DNA molecules; (3) according to the algorithms proposed in this paper, one can get the results of model checking of the several formulas, by reading the results of hybridization.

Experimental objective: To test the correctness, effectiveness and biological realizability of the new algorithms.

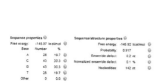
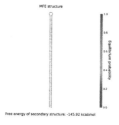
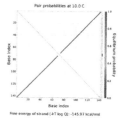

Fig. 2. checking the formula φ_1: the structural properties of encoding sequence

Fig. 3. (Chromatic) thermodynamic analysis for φ_1:minimum free energy structure

Fig. 4. (Chromatic) checking for φ_1:pairing probability in equilibrium

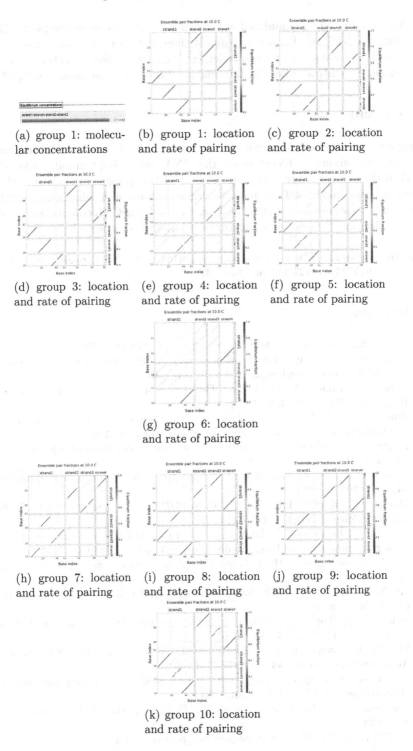

(a) group 1: molecular concentrations

(b) group 1: location and rate of pairing

(c) group 2: location and rate of pairing

(d) group 3: location and rate of pairing

(e) group 4: location and rate of pairing

(f) group 5: location and rate of pairing

(g) group 6: location and rate of pairing

(h) group 7: location and rate of pairing

(i) group 8: location and rate of pairing

(j) group 9: location and rate of pairing

(k) group 10: location and rate of pairing

Fig. 5. (Chromatic) checking for φ_1: the groups of sub-experimental results on base pairing and hybridizations

We have conducted the simulated experiments for φ_1. We have designed a DNA encoding via NUPAC. Figures 2, 3 and 4 show the thermodynamic analysis of the encoding sequence at 10 Celsius degree. We have checked whether or not the systematic FSA M_1 satisfies the formula φ_1. The results are shown in Fig. 5.

5   Conclusions

Early researches on DNA computing focus on the models and algorithms based on non autonomous. In recent years, the DNA computing technique has developed to the self-assembly. The main results of this paper are the Algorithm 3, which is based on the self assembly of sticker automata. With these algorithms at hands, we can conduct model checking for the basic CTL constructs via some DNA molecules. This is the main contribution of this paper.

Acknowledgment. This work has been supported by the NSFC project under Grant U1204608, 61572444, 61272022 and 61472372.

References

1. Clarke, E., et al.: Model Checking. MIT press, Cambridge (1999)
2. Pnueli, A.: The temporal logic of programs. In: Symposium on Foundations of Computer Science, Washington, DC, USA, pp. 46–57 (1977)
3. Benari, M., Pnueli, A., Manna, Z.: The temporal logic of branching time. Acta Informatica **20**(3), 207–226 (1983)
4. Emerson, E., Clarke, E.: Using branching time temporal logic to synthesize synchronization skeletons. Sci. Comput. Program. **2**(3), 241–266 (1982)
5. Adleman, L.: Molecular computation of solutions to combinatorial problems. Science **266**(5187), 1021–1023 (1994)
6. Lipton, R.: DNA solution of hard computational problems. Science **268**(5210), 542–545 (1995)
7. Ouyang, Q., Kaplan, P.D., Liu, S., et al.: DNA solution of the maximal clique problem. Science **278**(17), 446–449 (1997)
8. Shapiro, E., Benenson, Y., Adar, R., et al.: Programmable and autonomous computing machine made of biomolecules. Nature **414**(6862), 430–434 (2001)
9. Jin, X.: Probe machine. IEEE Trans. Neural Netw. Learn. Syst. **27**(7), 1405–1416 (2016)
10. Jin, X.: Forthcoming era of biological computer. Bull. Chin. Acad. Sci. **29**(1), 42–54 (2014). (in Chinese)
11. Emerson, E., Hager, K., Konieczka, J.: Molecular model checking. Int. J. Found. Comput. Sci. **17**(04), 733–741 (2006)
12. Zhu, W.-J., Zhou, Q.-L., Li, Y.-L.: LTL model checking based on DNA computing. Acta Electronica Sinica **44**(6), 1265–1271 (2016)
13. Zhu, W.-J., Zhou, Q.-L., Zhang, Q.-X.: A LTL model checking approach based on DNA computing. Chin. J. Comput. (2016)
14. Zimmermann, K., Ignatova, Z., Perez, M.: DNA Computing Models. Springer, New York (2008)
15. NUPACK (2015). http://www.nupack.org/partition/new

Two-Digit Full Subtractor Logical Operation Based on DNA Strand Displacement

Junwei Sun, Xing Li, Chun Huang, Guangzhao Cui, and Yanfeng Wang[✉]

College of Electrical and Electronic Engineering, Zhengzhou University of Light Industry, No. 5 Dongfeng Road, Zhengzhou 450002, China
yanfengwang@yeah.net

Abstract. DNA strand displacement has been widely used in designing the molecular logic circuit, nanomedicine and molecular automata and so on. In this article, the two-digit full subtractor is designed by DNA strand displacement reaction and has been verified by the simulation of DNA strand displacement. The accuracy of simulation results is further confirmed that DNA strand displacement is a valid method for the research of logical bio-chemical circuit. The multi-digit full subtractor could be used in biological computer in the future.

Keywords: DNA strand displacement · Two-digit full subtractor · Visual DSD

1 Introduction

DNA nanotechnology has become a reliable way to control matter in the nanoscale because of the specific of Watson-Crick base pairs [1–3]. DNA is an ideal nanoscale engineering material and has been applied widely in molecular device [4], logic circuit [5], nano-network [6], autonomous molecular walk [7,8], nano-medicine [9] and so on. DNA strand displacement is a kind of new DNA self-assembly method and has a series of the advantages.

AND gate, OR gate, and NOT gate were designed by the single strand nucleic acids, and the signal restoration function was demonstrated [10]. Three-input logic gate was developed by deoxyribozyme, and molecular full adder which consists of a seven logic gate array was constructed [11]. In 2010, Boolean circuits [12] were proposed to achieve a lot of functions, in which a latch circuit and a D flip-flop are designed. A simple and universal method was invented to establish logic gates by Qian and Winfree [13]. A 74L85 standard 4-bit magnitude comparator was simulated to prove its correctness [10]. The logic circuit [14] of the square root of a four-bit binary number was designed, which is useful for the next study. The implementation of logic AND gate by two grades strand displacement reaction was described to design circuits [15]. The patterns of logic AND gate and OR gate was put forward and confirmed by experiment [16].

DNA computing has been widely applied in DNA self-assembly technology [17], DNA strand displacement technology [18,19] and probe machine [20] and

© Springer Nature Singapore Pte Ltd. 2016
M. Gong et al. (Eds.): BIC-TA 2016, Part I, CCIS 681, pp. 21–29, 2016.
DOI: 10.1007/978-981-10-3611-8_3

so on. Compared with the past work [21,22], in this paper, the two-digit full subtractor is constructed for the first time. The circuit can achieve the two-digit subtraction function, which is different from the previous circuit. Many more complex circuits could be designed on the basis of this circuit. And these circuits could be applied to the biological computer in the future.

Based on DNA strand displacement molecular logic gates, a logical circuit of implementing binary two-digit subtractor is presented, which could be simulated in the programming language software. The paper is arranged as follows: the background of DSD and the seesaw motif of basic gates are described in the Sect. 2. The algorithm principle of binary two-digit subtractor and its dual-rail circuit are shown in the Sect. 3. The seesaw circuit and the simulation in the Visual DSD are shown in the Sect. 4. Finally, the conclusion about two-digit calculation is discussed in Sect. 5.

2   DSD and Seesaw Motif of Basic Gates

DNA strand displacement reaction is a process, which means that one single strand replaces another bounding single strand from complex. The single strand serves as the input signal and another bounding single strand from complex serves as output signal. The process of strand displacement and branch migration is shown in Fig. 1. Firstly, the process is initialed in a toehold which is short and usually consists of 4–6 base sequences [23–25,28–32]. Then branch migration is processed in the process. Finally, the output strand is released. T represent a short toehold domain and T* is the Watson-Crick complement pair of T. The strand S4L-S4-S4R-T-S5L-S5-S5R and S5L-S5-S5R-T-S6L-S6-S6R indicate input signal and output signal, respectively. S5L-S5-S5R is recognition domain. If the input strand and output strand have the same toehold domain, then the previous output could serve as the input of the next logic operation. This favorable condition is provided to construct cascade between front gates and back gates.

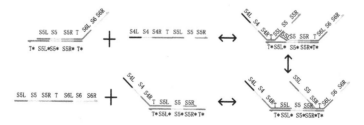

Fig. 1. The process of branch migration and strand displacement. T represents a short toehold domain and T* is the Watson-Crick complement pair of T. The strand S4L-S4-S4R-T-S5L-S5-S5R denotes input signal. The strand S5L-S5-S5R-t-S6L-S6-S6R indicates output signal. S5L-S5-S5R is recognition domain.

Boolean logic concerns the relationship of two numbers, which is a computing method. Two states are defined: digit "0" and digit "1", which often represent that the event is false and true, respectively. There are the basic logical operation, such as logic "AND", logic "OR" and logic "NOT".

The electronically logic gate can be transformed into an equivalent biochemical logic gate through the certain corresponding rules. The seesaw DNA motif of basic logic gates are shown in Fig. 2. An amplifying gate of one-input-three-outputs is shown in Fig. 2(a). Two-input-one-output molecular "OR" gate and "AND" gate are constructed (as shown in Fig. 2(c, d)) on the basis of the integrating gate (as shown in Fig. 2(b)). In the DNA gates, logic "0" and logic "1" are distinguished by high or low concentration.

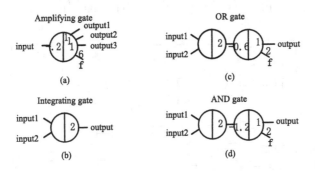

Fig. 2. The seesaw DNA motif of basic logic gates. (a) One-input-three-output amplifying gate. (b) Two-input-one-output integrating gate. (c, d) Abstract diagram of a seesaw OR and AND gate.

3   Binary Two-Digit Subtractor and Dual-Rail Circuit

One-bit half subtractor and one-bit full subtractor have been constructed, but they are unlikely to meet the needs of complying complex computations of biocomputer. Therefore, it is necessary strongly to design the complicated logic operation. Here, two-bit full subtractor (as shown in Fig. 3) is given to act as an example, two-digit are taken as the input signal and two outputs are produced in two-digit full subtractor. The truth table of two-digit full subtractor is given in Table 1. According to the calculating principle of two-digit subtractor operation, the corresponding logic circuit can be designed, as shown in Fig. 3. The logic circuit works from the left to the right. In the Fig. 3, the number x_2x_1 and y_2y_1 which are located at the left side are the input single, the number s_2s_1 and b_2 which are located at the right side are the output single. The number s_2s_1 and b_2 indicate the difference-bit and the borrow-bit, respectively.

If the input is absent in the response, the uncertain computation result will be produced. Here, the dual-rail logic operation is adopted to avoid the false output. In the dual-rail logic circuit, the original input is expressed by a pair

Table 1. Truth table of two-digit full subtractor

Input		Output		Input		Output	
x_2x_1	y_2y_1	s_2s_1	b_2	x_2x_1	y_2y_1	s_2s_1	b_2
00	00	00	0	10	00	10	0
00	01	11	1	10	01	01	0
00	10	10	1	10	10	00	0
00	11	01	1	10	11	11	1
01	00	01	0	11	00	11	0
01	01	00	0	11	01	10	0
01	10	11	1	11	10	01	0
01	11	10	1	11	11	00	0

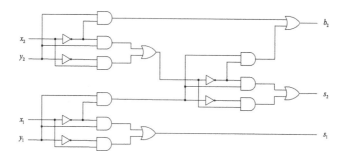

Fig. 3. The logic circuit of two-digit full subtractor operation. x_2x_1 and y_2y_1 are input signal. s_2s_1 and b_2 are output signal. s_2s_1 and b_2 indicate the difference-bit and the borrow-bit, respectively.

of inputs, which can be represented by logic ON and logic OFF, respectively. Taking the input x_1 as an example, if input x_1 doesnt take part in the reaction, then the input x_1^0 shows logic ON, meanwhile, the input x_1^1 shows logic OFF in the dual-rail logic circuit. In the dual-rail logic circuit, the AND, OR, or NOT logic function should be achieved by a pair of AND gate and OR gate. The dual-rail logic circuits of AND gate, OR gate, NAND gate and NOR gate are shown in Fig. 4(a–d), respectively. The dual-rail logic has been widely used to design DNA seesaw circuits. In this article, the two-bit full subtractor dual-rail logic circuit is designed in Fig. 4(e).

4   Seesaw Circuit and Simulation in Visual DSD

The dual-rail logic circuit should be transformed into an equivalent biochemical circuit through the certain corresponding rules. Two-inputs molecular logic OR gate and AND gate have been fabricated to design the DNA biochemical seesaw logic circuits. Then the seesaw biochemical logic circuit of two-digit full subtractor operation is shown in Fig. 5.

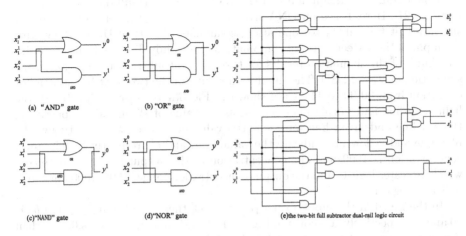

Fig. 4. The dual-rail logic circuits of basic gates. (a–d) The dual-rail logic circuits of AND gate, OR gate, NAND gate and NOR gate. (e) The two-bit full subtractor dual-rail logic circuit.

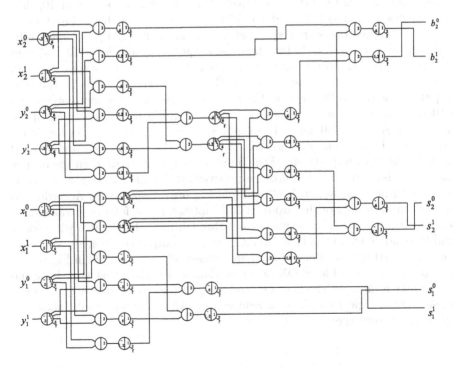

Fig. 5. The seesaw logic of two-digit full subtractor operation.

Visual DSD is a design and analysis tool for DNA strand displacement systems [26,27]. Here, based on DNA strand displacement, the reaction process of the two-digit full subtractor operation is simulated in visual DSD. Along with the input of the sixteen kinds of combinations we mainly discussed, there are sixteen kinds of the simulation results for two-digit full subtractor operation in the simulation of Visual DSD. The simulation results of the two-digit full subtractor operation from 00-00 to 11-11 are shown in Fig. 6(a–p). In the Fig. 6(a–p), the light blue line and purple lines represent the value of s_1^0 and s_1^1, respectively; the red line and green line represent the value of s_2^0 and s_2^1, respectively; the blue line and yellow line indicate the value of b_2^0 and b_2^1, respectively. The total concentration is 1000 nm. The concentration of the output is less than 100 nm which indicates logic 0, and the output concentration range is 900–1000 nm which indicates logic 1.

In the Fig. 6, if the input x_2x_1-y_2x_1 is 00-00, then the output s_2s_1 and b_2 is 00 and 0, respectively, as shown in Fig. 6(a). If the input x_2x_1-y_2x_1 is 00-01, then the output s_2s_1 and b_2 is 11 and 1 in Fig. 6(b), respectively. If the input x_2x_1-y_2x_1 is 00-10, then the output s_2s_1 and b_2 is 10 and 1 in Fig. 6(c), respectively. If the input x_2x_1-y_2x_1 is 00-11, then the output s_2s_1 and b_2 is 01 and 1 in Fig. 6(d), respectively. If the input x_2x_1-y_2x_1 is 01-00, then the output s_2s_1 and b_2 is 01 and 0 in Fig. 6(e), respectively. If the input x_2x_1-y_2x_1 is 01-01, then the output s_2s_1 and b_2 is 00 and 0 in Fig. 6(f), respectively. If the input x_2x_1-y_2x_1 is 01-10, then the output s_2s_1 and b_2 is 11 and 1 in Fig. 6(g), respectively. If the input x_2x_1-y_2x_1 is 01-11, then the output s_2s_1 and b_2 is 10 and 1 in Fig. 6(h), respectively. If the input x_2x_1-y_2x_1 is 10-00, then the output s_2s_1 and b_2 is 10 and 0 in Fig. 6(i), respectively. If the input x_2x_1-y_2x_1 is 10-01, then the output s_2s_1 and b_2 is 01 and 0 in Fig. 6(j), respectively. If the input x_2x_1-y_2x_1 is 10-10, then the output s_2s_1 and b_2 is 00 and 0 in Fig. 6(k), respectively. If the input x_2x_1-y_2x_1 is 10-11, then the output s_2s_1 and b_2 is 11 and 1 in Fig. 6(l), respectively. If the input x_2x_1-y_2x_1 is 11-00, then the output s_2s_1 and b_2 is 11 and 0 in Fig. 6(m), respectively. If the input x_2x_1-y_2x_1 is 11-01, then the output s_2s_1 and b_2 is 10 and 0 in Fig. 6(n), respectively. If the input x_2x_1-y_2x_1 is 11-10, then the output s_2s_1 and b_2 is 01 and 0 in Fig. 6(o), respectively. If the input x_2x_1-y_2x_1 is 11-11, then the output s_2s_1 and b_2 is 00 and 0 in Fig. 6(p), respectively. According to the simulation results of the two-digit full subtractor, the following conclusions can be obtained. (1) The output strand through fewer logic gates will sooner tend to steady state in the logic circuit. Thus, the output signal s_1, b_2 and s_2 in the same reaction time concentration are successively reduced. (2) In Fig. 6(c, e, h, g, o), two curves of logic ON occur overlap, which show that they have the same reaction rate. (3) The logic ON and logic OFF curves correctly express the stable state of logic 1 and logic 0, respectively. All simulation results show the high quality correctness.

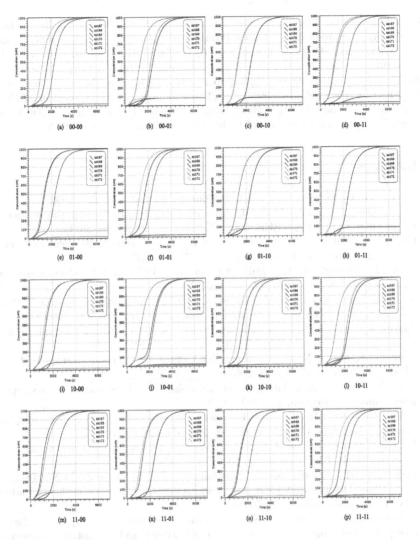

Fig. 6. The simulation in Visual DSD. (Color figure online)

5 Conclusion

Based on DNA strand displacement reaction, two-digit logic computing circuit has been constructed, which dedicates an approach of dynamic nanotechnology. Here, we have designed and acquired correct simulation result of two-digit full subtractor. Two-digit full subtractor can be applied to the biological computer. Although the dynamic nanotechnology currently faces tremendous challenges, this method of strand displacement still has a broad development prospect, which could be applied in the construction of logic circuits, molecular automata and nanomedicine and so on.

Acknowledgments. The work is supported by the State Key Program of the National Natural Science Foundation of China (Grant No. 61632002), the National Natural Science Foundation of China (Grant Nos. 61472371, 61472372, 61572446, 61602424 and 61603348), China Postdoctoral Science Foundation funded project (Grant No. 2015M570641 and 2016T90687), Basic and Frontier Technology Research Program of Henan Province (Grant No. 162300410220), Key Program of Higher Education of China Henan Province (Grant No. 17A120005) and the Science Foundation of for Doctorate Research of Zhengzhou University of Light Industry (Grant No. 2014BSJJ044).

References

1. Beaver, D.: Computing with DNA. J. Comput. Biol. **3**, 254–257 (1996)
2. Xu, J., Qiang, X., Yang, Y., et al.: An unenumerative DNA computing model for vertex coloring problem. IEEE Trans. Nanobiosci. **10**, 94–98 (2011)
3. Chen, Y.J., Dalchau, N., Srinivas, N., et al.: Programmable chemical controllers made from DNA. Nature Nanotechnol. **8**, 755–762 (2013)
4. Yurke, B., Turberfield, A.J., Mills, A.P., et al.: A DNA-fuelled molecular machine made of DNA. Nature **406**, 605–608 (2000)
5. Mao, C., LaBean, T.H., Reif, J.H., et al.: Logical computation using algorithmic self-assembly of DNA triple-crossover molecules. Nature **407**, 493–496 (2000)
6. Santini, C.C., Bath, J., Turberfield, A.J., et al.: A DNA network as an information processing system. Int. J. Mol. Sci. **13**, 5125–5137 (2012)
7. Shin, J.C.S., Pierce, N.A.: A synthetic DNA walker for molecular transport. J. Am. Chem. Soc. **126**, 10834–10835 (2004)
8. Lund, K., Manzo, A.J., Dabby, N., et al.: Molecular robots guided by prescriptive land-scapes. Nature **465**, 206–210 (2010)
9. Rahul, C., Jaswinder, S., Yan, L., Sherri, R., Hao, Y.: DNA self-assembly for nanomedicine. Adv. Drug. Deliver. Rev. **62**, 617–625 (2010)
10. Seelig, G., Soloveichik, D., Zhang, D.Y., Winfree, E.: Enzyme-free nucleic acid logic circuits. Science **314**, 1585–1588 (2006)
11. Lederman, H., Macdonald, J., Stephanovic, D., Stojanovic, M.N.: Deoxyribozymebased three-input logic gates and construction of a molecular full adder. Biochemistry **45**, 1194–1199 (2006)
12. Chiniforooshan, E., Doty, D., Kari, L., Seki, S.: Scalable, time-responsive, digital, energy-efficient molecular circuits using DNA strand displacement. In: Sakakibara, Y., Mi, Y. (eds.) DNA 2010. LNCS, vol. 6518, pp. 25–36. Springer, Heidelberg (2011). doi:10.1007/978-3-642-18305-8_3
13. Qian, L., Winfree, E.: A simple DNA gate motif for synthesizing large-scale circuits. J. R. Soc. Interface **8**, 1281–1297 (2011)
14. Qian, L., Winfree, E.: Scaling up digital circuit computation with DNA strand displacement cascades. Science **332**, 1196–1201 (2011)
15. Zhang, D.Y., Seelig, G.: Dynamic DNA nanotechnology using strand-displacement reactions. Nat. Chem. **3**, 103–113 (2011)
16. Zhang, C., Ma, L.N., Dong, Y.F., et al.: Molecular logic computing model based on DNA self-assembly strand branch migration. Chinese. Sci. Bull. **58**, 32–38 (2013)
17. Shi, X.L., Lu, W., Wang, Z.Y., Pan, L.Q., Cui, G.Z., Xu, J., LaBean, T.H.: Programmable DNA tile self-assembly using a hierarchical sub-tile strategy. Nanotechnology **25**(7), 075602 (2014)

18. Shi, X.L., Wang, Z.Y., Deng, C.Y., Song, T., Pan, L.Q., Chen, Z.H.: A novel bio-sensor based on DNA strand displacement. PLoS ONE **9**(10), e108856 (2014). doi:10.1371/journal.pone.0108856

19. Yang, J., Dong, C., Dong, Y.F., Liu, S., Pan, L.Q., Zhang, C.: Logic nanoparticle beacon triggered by the binding-induced effect of multiple inputs. ACS Appl. Mater. Interfaces **6**(16), 14486–14492 (2014)

20. Xu, J.: Probe machine. IEEE Trans. Neural Netw. Learn. Syst. **27**(7), 1405–1416 (2016)

21. Wang, Y., Tian, G., Hou, H., et al.: Simple logic computation based on the DNA strand displacement. J. Comput. Theor. Nanosci. **11**, 1975–1982 (2014)

22. Cui, G., Zhang, J., Cui, Y., et al.: DNA strand-displacement digital logic circuit with fluorescence resonance energy transfer detection. J. Comput. Theor. Nanosci. **12**, 2095–2100 (2015)

23. Zhang, D.Y., Winfree, E.: Control of DNA strand displacement kinetics using toehold exchange. J. Am. Chem. Soc. **131**, 17303–17314 (2009)

24. Zhang, D.Y.: Towards domain-based sequence design for DNA strand displacement reactions. In: Sakakibara, Y., Mi, Y. (eds.) DNA 2010. LNCS, vol. 6518, pp. 162–175. Springer, Heidelberg (2011). doi:10.1007/978-3-642-18305-8_15

25. Yurke, B., Mills, A.P.: Using DNA to power nanostructures. Genet. Program. Evol. Mach. **4**, 111 (2003). doi:10.1023/A:1023928811651

26. Lakin, M.R., Youssef, S., Polo, F., Emmott, S., et al.: Visual DSD: a design and analysis tool for DNA strand displacement systems. Bioinformatics **27**, 3211–3213 (2011)

27. Lakin, M.R., Petersen, R., Gray, K.E., Phillips, A.: Abstract modelling of tethered DNA circuits. In: Murata, S., Kobayashi, S. (eds.) DNA 2014. LNCS, vol. 8727, pp. 132–147. Springer, Heidelberg (2014). doi:10.1007/978-3-319-11295-4_9

28. Song, T., Pan, L.: Spiking neural P systems with request rules. Neurocomputing **193**(12), 193–200 (2016)

29. Song, T., Liu, X., Zhao, Y., Zhang, X.: Spiking neural P systems with white hole neurons. IEEE Trans. Nanobiosci. (2016). doi:10.1109/TNB.2016.2598879

30. Song, T., Pan, Z., Wong, D.M., Wang, X.: Design of logic gates using spiking neural P systems with homogeneous neurons and astrocytes-like control. Inf. Sci. **372**, 380–391 (2016)

31. Wang, X., Song, T., Gong, F., Pan, Z.: On the computational power of spiking neural P systems with self-organization. Scientific reports. doi:10.1038/srep27624

32. Shi, X., Wu, X., Song, T., Li, X.: Construction of DNA nanotubes with controllable diameters and patterns by using hierarchical DNA sub-tiles. Nanoscale **8**, 14785–14792 (2016). doi:10.1039/C6NR02695H

One-Bit Full Adder-Full Subtractor Logical Operation Based on DNA Strand Displacement

Yanfeng Wang, Xing Li, Chun Huang, Guangzhao Cui, and Junwei Sun[✉]

College of Electrical and Electronic Engineering,
Zhengzhou University of Light Industry,
No. 5 Dongfeng Road, Zhengzhou 450002, China
junweisun@yeah.net

Abstract. DNA nanotechnology has become a reliable, programmable control method, which can realize complex reaction networks nanostructures due to the accuracy and predictability complementary DNA base pairing. In this paper, one-bit full adder-full subtractor is constructed to achieve two kinds of functions which are full adder function and full subtractor function, respectively. Based on the cascaded DNA strand displacement reaction, the digital logic circuit is further translated into its corresponding dual-rail logic circuit and seesaw cascade logic circuit. The simulation results prove the feasibility and effectiveness of the designed circuit.

Keywords: DNA strand displacement · Full adder-full subtractor · Dual-rail circuit · Seesaw circuit

1 Introduction

DNA computing is a new field which combines computer science and molecular-biology subject. DNA acts as the computing tool, which has solved many problems, such as solving Hamition path, maximal clique problem [1–3]. DNA computing has merged a lot of molecule operation technology, such as self-assembly [4–6], fluorescence labeling [7–9] strand displacement [10–12] and probe machine [13]. DNA self-assembly technology and DNA stand displacement technology are two important technical support of DNA nanotechnology. DNA strand displacement technology is developed on the basis of DNA self-assembly technology. In recent years, DNA strand displacement [14–16] is a new method in the bio-computing, and has become a common method in DNA self-assembly. Based on the strand displacement cascade reaction [17], the dynamical connection adjacent logic modules [18–20] have been achieved, which makes it possible for the researcher to construct large-scale, complicated logic circuits [21]. Moreover, with the advantage of high-capacity information accumulation, high performance parallel computing, programming and simulating, it had acquired an in-depth study in the field of molecular computing, nano-machine, diagnosis and remedy of the disease. DNA strand displacement technology has the gigantic proficiency in

© Springer Nature Singapore Pte Ltd. 2016
M. Gong et al. (Eds.): BIC-TA 2016, Part I, CCIS 681, pp. 30–38, 2016.
DOI: 10.1007/978-981-10-3611-8_4

solving the math problem [22–24], managing the nano-machine and discussing the life course. Based on DNA strand displacement, the construction of the biochemistry logic circuits has significant research means by mastering the design procedures.

Compared with the previous work [25,26], the one-bit full adder-full subtractor logical operation is constructed for the first time in this paper. Based on the DNA strand displacement, there is the control terminal which concerns the function of the full adder-full subtractor. There are two kinds of function in the circuit, which are the full adder and the full subtroctor, respectively. The circuit could be applied to the construction of the biological computer in the future.

This paper is organized as follows. Firstly, the introduction is described in the Sect. 1. Then the strand displacement reaction mechanism is shown in the Sect. 2. The digit circuit and dual-rail circuit of the full adder-full subtractor is designed in the Sect. 3. The seesaw circuit and the simulation of the full adder-full subtractor are shown in the Sect. 4. Finally, the conclusion is given for the full adder-full subtractor.

2 The Background of DNA Strand Displacement

DNA strand displacement technology acts as an important technology of modern biological computing, which has been proved that it is a kind of nanoscale technologies to overcome circuit component miniaturization problem. DNA strand displacement response is a dynamic process and has the following three advantages. (1) DNA strand displacement response doesn't need special temperature requirements and can proceed in room temperature without annealing. (2) It is the spontaneous reaction without adding enzyme. (3) A dynamic cascade system can be constituted due to dynamic characteristics of DNA strand displacement response. The characteristics of DNA strand displacement technology provide a good way for building the nanoscale large-scale circuit.

In order to perform mathematical logic, DNA strand displacement cascade technology has been widely applied to the configuration of the basic DNA logic gates (AND gate, OR gate and NOT gate). DNA strand displacement reaction mechanism is shown in Fig. 1. In the Fig. 1, the domain t represents a short toehold and the domain t* is the complementary pairing of the domain t. The DNA single strand <a t b> and strand <b t c> represent input signal and output signal, respectively. The strand <b t> and strand {t*}[b t]<c> are recognition domain and the double strand complex, respectively. Firstly, the short toehold domain t of the strand <a t b> and toehold domain t* of the double strand complex have a DNA complementary pairing. Then the domain b of the DNA single strand <a t b> and domain b* of the double strand complex also conduct a DNA complementary pairing. Eventually, the output strand <b t c> falls off from the double strand complex and releases the molecule complex <a>[t b]:<b> [t]<c> The whole reaction process can be considered that a DNA single strand <a t b> replace of the DNA single strand <b t c>.

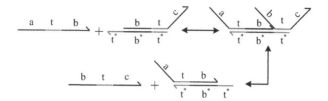

Fig. 1. The DNA strand displacement reaction process. The DNA single strand <a t b> and strand <b t c> represent input signal and output signal. The strand <b t> is recognition domain.

3   The Digit Circuit and Dual-rail Circuit

The full adder-full subtractor also is a combinational logic circuit which performs simple logic operations of four binary digits. The truth table of the full adder-full subtractor is given in Table 1. In the Table 1, there are sixteen kinds of conditions which achieve two kinds of functions. Boolean functions of logic circuit is constructed by "AND", "OR" and "NOT" gates. Based on the function of the truth table one-bit the full adder-full subtractor combinational logic circuit is shown in Fig. 2. The full adder-full subtractor logic circuit haves four inputs which are x_0, x_1, x_2 and y_0 in the left side of the logic circuit and two outputs which are y_1 and y_2 in the right side of the logic circuit, respectively. In the

Table 1. Truth table of the full adder-full subtractor.

Logical function	Input x_0	Input x_1	Input x_2	Input y_0	Output y_1	Output y_2
Full adder	0	0	0	0	0	0
	0	0	0	1	1	0
	0	0	1	0	1	0
	0	0	1	1	0	1
	0	1	0	0	1	0
	0	1	0	1	0	1
	0	1	1	0	0	1
	0	1	1	1	1	1
Full subtractor	1	0	0	0	0	0
	1	0	0	1	1	1
	1	0	1	0	1	1
	1	0	1	1	0	1
	1	1	0	0	1	0
	1	1	0	1	0	0
	1	1	1	0	0	0
	1	1	1	1	1	1

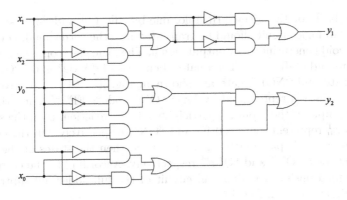

Fig. 2. Digital logic circuit of one-bit full adder-full subtractor. x_0, x_1, x_2 and y_0 are input signal, y_1 and y_2 are output signal. x_0 is the control terminal which concerns the function of the circuit. y_0 is the low level carry-bit or low level borrow-bit.

logic circuit, the input x_0 is the control terminal and concerns the function of the circuit. If the value of x_0 is "0", the logic circuit implements the function of full adder in which x_1 and x_2 are two addends, y_0, y_1 and y_2 indicate low level carry-bit the sum-bit and the high level carry-bit, respectively. On the other hand, the logic circuit achieves the function of full subtractor if the value of x_0 is "1". Under the circumstances, x_1 and x_2 are minuend and subtrahend, y_0, y_1 and y_2 indicate low level borrow-bit the difference-bit and the high level borrow-bit, respectively.

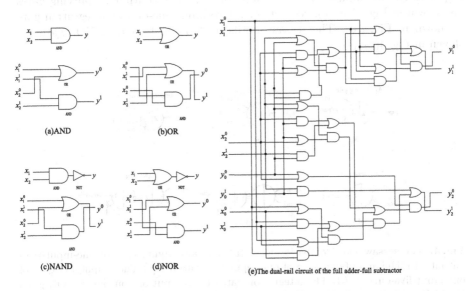

(a)AND   (b)OR

(c)NAND   (d)NOR   (e)The dual-rail circuit of the full adder-full subtractor

Fig. 3. The dual-rail logic circuits. (a) The dual-rail logic circuit of AND gate. (b) The dual-rail logic circuit of OR gate. (c) The dual-rail logic circuit of NAND gate. (d) The dual-rail logic circuit of NOR gate. (e) The dual-rail logic circuit of full adder-full subtractor.

On the basis of the given principle, one-bit the full adder-full subtractor combinational logic circuit should be translated into the corresponding dual-rail circuit to avoid generating error output signal. The logic gate consists of a pair of "AND" gate and "OR" gate. The dual-rail circuits of "AND" gate, "OR" gate, "NAND" gate and "NOR" gate are shown in Fig. 3(a)–(d), respectively. The input signal state is represented by logic "ON" and "OFF". Taking the input x_0 as an example, if the input x_0 participates in the reaction, then the states of the x_0^0 and x_0^1 represent logic "OFF" and "ON", respectively. On the contrary, if the input x_0 can't participate in the reaction, then the states of the x_0^0 and x_0^1 represent logic "ON" and "OFF" respectively. According to the corresponding logical relationship, the dual-rail circuit of the full adder-full subtractor is constructed, as shown in Fig. 3(e).

4   Seesaw Circuit and Simulation with Visual DSD

Based on DNA stand displacement response, DNA seesaw logic gates could be designed. The logic gates are divided into left side and right side, and are connected by a node, as shown in Fig. 4. In Fig. 4(a), the input acts as the input single strand <a t b>, the strand {t*}[b t]<c> is the gate note. The output 1 acts as the output strand <b t c>. And output 2 is other output strand. The red digit 0.6 is the threshold value. The value of fuel is two times of the total output value. The gates usually consist of amplifying gate which can produce multi-path outputs and integration gate which could receive multi-path inputs, respectively. One-input-four-output and one-input-five-output amplifying gates are shown in Fig. 4(b)–(c), respectively. Two-input-one-output integration gate is shown in Fig. 4(d). The seesaw motifs of "OR" gate and "AND" gate are shown in Fig. 4(e)–(f).

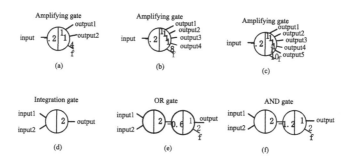

Fig. 4. The seesaw motif of basic gates. (a) The amplifying gate of one-input-two-output. (b) The amplifying gate of one-input-four-output. (c) The amplifying gate of one-input-five-output. (d) The integration gate of two-input-one-output. (e) OR gate. (f) AND gate. (Color figure online)

According to the seesaw circuit and the dual-rail logic circuit of full adder-full subtractor, the seesaw circuit of full adder-full subtractor is shown in Fig. 5, which could be simulated in the Visual DSD. There will be sixteen outputs which are produced along with the sixteen inputs. The simulation results of the full adder-full subtractor are shown in Fig. 6. In the Fig. 6, the blue curve and yellow curve represent the value of y_1^0 and y_1^1, respectively; the red line and green line separately indicate the value of y_2^0 and y_2^1, respectively In this paper, the total concentration of the reaction is 1000 nm. When the range is 0–100 nm, it expresses the logic "0". On the other hand, it expresses the logic "1" if the range is 900–1000 nm.

If the control terminal x_0 is "0", then the function of logic circuit is full adder whose simulation results are shown in Fig. 6(a)–(h). Under this cases, if the input signal $x_1x_2y_0$ is "000", then the output signal y_1y_2 is "00" in Fig. 6(a). If the input signal $x_1x_2y_0$ is "001", then the output signal y_1y_2 is "10" in Fig. 6(b). If the input signal $x_1x_2y_0$ is "010", then the output signal y_1y_2 is "10", as shown in Fig. 6(c). If the input signal $x_1x_2y_0$ is "011", then the output signal y_1y_2 is "01", as shown in Fig. 6(d). If the input signal $x_1x_2y_0$ is "100", then the output

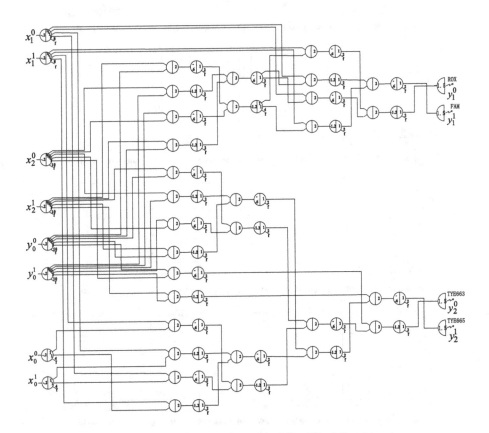

Fig. 5. The seesaw circuit of one-bit full adder-full subtractor.

signal y_1y_2 is "10" in Fig. 6(e). If the input signal $x_1x_2y_0$ is "101", then the output signal y_1y_2 is "01" in Fig. 6(f). If the input signal $x_1x_2y_0$ is "110", then the output signal y_1y_2 is "01", as shown in Fig. 6(g). If the input signal $x_1x_2y_0$ is "111", then the output signal y_1y_2 is "11", as shown in Fig. 6(h).

If the control terminal x_0 is "1", then the function of the logic circuit is full subtractor whose simulation results are shown in Fig. 6(i)–(p). If the input signal $x_1x_2y_0$ is "000", then the output signal y_1y_2 is "00", as shown in Fig. 6(i). If the input signal $x_1x_2y_0$ is "001", then the output signal y_1y_2 is "11" in Fig. 6(j). If the input signal $x_1x_2y_0$ is "010", then the output signal y_1y_2 is "11", as shown in Fig. 6(k). If the input signal $x_1x_2y_0$ is "011", then the output signal y_1y_2 is "01", as shown in Fig. 6(l). When the input signal $x_1x_2y_0$ is "100", the output signal

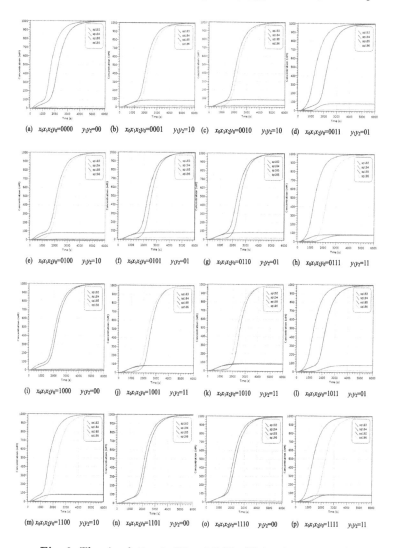

Fig. 6. The simulation in Visual DSD. (Color figure online)

y_1y_2 is "00", as shown in Fig. 6(m). If the input signal $x_1x_2y_0$ is "101", then the output signal y_1y_2 is "11" in Fig. 6(n). If the input signal $x_1x_2y_0$ is "110", then the output signal y_1y_2 is "11", as shown in Fig. 6(o). If the input signal $x_1x_2y_0$ is "111", then the output signal y_1y_2 is "01", as shown in Fig. 6(p).

According to the simulation results, the following conclusions can be obtained. The logic "ON" and logic "OFF" curves both enter into the stable area, which express the logic "1" and logic "0" correctly, respectively. The simulation results have a high validity.

5   Conclusion

In this paper, one-bit full adder-full subtractor logic circuit has been constructed by DNA strand displacement. Then the full adder-full subtractor combinational logic circuit has been converted to the corresponding the dual-rail logic circuit and the biochemical logic circuit. Finally, the seesaw logic circuit of the full adder-full subtractor is simulated in the visual DSD. The correctness of simulation results proves that the DNA strand displacement technique is a feasible method in the study of biochemical circuit. As a result of the limitation of the current scientific research platform and technology, the biochemical experiment also needs to continue to be explored, which will be the focus of the next research direction.

Acknowledgments. The work is supported by the State Key Program of the National Natural Science Foundation of China (Grant No. 61632002), the National Natural Science Foundation of China (Grant Nos. 61472371, 61472372, 61572446, 61602424 and 61603348), China Postdoctoral Science Foundation funded project (Grant Nos. 2015M570641 and 2016T90687), Basic and Frontier Technology Research Program of Henan Province (Grant No. 162300410220), Key Program of Higher Education of China Henan Province (Grant No. 17A120005) and the Science Foundation of for Doctorate Research of Zhengzhou University of Light Industry (Grant No. 2014BSJJ044).

References

1. Adleman, L.M.: Molecular computation of solutions to combinatorial problems. Science **226**, 1021–1024 (1994)
2. Carlson, R.: The changing economics of DNA synthesis. Nat. Biotechnol. **27**, 1091–1094 (2009)
3. Turberfield, A.J., Mitchell, J.C., Yurke, B., Mills Jr., A.P., Blakey, M.I., Simmel, F.C.: DNA fuel for free-running nanomachines. Phys. Rev. Lett. **90**, 118102-1–118102-4 (2003)
4. Yin, P., Choi, H.M.T., Calvert, C.R., Pierce, N.A.: Programming biomolecularself-assembly pathways. Nature **451**, 318–322 (2008)
5. Gothelf, K.V., LaBean, T.H.: DNA-programmed assembly of nanostructures. Org. Biomol. Chem. **3**, 4023–4037 (2005)
6. Shi, X.L., Lu, W., Wang, Z.Y., Pan, L.Q., Cui, G.Z., Xu, J., La Bean, T.H.: Programmable DNA tile self-assembly using a hierarchical sub-tile strategy. Nanotechnology **25**(7), 075602 (2014)

7. Zhang, D.Y., Turberfield, A.J., Yurke, B., Winfree, E.: Engineering entropy-drivenreactions and networks catalyzed by DNA. Science **318**, 1121–1125 (2007)
8. Seelig, G., Soloveichik, D., Zhang, D.Y., Winfree, E.: Enzyme-free nucleic acid logiccircuits. Science **314**, 1585–1588 (2006)
9. Chiniforooshan, E., Doty, D., Kari, L., Seki, S.: Scalable, time-responsive, digital, energy-efficient molecular circuits using DNA strand displacement. In: Sakakibara, Y., Mi, Y. (eds.) DNA 2010. LNCS, vol. 6518, pp. 25–36. Springer, Heidelberg (2011). doi:10.1007/978-3-642-18305-8_3
10. Srinivas, N., Ouldridge, T.E., Sulc, P., Schaeffer, J.M., Yurke, B., Louis, A.A., Doye, J.P.K., Winfree, E.: On the biophysics and kinetics of toehold-mediated DNA strand displacement. Nucleic Acids Res. **41**(22), 10641–10658 (2013)
11. Shi, X.L., Wang, Z.Y., Deng, C.Y., Song, T., Pan, L.Q., Chen, Z.H.: A Novel Bio-Sensor Based on DNA Strand Displacement. PLoS ONE **9**(10), e108856 (2014). doi:10.1371/journal.pone.0108856
12. Yang, J., Dong, C., Dong, Y.F., Liu, S., Pan, L.Q., Zhang, C.: Logic nanoparticle beacon triggered by the binding-induced effect of multiple inputs. ACS Appl. Mater. Interfaces **6**(16), 14486–14492 (2014)
13. Xu, J.: Probe machine. IEEE Trans. Neural Netw. Learn. Syst. **27**(7), 1405–1416 (2016)
14. Zhang, D.Y., Winfree, E.: J. Am. Chem. Soc. **131**, 17303–17314 (2009)
15. Soloveichik, D., Seelig, G., Winfree, E.: Proc. Nat. Acad. Sci. U.S.A. **107**, 5393–53989 (2010)
16. Phillips, A., Cardelli, L.: J. R. Soc. Interface **6** (2009). doi:10.1098/rsif.2009.0072. focus
17. Eckhoff, G., Codrea, V., Ellington, A.D., Chen, X.: J. Syst. Chem. **1**, 13 (2010). doi:10.1186/1759-2208-1-13
18. Qian, L., Winfree, E.: A simple DNA gate motif for synthesizing large-scale circuits. J. R. Soc. Interface **1**, 13 (2011). doi:10.1098/rsif.2010.0729
19. Lund, K., Manzo, A.J., Dabby, N., Michelotti, N., Johnson-Buck, A., Nangreave, J., Taylor, J.S., Pei, R., Stojanovic, M.N., Walter, N.G., Winfree, E., Yan, H.: Nature **465**, 206–210 (2010)
20. Qian, L., Soloveichik, D., Winfree, E.: Efficient turing-universal computation with DNA polymers. In: Sakakibara, Y., Mi, Y. (eds.) DNA 2010. LNCS, vol. 6518, pp. 123–140. Springer, Heidelberg (2011). doi:10.1007/978-3-642-18305-8_12
21. Gaber, R., Lebar, T., Majerle, A., Ster, B., Dobnikar, A., Bencina, M., Jerala, R.: Designable DNA-binding domain enable construction of logic circuit in mammaliancells. Nat. Chem. Biol. **10**, 203–208 (2014)
22. Zhang, Z., Li, J., Pan, L., Ye, Y., Zeng, X., Song, T., Zhang, X., Wang, E.K.: Anovel visualization of DNA sequences, reflecting GC-content. MATCH Commun. Math. Comput. Chem **72**, 533–550 (2014)
23. Zeng, X., Xu, L., Liu, X., Pan, L.: On languages generated by spiking neural P systems with weights. Inform. Sci. **278**, 423–433 (2014)
24. Zhang, X., Liu, Y., Luo, B., Pan, L.: Computational power of tissue P systems for generating control languages. Inform. Sci. **278**, 285–297 (2014)
25. Wang, Y., Tian, G., Hou, H., et al.: Simple logic computation based on the DNA strand displacement. J. Comput. Theor. Nanosci. **11**, 1975–1982 (2014)
26. Cui, G., Zhang, J., Cui, Y., et al.: DNA strand-displacement digital logic circuit with fluorescence resonance energy transfer detection. J. Comput. Theor. Nanosci. **12**, 2095–2100 (2015)

Logic Gate Based on Circular DNA Structure with Strand Displacement

Guangzhao Cui, Xi Wang, Xuncai Zhang$^{(\boxtimes)}$, Ying Niu, and Hua Liu

College of Electrical and Information Engineering,
Henan Key Lab of Information-based Electrical Appliances,
No. 5 Dongfeng Road, Zhengzhou 450002, China
zhangxuncai@163.com

Abstract. In this work, we fabricated two logic gates based on circular DNA structure – XOR gate and AND gate calculation model with the principle of complementary base pairing and the technology of fluorescence labeling. Whereafter, we constructed a simple half-adder model based on the two logic gates. This model is simple, but it can realize more complex logic operations in theory. And the experiment process is convenient to operate, the results are easy to realize.

Keywords: Logic gates · Circular DNA mode · DNA strand displacement · Fluorescence beacon · Half-adder

1 Introduction

Due to DNA has a unique ability to complementary base pairing and to produce a variety of reconfigurable DNA self-assembly structures. It is an ideal engineering material for molecular computing. Since 1994, Adleman [1] demonstrated the use of DNA strand displacement to perform logical operations by solving the Hamiltonian path problem. The idea of DNA computing has been leaded to, and since then, biological logic gates have been produced [2–4], such as common logic operations: OR, AND, NOT, XOR and so on [5,6], multi input logic circuit model [7], molecular switches, cascade amplifiers [8,9], programmable DNA tile self-assembly [10], logic nanoparticle beacon [11] and so on. At present, the computational functions based on biological systems have been applied in bioengineering and nanomedicine [12]. These systems include enzyme catalyzed [13], DNA reaction networks, DNAzyme facilitated reactions [14], memory system [15], neural networks [16], probe machine [17], disease diagnosis [18] and so no. Based on these natural dynamics systems, we can develop reliable constructs that perform logical operations after addition of nucleic acid inputs where strand displacement drives the calculation and production of the output.

In addition, various molecular operations, such as fluorescence techniques, self assembly techniques and strand displacement, have been utilized in the development of DNA computing. In this model, because of the fluorescence technique is easy to observe and detect advantage, DNA strand displacement with fluorescent

M. Gong et al. (Eds.): BIC-TA 2016, Part I, CCIS 681, pp. 39–46, 2016.
DOI: 10.1007/978-981-10-3611-8_5

labeling for constructing various molecular computing models develops rapidly [19]. DNAzymes in which the presence or absence of the fluorescence resonance energy transfer (FRET) signal was used as output to accomplish NOT, AND, and XOR logical operations. Fluorescence quenching and releasing were used as readout of the structures that were combined for constructing logic systems [20]. When the fluorescence is quenching, we customary consider as the output is 0. And when fluorescence is releasing, we customary consider as the output is 1. DNA strand displacement was used to initiate the release of entrapped molecules based on the logic computation [21–27], and in another study an automated DNA transporter that delivered a DNA strand in a programmed pattern was developed [22]. DNA strand branch migration has accelerated the development of research parallel computing, cryptography and nanoelectronics. And the DNA strand displacement with fluorescent technology will be utilized to design more complex structure, also came to widely use in the field of electronic calculation, such as logic gate and logic circuit.

In this paper, a series of logical components are constructed by using the principle of Watson-Crick complementary base pairing, DNA stand displacement and the technology of fluorescence labeling. These components introduced into the DNA strands worked as the input, and the output of the logic module is reading by the fluorescence detection technology. These structures are simple and stable. In addition, on this basis, we constructed a half-adder model. This model is simple, but provides important support to build more complex molecular logic circuit.

2   Design and Construction of Logic Gate Model

Here, we use a DNA circular containing complementary strand a/a* and two single DNA strand to form a basic structure. This structure can report a rational designed of two logic models – XOR gate and AND gate – based on the principle of Watson-Crick complementary base pairing, DNA stand displacement and the technology of fluorescence labeling.

2.1   Principle of the Proposed Method: XOR Gate

We fabricated a XOR logic computing model with Watson-Crick complementary base pairing. First, we designed two DNA signal strands ⟨ab∗⟩ and ⟨a∗e∗⟩, with a DNA circular containing complementary strand [a/a*] served as the basic device. And ⟨a∗⟩, ⟨a⟩ was labeled by a corresponding quencher with a fluorophore on their end. The mode is shown in Fig. 1.

Then, we design the XOR gate based on the basic structure. And the mechanism of the XOR gate computing model is shown in Fig. 2. Because when the quencher is close to the fluorophore, fluorescence is quenching and when the quencher is separate to the fluorophore, fluorescence is releasing. So, we record the fluorescence intensity. If the fluorescence signal is observed, output Y1 = 1, otherwise, Y1 = 0.

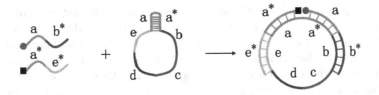

Fig. 1. The process of the basic device used for XOR gate

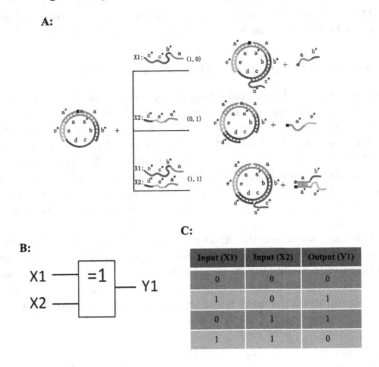

Fig. 2. (A) Schematic representation of XOR gate logic computing model. (B) XOR gate logic computing model electrical symbol defining inputs X1 and X2 and the output Y1. (C) Truth table of XOR gate logic computing model.

In the $(0, 0)$ state, where neither X1 nor X2 is present, there is no fluorescence signal been observed. So, the output reading is 0.

In the $(1, 0)$ state, X1 is added to the logic computing system. The X1 strand and the basic device form a double strands structure a/a*, b/b*, c/c*. At the same time, X1 displace the single stranded $\langle ab* \rangle$. At the new model, fluorescent groups and quencher BHQ wasn't present. There is fluorescence signal be observed. Consequently, the output reading is 1.

In the $(0, 1)$ state, only X2 is added to the system. Using base complementation pairing rule, the X2 strand could be combined with the basic mode to form a new structure. The single strand $\langle a * e* \rangle$ is replaced, at the end of $\langle a* \rangle$, the quencher BHQ and the fluorescent groups were separated. So, there is fluorescence signal be observed. Consequently, the output reading is 1.

In the (1, 1) state, both X1 and X2 are added to the system. This makes single strand ⟨ab∗⟩ and ⟨a ∗ e∗⟩ are displaced, and they could hybridized complementary with a form a double strands structure a/a*. The fluorescent was present, however, the quencher BHQ was present also, and it was approached with the end of the strand a fluorescent groups. The fluorescence is quenching. Accordingly, the fluorescence signal is not observed and the output reading is 0.

In conclusion, only input X1 or input X2 the output reading is 1, otherwise, the output reading is 0. So, the logic computing we have designed is an XOR gate. The electrical symbol of the XOR logic computing model is shown in Fig. 2(B) and (C) is the truth table. The logical expression is Y1 = (X1) * X2 + X1 * (X2).

2.2   Principle of the Proposed Method: AND Gate

First, we designed two DNA signal strands ⟨a∗g∗e∗⟩ and ⟨a∗f∗h∗⟩, with a DNA circular containing complementary strand a/a. Both ⟨a∗⟩ and ⟨a⟩ were labeled with a corresponding quencher and a fluorophore on their end, respectively. Then, adding a single DNA strand ⟨a ∗ fh⟩ form a double strands structure (a/a*, f/f*, h/h*). In the new circular structure add a DNA strand ⟨ap⟩, and at the end of a label a fluorophore. With the same principle, add the single strand ⟨aeg⟩ and the DNA strand ⟨a ∗ q⟩ with a corresponding quencher on its end in every new structure according to the same order. At the last, the basic model is shown in Fig. 3.

The following, we design the AND gate based on the basic device. And the mechanism of the XOR gate computing model is shown in Fig. 2. The result of the AND gate when we add two single strands X1X2, their base sequence same as the strands, of XOR gate. The quencher is close to the fluorophore, fluorescence is quenching and when the quencher is separate to the fluorophore, fluorescence

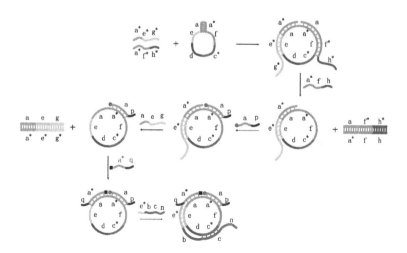

Fig. 3. The process of the basic device used for AND gate.

is releasing. So, we record the fluorescence intensity. If the fluorescence signal is observed, the output Y2 = 1, otherwise, Y2 = 0.

In the (0, 0) state, where neither X1 nor X2 is present, there is no fluorescence signal is observed. So, the output reading is 0.

In the (1, 0) state, only X1 is added to the system. The X1 strand and the basic device form a double strands structure [n/n*, c/c*, b/b*], but the fluorescence not released, so the output reads 0.

In the (0, 1) state, X2 is added to the logic computing system. There is no structure could hybridized complementary with the X2, so the quencher is close to the fluorophore, fluorescence is quenching and the output reading is 0.

In the (1, 1) state, both X1 and X2 are added to the system. Because X1 could hybridized complementary with the basic model and getting the new structure could hybridized complementary with the single strand $\langle d * e * a* \rangle$. The single strand $\langle a * q \rangle$ is replaced. At the ends of the strand a* quencher BHQ with the strand a fluorescent groups was separated, and the fluorescence signal is observed. Consequently, the output reads 1.

In conclusion, as long as any one input is 1, the output reads 0. Only both input X1 and X2, the output reads 1. So, the logic computing we have designed is an AND gate. Figure 3(B) express the electrical symbol of the AND logic computing model and the truth table is shown in Fig. 3(C). The logical expression is Y2 = X1 * X2 (Fig. 4).

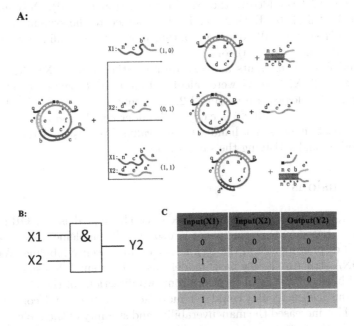

Fig. 4. (A) Schematic representation of AND gate logic computing model. (B) AND gate logic computing model electrical symbol defining inputs X1 and X2 and the output Y2. (C) Truth table of AND gate logic computing model.

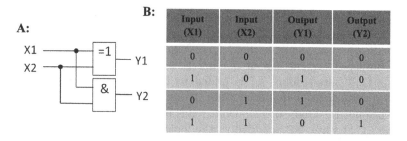

Fig. 5. (A) Half-adder logic computing model electrical symbol defining inputs X1 and X2 and the output Y1, Y2. (B) Truth table of half-adder logic computing model.

3   Result and Discussion

In this article, we use a DNA circular containing complementary strand [a/a*] and two single DNA strand to form a basic structure, and we designed two different basic device. Then add the X1 and X2 to the basic model to fabricate two logic gates – XOR gate and AND gate for calculation with the principle of complementary base pairing and the technology of fluorescence labeling. Using these logic computing gates could fabricate a simple half-adder, Fig. 5(A) express the electrical symbol of the half-adder model and the truth table is shown in Fig. 5(B). Only X1 is added to the system, the output is (1, 0). Only input X2, the output is still (1, 0). Both X1 and X2 are added to the system, the output is (0, 1). This simple half-adder computing model could realize two a binary encoding addition circuit in theory.

Half-adder has two inputs and two outputs, the input is X1, X2, and the output is Y1, Y2. X1 and X2 were calculated after XOR logic gate getting Y1, and getting AND logic gate getting Y2. We count up X1 and X2 getting the output, of which Y1 is and Y2 is carry. Half-adder could produce binary value, but for its part, it does not handle binary value. We designed the molecular "half-adder" model satisfying the same theory.

4   Conclusions

In summary, we achieve a rational designed of two logic models — XOR gate and AND gate — based on the principle of Watson-Crick complementary base pairs, DNA stand displacement and the technology of fluorescence labeling. When the circular DNA structure as the basic model was added some DNA signal strands, they could begin biochemical reaction from two directions of the circular structure, and the fuel molecules could get more accurate fixed and control in the structure. This increased the maneuverability and stability of the molecular logic operation. At the last, we constructed a simple half-adder model, which achieved the half plus operation based on DNA strand displacement. The half-adder logic model is simple, but it can realize more complex logic operations in theory. Though the model we fabricated is ideally, it is easy to be operated in biological experiment. However, in the actual biological experiment, there are still some uncontrollable factors, such as temperature, mismatch and so on. Firstly, temperature would have an influence on the biological reaction. For example, the reaction would inadequately under low temperature. So, the fluorescence would not be released completely in the result of Yi (i = 1, 2), such that the output reads 1 while we record the fluorescence intensity produce in the Yi. In addition, it would also form many not ideal products. We will adjust some parameters include temperature and material concentration to achieve this model. In the future, we hope to verify the feasibility of the model by biological experiments.

Acknowledgments. This work was supported by the National Natural Science Foundation of China (Grant Nos. 61602424, 61472371, 61472372, 61572446), Basic and Frontier Technology Research Program of Henan Province (Grant No. 142300413214), Program for Science and Technology Innovation Talents in Universities of Henan Province (Grant No. 15HASTIT019), and Young Backbone Teachers Project of Henan province (Grant No. 2013GGJS-106).

References

1. Adleman, L.M.: Molecular computations to combinatorial problems. Sci. New. Ser. **266**(5187), 1021–1024 (1994)
2. Katsikis, G., Cybulski, J.S., Prakash, M.: Synchronous universal droplet logic and control. Nat. Phys. **11**(7), 588–596 (2015)
3. Kramer, B.P., Fischer, C., Fussenegger, M.: BioLogic gates enable logical transcription control in mammalian cells. Biotechnol. Bioeng. **87**(4), 478–484 (2004)
4. Yong, L., Wang, L., Hea, K.: A biomimetic colorimetric logic gate system based on multi-functional peptide-mediated gold nanoparticle assembly. Nanoscale **8**(16), 8591–8599 (2016)
5. Fu, X.F., Sun, W., Guo, R.: Molecular logic function materials. Progr. Chem. **21**(5), 957–963 (2009)
6. Arun, V., Shukla, N.K., Singh, A.K.: Design and performance analysis of multiple all optical logic gates in a single photonic circuit. Opt. Quantum Electron. **48**(1), 236–244 (2016)
7. Bhoj, A.N., Simsir, M.O., Jha, N.K.: Fault models for logic circuits in the multigate era. IEEE Trans. Nanotechnol. **1**(11), 182–193 (2012)
8. Graugnard, E., Kellis, D.L., Bui, H., Barnes, S., Hughes, W.L., Yurke, B.: DNA-controlled excitonic switches. Nano Lett. **12**(47), 2117–2122 (2012)
9. Zhang, C., Wu, L., Yang, J., Liu, S., Xu, J.: A molecular logical switch beacon controlled by thiolated DNA signals. Chem. Commun. **3**(49), 11308–11310 (2013)
10. Shi, X.L., Lu, W., Wang, Z.Y., Pan, L.Q., Cui, G.Z., Xu, J., LaBean, T.H.: Programmable DNA tile self-assembly using a hierarchical sub-tile strategy. Nanotechnology **25**(7), 075602 (2014)
11. Yang, J., Dong, C., Dong, Y.F., Liu, S., Pan, L.Q., Zhang, C.: Logic nanoparticle beacon triggered by the binding-induced effect of multiple inputs. ACS Appl. Mater. Interfaces **6**(16), 14486–14492 (2014)
12. Song, T., Pan, L.: Spiking neural P systems with request rules. Neurocomputing **193**(2), 193–200 (2016)
13. Song, T., Liu, X., Zhao, Y., Zhang, X.: Spiking neural P systems with white hole neurons. IEEE Trans. Nanobiosci. (2016). doi:10.1109/TNB.2016.2598879

14. Song, T., Pan, Z., Wong, D.M., Wang, X.: Design of logic gates using spiking neural P systems with homogeneous neurons and astrocytes-like control. Inf. Sci. **372**, 380–391 (2016)
15. Wang, X., Song, T., Gong, F., Pan, Z.: On the computational power of spiking neural P systems with self-organization. Sci. Rep. doi:10.1038/srep27624
16. Shi, X., Wu, X., Song, T., Li, X.: Construction of DNA nanotubes with controllable diameters and patterns by using hierarchical DNA sub-tiles. Nanoscale. doi:10.1039/C6NR02695H
17. Fan, W.P., Bu, W.B., Shi, J.L.: On the latest three-stage development of nanomedicines based on upconversion nanoparticles. Adv. Mater. **28**(21), 3987–4011 (2016)
18. Vickery, A., Mulholland, A.J., Kamp, V.: On the temperature dependence of enzyme-catalyzed rates. Biochemistry **55**(12), 1681–1688 (2016)
19. Zhang, C., Yang, J., Jiang, S.X., Liu, Y., Yan, H.: DNAzyme-based logic gate-mediated DNA self-assembly. Nano Lett. **16**(1), 736–741 (2016)
20. Jing, Y., Dong, Y.F., Pan, L.Q.: Logic nanoparticle beacon triggered by the binding-induced effect of multiple inputs. ACS Appl. Mater. **6**(16), 14486–14492 (2014)
21. Chen, C.W.: Segmentation of DNA using simple recurrent neural network. Knowl. Based Syst. **1**(26), 271–280 (2012)
22. Xu, J.: Probe machine. IEEE Trans. Neural Netw. Learn. Syst. **27**(7), 1405–1416 (2016)
23. Zhu, Q.C., Liu, G., Kai, M.: DNA aptamers in the diagnosis and treatment of human diseases. Molecules **20**(12), 20979–20997 (2015)
24. Frezza, B.M., Cockroft, S.L., Ghadiri, M.R.: Modular multi-level circuits from immobilized DNA-based logic gates. J. Am. Chem. Soc. **129**(48), 14875–14879 (2007)
25. Zhou, X., Wu, X., Yoon, J.: A dual FRET based fluorescent probe as a multiple logic system. Chem. Commun. (Camb.) **51**(1), 111–113 (2015)
26. Li, W., Zhang, F., Yan, H., Liu, Y.: DNA based arithmetic function: a half adder based on DNA strand displacement. Nanoscale **8**(6), 3775–3784 (2016)
27. Marco, B., Eugenia, O.M.: Programming self-assembly of DNA tiles. Fundamenta Informaticae **143**(1–2), 35–49 (2016)

The Working Operation Problem Based on Probe Machine Model

Jing Yang[✉] and Zhixiang Yin

School of Science, Anhui University of Science and Technology,
Huainan 232001, Anhui, China
junweisun@yeah.net

Abstract. The working operation problem is an old problem that it is difficult to effectively solve the combinatorial mathematics. So far this problem has not been completely effectively solved, and it is an non-deterministic polynomial (NP)-complete problem. This paper mainly uses the probe machine model and combines the advantages of the nanometer-material to design a computing model for the working operation problem. It structures a database of the vertex and edge, then encodes as a probe library. Using computing platforms to get the solution to be tested, and finding all vertices of the directed Hamilton path which is the solution of the problem. The probe machine is a parallel computing model starting from the bottom; thereby it can improve the effectiveness of the calculation in theory.

Keywords: Probe machine · NP-complete problem · Working operation problem

1 Introduction

In 2016, Xu [1] and his research team reported major breakthrough article "Probe Machine" at the IEEE transactions on neural networks and learned system journal in computer science. This paper presents the first computing model beyond Turing machine [2] that is called the probe machine. It is computing model from the underlying whole of parallel. It is just one probe operation to find all solutions of problems for the NP-complete problem, while the computer can not handle today, such as Hamilton Problems, Vertex graph coloring problem, and so on. All NP-complete problems based on the Turing machine are equivalent in polynomial time, which means that it has no NP-completely problem puzzled mankind in the probe model. Some peering works on DNA computing can be found in [6–8].

The probe machine is divided into two types of transfer and connection. The probe machine is composed by the database, the probe libraries, data controller, the controller probe, probe computing, computing platform, the detector, the true solution, and residual memory support recycling. In order to composite nano-particles and DNA molecules as data and make use of the DNA molecule

© Springer Nature Singapore Pte Ltd. 2016
M. Gong et al. (Eds.): BIC-TA 2016, Part I, CCIS 681, pp. 47–53, 2016.
DOI: 10.1007/978-981-10-3611-8_6

as probe, the probe machine of connection type will be introduced. So it is the nanometer DNA computer. The difference with the Turing machine is: the data of the probe machine is free on placement pattern space, and it can be directly processed information between any pair of data, which indicates a powerful parallelism with the increase of the size of the data, with the increasing size of data, and the information processing capabilities dramatically.

The working operation problem for the production process is an important problem for the organization. It is a variety of parts, and how to arrange the appropriate equipment and decided on their order processing should be firstly considered. To enhance efficiency, it is beneficial for full using the equipment and shortening the production cycle. Here, we introduce a variety of jobs on a single machine production working operation problem.

We can suppose machine that it must manufacture a variety of parts J_1, $J_2,...,J_n$. For example, in a factory, each job J_i is a type of mold. In order to manufacture next job, machine must be adjusted after a job. If the adjustment time is t_{ij} from J_i to J_j parts, we seek a machining order that the entire machinery of the adjustment period is least. In fact, this problem seeks for the smallest weight to the directed Hamilton path in a weighted directed graph. At present, there is no known effective method. First we have to translate the problem into the directed graph G:

(1) The job $J_i, i = 1, 2, \cdots, n$ is represented vertex v_i of the directed graph G.
(2) A is an arc set of the directed graph G, and $(v_i, v_j) \in A$ if and only if $t_{ij} \leq t_{ji}$.
(3) Empowering t_{ij} to arc (v_i, v_j).

Thus, a working operation problem is corresponding with a directed Hamilton path of the minimum weights sum of directed weighted graph. The vertex order of the directed Hamilton path is corresponding to processing the order of the job.

This paper attempts to use the connection type probe computing model for working operation problem. Since the underlying model is an efficient full parallel resistance, it can be more effective for working operation problem.

2   The Probe Computing Principles

The probe machine includes nine sections, which are $X, Y, \sigma_1, \sigma_2, \tau, \lambda, \eta, Q, C$, respectively. The database X includes n data pool $X_1, X_2, X_3...X_n$. Each data pool X_i stores huge element x_i. Each cell consists of data and data fiber. And data cell has only one, but the data types of fibers has p_i, as shown in Fig. 1.

The probe of biological computing is used to detect a nucleotide sequence, wherein the molecular beacon has been widely used and developed as a new type of fluorescent probe in recent years [3–5]. The probe machine is similar to an existing probe meaning, but it is an abstract concept. If x_i^l and x_t^a can be the probe, it can be connected with the data elements x_i^l and x_t^a by connected probe

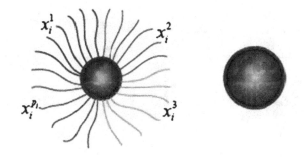

Fig. 1. The structure of data cell

$\tau^{x_i^l x_t^a}$. It is named operator connection, denoted by $\tau^{x_i^l x_t^a}$. Its direction is from x_i to x_j. According to the data types of fiber, we structure the probe pool Y_{it}, and different probe pools constitute a probe library Y (Fig. 2).

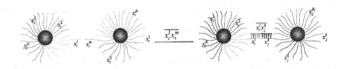

Fig. 2. The diagram of the connect operator process

The data controller σ_1 and the probe controller σ_2 respectively take the required number of data and probes into the computing platform λ. Be probe operation, and then through the detector η. Will be the result, respectively, in the true solution storage Q or residual limb collector C.

3 The Working Operation Problem Description

The paper uses a specific example to illustrate the molecular processes operating methods of the problem. Assuming that a machine can product 5 jobs $J_1, J_2, \cdots, J_5$. End processing needs change after J_i in order to process J_j. We know that the time required when we change from the mold of J_i to J_j are shown in the adjust matrix. First of all, we make the working operating problem matching to the graph G. For the encoding operation and convenience, we consider a simple working operating problem. Even to the DNA computing, the problem is still difficult. Although the figure can easily see that the best sort of work, but with our approach, the more complex plans can also be calculated, and it is almost difficult. If the degree of difficulty on the difference, it is only in the encoding and molecular aspects of the operation of the pilot in a little more trouble. We introduce the above-mentioned algorithm corresponding to the molecular steps.

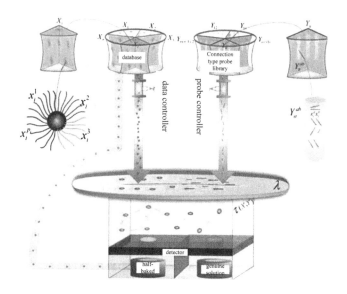

Fig. 3. A structure model for the connection type of probe machine

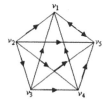

	J_1	J_2	J_3	J_4	J_5
J_1	0	6	4	5	1
J_2	2	0	1	3	2
J_3	3	4	0	1	2
J_4	1	5	6	0	1
J_5	1	3	4	3	0

Fig. 4. The graph of working operation problem and its adjust matrix

Algorithm
Step1 Structure database X.

$$X = \bigcup_{i=1}^{n} E^2(v_i)$$

Among them $E^2(v_i)$ is a set of directed two long that v_i is the center. Any directed two long $(v_l v_i v_j, i \neq l, j, l \neq j)$ is named x_{ilj}, and every x_{ilj} has two data fibers, be named x_{ilj}^l, x_{ilj}^j. Its direction is from v_l through v_i to v_j. In this example, database is:

$$X = \bigcup_{i=1}^{n} E^2(v_i), i = 1, 2, 3, 4, 5$$

$$E^2(v_1) = \{x_{125}, x_{135}, x_{145}\}$$

$$E^2(v_3) = \{x_{324}, x_{321}, x_{325}\}$$

$$E^2(v_4) = \{x_{431}, x_{421}, x_{435}, x_{425}\}$$
$$E^2(v_5) = \{x_{541}, x_{531}, x_{521}\}$$

Structure database according to Fig. 3. There have 13 types data, and 13 types data fibers, among that the length of data fiber is directly proportional to the weight in the examples.

Structure of 13 types of nanometer particles (2.5 nm) as 13 types data cell. Code DNA sequence for 13 type data fibers, and then synthesize corresponding DNA strands. Thus, DNA strands (data fibers) embed in the corresponding nanometer particles (data cell).

$$\Im(x_{125}) = x_{125}^5, \Im(x_{135}) = x_{135}^5, \Im(x_{145}) = x_{145}^5, \Im(x_{324}) = x_{324}^4, \Im(x_{321}) = x_{321}^1$$

$$\Im(x_{325}) = x_{325}^5, \Im(x_{431}) = x_{431}^1, \Im(x_{421}) = x_{421}^1, \Im(x_{435}) = x_{435}^5, \Im(x_{425}) = x_{425}^5$$

$$\Im(x_{541}) = x_{541}^1, \Im(x_{531}) = x_{531}^1, \Im(x_{521}) = x_{521}^1$$

Step2 Structure probe library based on the conditions of the probe.

In the example, to avoid small elements gathered by the probe after the operation, and affect the calculation, design of probe conditions between two elements is:

Between data x_{ilj}, x_{tab}, the probe need to meet and only meet one of the following conditions

$$(1)\ |\{i, l, j\} \bigcap \{t, a, b\}| = |\{l.j\} \bigcap \{a, b\}| = 1$$

$$(2)\ t \in \{l, j\}, i \in \{a, b\}, and |\{l, j\} \bigcap \{a, b\}| = 0$$

Structure the corresponding probe pool for the different data fibers, and structure a probe library. The structure of the probe is on the basis of the Xu Jin's probe principle [1].

These probe libraries include 31 probes.

$$Y_{13} = \{\overline{x_{321}^1 x_{125}^5}, \overline{x_{321}^1 x_{135}^5}, \overline{x_{321}^1 x_{145}^5}$$

$$Y_{14} = \{\overline{x_{431}^1 x_{125}^5}, \overline{x_{431}^1 x_{135}^5}, \overline{x_{431}^1 x_{145}^5}, \overline{x_{421}^1 x_{125}^5}, \overline{x_{421}^1 x_{135}^5}, \overline{x_{421}^1 x_{145}^5}$$

$$Y_{15} = \{\overline{x_{541}^1 x_{125}^5}, \overline{x_{541}^1 x_{135}^5}, \overline{x_{541}^1 x_{145}^5}, \overline{x_{531}^1 x_{125}^5}, \overline{x_{531}^1 x_{135}^5}, \overline{x_{531}^1 x_{145}^5},$$
$$\overline{x_{521}^1 x_{125}^5}, \overline{x_{521}^1 x_{135}^5}, \overline{x_{521}^1 x_{145}^5}, \overline{x_{125}^5 x_{541}^1}, \overline{x_{135}^5 x_{541}^1}, \overline{x_{145}^5 x_{541}^1},$$
$$\overline{x_{125}^5 x_{531}^1}, \overline{x_{135}^5 x_{531}^1}, \overline{x_{145}^5 x_{531}^1}, \overline{x_{125}^5 x_{521}^1}, \overline{x_{135}^5 x_{521}^1}, \overline{x_{145}^5 x_{521}^1}\}$$

$$Y_{34} = \{\overline{x_{324}^4 x_{431}^1}, \overline{x_{324}^4 x_{435}^5}, \overline{x_{324}^4 x_{421}^1}, \overline{x_{324}^4 x_{425}^5}\}$$

$$Y_{35} = \{\overline{x_{325}^5 x_{531}^1}, \overline{x_{325}^5 x_{541}^1}, \overline{x_{325}^5 x_{521}^1}\}$$

$$Y_{45} = \{\overline{x_{435}^5 x_{541}^1}, \overline{x_{435}^5 x_{531}^1}, \overline{x_{435}^5 x_{521}^1}, \overline{x_{425}^5 x_{541}^1}, \overline{x_{425}^5 x_{531}^1}, \overline{x_{425}^5 x_{521}^1}\}$$

Step3 Perform the operation and obtain the feasible solution. After testing platform, we get all the solution of a problem.

The probe machine takes the required number of data, the probe from the probe pool in the database, the probe library for the quantity of data using the data controller σ_1, and the probe controller σ_2, and putting into the computing platform, respectively. Then performing the operation. Through the specific hybridization reaction between DNA molecules, under the effect of computing platform, a variety of types of data aggregations are formatted. Get all of the possible solutions.

Step4 Test solution. Detector puts polymers into the memory of the true solution, and puts the rest of the polymer in the remnants of collector. Due to the design of the data fiber, making its length is proportional to the weight of sample, finally formed by detecting the order of working operation problem (Fig. 4).

$$J_2 \to J_3 \to J_4 \to J_5 \to J_1$$

4   Conclusion

The probe machine model is a mathematical model, and its data storage form make it has strong parallelism. To deal with the problem of the working operation problem, after a probe operation we can obtain all possible solutions. Compared with other models, the model greatly reduces the complexity of the operation process. Probe machine model expands the traditional notions of calculation as a new research direction, and owns a profound meaning relative to the computer and other subjects. However, we still face so many challenging problems in the question of what kind of material in this model.

Acknowledgment. This work is supported CNSF (Grant number: 61672001).

References

1. Xu, J.: Probe machine. IEEE T. Neur. Net. Lear. **27**(7), 1405–1416 (2016)
2. Turing, A.: On computable numbers, with an application to the Entscheidungsproblem. P. Lond. Math. Soc. **2**(1), 230–265 (1937)
3. Zhang, C., Yang, J., Xu, J.: Self-assembly of DNA/nanoparticles molecular logic calculation model. Chin. Sci. Bull. **27**, 2276–2282 (2011)
4. Xu, J., Li, Z.P., Zhu, E.Q.: Research progress of maximum plane graph theory. Chin. J. Comput. **8**, 1680–1704 (2015)
5. Huang, X.H., Yin, Z.X., Zhi, L.Y.: Molecularbeacon based on DNA computing model for 0–1 programming problem. In: Bio-inspired Computing, pp. 1–5 (2009)

6. Shi, X., Wang, Z., Deng, C., Song, T., Pan, L., Chen, Z.: A novel bio-sensor based on DNA strand displacement. PloS ONE 9(10), e108856 (2014)
7. Shi, X., Chen, C., Li, X., Song, T., Chen, Z., Zhang, Z., Wang, Y.: Size controllable DNA nanoribbons assembled from three types of reusable brick single-strand DNA tiles. 11(43), 8484–8492 (2015)
8. Shi, X., Wu, X., Song, T., Li, X.: Construction of DNA nanotubes with controllable diameters and patterns by using hierarchical DNA sub-tiles. Nanoscale. doi:10.1039/C6NR02695H

Matrix Flat Splicing Systems

Rodica Ceterchi[1], Linqiang Pan[2]($\boxtimes$), Bosheng Song[3], and K.G. Subramanian[4]

[1] Faculty of Mathematics and Computer Science, University of Bucharest,
14 Academiei Street, 010014 Bucharest, Romania
[2] School of Electric and Information Engineering,
Zhengzhou University of Light Industry, Zhengzhou 450002, Henan, China
lqpan@mail.hust.edu.cn
[3] Key Laboratory of Image Information Processing and Intelligent Control of
Education Ministry of China, School of Automation,
Huazhong University of Science and Technology, Wuhan 430074, Hubei, China
[4] Department of Mathematics, Madras Christian College, Chennai 600059, India

Abstract. In dealing with the problem of modelling DNA recombination, the operation of splicing on linear and circular strings of symbols was introduced. Inspired by splicing on circular strings, the operation of flat splicing on a pair of strings (u, v) was considered. This operation involves "cutting" u at a specified position and "inserting" v into it, with v having a pre-specified prefix as well as suffix defined by a flat splicing rule. In this work, we consider a well-known technique in formal language theory, known as "matrix of rules", and introduce matrix of flat splicing rules and thus define matrix flat splicing system ($MFSS$). Some results on the language generative power of $MFSS$ are provided. An application of $MFSS$ in the generation of chain code pictures is also pointed out.

Keywords: Splicing on strings · Flat splicing · Matrix of rules · Formal language

1 Introduction

In proposing an abstract model of the recombinant behaviour of DNA molecules under restriction enzymes and a ligase, Head introduced the operation of splicing on strings of symbols in his seminal work [7]. The idea of splicing is to "cut" two strings at specified positions and "paste" the resulting prefix fragment of one of these with the suffix fragment of the other, thereby yielding a new string. This study opened up an extensive investigation by many researchers, establishing several language theoretic results of interest and importance [8]. Head also introduced the splicing operation on circular words [9], in view of the fact that DNA molecules can occur in circular form as well.

Motivated by the splicing operation on circular strings, Berstel et al. [1] introduced a specific type of splicing, called *flat splicing on words*, which involves "cutting" a word α in a specified position leaving a prefix α_1 and a suffix α_2 so that $\alpha = \alpha_1\alpha_2$ and "inserting" another word β between α_1 and α_2, as directed by

M. Gong et al. (Eds.): BIC-TA 2016, Part I, CCIS 681, pp. 54–63, 2016.
DOI: 10.1007/978-981-10-3611-8_7

a flat splicing rule, which requires β to have certain pre-specified prefix and suffix. Berstel et al. [1] have made an elaborate study on the effect of this operation by defining a flat splicing system (FSS).

In formal language theory, regulating rewriting with different control mechanisms has been investigated extensively (see [3, 14]). Matrix grammar (see [4, 18]) is one such mechanism, where matrices of rules are finite sequences of rules, which are specified and in a successful derivation, any of these sequences of rules has to be applied in every derivation step of the matrix grammar.

In this work, we consider matrices of flat splicing rules and a new variant of systems, called *matrix flat splicing systems* (in short, $MFSS$), is proposed. We exhibit the generative power of $MFSS$ by certain comparison results. We also indicate an application of this system in the generation of chain code pictures [6, 11, 13, 19] made of unit horizontal and vertical segments in the two-dimensional plane.

2   Preliminaries

For notions and results on formal grammars and languages we refer to [17]. In what follows, we introduce some preliminaries used in this work.

A *word* w is a finite sequence of symbols belonging to a finite set V, called an *alphabet* in formal language theory. We denote by V^*, the set of all words over V, including the empty word λ and $V^+ = V^* - \{\lambda\}$. The number of symbols in w counting repetitions is the *length* $|w|$ of a word w. Obviously, $|\lambda| = 0$.

We recall the notion of flat splicing on words [1]. A flat splicing rule r is of the form $(\alpha|\gamma - \delta|\beta)$, where $\alpha, \beta, \gamma, \delta$ are words over an alphabet V. For two words $w_1 = u\alpha\beta v$, $w_2 = \gamma x\delta$, an application of the flat splicing rule $r = (\alpha|\gamma - \delta|\beta)$ to the pair (w_1, w_2) yields the word $w = u\alpha\gamma x\delta\beta v$ and we write $(w_1, w_2) \vdash_r w$. In other words, the second word w_2 is inserted between α and β in the first word w_1 as a result of applying the rule r. When $\alpha = \beta = \gamma = \delta = \lambda$, the flat splicing rule is $(\lambda|\lambda - \lambda|\lambda)$ and an application of this kind of rule allows insertion of any word v into any other word u and anywhere in u. A flat splicing rule $r = (\alpha|\gamma - \delta|\beta)$, where $\alpha, \beta, \gamma, \delta$ are letters in V or the empty word, is called *alphabetic*.

A flat splicing system (FSS) is a triple $S = (\Sigma, I, R)$, where Σ is an *alphabet*, I, called *initial set*, is a set of words over Σ, and R is a finite set of flat splicing rules [1]. The FSS S is respectively called *finite*, *regular* or *context-free* according as I is a finite set, regular set or a context-free language.

For any two words $u, v \in L$ and any rule $r \in R$, we write $(u, v) \vdash_r w$, if the rule r is applicable to the pair (u, v) and if the word w is obtained by applying the rule r to the pair (u, v). The language L generated by S is the smallest language containing I and such that for any two words $u, v \in L$, the word w is also in L, if $(u, v) \vdash_r w$. When all the flat splicing rules are alphabetic, the FSS is called an *alphabetic flat splicing system* ($AFSS$). The families of languages generated by FSS and $AFSS$ are respectively denoted by $\mathcal{L}(FSS, X)$ and $\mathcal{L}(AFSS, X)$ for $X = FIN, REG$ or CF according as the initial set is finite, regular or context-free.

We illustrate an alphabetic flat splicing system and its work with an example.

Example 1. Consider the alphabetic flat splicing system

$$\mathcal{S}_1 = (\{a, b, c, d\}, \{a, b, dcd\}, \{r_1, r_2, r_3, r_4\}),$$

where $r_1 = (d|a - \lambda|c), r_2 = (a|a - \lambda|c), r_3 = (c|b - \lambda|d), r_4 = (c|b - \lambda|b)$.

Initially, the rule r_1 or r_3 is applicable to the pair of words (dcd, a). Application of the rule r_1 inserts a (the only axiom which begins with a) between d and c in the first word dcd yielding $dacd$. Likewise, applying the rule r_3 to the pair (dcd, b) yields $dcbd$. Application of r_2 to the pair $(dacd, a)$ inserts a between a and c in $dacd$ yielding da^2cd while the application of r_4 to the pair $(dcbd, b)$ inserts b between c and b in $dcbd$ yielding dcb^2d. Thus, proceeding in this way, the words generated will be of the form da^ncb^md, $n, m \geq 0$. The language generated by $\mathcal{S}_1$ is $L_1 = \{a, b\} \cup \{da^ncb^md \mid n, m \geq 0\}$.

The following result [1] on alphabetic flat splicing system shows the power of alphabetic context-free flat splicing system.

Theorem 1. *[1] The language generated by an alphabetic flat splicing system with context-free initial set is context-free.*

3　Matrix Flat Splicing System

We now introduce matrix flat splicing system consisting of matrices of flat splicing rules.

Definition 1. *A matrix flat splicing system of degree $n \geq 1$ (each matrix has at the most n flat splicing rules) (M_nFSS) is a triple $\mathcal{S} = (\Sigma, I, M)$, where*

– *Σ is an alphabet;*
– *I, called initial set, is a set of words over Σ;*
– *M is a finite set of matrices which are finite sequences of flat splicing rules.*

The M_nFSS $\mathcal{S}$ is respectively called *finite*, *regular* or *context-free* according as I is a finite set, regular set or a context-free language.

Given words $u, v_1, \cdots, v_n$ and any matrix rule $r \in M$, with $r = [r_1, \cdots, r_n]$ we write $(u, v_1, \cdots, v_n) \vdash_r w$, if $(u, v_1) \vdash_{r_1} w_1$, and for $1 \leq i \leq (n-2)$, $(w_i, v_{i+1}) \vdash_{r_{i+1}} w_{i+1}$, and $(w_{n-1}, v_n) \vdash_{r_n} w_n = w$.

The language L generated by $\mathcal{S}$ is the smallest language containing I and such that for any two words $u, v \in L$, the word w is also in L if $(u, v) \vdash_r w$, for $r \in M$. When all the flat splicing rules in every matrix $r \in M$ are alphabetic, the M_nFSS is called an *alphabetic matrix flat splicing system* (AM_nFSS). The families of languages generated by M_nFSS and AM_nFSS are respectively denoted by $\mathcal{L}(M_nFSS, X)$ and $\mathcal{L}(AM_nFSS, X)$ for $X = FIN, REG$ or CF according as the initial set is finite, regular or context-free.

Remark 1. By definition, for $X = FIN, REG$, the inclusions $\mathcal{L}(M_nFSS, X) \subseteq \mathcal{L}(M_{n+1}FSS, X)$ and $\mathcal{L}(AM_nFSS, X) \subseteq \mathcal{L}(AM_{n+1}FSS, X)$ are clear. It remains to explore whether the inclusions are proper.

We illustrate (alphabetic) matrix flat splicing systems and their works with examples.

Example 2. Consider an AM_2FSS $\mathcal{S}_2 = (\{a, b, c, d\}, \{a, b, dabcbad\}, \{r_1, r_2\})$, where for $i \in \{1, 2\}$, $r_i = [r_{i1}, r_{i2}]$ with the flat splicing rules

$$r_{11} = (d|a - \lambda|a), r_{12} = (a|a - \lambda|d), r_{21} = (\lambda|b - \lambda|c), r_{22} = (c|b - \lambda|\lambda).$$

Application of the matrix rule $r_1 = [r_{11}, r_{12}]$ to $(dabcbad, a, a)$ yields the word da^2bcba^2d as follows. The rule $r_{11} = (d|a - \lambda|a)$ is applied to $(dabcbad, a)$ yielding the word da^2bcbad. Then the rule $r_{12} = (a|a - \lambda|d)$ is applied to (da^2bcbad, a) to yield da^2bcba^2d so that $(dabcbad, a, a) \vdash_{r_1} da^2bcba^2d$. Likewise, $(dabcbad, b, b) \vdash_{r_2} dab^2cb^2ad$. The process can be continued to yield the language $L_2 = \{a, b\} \cup \{da^nb^mcb^ma^nd \mid n, m \geq 1\}$.

Example 3. Consider the M_2FSS $\mathcal{S}_3 = (\{a, b, c, x, y\}, \{c, ab, xy\}, \{r_1, r_2\})$ where the matrix rule $r_1 = [(x|ab - \lambda|y), (b|c - \lambda|y)], r_2 = [(a|ab - \lambda|b), (b|c - \lambda|c)]$. We note that initially, only derivation $(xy, ab, c) \vdash_{r_1} xabcy$ is possible. Subsequently, for $n > 1$, $(xa^{(n-1)}b^{(n-1)}c^{(n-1)}, ab, c) \vdash_{r_2} xa^nb^nc^ny$. The language generated by $\mathcal{S}_3$ is $L_3 = \{ab, c\} \cup \{xa^nb^nc^ny \mid n \geq 0\}$.

Theorem 2. $\mathcal{L}(AM_2FSS, FIN) - \mathcal{L}(AFSS, CF) \neq \emptyset$.

Proof. Consider the language $L_4 = \{ab, c\} \cup \{a^nb^nc^n \mid n \geq 1\}$ over the alphabet $\{a, b, c\}$. This language is generated by an AM_2FSS with a finite initial set $\{abc, ab, c\}$ and matrix rule $r = [r_1, r_2]$ where $r_1 = (a|a - b|b), r_2 = (b|c - \lambda|c)$. Initially, only derivation $(abc, ab, c) \vdash_r aabbcc$ is possible. Subsequently, for $n > 2$, $(a^{(n-1)}b^{(n-1)}c^{(n-1)}, ab, c) \vdash_r a^nb^nc^n$. On the other hand, L_4 cannot be generated by any $AFSS$ with context-free initial set since by Theorem 1, the language generated by such a system can only be context-free while L_4 is a non-context-free language.

Corollary 1. $\mathcal{L}(AM_2FSS, FIN) - CF \neq \emptyset$.

Proof. The language L_4 in the proof of Theorem 2 is in $\mathcal{L}(AM_2FSS, FIN)$ as shown in the proof of Theorem 2, but it is not in CF.

Theorem 3. $\mathcal{L}(AFSS, FIN) = \mathcal{L}(AM_1FSS, FIN) \subset \mathcal{L}(AM_2FSS, FIN)$.

Proof. The equality in the statement follows by noting that every alphabetic flat splicing rule r can be considered as a matrix rule $[r]$. The inclusion $\mathcal{L}(AM_1FSS, FIN) \subseteq \mathcal{L}(AM_2FSS, FIN)$ holds by definition. The proper inclusion can be seen as follows: The language L_4 in the proof of Theorem 2 is in $\mathcal{L}(AM_2FSS, FIN)$ but not in $\mathcal{L}(AFSS, CF)$ as shown in the proof of Theorem 2. Also $\mathcal{L}(AFSS, FIN) \subseteq \mathcal{L}(AFSS, CF)$ as $FIN \subset CF$ and hence L_4 is not in $\mathcal{L}(AFSS, FIN)$ and hence not in $\mathcal{L}(AM_1FSS, FIN)$.

Theorem 4. *For $n \geq 3$, $\mathcal{L}(AM_{n-1}FSS, FIN) \subset \mathcal{L}(AM_nFSS, FIN)$.*

Proof. The inclusion follows from the definition. To prove the proper inclusion, we consider the language

$$L_n = \{a_{2n-1}\} \cup \{a_{2i-1}a_{2i} \mid 1 \leq i \leq (n-1)\}$$

$$\cup \{a_1^p a_2^p a_3^p a_4^p \cdots a_{2n-2}^p a_{2n-1}^p \mid p \geq 1\}$$

over the alphabet $\Sigma = \{a_i \mid 1 \leq i \leq (2n-1)\}$. This language is generated by an AM_nFSS $S_n = (\Sigma, I, M)$, where $I = \{a_{2n-1}, a_1a_2a_3a_4 \cdots a_{2n-3}a_{2n-2}a_{2n-1}\} \cup \{a_{2i-1}a_{2i} \mid 1 \leq i \leq (n-1)\}$ and $M = \{r\}$, $r = [(a_1|a_1 - a_2|a_2), (a_3|a_3 - a_4|a_4), \cdots, (a_{2n-3}|a_{2n-3} - a_{2n-2}|a_{2n-2}), (a_{2n-1}|a_{2n-1} - \lambda|\lambda)]$. Note that the matrix r is a sequence of n alphabetic flat splicing rules.

Initially, the only possibility of derivation is

$$(a_1a_2a_3a_4 \cdots a_{2n-3}a_{2n-2}a_{2n-1}, a_1a_2, a_3a_4, \cdots, a_{2n-3}a_{2n-2}, a_{2n-1})$$

$$\vdash_r a_1^2 a_2^2 a_3^2 a_4^2 \cdots a_{2n-3}^2 a_{2n-2}^2 a_{2n-1}^2.$$

The process can be continued and subsequently, for $p > 2$, we have

$$(a_1^{(p-1)} a_2^{(p-1)} a_3^{(p-1)} a_4^{(p-1)} \cdots a_{2n-3}^{(p-1)} a_{2n-2}^{(p-1)} a_{2n-1}^{(p-1)},$$

$$a_1a_2, a_3a_4, \cdots, a_{2n-3}a_{2n-2}, a_{2n-1})$$

$$\vdash_r a_1^p a_2^p a_3^p a_4^p \cdots a_{2n-3}^p a_{2n-2}^p a_{2n-1}^p.$$

It can be seen that no other derivation step is possible. Hence

$$L_n \in \mathcal{L}(AM_nFSS, FIN).$$

On the other hand, $L_n \notin \mathcal{L}(AM_{(n-1)}FSS, FIN)$. This can be seen as follows. Assume the contrary, it is clear from the language L_n that the word $a_1a_2a_3a_4 \cdots a_{2n-3}a_{2n-2}a_{2n-1}$ has to be in the axiom. So, in order to generate words of L_n of the form $a_1^p a_2^p a_3^p a_4^p \cdots a_{2n-3}^p a_{2n-2}^p a_{2n-1}^p$ for $p > 1$, insertion of a_i, $1 \leq i \leq (2n-1)$ in a previously generated word of a similar form $a_1^q a_2^q a_3^q a_4^q \cdots a_{2n-3}^q a_{2n-2}^q a_{2n-1}^q$, $q < p$ has to be done by a matrix or a finite sequence of at the most $(n-1)$ alphabetic flat splicing rules. This would mean that at the most only $(n-1)$ insertions can be done and also insertion of a word of the form $a_{2i-1}^r a_{2i}^r$, for some $r \geq 0$, can be done only between a_{2i-1} and a_{2i}. But $a_1^q a_2^q a_3^q a_4^q \cdots a_{2n-3}^q a_{2n-2}^q a_{2n-1}^q$ has $(n-1)$ such pairs and another letter (namely, a_{2n-1}) at the end, which means that there are at the most $n-1$ rules in a matrix, the word $a_1^p a_2^p a_3^p a_4^p \cdots a_{2n-3}^p a_{2n-2}^p a_{2n-1}^p$ cannot be generated from a previously generated word.

Regulated rewriting [3,14] is an intensively investigated area of formal language theory with different methods and techniques developed for controlling the application of rules in a context-free grammar. Matrix grammar [18] is such a mechanism defining a family of languages richer than the context-free languages.

Simple matrix grammars of degree $n \geq 1$ $(n - SMG)$ [10] constitute a subfamily of matrix grammars investigated by many researchers (see, for example, [5,10,16]). It is known [10] that there is a hierarchy of classes of languages generated by simple matrix grammars. More precisely, the family of languages generated by simple matrix grammars of degree $n \geq 1$ is denoted by $\mathcal{S}(n)$, the language $L_n = \{a_1^k a_2^k \cdots a_n^k b^k c_n^k c_{n-1}^k \cdots c_1^k \mid k \geq 1\}$, where $a_1, \cdots, a_n, b, c_1, \cdots, c_n$ are distinct symbols, is in $\mathcal{S}(n + 1)$ but not in $\mathcal{S}(n)$ [10]. In what follows, we now show that $\mathcal{L}(AM_{n+1}FSS, FIN)$ contains a language not generated by any simple matrix grammar of degree n.

Theorem 5. *For $n \geq 1$, $\mathcal{L}(AM_{n+1}FSS, FIN) - \mathcal{S}(n) \neq \emptyset$.*

Proof. Let $L_n = \{a_1^k a_2^k \cdots a_n^k b^k c_n^k c_{n-1}^k \cdots c_1^k \mid k \geq 1\}$. We first consider the case when n is even, $n = 2m$, $m \geq 1$. We prove the result by constructing a $M_{2m+1}FSS$ $\mathcal{S} = (\Sigma, I, M)$ generating $L = L_{2m} \cup \{a_{2i-1}a_{2i}, b, c_{2i}c_{2i-1} \mid 1 \leq i \leq m\}$, where $\Sigma = \{a_1, \cdots, a_{2m}, b, c_1, \cdots, c_{2m}\}$, $I = \{a_1 a_2 \cdots a_{2m-1} a_{2m} b c_{2m} c_{2m-1} \cdots c_2 c_1, a_{2i-1} a_{2i}, b, c_{2i} c_{2i-1} \mid 1 \leq i \leq m\}$, and M consists of the matrix flat splicing rule

$$r = [(a_1|a_1 - a_2|a_2), \cdots, (a_{2m-1}|a_{2m-1} - a_{2m}|a_{2m}), (b|b - \lambda|\lambda),$$

$$(c_{2m}|c_{2m} - c_{2m-1}|c_{2m-1}), \cdots, (c_2|c_2 - c_1|c_1)].$$

It can be seen that the $M_{2m+1}FSS$ $\mathcal{S}$ generates the language L but L cannot be generated by any SMG of degree $n = 2m$, which can be shown by an argument closely analogous to the proof showing L_n is not in $\mathcal{S}(n)$ [10].

The proof for the case when n is odd, $n = 2m - 1$, $m \geq 1$ is similar. Now $L = L_{2m-1} \cup \{a_{2i-1}a_{2i}, a_{2m-1}b, c_{2i}c_{2i-1} \mid 1 \leq i \leq m - 1\}$ and

$$I = \{a_1 a_2 \cdots a_{2m-2} a_{2m-1} b c_{2m-1} c_{2m-2} \cdots c_2 c_1, a_{2i-1} a_{2i},$$

$$a_{2m-1}b, c_{2i}c_{2i-1} \mid 1 \leq i \leq m - 1\}.$$

Also M consists of the matrix flat splicing rule

$$r = [(a_1|a_1 - a_2|a_2), \cdots, (a_{2m-3}|a_{2m-3} - a_{2m-2}|a_{2m-2}), (a_{2m-1}|a_{2m-1} - b|b),$$

$$(c_{2m-1}|c_{2m-1} - \lambda|\lambda), (c_{2m-2}|c_{2m-2} - c_{2m-3}|c_{2m-3}), \cdots, (c_2|c_2 - c_1|c_1)].$$

It can be again seen that the $M_{2m}FSS$ $\mathcal{S}$ generates the language L but L cannot be generated by any SMG of degree $n = 2m - 1$ [10].

Right-linear simple matrix grammars $(RLSMG)$ [10,15] form a subclass of simple matrix grammars and the family of languages of $RLSMG$ of degree $n \geq 1$ is denoted by $\mathcal{R}(n)$. It is known that the language $L_n' = \{a_1^k a_2^k \cdots a_{n+1}^k \mid k \geq 1\}$ where $a_1, \cdots, a_{n+1}$ are distinct symbols, is in $\mathcal{R}(n + 1)$ but not in $\mathcal{R}(n)$ [10]. In what follows, we show that there is a language generated by an $AMFSS$ which does not belong to $\mathcal{R}(n)$.

Theorem 6.

(i) For even n, $AM_{\frac{n}{2}+1}FSS - \mathcal{R}(n) \neq \emptyset$.
(ii) For odd n, $AM_{\frac{n+1}{2}}FSS - \mathcal{R}(n) \neq \emptyset$.

Proof. Let $L'_n = \{a_1^k a_2^k \cdots a_{n+1}^k \mid k \geq 1\}$, where $a_1, \cdots, a_{n+1}$ are distinct symbols. Let $n = 2m$, $m \geq 1$. Consider the language

$$L' = L'_{2m} \cup \{a_1 a_2, \cdots, a_{2m-1} a_{2m}, a_{2m+1}\}.$$

We construct a $M_{m+1}FSS$ $\mathcal{S} = (\Sigma, I, M)$ generating L'. Let $\Sigma = \{a_1, \cdots, a_{2m+1}\}$ and

$$I = \{a_1 a_2 \cdots a_{2m-1} a_{2m} a_{2m+1}, a_{2i-1} a_{2i}, a_{2m+1} \mid 1 \leq i \leq m\}.$$

Let M consist of the matrix flat splicing rule

$$r = [(a_1 | a_1 - a_2 | a_2), \cdots, (a_{2m-1} | a_{2m-1} - a_{2m} | a_{2m}), (a_{2m} | a_{2m+1} - \lambda | a_{2m+1}).$$

It can be seen that the $M_{m+1}FSS$ $\mathcal{S}$ generates the language L' but L' cannot be generated by any $RLSMG$ of degree $n = 2m$, which can be shown by an argument closely analogous to the proof showing L'_n is not in $\mathcal{S}(n)$ [10].

The proof for the case when n is odd, $n = 2m - 1$, $m \geq 1$ is similar. Now $L' = L'_{2m-1} \cup \{a_{2i-1} a_{2i} \mid 1 \leq i \leq m\}$ and $I = \{a_1 a_2 \cdots a_{2m-1} a_{2m}, a_{2i-1} a_{2i} \mid 1 \leq i \leq m\}$. Also M consists of the matrix flat splicing rule

$$r = [(a_1 | a_1 - a_2 | a_2), \cdots, (a_{2m-1} | a_{2m-1} - a_{2m} | a_{2m})].$$

It can be again seen that the $M_m FSS$ $\mathcal{S}$ generates the language L' but L' cannot be generated by any $RLSMG$ of degree $n = 2m - 1$ [10].

A new type of parallel rewriting system called grammar with linked nonterminals which uses context-free productions that replace a nonterminal with its connected instances, has been introduced in [12]. The family of languages generated by grammars with linked nonterminals of degree k is denoted by $\mathcal{L}(k - SN)$. In establishing a hierarchy result, it has been proved that the language $L_{k+1} = \{a_1^n a_2^n \cdots a_{k+1}^n \mid n \geq 1\}$, where $a_1, \cdots, a_{k+1}$ are distinct symbols, is not in $\mathcal{L}(k - SN)$ [12]. As done in Theorem 6, we can show that there is a language generated by an $AMFSS$ which does not belong to $\mathcal{L}(k - SN)$. We state the result in the following Theorem.

Theorem 7.

(i) For even k, $AM_{\frac{k}{2}+1}FSS - \mathcal{L}(k - SN) \neq \emptyset$.
(ii) For odd k, $AM_{\frac{k+1}{2}}FSS - \mathcal{L}(k - SN) \neq \emptyset$.

4   Application to Chain-Code Pictures

As early as 1982, Maurer et al. [13] introduced a picture generating model, called chain code picture grammar, where the chain code pictures are made of unit lines in the two-dimensional plane, with the pictures being drawn according to a sequence of instructions *left, right, up, down* represented by words over $\Sigma = \{l, r, u, d\}$. There has been a number of investigations on various properties of the chain-code pictures (e.g., see [2,6,11,19,20]). As an application of matrix flat splicing system, we indicate here the applicability of matrix flat splicing system with only alphabetic flat splicing rules in describing a chain code picture language consisting of diamond shaped chain code pictures with four equal size stair pattern in each side as shown in Fig. 1.

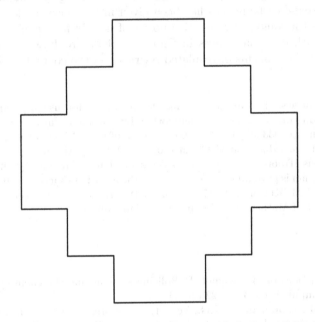

Fig. 1. A diamond shaped chain-code picture with four equal sized stairs

We note that description of such pictures in terms of a formal language of words over the symbols l, r, u, d is a context-sensitive language given by

$$L_c = \{u(ru)^n rr(dr)^n dd(ld)^n ll(ul)^n u \mid n \geq 1\}.$$

We give an AM_4FSS to generate L_c. The alphabet is $\{l, r, u, d\}$. The axioms are $ururrdrddldllulu, ru, dr, ld, ul$. The matrix alphabetic flat splicing rule is

$$r = [(u|r - u|r), (r|d - r|d), (d|l - d|l), (l|u - l|u)].$$

It can be seen that this AM_4FSS generates the language $L_c \cup \{ru, dr, ld, ul\}$. Except for the four words *ru, dr, ld, ul,* every word in this language corresponds to a diamond shaped chain code picture with four equal size stair pattern in each side. The drawn chain-code picture corresponding to the word $u(ru)^2rr(dr)^2dd(ld)^2ll(ul)^2u$ is shown in Fig. 1.

5 Conclusions and Discussions

In this work, a well-known technique in formal language theory, known as matrix of rules, has been introduced into flat splicing system, thus matrix flat splicing systems were defined. Some results on the language generative power of matrix flat splicing systems were presented. Matrix flat splicing systems were used to generate chain code pictures.

The language generative power of matrix flat splicing systems in comparison with context-free languages has been given in Corollary 1. It is of interest to investigate the language generative power of matrix flat splicing systems in comparison with other languages in Chomsky hierarchy. It will be of interest to study other mechanisms of regulated rewriting in the context of flat splicing systems.

Acknowledgments. The authors thank the reviewers for useful comments. The work of L. Pan and B. Song was supported by National Natural Science Foundation of China (61033003, 61320106005 and 61602192), Ph.D. Programs Foundation of Ministry of Education of China (20120142130008), the Innovation Scientists and Technicians Troop Construction Projects of Henan Province (154200510012). K.G. Subramanian is grateful to UGC, India, for the award of Emeritus Fellowship (No. F.6-6/2016-17/EMERITUS-2015-17-GEN-5933/(SA-II)) to him to execute his work in the Department of Mathematics, Madras Christian College.

References

1. Berstel, J., Boasson, L., Fagnot, I.: Splicing systems and the chomsky hierarchy. Theor. Comput. Sci. **436**, 2–22 (2012)
2. Ceterchi, R., Subramanian, K.G., Venkat, I.: P systems with parallel rewriting for chain code picture languages. In: Beckmann, A., Mitrana, V., Soskova, M. (eds.) CiE 2015. LNCS, vol. 9136, pp. 145–155. Springer, Heidelberg (2015). doi:10.1007/978-3-319-20028-6_15
3. Dassow, J., Păun, G.: Regulated Rewriting in Formal Language Theory. Springer, Berlin (1989)
4. Dassow, J., Fernau, H., Păun, G.: On the leftmost derivation in matrix grammars. Int. J. Found. Comput. S. **10**, 61–79 (1999)
5. Fernau, H.: Even linear simple matrix languages: formal language properties and grammatical inference. Theor. Comput. Sci. **289**, 425–456 (2002)
6. Gutbrod, R.: A transformation system for generating description languages of chain code pictures. Theor. Comput. Sci. **68**, 239–252 (1989)
7. Head, T.: Formal language theory and DNA: an analysis of the generative capacity of specific recombinant behaviours. B. Math. Biol. **49**, 735–759 (1987)

8. Head, T., Păun, G., Pixton, D.: Language theory and molecular genetics: generative mechanisms suggested by DNA recombination. In: Rozenberg, G., Salomaa, A. (eds.) Handbook of Formal Languages, vol. 2, pp. 295–358. Springer, Heidelberg (1997)
9. Head, T.: Splicing schemes and DNA. In: Rozenberg, G., Salomaa, A. (eds.) Lindenmayer Systems, pp. 371–383. Springer, Berlin (1992)
10. Ibarra, O.H.: Simple matrix languages. Inf. Contro. **17**, 359–394 (1970)
11. Kim, C., Sudborough, I.H.: The membership and the equivalence problem for picture languages. Theor. Comput. Sci. **52**, 177–191 (1987)
12. Klein, A., Kutrib, M.: Context-free grammars with linked nonterminals. Int. J. Found. Comput. S. **18**, 1271–1282 (2007)
13. Maurer, H.A., Rozenberg, G., Welzl, E.: Using string languages to describe picture languages. Inf. Contro. **54**, 155–185 (1982)
14. Meduna, A., Zemek, P.: Regulated Grammars and Automata. Springer, New York (2014)
15. Păun, G., Pérez-Jiménez, M.J.: dP automata versus right-linear simple matrix grammars. In: Dinneen, M.J., Khoussainov, B., Nies, A. (eds.) WTCS 2012. LNCS, vol. 7160, pp. 376–387. Springer, Heidelberg (2012). doi:10.1007/978-3-642-27654-5_29
16. Rosebrugh, R.D., Wood, D.: Image theorems for simple matrix languages and n-parallel languages. Math. Syst. Theor. **8**(2), 150–155 (1975)
17. Rozenberg, G., Salomaa, A. (eds.): Handbook of Formal Languages, vol. 1–3. Springer, Heidelberg (1997)
18. Salomaa, A.: Matrix grammars with a leftmost restriction. Inf. Contro. **20**, 143–149 (1972)
19. Sudborough, I.H., Welzl, E.: Complexity and decidability for chain code picture languages. Theor. Comput. Sci. **36**, 173–202 (1985)
20. Subramanian, K.G., Venkat, I., Pan, L.: P systems generating chain code picture languages. In: Proceedings of Asian Conference on Membrane Computing, Wuhan, pp. 115–123 (2012)

A Universal Platform for Building DNA Logic Circuits

Zicheng Wang[✉], Jian Ai, Yanfeng Wang, Guangzhao Cui, and Lina Yao

Henan Key Lab of Information-based Electrical Appliances,
School of Electrical and Information Engineering,
Zhengzhou University of Light Industry, Zhengzhou 450002, Henan, China
wzch@zzuli.edu.cn

Abstract. DNA strand displacement has great potential for use in logic circuits. In the paper, the two DNA-based logic circuits that behave as half-subtract and half-adder were implemented relying on strand displacement and fluorescence labeling technique. The half-adder and half-subtract were achieved by simply modifying the sequences of the input strands, while retaining the same DNA logical structure as a universal platform. By taking advantage of the branch migration mechanism, separation and combination of fluorescent group were controlled, two series of fluorescence signals were defined as the output signal. We simulated within the Visual DSD design tool which analyzes their performance and proves the correctness of the circuits. The system reported herein is rather concise compared to other molecular logic gate systems.

Keywords: DNA strand displacement · Universal platform · Fluorescence signal · Visual DSD

1 Introduction

As nanotechnology has become a principal research interest, molecular-scale devices that can be built by either top-down or bottom-up approach are widely studied. In recent years, DNA has been demonstrated as remarkable material in fabrication of arithmetic systems [1] and molecular logic computing, because of properties such as special recognition of target sequences, self-assembly into defined structures [2]. Meanwhile, DNA strand displacement is one of the basic DNA molecular computing technologies by virtue of its own energy level cause, highly specific hybridizations, sensitivity and accuracy to release and combination [3,4]. In 1994, Adleman in [5] introduced a DNA-based bio-computing system for solving famous mathematics traveling salesman problems. In 2011, Qian in [6,7] realized a four-bit binary square-root circuit that comprised 130 DNA strands and four interconnected neurons that can play mind-reading game by DNA strand displacement cascades, which has attracted great attention in the field of information computing. These demonstrated that DNA sequences can serve as elementary computing devices such as half-adder, half-subtract, full-adder, and full-subtract [8,9]. Simultaneously, as fluorescence technology rapid

© Springer Nature Singapore Pte Ltd. 2016
M. Gong et al. (Eds.): BIC-TA 2016, Part I, CCIS 681, pp. 64–71, 2016.
DOI: 10.1007/978-981-10-3611-8_8

development, the researchers tried to combine strand displacement with fluorescence technology to construct molecular devices. In 2003, Saghatelian in [10] established the DNA logic gates by using fluorescence technology and molecular operation for the first time. Fluorescent signals are used in the construction of logic gates since light can be recognized as the output signal. These techniques provide a new direction for the study of molecular devices in the future.

Most of the previous DNA logic operating methods, logic gates was used as an elementary unit to implement the logical circuits [11]. For instance: a half-adder can perform an addition operation on two binary digits by integration of an XOR gate and an AND gate in parallel to generate a Sum output and a Carry output, respectively. A half-subtract can perform a subtraction of two bits, which requires the combination of an XOR gate and an Inhibit gate to produce a Difference output and a Borrow output, respectively. But the half-adder and half-subtract have some limitations: (1) the inputs and logic gates for the required logical circuits are different from each other, (2) the reaction process is more complex, the reaction time is too long. So it is necessary to construct multi-functional molecular devices on a single bio-molecular platform.

In the paper, we achieved a half-adder and half-subtract on the same platform by simply modifying the inputs. The constructed systems in this study are based on the concept of molecular beacon [12] and DNA strand displacement. The simplicity and stability of this structure makes it easy to operate. The presence and absence of the single-stranded DNA are assigned as the respective inputs of 1 and 0, two series of fluorescence signals are defined as the output signal. We finally use this Visual DSD [13] software tool to analyze and simulate the DNA circuits in this paper.

2   Design and Construction of Half-adder and Half-subtract Model

2.1   Materials and Analysis

In this section, we present an universal platform architecture showed the Fig. 1 and implement the half-adder and half-subtract circuits on the base of the platform by using DNA strand displacement. The universal platform is formed of three DNA single strands with different direction and based on the principle of

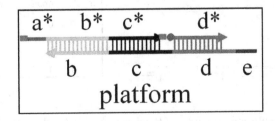

Fig. 1. A schematic representation of the universal platform.

Watson-Crick complementarity. Each strand has a direction from the 5-end to the 3-end. We think that the different letters represent different DNA domains that these domains between will not interfere with each other [14]. The domain b^* indicates the complementary domain of b that hybridizes with b. In addition, these short domain (a^*, e) are considered as toeholds. The toehold is extremely important component because it provides a DNA domain for the interaction between the input and the platform. Once the toehold domain (a, e^*) on the input strand binds to exposed toeholds on the platform (a^*, e); then, input toehold will initiate the reaction. Eventually, the reaction occurs through branch migration, which translates input strand into output strand.

In the platform, the $\langle d^* \rangle$ strand carries a Cy5 (red dye) at the 5'-end. The $\langle a^* \ b^* \ c^* \rangle$ strand is modified respectively with quencher at the 5'-end and at the 3'-end. Since the fluorescence resonance energy transfer (FRET) efficiency depends on the distance between donor and receptor pair. The DNA strand holds the fluorophore and the quencher in close proximity, leading the fluorescent signal is quenched. When the fluorophore and the quencher are separated by the strand displacement reaction, resulting in a high fluorescent signal [15]. Herein, the two input strands are designed to hybridize with the gate to cause an output change of fluorescence. The absence of the each input is considered as 0 and the presence of input is defined as 1. The output signal is defined depends on whether the last fluorescence signal was observed.

2.2   Design of Half-adder

The half-adder model is showed in the Fig. 2, the Input A $\langle e \ d \ c \ b \ a \rangle$ carries fluorophore (green dye) at the 3-end, the Input B $\langle a^* \ b^* \ c^* \ d^* \ e^* \rangle$ is only a pure single strand. Input A is complementary to the Input B completely. Furthermore, when the strand displacement reaction is completed and the balance is achieved. Then, the output has been read out. Herein, the high concentration green fluorescent signal on behalf of carry bit, the high concentration red fluorescent signal is read as the sum-bit.

In the (0, 0) state, neither Input A nor Input B is present, fluorophore of the platform stays near the quencher. Consequently, no fluorescent signal is released

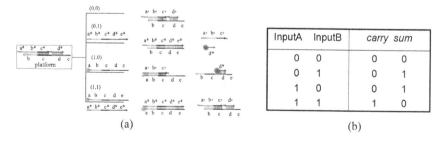

	(a)		(b)	
InputA	InputB		carry	sum
0	0		0	0
0	1		0	1
1	0		0	1
1	1		1	0

Fig. 2. (a) Implementation principles of the developed DNA half adder. (b) Truth table for half adder (Color figure online)

and the output reading is (0, 0). In the (0, 1) state, when Input B $\langle a^* \ b^* \ c^* \ d^* \ e^* \rangle$ is added, the branch migration is initiated when the toehold e^* binds to the exposed toehold e in the platform. As a result, forming a new complexes and displace single strand $\langle a^* \ b^* \ c^* \rangle$ and $\langle d^* \rangle$ from the platform. The fluorophore at the 5'-end of strand $\langle d^* \rangle$ shifts away from the quencher and releases a red fluorescence signal. Hence, the output reading is (0, 1).

In the (1, 0) state, when the Input A $\langle e \ d \ c \ b \ a \rangle$ is added, at first, the toehold in the Input A binds to the toehold a^* in the platform. This produces a double strand and releases another double strand. Since, forming the Input A-$\langle a^* \ b^* \ c^* \rangle$ duplex, the green fluorophore and the quencher stay together, so the green fluorescence is not observed. In contrast, the displacement reaction also leads to the red fluorophore separated from the platform, restoring the red high fluorescent signal. As a result, the output result is (0, 1).

In the (1, 1) state, both Input A and Input B coexist, the double strand of Input A-Input B is formed, because the Input A and Input B is favored over hybridization each other. Neither the $\langle a^* \ b^* \ c^* \rangle$ nor the $\langle d^* \rangle$ of gate is replaced by the Input A or the Input B. Therefore, the red fluorophore and the quencher still stay together in the gate duplex, so the red fluorescence is not observed. Because of the $\langle a^* \ b^* \ c^* \ d^* \ e^* \rangle$ strand does not carry quencher, the $\langle e \ d \ c \ b \ a \rangle$ strand carries fluorophore (green dye) at the 3-end, therefore we can observe the green fluorescence, so the final result reading is (1, 0).

2.3   Design of Half-subtract

The half-subtract model is showed in the Fig. 3, the Input A $\langle e \ d \ c \ b \ a \rangle$ carries quencher at the 5-end, the Input B $\langle a^* \ b^* \ c^* \ d^* \ e^* \rangle$ carries fluorophore (green dye) at the 3-end. Input A is complementary to the Input B completely. As the chemical reaction reaches equilibrium, the results will be read out. Eventually, in the half-subtract, the green fluorescent signal strand represents the borrow-bit, the red fluorescent signal strand represents the difference-bit.

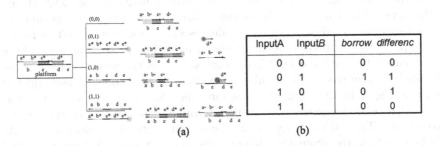

Fig. 3. (a) Implementation principles of the developed DNA-based half-subtract. (b) Truth table for half-subtract (Color figure online)

In the (0, 0) state, no input is added, consequently, no fluorescent signal is released. Both the borrow-bit and the difference-bit are read as 0, the output reading is (0, 0).

In the (0, 1) state, the $\langle d^* \rangle$ and $\langle a^* \, b^* \, c^* \rangle$ is released from the platform in the presence of Input B $\langle a^* \, b^* \, c^* \, d^* \, e^* \rangle$. Due to the presence of the toehold e in the platform, thus Input B prefers to hybridize with $\langle e \, d \, c \, b \rangle$ by the toehold (e, e^*), forming an Input B-$\langle e \, d \, c \, b \rangle$ duplex. The red fluorophore thus becomes far away from the quencher and exhibits red fluorescent signal. This green fluorescence is introduced simultaneously. So green fluorescence and red fluorescence can be observed at the same time. Thus, the output reading is (1, 1).

In the (1, 0) state, only the Input A $\langle e \, d \, c \, b \, a \rangle$ is present, the toehold a in the Input A first binds to the complementary toehold a^* in the platform. Finally, the strand displacement reaction results in the separation of the red fluorescence and the quencher, releasing the red fluorescent signal. The output reading is (0, 1).

In the (1, 1) state, both inputs are present, Input A and Input B have a higher probability to hybridize each other. When Input A and Input B are hybridized, fluorescence and quencher are brought in the vicinity, fluorophore on the Input B is quenched. Consequently, without any fluorescence signals are released and the output reading is (0, 0).

3   Result and Discussion

As mentioned above, we have theoretically verified the feasibility of half-adder and half-subtract. Next, we will prove the correctness of the molecular devices through the simulation with DSD [13]. Visual DSD is an implementation of a programming language for designing DNA circuits based on DNA strand displacement systems. The Visual DSD software can compile a number of DNA strand displacement into a set of chemical reactions for simulation. Herein we simulate the reaction process of half-adder and half-subtract in DSD. In the deterministic simulation plots, the abscissa represents the reaction time(s), and the ordinate represents the DNA strand concentration (nm), the upper left corner of the block diagram of different color corresponding to the DNA strand in the figure. The Output results in the designed half-adder and half-subtract where the output reading relies on the fluorescence. However, in DSD software we can prove the correctness of the theory by detecting the concentration of the strand connected with the final fluorescent signal, as the reactions reach equilibrium [16]. The stochastic simulation diagram of the model of half-adder is shown in Fig. 4. In the simulation diagram, the blue curve represents Input B $\langle a^* \, b^* \, c^* \, d^* \, e^* \rangle$, the green curve represents Input A $\langle e \, d \, c \, b \, a \rangle$ carrying green fluorescence. The red curve represents the output carrying red fluorescence. As can be seen from the simulation diagram Fig. 4(a) in the (0, 1) state, the initial concentration of the red curve is 0 nm, when the input strand $\langle a^* \, b^* \, c^* \, d^* \, e^* \rangle$ is added, it will be found that at first the red curve is rapidly increasing in the form of a slope. Because the input strand has just been added, the concentration is relatively large. After a period of time, along with the reaction, this input strand is gradually consumed, the rate of this reaction gradually slow. Thus, output concentration increase is relatively slow. Next when the strand displacement

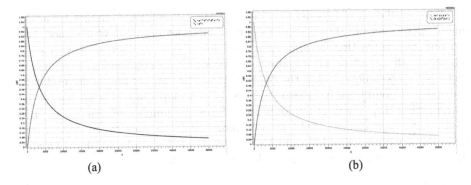

(a)   (b)

Fig. 4. A simulation diagram of the half-adder model. (a) the (0,1) state, (b) the (1,0) state. (Color figure online)

reaction is completed and toward equilibrium, the input strand is exhausted, the output strand remains stable [17]. This final equilibrium concentration is used as the output concentration. We see that the concentration of the output strand approaches 1 nM by the equilibrium of the simulation.

In the (1,0) state, when the input strand with green fluorescent signal is added, as time goes on, the concentration of green fluorescence gradually decreased and the concentration of red fluorescence increased gradually. The simulation process is similar to that of the (0, 1) state.

Figure 5 presents the simulation diagram of the model of half-subtract. In the (0, 1) state, the blue curve represents Input B $\langle a^* b^* c^* d^* e^* \rangle$, the green curve and red curve represent the output strand (Input B-$\langle e\, d\, c\, b \rangle$) and $< d* >$ respectively. In addition, it should be noted that the red curve and the green curve are completely overlapping, because of the output strand (Input B-$\langle e\, d\, c\, b \rangle$) and $\langle d^* \rangle$ are replaced at the same time. Other simulation principles are similar to the half adder. Figure 5(b) shows simulation diagram of the (1, 0) state.

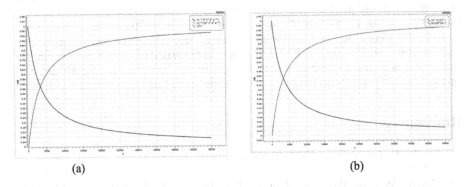

(a)   (b)

Fig. 5. A simulation diagram of the half-subtract model. (a) the (0,1) state, (b) the (1,0) state, the blue curve represents Input A $\langle e\, d\, c\, b\, a \rangle$ (Color figure online)

This simulation results demonstrate two DNA-based logic circuits for arithmetic operations and the correctness of molecular devices we have designed [18]. To our knowledge that computation time for circuits can be shown to scale linearly with circuit depth. However, in the study, the advantage of using the fluorescence technique is that the required two logic gates of half-adder and half-subtract are completed with same universal DNA platform and triggered by the same inputs [19]. There is no doubt, it reduces the number of reactive strands and circuit depth, making the circuits more easily to operate. In comparison with the previous half-adder and half-subtract, in this study, localized circuits have advantages with respect to both speed and stability.

4   Conclusions

In summary, a half-subtract and half-adder are designed by using the fluorescence technique and displacement of DNA strands successfully. In the study, the molecular devices overcome the limitations of the required two logic gates being achieved with different substrates or being triggered with different inputs. There is no doubt that the use of fluorescence as the signal evaluation makes it simple and flexible for the design of logic circuits to meet the arithmetic processing requirements. However, DNA strand displacement systems also have the disadvantages: for example, we know that DNA reactions happen in diffusion, perhaps not surprisingly, DNA strand displacement systems have their own leak reaction. Along with the increase of the system complexity, the leak phenomenon is more serious. Therefore, it should be noted that there is a long road ahead to integrate the developed molecular systems to compete with silicon-based technology. Although the developed half-adder and half-subtract are implemented in simulation stage, but these models provide a new method that makes DNA a highly promising for the implementation molecular devices on a single bio-molecular platform [20–24].

Acknowledgment. This work is supported by the NSFC (No. U1304620, 61472372, 61272022), Innovation Scientists and Technicians Troop Construction Projects of Henan (Grant No. 124200510017), and Innovation Scientists Technicians Troop Construction Projects of Zhengzhou (Grant No. 131PLJRC648), Basic and Frontier technologies Research Program of Henan Province (132300410183), Innovation Scientists and Technicians Troop Construction Projects of Henan Province (154200510012). Scientific Research Fund Project of Zhengzhou University of Light Industry (2014XJJ013).

References

1. Jin, X.: Probe machine. IEEE Trans. Neural Netw. Learn. Syst. **27**(7), 1405–1416 (2016)
2. Shi, X., Wei, L., Wang, Z., Pan, L., Cui, G., Jin, X., LaBean, T.H.: Programmable DNA tile self-assembly using a hierarchical sub-tile strategy. Nanotechnology **25**(7), 075602 (2014)

3. Shi, X., Wang, Z., Deng, C., Song, T., Pan, L., Chen, Z.: A novel bio-sensor based on DNA strand displacement. PLoS ONE **9**(10), e108856 (2014)
4. Yang, J., Dong, C., Dong, Y., Liu, S., Pan, L., Zhang, C.: Logic nanoparticle beacon triggered by the binding-induced effect of multiple inputs. ACS Appl. Mater. **6**(16), 14486–14492 (2014). doi:10.1371/journal.pone.0108856
5. Adleman, L.M.: Molecular computation of solutions to combinatorial problems. Science **266**(5187), 1021–1024 (1994)
6. Qian, L., Winfree, E.: Scaling up digital circuit computation with DNA strand displacement cascades. Science **332**(6034), 1196–1201 (2011)
7. Qian, L., Winfree, E., Bruck, J.: Neural network computation with DNA strand displacement cascades. Nature **475**(7356), 368–372 (2011)
8. Lin, H.Y., Chen, J.Z., Li, H.Y., Yang, C.N.: A simple three-input DNA-based system works as a full-subtractor. Sci. Rep. **5**(6), 2045–2322 (2015)
9. Yang, C.N., Hsu, C.Y., Chuang, Y.C.: Molecular beacon-based half-adder and half-subtractor. Chem. Commun. **48**(1), 112–114 (2012)
10. Saghatelian, A., Guckian, K.M., Thayer, D.A., et al.: DNA detection and signal amplification via an engineered allosteric enzyme. J. Am. Chem. Soc. **125**(2), 344–345 (2003)
11. Wang, Z., Zhang, W., Wang, Y., Cui, G.: A DNA code converter model for decimal numbers displaying. J. Comput. Theor. Nanosci. **562**, 447–455 (2015)
12. Xu, S.L., Li, H.L., Miao, Y.Q., et al.: Implementation of half adder and half subtractor with a simple and universal DNA-based platform. NPG Asia Mater. **5**, e76 (2013)
13. Matthew, L., Simon, Y.: Visual DSD: a design and analysis tool for DNA strand displacement systems. Bioinformatics **27**(22), 3211–3213 (2011)
14. Lakin, M.R., Yourssef, S., Cardelli, L., Phillips, A.: Abstractions for DNA circuit design. J. R. Soc. Interface **9**(68), 470–486 (2012)
15. Yang, J., Ma, J., Liu, S., Zhang, C.: A molecular cryptograph model based on structures of DNA self-assembly. Comput. Sci. Technol. **59**(11), 1192–1198 (2014)
16. Sun, J., Shen, Y.: Quasi-ideal memory system. IEEE Trans. Cybern. **45**(7), 1353–1362 (2015)
17. Sun, J., Quan, Y., Shen, Y.: Compound synchronization for four chaotic systems of integer order, fractional order. Europhys. Lett. **106**(4), 40005 (2014)
18. Sun, J., Shen, Y., Zhang, G., Xu, C., Cui, G.: Combination-combination synchronization among four identical or different chaotic systems. Nonlinear Dyn. **73**(3), 1211–1222 (2013)
19. Junwei, S., Guangzhao, C., Yanfeng, W., Yi, S.: Combination complexsynchronization of three chaotic complex systems. Nonlinear Dyn. **79**(2), 953–965 (2015)
20. Song, T., Pan, L.: Spiking neural P systems with request rules. Neurocomputing **193**(12), 193–200 (2016)
21. Song, T., Liu, X., Zhao, Y., Zhang, X.: Spiking neural P systems with white hole neurons. IEEE Trans. Nanobiosci. (2016). doi:10.1109/TNB.2016.2598879
22. Song, T., Pan, Z., Wong, D.M., Wang, X.: Design of logic gates using spiking neural P systems with homogeneous neurons and astrocytes-like control. Inf. Sci. **372**, 380–391 (2016)
23. Wang, X., Song, T., Gong, F., Pan, Z.: On the computational power of spiking neural P systems with self-organization. Sci. Rep. doi:10.1038/srep27624
24. Shi, X., Wu, X., Song, T., Li, X.: Construction of DNA nanotubes with controllable diameters and patterns by using hierarchical DNA sub-tiles. Nanoscale. doi:10.1039/C6NR02695H

Membrane Computing

A Hybrid "Fast-Slow" Convergent Framework for Genetic Algorithm Inspired by Membrane Computing

Zhongwei Li[1], Shengyu Xia[1], Yun Jiang[3], Beibei Sun[1], Yuezhen Xin[1], and Xun Wang[2(✉)]

[1] College of Computer and Communication Engineering,
China University of Petroleum, Qingdao 266580, Shandong, China
[2] The Center for Bioengineering and Biotechnology,
College of Chemical Engineering, China University of Petroleum,
Qingdao 266580, Shandong, China
wangsyun@upc.edu.cn
[3] School of Computer Science and Information Engineering,
Chongqing Technology and Business University, Chongqing 400067, China

Abstract. Genetic algorithm is a well known bio-inspired algorithm, which has been widely used to solve practical problems in real-life. The performance of the algorithm heavily depends on the convergence related to the values of parameters involved. It is formulated as a hard problem to select suitable values of mutation and crossover rates to achieve fast or slow convergence for unknown problems. As a new study of system framework inspired by cell model, membrane computing models is with a membrane structure having region segmentation, intrinsic discrete, non-deterministic, programmable and transparent features. In this paper, a hybrid "fast-slow" convergent framework for genetic algorithm inspired by membrane computing is proposed and applied to search optimal solution of 41 benchmark functions. It is obtained by the data experimental results that our method performs well in solving benchmark functions by achieving accuracy rate about 96%.

Keywords: Membrane computing · Genetic algorithm · Membrane structure · Convergence

1 Introduction

Genetic algorithm (GA) is bio-inspired intelligent algorithm abstracted from the human evolving process. Nowadays, the algorithm is known adaptive, heuristic, iterative, and has been applied in solving plenty of practical problems. The performance of GA heavily depends on the values of involved parameters, such as mutation rate and crossover rate of the population. The most intuitive case is that with different values, the convergence which is an important indicator of performance to test the algorithm, will be quite different. High convergence

© Springer Nature Singapore Pte Ltd. 2016
M. Gong et al. (Eds.): BIC-TA 2016, Part I, CCIS 681, pp. 75–84, 2016.
DOI: 10.1007/978-981-10-3611-8_9

rate does not mean it can search for the best solutions; while sometimes, slower convergence can get better results, but it means spending more time [1].

Due to the instability of the convergence, many researchers are focus on the precocious convergence of GA. It is proposed in [2] the genetic markers to actively avoid convergence to a particular rooted tree structure. This is achieved by maintaining a number of unique genetic markers in the population. After that, the structure fitness sharing (SFS) algorithm proposed in [3,4] is taken as a possible way to attempt to promote diversity based on tree structure. Motivated by the fitness sharing concept, it uses labels on tree structures to decrease the fitness of structures that are over-represented in the population. Generally speaking, most of the researches solve this problem by optimizing algorithm and intermediate data processing.

Membrane computing, initialed by Gh Paun in 1998 is known as new branch of natural computing [5]. The systems investigated in the framework of membrane computing is called P systems, and plenty of P systems have been developed, including cell-like P systems, tissue P systems and spiking neural P systems [6–20]. In this work, we propose a new model inspired from membrane computing models to achieve "fast-slow" convergence rate of GA in the membrane structure. The obtained algorithm is a new candidate in membrane algorithm, and many researchers have done good works on it. Currently, membrane computing has been used in optimization field [31], Systems and Synthetic Biology [21], Troubleshooting [36], economics [37] and linguistics [38]. These experiments demonstrate that applying Membrane Algorithm to optimize Genetic Algorithm is feasible. We developed here a thread control process following the Nested Membrane System [24] to searching optimal solution, where a single GA is used in each membrane and performs as a thread in the program [22]. After one iteration (evolution), the population will produce the best individual. Under the control of the communication rule [23,36], the efficiency of searching optimal solution gets a big promotion, when the problem has no solving information. It is obtained by the data experimental results that our method performs well in solving 41 benchmark functions by achieving accuracy rate about 96%.

2   Related Technologies

2.1   Genetic Algorithm

Genetic Algorithm (GA) was first proposed by J. Holland in 1975 [26]. It is a type of heuristic random search method inspired by natural selection and genetic mechanism of biological evolution law (survival of the fittest). It contains feature is the direct operating to the structured objects without the delimitation of derivation and continuity of function. It is inherent implicit parallelism and better global optimization and it can automatically obtain and guide optimized searching space for adjusting the search direction.

In general computing process, GA is started with setting the potential solution (population), and a population is consists of genes encoded by a certain number of individuals (individual). It is needed initially to encode individuals for simplify computer operation, such as binary encoding. After producing the first generation of populations, each generation produce more good approximate solution in accordance with the principle of survival of the fittest. In each generation, select individual according to the individual's fitness size, and then generate a population representative of the new solution set by genetic operators combined with cross and mutation. This process will lead new population to be more adapted to the environment, and the last population of the best individual can be the approximate optimal solution after decoding [25].

2.2   Membrane Computing Inspired Algorithm

Membrane Computing is a new branch of natural computing. It is originated from natural cells, and the structure also builds on the biological cells. The systems investigated in membrane computing are named P systems, which is defined as a series of membrane structures containing chemical substances (limited number), catalyst and rules (including the rules of the reaction, membrane transport rules etc.). It is shown in Fig. 1 the membrane structure of the P systems. Like in real biological cells, when the reactants (sometimes catalyst) are contact with each other, the chemical reaction will occur. Due to the random applications of rules, the calculation will be uncertain, in the other words, the repetition of the same question may lead to multiple solutions. When the computation of the P system is completed, the chemicals exist out of the outermost membrane will reach steady state, which means no reaction will continue.

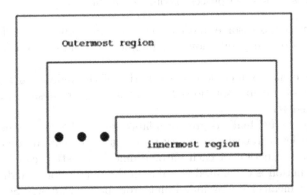

Fig. 1. Membrane structure.

A membrane algorithm framework consists of three different kinds of components:

- A number of regions which are separated by nested membranes (Fig. 1).
- For every region, a subalgorithm and a few tentative solutions of the optimization problem to be solved.
- Solution transporting mechanisms between adjacent regions.

There are three basic types of membrane system: Cell-like P system, Tissue P system, spiking neural P systems [29,32,35]. We consider here a cell-like membrane structure named Nested Membrane System, which is a friendly model for programming. The structure is used by Nishida to solve the TSP problem [30,31], and have been applied for data optimization [31].

We denote by S a feasible solution of the problem, which is distributed differences in different membranes. The communication rules means that the membrane sends some solutions into the outer membrane which directly contains it. The rule can be written as follows.

$$\{a_{max1}, a_{max2}, \ldots, a_{maxn}\}_i - \{\}_i a_{max1}, a_{max2}, \ldots, a_{maxn} \tag{1}$$

It is denoted by i the membrane i, and by $amax_1, amax_2, \ldots, amax_n$ the n best solutions in the region $1, 2, \ldots, n$, respectively. The model converges very fast because of the communication between membranes. In terms of realization of membrane computing, some associated simulation software have been released.

3   The Model and Data Experiments

3.1   GA Program

We design a basic GA program to run the dimensional function. In the program, we can set initial conditions to control the convergence rate. Every gene contains the potential solution and the threshold. In order to simplify the crossing and mutation process, encoding process is omitted as in [33].

- Chromosome: Chromosome and can be called individuals, a certain number of individuals of the population, the number of groups of individuals called population size.
- Gene: Gene elements include characteristics of the individual genes. In this paper, a set of possible solutions $S = (x1, x2, x3)$ are designed and each of them is called gene.
- Fitness: Each individual's degree of adaptation to the environment is called fitness. In order to reflect the ability to adapt to the chromosome, the introduction of the function of each chromosome in question can be measured. Here, the function is calculated to value in the population of individuals.
- Select: Select means winning individuals from population, and Selecting operation is based on the population of individual fitness assessment.
- Cross: Genetic recombinant (plus variation) play a central role in the process of evolution is a genetic recombinant organisms (plus variation). Because of giving up Genes encoding process gene cross is implemented by exchanging a random parameter of two genes.
- Variation: The basic contents of the gene mutation operator are the value of a population of some individual strings locus for change. Here we use Real value variation.

3.2 Membrane Structure

The nested membrane structure of degree m is selected, which means the number of membrane is m. The value of m is set to be 5 or 6 here, and in each membrane, GA is performed with different mutation and crossover rates. All of the GA run the same function. Because of the lightweight program, we set each GA as a thread [34]. The data communication rule works in neighbor membrane. The communication process looks as follows (current membrane is the middle membrane):

1. Each membrane start GA thread
2. Suspend thread every 50 iteration
3. Monitoring inner membrane
   If (inner membrane has no request for communication):
   3.1 Compared with the individual of the outer membrane
   3.2 Suspend outer membrane
   3.3 Replace the best individual of outer membrane
   3.4 Reuse thread
   3.5 Judge the outer membrane to reuse (avoid the thread to be suspended before reaching 50 iteration by inner membrane)
   Else: wait for the inner membrane
4. The best individual in the outmost becomes the output of the algorithm

The individual are modified only when both of the membranes have been suspended. In order to avoid deadlocks, the inner membrane has higher priority than the outer membrane.

3.3 Data Experiments

It is tested the proposed method by solving 41 benchmark functions. In the step of initialization, we created 5 GA and set different initialization information. The iteration is set to be 10000 for each GA. We controlled convergence rates by changing number of individuals, cross rate and variation rate (Table 1).

Table 1. The values of involved parameters in the GA in different regions

Population	Iterations	Cross	Variation
1000	10000	0.8	0.08
1000	10000	0.6	0.01
500	10000	0.8	0.08
500	10000	0.6	0.01
800	10000	0.8	0.1

The interface of the software is shown in Fig. 2.

The tested functions are listed in Table 2.

It is obtained by the data experimental results that our method performs well in solving benchmark functions by achieving accuracy rate about 96%.

We exam the formulas the help of the model (Table 3).

Table 2. The list of tested benchmark functions

Formula	
Ackley's function (Ak)	$f(x,y) = -20\exp(-0.2\sqrt{0.5(x^2+y^2)}) - \exp(0.5(\cos(2(\pi)x) + \cos(2(\pi)y))) + e + 20$
Sphere function (Sh)	$f(x) = \sum_{i=1}^{n} x_i^2$
Rosenbrock function (Rbk)	$f(x) = \sum_{i=1}^{n-1}[100(x_{i+1} - x_i^2) + (x_i - 1)^2]$
Beale's function (Bl)	$f(x,y) = (1.5-z+xy)^2 + (2.25-x+xy^2)^2 + (2.625-x+xy^3)^2$
GoldsteinPrice function (GP)	$f(x,y) = (1 + (x+y+1)^2(19 - 14x + 3x^2 - 14y + 6xy + 3y^2)) \times (30 + (2x-3y)^2(18-32x+12x^2+48y-36xy+27y^2))$
Booth's function (Bt)	$f(x,y) = (x+2y-7)^2 + (2x+y-5)^2$
Bukin function N.6 (BN.6)	$f(x,y) = 100\sqrt{|y - 0.01x^2|} + 0.01|x+10|$
Matyas function (Mt)	$f(x,y) = 0.26(x^2+y^2) - 0.48xy$
Levi function N.13 (LN.13)	$f(x,y) = \sin^2(3\pi x) + (x-1)^2(1+\sin^2(3\pi y)) + (y-1)^2(1+\sin^2(2\pi y))$
Three-hump camel function(Thc)	$f(x,y) = 2x^2 - 1.05x^4 + \frac{x^6}{6} + xy + y^2$
Easom function (Es)	$f(x,y) = -\cos x \cos y \exp(-((x-\pi)^2 + (y-\pi)^2))$
Cross-in-tray function (Ct)	$f(x,y) = -0.0001(|\sin x \sin y \exp(|100 - \frac{\sqrt{x^2+y^2}}{\pi}|)| + 1)^{0.1}$
Eggholder function (Ehd)	$f(x,y) = -(y+47)\sin(\sqrt{|\frac{x}{2} + (y+47)|}) - x\sin(\sqrt{|x - (y+47)|})$
Holder table function (Ht)	$f(x,y) = -|\sin x \cos y \exp(|1 - \frac{\sqrt{x^2+y^2}}{\pi}|)|$
McCormick function (McC)	$f(x,y) = \sin(x+y) + (x-y)^2 - 1.5x + 2.5y + 1$
Schaffer function N. 2 (Scf.2)	$f(x,y) = 0.5 + \frac{\sin^2(|x^2-y^2|)-0.5}{(1+0.001(x^2+y^2))^2}$
Schaffer function N. 4 (Scf.4)	$f(x,y) = 0.5 + \frac{\cos^2(\sin(|x^2-y^2|))-0.5}{(1+0.001(x^2+y^2))^2}$
Hump Functions (Hmp)	$f(x) = 4x_1^2 - 2.1x_1^4 + x_1^6/3 + x_1x_2 - 4x_2^2 + 4x_2^4$
Rastrigin function (Rst)	$f(x) = An + \sum_{i=1}^{n}(x_i^2 - A\cos(2\pi x_i))$
Colville function (Clv)	$f(x) = 100(x_1^2 - x_2)^2 + (x_1 - 1)^2 + (x_3 - 1)^2 + 90(x_3^2 - x_4)^2 + 10.1((x_2 - 1)^2 + (x_4 - 1)^2) + 19.8(x_2^- 1)(x_4 - 1)$
Griewank function (Gwk)	$f(x) = \sum_{i=1}^{n}\frac{x_i^2}{4000} - \prod_{i=1}^{n}\cos(\frac{x_i}{\sqrt{i}}) + 1$
Schwefel function (Swf)	$f(x) = -\sum_{i=1}^{n} x_i \sin(\sqrt{|x_i|})$
Shubert function (Shb)	$f(x) = (\sum_{i=1}^{5} i\cos((i+1)x_1+i))(\sum_{i=1}^{5} i\cos((i+1)x_2+i))$
Sum Squares function (SSq)	$f(x) = \sum_{i=1}^{n} ix_i^2$
Zakharov function (Zkr)	$f(x) = \sum_{i=1}^{n} x_i^2 + (0.5\sum_{i=1}^{n} ix_i)^2 + (0.5\sum_{i=1}^{n} ix_i)^4$
Generalized Rastrigins function (GR)	$f(x) = \sum_{i=1}^{n}[x_i^2 - 10\cos(2\pi x_i) + 10]$
Styblinski-Tang function (SbT)	$f(x) = 0.5(\sum_{i=1}^{n} x_i^4 - 16x_i^2 + 5x_i)$
Michaelwiczs function (Mcw)	$f(x,y) = -\sin x \sin^{20}(\frac{x^2}{\pi}) - \sin y \sin^{20}(\frac{2y^2}{\pi})$
Six-hump camel back function (Shcb)	$f(x,y) = (4 - 2.1x^2 + \frac{1}{3}x^4)x^2 + xy + 4(y^2 - 1)y^2$
Xin-She Yangs functions (XSY)	$f(x) = (\sum_{i=1}^{n}|x_i|)\exp(-\sum_{i=1}^{n}\sin(x_i^2))$
J.D. Schaffer function (JDS)	$f(x) = \frac{\sin^2(\sqrt{(x_1^2+x_2^2)})-0.5}{[1+0.001(x_1^2+x_2^2)]^2} - 0.5$
Quartic Function i.e. Niose (Qie)	$f(x) = \sum_{i=1}^{n} ix_i^4 + random[0,1)$
Step function (Step)	$f(x) = \sum_{i=1}^{n}(|x_i + 0.5|)^2$
Schwefels Problem 2.21 (Swf2.21)	$f(x) = \max_{i=1}^{n}\{|x_i|\}$
Schwefels Problem 2.22 (Swf2.22)	$f(x) = \sum_{i=1}^{n}|x_i| + \prod_{i=1}^{n}|x_i|$
Schwefels Problem 1.2 (Swf1.2)	$f(x) = \sum_{i=1}^{n}(\sum_{j=1}^{n} x_j)^2$

Table 3. The values of parameters in tested benchmark functions

Formula	Search domain	Minimum	Result	Deviation
Ak	[−10,10] n = 2	0	0	0
Sh	[−10,10] n = 2	0	0	0
	[−10,10] n = 30	0	0	0
Rbk	[−10,10] n = 2	0	0	0
	[−512,512] n = 10	0	0	0
Bl	[−10,10]	0	0	0
GP	[−2,2]	3	0	Err
Bt	[−10,10]	0	0	0
BN.6	[−15,15]	0	0	0
Bt	[−10,10]	0	0	0
Mt	[−10,10]	0	0	0
Es	[−100,100]	−1	−0.98564252	1.5%
LN.13	[−10,10]	0	0	0
The	[−10,10]	0	0	0
Ct	[−10,10]	−2.06261	−2.07697545	0.69%
Ehd	[−512,512]	−959.6407	−954.20825867	0.566%
Ht	[−10,10]	−19.2085	−19.12593522	0.43%
McC	[−3,4]	−1.9133	−1.89645318	0.88%
Scf. 2	[−5,5]	0	0	0
Scf. 4	[−5,5]	0.292579	0	Err
Hmp	[−5,5] n = 2	0	0	0
Rst	[−5.12,5.12] n = 2, A = 10	0	0	0
	[−5.12,5.12] n = 10, A = 10	0	0	0
Clv	[−10,10] n = 4	0	0	0
	[−10,10] n = 10	0	0	0
Gwk	[−600,600] n = 2	0	0	0
	[−600,600] n = 10	0	0	0
Swf	[−500,500] n = 2	837.9658	837.96552803	$3.24e^{-7}$
	[−500,500] n = 10	0	0	0
Shb	[−10,10] n = 3	−186.7309	−186.72187594	0.0048%
SSq	[−10,10] n = 2	0	0	0
	[−10,10] n = 30	0	0	0
Zkr	[−5,10] n = 2	0	0	0
	[−5,10] n = 10	0	0	0
GR	[−5.12,5.12] n = 2	0	0	0
	[−5.12,5.12] n = 10	0	0	0
SbT	[−5,5] n = 2	(−78.33234,−78.33232)	−78.322614322	0.023%
	[−5,5] n = 10	(−391.6617,−391.6616)	−391.59810786	0.0162%
Mcw	[0,5] m = 10, n = 2	−1.8013	−1.80120638	0.0052%
Shcb	[−3,3]	−1.0316	1.03052387	0.10%
XSY	[−2,2] n = 2	0	0	0
JDS	[−100,100]	−1	0.99022143	0.978%
Qie	[−1.28,1.28]	0	0	0
Step	[−100,100] n = 3	0	0	0
	[−100,100] n = 10	0	0	0
Swf2.21	[−100,100] n = 3	0	0	0
	[−100,100] n = 100	0	0	0
Swf2.22	[−10,10] n = 3	0	0	0
	[−10,10] n = 10	0	0	0
Swf1.2	[−100,100] n = 3	0	0	0

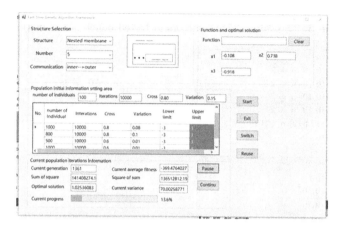

Fig. 2. Fast-slow GA framework.

4   Conclusion

In this paper, a hybrid "fast-slow" convergent framework for genetic algorithm inspired by membrane computing is proposed. Such framework incorporates basic Cell-like P System and GA. Several basic features like compartmentalization, communication among compartments, dynamic membrane structure help GA to combine the convergence. It is tested the proposed method by solving 41 benchmark functions. It is found that our method performs well in solving benchmark functions by achieving accuracy rate about 96%.

Compared with these results, we can find the algorithm show good performance for searching optimal solution. It combines the potential results of different GA and provides a method to solve premature convergence. It also reduces the influence of the initialization to GA. On the other hand, the communication rule can be optimized, and the present paper control the data transmission by making use of thread control inspired by Nested membrane structure.

Membrane algorithms inherit the parallelism of P system. In the further study, the algorithms will be naturally implemented on a parallel hardware. The parallelism is simulated in a common serial machine. The GA in each membrane is not true parallel processing and it is also the difficulty of the application of membrane computing, even if the algorithm running in a cluster, because the communication costs is too high to optimization. So, there are still many improvements to do if the framework in this paper runs on a parallel hardware, such as GPU. We hope other membrane structure such as spiking neural P systems [39] can also be applied if the threads control method is well designed. It is of interests to replace GA in each membrane by some other intelligent algorithms, such as PSO, simulated annealing. As well, some other membrane structures, for instance, star membrane structure, and rooted membrane structure can be expanded to our hybrid framework.

Acknowledgment. This work was supported by National Natural Science Foundation of China (61402187, 61502535, 61572522, 61502063 and 61572523), China Postdoctoral Science Foundation funded project (2016M592267), Program for New Century Excellent Talents in University (NCET-13-1031), 863 Program (2015AA020925), Natural Science Foundation Project of CQ CSTC (No. cstc2012jjA40059), and Fundamental Research Funds for the Central Universities (247201607005A).

References

1. Lin, F., Zhou, C., Changm K.: Convergence rate analysis of allied genetic algorithm. In: IEEE Conference on Decision and Control, pp. 786–791 (2010)
2. Burks, A.R., Punch, W.F.: An efficient structural diversity technique for genetic programming. In: ACM Conference on Genetic and Evolutionary Computation, pp. 991–998 (2015)
3. Hu, J., Seo, K., Li, S., et al.: Structure fitness sharing (SFS) for evolutionary design by genetic programming. In: Genetic & Evolutionary Computation Conference, pp. 780–787 (2012)
4. Mckay, R.I.: Fitness sharing in genetic programming. In: Genetic and Evolutionary Computation Conference, pp. 10–12 (2000)
5. Paun, G.: Membrane Computing: An Introduction (2002)
6. Song, T., Pan, L., Wang, J., Venkat, I., Subramanian, K., Abdullah, R.: Normal forms of spiking neural P systems with anti-spikes. IEEE Trans. NanoBiosci. **11**(4), 352–359 (2012)
7. Padmavati Metta, V., Kelemenova, A.: Universality of spiking neural P systems with anti-spikes. New Math. Nat. Comput. **8**(3), 281–283 (2014)
8. Krithivasan, K., Metta, V.P., Garg, D.: On string languages generated by spiking neural P systems with anti-spikes. Int. J. Found. Comput. Sci. **22**(1), 15–21 (2011)
9. Song, T., Wang, X., Zhang, Z., Chen, Z.: Homogenous spiking neural P systems with anti-spikes. Neural Comput. Appl. doi:10.1007/s00521-013-1397-8
10. Song, T., Liu, X., Zeng, X.: Asynchronous spiking neural P systems with anti-spikes. Neural Process. Lett. **42**(3), 633–647 (2014)
11. Jiang, K., Pan, L.: Spiking neural P systems with anti-spikes working in sequential mode induced by maximum spike number. Neurocomputing **171**(1), 1674–1683 (2015)
12. Metta, V.P., Raghuraman, S., Krithivasan, K.: Spiking neural P systems with cooperating rules. In: Gheorghe, M., Rozenberg, G., Salomaa, A., Sosík, P., Zandron, C. (eds.) CMC 2014. LNCS, vol. 8961, pp. 314–329. Springer, Heidelberg (2014). doi:10.1007/978-3-319-14370-5_20
13. Metta, V.P., Raghuraman, S., Krithivasan, K.: Small universal spiking neural P systems with cooperating rules as function computing devices. In: Gheorghe, M., Rozenberg, G., Salomaa, A., Sosík, P., Zandron, C. (eds.) CMC 2014. LNCS, vol. 8961, pp. 300–313. Springer, Heidelberg (2014). doi:10.1007/978-3-319-14370-5_19
14. Song, T., Xu, J., Pan, L.: On the universality and non-universality of spiking neural P system with rules on synapses. IEEE Trans. NanoBiosci. **14**(8), 960–966 (2015)
15. Song, T., Pan, L.: Spiking neural P systems with rules on synapses working in maximum spiking strategy. IEEE Trans. Nanobiosci. **14**(4), 465–477 (2015)
16. Song, T., Pan, L.: Spiking neural P systems with rules on synapses working in maximum spikes consumption strategy. IEEE Trans. Nanobiosci. **14**(1), 38–44 (2015)
17. Song, T., Zou, Q., Liu, X., Zeng, X.: Asynchronous spiking neural P systems with rules on synapses. Neurocomputing **151**, 1439–1445 (2015)

18. Zhang, X., Zeng, X., Pan, L.: Weighted spiking neural P systems with rules on synapses. Fundamenta Informaticae **134**(1–2), 201–218 (2014)
19. Ionescu, M., Paun, G., Pérez-Jiménez, M.J., Yokomori, T.: Spiking neural dP systems. Fundamenta Informaticae **111**(4), 423–436 (2011)
20. Song, T., Pan, L.: Spiking neural P systems with request rules. Neurocomputing (2016). doi:10.1016/j.neucom.2016.02.023
21. Graham, S., Saxton, J., Woodward, M., et al.: Applications of membrane computing in systems and synthetic biology. Emergence Complex. Comput. **7**(09), S624 (2013)
22. Moon, S., Chang, B.M.: A thread monitoring system for multithreaded java programs. ACM Sigplan Not. Homepage **41**(5), 21–29 (2006)
23. Wang, X., Song, T., Gong, F., Zheng, P.: On the computational power of spiking neural P systems with self-organization. Sci. Rep. doi:10.1038/srep27624
24. Leporati, A., Pagani, D.: A membrane algorithm for the min storage problem. In: Hoogeboom, H.J., Păun, G., Rozenberg, G., Salomaa, A. (eds.) WMC 2006. LNCS, vol. 4361, pp. 443–462. Springer, Heidelberg (2006). doi:10.1007/11963516_28
25. Pezzella, F., Morganti, G., Ciaschetti, G.: A genetic algorithm for the flexible job-shop scheduling problem. Comput. Oper. Res. **35**(10), 3202–3212 (2008)
26. Goldberg, D.E.: Genetic algorithm in search
27. Paun, G., Rozenberg, G.: A guide to membrane computing. Theor. Comput. Sci. **287**(1), 73–100 (2002)
28. Paun, G.: Computing with Membranes, Working with Computers, pp. 108–143. National Computing Centre Limited (1982)
29. Ionescu, M., Paun, G., Yokomori, T.: Spiking neural P systems with an exhaustive use of rules. Int. J. Unconventional Comput. **3**, 135–153 (2007)
30. Nishida, T.Y.: Membrane algorithms. In: Freund, R., Păun, G., Rozenberg, G., Salomaa, A. (eds.) WMC 2005. LNCS, vol. 3850, pp. 55–66. Springer, Heidelberg (2006). doi:10.1007/11603047_4
31. Huang, L., Wang, N.: An optimization algorithm inspired by membrane computing. In: Jiao, L., Wang, L., Gao, X., Liu, J., Wu, F. (eds.) ICNC 2006. LNCS, vol. 4222, pp. 49–52. Springer, Heidelberg (2006). doi:10.1007/11881223_7
32. Gutierrez-Naranjo, M.A., Perez-Jimenez, M.J., Ramrez-Martnez, D.: A software tool for verification of spiking neural P systems. Nat. Comput. **7**(4), 485–497 (2008)
33. Wu, Y., Tang, Y., Han, B., et al.: A topology analysis and genetic algorithm combined approach for power network intentional islanding. Int. J. Electr. Power Energy Syst. **71**, 174–183 (2015)
34. Nowotniak, R., Kucharski, J.: GPU-based tuning of quantum-inspired genetic algorithm for a combinatorial optimization problem. Bull. Pol. Acad. Sci. Tech. Sci. **60**(2), 323–330 (2012)
35. Song, T., Pan, L.: Spiking neural P systems with rules on synapses working in maximum spiking strategy. IEEE Trans. Nanobiosci. **14**(1), 465–477 (2015)
36. Wang, T., Zhang, G., Zhao, J., et al.: Fault diagnosis of electric power systems based on fuzzy reasoning spiking neural P systems. IEEE Trans. Power Syst. **30**, 1182–1194 (2014)
37. Un, G., Un, R.: Membrane computing and economics: numerical P systems. Fundamenta Informaticae **73**(1–2), 213–227 (2006)
38. Ciobanu, G., Păun, G., Prez-Jimnez, M.J.: Applications of membrane computing. Nat. Comput. **287**(1), 73–100 (2006)
39. Zhang, G., Rong, H., Neri, F.: An optimization spiking neural P system for approximately solving combinatorial optimization problems. Int. J. Neural Syst. **24**(5), 1440006 (2014)

An Image Threshold Segmentation Algorithm with Hybrid Evolutionary Mechanisms Based on Membrane Computing

Shuo Liu[1], Kang Zhou[2(✉)], Shan Zeng[1], Huaqing Qi[1], and Tingfang Wu[1,3]

[1] Department of Math and Computer, Wuhan Polytechnic University,
Wuhan 430023, Hubei, China
liushuo1979@hotmail.com, zengshan1981@whpu.edu.cn, qihuaqing@sohu.com
[2] Department of Economics and Management, Wuhan Polytechnic University,
Wuhan 430023, Hubei, China
zhoukang_wh@163.com
[3] Key Laboratory of Image Information Processing and Intelligent Control,
School of Automation, Huazhong University of Science and Technology,
Wuhan 430074, Hubei, China
tfwu@hust.edu.cn

Abstract. Focused on the contradiction between selective pressure and population diversity in the optimization algorithm using hybrid evolutionary mechanisms, this paper proposes a membrane image threshold segmentation algorithm based on the idea of membrane computing. The proposal uses a hybrid tissue P system of three one-level-membrane-structure (OLMS) membranes in which genetic algorithm (GA) and particle swarm optimal algorithm (PSO) are used as evolution operator. The proposed algorithm uses the communication rules and transfer rules to establish the interactions among the membranes, and then enhances the diversity of population in the system and improves the convergence of the algorithm. After comparing with the conventional methods, simulation results and dynamic behavior analysis show that the proposal evidently improve the validity and feasibility of the image segmentation algorithm.

Keywords: Membrane computing · Tissue P system · Threshold segmentation

1 Introduction

Image segmentation is critical for the digital image processing, and is the first step to analyze image [1]. The quality of image segmentation directly affects the effect of the subsequent processing of image processing. The current methods of image segmentation mainly include threshold method, edge test [2], region growing method [3], morphology watershed method, and etc.

Image threshold segmentation is an important segmentation technology [4]. The basic idea regards the image as two parts: the object and background, using

© Springer Nature Singapore Pte Ltd. 2016
M. Gong et al. (Eds.): BIC-TA 2016, Part I, CCIS 681, pp. 85–94, 2016.
DOI: 10.1007/978-981-10-3611-8_10

the gray value difference between the object and background, select a suitable gray value as a threshold, for each pixel in the image by gray value attributable to the object and the background of two parts.

Based on the maximum class square error method, Otsu proposes an algorithm to calculate the single threshold. Not related to the specific content of the image but based on pixel gray level statistics, So it has stronger robustness, and has been applied in many fields, such as medical [5], infrared image [6] and so on. Single threshold Otsu method only considers the gray information of the image, but does not take into account the spatial position of the pixels, the image segmentation effect is not obvious in double peak image. In 1979, a two-dimensional segmentation method was proposed, which became a hot issue in the study [7,8]. As the single threshold is extended to multi-threshold, due to the increase of the dimension, the traversing method to select threshold is larger, and the computation complexity increases exponentially. Then how to efficiently calculating the optimal threshold value becomes the key of the algorithm. Swarm intelligence evolution algorithm is introduced to find the optimal threshold, such as the genetic algorithms [9], particle swarm optimization algorithm [10], and etc.

But for intelligent algorithms, the efficiency of the algorithm mostly depends on the configuration parameters and the initial solution. At the same time, intelligent algorithm is easy to fall into local optimum, and thus can not find the global optimal solution. Many scholars had done related work [11,12] to improve the algorithm. Membrane Computing is a novel distributed parallel computing model. It is a abstract computational model based on the most basic unit of life cells, and first formally proposed by the European Academy of Sciences Gheorghe Păun in his research report at Turku computer center [13]. Since then, many scholars began to engage in related research [26–29] [30].

The purpose of membrane computing is to abstract a new calculation model from cells, particularly in the cell membrane, with its structure and function, called a membrane system [19,20]. Membrane computing includes the three elements: membrane structures, objects and evolution of the rules [14,21]. The object of tissue-like P systems is the mechanism in which multiple cells that each cell can have its own objects and evolutionary rules, through mutual cooperation and communication with each other, together to complete the calculation. This parallel multiple evolutionary mechanism provides a feasible solution to solve the problem: convergence to local optimal due to lack of population diversity. There is a wide range of applications, such as the gradient edge detection [15], multimodal image registration [16], coal sorting robots [17]and so on. There are some works [23–27] on evolutionary optimization.

2   Principle of Threshold Images Segmentation

For a digital image, the variance is a measure of the uniformity of the gray level distribution. Bigger the variance is, more evident the difference between the various parts of the image is. It means that in the image segmentation, as part of the target is divided into background or part of the background wrong into target, this will lead to the two part of the difference is smaller, so the maximum variance in image segmentation means that the probability of fault points minimum. Based on the principle, a threshold image segmentation algorithm is proposed by Otus. In later studies, to consider both grey value and the corresponding spatial location relationship, two-dimensional threshold image segmentation algorithm is proposed.

For a digital image with size $M * N$, for each pixel, its pixel gray value and neighborhood gray value are L, define a binary array (i, j), of which i is the pixel gray value, j is the average gray value of corresponding $(3 * 3)$ neighborhood; n_{ij} is the number of the pixel which have the same binary array (i, j).

The relative probability is:

$$p_{i,j} = \frac{n_{i,j}}{M \cdot N};$$

(1)

Assume that the object and background as I_0 and I_1, s is the threshold of pixel gray value and t is the gray value threshold of neighborhood.

Two classes of the probability are:

$$P_0(s,t) = \sum_{i=1}^{s}\sum_{j=1}^{t} P_{i,j}$$

(2)

$$P_1(s,t) = \sum_{i=s+1}^{L}\sum_{j=t+1}^{L} P_{i,j}$$

(3)

Two classes of the corresponding mean vector are:

$$\mu_0 = (\mu_{0i}\ \mu_{0j})^T = \left(\sum_{i=1}^{s}\sum_{j=1}^{t}\frac{i \cdot P_{i,j}}{P_0}\ \sum_{i=1}^{s}\sum_{j=1}^{t}\frac{j \cdot P_{i,j}}{P_0}\right)^T$$

(4)

$$\mu_1 = (\mu_{1i}\ \mu_{1j})^T = \left(\sum_{i=1}^{L}\sum_{j=1}^{L}\frac{i \cdot P_{i,j}}{P_1}\ \sum_{i=1}^{L}\sum_{j=1}^{L}\frac{j \cdot P_{i,j}}{P_1}\right)^T$$

(5)

The population mean vector is

$$mu_T = (\mu_{Ti}\ \mu_{Tj})^T = \left(\sum_{i=1}^{L}\sum_{j=1}^{L} i \cdot P_{i,j}\ \sum_{i=1}^{L}\sum_{j=1}^{L} j \cdot P_{i,j}\right)^T$$

(6)

Ignoring the influence of noise and other, we can do the assumptions as the following:

$$P_0 + P_1 \approx 1, \mu \approx P_0\mu_0 + P_1\mu_1$$

(7)

Use the trace of matrix Sb(s,t) as the discrete degree measure, then

$$R = P_0[(\mu_{0i} - \mu_{Ti})^2 + (\mu_{0j} - \mu_{Tj})^2] + P_1[(\mu_{1i} - \mu_{Ti})^2 + (\mu_{1j} - \mu_{Tj})^2]$$

(8)

So the best optional threshold value (s, t) should meet the following equation:

$$(s^*, t^*) = arg \max_{1 \leq s, t \leq L} (R) \tag{9}$$

How to ascertain the optimal threshold is the key for the algorithm. Due to the adoption of the two-dimensional data, the calculation amount and difficulty are increased. How to solve the large data optimization, based on membrane computing framework we proposed a hybrid evolutionary mechanism of two-dimensional segmentation algorithm. Using membrane parallel evolution and exchange of information, this work maintains the diversity algorithm object, and overcomes the algorithm falling into a local optimum.

3 Threshold Segmentation Membrane Algorithm

The 3-degree tissue-link membrane system is defined as [17, 21, 22]:

$$\prod = (O, \sigma_1, \sigma_2, \sigma_3, syn, i_0);$$

Therein to,

(1) O is a finite non-empty alphabet, and its elements is the object of membrane system, in this paper the object indicates the image grey value corresponding to the binary code set.

(2) σ_i shows the ith cell as follows: $\sigma_i = (Q_i, R_i)$, Q_i shows the object of ith cell. R_i expresses the evolution rules, evolution rule of cell σ_1, σ_2 is the particle swarm algorithm, and evolution rule of cell σ_3 is the genetic algorithm.

(3) Syn indicates the connections between cells, and this cells can communicate. Between three cells can be two-way information transmission, which form a network structure.

(4) i_0 shows the output cell label. Here $i_0 = 0$, that means cells will send optimal solution to the environment.

(5) System input is the parameters and initial solution configuration for various evolutionary algorithm; System downtime rule is to meet the maximum number of iterations; System output is the global optimal solution to the environment.

3.1 Object of the Tissue-Link Membrane System

The tissue-link P system is to solve the given optimization, so all the objects of the membrane system is feasible solution set. Considering the characteristics of digital image grey value, all objects in this work use binary coding.

Assume that the object number in the whole system is N, and the dimension of each solution is D, all objects in the cells constitute a $N * D$ matrix:

$$\begin{pmatrix} pop_{11} & pop_{12} & \cdots & pop_{1D} \\ pop_{21} & pop_{22} & \cdots & pop_{2D} \\ \cdots & \cdots & \cdots & \cdots \\ pop_{N1} & pop_{N2} & \cdots & pop_{ND} \end{pmatrix}$$

All objects are averagely assigned to three membranes. Membrane $1, 2$ as the auxiliary membrane, is to increase the diversity of population; Membrane 3 as the main membrane, focuses on the local optimization. For each object, the relative object function value is its fitness value. In the iterative process, the optimal solution of whole system was sent to environment, called the global optimal, denoted as Z_{best}.

3.2   Hybrid Evolutionary Rule and Communication Rules

Three membranes with intelligent optimization rules, due to their respective different purposes, are different in specific evolutionary rules. The main function of auxiliary membrane is used to keep the diversity of population, and expand the search space, then reduce the probability that fall into local optimum, and improve the ability of global optimization. The particle swarm algorithm is simple and can be quick calculated. Therefore parameter configuration can be used to expand the search space so as to maintain the population diversity. The main function of main membrane focuses on the strong local search ability, and this can effectively solve the optimal solution in the space.

Genetic algorithm has the strong optimal ability, through the parameter configuration, we can strengthen its local optimization ability. Through information exchange between the main membrane and the auxiliary membrane, the advantages of different algorithms are played, and the efficiency of the system can be great optimized by using the hybrid evolution rules.

The evolution rules of the membrane 1: The global PSO. The global particle swarm optimal intelligence algorithm is used as evolution rules of membrane 1. In the particle location update formula, as $C1 = 0$, the particles have not the cognitive ability, and become only a social model, called global PSO algorithm. The particle has the ability to expand the search space, and has the greatest protection for the whole population diversity.

Location update function is shown as follows:

$$V_{k+1} = c_2 r_2 (G_{best} - X_k) \tag{10}$$

$$sig(V_k) = \frac{1}{1 + exp(-V_k)} \tag{11}$$

$$X_{k+1} = \begin{cases} 0 & sig(V_k) < rand \\ 1 & sig(V_k) \geq rand \end{cases} \tag{12}$$

Therein to, c_2 is learning factor, and r_2 is random number. G_{best} is the current optimal location of the global, X_k is the kth iterations of the particle position, V_k is the kth iterations of the particle velocity. After each iteration of the fixed number, Membrane 1 output to the membrane 3 T of the best particle, to the membrane 2 output T of the suboptimal particle. To ensure that the same size of the particles, before the next iteration, through the roulette way to select fixed particles into the next iteration.

The evolution rules of the membrane 2: PSO with inertia weight. At the international conference on evolutionary computation, some researchers corrected the basic location and velocity formula in 1998. Inertia weighting factor had been introduced. The value of inertia weighting factor is bigger, then global optimization capability is stronger, as well as local optimization ability weaker, and vice versa.

The 2th Membrane mainly give the diversity of particles to the main Membrane, so the weight sets up by using linear growth, then enhance global optimization ability, and consider the global optimal solution. The new formula of velocity is given as follows:

$$V_{k+1} = \omega \cdot V_k + c_1 r_1 (P_{best} - X_k) + c_2 r_2 (G_{best} - X_k) \tag{13}$$

$$\omega = \omega_{win} + n \cdot (\frac{\omega_{max} - \omega_{win}}{N}) \tag{14}$$

Particles location update formula same as membrane 1. After each iteration of the fixed number, membrane 2 give the number T of the optimal particle to the membrane 3, and give the number T of the suboptimal particle to the membrane 2. To ensure that the same size of the particles, before the next iteration, through the roulette way to select fixed particles into the next iteration.

The evolution rules of the membrane 3: The Standard GA. The rule of Membrane 3 is standard genetic algorithm: elite strategy choice, two-point crossover and random mutation. After each iteration of the fixed number, it accept $2T$ object from the auxiliary membrane, and with the original object which constitute a set of selected object. Keep the best T objects, and select the rest of the object through the form of the roulette wheel based on fitness values. So it can not only retain the best object of the whole system, but also keep the diversity of the population under large probability.

4   Experiment Analysis

4.1   Data Sets Used in the Experiments

The paper uses 3 typical images to carry out the experiment. Digital image corresponding to the experiment and the relative data characteristics are shown below (Table 1) (Fig. 1).

Table 1. Data sets used in the experiments

Data sets	Type	Col of data	Row of data	No. of data
Lena	jpg	240	240	57600
Rice	png	256	256	65536
Cameraman	jpg	330	314	103620

(a) lena   (b) rice   (c) cameraman

Fig. 1. There experiment images

4.2 Parameter Configuration in Experiments

The parameter configuration are as follows: each membrane has 50 objects, the largest number of iterations is 300; Membrane 1 uses the global particle swarm optional algorithm, $C1 = 2$; Membrane 2 use the global particle swarm optional algorithm, $C1 = C2 = 2$; The crossover probability and mutation probability of the genetic algorithm is $p_c = 0.8$ and $p_m = 0.003$. Each iteration 5 times, an information communication is active.

4.3 Algorithm Analysis and Comparison

In order to evaluate the characteristics of the algorithm, the two kinds of measure factors used in this work are the diversity and convergence. Population diversity is mainly used to evaluate the individuals difference degree, in the iteration of the algorithm, the diversity of population is important for preventing the algorithm from falling into local optimum.

Based on the Statistical diffusion theory, the function used to measure the particle diversity is [18].

$$D_{bc} = \frac{1}{n-1}(\frac{\sum_i S_i^2}{L} - \frac{s^2}{L \cdot n}) \tag{15}$$

Therein to, n is the population number, L is the dimension of the particles; S_i is the number of 1 in the binary digits for the ith particle; S is the number of 1 for all particles in the binary. D_{bc} relative change rate reflect species diversity change rate.

Convergence is one of the important factors that determines the algorithm performance. In this paper, we use the best individual fitness and the average individual fitness to test and analyze the convergence of the algorithm. The defines are respectively given as follows:

$$C_{fb} = max(f_i(x))(i = 1, 2, \cdots, n) \tag{16}$$

$$C_{fa} = \frac{\sum_{i=1}^{n} f_i(x)}{n} \tag{17}$$

The numerical change shows the capabilities of exploration and development (Fig. 2).

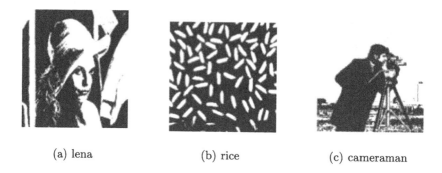

(a) lena   (b) rice   (c) cameraman

Fig. 2. The segmentation image

5   Conclusion

Focused on the contradiction between selective pressure and population diversity in the optimization algorithm, using hybrid evolutionary mechanisms, this paper proposes a membrane image threshold segmentation algorithm based on the idea of membrane computing. The proposal uses a hybrid tissue P system consisting of OLMS membranes in which GA and PSO are used as evolution operator. The proposed algorithm uses the communication rules and transfer rules to establish the interactions among the membranes, and then enhances the diversity of population in the system and improves the convergence of the algorithm. After comparing with the conventional methods, simulation results and dynamic behavior analysis show that the proposal evidently improve the validity and feasibility of the image segmentation algorithm.

There are several further problems which deserve be considered. An interesting and important research line is how to proved the advantage of the membrane computing than others.

Acknowledgments. The work was supported by National Natural Science Foundation of China (Grant No. 61179032 and 61303116), the Special Scientific Research Fund of Food Public Welfare Profession of China (Grant No. 2015130043), the Research and Practice Project of Graduate Education Teaching Reform of Polytechnic University (YZ2015002), the Scientific research project of Wuhan Polytechnic University (2016Y01), the science and technology research project of the Hubei province (B201601).

References

1. Gonzalez, C., Woods, E.: Digital Image Processing, 2nd edn. Electronic Industry Press, Beijing (2007)

2. Fu, Z.C., Li, X.Q.: Based on the radial edge detection and segmentation of tongue like a Snake model. Chin. J. Image Graph. **4**, 688–699 (2009)

3. Yu, C.C., Chen, J.: Based on adaptive threshold and region growing SD - OCT sugar net light spot image segmentation. J. Comput. Sci. **B11**, 123–125 (2015)

4. Dong, L.J.: Review the image threshold technology, classification and evaluation. J. Shenyang Univ. **4**, 8–11 (2004)

5. Shen, X.J., Pan, H., Chen, H.P.: Medical images based on one-dimensional Otsu threshold segmentation algorithm. J. Jilin Univ. (Sci. Ed.) **2**, 344–348 (2016)

6. Zhou, L.P., Chen, Z.: Based on the improved Otsu algorithm of pig ears thermal infrared image characteristic area detection. J. Agric. Mach. **4**, 228–232 (2016)

7. Wang, Y.B., Chen, J.R.: Two-dimensional Otsu threshold segmentation algorithm is improved and the application. Comput. Simul. **4**, 263–267 (2008)

8. Fan, J.L., Zhao, F.: The gray image threshold segmentation method of two-dimensional Otsu curve. J. Electron. **4**, 751–756 (2007)

9. Tian, Y., Yuan, W.Q.: The application of genetic algorithm in image processing. Chin. J. Image Graph. **3**, 389–397 (2007)

10. Tang, Y.G., Liu, D., Guan, X.P.: The two-dimensional Otsu method based on particle swarm and fast image segmentation. Control and Decision Making, pp. 202–206 (2007)

11. Jiang, W.J.: High-speed data acquisition based on improved ant colony algorithm fuzzy region segmentation image. Comput. Simul. **12**, 377–381 (2015)

12. He, C.H., Hu, Y.C.: Based on the improved genetic algorithm of automatic threshold image segmentation method. Comput. Simul. **2**, 312–315 (2011)

13. Zhang, G.X., Pan, L.P.: A new branch of natural computation: membrane computing. J. Comput. **2**, 208–214 (2010)

14. Pan, L.Q., Song, T.: Cell calculation progress and future. Proc. Chin. Acad. Sci. **1**, 115–123 (2014)

15. Xie, P.J., Ji, S.M.: A gradient edge detection algorithm based on membrane computing. J. Comput. Appl. Softw. **2**, 161–163 (2016)

16. Li, Z.Y., Zhang, C.F.: Based on membrane computing research of multimodal image registration algorithm. J. Xihua Univ. (Nat. Sci. Ed.) **5**, 7–15 (2015)

17. Paun, G.: Membrane Computing-An Introduction. Springer, Berlin (2002). (Chinese translation, L.Q. Pan, X.X. Zeng, T. Song)

18. Zhang, G.X., Cheng, J.X., Wang, T.: Membrane Computing: Theory and Applications. Science Press, Beijing (2014)

19. Zhang, G.X., Pan, L.Q.: A survey of membrane computing as a new branch of natural computing. Chin. J. Comput. **33**(2), 208–214 (2010)

20. Song, T., Pan, L.: Spiking neural P systems with request rules. Neurocomputing **193**(12), 193–200 (2016)

21. Song, T., Pan, Z., Wong, D.M., Wang, X.: Design of logic gates using spiking neural P systems with homogeneous neurons and astrocytes-like control. Inf. Sci. **372**, 380–391 (2016)

22. Shi, X., Wu, X., Song, T., Li, X.: Construction of DNA nanotubes with controllable diameters and patterns by using hierarchical DNA sub-tiles, Nanoscale. doi:10.1039/C6NR02695H

23. Zhang, X.Y., Tian, Y., Jin, Y.C.: A knee point driven evolutionary algorithm for many-objective optimization. IEEE Trans. Evol. Comput. **19**(6), 761–776 (2015)

24. Zhang, X.Y., Tian, Y., Cheng, R., Jin, Y.C.: An efficient approach to non-dominated sorting for evolutionary multi-objective optimization. IEEE Trans. Evol. Comput. **19**(2), 201–213 (2015)

25. Song, T., Gong, F., Liu, X.Y., Zhao, Y.Z., Zhang, X.Y.: Spiking neural P systems with white hole neurons. IEEE Trans. Nanobiosci. (2016, in press). doi:10.1109/TNB.2016.2598879

26. Zhang, X.Y., Pan, L.Q., Păun, A.: On universality of axon P systems. IEEE Trans. Neural Netw. Learn. Syst. **26**(11), 2816–2829 (2015)

27. Zhang, X.Y., Liu, Y.J., Luo, B., Pan, L.Q.: Computational power of tissue P systems for generating control languages. Inf. Sci. **278**(10), 285–297 (2014)

28. Zeng, X.X., Xu, L., Liu, X.R., Pan, L.Q.: On languages generated by spiking neural P systems with weights. Inf. Sci. **278**, 423–433 (2014)

29. Wang, X., Song, T., Gong, F., Zheng, P.: On the computational power of spiking neural P systems with self-organization, Scientific reports (2016). doi:10.1038/srep27624

K-Medoids-Based Consensus Clustering Based on Cell-Like P Systems with Promoters and Inhibitors

Xiyu Liu, Yuzhen Zhao[✉], and Wenxing Sun

School of Management Science and Engineering,
Shandong Normal University, Jinan 250014, China
sdxyliu@163.com, zhaoyuzhen_happy@126.com, 373253360@qq.com

Abstract. Consensus clustering is a class of robust clustering algorithms, which obtain the finally clustering results based on multiple existing basic partitionings. In this study, we introduce the K-medoids algorithm and the cell-like P systems with promoters and inhibiters (a class of parallel and distributed computing models) to the consensus clustering, and propose the K-medoids-based consensus clustering based on the cell-like P system with promoters and inhibiters. Through the experiment, the proposed consensus clustering algorithm can obtain high quality clustering results in a short time. This study improves the result in *TKDE, 2015, 2, 155–169*.

Keywords: Consensus clustering · K-medoids · P system · Membrane computing

1 Introduction

Information plays an important rule in each field in modern society. It is an important problem that how to analyze data and extract useful information from the huge amounts of data. Clustering analysis is a class of important data analysis methods, which can reveal the relationship between data objects and data objects, data objects and data features, data features and data features. Although there are many traditional clustering algorithms, they have three limitations: (1) The clustering results largely depend on the parameters settings and the initialization. (2) Most clustering algorithms can not judge the real clustering numbers. (3) Different clustering algorithms may generate different clustering results through different clustering algorithms. Consensus clustering is proposed make up the above limitations [1]. A consensus clustering algorithm contains two phases: the generation of several basic partitionings of data set (each basic partitioning is a clustering result of the data set by a certain clustering algorithm), and the aggregation of these basic partitionings. It aggregates several basic partitionings obtained by common clustering algorithms, and obtains the finally result which is better than all these partitionings. Many improvements are proposed from these two aspects [2–8].

© Springer Nature Singapore Pte Ltd. 2016
M. Gong et al. (Eds.): BIC-TA 2016, Part I, CCIS 681, pp. 95–108, 2016.
DOI: 10.1007/978-981-10-3611-8_11

The basic partitionings are usually generated by simple algorithms such as K-means algorithm, because of the low time complexity of these algorithms [9]. However, K-means algorithm is sensitive to the outlier. How to generate higher quality clustering result in a shorter time is an important topic in consensus clustering. In this study, we use K-medoids algorithm to increase the robustness, and the parallel and distributed computing model: cell-like P systems with promoters and inhibiters to decrease the time complexity [10,11].

Membrane computing is a novel research branch of bio-inspired computing, initiated by Păun in 2002, which seeks to discover new computational models from the study of biological cells, particularly of the cellular membranes [11,12]. The obtained models are distributed and parallel bio-inspired computing devices, usually called P systems. There are three mainly investigated P systems, cell-like P systems [11], tissue P systems [13], and neural-like P systems (also known as spiking neural P systems) [14] (and their variants, see e.g. [15–24]). P systems are known as powerful computing models, are able to do what Turing machines can do efficiently [25–31]. The parallel evolution mechanism of variants of P systems, such as numerical P systems [32,33], spatial P systems [34], spiking neural P systems with anti-spikes [35], has been found to perform well in doing computation, even solving computational hard problems [36–38]. Cell-like P systems with promoters and inhibiters are abstracted based on the structure and function of the living cell, which have three main components, the membrane structure, multisets of objects evolving in a synchronous maximally parallel manner, and evolution rules. Objects in P system evolve in a maximum parallel mechanism, regulating by promoters and inhibiters, such that the systems do computation efficient [39].

In this study, a consensus clustering based on the K-medoids algorithm and the cell-like P systems with promoters and inhibiters is proposed (CPPI-KMCC algorithm, for short). Specifically, the r basic partitionings are obtained in r membranes in parallel, and the finally partitioning is obtained in membrane n. Experimental results based on Iris database of UC Irvine Machine Learning Repository [40] shows that the proposed algorithm can obtain more accurate and stable results in data clustering.

2   Preliminaries

In this section, we recall some basic concepts and notions in K-medoids algorithm, consensus clustering, and cell-like P systems with promoters and inhibiters.

2.1   The K-Medoids Algorithm

The K-medoids algorithm, which is more robust to outliers and noise, is a one of the classical partitioning algorithm of clustering improved by the K-means algorithm [10].

Let $X = \{x_1, x_2, \cdots, x_n\}$ denotes a data set with n objects. A medoid is one object of a cluster with the minimal total distance to all other objects. By distributing all non-medoid objects to the nearest medoid, all objects are clustered into K clusters $C = \{C_1, C_2, \cdots, C_K\}$. The clusters have the three following properties:

- $C_i \neq \phi, 1 \leq i \leq K$;
- $\bigcup_{i=1}^{K} C_i = X$;
- $C_i \cap C_j = \phi, i \neq j, 1 \leq i, j \leq K$.

What's more, objects in the same cluster are similar to each other, and objects from distinct clusters are different from each other. The distance needs to be defined in order to find the solution. In the literatures various alternatives have been reported to approach this task. It can choose one according to the request.

The K-medoid algorithm has some specific methods. Partitioning around medoids (PAM) is a representative one.

The steps of the PAM are as follows:

- Select K objects as medoids arbitrarily from all the objects as the initial K clusters.
- Distribute the remaining objects to their most similar cluster with the shortest distance.
- Randomly select non-medoid object O'.
- Compute the distance of O' and all the other objects in the belonging cluster.
- Set O' as the new medoid if the total distance in the belonging cluster is decreased.
- Repeat the steps 2 to 5 above until all medoids don't change anymore.

So given arbitrary n objects, they can be clustered into K clusters using the K-mediods algorithm.

2.2 The Consensus Clustering

Let $X = \{x_1, x_2, \cdots, x_n\}$ denotes a data set with n objects. These n objects can be clustered into K clusters $C = \{C_1, C_2, \cdots, C_K\}$ by some clustering algorithm, which is called a partitioning of this data set. Given r basic partitionings $\prod = \pi_1, \pi_2, \cdots, \pi_r$ of a data set X, consensus clustering aims to find a consensus partitioning π which meets:

$$max\Gamma(\pi, \Pi) = \Sigma_{i=1}^{r} w_i U(\pi, \pi_i), \tag{1}$$

where, Γ is the consensus function, U is the utility function, w_i is the weight of basic partitioning π_i with $\sum_{i=1}^{r} w_i = 1$. Or meets:

$$min\Gamma(\pi, \Pi) = \Sigma_{i=1}^{r} w_i D(\pi, \pi_i), \tag{2}$$

where, D is the distance function.

In this study, we use the method proposed in [9] to find the cluster π.

The initial data set X is transformed into a binary data set $\chi^{(b)} = \{x_l^{(b)} | l = 1, 2, \cdots, n\}$, which is derived from the r basic partitionings:

$$x_l^{(b)} = <x_{l,1}^{(b)}, \cdots, x_{l,i}^{(b)}, \cdots, x_{l,r}^{(b)}>, \text{with}$$

$$x_{l,i}^{(b)} = <x_{l,i1}^{(b)}, \cdots, x_{l,ij}^{(b)}, \cdots, x_{l,iKi}^{(b)}>, \text{and}$$

$$x_{l,ij}^{(b)} = \begin{cases} 1, \text{if } x_l \text{ belongs to the } j\text{-}th \text{ cluster} \\ \quad \text{in the } i\text{-}th \text{ basic partitioning,} \\ 0, \text{otherwise} \end{cases}$$

The finally clustering result can be obtained by clustering this new data set $\chi^{(b)}$.

In this study, we use the squared Euclidean distance to compute the distance between two objects.

2.3   Cell-like P System with Promoters and Inhibitors

A cell-like P system with promoters and inhibitors consists of three main components: the hierarchical membrane structure, objects and evolution rules. By membranes, a cell-like P system with promoters and inhibitors is divided into separated regions. Objects, information carriers, and evolution rules (by which objects can evolve to new objects) present in these regions. Objects are represented by characters or strings of symbols. Evolution rules are executed in the uncertainty and maximum parallelism way in each membrane.

The definition of cell-like P system with promoters and inhibitors is as follows. A cell-like P system of degree m is of the form

$$\Pi = (O, \mu, w_1, w_2, \ldots, w_m, R_1, \ldots, R_m, \rho, i_{out}),$$

where

(1) O is the alphabet which includes all objects of the system.
(2) μ is the membrane structure.
(3) w_i is the initial objects in cell i, object λ shows that there is no object in cell i.
(4) R_i is the set of rules in cell i with the form of $(u \rightarrow v)_\alpha$, where u is a string composed of objects in O and v is a string over $\{a_{here}, a_{out}, a_{in_j} | a \in O, 1 \leq j \leq t\}$. ($a_{here}$ means object a remains in membrane i in which $here$ can be omitted; a_{out} means object a goes into the outer layer membrane. And a_{in_j} means object a goes into the inner layer membrane j.) $\alpha \in \{z, z'\}$ is a promoter or an inhibitor. A rule can execute only when promoter z appears and stop only when inhibitor z' appears.
(5) ρ_l defines the partial order relationship of the rules, i.e., higher priority rule means the rule should be executed with higher priority.
(6) i_{out} is where the computation result is placed.

In the system, evolution rules are executed in the maximum parallel way and in the uncertain way in each membrane. If more than one rule can possibly be used but the objects in the membrane can only support some of them, then the maximal number of rules will be used. For more details one can refer to [11].

3 The K-Medoids-Based Consensus Clustering Based on Cell-like P Systems with Promoters and Inhibitors

In this section, a consensus clustering based on the K-medoids algorithm and the cell-like P systems with promoters and inhibitors is proposed, where promoters and inhibitors are utilized to regulate parallelism of objects evolution. The obtained algorithm is shortly called CPPI-KMCC.

Before introducing CPPI-KMCC, two distance matrixes are defined.

$$D'_{nn} = \begin{pmatrix} f'_{11} & f'_{12} & \cdots & f'_{1n} \\ f'_{21} & f'_{22} & \cdots & f'_{2n} \\ & \cdots & & \\ f'_{n1} & f'_{n2} & \cdots & f'_{nn} \end{pmatrix}, \tag{3}$$

where f'_{ij} is the distance between the objects x_i and x_j. Specific calculation method is selected depending on the type of object. Specifically, the element f_{ij} of matrix D_{nn} is obtained by multiplying f'_{ij} for 100 times and rounding off, thus getting an integer. The distance matrix D_{nn} is as follows:

$$D_{nn} = \begin{pmatrix} f_{11} & f_{12} & \cdots & f_{1n} \\ f_{21} & f_{22} & \cdots & f_{2n} \\ & \cdots & & \\ f_{n1} & f_{n2} & \cdots & f_{nn} \end{pmatrix}. \tag{4}$$

3.1 The Cell-like P System for CPPI-KMCC

The membrane structure used as the framework for CPPI-KMCC is shown in Fig. 1.

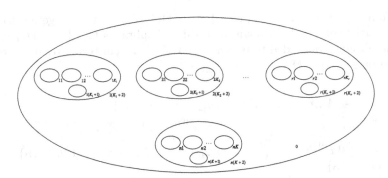

Fig. 1. Membrane structure for CPPI-KMCC

The dataset of objects to be dealt with is placed in membrane 0. The r basic partitionings are generated in membranes $K_1 + 2, K_2 + 2, \cdots, K_r + 2$ by K-medoids algorithm in parallel. And all these basic partitionings information are put into membrane $K + 2$ to process the consensus clustering.

The cell-like P system with promoters and inhibitors for CPPI-KMCC is as follows.

$$\Pi = (O, \mu, w_{ij}, R_{ij}, i_{in}, i_{out}), \ i, j = 1, 2, \cdots, r, n,$$

where,

- $O = \{a_i, U_{ij}, W_{ij}, W'_{ij}, \beta_j, A_{ij}, \delta, D_{ij}, e, \psi, \theta, \alpha, a_{ij}, O_i, \delta_i, \zeta_i, s, s', \eta, \sigma, b_i, S_{ij}\};$
- $\mu = [_0[_{i(K_i+2)}[_{i1}]_{i1}[_{i2}]_{i2} \cdots [_{i(K_i+1)}]_{i(K_i+1)}]_{i(K_i+2)}]_0, \ i = 1, 2, \cdots, r, n;$
- $w_0 = w_{n(K_n+1)} = \lambda,$
  $w_{i(K_i+2)} = w_{n(K+2)} = \beta_1, \beta_2, \cdots, \beta_{K_i}, \delta^{K_i}, e \ (i = 1, 2, \cdots, r),$
  $w_{ij} = \delta_1 \ (i = 1, 2, \cdots, r; \ j = 1, 2, \cdots, K_i + 1),$
  $w_{nj} = \delta_1 \ (j = 1, 2, \cdots, K);$
- $i_{in} = 0;$
- $i_{out} = n + 2;$
- R_{ij} is the set of rules in membrane ij.

$R_0:$
$$\begin{cases} r_1 = \{a_i U_{ij}^{W_{ij}} \to (a_i)_{in_{1(K_1+2),2(K_2+2),\cdots,r(K_r+2),n(K_n+2)}} U_{ij}^{W_{ij}} {}_{in_{1(K_1+2),2(K_2+2),\cdots,r(K_r+2)}} \\ \quad |i,j = 1, 2, \cdots, n\} \\ r_2 = \{W'_{ij} \to (W_{ij})_{in \ n(K+2)} | i,j = 1, 2, \cdots, n\} \end{cases}$$

Objects a_i and $U_{ij}^{W_{ij}}$ are put into membrane 0 to start the computational process. Object a_i means the i-th data in the data set, and object $U_{ij}^{W_{ij}}$ means the distance between the i-th data a_i and the j-th data a_j is W_{ij}. Rule r_1 is executed to send copies of a_i to membranes $1(K_1 + 2), 2(K_2 + 2), \cdots, r(K_r + 2), n(K_n + 2)$, and copies of W_{ij} to membranes $1(K_1 + 2), 2(K_2 + 2), \cdots, r(K_r + 2)$.

The Generation of Basic Partitionings

Rules in membranes $11, 12, \cdots, 1K_1, 1(K_1 + 1), 1(K_1 + 2)$ work together to give a basic partitioning by K-medoids algorithm. Membranes $11, 12, \cdots, 1K_1$ represent the K_1 clusters needed to be generated. And the clustering result is stored in membrane $1(K_1 + 1)$.

$R_{1(K_1+2)}:$
$$\begin{cases} r_1 = \{a_i \beta_j \to A_{ji} A_{ji \ in_j} | i = 1, 2, \cdots, n; j = 1, 2, \cdots, K_1\} \\ r_2 = \{a_{i\delta^{K_1} A_{1i_1} A_{2i_2} \cdots A_{K_1 i_{K_1}}} U_{ii_1}^{W_{ii1}} U_{ii_2}^{W_{ii2}} \cdots U_{ii_{K_1}}^{W_{iiK_1}} \neg D_{i1}^{W_{ii1}} D_{i2}^{W_{ii2}} \cdots D_{i(K_1)}^{W_{iiK_1}}} \to \\ \quad a_i D_{i1}^{W_{ii1}} D_{i2}^{W_{ii2}} \cdots D_{iK_1}^{W_{iiK_1}} | i = 1, 2, \cdots, n; i_1, i_2, \cdots, i_{K_1} = 1, 2, \cdots, n\} \\ r_3 = \{\delta^{K_1} \to \lambda\} \\ r_4 = \{a_{i\neg D_{ik}} \to a_i \ in_k | i = 1, 2, \cdots, n; k = 1, 2, \cdots K_1\} \\ r_5 = \{D_{i1} D_{i2} \cdots D_{iK_1} \to \lambda | i_1, i_2, \cdots, i_{K_1} = 1, 2, \cdots, n\} \\ r_6 = \{D_{ij} \to \lambda | i = 1, 2, \cdots, n; j = 1, 2, \cdots, K_1\} \\ r_7 = \{e^i \psi^j \to \theta_{in_{1,2,\cdots,K_1}} | i = 1, 2, \cdots, n; \psi = 0, 1, \cdots k - 1\} \bigcup \{\psi^k \to \alpha_{in_{1,2,\cdots,K_1}}\} \\ r_8 = \{a_{ik} \to a_{ik \ in_{1(K_1+2)}} | i = 1, 2, \cdots, n; k = 1, 2, \cdots K_1\} \\ r_9 = \{W'_{ij} \to (W'_{ij})_{out} | i, j = 1, 2, \cdots, n\} \end{cases}$$
$\rho_1 > \rho_2 > \rho_3 > \rho_4 > \rho_5 > \rho_6 > \rho_7 > \rho_8 = \rho_9$

In the initial state, objects $\beta_1, \beta_2, \cdots, \beta_{K_1}$ are in membrane $1(K_1 + 2)$ to show K_1 medoids are needed. Rule r_1 is executed to choose K_1 medoids and put them to membranes $11, 12, \cdots, 1K_1$ for the K_1 clusters. Rule r_2 is executed to generate W_{ij} distance objects D_{ij}, which means the distance between object a_i and the j-th medoid is W_{ij}. Rule r_5 is executed to dissolve the same part of $D_{i1}D_{i2}\cdots D_{iK_1}$. When a D_{ik} is disappeared, which means the distance between a_i and the k-th cluster is the shortest one, object a_i is sent to membrane k. Rules r_3 and r_6 is executed to dissolve the useless objects. Rule r_7 is executed to send an object θ to each of membranes $11, 12, \cdots, 1K_1$ to start the computation in membranes $11, 12, \cdots, 1K_1$.

When all medoids in the K_1 clusters are not changed, which means the clusters are obtained, an object α is sent to these K_1 membranes by rule r_7.

Rule r_8 is executed to send objects a_{ik} to membrane $1(K_1 + 2)$, which means a_i belongs to the k-th cluster.

$R_{1k}, k = 1, 2, \cdots, K_1$:

$$
\left\{
\begin{aligned}
r_1 &= \{(a_i)_\alpha \to a_{ik\ out} | i = 1, 2, \cdots, n;\ k = 1, 2, \cdots K_1\} \\
r_2 &= \{(\theta A_{jh})_{\neg a_i} \to A_{jh}\psi_{out}(A_{jh})_{out}\delta_{out}\#|i, h = 1, 2, \cdots, n; j = 1, 2, \cdots, K_1\} \\
r_3 &= \{\theta\delta_i a_i \to \theta\zeta_i O_i | i = 1, 2, \cdots, n\} \bigcup \{(\theta\delta_i)_{\neg a_i} \to \theta\delta_{i+1} | i = 1, 2, \cdots, n\} \\
r_4 &= \{(a_j)_{O_i A_{hp}} \to b_j s^{w_{ij}} s'^{w_{pj}} | i, j, p = 1, 2, \cdots, n;\ h = 1, 2, \cdots, K_1\} \\
r_5 &= \{ss' \to \lambda\} \\
r_6 &= \{s'^t O_i A_{hp} \to a_p A_{hi} \eta | i, p = 1, 2, \cdots, n;\ h = 1, 2, \cdots, K_1\} \\
&\quad \bigcup\{s^t O_i A_{hp} \to a_i A_{hp}\sigma | i, p = 1, 2, \cdots, n;\ h = 1, 2, \cdots, K_1\} \\
r_7 &= \{b_i \to a_i | i = 1, 2, \cdots, n\} \\
r_8 &= \{\zeta_i \to \delta_{i+1} | i = 1, 2, \cdots, n\} \\
r_9 &= \{\eta^i \sigma^j \to e_{out} | i = 1, 2, \cdots, n;\ j = 0, 1, \cdots, n\} \\
&\quad \bigcup\{(\sigma^j)_{\neg \eta^j} \to \psi_{out} | i, j = 1, 2, \cdots, n\} \\
r_{10} &= \{a_i \to (a_i)_{out} | i = 1, 2, \cdots, n\} \\
r_{11} &= \{\delta_{n+1} A_{jp}\theta \to (\delta)_{out}(A_{jp})_{out}\delta_1 A_{jp}\#|j = 1, 2, \cdots, K_1;\ p = 1, 2, \cdots, n\} \\
&\quad \bigcup\{(A_{jp}\theta)_{\delta_{n+1}} \to (\delta)_{out}(A_{jp})_{out}\delta_1 A_{jp}\#|j = 1, 2, \cdots, K_1; p = 1, 2, \cdots, n\}
\end{aligned}
\right.
$$

$\rho_1 > \rho_2 > \rho_3 > \rho_4 > \rho_5 > \rho_6 > \rho_7 > \rho_8 > \rho_9 = \rho_{10} = \rho_{11}$

The best medoid is found in the membrane. The process starts with a_1 controlled by the auxiliary object δ_1. If a_1 does not in the membrane, auxiliary object δ_1 is changed to δ_2 to check a_2. Otherwise, a_1 is changed to O_1 to show that a_1 is set as the new medoid by rule r_3. Rule r_4 is executed to calculated the distance sum between the new medoid and all the other objects a_j. The distance sum value are stored by the number of object s. Similarly, the distance sum between the old medoid and all the other objects a_j value are stored by the number of object s'. Rule r_5 is executed to dissolve objects s and s'. Rule r_6 is executed to compare the two medoids. If s' are still in the membrane, which means the new medoid can reduce the distance sum, object a_1 is set as the new medoid. If s are still in the membrane, which means the new medoid cannot reduce the distance sum, the medoid is still the old one. Rule r_8 is executed to generate δ_2 to check the object a_2. And so on, until all objects in this membrane are all checked, and the best medoid will be found. If the medoid in this membrane is changed, an object e is sent out. If the medoid in this membrane is not changed, an object ψ is sent out. Lastly, rules r_9 and r_10 are executed to return the objects in this membrane to the initial state, and put the information of the medoid out. Object $\#$ is generated to stop the computational process.

When the clustering process is over, an object α is sent to this membrane. Rule r_1 is executed to send an object a_{ik} to show that a_i belongs to the k-th membrane.

The structure and rules in $i1, i2, \cdots, iK_i, i(K_i + 1), i(K_i + 2)$ are similar. Therefore, the rules are not listed in detail.

$R_{1(K_1+1)}$:
W_{ij}^r
$$\begin{cases} r_1 = \{(a_{ik}a_{jk})_{\neg S_{ij}} \to a_{ik}a_{jk}S_{ij} | i,j = 1,2\cdots,n; \ k = 1,2,\cdots,K_1\} \\ r_2 = \{a_{ij} \to \lambda | i,j = 1,2,\cdots,n\} \\ r_3 = \{W_{ij}S_{ij} \to \lambda | i,j = 1,2,\cdots,n\} \\ r_4 = \{W_{ij} \to (W'_{ij})_{out} | i,j = 1,2,\cdots,n\} \end{cases}$$

If a_{ik} and a_{jk} are in this membrane, which means a_i and a_j both belongs to the k-th cluster, an object S_{ij} is generated. In the initial state, $K_1 \ W_{ij}$ are in this membrane to show that the initial distance between a_i and a_i is K_1. Rule r_3 is executed to dissolve W_{ij} and S_{ij}. Rule r_4 is executed to put out the result.

The Consensus Process

$R_{n(K+2)}$:
$$\begin{cases} r_1 = \{a_i\beta_j \to A_{ji}A_{ji} \ _{in_j} | i = 1,2,\cdots,n; j = 1,2,\cdots,K\} \\ r_2 = \{a_{i\delta^{K_1}A_{1i_1}A_{2i_2}\cdots A_{Ki_K}U_{ii_1}^{W_{ii_1}}U_{ii_2}^{W_{ii_2}}\cdots U_{ii_K}^{W_{ii_K}}\neg D_{i1}^{W_{ii_1}}D_{i2}^{W_{ii_2}}\cdots D_{i(K)}^{W_{ii_K}}} \to \\ \quad a_i D_{i1}^{W_{ii_1}}D_{i2}^{W_{ii_2}}\cdots D_{iK}^{W_{ii_K}} | i = 1,2,\cdots,n; i_1, i_2, \cdots, i_K = 1,2,\cdots,n\} \\ r_3 = \{\delta^K \to \lambda\} \\ r_4 = \{a_{i\neg D_{ik}} \to a_i \ _{in_k} | i = 1,2,\cdots,n; k = 1,2,\cdots K\} \\ r_5 = \{D_{i1}D_{i2}\cdots D_{iK} \to \lambda | i_1, i_2, \cdots, i_K = 1,2,\cdots,n\} \\ r_6 = \{D_{ij} \to \lambda | i = 1,2,\cdots,n; j = 1,2,\cdots,K\} \\ r_7 = \{e^i\psi^j \to \theta_{in_{1,2,\cdots,K}} | i=1,2,\cdots,n; \psi = 0,1,\cdots k - 1\} \bigcup \{\psi^k \to \alpha_{in_{1,2,\cdots,K}}\} \\ r_8 = \{a_{ik} \to a_{ik} \ _{in_{n(K+2)}} | i = 1,2,\cdots,n; k = 1,2,\cdots K\} \end{cases}$$
$\rho_1 > \rho_2 > \rho_3 > \rho_4 > \rho_5 > \rho_6 > \rho_7 > \rho_8 = \rho_9$

$R_{nk}, k = 1, 2, \cdots, K$:

$$\left\{ \begin{array}{l} r_1 = \{(a_i)_\alpha \to a_{ik\ out} | i = 1, 2, \cdots, n; k = 1, 2, \cdots K\} \\ r_2 = \{(\theta A_{jh})_{\neg a_i} \to A_{jh}\psi_{out}(A_{jh})_{out}\delta_{out}\# | i, h = 1, 2, \cdots, n; j = 1, 2, \cdots, K\} \\ r_3 = \{\theta\delta_i a_i \to \theta\zeta_i O_i | i = 1, 2, \cdots, n\} \bigcup \{(\theta\delta_i)_{\neg a_i} \to \theta\delta_{i+1} | i = 1, 2, \cdots, n\} \\ r_4 = \{(a_j)_{O_i A_{hp}} \to b_j s^{w_{ij}} s'^{w_{pj}} | i, j, p = 1, 2, \cdots, n; h = 1, 2, \cdots, K\} \\ r_5 = \{ss' \to \lambda\} \\ r_6 = \{s'^t O_i A_{hp} \to a_p A_{hi}\eta | i, p = 1, 2, \cdots, n; h = 1, 2, \cdots, K\} \\ \quad\quad \bigcup\{s^t O_i A_{hp} \to a_i A_{hp}\sigma | i, p = 1, 2, \cdots, n; h = 1, 2, \cdots, K\} \\ r_7 = \{b_i \to a_i | i = 1, 2, \cdots, n\} \\ r_8 = \{\zeta_i \to \delta_{i+1} | i = 1, 2, \cdots, n\} \\ r_9 = \{\eta^i \sigma^j \to e_{out} | i = 1, 2, \cdots, n; j = 0, 1, \cdots, n\} \\ \quad\quad \bigcup\{(\sigma^j)_{\neg\eta^j} \to \psi_{out} | i, j = 1, 2, \cdots, n\} \\ r_{10} = \{a_i \to (a_i)_{out} | i = 1, 2, \cdots, n\} \\ r_{11} = \{\delta_{n+1} A_{jp}\theta \to (\delta)_{out}(A_{jp})_{out}\delta_1 A_{jp}\# | j = 1, 2, \cdots, K; p = 1, 2, \cdots, n\} \\ \quad\quad \bigcup\{(A_{jp}\theta)_{\delta_{n+1}} \to (\delta)_{out}(A_{jp})_{out}\delta_1 A_{jp}\# | j = 1, 2, \cdots, K; p = 1, 2, \cdots, n\} \end{array} \right.$$

$\rho_1 > \rho_2 > \rho_3 > \rho_4 > \rho_5 > \rho_6 > \rho_7 > \rho_8 > \rho_9 = \rho_{10} = \rho_{11}$

$R_{n(K+1)}$:

ϕ

Rules in this process are similar with the process in the basic partitionings, therefore, the details are not listed.

3.2 Time Complexity Analysis

In this subsection, the time cost in the worst case of CPPI-KMCC is analyzed.

The computational process begins when the data set and the distance information are put into membrane 0.

1 step is needed to send copies of the data set to membranes $1(K_1 + 2), 2(K_2 + 2), \cdots, r(K_r + 2), n(K + 2)$, and send copies of the distance information to membranes $1(K_1 + 2), 2(K_2 + 2), \cdots, r(K_r + 2)$.

Then, rules in membranes $1(K_1 + 2), 2(K_2 + 2), \cdots, r(K_r + 2)$ work in parallel to generate the r basic partitionings.

In membrane $i(K_i + 2)$, 1 step is needed to choose the K_i medoids randomly. 1 step is needed to generate the distance objects between each a_i and the j-th medoids. 1 step is needed to dissolve the auxiliary objects δ. 2 steps are needed to put the object a_i to its nearest cluster. 1 step is needed to dissolve the auxiliary objects D_{ij}. 1 step is needed to send an object θ to membranes $1, 2, \cdots, K_1$ to active the computational process in these membranes.

In each membrane $1, 2, \cdots, K_i$, each objects a_i is compared with the current medoids, if the distance sum between some a_i and the other objects is smaller than the distance sum between the current medoids and the other objects, this a_i is the new medoids. The comparison is made from a_1 to a_n, which is controlled by the auxiliary objects δ_i. Each comparison need 6 steps if a_i is in this membrane, and 1 step if a_i is not in this membrane. 1 step is needed to dissolve the auxiliary objects, return the objects in this membrane to the initial state, and send an object e to show the new medoid has been found.

Then, rules in membrane $i(K_i + 2)$ runs to redistribute objects a_i to its nearest medoids, and the best medoid of each cluster is refound.

Suppose at the Ith iteration, $K_i \psi$ are sent to membrane $i(K_i + 2)$ to show that all medoids are not changed. An object α is sent to membranes $1, 2, \cdots, K_i$. And 2 steps are needed to put objects a_{ik} out, which means a_i belongs to the kth cluster.

4 steps are needed in membrane $i(K_i+1)$ to generate the distance information between each object in the new binary data set. And 2 steps are needed to transfer these objects to membrane $n(K + 2)$ to active the consensus clustering process.

The total time complexity is: $1 + (7 + 6n) + (6 + 6n) * (I - 1) + (6 + 2) + 4 + 2 + (7 + 6n) + (6 + 6n) * (I - 1) + (6 + 2) = 12nI + 12I + 25 = O(nI)$, while the time complexity of in [9] is $O((d + 1)InrK)$ (d is the number of data dimensions.).

4   Experiments and Analysis

Breast Cancer Database

The breast cancer database of UC Irvine Machine Learning Repository is used as an experiment [40]. This database contains 699 records, and each record contains 10 attribute values and the corresponding breast cancer class (benign, or malignant). 16 records containing the missing attributes are removed in this experiment. The left 683 records are numbered from 1 to 683 following the order. All records are divided into two classes.

Firstly, the K-medoids algorithm is used to cluster this database. Because we don't know the right clustering numbers, the K is set 2, 3 and 4, respectively. The clustering results are shown in Table 1. All experiments are done ten times. And these 30 cluster results are used as the basic partitionings to do the K-medoids-based consensus clustering. The clustering results are shown in Table 2.

Table 1. The clustering accuracy by the K-medoids algorithm with different K values for 10 times

The value of K	1	2	3	4	5
2	0.959004392	0.959004392	0.959004392	0.959004392	0.959004392
3	0.884333821	0.692532943	0.904831625	0.834553441	0.869692533
4	0.535871157	0.812591508	0.811127379	0.639824305	0.655929722
The value of K	6	7	8	9	10
2	0.959004392	0.959004392	0.959004392	0.959004392	0.959004392
3	0.7715959	0.890190337	0.884333821	0.802342606	0.834553441
4	0.578330893	0.720351391	0.65885798	0.79795022	0.696925329

Table 2. The clustering accuracy by the K-medoids-based consensus algorithm with different K values for 10 times

The value of K	1	2	3	4	5
2	0.959004392	0.959004392	0.959004392	0.959004392	0.959004392
3	0.959004392	0.734992679	0.959004392	0.959004392	0.959004392
4	0.959004392	0.959004392	0.959004392	0.959004392	0.959004392
The value of K	6	7	8	9	10
2	0.959004392	0.959004392	0.959004392	0.959004392	0.959004392
3	0.959004392	0.734992679	0.959004392	0.959004392	0.959004392
4	0.959004392	0.734992679	0.959004392	0.959004392	0.959004392

We can see from this figure, if the clustering numbers of the K-medoids algorithm are set correctly, the results are good. However, if the clustering numbers are set incorrectly, the results are unstable, and the results are bad sometimes. We use the 30 results as 30 basic partitionings, and do K-medoids-based consensus clustering, the clustering results are better and stable, even if half basic partitionings are not so good and the clustering numbers are set incorrectly. The consensus clustering can improve the clustering accuracy compared to the basic algorithms.

Iris Database

The Iris database of UC Irvine Machine Learning Repository is used as an experiment [40]. This database contains 150 records. The 150 records are numbered from 1 to 150 following the order. Each record contains four Iris attribute values and the corresponding Iris species. All records are divided into three species, data from 1 to 50, data from 51 to 100 and data from 101 to 150, respectively.

Firstly, the K-medoids algorithm is used to cluster this database. Because we don't know the right clustering numbers, the K is set 3 and 4, respectively. All experiments are done ten times. And these 20 cluster results are used as the basic partitionings to do the K-medoids-based consensus clustering. The clustering results are shown in Fig. 2.

We can see from this figure, if the clustering numbers of the K-medoids algorithm are set correctly, the results are good. However, if the clustering numbers are set incorrectly, the results are unstable, and the results are bad sometimes. We use the 20 results as 20 basic partitionings, and do K-medoids-based consensus clustering, the clustering results are better and stable, even if half basic partitionings are not so good. The consensus clustering can improve the clustering accuracy compared to the basic algorithms.

Then, we use the K-means-based consensus clustering to cluster this database, the results are shown in Fig. 3.

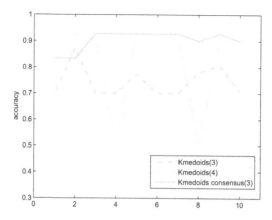

Fig. 2. The clustering accuracy comparison

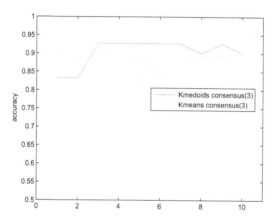

Fig. 3. The clustering accuracy comparision

We can see from this figure, the clustering results obtained by K-medoids-based consensus clustering are better than K-means-based consensus clustering in most cases. The comparison is more remarkable when noises or outliers are in the databases.

5   Conclusions

With the advent of the era of big data, the traditional way of data processing is more and more difficult to meet people's requirement. Consensus clustering as a new clustering thoughts, can obtain robust results. However, the time complexity of consensus clustering is usually high. Profit from the great parallelism, P system can decrease the time complexity of computing and improve the computational efficiency. Recent years, as a new biological computing method, the theory of membrane computing has been adequately studied. In this study, a K-medoids-based consensus clustering based on the cell-like P system with promoters and inhibiters is proposed. The clustering results are more accurate, and the time complexity is lower through experiments. In previous studies, simple algorithms are used as basic algorithms in the consensus algorithm considering the time complexity. In the future, complicated algorithms can be used as basic algorithms because of the parallel computational models: P systems. The accuracy can be further improved. And P system can be used in other clustering algorithms.

Acknowledgment. This work is supported by the Natural Science Foundation of China (Nos. 61170038, 61472231, 61402187, 61502535, 61572522 and 61572523).

References

1. Strehl, A., Ghosh, J.: Cluster ensembles-a knowledge reuse framework for combining multiple partitions. J. Mach. Learn. Res. **3**(12), 583–617 (2002)
2. Sandro, V., Jose, R.: A survey of clustering ensemble algorithm. Int. J. Pattern Recogn. Artif. Intell. **25**(3), 337–372 (2011)
3. Abdala, D.D., Wattuya, P., Jiang, X.: Ensemble clustering via random walker consensus strategy. In: International Conference on Pattern Recognition, pp. 1433–1436 (2010)
4. Zhou, P., Du, L., Wang, H., Shi, L., Shen, Y.: Learning a robust consensus matrix for clustering ensemble via Kullback-Leibler divergence minimization. In: International Conference on Artificial Intelligence, pp. 4112–4118 (2015)
5. Huang, D., Lai, J., Wang, C.: Robust ensemble clustering using probability trajectories. IEEE Trans. Knowl. Data Eng. **28**(5), 1312–1326 (2016)
6. Xanthopoulos, P.: A review on consensus clustering methods. Optim. Sci. Eng. **8**(5), 553–566 (2014)
7. Mirkin, B.G., Shestakov, A.: Least square consensus clustering: criteria, methods, experiments. Adv. Inf. Retr. **7814**, 764–767 (2013)
8. Saeed, F., Salim, N., Abdo, A.: Voting-based consensus clustering for combining multiple clusterings of chemical structures. J. Cheminform. **4**(1), 165–178 (2012)
9. Wu, J., Liu, H., Xiong, H., Cao, J., Chen, J.: K-means-based consensus clustering: a unified view. IEEE Trans. Knowl. Data Eng. **27**(1), 155–169 (2015)
10. Kaufman, L., Rousseeuw, P.J.: Finding Groups in Data. An Introduction to Cluster Analysis. Wiley, New York (1990)
11. Păun, G.: Computing with membranes. J. Comput. Syst. Sci. **61**(1), 108–143 (2000)
12. Păun, G., Rozenberg, G., Salomaa, A.: The Oxford Handbook of Membrane Computing. Oxford University Press, Oxford (2010)
13. Marti, C., Păun, G., Pazos, J.: Tissue P systems. Theoret. Comput. Sci. **296**(2), 295–326 (2003)
14. Ionescu, M., Păun, G., Yokomori, T.: Spiking neural P systems. Fundamenta Informaticae **71**(2), 279–308 (2006)
15. Song, T., Wang, X.: Homogenous spiking neural P systems with inhibitory synapses. Neural Process. Lett. **42**(1), 199–214 (2015)
16. Song, T., Pan, L.: Spiking neural P systems with rules on synapses working in maximum spikes consumption strategy. IEEE Trans. Nanobiosci. **14**(1), 38–44 (2015)
17. Song, T., Pan, L.: Spiking neural P systems with rules on synapses working in maximum spiking strategy. IEEE Trans. Nanobiosci. **14**(4), 465–477 (2015)

18. Cavaliere, M., Ibarra, O.H., Păun, G., Egecioglu, O., Ionescu, M., Woodworth, S.: Asynchronous spiking neural P systems. Theoret. Comput. Sci. **410**(24), 2352–2364 (2009)
19. Song, T., Pan, L.: Spiking neural P systems with request rules. Neurocomputing **193**(12), 193–200 (2016)
20. Song, T., Zheng, P., Wong, M.L.D., Wang, X.: Design of logic gates using spiking neural P systems with homogeneous neurons and astrocytes-like control. Inf. Sci. **372**, 380–391 (2016). doi:10.1016/j.ins.2016.08.055
21. Song, T., Liu, X., Zhao, Y., Zhang, X.: Spiking neural P systems with white hole neurons. IEEE Trans. Nanobiosci. (2016). doi:10.1109/TNB.2016.2598879
22. Zhang, X., Pan, L., Păun, A.: On the universality of axon P systems. IEEE Trans. Neural Netw. Learn. Syst. **26**(11), 2816–2829 (2015)
23. Zeng, X., Zhang, X., Song, T., Pan, L.: Spiking neural P systems with thresholds. Neural Comput. **26**(7), 1340–1361 (2014)
24. Zhang, X., Wang, B., Pan, L.: Spiking neural P systems with a generalized use of rules. Neural Comput. **26**(12), 2925–2943 (2014)
25. Zeng, X., Zhang, X., Pan, L.: Homogeneous spiking neural P systems. Fundamenta Informaticae **97**(1), 275–294 (2009)
26. Song, T., Zou, Q., Zeng, X., Liu, X.: Asynchronous spiking neural P systems with rules on synapses. Neurocomputing **151**(1), 1439–1445 (2015)
27. Ibarra, O.H., Păun, A., Rodríguez-Patón, A.: Sequential SNP systems based on min/max spike number. Theoret. Comput. Sci. **410**(30), 2982–2991 (2009)
28. Song, T., Xu, J., Pan, L.: On the universality and non-universality of spiking neural P systems with rules on synapses. IEEE Trans. Nanobiosci. **14**(8), 960–966 (2015)
29. Wang, X., Song, T., Gong, F., Zheng, P.: On the computational power of spiking neural P systems with self-organization. Sci. Rep. **6**, 27624 (2016). doi:10.1038/srep27624
30. Zhang, X., Liu, Y., Luo, B., Pan, L.: Computational power of tissue P systems for generating control languages. Inf. Sci. **278**(10), 285–297 (2014)
31. Zeng, X., Xu, L., Liu, X., Pan, L.: On languages generated by spiking neural P systems with weights. Inf. Sci. **278**(10), 423–433 (2014)
32. Romero-Campero, F.J., Pérez-Jiménez, M.J.: Modelling gene expression control using P systems: the Lac Operon, a case study. Biosystems **91**(3), 438–457 (2008)
33. Bel Enguix, G.: Preliminaries about some possible applications of P systems in linguistics. In: PĂun, G., Rozenberg, G., Salomaa, A., Zandron, C. (eds.) WMC 2002. LNCS, vol. 2597, pp. 74–89. Springer, Heidelberg (2003). doi:10.1007/3-540-36490-0_6
34. Enguix, G.B.: Unstable P systems: applications to linguistics. In: Mauri, G., Păun, G., Pérez-Jiménez, M.J., Rozenberg, G., Salomaa, A. (eds.) WMC 2004. LNCS, vol. 3365, pp. 190–209. Springer, Heidelberg (2005). doi:10.1007/978-3-540-31837-8_11
35. Song, T., Liu, X., Zeng, X.: Asynchronous spiking neural P systems with anti-spikes. Neural Process. Lett. **42**(3), 633–647 (2015)
36. Díaz-Pernil, D., Berciano, A., Pena-Cantillana, F., GutiéRrez-Naranjo, M.A.: Segmenting images with gradient-based edge detection using membrane computing. Pattern Recogn. Lett. **34**(8), 846–855 (2013)
37. Song, T., Zheng, H., He, J.: Solving vertex cover problem by tissue P systems with cell division. Appl. Math. Inf. Sci. **8**(1), 333–337 (2014)
38. Păun, G., Păun, R.: Membrane computing and economics: numerical P systems. Fundamenta Informaticae **73**(1, 2), 213–227 (2006)
39. Păun, G.: A quick introduction to membrane computing. J. Log. Algebr. Program. **79**(1), 291–294 (2010)
40. http://archive.ics.uci.edu/ml

Fault Classification of Power Transmission Lines Using Fuzzy Reasoning Spiking Neural P Systems

Kang Huang, Gexiang Zhang[(✉)], Xiaoguang Wei, Haina Rong, Yangyang He, and Tao Wang

School of Electrical Engineering, Southwest Jiaotong University, Chengdu 610031, People's Republic of China
zhgxdylan@126.com

Abstract. This paper presents an approach for classifying different types of faults occurring in power transmission lines by integrating Fuzzy Reasoning Spiking Neural P Systems (FRSNPS) with wavelet transform and singular value decomposition. This is the first attempt to extend the application of FRSNPS from fault section identification to fault classification. The effectiveness of the introduced method is verified by various cases of fault types in power transmission lines.

Keywords: Membrane computing · Fuzzy reasoning spiking neural P systems · Fault classification

1 Introduction

Membrane computing, formally introduced by Păun in [1], is an attractive research field of computer science aiming at abstracting computing models, called membrane systems or P systems, from the structure and functioning of living cells, as well as from the way the cells are organized in tissues or high order structures [2–4]. A spiking neural P system (SNPS), introduced in [5], is the type of P system inspired by the neurophysiological behavior of neurons sending electrical impulses (spikes) along axons from presynaptic neurons to postsynaptic neurons [6,7,9]. SNPS is a kind of distributed and parallel computing models with good understandability and dynamics, which makes it become a hot topic in membrane computing [8,10].

Until now, there are only several investigations focusing on the applications of SNPS [13]. In [11], an optimization neural P system was proposed to solve well-known NP complete combinatorial optimization problems. In [12], SNPS was used to represent fuzzy knowledge. In addition, spiking neural P systems combining fuzzy reasoning (FRSNPS) were presented to diagnose the faults occurring in power systems with uncertainty and incompleteness [14–19]. The use of FRSNPS for fault diagnosis focused on only fault element diagnosis. These applications indicate that FRSNPS has good characteristics, such as strong capability

© Springer Nature Singapore Pte Ltd. 2016
M. Gong et al. (Eds.): BIC-TA 2016, Part I, CCIS 681, pp. 109–117, 2016.
DOI: 10.1007/978-981-10-3611-8_12

to set up complicated logical relationships and intuitive visualization, for solving real-life problems. So this paper discusses the application of FRSNPS to fault classification.

Fault classification is the most important task involved in power transmission line protection, which must be accomplished as fast and accurate as possible to isolate the system from fault point and recover power supply after a fault occurs. Because of the strict requirements and its significance, much attention has been paid to fault classification in the past years. Traditional methods for fault classification are mostly based on power frequency component, which are limited with respect to protection speed and susceptible to many factors, such as fault types, fault resistance, fault locations and fault inception angles [20–23]. The transient components with abundant fault information, generated by faults, was analyzed by using wavelet transform [36–39] and fuzzy logic [24–27] and artificial neural networks [31,33–35]. The main disadvantages of these techniques are that they require numerous training samples or that the inference process is a black-box operation, which are not easily understood [40]. Thus, fault classification is still a challenging problem and an ongoing research topic in power systems.

This paper presents a fault classification scheme with FRSNPS to build a fault classification model to identify fault types on the basis of fault features. Extensive experiments verify the feasibility.

2   Fault Classification with FRSNPS

2.1   Fuzzy Production Rules of Fault Classification

When a fault occurs in the power transmission lines, the fault component current of the fault phase has a dramatic change, while the fault component current of the sound phases slightly changes. So the wavelet singular value of a fault phase is much larger than that without any fault and the wavelet singular value of a sound phase is very small. The zero sequence current is theoretically zero to phase to phase faults and three phase fault. The zero sequence current is large to ground faults. Thus, the wavelet singular value of the fault component zero-sequence current to ground fault is much larger than that without any fault. The wavelet singular value of the fault component zero-sequence current of phase to phase fault is very small. It is noting that *large* and *small* mentioned above are fuzzy knowledge representing transient feature values. Thus, the fuzzy production rules of fault classification are described as follows.

R_1: IF (s_0 is *large*) THEN (*Grounded fault*)
R_2: IF (s_0 is *small*) THEN (*Phase-to-Phase fault*)
R_3: IF (s_a is *large*) AND (s_b is *small*) AND (s_c is *small*) AND (*Grounded fault*) THEN A_g
R_4: IF (s_a is *small*) AND (s_b is *large*) AND (s_c is *small*) AND (*Grounded fault*) THEN B_g

R_5: IF (s_a is *small*) AND (s_b is *small*) AND (s_c is *large*) AND (*Grounded fault*) THEN C_g

R_6: IF (s_a is *large*) AND (s_b is *large*) AND (s_c is *small*) AND (*Grounded fault*) THEN AB_g

R_7: IF (s_a is *small*) AND (s_b is *large*) AND (s_c is *large*) AND (*Grounded fault*) THEN BC_g

R_8: IF (s_a is *large*) AND (s_b is *small*) AND (s_c is *large*) AND (*Grounded fault*) THEN CA_g

R_9: IF (s_a is *large*) AND (s_b is *large*) AND (s_c is *small*) AND (*Phase-to-Phase fault*) THEN AB

R_{10}: IF (s_a is *small*) AND (s_b is *large*) AND (s_c is *large*) AND (*Phase-to-Phase fault*) THEN BC

R_{11}: IF (s_a is *large*) AND (s_b is *small*) AND (s_c is *large*) AND (*Phase-to-Phase fault*) THEN CA

R_{12}: IF (s_a is *large*) AND (s_b is *large*) AND (s_c is *large*) AND (*Phase-to-Phase fault*) THEN ABC.

The normalized wavelet singular values obtained by wavelet transform and SVD, s_a, s_b, s_c and s_0, are crisp and need to be fuzzified before they are used as the inputs of fault classification models based on rFRSNPS. On the basis of data analysis, two fuzzy sets are chosen for the normalized values s_a, s_b and s_c designated as *large* and *small*. Similarly, two fuzzy sets are used for the normalized value s_0 designated as *large* and *small*. The membership functions, which are shown in Fig. 1, are defined for the four normalized values according to data analysis of different fault samples. For s_a, s_b, and s_c, *small* expresses any value less than 0.5, while *large* reflects any value greater than 0.5. *small* in the functions of s_0 indicates any value less than 0.001, while *large* indicates the value greater than 0.001.

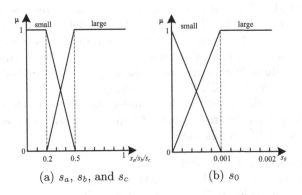

(a) s_a, s_b, and s_c (b) s_0

Fig. 1. Fuzzy membership functions.

2.2 Fault Classification Models

On the basis of fuzzy production rules, fault classification model with rFRSNPS can be built and are shown in Fig. 2, where A_l, A_s, B_l, B_s, C_l, C_s, 0_l and 0_s represent propositions "s_a is *large*", "s_a is *small*", "s_b is *large*", "s_b is *small*", "s_c is *large*", "s_c is *small*", "s_0 is *large*", "s_0 is *small*", respectively. The rFRSNPS for fault classification is described as follows:

$$\Pi_1 = (O, \sigma_1, \sigma_2, \ldots, \sigma_{32}, syn, in, out)$$

where

(1) $O = \{a\}$ is the singleton alphabet (a is called spike);
(2) $\sigma_1, \ldots, \sigma_{20}$ are proposition neurons corresponding to the propositions with fuzzy truth values $\theta_1, \ldots, \theta_{20}$;
(3) $\sigma_{21}, \ldots, \sigma_{32}$ are rule neurons, where σ_{21}, σ_{22} are *general* rule neurons, $\sigma_{23}, \ldots, \sigma_{32}$ are *and* rule neurons;
(4) $syn = \{(1,21), (2,22), (3,23), (3,26), (3,28), (3,29), (3,31), (3,32), (4,24),$
    $(4,25), (4,27), (4,30), (5,24), (5,26), (5,27), (5,29), (5,30), (5,32), (6,23),$
    $(6,25), (6,28), (6,31), (7,25), (7,27), (7,28), (7,30), (7,31), (7,32), (8,23),$
    $(8,24), (8,26), (8,29), (9,23), (9,24), (9,25), (9,26), (9,27), (9,28), (10,29),$
    $(10,30), (10,31), (10,32), (21,9), (22,10), (23,11), (24,12), (25,13), (26,14),$
    $(27,15), (28,16), (29,17), (30,18), (31,19), (32,20)\}$;
(5) $in = \{\sigma_1, \ldots, \sigma_8\}$;
(6) $out = \{\sigma_{11}, \ldots, \sigma_{20}\}$.

3 Experiments

The two-machine three-phase power system, which is shown in Fig. 3, is simulated on PSCAD/EMTDC for producing fault samples to test the performance of the introduced approach. The Bergeron line model of PSCAD/EMTDC is considered for transmission lines. Power system parameters are given in Table 1. Wavelet transform [29] and singular value decomposition [30] are used to obtain wavelet singular values. Fuzzy reasoning algorithm [14,15] is applied to inference classification model with FRSNPS. The sampling frequency is set to 50 kHz, and the mother wavelet "db3" and 8-scaled wavelet transform are chosen. The test cases are considered for different values of fault resistance, fault location, fault inception angles [23,42], as follows:

(1) Fault resistance: 0, 50, 100 and 200 ohms.
(2) Fault location: 0, 50, 100, 150 and 200 km from the bus.
(3) Fault inception angles: 0, 30, 60, 90, 120 and 150°.

We use one sample as the example to illustrate the classification process, which are described as follows:

Case 1: The fault is A_g fault.

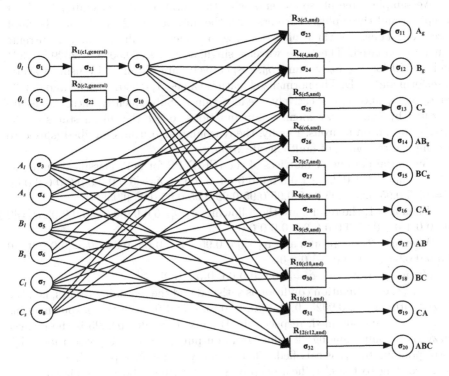

Fig. 2. Fault classification models with rFRSNPS.

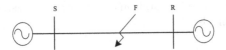

Fig. 3. Simplified model of the transmission line.

Table 1. Power system parameters considered in the experiments

Source data at sending ends		Transmission line data	
Positive-sequence impedance	$9.19 + j52.1$ (Ω)	Length	200 (km)
Zero-sequence impedance	$6.69 + j37.9$ (Ω)	Voltage (kV)	500
Frequency	50 (Hz)	Positive-sequence impedance	$3.92 + j56.0$ (Ω)
Source data at receiving ends		Zero-sequence impedance	$36.6 + j172$ (Ω)
Positive-sequence impedance	$8.19 + j42.1$ (Ω)	Positive-sequence capacitance	13.5 (nF/km)
Zero-sequence impedance	$6.47 + j33.3$ (Ω)	Zero-sequence capacitance	9.20 (nF/km)
Frequency	50 (Hz)		

We sample three phase currents with the duration 1/4 cycle after the fault inception and three phase currents with the duration 15–20 ms before the fault inception. Thus, the three phases and zero-sequence fault component currents can be calculated. Then, the wavelet singular values, 20.5098, 1.2329, 1.2341 and 7.6589 for S_a, S_b, S_c and S_0, respectively, are obtained by using wavelet transform and SVD. The normalized feature values, 1, 0.0601, 0.0602 and 0.3734 for s_a, s_b, s_c and s_0, respectively, are also gained. Subsequently, these values are fuzzified by using fuzzy membership functions to get the initial states of the input proposition neurons. Finally, the reasoning algorithm described is used to accomplish reasoning of fault classification.

The initial parameter matrices of the rFRSNPS for fault classification are as follows: θ_0=[1 0 1 0 0 1 0 1 0 0 0 0 0 0 0 0 0 0 0 0], δ_0=[0 0 0 0 0 0 0 0 0 0 0 0], C=[0.95 0.95 0.95 0.95 0.95 0.95 0.95 0.95 0.95 0.95].

When $g = 1$, the results are the following: δ_1=[1 0 0 0 0 0 0 0 0 0 0 0], θ_1=[0 0 1 0 0 1 0 1 0.95 0 0 0 0 0 0 0 0 0 0 0].

When $g = 2$, the results are: δ_2=[0 0 0.95 0 0 0 0 0 0 0 0 0], θ_2=[0 0 0 0 0 0 0 0 0 0 0.9025 0 0 0 0 0 0 0 0 0].

When $g = 3$, we get: δ_3=[0 0 0 0 0 0 0 0 0 0 0 0].

Thus, the termination condition is satisfied and the reasoning results, i.e., the fuzzy truth values, 0.9025, 0, 0, 0, 0, 0, 0, 0, 0 and 0, from the output neurons $\sigma_{11}, \ldots, \sigma_{20}$, are obtained, respectively. Because the value 0.9025 is the highest fuzzy truth values among all values from output neurons, the proposition "A_g" corresponding to σ_{11} is satisfied. That is to say, the fault type is A_g.

According to the classification processes described above, the classification results of 1200 simulations for various values of fault resistance and various fault locations, and various fault inception angles is shown in Table 2. It can be seen that the method presented in this paper achieves good results with high accuracy, and is immune to various fault conditions, such as fault resistance, fault locations and fault inception angels.

Table 2. Classification results of 1200 independent simulations

Fault types		Number of samples	Misclassification	Accuracy
Single-phase-to-ground fault	A_g	120	0	100%
	B_g	120	0	100%
	C_g	120	0	100%
Double-phase-to-ground fault	AB_g	120	0	100%
	BC_g	120	0	100%
	CA_g	120	0	100%
Phase-to-phase fault	AB	120	0	100%
	BC	120	0	100%
	CA	120	0	100%
Three phase fault	ABC	120	0	100%
Total		1200	0	100%

4   Conclusions

In this paper, an approach combining wavelet transform, singular value decomposition and fuzzy reasoning spiking neural P systems was presented to classify ten types of short-circuit faults occurring in power system transmission lines. A case considering fault inception angles, various fault resistance and fault locations was used to carry out the experiments to show the feasibility.

Acknowledgment. This work is supported by the National Natural Science Foundation of China (61672437, 61373047).

References

1. Păun, G.: Computing with membranes. J. Comput. Syst. Sci. **61**(1), 108–143 (2000)
2. Zhang, G.X., Cheng, J.X., Wang, T., Wang, X.Y., Zhu, J.: Membrane Computing: Theory and Applications. Science Press, Beijing (2015)
3. Zhang, G., Gheorghe, M., Pan, L., Pérez-Jiménez, M.J.: Evolutionary membrane computing: a comprehensive survey and new results. Inf. Sci. **279**, 528–551 (2014)
4. Zhang, G., Cheng, J., Gheorghe, M., Meng, Q.: A hybrid approach based on differential evolution and tissue membrane systems for solving constrained manufacturing parameter optimization problems. Appl. Soft Comput. **13**(3), 1528–1542 (2013)
5. Ionescu, M., Păun, G., Yokomori, T.: Spiking neural P systems. Fundamenta Informaticae **71**(2–3), 279–308 (2006)
6. Song, T., Pan, L.Q., Păun, G.: Asynchronous spiking neural P systems with local synchronization. Inf. Sci. **219**, 197–207 (2013)
7. Zeng, X., Zhang, X., Song, T., Pan, L.: Spiking neural P systems with thresholds. Neural Comput. **26**, 1340–1361 (2014)
8. Song, T., Pan, Z., Wong, D.M., Wang, X.: Design of logic gates using spiking neural P systems with homogeneous neurons and astrocytes-like control. Inf. Sci. **372**, 380–391 (2016)
9. Wang, X., Song, T., Gong, F., Zheng, P.: On the computational power of spiking neural P systems with self-organization. Sci. Rep. **6**, 27624 (2016). doi:10.1038/srep.27624
10. Cabarle, F.G.C., Adorna, H.N., Martínez, M.A., Pérez-Jiménez, M.J.: Improving GPU simulations of spiking neural P systems. Roman. J. Inf. Sci. Technol. **15**(1), 5–20 (2012)
11. Zhang, G.X., Rong, H.N., Neri, F., Pérez-Jiménez, M.J.: An optimization spiking neural P system for approximately solving combinatorial optimization problems. Int. J. Neural Syst. **24**(5), 1–16 (2014). 1440006
12. Wang, J., Shi, P., Peng, H., Pérez-Jiménez, M.J., Wang, T.: Weighted fuzzy spiking neural P systems. IEEE T Fuzzy Syst. **21**(2), 209–220 (2013)
13. Wang, T., Zhang, G.X., Pérez-Jiménez, M.J.: Fuzzy membrane computing: theory and applications. Int. J. Comput. Commun. **10**(6), 904–935 (2015)
14. Peng, H., Wang, J., Pérez-Jiménez, M.J., Wang, H., Shao, J., Wang, T.: Fuzzy reasoning spiking neural P system for fault diagnosis. Inf. Sci. **235**(20), 106–116 (2013)

15. Wang, T., Zhang, G.X., Zhao, J.B., He, Z.Y., Wang, J., Pérez-Jiménez, M.J.: Fault diagnosis of electric power systems based on fuzzy reasoning spiking neural P systems. IEEE Trans. Power Syst. **30**(3), 1182–1194 (2015)

16. Xiong, G.J., Shi, D.Y., Zhu, L., Duan, X.Z.: A new approach to fault diagnosis of power systems using fuzzy reasoning spiking neural P systems. Math. Probl. Eng. **2013**, 1–13 (2013). Article ID 815352

17. Tu, M., Wang, J., Peng, H., Shi, P.: Application of adaptive fuzzy spiking neural P systems in fault diagnosis of power systems. Chin. J. Electron. **23**(1), 87–92 (2014)

18. Wang, T., Zhang, G.X., Rong, H.N., Pérez-Jiménez, M.J.: Application of fuzzy reasoning spiking neural P systems to fault diagnosis. Int. J. Comput. Commun. **9**(6), 786–799 (2014)

19. Wang, T., Zhang, G.X., Pérez-Jiménez, M.J., Cheng, J.: Weighted fuzzy reasoning spiking neural P systems: application to fault diagnosis in traction power supply systems of high-speed railways. J. Comput. Theoret. Nanosci. **12**(7), 1103–1114 (2015)

20. Silva, K.M., Souza, B.A., Brito, N.S.D.: Fault detection and classification in transmission lines based on wavelet transform and ANN. IEEE Trans. Power Deliv. **21**(4), 2058–2063 (2006)

21. Gaoda, A.M., Salama, M.M.A., Sultan, M.R., Chikhani, A.Y.: Power quality detection and classification using wavelet-multiresolution signal decomposition. IEEE Trans. Power Deliv. **14**(4), 1469–1476 (1999)

22. Littler, T.B., Morrow, D.J.: Wavelets for the analysis and compression of power system disturbances. IEEE Trans. Power Deliv. **14**(2), 358–364 (1999)

23. He, Z.Y., Fu, L., Lin, S., Bo, Z.Q.: Fault detection and classification in EHV transmission line based on wavelet singular entropy. IEEE Trans. Power Deliv. **25**(4), 2156–2163 (2010)

24. Wang, H.S., Keerthipala, W.W.L.: Fuzzy-neuro approach to fault classification for transmission line protection. IEEE Trans. Power Deliv. **13**(4), 1093–1104 (1998)

25. Youssef, O.A.S.: Combined fuzzy-logic wavelet-based fault classification technique for power system relaying. IEEE Trans. Power Deliv. **19**(2), 582–589 (2004)

26. Reddy, M.J., Mohanta, D.K.: Adaptive-neuro-fuzzy inference system approach for transmission line fault classification and location incorporating effects of power swings. IET Gener. Transm. Distrib. **2**(2), 235–244 (2008)

27. Vasilic, S., Kezunovic, M.: Fuzzy ART neural network algorithm for classifying the power system faults. IEEE Trans. Power Deliv. **20**(2), 1306–1314 (2005)

28. Suonan, J.L., Zhang, J.K., Liu, H., et al.: A new method for fault components extraction and fault phases selection. Autom. Electr. Power Syst. **27**(16), 58–61 (2003)

29. Mallat, S.G.: A theory for multiresolution signal decomposition: the wavelet representation. IEEE Trans. Pattern Anal. **11**(7), 674–693 (1989)

30. Hou, Z.J.: Adaptive singular value decomposition in wavelet domain for image denoising. Pattern Recogn. **36**(8), 1747–1763 (2003)

31. Lin, W.M., Yang, C.D., Lin, J.H., Tsay, M.T.: A fault classification method by RBF neural network with OLS learning procedure. IEEE Trans. Power Deliv. **16**(4), 473–477 (2001)

32. Zhang, J., Wang, X.G., Li, Z.L.: Application of neural network based on wavelet packet-energy entropy in power system fault diagnosis. Power Syst. Technol. **30**(5), 72–75 (2006)

33. Mahanty, R.N., Gupta, P.B.D.: Application of RBF neural network to fault classification and location in transmission lines. IET Gener. Transm. Distrib. **20**(2), 1306–1314 (2005)

34. Li, D.M., Liu, Z.G., Su, Y.X., Cai, J.: Fault recognition based on multi-wavelet packet and artificial network. Electr. Power Autom. Equip. **29**(1), 99–103 (2009)

35. Yang, G.L., Le, Q.M., Yu, W.Y., Wang, Z.M., Zhang, Q.M., Zhou, L.: A fault classification method based on wavelet neural networks and fault record data. Proc. CSEE **26**(10), 99–103 (2006)

36. Pradhan, A.K., Routray, A., Pati, S., Pradhan, D.K.: Wavelet fuzzy combined approach for fault classification of a series-compensated transmission line. IEEE Trans. Power Deliv. **19**(4), 1612–1618 (2004)

37. He, Z.Y., Chen, X.Q., Luo, G.M., Qian, Q.Q.: Faulted phase selecting method of transmission lines based on wavelet entrophy weight of transient current. Autom. Electr. Power Syst. **30**(21), 39–43 (2006)

38. Youssef, O.A.S.: New algorithm to phase selection based on wavelet transforms. IEEE Trans. Power Deliv. **17**(4), 908–914 (2002)

39. Duan, J.D., Zhang, B.H., Zhou, Y., Luo, S.B., Ren, J.F., Hang, N.S., Diao, P.: Transient-based faulty phase selection in EHV transmission lines. Proc. CSEE **26**(3), 1–6 (2006)

40. Yang, J.W., He, Z.Y.: Study on recognition of fault transients using hybrid fuzzy petri net. Power Syst. Technol. **36**(2), 250–256 (2012)

41. Bo, Z.Q., Agganval, R.K., Johns, A.T., Yu, H., Song, Y.H.: A new approach to phase selection using fault generated high frequency noise and neural networks. IEEE Trans. Power Deliv. **12**(1), 106–115 (1997)

42. Lin, S., He, Z.Y., Zang, T.L., Qian, Q.Q.: Novel approach of fault type classification in transmission lines based on rough membership neural networks. Proc. CSEE **30**(28), 72–79 (2010)

Membrane Algorithm with Genetic Operation and VRPTW-Based Public Optimization System

Yingying Duan[1,3], Kang Zhou[1,2,3(✉)], Huaqing Qi[1,3], and Zhiqiang Zhang[2,3]

[1] School of Math and Computer,
Wuhan Polytechnic University, Wuhan 430023, China
dybngduan@163.com, zhoukang_wh@163.com, qihuaqing@sohu.com
[2] Department of Economics and Management,
Wuhan Polytechnic University, Wuhan 430023, China
zhiqiangzhang@hust.edu.cn
[3] Key Laboratory of Image Information Processing and Intelligent Control,
School of Automation, Huazhong University of Science and Technology,
Wuhan 430074, China

Abstract. That combining membrane computing with optimization technology offers a new information interaction model for the research of problems in optimization filed. Based on this, a membrane algorithm owned six basic membranes is proposed to solve the defects of the slow convergence and the small diversity in solving vehicle routing problem with time window. In order to further improve the efficiency and the precision, some new rules are designed: for the former problem, a node classifier is introduced to improve the efficiency by filtering directly a plenty of in-feasible solutions; two methods for the latter problems: an uncertain segment crossover is designed in the corresponding membrane in order to explore directly two feasible segments and segment-node insertion operation is introduced in order to make two individuals inserted synchronously another path. In order to verify the effectiveness of the algorithm, a series of experiments are designed. Known through the results of experiments that these two properties of membranes make the search ability of the algorithm improving quickly for local and global exploration and node classifier improves effectively the running efficiency of this algorithm, which proves that membrane algorithm can accelerate the convergence speed and increase diversity of population.

Keywords: Membrane computing · IUOX · PMX · Node classifier · VRPTW

1 Introduction

The vehicle routing problem (VRP) is proposed by Dantzig and Ramser in 1959, which is an important research topic in management science. Vehicle routing problem with time windows (VRPTW) is an expand of VRP, which adds time windows to each client on the basis of VRP and specifies that each vehicle must

© Springer Nature Singapore Pte Ltd. 2016
M. Gong et al. (Eds.): BIC-TA 2016, Part I, CCIS 681, pp. 118–132, 2016.
DOI: 10.1007/978-981-10-3611-8_13

be visited within this window. So far, VRPTW has important theoretical and practical significance in logistic research area such as rail distribution system, the layout of public traffic transport routing, the mail and newspaper delivery system and so on. Therefore it has important theoretical and practical significance in logistic research area. However, because VRPTW is the different premutation and combination of all clients under max-load and time windows constraints, the consuming time can be grow exponentially as the scales increases such as the computational complexity of this problem is $O(MN^2)$ (where M is the size of population and N is the number of clients), promptly, showing that this problem is an NP-hard problem. Therefore, this problem has caused more attentions among many scholars, for example, references [1,2] respectively researched the impact of congestion avoidance and a dynamic constraint for VRPTW with time-dependent; These constraints for VRPTW are to be more realistic close to real life.

Based on the difficulty in solving NP-hard problem through exact algorithms, some heuristic algorithms are used to optimize this problem, such as [3,4] are respectively introduced an improved ant colony algorithm and an adaptive cauchy differential evolution algorithm to VRPTW, and reference [5] proposed an uniform crossover to make GA exploring quickly a better search space in order to improve the precision of solutions; However these algorithms have existed different deficiencies, for example, the lower efficiency and poor precision, especially traditional genetic algorithm. Therefore the paper tries to use a new scheme to improve the performance of the algorithm.

As the research has advanced, a new filed-membrane computing-is explored to solve some practical problems based on its parallelism and closure. With the development of this filed, many researches about P system began to rise, for example, P system with minimal parallelism is used in [6], Alhazov studied trading polarizations in P system with active membranes in [7–10], reference [11] researched computational complexity of tissue-like P system, and reference [12] studied Tissue P system with cell separation, Spiking Neural P system with different operation are researched contained neuron division and budding [13], astrocytes [14], exhaustive use of rules [15] and sequential spiking for normal forms for some classes [16], references [17–19] introduced asynchronous spiking neural P systems. Based on these properties, membrane algorithm was introduced by Nishida [20], references [21,22] analyzed its diversity, convergence and implementation, which shows that membrane computing can solve effectively some problems than other technologies.

Aiming at above introduction, membrane computing is considered to solve discrete optimization problems based on this state that all membranes in P system can execute synchronously thus reducing time complexity; According to the characteristics of global search for genetic algorithm, the paper proposed a new membrane algorithm with GA evolution mechanism (MGA) to deal with these problems. In order to better optimize this problem, two improved strategies are introduced to this mechanism on the basis of membrane algorithm: (a) a node classifier is added to mem. 1 for ameliorating the efficiency; (b) double crossover mechanisms are respectively introduced to mem. 3 and mem. 4 thus expanding the search scope of population.

The paper is organized as follows: in Sect. 2, the definition and mathematical model are introduced; Sect. 3 is devoted to the object and evolution rules; Sect. 4 addresses the experimental design, computational results are presented based on some standard data set. Finally, conclusions are presented in Sect. 6.

2   Definition and Mathematical Mode for VRPTW

2.1   Definition for VRPTW

The VRPTW can be defined as a problem of designing an optimal set of routes that services all customers. Each customer is visited only once by exactly one vehicle with a given time interval; all routes start and end at the depot, and total demands of all customers on one particular route must not exceed the capacity of the vehicle. Let the number of depot be 0, client number is labeled as $1, 2, \ldots, n$ and variant is defined as

$$x_{ijk} = \begin{cases} 1, if\ exist\ an\ edge\ from\ i\ to\ j\ serviced\ by\ vehicle\ k, \\ 0, else, not\ exist. \end{cases} \quad (1)$$

And the time t_j of arriving v_j is described as:

$$t_j = \sum_{i=0}^{N} \sum_{k=1}^{K} x_{ijk}(max(t_i, e_i) + t_{ij} + s_i), \quad j \in 1, 2, \ldots, N \quad (2)$$

Where t_{ij} is the time computed from v_i to v_j, $s_i(s_0 = 0)$ is the service time of loading or unloading for v_i, $max(t_i, e_i)$ represents a starting service time for v_i, set $N = N + i(i = 1, \ldots, n)$.

2.2   Mathematical Model for VRPTW

Mathematically, it can be described as $G = (V, A)$, where V represents a node set, $A = \{(i, j)|i, j \in V\}$ is an edge set. For VRPTW, 0 stands for a central depot owned q vehicles that are responsible for n customers to carry out the work of distribution of goods, $g_i(i = 1, \ldots, n)$ is the demand of v_i, $[e_i, l_i]$ is a time window of v_i that the serviced time of each customer is not earlier than e_i and can not be later than l_i. The objective is to determine a feasible route schedule that primarily minimizes the total travel distance.

$$Min\ Z = \sum_{k \in V} \sum_{i \in N} \sum_{j \in N} C_{ij} x_{ijk} \quad (3)$$

Subject to:

$$\sum_{i \in V} y_{ijk} = \sum_{j \in V} y_{jik}$$

$$\sum_{i \in V'} y_{0ik} = \sum_{j \in V'} y_{j0k} = 1$$

$$\sum_{k \in K} \sum_{j \in N} y_{ijk} \leq 1, \quad \forall k \in K$$

$$\sum_{i \in C} d_i \sum_{j \in N} y_{ijk} \leq q, \quad \forall k \in K$$

$$\sum_{j \in N} x_{0jk} = 1, \quad \forall k \in K$$

$$\sum_{i \in N} x_{ihk} = \sum_{j \in N} x_{hjk}, \quad \forall h \in C, \ \forall k \in V$$

$$\sum_{i \in N} y_{i,n+1,k} = 1, \quad \forall k \in V$$

$$e_i \sum_{j \in V} y_{jik} \leq a_{ik} \leq l_i \sum_{j \in V} y_{jik}$$

$$a_{ik} + s_i + c_{ij} - a_{jk} \leq (1 - y_{ijk}), \quad \forall i, j \in V'$$

$$y_{ijk} \in \{0, 1\}$$

Where, C_{ij} is the transportation cost; formula (3) is the minimum total distance of all routes; constraint (1) shows the connectivity of each path; constraint (2) expresses each vehicle must start from certral depot and end at the depot; constraint (3) ensures that each customer is visited at most once by vehicle k; constraint (4) shows that the demand of each client is less than the remain of vehicle; constraint (5)–(7) ensures that the path continuity; constraint (8) and (9) ensure the constraint condition of time window for each client; constraint (10) is that if $x_{kij} = 1$, then v_i and v_j are visited by vehicle k;

3 Membrane Algorithm with GA Evolution Machanism

Based on the case that the capability of traditional algorithm lacks power for keeping a kind of a balance between the diversity and the convergence as well as between global optimum and local optimum when solving optimization problem, MGA is proposed. Evolution mechanism of genetic algorithm designed as rules of membranes also merges both the distribution and the parallelism. In paper, membrane structure, objects and rules are designed in detail as Sect. 3.1–3.3.

3.1 Membrane Configuration of MGA

According to the property of VRPTW and the evolution characteristic of genetic algorithm, the paper designs six membranes in membrane configuration, where mem. 0 records a global optimal solution x_{gbest}, mem. 1 is used to execute node classifier operation, mem. 2 is used for initialing population, mem. 3 executes unified order crossover operation, mem. 4 is designed as partially mapped crossover, mem. 5 is regarded as mutation operation and mem. 6 executes copy operation, where mem. i represents membrane number such as mem. 1 is membrane 1, others similar. Therefore, the system $\prod$ of MGA is designed as follows.

$$\prod = (O, \sigma_1, \sigma_2, \sigma_3, \sigma_4, \sigma_5, \sigma_6, syn, i_0) \tag{4}$$

where,

(1) $O = \{a\}$, $a \in [1, N]$, N is the number of clients;
(2) $syn = \{(1,3), (1,4), (1,5), (2,3), (2,4), (2,5), (3,2), (4,2), (5,2), (2,6)\}$;
(3) $i_0 = 0$ is output membrane number;
(4) σ_i ($i = 1, \ldots, 6$) represents the ith cell, which is expressed by:

$$\sigma_i = (Q_i, s_{i,0}, \omega_{i,0}, R_i) \tag{5}$$

In formula (5),

(a) $Q_i = (s_{i,0}, s_{i,1}, \ldots, s_{i,t_{max}})$, $s_{i,j}$ is the jth iterations of the ith cell, t_{max} is max iterations.
(b) $s_{i,0}$ is an initial statue, initial objects of mem. 1, mem. 2, 3, 4 is an empty set;
(c) R_i is a limited rule set contained the evolved rules and the transported rules;

In order to clearly to express this system, the paper uses the form of picture to express it, it is described as Fig. 1 following.

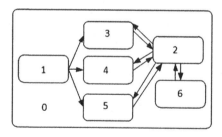

Fig. 1. The framework of MGA.

Seen from Fig. 1 that the transport rules between membranes is as: Initial population are firstly produced in mem. 2 before l_1 chromosomes are sent to mem. 3, l_2, l_3, l_4($l_4 = S - l_1 - l_2 - l_3$) chromosomes selected using roulette method are respectively sent to mem. 4, 5, 6, and then the classed results of mem. 1 are respectively sent to mem. 3, 4, 5 before executing operation according to the rules of each membrane. These individuals of four membranes are synchronously resent to mem. 2 after the completion of evolution.

3.2   Coding for Objects

Based on this case that VRPTW is multiple vehicles routing optimization problem with constraints, the solutions is as an object of MGA which is formed by applying combinatorial arrangement of data structure for all clients under satisfying max load and time window. In the algorithm, an object is encoded by selecting natural number where each object is expressed by using the form of $X_i^t = \{x_{i1}^t, x_{i2}^t, \ldots, x_{iN}^t\}$, $\omega_i = (X_{1i}, X_{2i}, \ldots, X_{ni})$ is object multiple sets of the ith membrane, and $x_{ij} \in [1, N]$, X_{ni} is a code of kth object in mem. i.

3.3   The Rules in Membranes

To ensure the corrected evolution of all objects in each membrane, some rules is designed according to evolution mechanism of MGA. Based on this, the rules are divided two classes: (1) Evolution rules: mem. 1 executes node classifier rules; mem. 2 is used to produce initial population, mem. 3 and mem. 4 execute respectively crossover rules, mem. 5 is used to make mutation rules and mem. 6 is designed as copy rules; (2) Transportation rules.

3.3.1   Rules in Membrane 1: Node Classifier Mechanism

In order for further improving the running efficiency on the basis of improving efficiency by using the parallelism between membranes, a node classifier mechanism is introduced to mem. 1. This mechanism is that v_i is classed into a set owned similar time window with other nodes according to its window thus avoiding the disadvantage of a plenty of selecting infeasible solutions and then improving the running efficiency of the algorithm.

   According to the characteristic of VRPTW, node classifier is introduced from the following six types.

Definition. Let T be a set after the classification. Under satisfying max load, for all to meet $v \in V$, obtain:

C_1: In node classifier, for time window $[e_i, l_i]$: If $l_i > Node[i-1].car_time$, then $v(x + v_i, v_i, y) \to v(x, v_i, y + v_i)$; else, v_i is directly deleted.
C_2: For PMX, execute the rules $v_1(x + s_1, s_1, y) \to v_2(x_1 + s_2, s_2, y_1)$ and $v_2(x + s_2, s_2, y) \to v_1(x_2 + s_1, s_1, y_2)$, that all segments in Node Classifier satisfy $s_1 \in [e_{x_2}, l_{y_3}]$ and $s_2 \in [e_{x_1}, l_{y_1}]$ can execute PMX operation.
C_3: For IUOX, if all nodes belonged to s_1 and s_2 satisfy the requirement and of inserting R_2 and R_1 in Node Classifier, then the rules $v_1(x + a, a, y) \to v_2(x_2 + a, a, y_2)$ and $v_2(x_2 + b, b, y_2) \to v_1(x_1 + b, b, y_1)$ can be executed, where $a \in s_1$ and $b \in s_2$.
C_4: Initialize routing structure car_client, for arbitrary window $[e_i, l_i]$, $[e_{i+1}, l_{i+1}]$ and $e_{i+1} > l_i$: if select tail insertion operation, then these clients of Node Classifier that latest service $l_k(k \in [0, i))$ is less than e_{i+1} are directly deleted.

Seen from the above six properties that C_1 shows that latest service time of node v_i is larger than depart time of previous node c_{i-1}; C_2 and C_3 express that different crossover operations are executed under the premise of satisfying constraints of the exchange; C_4 illustrates that the probability is very small that a node of T_i is inserted to the back of a node of $T_k (k > i)$ in node classifier.

Analysis from the complexity after improving that since the archive size is usually chosen proportional to the population size M, that each client v_k is inserted to current route R_i needs to judge N times, the overall complexity of traditional GA is $O(M * N)$ without introducing node classifier. However, after adding to this mechanism, because these nodes inserted effectively current position p_{ij} must be at a certain range, promptly, the number of nodes selected to insert to p_{ij} is $log_{T_i}(N)$, the computational complexity for MGA is $O(M * log_{T_i}(N))$. According to above analysis, running efficiency gets improving thus proving that this mechanism is effective to solve efficiency problem.

3.3.2 Operation of Membrane 2: Initialization Population

Due to the idea that MGA is regarded as multi-population algorithm, S objects need to be produced by applying the corresponding technology. In order for making the algorithm producing multiple objects in the closed and independent domain, mem. 2 is used as a computing device for obtaining objects and stores new object set after updating through every generation. The steps are designed as $(a) - (e)$.

(a) Let population scale be S, v_i is the ith client, s is the sth object.
(b) Obtain classification set T and then $F = T$ and $s + +(s = 0)$ after calling the rules of mem. 1.
(c) v_i is selected from set F and then adjust whether v_i is inserted to route r_k according to C1-C6: if possible, execute this operation using tail operation; Else, turn(d).
(d) Reopen a route r_j under the premise of not inserting into any route and v_i is inserted to route r_j, continue until set F is an empty set, over.
(e) If $s > S$, then complete initialization, over; Else, turn (b).

Analyzing from rules (a)–(e) that the method of obtaining objects is that firstly initial the number of vehicles n computed according to the requirement of load VRPTW before this n clients stored in the front row of node classifier are randomly inserted to n routes, and then other clients beyond above clients are respectively inserted to above routes using tail insertion, if not satisfy, then reopen a new route, which expresses that this way both avoids this defect of applying a plenty of space in obtaining objects and improves the convergence speed thus proving the great feasibility of this mechanism.

3.3.3 Rules in Membrane 3: Unified Order Crossover (IUOX)

Because that the span of windows for two segments not existed in the same domain leads to the larger probability of the un-success for segments crossover when the nodes based on time window are doing segment crossover, a segment-point insertion is proposed through the characteristic of this problem. The definition and the evolution rules are respectively introduced as follows.

(a) **Definition.** Two crossover segments s_1 and s_2 are randomly elected from routes R_1 and R_2 after randomly selecting routes R_1 and R_2 before executing $R_2 = R_2 - \{s_1\}$ and $R_1 = R_1 - \{s_2\}$ and then R_1 and R_2 after deleting segment s_2 and s_1 are recomputed arrival time of each v_i for every route and then execute two operations $R_2 = R_2 + \{s_1\}$ and $R_1 = R_1 + \{s_1\}$, promptly, obtain R_1' and R_2'.

Where $R = R + \{s\}$ is that segment s is inserted to route R and $R = R - \{s\}$ represents that segment s is deleted from route R;

(b) Evolution rules for IUOX

$$r_1 : \{x_{11}, x_{12}, \ldots, x_{1i}, x_{1(1+l)}, \ldots, x_{1N}\} \to \{x_{11}, x_{2(j+l)}, \ldots, x_{12}, x_{2j}, \ldots, x_{1N}\} \tag{6}$$

$$r_2 : \{x_{21}, x_{22}, \ldots, x_{2j}, x_{2(j+l)}, \ldots, x_{2N}\} \to \{x_{21}, x_{22}, \ldots, x_{1i}, x_{1(i+1)}, \ldots, x_{2N}\} \tag{7}$$

Where $s_1 = (x_{1i}, x_{1(i+1)}, \ldots, x_{1(i+l)})$ and $s_2 = (x_{2j}, x_{2(j+1)}, \ldots, x_{2(j+l)})$ are two crossover segments.

Based on the above analysis, IUOX must make two segments inserting into current route thus greatly improving the evolution efficiency of this algorithm and then proving the effectiveness of this evolution mechanism.

3.3.4 Rules in Membrane 4: Partially Mapped Crossover (PMX)

Because of the existence of the span of window, a double-uncertain segments crossover is proposed to evolve with a smaller probability in order to ensure the feasibility of objects. Based on this, its definition and evolution rules are introduced as $a. - c.$

a. **Definition.** s_1 is arbitrarily selected from route R_1 after routes R_1 and R_2 are selected and then s_2 is selected from R_2 under the premise of double constraints about the remain of vehicle and time window of R_1, promptly, obtain R_1' and R_2' after exchanging s_1 and s_2.

Summary from proposition that rules of PMX is designed as:

(a) Crossover Rules for object X_1

$$r_3 : x_1 u_1 y_1 \to x_1 u_2 y_1 \tag{8}$$

(b) Crossover Rules for object X_2

$$r_4 : x_2 u_2 y_2 \to x_2 u_1 y_2 \tag{9}$$

Analysis from the operation process of PMX that this method can make more excellent segments from parents passed on to next generation thus motivating individual to move toward the direction of the optimum and then improving the precision of the algorithm on the basis of multiple membranes.

3.3.5   Rules in Membrane 5: Mutation Operation

Mutation mechanism is designed in mem. 5 in order to expand the search scope of population, the rule is introduced as follows.

$$r_5 : \{x_{11}, x_{12}, \ldots, x_{1k}, \ldots, x_{1m}, \ldots, x_{1N}\} \rightarrow \{x_{11}, x_{12}, \ldots, x_{1m}, \ldots, x_{1k}, \ldots, x_{1N}\} \tag{10}$$

Study from rule r_5, that mutation mechanism makes a blind search in current space makes the diversity of population expanding thus improving the precision of solutions at a certain extent, promptly, proving that the effectiveness of this mutation mechanism introduced by membrane 5.

3.3.6   Rules for Membrane 6: Copy Rules

Because the evolved direction of population is directed toward the optimal solution space, the cope rule is proposed and the rule is designed as: where $s_{i,j} = s'_{i,j}$.

$$r_6 : s_{i,j} \rightarrow s'_{i,j} \tag{11}$$

Analysis from formula (11) that elite selection strategy can make optimal objects from parents copying to next generation thus ensuring that these object sets of membranes continuously evolves toward an optimal space with a better trend and then improving the convergence speed of the algorithm, promptly, proving that the efficiency of this rules for MGA.

3.4   Transportation Mechanism of MGA

Based on the restrictions that the evolution of some objects of current membrane can successfully execute after obtaining the source of other membranes, some communications are built between membranes. These rules are introduced as follows.

M1: Transport for Objects from mem. 2 to mem. 3, 4, 5, 6

$$r_7 : s_{i,j} \rightarrow (s_{i,j}, go) \tag{12}$$

M2: Design for set T from mem. 1 to mem. 3,4,5

$$r_8 : T \rightarrow (T, go) \tag{13}$$

M3: Rules for objects from mem. 3, 4, 5, 6 to mem. 2, where $s'_{1,(i,j)}$ represents the objects after evolving in mem. 3, 4, 5, 6 by using the rules of four membranes.

$$r_9 : s'_{k,(i,j)} \rightarrow (s'_{k,(i,j)}, go) \tag{14}$$

where k stands for a membrane labeled as k and k can be given these values such as 1, 2, 3, 4.

M4: Rules for local optimum from mem. 2 to mem. 0

$$r_{13} : x_{lbest} \rightarrow (x_{lbest}, go) \tag{15}$$

M5: Rules for global optimum in mem. 0

$$r_{14} : x_{gbest} \rightarrow (x_{gbest}, out) \tag{16}$$

3.5   Termination Condition and Output

For MGA, in order to ensure the convergence at the process of program running, the paper designs the following termination criterions:

(1) The program has achieved termination status when the value of the optimal solution is equal to the one of standard database;
(2) In order to the running time of the algorithm, adjust that the algorithm also gets stopping when the ratio is controlled within 10%, where $ratio = (fit_{current} - optimum)/optimum\%100$ and current solution $fit_{current}$ remains unchanged in a certain number of iterations.

Seen that the algorithm terminated immediately just meeting any one of these two conditions.

For output domain, it is specified as environment area of mem. 0, promptly, the optimum of mem. 0 is a final output result of MGA.

4   Application of MGA in VRPTW

Based on the effect that MGA is applied to optimize the route for some practice problems, MGA is adopted to deal with vehicle route problem with time window. In order to make the algorithm optimizing current objects in solving the process of VRPTW, the detailed steps are designed as follows.

Step 1: Construct membrane system; Initialization population using the rules of mem. 2.

Step 2: Local optimum P_i and global optimum P_g are respectively computed after compute the fitness of individual.

Step 3: For mem. 3, two objects are randomly selected using formula (23) from current population and do segment-point crossover operation using IUOX according to the crossover rules of this mechanism.

Step 4: For mem. 4, two objects are picked using roulette method and then evolve by adopting an uncertain crossover method through the evolution rules of this membrane.

Step 5: For mem. 5, v_i recorded its position p_1 is selected in node classifier and an inserted set T of v_i is obtained and then adjust whether T is an empty or not: if not, k is obtained from set T and then adjust whether the node of p_k is inserted into the p_1 or not: if possible, then insert; else, directly discard. Repeat Step 5, until reaching termination condition, over.

Step 6: For mem. 6, l_4 objects are synchronously selected using formula (23) to directly enter into the next generation by adopting the rules of membrane 6

Step 7: These objects from membrane 3, 4, 5, 6 are synchronously sent to membrane 2, turn Step 2, continue until getting stop condition.

Table 1. Different benchmarks with time windows: comparison with best known.

	GAMC	Best known		GAMC	Known		GAMC	Known
B = 25								
C101	191.30	191.3	R101	709.94	617.1	RC101	597.14	461.0
C103	277.76	190.3	R103	571.04	454.6	RC103	515.39	332.8
C104	206.70	186.9	R104	451.17	416.9	RC104	498.19	306.6
C201	295.66	214.7	R201	533.04	463.3	RC201	415.55	360.2
C202	221.87	214.7	R202	480.87	410.5	RC202	412.67	338.1
C203	231.81	214.7	R203	401.43	391.4	RC203	438.87	326.9
C204	277.65	213.1	R204	368.75	355.0	RC204	318.89	299.0
Average	239.05	202.0		524.98	456.98		454.26	347.05
B = 50								
C101	537.84	362.4	R101	1085.29	1044.0	RC101	2264.97	944.0
C102	524.02	361.4	R102	912.050	909.0	RC102	2111.22	822.5
C103	417.72	361.4	R103	1148.14	772.9	RC103	2205.61	710.9
C104	483.54	358.0	R104	894.76	625.4	RC104	1513.28	545.8
C201	669.49	360.2	R201	943.29	791.9	RC201	1306.95	684.8
C202	781.31	360.2	R202	790.91	698.5	RC202	1185.83	613.6
C203	489.9	359.8	R203	871.96	605.3	RC203	1247.58	553.3
C204	556.98	350.1	R204	990.05	506.4	RC204	1695.48	444.2
Average	557.6	359.18		954.55	744.17		691.36	664.8

5   Simulation Experiment

In order for verifying the performance of the algorithm, MGA is selected to use the data of 100 scales for testing VRPTW, which mainly evaluates the diversity of population and the ability of global convergence. The flat of this experiment select dual-core Intel, 2.30 GHz, 4.00 GB memory based on Windows 10 system and select VC6.0++ to encode. In experiment parts, the parameters is tuned according to the method [10] and MGA is compared with GA and database, and then the experiment results focus on the research in order to thoroughly analysis the comprehensive performance.

5.1   Results for Parameters Tuning

Analysis through the theory of optimization algorithm that the value for each parameter has an effect on the optimization of MGA, promptly, the better parameters can promote this optimization. Therefore, these parameters are tuned by using this method in reference [10]. All results by tuning are designed as: crossover rate PC is designed as 0.75, mutation rate PM is obtained as 0.20,

Table 2. Comparison results under clients 100 for MGA and GA.

Network scales	Optimum		Average		Time		Ratio (%)
	MGA	GA	MGA	GA	MGA	GA	MGA/GA
$C101$	3161.02	3731.12	3330.42	4036.90	81.88	101.32	−0.180
$C102$	3412.38	3386.32	3644.89	3459.1	220.68	261.57	0.007
$C103$	3488.55	3521.07	3658.13	3698.27	122.25	369.52	−0.009
$C104$	3445.99	3613.07	3881.76	3780.31	506.73	598.34	−0.048
$C201$	2612.29	3013.13	2921.34	3103.10	131.89	164.21	−0.153
$C202$	2928.49	3413.63	3600.93	3510.30	145.42	201.79	−0.165
$C203$	3331.47	3521.36	3796.58	3591.41	285.98	274.01	−0.056
$C204$	3376.85	3247.25	3600.63	3613.28	542.10	437.07	0.038
$R101$	3124.77	3341.71	3527.19	3987.41	261.32	332.20	−0.069
$R102$	2902.94	3287.19	3316.54	3758.19	198.24	241.32	−0.123
$R103$	2662.68	3103.31	3131.29	3151.90	318.79	351.40	−0.165
$R104$	2788.43	2896.46	2937.85	3125.61	234.19	296.51	−0.038
$R201$	2253.78	2431.67	2693.77	2510.01	174.95	210.30	−0.078
$R202$	2307.27	2354.01	2420.62	2409.31	198.72	231.17	−0.020
$R203$	2410.39	2517.89	2855.91	2597.06	302.33	392.19	−0.044
$R204$	2594.80	2630.34	2778.95	2725.07	368.53	413.07	0.109
$RC101$	3775.05	4103.41	3937.77	4209.17	93.35	127.01	−0.041
$RC102$	3705.93	4038.25	3959.37	4137.06	158.17	211.15	−0.089
$RC103$	3569.42	3845.03	3581.23	3945.17	231.03	298.13	−0.077
$RC104$	3319.85	3590.48	3331.01	3658.93	380.902	411.03	−0.081
$RC201$	2778.42	2913.52	2977.71	3014.30	174.84	201.36	−0.048
$RC202$	2850.69	2985.04	3009.52	3128.69	186.27	213.14	−0.047
$RC203$	2821.21	3045.97	3205.78	3379.23	306.60	331.07	−0.079
$RC204$	3407.26	3564.41	3583.31	3610.73	441.86	479.13	−0.046
Average	3042.93	3253.98			252.79	297.83	8.6%

population size S is computed as 500, iter_max D is tuned as 1000, and the algorithm runs 30 times where R expresses operation times.

5.2   Analysis of Experiment Results for Different Scales

To obtain effectively experiment results for proving the performance contained computing ability and optimized one when solving problem using MGA in an optimization field, some scales are firstly tested before the performance for MGA is optimized to the best state and then a large scale instance is tested in order to verify its advantage after deviated ratio is controlled to a smaller range when testing some small scale data. These results are as Tables 1 and 2.

By analyzing experiment results of three above types with a quantitative approach in Table 1, with the application of 25 scales, that the averages of optimums for three types of problems are respectively 239.05, 524.98 and 454.26

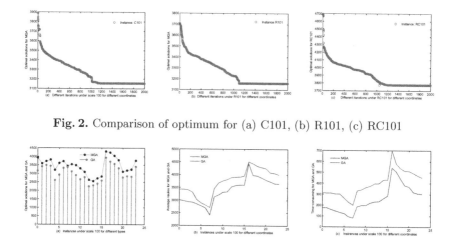

Fig. 2. Comparison of optimum for (a) C101, (b) R101, (c) RC101

Fig. 3. Comparison of optimum, average and time for scale 100 in (a)–(c)

and the averages of optimums in database are severally 202.0, 456.98 and 347.05 illustrates that the deviated ratio between MGA and database is respectively 18.3%, 14.8% and 30.8%, which shows that the algorithm can correctly adduce populations evolving toward the direction of the best domains in small scales; With the resurrect of 50 scales in Table 2, that the averages of optimums of three instances are respectively 557.6, 954.55 and 691.36 shows that deviated ratios about three indicators are aptly 55.4%, 28.2% and 3.9% computed by comparing with database, which shows that the performance of the algorithm has been improved and this ratio can be controlled within a certain error range thus illustrating that it can search a good solution under the premise of the limited time, promptly, proving the feasibility of MGA for solving large scales problems.

In order to directly express the results in above tables, the paper are designed two graphs as Figs. 2 and 3 where Fig. 2 is the curves of optimum for C101, R101 and RC101 under 2000 iterations and Fig. 3 is the graphics of the optimum of 24 instances, average values and time where for average and time, the former eight instances are in the descending order, middle eight instances are in ascending and last eight instances are descending in order to the effect of graph. Analysis from Figs. 2 and 3(a)–(c) that the comprehensive performance of MGA is better than GA; For the total results for these three instances.

The performance with which MGA is applied to test the data of a large scale is verified by using the instance of 100 scales and the experiment results are proved by analysing according to Tables 1 and 2, Figs. 1 and 2.

6   Conclusion

Considering the efficiency about NP-hard optimization problems, membrane algorithm is regarded as the best choose for the defects. MGA is an optimization algorithm that improved genetic algorithm is embedded in membrane computing based on bionic cell. Communication cooperation mechanism between membranes is regarded as crucial problems thus initially solving the problem of the low convergence and the small diversity. Obtaining the following conclusions: (1) In the study of the algorithm efficiency, node classifier is used to make process of single membrane evolving in high reliability, accurate positioning and fast processing speed; (2) In the study of improving precision, that crossover mechanism and mutation one make the algorithm converging quickly and the diversity increasing fleetly; (3) Transportation rules between membranes can make objects evolving smoothly and efficiently so as to improve the performance of membrane algorithm.

Verification through these results indicates that in precision aspect, the accuracy of MGA increases by 15.3 percentage points so as to prove that the independent evolution of membranes and the communication mechanism between membranes can achieve the higher precision; In time efficiency aspect, this mechanism makes the algorithm increasing by 7.8 percentage points, which proves that MGA fully demonstrates the optimized abilities and computing power.

Acknowledgments. This project was supported by National Natural Science Foundation of China (Grant No. 61179032), the Special Scientific Research Fund of Food Public Welfare Profession of China (Grant No. 201513004-3) and the Research and Practice Project of Graduate Education Teaching Reform of Wuhan Polytechnic University (YZ2015002).

References

1. Kok, A.L., Hans, E.W., Schutten, J.M.: Vehicle routing under time-dependent travel times: the impact of congestion avoidance. Comput. Oper. Res. **39**(5), 910–918 (2012)
2. Haghani, A., Jung, S.: A dynamic vehicle routing problem with time-dependent travel times. Comput. Oper. Res. **32**(11), 2959–2986 (2005)
3. Qi, C., Sun, Y.: An improved ant colony algorithm for VRPTW. IN: Computer Science and Software Engineering, pp. 455–458 (2008)
4. Taner, F., Galic, A., Caric, T.: Solving practical vehicle routing problem with time windows using metaheuristic algorithms. PROMET-traffic Transp. **24**(4), 343–351 (2012)
5. Bate, S.T., Jones, B.H.: A review of uniform cross-over designs. J. Stat. Plan. Inference **138**(2), 336–351 (2008)
6. Ciobanu, G., Pan, L., Păun, G.: P systems with minimal parallelism. Theoret. Comput. Sci. **378**(1), 117–130 (2007)
7. Alhazov, A., Pan, L., Păun, G.: Trading polarizations for labels in P systems with active membranes. Acta Informatica **41**, 111–144 (2004)
8. Pan, L., Ishdorj, T.: P Systems with active membranes and separation rules. J. Univers. Comput. Sci. **10**, 630–649 (2004)
9. Pan, L., Alhazov, A.: Solving HPP and SAT by P systems with active membranes and separation rules. Acta Informatica **43**(2), 131–145 (2006)
10. Pan, L., Alhazov, A., Ishdorj, T.: Further remarks on P systems with active membranes, separation, merging, and release rules. Soft Comput. **9**(9), 686–690 (2004)

11. Pan, L., Perezjimenez, M.J.: Computational complexity of tissue-like P systems. J. Complex. **26**(3), 296–315 (2010)
12. Zhang, X., Wang, S., Niu, Y., Pan, L.: Tissue P systems with cell separation: attacking the partition problem. Sci. China Inf. Sci. **54**(2), 293–304 (2011)
13. Pan, L., Păun, G., Perezjimenez, M.: Spiking neural P systems with neuron division and budding. Sci. China Ser. F: Inf. Sci. **54**(8), 1596–1607 (2011)
14. Pan, L., Wang, J., Hoogeboom, H.: Spiking neural P systems with astrocytes. Neural Comput. **24**(3), 805–825 (2012)
15. Zhang, X., Zeng, X., Pan, L.: On string languages generated by spiking neural P systems with exhaustive use of rules. Nat. Comput. **7**(4), 535–549 (2008)
16. Song, T., Pan, L., Jiang, K.: Normal forms for some classes of sequential spiking neural P systems. IEEE Trans. Nanobiosci. **12**(3), 255–264 (2013)
17. Pan, L., Păun, G.: Spiking neural p systems with anti-spikes. Int. J. Comput. Commun. Control **4**(3), 273–282 (2009)
18. Zhang, X., Zeng, X., Pan, L.: On languages generated by asynchronous spiking neural P systems. Theoret. Comput. Sci. **410**(26), 2478–2488 (2009)
19. Song, T., Zou, Q., Liu, X.: Asynchronous spiking neural P systems with rules on synapses. Neurocomputing **151**, 1439–1445 (2015)
20. Nishida, T.Y.: An application of P-system: a new algorithm for NP-complete optimization problems. In: Cybernetics and Informatics, pp. 109–112 (2004)
21. Zhang, G., Liu, C., Gheorghe, M.: Diversity and convergence analysis of membrane algorithm. In: Theories and Applications, pp. 596–603 (2010)
22. Zhang, X., Wang, B., Ding, Z.: Implementation of membrane algorithms on GPU. J. Appl. Math. (2014). Conference Series, 8005: 8 (2011)

An Immune Algorithm Based on P System for Classification

Lian Ye[1,2(✉)] and Ping Guo[1,2]

[1] College of Computer Science, Chongqing University, Chongqing 400044, China
{ylredleaf,guoping}@cqu.edu.cn
[2] Chongqing Key Laboratory of Software Theory and Technology,
Chongqing 400044, China

Abstract. The membrane system and artificial immune system are both a branch of natural computing, which has attracted much attention in various disciplines. Inspired from the structure and inherent mechanism of membrane computing and immune computing, a membrane system based on immune mechanism algorithm is proposed to deal with classification problems. The approach contains three important stages: firstly, the candidate cells are generated by selecting from the gene pool randomly; then, calculate the affinity of the candidate cell with each element in the self-set to construct the classifier; finally, input the un-label cells into the detectors to test the performance of the classifier.

Keywords: Membrane computing · Immune algorithm · Negative selection · Classifier

1 Introduction

Natural Computing is a discipline whose aim is the study and implementation of the dynamic processes that occur in the living nature and that are likely to be interpreted as calculation procedures. Membrane computing (P systems) was initiated by Păun, which is a class of powerful computing model abstracted from the way that the living cells process chemical compounds, energy and information in their compartmental structures [1].

As a model of computation with universality property, membrane computing is so computationally efficient that it can solve difficult computational NP-complete problems in a polynomial time by creating exponentially membranes [2]. SAT problem was solved by the splitting rule of membrane system [3]. [4] gives a family of P systems to solve All-SAT problem with simplified membrane structure and few evolution rules based on the character of membrane division and parallel processing in the P systems.

Artificial immune systems (AIS) can be defined as computational systems inspired by theoretical immunology, observed immune functions, principles, and mechanisms to solve problems [5]. Negative selection is one of the most discussed algorithms in artificial immune system [6].

© Springer Nature Singapore Pte Ltd. 2016
M. Gong et al. (Eds.): BIC-TA 2016, Part I, CCIS 681, pp. 133–141, 2016.
DOI: 10.1007/978-981-10-3611-8_14

In this paper, based on a combination of membrane system and artificial immune systems, we proposed immune classification algorithm by a membrane system. In this system, a set of detectors are created by the given rules firstly, then this collection of detectors called classifier will be used to recognize the category of the unknown objects. It can be also used in some pattern identification and combinatorial optimization problems.

The paper is organized as follows. Section 2 describes the foundation of membrane system and negative selection algorithm. The details of Π_{NS}, including the membrane structure, evolving rules and analyses are proposed in Sect. 3. The conclusions and further researches are then discussed in Sect. 4.

2   Related Works

Membrane Computing devices are generically called P systems. They constitute a theoretical computing model of a distributed, parallel and non-deterministic type.

2.1   Cell-Like P System

The main syntactic ingredients of a cell-like P system are the membrane structure shown in Fig. 1, the multi-sets, and the evolution rules. The semantics of the systems are defined through a nondeterministic and synchronous model, by introducing the concepts of configuration, transition step, and computation.

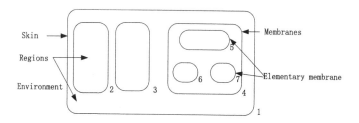

Fig. 1. The structure of cell-like P system

A basic transition P system of degree $m \geq 1$ is a tuple,

$$\Pi = (O, \mu, \omega_1, \cdots, \omega_m, (R_1, \rho_1), (R_2, \rho_2), \cdots, (R_m, \rho_m), i_o) \qquad (1)$$

where,

(i) O is the alphabet of the system;

(ii) μ is a membrane structure consisting of m membranes, which are labeled by numbers in the set $\{1, \cdots, m\}$;

(iii) $\omega_1 \cdots \omega_m$ are multi-sets, representing the objects initially presented in the regions $(1, \cdots, m)$ of the system;

(iv) $R_1, \cdots, R_m$ are finite sets of evolution rules associated with the regions $(1, \cdots, m)$ of μ; $(\rho_1, \cdots, \rho_m)$ are strict partial order relations defined over $(R_1, \cdots, R_m)$ respectively, specifying a priority relation among the evolution rules; The rule can be described as the form $(u \rightarrow v, \rho_i)$, where, $u \rightarrow v$ is rewrite rule, and $\rho_i (1 \leq i \leq m)$ indicate the priority.

(v) i_o is indicating the output region.

The cell division in P systems plays in a crucial role for generating exponential work space in linear time. Here we consider the following cell membrane interaction operation to formalize in P systems area.

2.2 Negative Selection

The immune algorithm called negative selection was first developed by Forrest [6] for real-time detection of computer virus. In this algorithm, T cells are randomly generated to detect foreign antigens without reacting to self-cells in the thymus. Hence, the mature T cells leaving the thymus will not match the self-cells and will therefore only match the non-self cells. The basic concept of a negative selection algorithm is shown in Fig. 2.

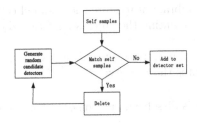

Fig. 2. Negative selection algorithm

3 Π_{NS} for Classification

The P system named Π_{NS} is proposed to create the classifier which will classify the un-label objects. The details of the system will be given in this section.

3.1 Definition

Π_{NS} for classification can defined as:

$$\Pi_{NS} = (O, \mu, \omega_1, \cdots, \omega_m, R, i_o) \tag{2}$$

I. O is a finite and non-empty alphabet of objects.
$O = \{\Psi_1, \Psi_2, \beta, \gamma, \gamma', \lambda, \delta, \phi, \phi_s, \phi_{ss}, \phi_c, \phi_{cc}, \eta, \eta_0, \eta', \eta_i, \eta_{ii}\}$
$\cup \{\xi_i, 0 \leq i \leq 26\} \cup \{a_j, b_j, \cdots, z_j, 1 \leq j \leq k\}$

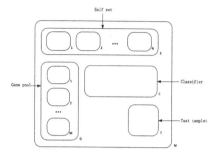

Fig. 3. Initial membrane structure

II. μ is the membrane structure composed of four main membranes in the skin membrane shown in Fig. 3. The membrane G represents gene pool to store the different gene segments as the initial multi-sets which should be placed. The membrane S represents the self-set to store the autologous cells which should also be placed at first, the number of these cells is define as $(2^k - 1)$. The membrane C denotes as classifier which is used to retain the detectors, it is empty at the beginning. The membrane T is the templte of a membrane to generate new membrane u to store the un-label cells.

III. ω_i is multi-sets, representing the objects for i record of the data set in the regions i.

IV. The rules in R should have priority, and the explanations of some rules are given here, k indicates the priority:

- $[_h u\delta]_h \rightarrow v, k$
  The membrane h is dissolved, and the object u is replaced with object v.
- $[_h u \rightarrow v]_h, k$
  In the region named h, remove the multi-set of objects specified by u, and to introduce the objects specified by v.
- $[_h u \rightarrow (v, in_j)]_h, k$
  The object v should be moved into the membrane j which is the upper membrane that has not been dissolved, and the object u will be removed from membrane h.
- $[_h u \rightarrow (v, out)]_h, k$
  The object v will be moved to the region immediately outside membrane h.
- $[_h u \rightarrow [_h v]_h]_h, k$
  The object u will be replaced with a new membrane containing object v.
- $[_{h1} u]_{h1} \rightarrow [_{h2} u]_{h2} [_{h2} u]_{h2}$
  All objects and membranes in the original membrane will be duplicated and appear in the two new membranes.
- $u_j [_h]_h [_j]_j \rightarrow [_j v[_h]_h]_j$
  The membrane will be filtered into j_{th} membrane by u_j, and u_j be replaced with symbol v.

V. i_o is the skin membrane to output the result.

The value of k is smaller, and the priority of the corresponding rule is higher. When k = 1, the corresponding rule will have the highest priority.

All of the rules that can be applied must be applied simultaneously. The marked output membranes are never dissolved.

3.2 Rule Set

The rules of P system Π_{NS} in each membrane are as follows:

(1) The rule set in the skin membrane called R_M. In this set, $r_1 \sim r_7$ are used in generation phase, $r_8 \sim r_{37}$ are used in testing phase. In generation phase, The number of new cell is determined by the number of symbol ϕ denoted as N. The symbol ϕ_{ss} is used to send detectors into self set. The key point of this process is that leaving only one cell in skin membrane, the others all sending into membrane S. In testing phase, The symbol L represents number of detectors to be generated. The symbol K represents the count of each attribute. The priority of r_9 is lower than that of $r_1 2 \sim r_{37}$, in other words, sending the objects into membrane u before duplicating membrane u.

r_1: $\Psi_1 \rightarrow \phi^N (\xi_0 \xi_1 \cdots \xi_M, in_G)$

r_2: $\phi[_0]_0 \rightarrow \phi_s[_0]_0[_0]_0$

r_3: $\phi_s^N \rightarrow \phi_{ss}^N$

r_4: $\phi_{ss}^N[_0]_0 \rightarrow (\eta[_0]_0, in_s)$

r_5: $\gamma \rightarrow \gamma' \Psi_1([_0]_0, in_C), 2$

r_6: $\gamma'^L \Psi_1 \rightarrow \natural, 1$

r_7: $\beta \rightarrow \Psi_1(\eta'', in_0)$

r_8: $\Psi_2[_T]_T \rightarrow \phi^{L-1}[_T]_T[_u]_u$

r_9: $\phi[_u]_u \rightarrow \phi_c[_u]_u[_u]_u, 2$

r_{10}: $\phi_c^{L-1} \rightarrow \phi_{cc}^L$

r_{11}: $\phi_{cc}[_u]_u \rightarrow (\eta_0[_u]_u, in_C)$

r_{12}: $a_j \rightarrow (a_j, in_u), 1; (1 \le j \le K)$

r_{13}: $b_j \rightarrow (b_j, in_u), 1; (1 \le j \le K)$

$\cdots$

r_{37}: $z_j \rightarrow (z_j, in_u), 1; (1 \le j \le K)$

(2) The rule set in membrane G called R_G. The symbol M represents the number of attributes in the data set, its max value is 26. The symbol ξ_0 was generated a new candidate cell. The membrane 0 will be out of membrane G after that all the values have been sent into the membrane by $r_4 \sim r_{29}$.

r_1: $\xi_i \rightarrow (\xi_i, in_i), 1; (1 \le i \le M)$

r_2: $\xi_0 \rightarrow [_0]_0, 1$

r_3: $\phi^M[_0]_0 \rightarrow ([_0]_0, out_G)$

r_4: $a_j \rightarrow \phi(a_j, in_0), 1; (1 \le j \le K)$

r_5: $b_j \rightarrow \phi(b_j, in_0), 1; (1 \le j \le K)$

$\cdots$

r_{29}: $z_j \rightarrow \phi(z_j, in_0), 1; (1 \le j \le K)$

(3) The rule set in gene membrane of membrane G called R_{gi}, $1 \leq i \leq M$. The symbol ξ_i releases an attribute value randomly out of corresponding membrane i.

$r_1: \xi_1 a_j \rightarrow a_j(a_j, out_1); (1 \leq j \leq K)$
$r_2: \xi_2 b_j \rightarrow b_j(b_j, out_2); (1 \leq j \leq K)$
$\cdots$

$r_{26}: \xi_{26} z_j \rightarrow z_j(z_j, out_{26}); (1 \leq j \leq K)$

(4) The rule set in membrane S called R_S. The symbol N represents the number of self cells. The symbol β represents that the corresponding attribute from the two cells are matched. The symbol γ represents that the two cells are not matched.

$r_1: \eta \eta_i \rightarrow \eta_{ii}; (1 \leq i \leq N)$
$r_2: \eta_{ii}[_i]_i \rightarrow [_i]_i \eta_i([_i \eta']_i, in_0); (1 \leq i \leq N)$
$r_3: \beta^2 \rightarrow \beta\gamma, 1$
$r_4: \beta\gamma^{M-1} \rightarrow (\beta, out_S), 2$
$r_5: \gamma^M \rightarrow (\gamma, out_S)$

(5) The rule set in self membrane of membrane S called R_{si}, $1 \leq i \leq N$. Dissolve the membrane to release the object into outer membrane.

$r_1: \eta' \rightarrow \gamma\delta$

(6) The rule set in membrane 0 called R_0. $r_1 \sim r_{26}$ are matching rules for the affinity measure. The symbol m is a threshold of the affinity. If the number of matched attributes is greater than the threshold, it will release a symbol β out of membrane, otherwise it will release a symbol γ.

$r_1: a_j^2 \rightarrow \beta; (1 \leq j \leq K)$
$r_2: b_j^2 \rightarrow \beta; (1 \leq j \leq K)$
$\cdots$

$r_{26}: z_j^2 \rightarrow \beta; (1 \leq j \leq K)$
$r_{27}: \gamma \rightarrow \gamma^2, 3$
$r_{28}: \beta^m \gamma^2 \rightarrow \eta''(\beta, out_0), 1$
$r_{29}: \gamma^2 \rightarrow \eta''(\gamma, out_0), 1$
$r_{30}: \beta \rightarrow \lambda|_{\eta''}, 1$
$r_{31}: a_j \rightarrow \lambda|_{\eta''}, 1; (1 \leq j \leq K)$
$r_{32}: b_j \rightarrow \lambda|_{\eta''}, 1; (1 \leq j \leq K)$
$\cdots$

$r_{56}: z_j \rightarrow \lambda|_{\eta''}, 1; (1 \leq j \leq K)$
$r_{57}: \eta'' \rightarrow \delta, 2$
$r_{58}: \eta' \rightarrow \gamma\delta$

(7) The rule set in membrane C called R_C. The copies of unlabel cell are sent into each detector in this membrane. The symbol Z represents the self cell and the symbol Y represents the non-self cell. The result will be sent out of this membrane into skin membrane.

$r_1: \eta_0[_0]_0 \rightarrow [_0]_0([_0\eta']_0, in_u)$
$r_2: \beta^2 \rightarrow \beta\gamma, 1$
$r_3: \beta\gamma^{N-1} \rightarrow (Y, out_C), 2$
$r_4: \gamma^N \rightarrow (Z, out_C)$

(8) The rule set in membrane T and u called R_T. Each unknown cell is sent into the copy of membrane T saved as membrane u. The match procedure is the same with R_0. If the affinity of the two cell is greater than the threshold, it will release a symbol β out of membrane, otherwise it will release a symbol γ.

$$r_1: a_j^2 \rightarrow \beta; (1 \leq j \leq K)$$
$$r_2: b_j^2 \rightarrow \beta; (1 \leq j \leq K)$$
...

$$r_{26}: z_j^2 \rightarrow \beta; (1 \leq j \leq K)$$
$$r_{27}: \gamma \rightarrow \gamma^2, 3$$
$$r_{28}: \beta^m \gamma^2 \rightarrow \eta''(\beta, out_u), 1$$
$$r_{29}: \gamma^2 \rightarrow \eta''(\gamma, out_u), 1$$
$$r_{30}: \beta \rightarrow \lambda|_{\eta''}, 1$$
$$r_{31}: a_j \rightarrow \lambda|_{\eta''}, 1; (1 \leq j \leq K)$$
$$r_{32}: b_j \rightarrow \lambda|_{\eta''}, 1; (1 \leq j \leq K)$$
...

$$r_{56}: z_j \rightarrow \lambda|_{\eta''}, 1; (1 \leq j \leq K)$$
$$r_{57}: \eta'' \rightarrow \delta, 2$$

3.3   Algorithm Implementation

Π_{NS} contains three important phases: generate the candidate detectors randomly; calculate the affinity of the detector to decide whether deleted or converted into immune cell in classifier; test the performance of the classifier.

In skin membrane M, when it receives the starting symbol Ψ_1, the rule ($r_1 \in R_M$) will send symbols into membrane G to produce a new elementary membrane called the candidate cell. In skin membrane G, the new membrane marked zero for a candidate detector by rule ($r_2 \in R_G$). The symbol $\xi_i (1 \leq i \leq M)$ is sent into membrane ($1 \leq i \leq M$) in order to release a random attribute value by the rules ($r_1 \sim r_{26} \in R_{gi}$), the detector will be out of the gene pool by rule ($r_3 \in R_G$).

The candidate cell will be replicated by membrane separation. The affinity of each self cell in self set with the candidate cell must be calculated. Suppose the number of self cells is $N (N = 2^k - 1)$, the symbol ϕ controls the times of replication to produce N copies which will be sent into membrane S by the rules ($r_2 \sim r_4 \in R_M$). Only one membrane will be left in the skin membrane waiting for the next operation.

In membrane S, once the symbol η sent in, the rule ($r_1, r_2 \in R_S$) will send the copy of each self cell into the candidate cell. Then the membranes i will dissolve and release the objects into membrane zero. Next, the rules ($r_1 \sim r_{26} \in R_0$) may be reacted or not. There are ($M + 1$) kinds of possibility. If one attribution is equivalent, it will produce one β. The symbol γ is as a time slice, its count will be two by the rule $r_{27}.m$ is the affinity to determine the similarity of two cells according to the specific problem ($1 \leq m \leq M$). The final output is β or γ representing matched or not matched respectively.

In the skin membrane, the symbol γ means that the new cell can not be recognized by the self set and can join to the classifier by rule ($r_5 \in R_M$). The symbol β means that the new cell can be recognized and must be deleted and start the next round search of by rules ($r_7 \in R_M$ and $r_{57} \in R_0$). L indicates the number of detectors to be generated, the search process will stop until the termination symbol $\sharp$.

When the classifier is generated, the classification performance of that must be tested. In the testing process, input the symbol Ψ_2 from the environment to start the detection, then apply the rule ($r_8 \in R_M$) to generate membrane u to store the unlabel cell by rules ($r_{12} \sim r_{37} \in R_M$). Then replicate the membrane u and send them into membrane C by rule ($r_9 \sim r_{11} \in R_M$). The replication process and matching process are similar to the process of affinity testing in generation of detector.

In membrane C, the rules ($r_3 \sim r_4 \in R_C$) are applied to release the symbol Y which means that the cell is allogeneic or Z which means that the cell is autologous.

3.4   Analyses

Π_{NS} is a P system of immune algorithm for classification. The key issues of the classification problem are implemented in three membranes. Therefore, the data of practical problems in real life can be transferred into objects in the specific membrane. The membrane G represents gene pool to store the different gene segments as the initial multi-sets, in other words, which contains the range of values for each attribute and the values must be the discrete numerical. The membrane S represents the self-set to store the autologous cells. Typically, all the data is divided into two sets: training set and testing set. The records of training set are transferred and placed in the membrane S in advance. If the new candidate cell is recognized by the cells of training set, that means they are the same kind, otherwise, they belong to different kinds, and the candidate cell will be converted to detector and sent to the membrane C which denotes as classifier. When the classifier is generated, it can be used to differentiate the objects without class label. The performance of the classifier can be tested by the data of testing set.

The simulation of Π_{NS} based on negative selection was validated using iris data set from UCI Machine Learning Repository [7]. The initial data of iris data set was preprocessed. In the experimentations, the affinity of two different cell is 75%. According to the thought of membrane calculation, both in the detector generation phase and in the testing phase, the matching process between self cell with detector and the testing cell with detector are asynchronous execution. It means that this system converts serial execution of the basic algorithm to parallel execution, decreases the algorithm execution time. The classification accuracy is improved with the increase of the number of detectors and the accuracy of classification is sufficiently comparable to other top classification algorithm.

4   Conclusion

In this paper, we have proposed Π_{NS} for classification based on immune algorithm of immune system. The important advantage of the system is the parallelism which is inherent character of membrane system. In standard negative selection algorithm, the operate to calculate the affinity of two cells both in searching the immune cell and testing the unlabel cell is serial process. However, the candidate cell will be duplicated to match the self cells or detectors at the same time. It could be increase the searching speed. There are still some problem to solve, from which the most important is ignoring noise in data and increasing efficiency of algorithm when using data sets containing patterns not uniformly distributed within different classes.

References

1. Păun, G.: Computing with membranes. J. Comput. Syst. Sci. **61**(1), 108–143 (2000)
2. Calude, C.S., Paun, G.: Bio-steps beyond turing. Biosystems **77**(1C3), 175–194 (2004)
3. Obtulowicz A.: Deterministic P system for solving SAT problem. J. Inf. Sci. Technol. Roman. **4**(1-2), 195–202 (2001)
4. Ping, G., Jinfang, J., Haizhu, Z.: Solving All-SAT problems by P systems. Chin. J. Electron. **24**(4), 744–749 (2015)
5. de Castro, L.N., Timmis, J.: Artificial immune systems as a novel soft computing paradigm. Soft Comput. **7**, 526–544 (2003)
6. Forrest, S., Perelson, A.S., Allen, L.: Self-nonself discrimination in a computer. In: IEEE Computer Society Symposium on Research in Security and Privacy, Los Alamitos, pp. 202–212 (1994)
7. Frank, A., Asuncion, A.: UCI machine learning repository. School of Information and Computer Sciences, University of California, Irvine, CA (2010). http://archive. ics.uci.edu/ml

Simulation of Fuzzy *ACSH* on Membranes with Michaelis-Menten Kinetics

J. Philomenal Karoline, P. Helen Chandra[✉],
S.M. Saroja Theerdus Kalavathy, and A. Mary Imelda Jayaseeli

Jayaraj Annapackiam College for Women (Autonomous),
Periyakulam, Theni District, Tamilnadu, India
philoharsh@gmail.com, chandrajac@yahoo.com, kalaoliver@gmail.com,
imeldaxavier@gmail.com

Abstract. Various models have been used to represent natural phenomenon in order to gain insight on what stability is. A computing model called Fuzzy abstract rewriting system on multisets, close to reality is recently designed by introducing fuzziness on computation [1]. As an extension of this model a device named Fuzzy Artificial cell system with proteins on membrane is developed and the corresponding structure is analyzed on its parameters [2]. The aim of the present study is to investigate how the choices made in a simulation affect its accuracy and therefore the reliability of the result.

Keywords: P system · Artificial cell system · Fuzzy *ACS* · Proteins on membranes · Michaelis-menten behaviour · Simulation

1 Introduction

Fuzzification of membrane systems and their evolution rules which is motivated by some practical applications is a quite recent development. Rigid mathematical models employed in biology are not completely adequate for the interpretation of biological information. This fact has led to the adoption of fuzzy models and methodologies. Also it has been shown that P systems with fuzzy multiset rewriting rules are equivalent to fuzzy Turing machines. Suzuki and Tanaka [3] have introduced the multiset Rewriting system, called Abstract Rewriting System on Multisets ($ARMS$). Based on this system, they have developed a molecular computing model called Artificial Cell System which consists of a multiset of symbols, a set of rewriting rules and membranes [3,4]. These correspond to a class of P systems which are parallel molecular computing models proposed by Paun [5] and are based on the processing of multisets of objects in cell-like membrane structures [5].

On the other hand, P system with proteins on membranes has been introduced and the power of the system is examined in [6,7]. Following chemical reactions, the kinetics of the sulfoxidation reactions, analogous to biological systems

© Springer Nature Singapore Pte Ltd. 2016
M. Gong et al. (Eds.): BIC-TA 2016, Part I, CCIS 681, pp. 142–154, 2016.
DOI: 10.1007/978-981-10-3611-8_15

were carried out by Jayaseeli and Rajagopal [8]. The computational studies of the work mentioned above, based on membrane computing has been proposed and *Kinetic ARMS* in Artificial Cell System with hierarchically structurable membrane ($KACSH$) is developed in [9].

Recently we have proposed a computing device that is based on Abstract Rewriting systems on multisets closely related to P system with fuzzy multiset rewriting rules and fuzzy data [1]. As an extension of this model, we have developed a new system called $FACSP$ (*Fuzzy ARMS* in Artificial Cell System with proteins on membranes) and its behaviour has been studied in [2].

Models of chemically reacting systems have traditionally been simulated by solving a set of ordinary differential equations. Many researches have conducted numerical simulation to establish the simulation conditions and the impact on simulation results. In this paper, the continuous interaction of the system with environment, an operating function from kinetic equilibrium is established. A series of eigenvalues (λ) that satisfy the equation using the corresponding rate of reactions, complexes, oxidant, substrates and the significants according to the real and imaginary parts of the eigen values are obtained.

2 Preliminaries

2.1 Kinetic Studies of the Sulfoxidation Reactions [8]

In many biomimetic approaches, the study of enzymatic reactions are carried out kinetically. Jeyaseeli and Rajagopal [8] followed the spectrophotometric kinetic studies of [Iron(III)-salen] complexes catalysed H_2O_2 oxidation of organic sulfides. When the rate of reaction (k) is plotted against substrate concentration ($[S]$), a saturation kinetics called Michaelis-Menten behaviour is followed. They have proposed mechanisms based on the results of rate of reactions under various experimental conditions.

2.2 P System with Proteins on Membranes [7]

A system with proteins on membranes is of the form

$$\Gamma = \{O, P, \mu, w_1/z_1, \cdots, w_m/z_m, E, R_1, \cdots, R_m, i_0\}$$

where

- m is the degree of the system (the number of membranes)
- O is the set of objects
- P is the set of proteins (with $O \cap P = \phi$)
- μ is the membrane structure
- $w_i, i = 1$ to m are the (strings representing the) multisets of objects present in the m regions of μ
- $z_i, i = 1$ to m are the multisets of proteins present on the membranes of μ
- $E \subseteq O$ is the set of objects present in the environment (in an arbirarily large number of copies each)

- R_i are finite sets of rules associated with the m membranes of μ
- $i_0 \in \{1, 2, \cdots, m\}$ is the label of the output membrane.

Reaction rules are applied in the following manner: In each step, a maximal multiset of rules is used, that is, no other rule is applicable to the objects and the proteins which remain unused by the chosen multiset. At each step we have the condition that each object and each protein can be involved in the application of at most one rule, but the membranes are not considered as involved in the rule applications except the division rules, hence the same membrane can appear in any number of rules of types 1–5 at the same time [7]. By halting computation, we understand a sequence of configurations that ends with a halting configuration (there is no rule that can be applied considering the objects and proteins present at that moment in the system). With a halting computation, we associate a result in the form of the multiplicity of objects present in region i_0 at the moment when the system halts. We denote by $N(\Pi)$ the set of numbers computed in this way by a given system Π. We denote in the usual way by $NOP_m(pro_r; list\ of\ types\ of\ rules)$ the family of sets of numbers $N(\Pi)$ generated by systems with at most m membranes using rules as specified in the *list of types of rules*, and with at most r proteins present on a membrane. When parameters m or r are not bounded, we use $*$ as a subscript.

2.3   Fuzzy Artificial Cell System with Proteins on Membranes [2]

Definition. A *Fuzzy ACS* with Proteins on membranes $FACSP$ is a construct,

$$\Gamma = \{O, P, \mu, w_1/z_1, \cdots, w_m/z_m, E, (R_p, \rho), i_0, J, \omega\}$$

where

- m is the degree of the system (the number of membranes)
- O is the set of objects
- P is the set of proteins (with $O \cap P = \phi$)
- μ is the membrane structure
- $w_i, i = 1$ to m are the (strings representing the) multisets of objects present in the m regions of μ
- $z_i, i = 1$ to m are the multiset of proteins (biological catalysts) present on the membranes of μ
- E is the set of objects present in the environment (in an arbitarily large number of copies each)
- R_p are finite sets of Fuzzy multiset evolution rules, $p = 1$ to m of μ
- ρ is the partial order relation over R_p
- $i_0 \in \{1, 2, \cdots, m\}$ is the elementary membrane (output)
- $J = \{R_{pi} \in R_p/1 \leq i \leq q\}, q = $ cardinality of R_p
- $\omega : J \to [0, 1]$ is the membership function s.t. $\omega(R_{pq}) = i, i \in [0, 1]$.

The rules are used in the non-deterministic maximally parallel way:

The same rules are applied to every membrane. There are no rules specific to a membrane. All the rules are applied in parallel. In every step, all the rules are applied to all objects in every membrane that can be applied. If there are more than one applicable rule that can be applied to an object and protein then one rule is selected randomly. If a membrane dissolves, then all the objects in its region are left free in the region immediately above it. All objects and proteins not specified in a rule and which do not evolve are passed unchanged to the next step. At each step we have the condition that each object and each protein can be involved in the application of at most one rule, but the membranes are not considered as involved in the rule applications except the division rules, hence the same membrane can appear in any number of rules at the same time.

By halting computation, we understand a sequence of configurations that ends with a halting configuration (there is no rule that can be applied considering the objects and proteins present at that moment in the system). With a halting computation we associate a result in the form of the multiplicity of objects present in region i_0 at the moment when the system halts.

A *Fuzzy ACS* with proteins on membranes generates a language $L(FACSP)$ as follows: An object $x \in O^*$ which is present in the region i_0 at the moment when the system halts is said to be in $L(FACSP)$ iff it is derivable from any object $S \in O$ and the grade of membership $\omega_{L(FACSP)}(x)$ is greater than 0, where

$$\omega_{L(FACSP)}(x) = \left(\begin{matrix} max \\ 1 \leq k \leq n \end{matrix}\right)\left[\left(\begin{matrix} min \\ 1 \leq i \leq l_k \end{matrix}\right)?\omega(R_i^k)\right],$$

$x \in O^*$ and n is the number of different derivatives that x has in $FACSP$, l_k is the length of the kth derivative chain, R_i^k denotes the label of the ith multiset evolution rule used in the kth derivative chain, $i = 1, 2, \ldots, l_k$.

Clearly, $\omega_{L(FACSP)}(x)$ = Strength of the strongest derivative chain for S to x for all $x \in O^*$.

We denote in the usual way by $FACSP_m(pro_r; list\ of\ types\ of\ rules)$ the family of languages $L(FACSP)$ generated by systems Π with at most m membranes, using rules as specified in the *list of types of rule* and with at most r proteins present on a membrane. When parameters m or r are not bounded, we use $*$ as a subscript.

3   Simulation of *FACSP*

The mathematical simulation pattern of rate constants (k) with substrate concentrations are analysed.

3.1   FACSP in Oxidation of Sulfides

Process. We describe the formation of intermediate between complex and the oxidant.

(a) $Z + X(F3)X \rightarrow X(F4O)X$;
  $X(F4O)X + Y\text{-}RSR' \rightarrow X(F3)X + Y\text{-}RSOR'$

Hydrogen Peroxide Z	Fe(III) Salen Complex X(F3)X	Fe(IV) Oxo Salen Complex X(F4O)X

Fe(IV) Oxo Salen Complex X(F4O)X	Phenyl Methyl Sulfide Y-RSR*	Fe(III) Salen Complex X(F3)X	Phenyl Methy Sulfoxide Y-RSOR*

R–C₆H₅ , R'–CH₃

R=C_6H_5 , R'=CH_3

A simple abstract reaction scheme is followed.

Case $I : X = H$

Following convention is used to do the computation.
$Y = H = L, Y = OCH_3 = M, Y = CH_3 = N,$
$Y = F = P, Y = Cl = Q, Y = Br = U, Y = NO_2 = V.$
Now (a) will have the following reaction rules

1. $Z + H(F3)H \rightarrow H(F4O)H$;
   $H(F4O)H + L\text{-}RSR' \rightarrow H(F3)H + L\text{-}RSOR'$
2. $Z + H(F3)H \rightarrow H(F4O)H$;
   $H(F4O)H + M\text{-}RSR' \rightarrow H(F3)H + M\text{-}RSOR'$
3. $Z + H(F3)H \rightarrow H(F4O)H$;
   $H(F4O)H + N\text{-}RSR' \rightarrow H(F3)H + N\text{-}RSOR'$
4. $Z + H(F3)H \rightarrow H(F4O)H$;
   $H(F4O)H + P\text{-}RSR' \rightarrow H(F3)H + P\text{-}RSOR'$
5. $Z + H(F3)H \rightarrow H(F4O)H$;
   $H(F4O)H + Q\text{-}RSR' \rightarrow H(F3)H + Q\text{-}RSOR'$
6. $Z + H(F3)H \rightarrow H(F4O)H$;
   $H(F4O)H + U\text{-}RSR' \rightarrow H(F3)H + U\text{-}RSOR'$
7. $Z + H(F3)H \rightarrow H(F4O)H$;
   $H(F4O)H + V\text{-}RSR' \rightarrow H(F3)H + V\text{-}RSOR'$

3.2   Behaviour of FACSP

Consider the $FACSP$

$$\Gamma = (O, P, \mu, w_1/z_1, w_2/z_2, E, (R_p, \rho), i_0, J, \omega)$$

where

- $O = \{Z, A_1, B, S_i, P_i, i = 1, \ldots, 7\}$,
- $P = \{A_1, B\}$,
- $\mu = [_1[_2]_2]_1$,
- w_1, w_2 are the multisets of objects present in the regions $1, 2$ of μ, $w_1 = \{Z, S_i, i = 1, \ldots, 7\}, w_2 = \{\phi\}$,
- z_1, z_2 are the multisets of proteins present on the membranes $1, 2$ of μ, $z_1 = \{A_1\}, z_2 = \{\phi\}$,
- $E = \{\phi\}$,
- R_p are finite sets of Fuzzy multiset evolution rules, $p = \{1, 2\}$
- $\rho = \phi$,
- $i_0 = 2$ is the output membrane,
- $J = \{R_{pi} \in R_p/q = 1 \le i \le q\}$, $q = $ cardinality of R_p,
- $\omega : J \to [0, 1]$ is the membership function s.t. $\omega(R_{pq}) = i, i \in [0, 1]$, where

$$\omega_{L(FACSP)}(x) = \begin{pmatrix} max \\ 1 \le k \le n \end{pmatrix} \left[\begin{pmatrix} min \\ 1 \le i \le l_k \end{pmatrix} ?\omega(R_i^k) \right]$$

and $x \in O^*$

$R_p = \{R_1, R_2\}$ consists the following evolution rules.

$$R_1 = \begin{cases}
R_{11} : [_1 A_1 | Z]_1 \quad \to [_1 B | \phi]_1; \\
\quad [_1 B | S_1]_1 \quad \to [_1 A_1 | \quad [_2 \quad |P_1]_2]_1 \\
\quad \text{with } \omega(R_{11}) = 0.0025 \\
\\
R_{12} : [_1 A_1 | Z]_1 \quad \to [_1 B | \phi]_1; \\
\quad [_1 B | S_2]_1 \quad \to [_1 A_1 | \quad [_2 \quad |P_2]_2]_1 \\
\quad \text{with } \omega(R_{12}) = 0.01 \\
\\
R_{13} : [_1 A_1 | Z]_1 \quad \to [_1 B | \phi]_1; \\
\quad [_1 B | S_3]_1 \quad \to [_1 A_1 | \quad [_2 \quad |P_3]_2]_1 \\
\quad \text{with } \omega(R_{13}) = 0.0059 \\
\\
R_{14} : [_1 A_1 | Z]_1 \quad \to [_1 B | \phi]_1; \\
\quad [_1 B | S_4]_1 \quad \to [_1 A_1 | \quad [_2 \quad |P_4]_2]_1 \\
\quad \text{with } \omega(R_{14}) = 0.0016 \\
\\
R_{15} : [_1 A_1 | Z]_1 \quad \to [_1 B | \phi]_1; \\
\quad [_1 B | S_5]_1 \quad \to [_1 A_1 | \quad [_2 \quad |P_5]_2]_1 \\
\quad \text{with } \omega(R_{15}) = 0.0011 \\
\\
R_{16} : [_1 A_1 | Z]_1 \quad \to [_1 B | \phi]_1; \\
\quad [_1 B | S_6]_1 \quad \to [_1 A_1 | \quad [_2 \quad |P_6]_2]_1 \\
\quad \text{with } \omega(R_{16}) = 0.0009 \\
\\
R_{17} : [_1 A_1 | Z]_1 \quad \to [_1 B | \phi]_1; \\
\quad [_1 B | S_7]_1 \quad \to [_1 A_1 | \quad [_2 \quad |P_7]_2]_1 \\
\quad \text{with } \omega(R_{17}) = 0.00027
\end{cases}$$

$R_2 = \phi$.

In its initial configuration, the system contatins 2 membranes with 8 objects $\{Z, S_i, i = 1, ..., 7\}$ and a biological protein A_1 on membrane 1. It has two steps. In the first step, any one of the 7 rules is selected randomly. Let the rule R_{11} be applied. Then the protein A_1 is changed into B. In the second step, the protein change back from B to A_1 and the object S_1 evolved into P_1 and move to membrane 2. Since there is no rule that can transform the object in membrane 2 further, the process halts. The resulting object in the output membrane 2 is P_1.

$$\begin{matrix} max \\ 1 \le k \le n \end{matrix} \left[\begin{matrix} min \\ 1 \le i \le l_1 \end{matrix} (0.0025) \right] = 0.0025;$$

$$\omega_{L(FACSP)}(P_1) = 0.0025$$

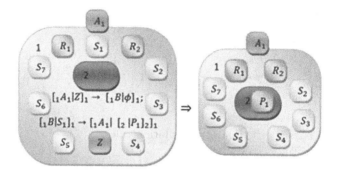

FACSP

Similar process will be done when other rules are applied. As a result, the membership values $\omega_{L(FACSP)}(P_i)$ for $i = 1$ to 7 are obtained. Hence $L(FACSP) = \{P_i / i = 1 \text{ to } 7\}$.

We obtain different languages with corresponding membership values for different complexes $(A_i, i = 1 \text{ to } 7)$. The membership values for different complexes are tabulated as follows (Table 1).

We denote by $FACSP_2(pro_1; 7ffp)$ the family of languages $L(FACSP)$ generated by Γ with atmost 2 membranes using rules as specified in the $7ffp$ rules and with atmost one protein.

3.3 Mathematical Modeling and Simulation of FACSP

Chemical equations are commonly written in the following way:

$$A + B \longrightarrow C + D$$

indicating that species A and B react together to form species C and D. From the chemical equation we can easily write the rate equation. It is important to note

Table 1. Membership values $\omega_{L(FACSP)}(P_i) = \omega(P_i)$.

Complex	$\omega(P_1)$	$\omega(P_2)$	$\omega(P_3)$	$\omega(P_4)$	$\omega(P_5)$	$\omega(P_6)$	$\omega(P_7)$
A_1	0.0025	0.01	0.0059	0.0016	0.0011	0.0009	0.00027
A_2	0.006	0.034	0.023	0.0054	0.0028	0.0029	0.0009
A_3	0.0055	0.023	0.019	0.0062	0.0025	0.0026	0.0008
A_4	0.0017	0.0025	0.0019	0.0009	0.00084	0.00072	0.00023
A_5	0.00089	0.0018	0.00096	0.00062	0.00051	0.0004	0.00017
A_6	0.015	0.066	0.043	0.011	0.008	0.0065	0.0021
A_7	0.00053	0.0011	0.00076	0.00042	0.0004	0.0003	0.00019

that most chemical systems are assumed to follow mass action kinetics, meaning that the reaction rate is proportional to the concentration of the reactants.

$$-[\dot{A}] = -r_a = k[A][B]$$

Here $[A]$ represents the concentration of species A, r_a is the reaction rate and k is the rate constant of the reaction. r_a is by convention negative since A is being consumed in the reaction. Now we describe the natural phenomenon of Fuzzy *ACS* in oxidation of sulfides. The mathematical model [10] is used because of its theoretical simplicity. The mathematical modeling of $FACSP$ is given below.

$$[_1A_1|Z]_1 \underset{k_{-1}}{\overset{k_1}{\longrightarrow}} [_1B|\phi]_1 \tag{1}$$

$$[_1B|S_1]_1 \underset{k_2}{\rightarrow} [_1A_1|[_2|P_1]_2]_1 \tag{2}$$

In Eqs. (1) and (2), $k_i, i = 1, 2$ are the reaction rate for each individual reaction, while Z, A_1, B, S_1 and P_1 are species. The molar concentration of A_1 is denoted by $[A_1]$ likewise for the other species. The equations for the evolution of $[A_1]$ and $[S_1]$ are as follows.

$$d[A_1]/dt = k_2[B][S_1] - k_1[Z][A_1] \tag{3}$$

$$d[S_1]/dt = -k_2[B][S_1] \tag{4}$$

The above equations are of the form

$$d[A_1]/dt = F_1([A_1], [S_1])$$
$$d[S_1]/dt = F_2([A_1], [S_1])$$

where

$$F_1([A_1], [S_1]) = k_2[B][S_1] - k_1[Z][A_1]$$
$$F_2([A_1], [S_1]) = -k_2[B][S_1]$$

Equilibria. The equilibria of (3) and (4) is given by solving the system

$$k_2[B][S_1] - k_1[Z][A_1] = 0 \qquad (5)$$

$$- k_2[B][S_1] = 0 \qquad (6)$$

From (5)

$$k_2[B][S_1] = k_1[Z][A_1]$$

$$[B] = (k_1[Z][A_1])/(k_2[S_1]) \qquad (7)$$

(5)–(6) gives

$$2k_2[B][S_1] - k_1[Z][A_1] = 0$$
$$k_1[Z][A_1] = 2k_2[B][S_1]$$

$$[A_1] = (2k_2[B][S_1])/(k_1[Z]) \qquad (8)$$

$$[S_1] = (k_1[Z][A_1])/(2k_2[B]) \qquad (9)$$

From Eq. (5), we obtain
$S_1 = \alpha(A_1)$ where $\alpha = k_1[Z]/k_2[B]$

$$([A_1], [S_1]) = ([A_1], \alpha[A_1])$$

From Eq. (6),
$$([A_1], [S_1]) = (0, 0)$$

Hence $(0, 0)$ and $([A_1], \alpha[A_1])$ are the equilibrium of the system.

Stability. To evaluate stability, we evaluate the Jacobian at the stationary state.

$$\partial(F_1)/\partial[A_1] = -k_1[Z]; \quad \partial(F_1)/\partial[S_1] = k_2[B];$$
$$\partial(F_2)/\partial[A_1] = 0; \quad \partial(F_2)/\partial[S_1] = -k_2[B]$$

$$J = \begin{pmatrix} \partial(F_1)/\partial[A_1] & \partial(F_1)/\partial[S_1] \\ \partial(F_2)/\partial[A_1] & \partial(F_2)/\partial[S_1] \end{pmatrix} = \begin{pmatrix} -k_1[Z] & k_2[B] \\ 0 & -k_2[B] \end{pmatrix}$$

$$Trace\, J = -(k_1[Z] + k_2[B])$$

The eigen value equation or characteristic equation is applied in order to evaluate the stationary state.

$$det(J - \lambda I) = 0$$

Arranging these values into matrix form gives

$$\begin{pmatrix} -k_1[Z] - \lambda & k_2[B] \\ 0 & -k_2[B] - \lambda \end{pmatrix} = 0$$

i.e.,

$$\lambda^2 + (k_1[Z] + k_2[B])\lambda + k_1k_2[Z][B] = 0$$

Using Eq. (7)

$$[S_1]\lambda^2 + ([S_1] + [A_1])k_1[Z]\lambda + k_1^2[Z]^2[A_1] = 0 \tag{10}$$

Here we state that,

$$k_1 = 2.5 \times 10^{-3}, [Z] = 5 \times 10^{-3}, [S_1] = i \times 10^{-3}, i = 0, 2, 4, 10, [A_1] = 2 \times 10^{-4}$$

Solving the quadratic Eq. (10) for different values of $[S_1]$ using MATLAB, eigen values of the Jacobian matrix are obtained.

The eigen values for different catalysts for the sulfoxidation reactions are tabulated in Table 2. From the data collected, all Eigen values are real and negative since $\lambda_1 < 0$ and $\lambda_2 < 0$. Thus the system is stable. The changes for the eigen values with substrate concentrations are plotted.

Table 2. Eigen values for different catalysts

		A_1	A_2	A_3	A_4	A_5	A_6	A_7
s_1	λ_1	-1.25	-3	-2.75	-85	-44.5	-7.5	-26.5
	λ_2	0	0	0	0	0	0	0
s_2	λ_1	-0.05	-0.0017	-0.00115	-0.0125	-0.9	-0.0033	-0.55
	λ_2	-0.005	-0.00017	-0.000115	-0.00125	-0.09	-0.00033	-0.055
s_3	λ_1	-0.0295	-0.00115	-0.095	-0.95	-0.48	-0.00215	-0.38
	λ_2	-0.00148	-0.000058	-0.00475	-0.0475	-0.024	-0.000108	-0.019
s_4	λ_1	-0.8	-0.027	-0.95	-0.0475	-0.31	-0.055	-0.21
	λ_2	-0.0267	-0.0009	-0.48	-0.024	-0.0103	-0.00183	-0.007
s_5	λ_1	-0.55	-0.014	-0.0125	-0.42	-0.255	-0.04	-0.2
	λ_2	-0.0138	-0.00035	-0.00031	-0.0105	-0.0064	-0.001	-0.005
s_6	λ_1	-0.45	-0.0145	-0.013	-0.36	-0.2	-0.0325	-0.15
	λ_2	-0.009	-0.00029	-0.00026	-0.0072	-0.004	-0.00065	-0.003
s_7	λ_1	-0.135	-0.45	-0.4	-0.00115	-8.5	-0.0105	-9.5
	λ_2	-0.0023	-0.0075	-0.0067	-0.000019	-0.142	-0.00017	-0.158

When the concentration of the substrate (sulfides) increases there is an increase in rate constant and attains saturation at higher concentration (Fig. 1). When these results are examined mathematically using Fuzzy *ACSH* on membranes there is a consistancy between the pattern of plots obtained for kinetic results. As the concentration of the substrate increases, the eigen values first decreases and increases. It becomes constant at higher rate constant. This behaviour can be correlated to the saturation kinetics of chemical reactions. The pattern is shown in figure (Figs. 2 and 3).

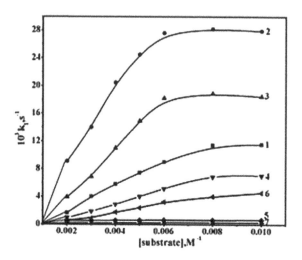

Fig. 1. k_1 vs. [substrate] for complex 1 catalyzed H_2O_2 oxidation of 1–7

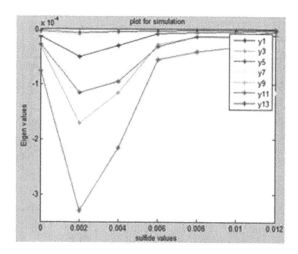

Fig. 2. (S, λ_1)

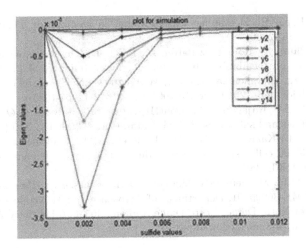

Fig. 3. (S, λ_2)

4 Conclusion

The new membrane computing model $FACSP$ (Fuzzy $ARMS$ in Artificial Cell System with Proteins on membranes) is analysed in its environment. The stability and equilibrium of the system are determined. The eigen values and the critical points of different catalysts for the sulfoxidation reactions are obtained. A mathematical approach is constructed to show the consistency of Fuzzy $ACSH$ on membranes with the Michaelis-Menten kinetics. It is interesting to note that there is a correlation between the two types of plots.

References

1. Chandra, P.H., Kalavathy, S.M.S.T., Jayaseeli, A.M.I., Karoline, J.P.: Mechanism of fuzzy *ARMS* on chemical reaction. In: Snášel, V., Abraham, A., Krömer, P., Pant, M., Muda, A.K. (eds.) Innovations in Bio-Inspired Computing and Applications. AISC, vol. 424, pp. 43–53. Springer, Heidelberg (2016). doi:10.1007/978-3-319-28031-8_4
2. Chandra, P.H., Kalavathy, S.M.S.T., Jayaseeli, A.M.I., Karoline, J.P.: Fuzzy ACS with biological catalysts on membranes in chemical reactions. J. Netw. Innov. Comput. **4**, 143–151 (2016). MIR Labs, USA
3. Suzuki, Y., Tanaka, H.: Symbolic chemical system based on abstract rewriting system and its behaviour pattern. J. Artif. Life Robot. **1**, 211–219 (1997). Springer-Verlag
4. Suzuki, Y., Fujiwara, Y., Takabayashi, J., Tanaka, H.: Artificial life applications of a class of P systems: abstract rewriting systems on multisets. In: Calude, C.S., Păun, G., Rozenberg, G., Salomaa, A. (eds.) WMC 2000. LNCS, vol. 2235, pp. 299–346. Springer, Heidelberg (2001). doi:10.1007/3-540-45523-X_16
5. Păun, G.: Membrane Computing: An Introduction. Springer-Verlag, Berlin (2002)

6. Păun, P., Popa, B.: P systems with proteins on membranes. Fundam. Inform. **72**(4), 467–483 (2006)
7. Sosík, P., Păun, A., Rodríguez-Patón, A., Pérez, D.: On the power of computing with proteins on membranes. In: Păun, G., Pérez-Jiménez, M.J., Riscos-Núñez, A., Rozenberg, G., Salomaa, A. (eds.) WMC 2009. LNCS, vol. 5957, pp. 448–460. Springer, Heidelberg (2010). doi:10.1007/978-3-642-11467-0_30
8. Jayaseeli, A.M.I., Rajagopal, S.: [Iron(III)-salen] ion catalyzed H_2O_2 oxidation of organic sulfides and sulfoxides. J. Mol. Catal. Chem. **309**, 103–110 (2009)
9. Chandra, P.H., Kalavathy, S.M.S.T., Jayaseeli, A.M.I.: Mechanism of sulfoxidation in artificial cell system. In: Proceedings of Asian Conference on Membrane Computing. IEEE (2014)
10. McDowell, M.P.: Mathematical Modeling of the Brusselator. Prepared for: Powers, J.M. AME 36099–01, Department of Aerospace and Mechanical Engineering, University of Notre Dame, Notre Dame, Indiana 46556, 6 February 2008. http://www3.nd.edu/powers/mcdowell.pdf

A Family P System of Realizing RSA Algorithm

Ping Guo[1,2(✉)] and Wei Xu[1,2]

[1] College of Computer Science, Chongqing University, Chongqing 400044, China
guoping@cqu.edu.cn, xuwei8091@163.com
[2] Chongqing Key Laboratory of Software Theory and Technology,
Chongqing 400044, China

Abstract. P system is a new kind of distributed parallel computing model, and many variants of it are proposed to solve the problems such as NP problems, arithmetic operation, image processing. RSA is a classic asymmetric encryption algorithm which plays a very import role in the field of the information security and it is used widely in data transmission and digital signature. This paper is based on P system to realize the RSA algorithm in parallel which includes key generation and encryption & decryption, then a cell-like RSA P system Π_{RSA} is designed from this. An instance is given to illustrate the feasibility and effectiveness of our designed P systems.

Keywords: RSA · Cell-like P system · Membrane computing

1 Introduction

RSA algorithm [1] is a classic asymmetric encryption algorithm which has been used widely in the data transmission and the digital signature. Many researches have made improvements and breakthroughs on the basis of it and a variety of RSA variants are designed. In [2], authors presented an electronic cash scheme using the modulus $N = p^2q$. And Takagi in [3] introduced the CRT variant of RSA, where the RSA modulus of the form $N = p^rq$. In addition RSA is also used for different application scenarios. Reference [4] applies it in Cloud data auditing and propose a concrete ID-CDIC construction from RSA signature. Reference [5] proposed a new CEMBS-constructing method based on RSA signature.

Membrane computing, also called P systems, is a branch of natural computing and abstracts computing models from the architecture and the functioning of living cells. It is a distributed parallel computing model, and based on maximal parallelism and non-determinism of evolutionary rules in P system, it has been proved that membrane computing has the same equivalent computing power as Turing machine. Up to now, many different P systems are proposed to solve the problems in the field of computer science. References [6,7] are used for solving SAT problem, References [8,9] are applied in solving image processing problem, References [10,11] presents some P systems for solving problems in the field of graph theory, and References [12,13] are used for multi-objective optimization.

© Springer Nature Singapore Pte Ltd. 2016
M. Gong et al. (Eds.): BIC-TA 2016, Part I, CCIS 681, pp. 155–167, 2016.
DOI: 10.1007/978-981-10-3611-8_16

Focus on realizing RSA algorithm in parallel, this paper designs a P system Π_{RSA} which includes two sub P systems: the key generation P system and the encryption & decryption P system. The remainder of this paper is organized as follows: The second section we give descriptions of the RSA algorithm which is designed based on the maximal parallelism. The P systems designed for realizing RSA algorithm are discussed in the third section. The fourth section gives an instance to show the implementation of the P systems. And the conclusions are drawn in the final section.

2   RSA Algorithm

Figure 1 shows the process of single RSA algorithm which includes two parts [1]. One is the process to generate private and public key pairs. The other is to do encryption and decryption.

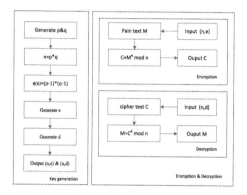

Fig. 1. The process of RSA algorithm

(1) In the key generation process, (n, e) is the public key pair and (n, d) is the private key where

$$1 < e < \phi(n), gcd(e, \phi(n)) = 1 \tag{1}$$

where $\phi(n) = (p - 1) \times (q - 1)$.

$$d \equiv e^{-1}(mod\ \phi(n)) \tag{2}$$

In this paper, we detailedly designs the RSA algorithm in more consideration of parallelism. The key generations can be done in two steps as follows.

(i) Generating three big primes p & q & e in parallel.

To meet Eq. (1), we can just generate a prime not more than $\phi(n)$ as e. So we can generate three big random primes p & q & e in parallel. An algorithm designed for generating p & q is to loop to generate a big number util the number is a prime. The input is a list of placeholders $h_n b_{n-1} b_{n-2} \ldots b_1 e_0$ and the output is a random prime who has d digits. In the input e_0 is the lowest digit which is selected from the set $\{1, 3, 5, 7, 9\}$, b_i represents the number in the ith digit and h_n is the highest digit which meets the condition $h_n \neq 0$. Additionally, the method to generate the primes e can be to generate a number whose digits no more than the sum digits of p & q, so just apply the same algorithm and replace h_n with b_n as the input. In this way, we can generate a number who has n or no more than n digits by select number of each digit in parallel, the complexity of the number generation can be $O(1)$.

After we get the number, the prime judgement is needed. Since the number we generated is an odd and the odd prime can only be divide by 3 or the number in the format of $6i \pm 1$, so we judge the prime by trial division where the divisors is the number 3 or the number in the format of $6i \pm 1$ enumerated from the square estimate root of the number down to 1. In addition, we have a conclusion that between the two numbers $10^k + 1$ and $10^k + 3$, one is always in the format of $6i - 1$, the other is $6i + 1$. So the square root of a number a can be estimated by $10^{\lfloor a/2 \rfloor + 1}$. So the complexity of prime judgement is $O(10^{log_{10}(a)/2}/6)$ where a is the number we generated.

In this way, the complexity of random prime generations is $O(k \times 10^{log_{10}(a)/2}/6)$ where k is the times of the random number generations.

(ii) Two multiplications for calculating n & $\phi(n)$, and then we get the decryption key d in Eq. (2) by the extended Euclid. And the complexity of the extended Euclid is $O(log(n))$ where n is the number equals $p \times q$.

So the complexity of the key generation is $O(k \times 10^{log_{10}(a)/2}/6 + O(log(n)))$.

(2) The process of decryption and encryption have the same operations. If we have a message M, the ciphertext C can be calculated by the following formula:

$$C = M^e (mod\ n) \tag{3}$$

Similarly, the plain text can also be calculated by the similar formula:

$$M = C^e (mod\ n) \tag{4}$$

In this paper, the algorithm we used to do the decryption and encryption is the fast modular multiplication and the complexity is $O(log(e))$.

3 Design of the P System

Cell-like P systems [14] is a hierarchically arranged set of membranes which are usually identified by Labels from a given set and contained in a distinguished external membrane. In this section, we discuss the design of a RSA P system based on the algorithm mentioned in Sect. 2 and the cell-like P system.

3.1   The Definition of the RSA P System

According to [14], the RSA P system can be defined as formula (5).

$$\Pi_{rsa} = (O, \mu, \omega, R, \rho, A_1) \tag{5}$$

where,

(1) O is a finite and non-empty alphabet of objects, including

$$\{a_i, b_i, c_i, m_i, n_i, x_i, d_i, p_i, q_i, h_i, g_i, s_i, e_i, e_0, f, d, s', t, t_1,$$
$$t_2, t_3, t_4, t_5, t_6, t_7, t_8, t_9, t_{10}, t_{11}, t_{12}, t_{13}, t_{14}, u, v, p', q', e',$$
$$\#_1, \#_2, \#_3, -, o_-, o_+, o_\times, o_\div\}$$

including:
   (i) $a_i, b_i, c_i, m_i, n_i, x_i, d_i, p_i, q_i, h_i, g_i, s_i, e_i$ which are used for representing number in hybrid encoding [15]. In the following parts, we will use $N(x)$ to represent a number, and mark the multiset $\{x_0^{k_0} x_1^{k_1} x_2^{k_2} \ldots x_n^{k_n}\}$ $(N(x) = k_0 * 10^0 + k_1 * 10^1 + k_2 * 10^2 + \ldots + k_n * 10^n)$ as x. If $N(x) = 23$, then $x = \{x_1^2 x_0^3\}$ will represents 23 in the hybrid encoding.
   (ii) i, j, k in rules are used as index, which represents all the integers in [0,1000].
   (iii) $-, o_-, o_+, o_\times, o_\div$ which represents minus sign and four operations.
   (iv) the other objects which control the evolution of the P system.
(2) μ is the initial structure of our P system as shown in Fig. 2.
   where,
   – A_2 and its sub membranes are used for key generation, see Sect. 3.2;
   – Rules in A_3 are used for encryption and decryption, see Sect. 3.3;
   – A_1 is used for controlling and coordinating its sub membranes to achieve the RSA, see Sect. 3.4.
(3) ω is a collection of multisets in the initial configuration. Where:

$$\omega_{A_1} = \phi, \ \omega_{A_2} = \phi, \ \omega_{A_3} = \phi$$

(4) In R, there are five types of rules:
   (i) $u \to v, k$. This rule means object u evolves to object v. And the k indicates the priority; the smaller value k is set, the higher the priority of the rule is.
   (ii) $u \to v|_w, k$. This rule means object u evolves to object v when multiset w appears in the membrane. In the rule, the w indicates rule can only be applied in the presence of multiset w.
   (iii) $u \to v_1(v_2, in/out), k$. This rule means object u evolves to object v_1, at the same time generates object v_2 which stays in or is sent into or outer the membrane.
   (iv) $u \to v_1(v_2, in/out)|_w, k$. This rule means object u evolves to object v_1 when multiset w appears in the membrane, at the same time generates object v_2 which stays in or is sent into or outer the membrane.

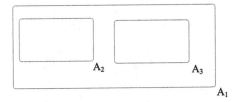

Fig. 2. The initial configuration of the RSA P system

(v) $[u]_i \rightarrow [v_1]_i[v_2]_i$. This rule generates two copies of membranes i. The multiset u will separately evolve to multiset v_1 and multiset v_2 in each membrane, meanwhile other objects and sub membranes do not have any changes.

(5) The final result can be found in membrane A_1 when the whole system halts.

In addition, there are many arithmetic operations in A_2 & A_3, so we need an arithmetic membrane to provide addition, subtraction, multiplication and division functions. Since the focus of this paper is to realize RSA algorithm and many arithmetic P systems have been designed [16, 17], we don't specially design an arithmetic sub P system separately, and we just define a membrane M_C is one of these arithmetics. We define that the input of M_C is two multisets a, b which represents the two operands $N(a), N(b)$ and an operator of the multiset $\{o_-, o_+, o_\times, o_\div\}$. Then the output of M_C is the multiset c represented the result, the multiset m represented remainders which may exists and the object $-$ which occurs when the result is a negative number.

The next will introduce each membrane and its rules, for more convenience in narration, the copies of the object x is denoted by $|x|$.

3.2 Key Generation Membrane A_2

The Key Generation Membrane A_2 has some sub membranes and the initial structure of it is as shown in Fig. 3, where the rules is designed according to the algorithm in Sect. 2.

Random Prime Integer Generation Membrane M_1, M_2, M_3. The membrane M_1, M_2 & M_3 has the same rules, they each accept the object $h_n b_{n-1} b_{n-2} \ldots b_1 e_0$ with an object t to generate a random prime integer, and then send out the result objects as p, q and e separately. The rules are:

r_1: $(b_i \rightarrow b_i \,|_t, 1)$ r_2: $(b_i \rightarrow b_i a_i \,|_t, 1)$

r_3: $(b_i \rightarrow b_i a_i^2 \,|_t, 1)$ r_4: $(b_i \rightarrow b_i a_i^3 \,|_t, 1)$

r_5: $(b_i \rightarrow b_i a_i^4 \,|_t, 1)$ r_6: $(b_i \rightarrow b_i a_i^5 \,|_t, 1)$

r_7: $(b_i \rightarrow b_i a_i^6 \,|_t, 1)$ r_8: $(b_i \rightarrow b_i a_i^7 \,|_t, 1)$

r_9: $(b_i \rightarrow b_i a_i^8 \,|_t, 1)$ r_{10}: $(b_i \rightarrow b_i a_i^9 \,|_t, 1)$

r_{11}: $(e_0 \rightarrow e_0 a_0^1 \,|_t, 1)$ r_{12}: $(e_0 \rightarrow e_0 a_i^3 \,|_t, 1)$

r_{13}: $(e_0 \rightarrow e_0 a_0^5 \,|_t, 1)$ r_{14}: $(e_0 \rightarrow e_0 a_0^7 \,|_t, 1)$

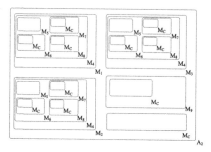

Fig. 3. The initial structure of membrane A_2

r_{15}: $(e_0 \rightarrow e_0 a_i^9 \mid_t, 1)$

r_{16}: $(h_i \rightarrow h_i a_i \mid_t, 1)$

r_{17}: $(h_i \rightarrow h_i a_i^2 \mid_t, 1)$

r_{18}: $(h_i \rightarrow h_i a_i^3 \mid_t, 1)$

r_{19}: $(h_i \rightarrow h_i a_i^4 \mid_t, 1)$

r_{20}: $(h_i \rightarrow h_i a_i^5 \mid_t, 1)$

r_{21}: $(h_i \rightarrow h_i a_i^6 \mid_t, 1)$

r_{22}: $(h_i \rightarrow h_i a_i^7 \mid_t, 1)$

r_{23}: $(h_i \rightarrow h_i a_i^8 \mid_t, 1)$

r_{24}: $(h_i \rightarrow h_i a_i^9 \mid_t, 1)$

r_{25}: $(t \rightarrow t_3, 2)$

r_{26}: $(a_i \rightarrow a_i(a_i \ in \ M_4) \mid_{t_3}, 1)$

r_{27}: $(t_3 \rightarrow (t \ in \ M_4), 2)$

r_{28}: $(a_i \rightarrow (p_i, \ out) \mid_{p't_1}, 1)$

r_{29}: $(a_i \rightarrow (q_i, \ out) \mid_{q't_1}, 1)$

r_{30}: $(a_i \rightarrow (e_i, \ out) \mid_{e't_1}, 1)$

r_{31}: $(b_i \rightarrow \lambda \mid_{t_1}, 1)$

r_{32}: $(h_i \rightarrow \lambda \mid_{t_1}, 1)$

r_{33}: $(e_0 \rightarrow \lambda \mid_{t_1}, 1)$

r_{34}: $(t_1 \rightarrow \lambda, 2)$

r_{35}: $(p' \rightarrow (p' \ out) \mid_{t_1}, 1)$

r_{36}: $(q' \rightarrow (q' \ out) \mid_{t_1}, 1)$

r_{37}: $(e' \rightarrow (e' \ out) \mid_{t_1}, 1)$

r_{38}: $(a_i \rightarrow \lambda \mid_{t_2}, 1)$

r_{39}: $(t_2 \rightarrow t, 2)$

Where $r_1 \sim r_{24}$ are used to generate the number in each digit, $r_{25} \sim r_{27}$ are used to send the generated number into M_4 to do prime judgement, $r_{28} \sim r_{30}$ send out the prime number and the other rules are used to clear objects and control the evolution.

Prime Judgment Membrane M_4. Membrane M_4 and its sub membranes are designed to judge whether a number is a prime number, it accepts the multiset a and an object t, and output an object t_1 if the number is a prime number, otherwise output an object t_2. The process of the membrane includes three steps:

1. To estimate the square root of the number in M_5, the rules are

r_{40}: $(t \rightarrow b_0 t_0, 1)$

r_{41}: $(a_i \rightarrow \lambda \mid_{t_i}, 1)$

r_{42}: $(t_i \rightarrow d t_{i+1} \mid_{a_j}, 2)$

r_{43}: $(t_i \rightarrow e', 3)$

r_{44}: $(b_i d^2 \rightarrow b_i + 1, 1)$

r_{45}: $(b_i \rightarrow (b_{i+1} \ out) \mid_{e'}, 1)$

r_{46}: $(d \rightarrow \lambda \mid_{e'}, 1)$

r_{47}: $(e' \rightarrow (t_3 \ out), 2)$

2. The membrane M_6, M_7 & M_8 are used to do trial division, and they separately judge the number is a multiple of 3 or the number can be in the format $6i + 1, \ 6i - 1$. The rules are:

r_{48}: $(a_i \rightarrow a_i(a_i \ in \ M_c) \mid_{ft_1}, 1)$

r_{49}: $(b_i \rightarrow b_i(b_i \ in \ M_c) \mid_{ft_1}, 1)$

r_{50}: $(f \rightarrow d(o_{\div} \ in \ M_c) \mid_{t_1}, 2)$

r_{51}: $(t_1 \rightarrow t_3 \mid_{m_i}, 1)$

r_{52}: $(t_1 \rightarrow t_2 \mid_{e'}, 2)$

r_{53}: $(c_i \rightarrow \lambda \mid_{t_3}, 1)$

$r_{54}: (m_i \rightarrow \lambda \mid_{t_3}, 1)$ $r_{55}: (b_i \rightarrow (a_i \ in \ M_c) \mid_{t_3}, 1)$

$r_{56}: (d \rightarrow f(o\_b_0^6 \ in \ M_C) \mid_{t_3}, 1)$ $r_{57}: (t_3 \rightarrow t_4, 2)$

$r_{58}: (a_i \rightarrow \lambda \mid_-, 1)$ $r_{59}: (b_i \rightarrow \lambda \mid_-, 1)$

$r_{60}: (c_i \rightarrow \lambda \mid_-, 1)$ $r_{61}: (ft_4- \rightarrow s'(t_1 \ out), 3)$

$r_{62}: (t_4 \rightarrow t_1 \mid_{c_0^2}, 4)$ $r_{63}: (t_4 \rightarrow t_1 \mid_{c_i}, 4)$

$r_{64}: (t_4 \rightarrow t_4- \mid_{c_0}, 5)$ $r_{65}: (c_i \rightarrow b_i \mid_f, 6)$

$r_{66}: (a_i \rightarrow \lambda \mid_{t_2}, 1)$ $r_{67}: (b_i \rightarrow \lambda \mid_{t_2}, 1)$

$r_{68}: (c_i \rightarrow \lambda \mid_{t_2}, 1)$ $r_{69}: (m_i \rightarrow \lambda \mid_{t_2}, 1)$

$r_{70}: (d \rightarrow \lambda \mid_{t_2}, 1)$ $r_{71}: (t_2 \rightarrow s'(t_2 \ out), 3)$

$r_{72}: (a_i \rightarrow \lambda \mid_{s't_4e'}, 1)$ $r_{73}: (b_i \rightarrow \lambda \mid_{s't_4e'}, 1)$

$r_{74}: (c_i \rightarrow \lambda \mid_{s't_4c_i}, 1)$ $r_{75}: (s't_2 \rightarrow (e' \ out), 2)$

$r_{76}: (s'ft_4- \rightarrow (e' \ out), 2)$ $r_{77}: (s'^2 \rightarrow \lambda, 1)$

3. The membrane M_4 is used to control the evolution.
   (i) Accepting the multiset a and an object t, then send them into M_5 to do the estimation.

   $r_{78}: (a_i \rightarrow a_i(a_i \ in \ M_5) \mid_t, 1)$ $r_{79}: (t \rightarrow (t \ in \ M_5), 2)$

   (ii) After the estimate in the M_5, transfer the result into M_6, M_7 & M_8:

   $r_{80}: (a_i \rightarrow (a_i \ in \ M_6)(a_i \ in \ M_7)(a_i \ in \ M_8) \mid_{t_3}, 1)$

   $r_{82}: (b_i \rightarrow (b_i \ in \ M_7)(b_i \ in \ M_7) \mid_{t_3}, 1)$

   $r_{83}: (t_3 \rightarrow (b_0^3t_1 \ in \ M_6)(b_0t_1 \ in \ M_7)(b_0^3t_1 \ in \ M_7), 2)$

   (iii) For the result of the prime judgement:
   (1) If the object sent from M_6, M_7 & M_8 are all t_1, which indicates that the numbers are all prime numbers, we send out the object t_1, and send an object s' into M_6, M_7 & M_8 to clear the temporary object s'. Rules are:

   $r_{84}: (t_1^3 \rightarrow (s' \ in \ M_6)(s' \ in \ M_7)(s' \ in \ M_8)(t_1 \ out), 1)$

   (2) If any output of the membrane M_6 & M_7 & M_8 is an object t_2, we will send an object s' to each of the other membranes to stop their evolution, then send out the sign object t_2.

   $r_{85}: (t_1 \rightarrow \lambda \mid_{t_2}, 1)$ $r_{86}: (t_2 \rightarrow e' \mid_e, 1)$

   $r_{87}: (t_2^3 \rightarrow e'^3(s' \ in \ M_6)(s' \ in \ M_7)(s' \ in \ M_8), 2)$

   $r_{88}: (t_2^2 \rightarrow e'^2(s' \ in \ M_6)(s' \ in \ M_7)('s \ in \ M_8), 3)$

   $r_{89}: (t_2 \rightarrow e'(s' \ in \ M_6)(s' \ in \ M_7)(s' \ in \ M_8), 4)$

   $r_{90}: (e'^3 \rightarrow (t_2 \ out), 1)$

Extended Euclidean Membrane M_9. Membrane M_9 is designed according to the Extended Euclidean algorithm, and it accepts the multiset $a \bigcup n \bigcup \{tf\}$ from the outer membrane and output the reverse of $N(a)$ to $N(n)$. The main rules are:

$r_{91}: (a_i \rightarrow a_i(a_i \ in \ M_C) \mid_t, 1)$ $r_{92}: (n_i \rightarrow n_i(b_i \ in \ M_C) \mid_t, 1)$

$r_{93}: (f \rightarrow f(o\div \ in \ M_C) \mid_t, 1)$ $r_{94}: (t \rightarrow t_1, 2)$

$r_{95}: (t_1 \rightarrow t_2 \mid_{m_i}, 1)$ $r_{96}: (e' \rightarrow \lambda, 3)$

$r_{97}: (a_i \rightarrow (a_i \ in \ M_C) \mid_{t_2}, 1)$ $r_{98}: (m_i \rightarrow m_i(b_i \ in \ M_C) \mid_{t_2}, 1)$

$r_{99}: (c_i \rightarrow \lambda \mid_{t_2}, 1)$ $r_{100}: (f \rightarrow f(o\_ \ in \ M_C) \mid_{t_2}, 1)$

$r_{101}: (t_2 \rightarrow t_3, 2)$ $r_{102}: (t_3 \rightarrow t_4 \mid_{e'}, 1)$

$r_{103}: (c_i \rightarrow (a_i \ in \ M_C) \mid_{t_4}, 1)$ $r_{104}: (n_i \rightarrow a_i(b_i \ in \ M_C) \mid_{t_4}, 1)$

r_{105}: $(f \rightarrow f(o_{\div} \ in \ M_C) \ |_{t_4}, 1)$ r_{106}: $(m_i \rightarrow n_i \ |_{t_4}, 1)$

r_{107}: $(t_4 \rightarrow t_5, 2)$ r_{108}: $(t_5 \rightarrow t_6 \ |_{e'}, 1)$

r_{109}: $(c_i \rightarrow (a_i \ in \ M_C) \ |_{t_6}, 1)$ r_{110}: $(h_i \rightarrow h_i(b_i \ in \ M_C) \ |_{t_6}, 1)$

r_{111}: $(m_i \rightarrow \lambda \ |_{t_6}, 1)$ r_{112}: $(f \rightarrow f(o_{\times} \ in \ M_C) \ |_{t_6}, 1)$

r_{113}: $(t_6 \rightarrow t_7, 2)$ r_{114}: $(t_7 \rightarrow t_8 \ |_{e'}, 1)$

r_{115}: $(c_i \rightarrow (b_i \ in \ M_C) \ |_{t_8}, 1)$ r_{116}: $(g_i \rightarrow (a_i \ in \ M_C) \ |_{t_8}, 1)$

r_{117}: $(uv \rightarrow - \ |_{t_8}, 1)$ r_{118}: $(fv \rightarrow (o_+ \ in \ M_C) \ |_{t_8}, 2)$

r_{119}: $(fu \rightarrow -(o_+ \ in \ M_C) \ |_{t_8}, 2)$ r_{120}: $(f \rightarrow (o_- \ in \ M_C) \ |_{t_8}, 3)$

r_{121}: $(h_i \rightarrow g_i \ |_{t_8}, 1)$ r_{122}: $(v \rightarrow u \ |_{t_8}, 1)$

r_{123}: $(x_i \rightarrow h_i \ |_{t_8}, 1)$ r_{124}: $(- \rightarrow v \ |_{t_8}, 1)$

r_{125}: $(t_8 \rightarrow t_9, 4)$ r_{126}: $(t_8 \rightarrow t_9 \ |_{e'}, 1)$

r_{127}: $(-^2 \rightarrow \lambda \ |_{t_9.}, 1)$ r_{128}: $(t_9 \rightarrow t, 2)$

r_{129}: $(t_1 \rightarrow t_{10} \ |_{e'}, 2)$ r_{130}: $(a_i \rightarrow \lambda \ |_{t_{10}}, 1)$

r_{131}: $(n_i \rightarrow \lambda \ |_{t_{10}}, 1)$ r_{132}: $(c_i \rightarrow \lambda \ |_{t_{10}}, 1)$

r_{133}: $(g_i \rightarrow \lambda \ |_{t_{10}}, 1)$ r_{134}: $(h_i \rightarrow \lambda \ |_{t_{10}}, 1)$

r_{135}: $(u \rightarrow \lambda \ |_{t_{10}}, 1)$ r_{136}: $(v \rightarrow \lambda \ |_{t_{10}}, 1)$

r_{137}: $(t_{10} \rightarrow t_{11} \ |_-, 2)$ r_{138}: $(x_i \rightarrow (a_i \ in \ M_C) \ |_{t_{11}}, 1)$

r_{139}: $(b_i \rightarrow b_i(b_i \ in \ M_C) \ |_{t_{11}}, 1)$ r_{140}: $(f \rightarrow f(o_- \ in \ M_C) \ |_{t_{11}}, 1)$

r_{141}: $(t_{11} \rightarrow t_{12}, 2)$ r_{142}: $(t_{12} \rightarrow t_13 \ |_{e'}, 1)$

r_{143}: $(c_i \rightarrow x_i \ |_{t_{13}}, 1)$ r_{144}: $(t_{13} \rightarrow t_{10}, 2)$

r_{145}: $(t_{10} \rightarrow t_{14}, 3)$ r_{146}: $(x_i \rightarrow (x_i \ out) \ |_{t_{14}}, 1)$

r_{147}: $(b_i \rightarrow \lambda \ |_{t_{14}}, 1)$ r_{148}: $(f \rightarrow \lambda \ |_{t_{14}}, 1)$

Key Generation Membrane A_2. The membrane A_2 accepts the objects from A_1, and control the process of key generation. It has four steps, including:

(1) Sending the objects from A_1 into M_1, M_2 & M_3, to generate the multisets p, q & e representing three primes $N(p), N(q)$ & $N(e)$, the rules are:

r_{149}: $(i \rightarrow (h_i b_{i-1} b_{i-2} \ldots b_1 e_0 \ in \ M_1) \ |_{\#_1}, 1)$ r_{150}: $(\#_1 \rightarrow (p't \ in \ M_1), 2)$

r_{151}: $(i \rightarrow (h_j b_{j-1} b_{j-2} \ldots b_1 e_0 \ in \ M_2) \ |_{\#_2}, 1)$ r_{152}: $(\#_2 \rightarrow (q't \ in \ M_2), 2)$

r_{153}: $(i \rightarrow (b_k b_{k-1} b_{k-2} \ldots b_1 e_0 \ in \ M_3) \ |_{\#_3}, 1)$ r_{154}: $(\#_3 \rightarrow (e't \ in \ M_3), 2)$

(2) The occurrence of the object p' & q' indicates that p & q are generated, rules $r_{155} \sim r_{157}$ are applied to send objects into M_C for the calculation of $N(n) = N(p) \times N(q)$. After that calculation, the object e' occurs, the result c_i evolves to n_i, and an object p_0 and an object q_0 are consumed. Then sending $p \bigcup q$ into M_C to calculate $N(m) = (N(p) - 1) \times (N(q) - 1)$, the rules are:

r_{155}: $(p_i \rightarrow p_i(p_i \ in \ M_C) \ |_{p'q'}, 1)$ r_{156}: $(q_i \rightarrow q_i(q_i \ in \ M_C) \ |_{p'q'}, 1)$

r_{157}: $(p'q' \rightarrow (o_{\times} \ in \ M_C), 2)$ r_{158}: $(c_i \rightarrow n_i \ |_{e'}, 2)$

r_{159}: $(e'p_0 q_0 \rightarrow p'q'f, 2)$ r_{160}: $(p_i \rightarrow \lambda \ |_f, 1)$

r_{161}: $(q_i \rightarrow \lambda \ |_f, 1)$ r_{162}: $(c_i \rightarrow m_i \ |_{e'f}, 1)$

(3) Sending m & e into M_9 to get d.

r_{163}: $(e'f \rightarrow t \ |_{e_0}, 1)$ r_{164}: $(m_i \rightarrow (m_i \ in \ M_9) \ |_t, 1)$

r_{165}: $(e_i \rightarrow e_i(e_i \ in \ M_9) \ |_t, 1)$ r_{166}: $(t \rightarrow (tf \ in \ M_9), 2)$

(4) Sending out the key pairs (n, e) and (n, d) into membrane A_2.

r_{167}: $(n_i \rightarrow (n_i \ out) \ |_{d0}, 1)$ r_{168}: $(e_i \rightarrow (e_i \ out) \ |_{d0}, 1)$

r_{169}: $(d_i \rightarrow (d_i \ out), 2)$

3.3 Encryption and Decryption Membrane A_3

Membrane A_3 is designed based on the fast modular multiplication algorithm. It accepts abc from outer membrane, and send out the result of $N(a)^{N(b)}\%N(c)$. The initial structure of A_3 is shown as Fig. 4.

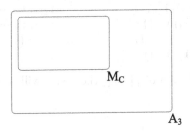

M_C

A_3

Fig. 4. The initial structure of membrane A_3

The rules of A_3 are:

r_{170}: $(t \rightarrow t_1 \,|_{b_i}, 1)$ $\qquad r_{171}$: $(b_i \rightarrow (a_i \; in \; M_C) \,|_{t_1}, 1)$

r_{172}: $(t_1 \rightarrow t_2(o \div b_0^2 \; in \; M_C), 2)$ $\qquad r_{173}$: $(c_i \rightarrow b_i \,|_{t_3}, 1)$

r_{174}: $(c_i \rightarrow b_i \,|_{t_4}, 1)$ $\qquad r_{175}$: $(e \rightarrow \lambda, 3)$

r_{176}: $(t_2 \rightarrow t_3 \,|_{m0}, 1)$ $\qquad r_{177}$: $(s_i \rightarrow (b_i \; in \; M_C) \,|_{t_3}, 1)$

r_{178}: $(a_i \rightarrow a_i(a_i \; in \; M_C) \,|_{t_3}, 1)$ $\qquad r_{179}$: $(t_3 \rightarrow t_5(o \times \; in \; M_C), 2)$

r_{180}: $(t_5 \rightarrow t_6 \,|_{e'}, 1)$ $\qquad r_{181}$: $(c_i \rightarrow (a_i \; in \; M_C) \,|_{t_6}, 1)$

r_{182}: $(n_i \rightarrow n_i(b_i \; in \; M_C) \,|_{t_6}, 1)$ $\qquad r_{183}$: $(t_6 \rightarrow t_7(o \div \; in \; M_c), 2)$

r_{184}: $(t_7 \rightarrow t_8 \,|_{e'}, 1)$ $\qquad r_{185}$: $(m_i \rightarrow s_i \,|_{t_8}, 1)$

r_{186}: $(c_i \rightarrow \lambda \,|_{t_8}, 1)$ $\qquad r_{187}$: $(t_2 \rightarrow t_4 \,|_{e'}, 2)$

r_{188}: $(t_4 \rightarrow t_8, 2)$ $\qquad r_{189}$: $(a_i \rightarrow (a_i b_i \; in \; M_C) \,|_{t_8}, 1)$

r_{190}: $(t_8 \rightarrow t_9(o \times \; in \; M_C), 2)$ $\qquad r_{191}$: $(t_9 \rightarrow t_{10} \,|_{e'}, 1)$

r_{192}: $(c_i \rightarrow (a_i \; in \; M_C) \,|_{t_{10}}, 1)$ $\qquad r_{193}$: $(n_i \rightarrow n_i(b_i \; in \; M_C) \,|_{t_{10}}, 1)$

r_{194}: $(t_{10} \rightarrow t_{11}(o \div \; in \; M_c), 2)$ $\qquad r_{195}$: $(t_11 1 \rightarrow t_{12} 2 \,|_{e'}, 1)$

r_{196}: $(m_i \rightarrow a_i \,|_{t_1 2}, 1)$ $\qquad r_{197}$: $(c_i \rightarrow \lambda \,|_{t_{12}}, 1)$

r_{198}: $(t_{12} \rightarrow t, 2)$ $\qquad r_{199}$: $(t \rightarrow t_{13}, 2)$

r_{200}: $(a_i \rightarrow \lambda \,|_{t_{13}}, 1)$ $\qquad r_{201}$: $(s_i \rightarrow (s_i \; out) \,|_{t_{13}}, 1)$

r_{202}: $(t_{13} \rightarrow \lambda, 2)$ $\qquad r_{203}$: $(n_i \rightarrow \lambda \,|_{t_{13}}, 1)$

3.4 Skin Membrane A_1

The function of membrane A_1 is to control and coordinate its sub membrane to achieve RSA algorithm, and start the evolution of the system according to the input of P system, including 2 aspects: send the input which are the digits of $N(p), N(q)$ & $N(e)$ into A_2 (the input should promise that the digits of $N(e)$ are less than the sum of digits of $N(p)$ and $N(q)$) and then send the message to be encrypted or decrypted with key pair into A_3. The main rules are:

(1) Sending three numbers and three sign objects into A_2:

r_{204}: $(i \to i \ in \ A_2 \mid_{\#_1}, 1)$ r_{205}: $(\#_1 \to \#_1 \ in \ A_2, 2)$

r_{206}: $(i \to i \ in \ A_2 \mid_{\#_2}, 1)$ r_{207}: $(\#_2 \to \#_2 \ in \ A_2, 2)$

r_{208}: $(i \to i \ in \ A_2 \mid_{\#_3}, 1)$ r_{209}: $(\#_3 \to \#_3 \ in \ A_2, 2)$

(2) According to the input object, send the (m, n, e) or (m, n, d) into A_3 to do encryption or decryption.

r_{210}: $(n_i \to n_i(n_i \ in \ A_3) \mid_u, 1)$ r_{211}: $(e_i \to e_i(b_i \ in \ A_3) \mid_u, 1)$

r_{212}: $(m_i \to (a_i \ in \ A_3) \mid_u, 1)$ r_{213}: $(u \to (ts_0 \ in \ A_3), 2)$

r_{214}: $(n_i \to n_i(n_i \ in \ A_3) \mid_v, 1)$ r_{215}: $(d_i \to d_i(b_i \ in \ A_3) \mid_v, 1)$

r_{216}: $(m_i \to (a_i \ in \ A_3) \mid_v, 1)$ r_{217}: $(v \to (ts_0 \ in \ A_3), 2)$

After the end of evolution of $\prod_{RSA}$, the result will be in the membrane A_1.

4   Instance

In this section, we will give an instance to show how the P system works on realizing RSA algorithm.

4.1   Key Generation

We assume that the digits of $N(p), N(q)$ & $N(e)$ are 2, 3, 3, then the input objects $\{2, \#_1, 2, \#_2, 3, \#_3\}$ will be sent into membrane A_1 in sequence. Rules $r_{204} \sim r_{209}$ of A_1 will be applied to send the objects into A_2 and then rules in A_2 are used to initialize the process of key generation with sending different placeholders into M_1, M_2 & M_3. The initialization structure is shown as Fig. 5.

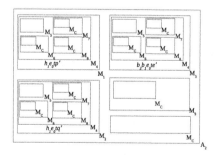 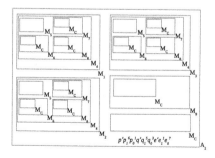

Fig. 5. The initial structure of generation

Fig. 6. Complete the generation of p & q & e

(1) Rules in M_1, M_2 & M_3 are used to generate p & q & e in parallel, and if we assume the primes we generated in M_1, M_2 & M_3 are 61 & 53 & 17, the objects generated in M_1, M_2 & M_3 will be $\{h_1 e_0 t_1 p a_1^6 a_0^1\}$, $\{h_1 e_0 t_1 q a_1^5 a_0^3\}$ & $\{b_2 b_1 e_0 t_1 e a_1^1 a_0^7\}$, then a_i will evolve to p_i, q_i & e_i and be sent out, the structure of membrane will be shown as Fig. 6.

(2) In the presence of p' & q', the multiset $p \bigcup q$ will be sent into membrane M_C to calculate $N(n) = 61 \times 53 = 3233$ and get the result multiset $\{n_3^3 n_2^2 n_1^3 n_0^3\}$. After the calculation the multiset $(p-1) \bigcup (q-1)$ will be sent into M_C to calculate $N(m) = 60 \times 52 = 3120$ which represents $\phi(N(n))$ in Sect. 2 and get the result $\{m_3^3 m_2 m_1^2\}$, see Fig. 7.

(3) After the calculation of $N(m)$, the multiset $e \bigcup m$ will be sent into membrane M_9 to calculate $N(d)$, the result $\{d_3^2 d_2^7 d_1^5 d_0^3\}$ which represents $N(d) = 2753$ can be seen in Fig. 8.

(4) The end of the evolution in M_9 is the end of the key generation, the objects $\{e_1 e_0^7 n_3^3 n_2^2 n_1^3 n_0^3 d_3^2 d_2^7 d_1^5 d_0^3\}$ which represents the key pairs (n, e) & (n, d) will be sent out to A_1, and redundant objects will be cleaned (Fig. 9).

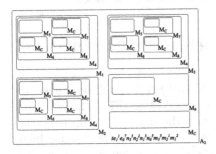

Fig. 7. After the calculation of m

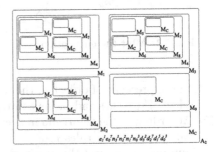

Fig. 8. After the calculation of d

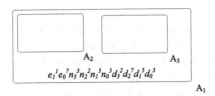

Fig. 9. Key generation completed

4.2 Encryption and Decryption

The algorithm of encryption is same with the decryption, and the only difference is that the input of encryption is e while the input of decryption is d. We take 65 for example to show the process of encryption, so the input of A_1 will be $\{m_1^6 m_0^5\} \bigcup \{u\}$ (Fig. 10).

$e_1{}^1e_0{}^7n_3{}^3n_2{}^2n_1{}^3n_0{}^3d_3{}^2d_2{}^7d_1{}^5d_0{}^3um_1{}^6m_0{}^5$

Fig. 10. The initial structure of encryption

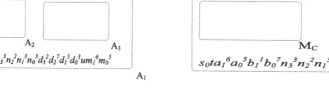

$s_0ta_1{}^6a_0{}^5b_1{}^1b_0{}^7n_3{}^3n_2{}^2n_1{}^3n_0{}^3$

Fig. 11. A_3 accepts objects and start the encryption

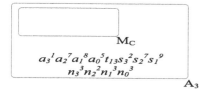

$a_3{}^1a_2{}^7a_1{}^8a_0{}^5t_{13}s_3{}^2s_2{}^7s_1{}^9$
$n_3{}^3n_2{}^2n_1{}^3n_0{}^3$

Fig. 12. After the encryption

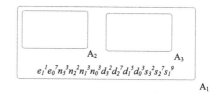

$e_1{}^1e_0{}^7n_3{}^3n_2{}^2n_1{}^3n_0{}^3d_3{}^2d_2{}^7d_1{}^5d_0{}^3s_3{}^2s_2{}^7s_1{}^9$

Fig. 13. After the encryption

(1) In the presence of object u, the multiset $n \bigcup m \bigcup e \bigcup \{u\}$ will be convert to $n \bigcup a \bigcup b \bigcup \{ts_0\}$ and be sent into A_3 to do encryption (Fig. 11).

(2) According to the algorithm in Sect. 2, we send the objects into M_C to do the calculations, and rules $r_{170} \sim r_{203}$ are used to complete the fast modular multiplication, and the result objects $\{s_3^2s_2^7s_1^9\}$ which represents $s = 2790$ can be seen in Fig. 12.

(3) After the encryption in A_3, all the result objects will be sent out to A_1 (Fig. 13).

5   Conclusions

In this paper, we give a solution to realize the RSA algorithm in parallel and design a P system Π_{RSA}, including structure and rules. Then an instance is given to describe the process of the calculation and illustrate the feasibility and effectiveness of our designed P system. But the foundation of the P system Π_{RSA} we designed in this paper is the RSA algorithm proposed in [1], although we make the process to generate a big prime more parallel, it is still the bottleneck in the realization of Π_{RSA}. On the other hand, the code we used in this paper is based on hybrid coding, which makes a large number of rules exist during the process, the use of other coding methods will effectively reduce the number of rules. We will do further research in these two directions.

References

1. Rivest, R.L., Shamir, A., Adleman, L.: A method for obtaining digital signatures and public-key cryptosystems. Commun. ACM **1**(2), 120–126 (1978)

2. Fujioka, A., Okamoto, T., Miyaguchi, S.: ESIGN: an efficient digital signature implementation for smart cards. In: Davies, D.W. (ed.) EUROCRYPT 1991. LNCS, vol. 547, pp. 446–457. Springer, Heidelberg (1991). doi:10.1007/3-540-46416-6_38

3. Takagi, T.: Fast RSA-type cryptosystem modulo $p^k q$. In: Krawczyk, H. (ed.) CRYPTO 1998. LNCS, vol. 1462, pp. 318–326. Springer, Heidelberg (1998). doi:10.1007/BFb0055738

4. Yu, Y., Xue, L., Man, H.A., et al.: Cloud data integrity checking with an identity-based auditing mechanism from RSA. Future Gener. Comput. Syst. **62**(C), 85–91 (2016)

5. Zhou, Y.B., Zhang, Z.F., Qing, S.H., et al.: A new CEMBS based on RSA signatures and its application in constructing fair exchange protocol. In: IEEE International Conference on E-Technology, E-Commerce and E-Service, pp. 558–562 (2004)

6. Wang, X., Song, T., Gong, F., Pan, Z.: On the computational power of spiking neural P systems with self-organization. Sci. Rep. doi:10.1038/srep27624

7. Song, B., Song, T., Pan, L.: Time-free solution to SAT problem by P systems with active membranes and standard cell division rules. Nat. Comput. **14**(4), 673–681 (2015)

8. Christinal, H.A., Díaz-Pernil, D., Jurado, P.R., Selvan, S.E.: Color segmentation of 2D images with thresholding. In: Mathew, J., Patra, P., Pradhan, D.K., Kuttyamma, A.J. (eds.) ICECCS 2012. CCIS, vol. 305, pp. 162–169. Springer, Heidelberg (2012). doi:10.1007/978-3-642-32112-2_20

9. Song, T., Pan, Z., Wong, D.M., Wang, X.: Design of logic gates using spiking neural P systems with homogeneous neurons and astrocytes-like control. Inf. Sci. **372**, 380–391 (2016)

10. Pan, L., Alhazov, A.: Solving HPP and SAT by P systems with active memabrabes and separation rules. Acta Informatica **43**, 131–145 (2006)

11. Ishii, K., Fujiwara, A., Tagawa, H.: Asynchronous P systems for SAT and Hamiltonian cycle problem. In: Nature and Biologically Inspired Computing, pp. 513–519. IEEE (2010)

12. Zhang, X., Tian, Y., Jin, Y.: A knee point driven evolutionary algorithm for many-objective optimization. IEEE Trans. Evol. Comput. **19**(6), 761–776 (2015)

13. Zhang, X., Tian, Y., Cheng, R., Jin, Y.: An efficient approach to non-dominated sorting for evolutionary multi-objective optimization. IEEE Trans. Evol. Comput. **19**(2), 201–213 (2015)

14. Puan, G.: Membrane Computing: An Introduction. Springer, Secaucus (2002)

15. Alhazov, A., Bonchi, C., Ciobanu, G., Isbasa, C.: Encodings and arithmetic operations in P systems. In: The Proceedings of Fourth Brainstorming Week on Membrane Computing, Sevilla, pp. 13–39 (2006)

16. Guo, P., Chen, H., Zhang, H.: An integrated P system for arithmetic operations. J. Comput. Theor. Nanosci. **12**(10), 3346–3356 (2015)

17. Guo, P., Chen, H., Zheng, H.: Arithmetic expression evaluations with membranes. Chin. J. Electron. **23**(CJE-1), 55–60 (2014)

A General Object-Oriented Description for Membrane Computing

Xiyu Liu, Yuzhen Zhao$^{(\boxtimes)}$, and Wenping Wang

School of Management Science and Engineering,
Shandong Normal University, Jinan 250014, China
sdxyliu@163.com, zhaoyuzhen_happy@126.com, 64759428@qq.com

Abstract. Membrane computing is a distributed and parallel bio-inspired computing paradigm providing new computing models. The computational model of membrane computing is called "P systems". Despite several P systems simulation tools have been built, the general object-oriented framework of P systems lacks. This study gives the computer storage structure of P systems, the object-oriented static model and the object-oriented dynamic model of membrane computing using Umlet. This study intuitively gives the concepts and operations involved in the membrane computing, which facilitates a better understanding of the thought of membrane computing, and provides support for research personnel having no membrane computing foundation.

Keywords: Membrane computing · P system · Object-oriented method · Modeling · UML

1 Introduction

Biological systems, such as cells, tissues, and human brains, have deep computational intelligences. Biologically inspired computing, or bio-inspired computing in short, focuses on abstracting computing ideas from biological systems to construct computing models and algorithms. Membrane computing is a novel research branch of bio-inspired computing, initiated by Gh. Păun in 2002, which seeks to discover new computational models from the study of biological cells, particularly of the cellular membranes [1,2]. The obtained models are distributed and parallel bio-inspired computing devices, usually called P systems. There are three mainly investigated P systems, cell-like P systems [1], tissue P systems [3], and neural-like P systems (also known as spiking neural P systems) [4] (and their variants, see e.g. [5–11]). P systems are known as powerful computing models, are able to do what Turing machines can do efficiently [12–16]. The parallel evolution mechanism of variants of P systems, such as numerical P systems [17,18], spatial P systems [19], spiking neural P systems with anti-spikes [20], has been found to perform well in doing computation, even solving computational hard problems [21–23].

The implement research of membrane computing contains three aspects: software, hardware and biochemical methods. Sixteen P systems softwares are listed

© Springer Nature Singapore Pte Ltd. 2016
M. Gong et al. (Eds.): BIC-TA 2016, Part I, CCIS 681, pp. 168–186, 2016.
DOI: 10.1007/978-981-10-3611-8_17

on the P systems webpage, in which P-Lingua and MeCoSim are the most popular ones [24]. The field-programmable gate arrays are used to carry out the reconfigurable hardware implementation of P systems [25]. Unicom u-tube and broth are used to realized the biochemical implementation scheme [26]. Due to the hardware and the biochemical methods need to consume large amounts of resources, the software simulation is currently the most common way to implement the membrane computing. Although several software simulation tools have been built, they give the functions in detail, while the general object-oriented framework of P systems is not given. Only the simulations of several specific P systems are given, therefore, when researchers want to simulate a new variety of P systems, they need to design themselves. If there is a description of all concepts and operations from a macroscopic perspective, the design process will become easier.

For this purpose, a general object-oriented description for membrane computing is given. The paper is organized as follows: The object-oriented description of membrane computing is introduced in Sect. 2. Section 3 gives the storage structure of P systems in computers. In Sects. 4 and 5, the object-oriented static model and the object-oriented dynamic model are constructed respectively. Finally, some conclusions are drawn in Sect. 6.

2   Preliminaries

In this section, some knowledge about Unified Modeling Language (UML) is introduced. For more detail, please refer [28].

The UML is a unified modeling language in the field of software engineering, which aims to provide a standard way to model and visualize the software development. UML defines five classes of diagrams.

(1) The use-case diagram: The use-case diagram describes the system function from the perspective of the users, and points out the operators of each function.
(2) The static diagram: (including the class diagram, the package diagram, and the object diagram)
the class diagram: The class diagram describes the static structure of the class in the system.
the package diagram: The package diagram is composed of packages and classes showing the relationship between the packages.
the object diagram: The object diagram is the instance of class diagram.
(3) The behavior diagram (including the state diagram and the activity diagram): The behavior diagram describes the exchange relationship composed by the system dynamic model and the objects.
the state diagram: The state diagram describes to state control flow.
the activity diagram: The activity diagram describes the workflow of the case.

(4) The interaction diagram (the sequence diagram and the cooperation diagram): The interaction diagram describes the interactions between objects. the sequence diagram: The sequence diagram describes a dynamic relationship between objects, emphasizes the order of the messages which are sent by objects, and shows the interaction between objects.
the cooperation diagram: The cooperation diagram describes the cooperative relationship between objects.

(5) The implementation diagram: the configuration diagram: The configuration diagram defines the physical architecture of software and hardware in the system.

3 The Object-Oriented Description of Membrane Computing

The object-oriented method is a programming paradigm which is based on the "objects". The object is a package composed of data attributes and the corresponding operations on these data. A group of objects with similar properties form a "class" [27].

The three main components: membranes, rules, and P system objects of the three main P systems: cell-like P system, tissue-like P system, and neural-like P system are described from the view of the object-oriented description.

(1) **P system object:** The characters or strings which are derived from chemical substances in cells are called *objects*. In this paper, they are called *P system objects* to differentiate them from objects in an object-oriented method. *Alphabet O contains all P system objects in a P system.*

(2) **Membrane:** *Membranes* divide the whole P system region into several *compartments*. *Multiset* of P system objects and rules are placed in compartments. Each compartment is a relatively independent computing unit. Each membrane has its label (the set of labels h is called H) and charge $(+, -, 0)$.

(3) **Rule:** *Rules* point out the operations that need to be executed on P system objects or membranes. By executing rules, the *configuration* of a P system is changed. Higher priority rules should be executed with higher priority if the priority of rules is defined.
There are several types of rules: evolution rules which change the kind or the number of P system objects in a certain compartment $(u \rightarrow v, u, v \in O^*)$, communication rules which change the compartment which the P system objects belong to $((u, out; v, in), u, v \in O^*)$, membrane creation rules which create new membranes $(a \rightarrow [b]_j^\alpha, a, b \in O, h \in H, \alpha \in \{+, -, 0\})$, membrane division rules which divide one membrane into two membranes $([_h a]_h^{\alpha_1} \rightarrow [_{h_1} b]_{h_1}^{\alpha_2} [_{h_2} c]_{h_2}^{\alpha_3}, h, h_1, h_2 \in H, \alpha_1, \alpha_2, \alpha_3 \in \{+, -, 0\}, a, b, c \in O)$, and membrane dissolution rules which dissolve membranes $([_h a]_h^\alpha \rightarrow b, h \in H, \alpha \in \{+, -, 0\}, a, b \in O)$.

(4) **Cell-like P system:** The *cell-like P system* is the basic membrane computing model. It simulates the structure and function of cells. All other membranes, rules, and P system objects are in a membrane called *skin membrane*. The membrane structure of a cell-like P system is a tree structure.

(5) **Tissue-like P system:** The *tissue-like P system* is an important extension of membrane computing model. It simulates the structure and function of tissues. Multiple cells are placed in one environment, and both the cells and the environment can have P system objects. The membrane structure is a graph structure.

(6) **Neural-like P system:** The *neural-like P system* is a relatively new proposed membrane computing model which is a hot area in membrane computing. The cells in this P system are neurons. *Spiking Neural P system, SN P system* for short, is the main kind of neural-like P system, which has only one P system object called *spike*. The execution of rules in SN P systems need several steps. If a rule in one neuron needs t steps to be executed, this neuron is closed during this period of time, which means this neuron cannot receive or emit spikes. If no rule in one neuron is executed at a time, this neuron is open.

In conclusion, the model of membrane computing: P system can be seen as a class which has several attributes, such as membrane structure, environment (the kind and number of objects in environment), rules, alphabet, multiset, configuration(the membrane structure and the multiset in each component). P system class has three subclasses: cell-like P system, tissue-like P system, and neural-like P system. The membrane structure and the objects of the P systems are changed through executing rules, therefore, three types of operations are defined: operation on membranes, operation on rules, and operation on P system objects. The details will be given in the following sections.

4   The Data Structure of Membrane Computing

In this section, the data structure of membrane computing is designed with the purpose of storing the alphabet, membrane, multiset, evolution rule, communication rule, membrane creation rule, membrane division rule, and membrane dissolution rule in computers.

(1) **Alphabet:** A *string array* is used to store all characters in a P system. The characters appear only in this array in the whole P system. In the following, the characters are represented by the serial number in the string array to save space. For instance, there is a string array $alphabet = [a, b, c, d, e]$ shown in Fig. 1, the five characters are represented by 1, 2, 3, 4 and 5. String 224 is used to show two a and one d.

(2) **Membrane:** *String arrays* of length 5 are used to store the relevant information as Figs. 2 and 3.

(3) **Multiset:** *String arrays* of length 2 are used to store the multiset as Fig. 4.

alphabet	a	b	c	d	e
serial number	1	2	3	4	5

Fig. 1. The data structure of the alphabet.

membrane label number	membrane charge	labels of the inner membranes	label of the outer membrane	status

Fig. 2. The data structure of the membrane for the cell-like P systems.

membrane label number	membrane charge	labels of membranes which have connections coming from the current membrane	labels of membranes which have connections going to the current membrane	status

Fig. 3. The data structure of the membrane for the tissue-like P systems and the neural-like P systems.

label number of the membrane	serial number of each object in this membrane

Fig. 4. The data structure of the multiset.

(4) **Rule type:** An *string array* is used to store all rules types used in a P system. Each string stores one type of rule. The strings appear only in this array in the whole P system. In the following, the strings are represented by the serial number in the string array to save space.

(5) **Evolution rule:** *String Arrays* of length 6 are used to store the evolution rule as Fig. 5.

(6) **Communication rule:** *String Arrays* of length 7 are used to store the communication rule as Fig. 6.

(7) **Membrane creation rule:** *String Arrays* of length 8 are used to store the membrane creation rule as Fig. 7.

(8) **Membrane division rule:** *String Arrays* of length 12 is used to store the membrane division rule which divides a membrane into two membranes as Fig. 8.

(9) **Membrane dissolution rule:** *String Arrays* of length 7 is used to store the membrane dissolution rule as Fig. 9.

label number of the membrane which this rule belongs to	serial number of this rule type	rule id	serial number of objects which are consumed by this rule	serial number of objects which are generated by this rule	priority

Fig. 5. The data structure of the evolution rule.

label number of the membrane which this rule belongs to	serial number of this rule type	label number of the membrane which communicates with the current membrane	rule id	serial number of objects which are transported from the current membrane by this rule	serial number of objects which are transported to the current membrane by this rule	priority

Fig. 6. The data structure of the communication rule.

label number of the membrane which this rule belongs to	serial number of this rule type	rule id	serial number of objects which are consumed by this rule	label of the created membrane	charge of the created membrane	serial number of objects which are generated by this rule	priority

Fig. 7. The data structure of the membrane creation rule.

label number of the membrane which this rule belongs to	charge of the membrane	serial number of this rule type	rule id	serial number of objects which are consumed by this rule	label of the first created membrane	charge of the first created membrane	serial number of objects which are generated by this rule and belong to the first created membrane	label of the second created membrane	charge of the second created membrane	serial number of objects which are generated by this rule and belong to the second created membrane	priority

Fig. 8. The data structure of the membrane division rule.

label number of the membrane which this rule belongs to	charge of the membrane	serial number of this rule type	rule id	serial number of objects which are consumed by this rule	serial number of objects which are generated by this rule	priority

Fig. 9. The data structure of the membrane dissolution rule.

5   An Object-Oriented Static Model of Membrane Computing

According to the object-oriented description of membrane computing, the P system class has three subclasses: cell-like P system class, tissue-like P system class, and neural-like P system class. These subclasses inherit the attributes of the P system class, and they have their own attribute: the membrane structure. Each P system class aggregates by membrane class, rule class, and object class.

The membrane class has eight attributes.

(1) **Label:** Label is used to distinguish different membranes.
(2) **Charge:** The charge of a membrane can be positive which is represented by "+", negative which is represented by "-", and neutral which is represented by "0".
(3) **Multiset:** Multiset shows the kind and the number of P system objects contained in this membrane.
(4) **InnerMembranes:** InnerMembranes show the labels of membranes which are in this membrane. (This is the attribute of the cell-like P systems.)
(5) **OuterMembrane:** The OuterMembrane shows the label of membrane which is outside this membrane. (This is the attribute of the cell-like P systems.)
(6) **ConnectToMembrane:** The ConnectToMembrane shows the labels of the membranes which have channels from the current membrane. (This is the attribute of the tissue-like P systems and the neural-like P systems.)
(7) **ConnectFromMembrane:** ConnectFromMembrane shows the labels of membranes which have channels to the current membrane. (This is the attribute of the tissue-like P systems and the neural-like P systems.)
(8) **Status:** Status shows at this step, this membrane is open or closed.

The rule class also has four attributes aims to make the operations easier.

(1) **Id:** Id uses to distinguish different rules.
(2) **RuleComparator:** RuleComparator is used to compare the priority and choose the rule with higher priority. Each rule is assigned a priority level represented by a positive integer. Bigger number means higher priority.

Object class has only one attribute: alphabet.

The class diagram is shown in Fig. 10. The relationship between the P system class and the cell-like P system class, the tissue-like P system class, the neural-like P system class is inheritance. The inheritance means a class (called subclass) inherits the attributes and operations of another class (called superclass), and the subclass can add its own attributes and operations or rewrite its superclass's operations. In UML diagram, the inheritance is represented by a solid line with a hollow triangular arrowhead, pointing from the subclass to the superclass. The relationship between the cell-like P system class, the tissue-like P system class, the neural-like P system class and the membrane class, the rule class, the object

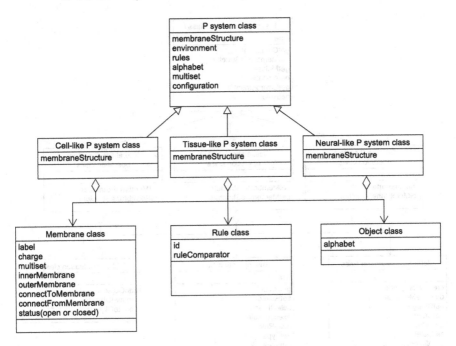

Fig. 10. The class diagram shows that the relationship between the P system class and the cell-like P system class, the tissue-like P system class, the neural-like P system class is inheritance, and the relationship between these three P system classes and the membrane class, the rule class, the object class are aggregation.

class are aggregation. The aggregation shows the relationship between the whole and the parts, while the whole and the parts are separable. In UML diagram, the aggregation is represented by a solid line with a arrow and a hollow diamond.

Figure 11 shows the relationship among operation classes. The P system operation class aggregates by cell-like P system operation class, tissue-like P system operation class, and neural-like P system operation class. Each of these three class aggregates by membrane operation class, rule operation class, and object operation class.

The P system operation class has six operations which are used to acquire information about a P system: get configuration, get membrane structure, get multiset, get alphabet, get environment, and get rules. The cell-like P system operation class, the tissue-like P system operation class, and the neural-like P system operation class inherit the operations from P system operation class, and they have their own operations: get membrane structure, and set membrane structure. Each P system operation class aggregates by membrane operation class, rule operation class, and object operation class.

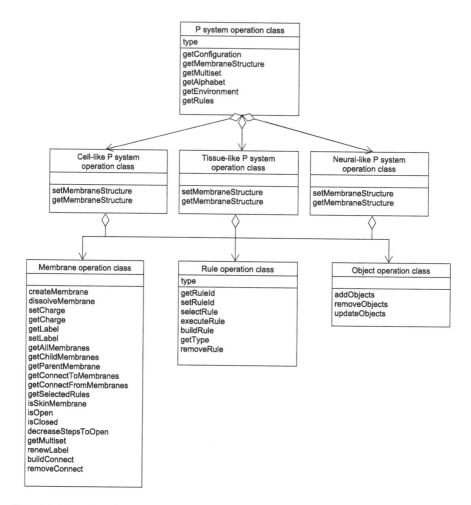

Fig. 11. The class diagram shows that relationship between the operation classes of P system.

The membrane operation class has twenty operations.

(1) **CreateMembrane:** A new membrane is created by the membrane creation rule.
(2) **DissolveMembrane:** The current membrane is dissolved, P system objects and the innermembranes in the current membrane enter into the outermembrane, and rules in the current membrane are removed.
(3) **SetCharge:** The charge of the current membrane is set.
(4) **GetCharge:** The charge of the current membrane is obtained.
(5) **SetLabel:** The label of the current membrane is set.
(6) **GetLabel:** The label of the current membrane is obtained.
(7) **GetAllMembranes:** All labels of membranes in a P system are obtained.

(8) **GetChildMembranes:** All labels of innermembranes in the current membrane are obtained.

(9) **GetParentMembrane:** The label of outermembrane in the current membrane is obtained.

(10) **GetChannelsToMembrane:** All membranes which are connected to the current membrane are obtained.

(11) **GetChannelsFromMembrane:** All membranes which are connected from the current membrane are obtained.

(12) **GetSelectedRules:** The id of rule which will be executed in the current membrane is obtained.

(13) **IsSkinMembrane:** Whether a membrane is the skin membrane or not is judged.

(14) **IsOpen:** Whether a neuron is open is judged.

(15) **IsClosed:** Whether a neuron is closed is judged.

(16) **DecreaseStepsToOpen:** This operation is used to record how many steps are needed to make a closed neuron open again.

(17) **GetMultiset:** Multiset of P system objects in the current membrane is obtained.

(18) **renewLabel:** The label of the current membrane is updated.

(19) **BuildChannel:** For dynamic membrane structure, a new channel between membranes is created.

(20) **RemoveChannel:** For dynamic membrane structure, a channel between membranes is melt.

The rule class has seven operations: getRuleId, setRuleId, selectRule, executeRule, buildRule, getType and removeRule.

The object class has three operations: add objects, remove objects, and update objects.

The relationship between the P system class, the P system operation class and the P system set class is shown in Fig. 12. The P system set class contains the whole set of P system. The P system operation depends on the P system. The dependence means the change of class A can make the change of the class B. It is said that class B depends on class A. In UML diagram, the dependence is represented by a imaginary line with a arrow, pointing from the class B to the class A.

6   Object-Oriented Dynamic Model of Membrane Computing

The object-oriented dynamic model of membrane computing describes the information transmission process between objects. In P system, changes are triggered by rules. In this section, the activity diagram and the sequence diagrams of four common rule operations are given.

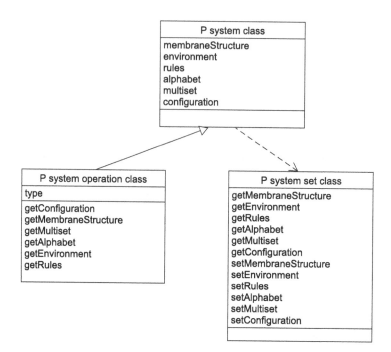

Fig. 12. The relationship between P system class, P system operation class and the P system set class. The relationship between P system class and the P system set class is unidirectional association.

6.1 The Activity Diagram

Figure 13 shows the workflow of the rules. The activity is controlled by rules. At the beginning, a rule is selected. The type of the selected rule is checked by "getType".

If the rule is an evolution rule, the objects which are consumed by this rule is removed from the system by "removeObjects", and then the objects which are generated by this rule is added to the system by "addObjects".

If the rule is a communication rule, the label number of the membrane which communicates with the current membrane is obtained by "getLabel". The objects which are transported from the current membrane are removed from the current membrane by "removeObjects", and these objects are added to the membrane which communicates with the current membrane by "addObjects". The objects which are transported to the current membrane are handle by opposite operations.

If the rule is a membrane creation rule, the objects which are consumed by this rule is removed from the system by "removeObjects", and then a new membrane is created by "createMembrane". The label and the charge of the new membrane are set by "setLabel" and "setCharge". Objects are added to the new membrane by "addObjects".

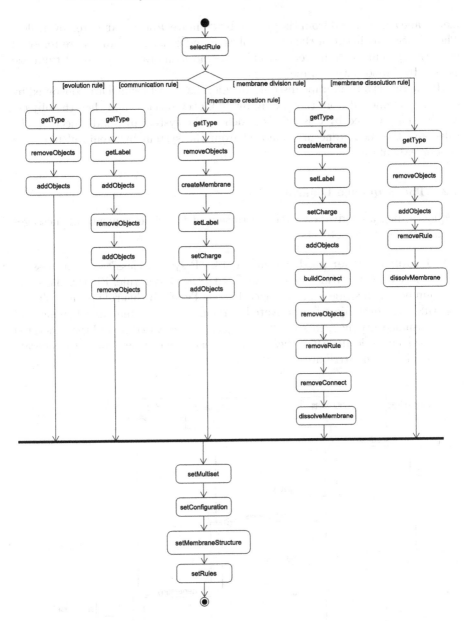

Fig. 13. The activity diagrams

If the rule is a membrane division rule, two new membranes are created by "createMembrane". The label and the charge of the new membranes are set by "setLabel" and "setCharge". Objects are added to the new membranes by "addObjects". The connections between the new membranes and other membranes are built by "buildConnect". The objects and the rules in the old

membrane are removed from the system by "removeObjects" and "removeRule".
The connections between the old membrane and other membranes are removed
from the system by "removeConnect". The old membrane is removed from the
system by "dissolveMembrane".

If the rule is a membrane dissolution rule, the objects which are consumed by
this rule is removed from the system by "removeObjects", and then the objects
which are generated by this rule is added to the system by "addObjects". The
rules and the membrane are removed from the system by "removeRule" and
"dissolveMembrane".

6.2   The Sequence Diagrams

Sequence diagrams give a visual description of the time sequence of messages
transmitted between objects.

(1) **Evolution rule:** As shown in Fig. 14, "P system class" sends a message
    "selectRule" to "Rule class" to deal with the chosen rule. Firstly, the serial
    number of this rule type is judged by "getType". If this rule is an evolution
    rule, "removeObjects" is activated to remove the P system objects which are
    consumed. At the next step, "addObjects" is activated to add the generated
    P system objects. After these steps, "generate()" is activated to generate
    new P system attributes.

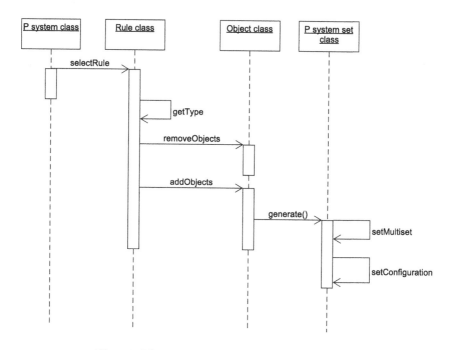

Fig. 14. The sequence diagrams of evolution rule

(2) **Communication rule:** As shown in Fig. 15, "P system class" sends a message "selectRule" to "Rule class" to deal with the chosen rule. Firstly, the serial number of this rule type is judged by "getType". If this rule is an communication rule, "getLabel" is used to obtain the label of the membrane which is communicated with the current membrane. The objects which are transported from the current membrane are removed from the current membrane by "removeObjects", and these objects are added to the membrane which communicates with the current membrane by "addObjects". The objects which are transported to the current membrane are handle by opposite operations. After these steps, "generate()" is activated to generate new P system attributes.

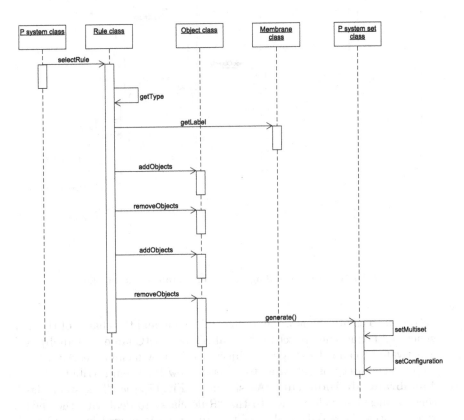

Fig. 15. The sequence diagrams of communication rule

(3) **Membrane creation rule:** As shown in Fig. 16, "P system class" sends a message "selectRule" to "Rule class" to deal with the chosen rule. Firstly, the serial number of this rule type is judged by "getType". If this rule is a membrane creation rule, "removeObjects" is activated to remove the P system objects which are consumed. At the next step, "createMembrane" is

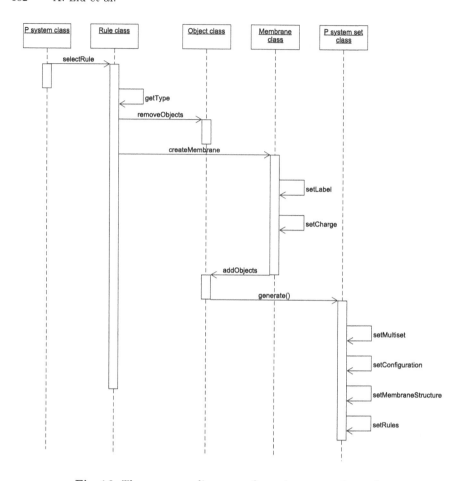

Fig. 16. The sequence diagrams of membrane creation rule

activated to create the new membrane. The label and the charge of the new generated membrane are set by "setLabel" and "setCharge". "addObjects" is activated to add the P system objects to the new membrane. After these steps, "generate()" is activated to generate new P system attributes.

(4) **Membrane division rule:** As shown in Fig. 17, the "P system class" sends a message "selectRule" to the "Rule class" to deal with the chosen rule. Firstly, the serial number of this rule type is judged by "getType". If this rule is a membrane division rule, two new membranes are created by "createMembrane". The label and the charge of the new membranes are set by "setLabel" and "setCharge". Objects are added to the new membranes by "addObjects". The connections between the new membranes and other membranes are built by "buildConnect". The objects and the rules in the old membrane are removed from the system by "removeObjects" and "removeRule". The connections between the old membrane and other

membranes are removed from the system by "removeConnect". The old membrane is removed from the system by "dissolveMembrane". After these steps, "generate()" is activated to generate new P system attributes.

(5) **Membrane dissolution rule:** As shown in Fig. 18, "P system class" sends a message "selectRule" to "Rule class" to deal with the chosen rule. Firstly, the serial number of this rule type is judged by "getType". If this rule is

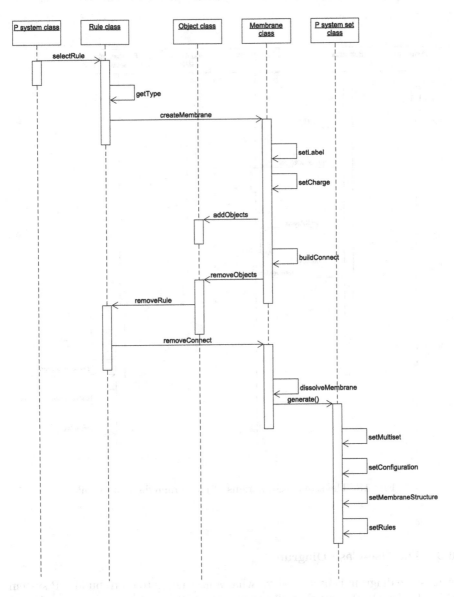

Fig. 17. The sequence diagrams of membrane division rule

a membrane dissolution rule, "removeObjects" is activated to remove the P system objects which are consumed. At the next step, "addObjects" is activated to add the generated P system objects. Because this rule is a membrane dissolution rule, "removeRule" is activated to remove all rules in this membrane, and then, "dissolveMembrane" is activated to dissolve this membrane. All P system objects enter into the outermembrane. After these steps, "generate()" is activated to generate new P system attributes.

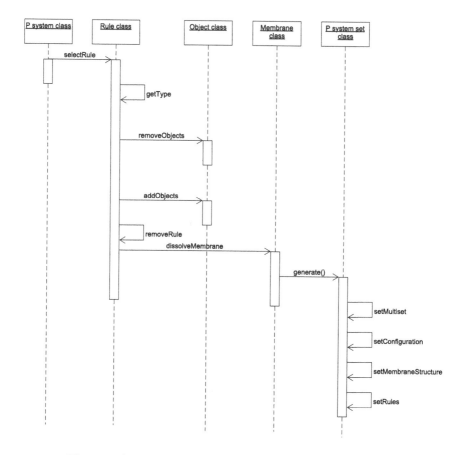

Fig. 18. The sequence diagrams of membrane dissolution rule

6.3   The Use-Case Diagram

A use-case diagram is used to show what a user needs to do to build a P system (Fig. 19). Due to the fact that all parameters of P systems and operations (rules) are packaged in the P system class and the P system operation class, respectively, what a user needs to do is to set the P system parameters, and the system will run itself to generate the computational result. The user does not need to know the programming details.

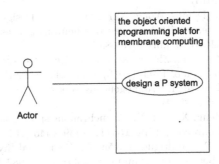

Fig. 19. The use-case diagram

7   Conclusion and Discussion

This paper analyzes membrane computing from the object-oriented method, gives a feasible scheme of storing P systems in computers, and builds object-oriented static model and the object-oriented dynamic model, which can help new researchers know membrane computing more quickly and roundly. In the further, the reusable components will be designed to make the realization of P systems easier.

Acknowledgment. This work was supported by National Natural Science Foundation of China (61472231, 61170038, 61402187, 61502283).

References

1. Păn, G.: Computing with membranes. J. Comput. Syst. Sci. **61**(1), 108–143 (2000)
2. Paun, G., Rozenberg, G., Salomaa, A.: The Oxford Handbook of Membrane Computing. Oxford University Press Inc., Oxford (2010)
3. Martín-Vide, C., Păun, G., Pazos, J.: Tissue P systems. Theor. Comput. Sci. **296**(2), 295–326 (2003)
4. Ionescu, M., Păun, G., Yokomori, T.: Spiking neural P systems. Fundam. Inform. **71**(2), 279–308 (2006)
5. Song, T., Wang, X.: Homogenous spiking neural P systems with inhibitory synapses. Neural Process. Lett. **42**(1), 199–214 (2015)
6. Song, T., Pan, L.: Spiking neural P systems with rules on synapses working in maximum spikes consumption strategy. IEEE Trans. Nanobiosci. **14**(1), 38–44 (2015)
7. Song, T., Pan, L.: Spiking neural P systems with rules on synapses working in maximum spiking strategy. IEEE Trans. Nanobiosci. **14**(4), 465–477 (2015)

8. Cavaliere, M., Ibarra, H., Păun, G., Woodworth, S., Egecioglu, O., Ionescu, M.: Asynchronous spiking neural P systems. Theor. Comput. Sci. **410**(24), 2352–2364 (2009)

9. Song, T., Pan, L.: Spiking neural P systems with request rules. Neurocomputing **193**(12), 193–200 (2016)

10. Song, T., Zheng, P., Dennis Wong, M.L., Wang, X.: Design of logic gates using spiking neural P systems with homogeneous neurons and astrocytes-like control. Inf. Sci. (2016). doi:10.1016/j.ins.2016.08.055

11. Song, T., Liu, X., Zhao, Y., Zhang, X.: Spiking neural P systems with white hole neurons. IEEE Trans. NanoBiosci. (2016). doi:10.1109/TNB.2016.2598879

12. Zeng, X., Zhang, X., Pan, L.: Homogeneous spiking neural P systems. Fundam. Inform. **97**(1), 275–294 (2009)

13. Song, T., Zou, Q., Zeng, X., Liu, X.: Asynchronous spiking neural P systems with rules on synapses. Neurocomputing **151**(1), 1439–1445 (2015)

14. Ibarra, O.H., Păun, A., Rodríguez-Patón, A.: Sequential SNP systems based on min/max spike number. Theor. Comput. Sci. **410**(30), 2982–2991 (2009)

15. Song, T., Xu, J., Pan, L.: On the universality and non-nniversality of spiking neural P systems with rules on synapses. IEEE Trans. Nanobiosci. **14**(8), 960–966 (2015)

16. Wang, X., Song, T., Gong, F., Zheng, P.: On the computational power of spiking neural P systems with self-organization. Sci. Rep. **6**, 27624 (2016). doi:10.1038/srep27624

17. Romero-Campero, F.J., Pérez-Jiménez, M.J.: Modelling gene expression control using P systems: the lac operon, a case study. BioSystems **91**(3), 438–457 (2008)

18. Enguix, G.B.: Preliminaries about some possible applications of P systems in linguistics. In: PĂun, G., Rozenberg, G., Salomaa, A., Zandron, C. (eds.) WMC 2002. LNCS, vol. 2597, pp. 74–89. Springer, Heidelberg (2003). doi:10.1007/3-540-36490-0_6

19. Enguix, G.B.: Unstable P systems: applications to linguistics. In: Mauri, G., Păun, G., Pérez-Jiménez, M.J., Rozenberg, G., Salomaa, A. (eds.) WMC 2004. LNCS, vol. 3365, pp. 190–209. Springer, Heidelberg (2005). doi:10.1007/978-3-540-31837-8_11

20. Song, T., Liu, X., Zeng, X.: Asynchronous spiking neural P systems with anti-spikes. Neural Process. Lett. **42**(3), 633–647 (2015)

21. Díaz-Pernil, D., Berciano, A., Pena-Cantillana, F., GutiéRrez-Naranjo, M.A.: Segmenting images with gradient-based edge detection using membrane computing. Pattern Recogn. Lett. **34**(8), 846–855 (2013)

22. Song, T., Zheng, H., He, J.: Solving vertex cover problem by tissue P systems with cell division. Appl. Math. Inform. Sci. **8**(1), 333–337 (2014)

23. Păun, G., Păun, R.: Membrane computing and economics: numerical P systems. Fundam. Inform. **73**(1–2), 213–227 (2006)

24. UCI Machine Learning Repository. http://ppage.psystems.eu/index.php/Software

25. Nguyen, V.T.: An Implementation of the Parallelism, Distribution and Nondeterminism of Membrane Computing models on Reconfigurable Hardware. University of South Australia, Adelaide (2010)

26. Zhang, G., Cheng, J., Wang, T., Wang, X., Zhu, J.: Membrane Computing: Theory and Applications. Science Press, Beijing (2015)

27. Rumbaugh, J., Blaha, M., Premerlani, W., Eddy, F., Lorensen, W.: Objectoriented Modeling and Design. PreNtice-Hall, Englewood Cliffs (1991)

28. Rumbaugh, J., Jacobson, I., Booch, G.: Unified Modeling Language Reference Manual. Pearson Higher Education, Upper Saddle River (2004)

Matrix Representation of Parallel Computation for Spiking Neural P Systems

Juan Hu[1], Guangchun Chen[1], Hong Peng[1(✉)], Jun Wang[2], Xiangnian Huang[1], and Xiaohui Luo[1]

[1] School of Computer and Software Engineering,
Xihua University, Chengdu 610039, Sichuan, China
ph.xhu@hotmail.com
[2] School of Electrical and Information Engineering,
Xihua University, Chengdu 610039, Sichuan, China

Abstract. Spiking neural P systems (in short, SN P systems) is a class of distributed parallel computing models. Parallel computation of matrix operations has been supported on some new computing devices such as GPU, which provides a promising way to simulate the parallel computation of SN P systems. In this paper a matrix representation method of parallel computation for SN P systems is developed. In firing mechanism of SN P systems, the delay factor plays the role of controlling the receiving of spikes in neurons and the opportunity of emitting the spikes after the firing. In order to achieve the parallel computation of SN P systems, several matrices or vectors are introduced to decompose the firing mechanism of neurons. The parallel computation procedure of SN P systems can be achieved by the operations of the matrices or vectors. Two examples are used to illustrate the parallel computation procedure using the matrix operations.

Keywords: P systems · Spiking neural P system · Parallel computing · Matrix representation

1 Introduction

Membrane computing initiated by Păun [1], was inspired from the structure and functioning of living cells as well as the interactions of living cells in tissues or higher order biological structures. Membrane computing is a class of distributed parallel computing models, known as P systems [2–7]. As one of main forms, spiking neural P systems (in short, SN P systems) were inspired by the neurophysiological behavior of neurons sending electrical impulses (spikes) along axons to other neurons under the framework of membrane computing [8]. A SN P system can be viewed as a net of neurons placed in the nodes of a directed graph whose arcs represent the synaptic connections among the neurons. The flow of information is inherently realized by the exciting of pulse potentials, which are encoded by the so-called spikes. The spikes, which are objects of a

© Springer Nature Singapore Pte Ltd. 2016
M. Gong et al. (Eds.): BIC-TA 2016, Part I, CCIS 681, pp. 187–199, 2016.
DOI: 10.1007/978-981-10-3611-8_18

unique type and are placed inside the neurons, can be sent from presynaptic to postsynaptic neurons according to specific firing/spiking rules. By applying a firing/spiking rule, some spikes are consumed and new spikes are produced, and the produced spikes are sent to all subsequent neurons. When a forgetting rule is applied, spikes are removed from neurons. More recently, a large number of variants of SN P systems have been proposed [8–19].

The parallel computation is an important feature of SN P systems, and it is attractive for the development of efficient algorithms in real-world applications. However, the parallel computation ability of SN P systems can not be implemented or simulated really because of the limitation of serial architecture of current computer. GPUs (Graphical Processing Units) and FPGA (Field-Programmable Gate Array) provided the implementation means of parallel computation, specially, parallel computation of matrix operations. In order to realize the parallel computation of SN P systems, a feasible way is to express its parallel computation procedure by matrix operations. For this, Zeng et al. [20] discussed matrix representations of two kinds of SN P systems without delay: SN P systems with extended rules and SN P systems with weights. Based on the matrix representations, Cabarle et al. [21–23] achieved the simulators of several SN P systems without delay. However, the delay is an important characteristic in firing mechanism of SN P systems. Therefore, it is an interesting topic how to build the matrix representation of SN P systems with delay because it is significant for implementation of their parallel computations on GPU/FPGA. This work focuses on the interesting issue and proposes a matrix representation method of SN P systems with delay. In order to decompose the firing mechanism of SN P systems, several matrices and vectors are introduced, such as rule delay matrix, spike consumption matrix, spike generation matrix and caching spike vector. Based on matrix operations, the matrices and vectors describe the firing mechanism of neurons in SN P systems, including the firing, spike consumption, time delay and emitting spike. The main contribution behind this work is that a matrix representation method of SN P systems (with delay) is developed.

The rest of this paper is organized as follows. First, we briefly review the definition of SN P systems in Sect. 2. The matrix representation method of SN P systems is discussed in Sect. 3. Two examples to illustrate the parallel computation procedure of SN P systems are provided in Sect. 4. The conclusions and future work on the topic are discussed in Sect. 5.

2   SN P Systems

In this section, we briefly review SN P systems in a computing version (i.e., able to take some inputs and provide some outputs). A more detailed description of SN P systems can be found in literatures [2, 8–10].

Definition 1. *A SN P system of degree $m \geq 1$, is a construct of the form*

$$\Pi = (A, \sigma_1, \sigma_2, \ldots, \sigma_m, syn, I, O)$$

where

(1) $A = \{a\}$ *is the singleton alphabet (the object a is called spike);*

(2) $\sigma_1, \ldots, \sigma_m$ *are neurons, of the form* $\sigma_i = (n_i, R_i)$, $1 \leq I \leq m$, *where*

   (i) $n_i \geq 0$ *is the initial number of spikes contained in neuron* σ_i;

   (ii) R_i *is a finite set of rules of the form*

$$E/a^c \rightarrow a^p; d$$

   where E is a regular expression over a, $c \geq 1$ *and* $p, d \geq 0$, *with* $c \geq p$; *if*
     $p = 0$, *then* $d = 0$.

(3) $syn \subseteq \{1, 2, \ldots, m\} \times \{1, 2, \ldots, m\}$ *with* $i \neq j$ *for all* $(i, j) \in syn$, $1 \leq i, j \leq$
   m *(synapses between neurons).*

(4) I *and* O *are input neuron set and output neuron set, respectively.*

A SN P system can be viewed as a directed graph in which the nodes denote its neurons and the arcs represent the synaptic connections among the neurons. Each neuron contains one or more spikes, or no spike. Under the control of firing/spiking rules, the spikes excited by a neuron will be transmitted into its subsequent neurons. The firing/spiking rules are of the form $E/a^c \rightarrow a^p; d$, where $d \geq 0$ is called the delay factor. If $p = d = 0$, $E/a^c \rightarrow a^p; d$ is written in the form $E/a^c \rightarrow \lambda$, known as forgetting rule. If $d = 0$, $E/a^c \rightarrow a^p; d$ can be written as a simple form, $E/a^c \rightarrow a^p$, called the firing/spiking rule without delay. Thus, SN P systems with the firing/spiking rules without delay is called SN P systems without delay in this work. The literature [20] has discussed matrix representation of SN P systems without delay. However, this paper focuses on matrix representation of SN P systems with delay.

The firing mechanism of neurons can be described as follows. If neuron σ_i contains k spikes, $a^k \in L(E)$, and $k \geq c$, then firing/spiking rule $E/a^c \rightarrow a^p; d$ can be applied. When the rule is applied, c spikes are consumed ($k - c$ spikes remain) and the neuron will produces p spikes after d time units. In case of no delay (i.e., $d = 0$), the produced spikes are emitted immediately. However, in the case of delay $d > 0$, delay mechanism will work as follows: if rule $E/a^c \rightarrow a^p; d$ in neuron σ_i is used at step t, the neuron is "closed" or "blocked" at steps $t, t+1, \ldots, t+d-1$, and it can not receive new spikes from other neurons; at step $t + d$, the neuron emits the produced spikes and becomes again open, hence it can receive the spikes from other neurons; the p spikes emitted by neuron σ_i are transmitted to all neurons σ_j such that $(i, j) \in syn$, hence each such neuron σ_j of them receives p spikes. A forgetting rule $a^c \rightarrow \lambda$ is applicable to a neuron whether the neuron contains exactly c spikes and then all c spikes are removed.

SN P systems are synchronized by a global clock, marking the time for the whole system. Besides, SN P systems are non deterministic because two rules $E_1/a^{c_1} \rightarrow a^{p_1}; d_1$ and $E_2/a^{c_2} \rightarrow a^{p_2}; d_2$ can have $L(E_1) \cap L(E_2) \neq \emptyset$. Therefore, it is possible that two or more rules of the system can be enabled in a neuron. In this case, one of them is non-deterministically chosen to be used. Moreover, in each time unit, if a neuron can use a rule, the rule must be used. Each neuron deals with its spikes in the sequential manner, only using one rule in each time unit, but the rules are used in parallel for all neurons of the system.

3   Matrix Representation of SN P Systems with Delay

Currently, parallel implementation of matrix operations has received an effective support on some new computing devices such as GPUs and FPGA. Therefore, an effective way to realize parallel computation of SN P systems is using the matrix operations to express its computing procedure. In this section, we will focus on the matrix representation of SN P systems with delay.

We assume the SN P system Π considered here has m neurons $\sigma_1, \sigma_2, \ldots, \sigma_m$ and n rules $r_1, r_2, \ldots, r_n$. Denote by $R_1, R_2, \ldots, R_n$ the firing rule sets of neurons $\sigma_1, \sigma_2, \ldots, \sigma_m$ respectively. We firstly define several matrices, vectors and operations as follows.

Definition 2 *(Relation Matrix). The relation matrix of Π, L, is defined by*

$$L = \left(l_{ij} \right)_{n \times m} \tag{1}$$

where

$$l_{ij} = \begin{cases} 1, \, if \, (i,j) \in syn \, and \, i \neq j \\ 0, \, elsewise \end{cases} \tag{2}$$

Matrix L describes relationship between neurons in Π. $l_{ij} = 1$ means a synapse connection from neuron σ_i to neuron σ_j where σ_j is a successor of σ_i. However, $l_{ij} = 0$ indicates no synapse connection from neuron σ_i to neuron σ_j. L is often asymmetric Maybe, this is, if $(i,j) \in syn$ then (j,i) is not necessarily be in syn.

Definition 3 *(Rule Delay Matrix). The rule delay matrix of Π, D, is defined by*

$$D = \left(\tau_{ij} \right)_{n \times m} \tag{3}$$

where

$$\tau_{ij} = \begin{cases} d_{ij}, \, if \, r_i \in R_j \\ 0, \quad elsewise \end{cases} \tag{4}$$

where d_{ij} is the delay of ith firing rule $E_{ij}/a^{s_{ij}} \to a^{p_{ij}}; d_{ij}$ in neuron σ_j.

Matrix D expresses the delay factors of firing rules in neurons of Π. The matrix will be used to control the waiting times until spikes are emitted after neurons fire.

Definition 4 *(Spike Consumption Matrix). The spike consumption matrix of Π, U, is defined by*

$$U = \left(u_{ij} \right)_{n \times m} \tag{5}$$

where u_{ij} expresses the number of the consumed spikes when ith firing rule $E_{ij}/a^{s_{ij}} \to a^{p_{ij}}; d_{ij}$ in neuron σ_j fires.

$$u_{ij} = \begin{cases} s_{ij}, \, if \, r_i \in R_j \\ 0, \quad elsewise \end{cases} \tag{6}$$

The matrix indicates that if firing rule $r_i : E_{ij}/a^{s_{ij}} \rightarrow a^{p_{ij}}; d_{ij}$ is enabled and applied and $r_i \in R_j$, then $u_{ij} = s_{ij}$; elsewise $u_{ij} = 0$.

Definition 5 *(Spike Generation Matrix). The spike generation matrix of Π, V, is defined by*

$$V = \left(v_{ij}\right)_{n \times m} \tag{7}$$

where v_{ij} denotes the number of the generated spikes after ith firing rule $E_{ij}/a^{s_{ij}} \rightarrow a^{p_{ij}}; d_{ij}$ in neuron σ_j fires.

$$v_{ij} = \begin{cases} p_{ij}, & if \ r_i \in R_j \\ 0, & elsewise \end{cases} \tag{8}$$

The matrix indicates that if $r_i \in R_j$ and firing rule $r_i : E_{ij}/a^{s_{ij}} \rightarrow a^{p_{ij}}; d_{ij}$ is applied, then $v_{ij} = p_{ij}$; elsewise $v_{ij} = 0$.

Definition 6 *(Countdown Operation). Suppose $T = (t_1, t_2, \ldots, t_m)$ is a vector, $t_i \in N, i = 1, 2, \ldots, m$. The countdown operation of T is defined by*

$$T^{\downarrow} = (t_1, t_2, \ldots, t_m)^{\downarrow} = (t_1^{\downarrow}, t_2^{\downarrow}, \ldots, t_m^{\downarrow}) \tag{9}$$

where

$$t_i^{\downarrow} = \begin{cases} t_i - 1, & if \ t_i \geq 1 \\ 0, & elsewise \end{cases} \tag{10}$$

In Definition 6, vector T is called waiting time vector, each of which indicates the waiting time of the corresponding neuron to be opened. In this work, rule delay matrix and countdown operation will be used to realize the delay mechanism of SN P systems.

Definition 7 *(Caching Spike Vector). The vector $W_k = (w_1^{(k)}, w_2^{(k)}, \ldots, w_m^{(k)})$ is called the caching spike vector at kth computing step, where $w_i^{(k)}$ is the number of the cached spikes in neuron σ_i at kth computing step, $i = 1, 2, \ldots, m$. Initially, let $W_0 = (0, 0, \ldots, 0)$.*

Definition 8 *(Waiting Time Vector). The vector $T_k = (t_1^{(k)}, t_2^{(k)}, \ldots, t_m^{(k)})$ is called the waiting time vector at kth computing step, where $t_i^{(k)}$ expresses the residual time that neuron σ_i waits for at kth computing step, $i = 1, 2, \ldots, m$. Initially, let $T_0 = (0, 0, \ldots, 0)$.*

Definition 9 *(Spiking Vector). The vector $X_k = (x_1^{(k)}, x_2^{(k)}, \ldots, x_m^{(k)})$ is called the spiking vector at kth computing step, where $x_i^{(k)}$ expresses the number of spikes to be sent in neuron σ_i at kth computing step. Initially, let $X_0 = (0, 0, \ldots, 0)$.*

Based on firing principle of neurons, $x_i^{(k)}$ can be computed by

$$x_i^{(k)} = \begin{cases} w_i^{(k)}, & if \ t_i^{(k)} = 0 \\ 0, & elsewise \end{cases} \tag{11}$$

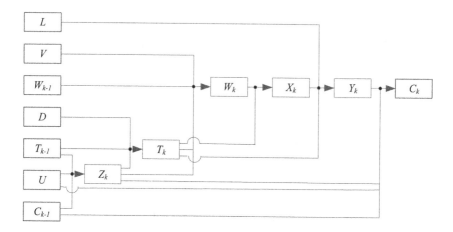

Fig. 1. The computing procedure of parallel computing for SN P systems.

where $w_i^{(k)}$ is the number of the cached spikes in neuron σ_i and $t_i^{(k)}$ denotes the residual time that neuron σ_i waits for at kth computing step, $i = 1, 2, \ldots, m$. For convenience, we formally denote $X_k = W_k \triangleright T_k$.

Definition 10 (*Receiving Vector*). *The vector* $Y_k = (y_1^{(k)}, y_2^{(k)}, \ldots, y_m^{(k)})$ *is called the receiving vector at kth computing step, where $y_i^{(k)}$ expresses the number of the spikes received in neuron σ_i at kth computing step. Initially, let $Y_0 = (0, 0, \ldots, 0)$.*

Based on firing principle of neurons, $y_i^{(k)}$ can be computed by

$$y_i^{(k)} = \begin{cases} X_k \cdot [L]_i, & \text{if } t_i^{(k)} = 0 \\ 0, & \text{elsewise} \end{cases} \tag{12}$$

where $[L]_i$ is ith column of relation matrix L, $i = 1, 2, \ldots, m$. For convenience, we formally denote $Y_k = (X_k \cdot L) \triangleright T_k$.

Definition 11 (*Configuration Vector*). *The vector* $C_k = (n_1^{(k)}, n_2^{(k)}, \ldots, n_m^{(k)})$ *is called the configuration vector of Π after kth computing step, where $n_i^{(k)}$ is the number of spikes contained in neuron σ_i after kth computing step, $i = 1, 2, \ldots, m$.*

Denote by vector $C_0 = (n_1^{(0)}, n_2^{(0)}, \ldots, n_m^{(0)})$ the initial configuration vector of Π, where $n_i^{(0)}$ is the initial number of spikes in neuron σ_i, $i = 1, 2, \ldots, m$. Therefore, computing procedure of SN P system Π can be expressed as $C_0 \overset{1}{\Rightarrow} C_1 \overset{2}{\Rightarrow} C_2 \overset{3}{\Rightarrow} \cdots \overset{k}{\Rightarrow} C_k \overset{k+1}{\Rightarrow} \cdots$.

Definition 12 (*Rule Firing Vector*). *The vector* $Z_k = (z_1^{(k)}, z_2^{(k)}, \ldots, z_n^{(k)})$ *is called the rule firing vector after kth computing step, where*

$$z_i^{(k)} = \begin{cases} 1, & \text{if rule } r_i \text{ fires and } t_i^{(k-1)\downarrow} = 0 \\ 0, & \text{elsewise} \end{cases} \tag{13}$$

Table 1. The parallel computation algorithm for SN P systems

Input: C_0, W_0, T_0, U, V, D and L;
Output: C_k;
Begin
for $k = 1, 2, \cdots$
$Z_k \leftarrow \overbrace{(C_{k-1}, U, T_{k-1}^{\downarrow})}$;
$T_k \leftarrow T_{k-1}^{\downarrow} + Z_k \cdot D$;
$W_k \leftarrow W_{k-1} - W_{k-1} \triangleright T_k + Z_k \cdot V$;
$X_k \leftarrow W_k \triangleright T_k$;
$Y_k \leftarrow (X_k \cdot L) \triangleright T_k$;
$C_k \leftarrow C_{k-1} - Z_k \cdot U + Y_k$;
end for
End.

Note that Z_k is an indicator vector, each component of which indicates whether the corresponding rule fires and opened.

Lemma 1. $Z_k = \overbrace{(C_{k-1}, U, T_{k-1}^{\downarrow})}$, where $\overbrace{(\cdot, \cdot, \cdot)}$ is called the firing operation.

Proof. According to firing mechanism of neurons, if the number of spikes contained in neuron σ_j meets regular expression E of rule r_i (related with C_{k-1} and U) and $t_i^{(k-1)\downarrow} = 0$, then $z_i^{(k)} = 1$; elsewise $z_i^{(k)} = 0$. Therefore, we have

$$Z_k = \overbrace{(C_{k-1}, U, T_{k-1}^{\downarrow})}.$$

Lemma 2. $T_k = T_{k-1}^{\downarrow} + \overbrace{(C_{k-1}, U, T_{k-1}^{\downarrow})} \cdot D$

Proof. Note that T_k is a waiting time vector, each component of which indicates whether the corresponding neuron is closed and has waiting time to be opened. According to firing mechanism of neurons, if a neuron is closed (after firing) and waits to open, then $t_{i,k} = t_{i,k-1} - 1$; if a neuron is enabled and fires and delay factor of the corresponding rule has $d_i > 0$, then $t_{i,k} = Z_i \cdot [D]_j$, where $[D]_j$ is jth column of D. Thus, Lemma 2 can be concluded by Lemma 1.

Lemma 3. $W_k = W_{k-1} - W_{k-1} \triangleright T_k + \overbrace{(C_{k-1}, U, T_{k-1}^{\downarrow})} \cdot V$

Proof. Note that W_k is a caching spike vector, each component of which indicates the number of spikes cached in the corresponding neuron. According to firing mechanism of neurons, $W_k = W_{k-1} - W' + W''$, where W' is the emitted spike vector and W'' is the spike vector to be cached at k computing step. By Definition 9, we have $W' = W_{k-1} \triangleright T_k$. Since V is the spike generation matrix, $W'' = Z_k \cdot V$ can be concluded by Definitions 9 and 12. Based on Lemma 1, we have $W'' = \overbrace{(C_{k-1}, U, T_{k-1}^{\downarrow})} \cdot V$.

Based on Lemma 2 and 3, we can conclude matrix representation of parallel computation for SN P systems as follows.

Theorem 1 *(Matrix Representation). The computation procedure of Π is given by*

$$C_k = C_{k-1} + ((W_k \triangleright T_k) \cdot L) \triangleright T_k - \overbrace{(C_{k-1}, U, T_{k-1}^{\downarrow})} \cdot U. \tag{14}$$

Proof Based on firing mechanism of neurons, $C_k = C_{k-1} + C' - C''$, where C' denotes the received new spike vector and C'' denotes the consumed spike vector at kth computing step. By Definitions 9 and 10, we have $C' = ((W_k \triangleright T_k) \cdot L) \triangleright T_k$. Note that U is spike consumption matrix. Based on Lemma 1, we have $C'' = Z_k \cdot U = \overbrace{(C_{k-1}, U, T_{k-1}^{\downarrow})} \cdot U$. Thus, the theorem is proven.

Based on Theorem 1, the developed parallel computing algorithm for SN P systems based on matrix operations is provided in Table 1 in an iteration algorithm, and its computing procedure is shown in Fig. 1.

4   Two Illustration Examples

In this section, we use two examples to illustrate parallel computation procedure of SN P systems with delay.

Example 1 SN P system Π_1, shown in Fig. 2, has three neurons ($\sigma_1, \sigma_2, \sigma_3$) and three rules ($r_1, r_2, r_3$). $R_1 = \{r_1\}$, $R_2 = \{r_2\}$ and $R_3 = \{r_3\}$.

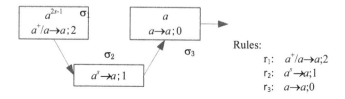

Fig. 2. SN P system Π_1 and its firing rules.

According to the Definitions 2, 3, 4 and 5, the relation matrix, rule delay matrix, spike consumption matrix and spike generation matrix of Π_1 are, respectively

$$L = \begin{pmatrix} 0 & 1 & 0 \\ 0 & 0 & 1 \\ 0 & 0 & 0 \end{pmatrix}, D = \begin{pmatrix} 2 & 0 & 0 \\ 0 & 1 & 0 \\ 0 & 0 & 0 \end{pmatrix}, U = \begin{pmatrix} 1 & 0 & 0 \\ 0 & s & 0 \\ 0 & 0 & 1 \end{pmatrix}, V = \begin{pmatrix} 1 & 0 & 0 \\ 0 & 1 & 0 \\ 0 & 0 & 1 \end{pmatrix}$$

Initially, $C_0 = (2s - 1, 0, 1)$, $W_0 = (0, 0, 0)$, $T_0 = (0, 0, 0)$. The parallel computation procedure of Π_1 is provided as follows.

Step (1) $Z_1 = \overbrace{(C_0, U, T_0^\downarrow)} = (1,0,1)$, $T_1 = T_0^\downarrow + Z_1 \cdot D = (2,0,0)$,
$W_1 = W_0 - W_0 \triangleright T_1 + Z_1 \cdot V = (1,0,1)$, $X_1 = W_1 \triangleright T_1 = (0,0,1)$,
$Y_1 = (X_1 \cdot L) \triangleright T_1 = (0,0,0)$, $C_1 = C_0 - Z_1 \cdot U + Y_1 = (2s - 2, 0, 0)$.

Step (2) $Z_2 = \overbrace{(C_1, U, T_1^\downarrow)} = (0,0,0)$, $T_2 = T_1^\downarrow + Z_2 \cdot D = (1,0,0)$,
$W_2 = W_1 - W_1 \triangleright T_2 + Z_2 \cdot V = (1,0,0)$, $X_2 = W_2 \triangleright T_2 = (0,0,0)$,
$Y_2 = (X_2 \cdot L) \triangleright T_2 = (0,0,0)$, $C_2 = C_1 - Z_2 \cdot U + Y_2 = (2s - 2, 0, 0)$.

Step (3) $Z_3 = \overbrace{(C_2, U, T_2^\downarrow)} = (0,0,0)$, $T_3 = T_2^\downarrow + Z_3 \cdot D = (0,0,0)$,
$W_3 = W_2 - W_2 \triangleright T_3 + Z_3 \cdot V = (1,0,0)$, $X_3 = W_3 \triangleright T_3 = (1,0,0)$,
$Y_3 = (X_3 \cdot L) \triangleright T_3 = (0,1,0)$, $C_3 = C_2 - Z_3 \cdot U + Y_3 = (2s - 2, 1, 0)$.

Step (4) $Z_4 = \overbrace{(C_3, U, T_3^\downarrow)} = (1,0,0)$, $T_4 = T_3^\downarrow + Z_4 \cdot D = (2,0,0)$,
$W_4 = W_3 - W_3 \triangleright T_4 + Z_4 \cdot V = (1,0,0)$, $X_4 = W_4 \triangleright T_3 = (0,0,0)$,
$Y_4 = (X_4 \cdot L) \triangleright T_4 = (0,0,0)$, $C_4 = C_3 - Z_4 \cdot U + Y_4 = (2s - 3, 1, 0)$.

Step (5) $Z_5 = \overbrace{(C_4, U, T_4^\downarrow)} = (0,0,0)$, $T_5 = T_4^\downarrow + Z_5 \cdot D = (1,0,0)$,
$W_5 = W_4 - W_4 \triangleright T_5 + Z_5 \cdot V = (1,0,0)$, $X_5 = W_5 \triangleright T_4 = (0,0,0)$,
$Y_5 = (X_5 \cdot L) \triangleright T_5 = (0,0,0)$, $C_5 = C_4 - Z_5 \cdot U + Y_5 = (2s - 3, 1, 0)$.

Step (6) $Z_6 = \overbrace{(C_5, U, T_5^\downarrow)} = (0,0,0)$, $T_6 = T_5^\downarrow + Z_6 \cdot D = (0,0,0)$,
$W_6 = W_5 - W_5 \triangleright T_6 + Z_6 \cdot V = (1,0,0)$, $X_6 = W_6 \triangleright T_5 = (1,0,0)$,
$Y_6 = (X_6 \cdot L) \triangleright T_6 = (0,1,0)$, $C_6 = C_5 - Z_6 \cdot U + Y_6 = (2s - 3, 2, 0)$.

According to parallel computing algorithm described above, we easily obtain the computing results in the subsequent steps. Table 2 gives the computing results of Π_1 in the first 15 steps.

Example 2 SN P system Π_2, shown in Fig. 3, has six neurons ($\sigma_1, \sigma_2, \sigma_3, \sigma_4, \sigma_5, \sigma_6$) and eleven rules ($r_1, r_2, r_3, r_4, r_5, r_6, r_7, r_8, r_9, r_{10}, r_{11}$). $R_1 = \{r_1, r_2, r_3\}$, $R_2 = \{r_4, r_5\}$, $R_3 = \{r_6\}$, $R_4 = \{r_7\}$, $R_5 = \{r_8\}$ and $R_6 = \{r_9, r_{10}, r_{11}\}$.

Based on the definitions above, the relation matrix, rule delay matrix, spike consumption matrix and spike generation matrix of Π_2 are, respectively

$$L = \begin{pmatrix} 0 & 1 & 1 & 0 & 0 & 0 \\ 1 & 0 & 0 & 0 & 0 & 1 \\ 1 & 0 & 0 & 1 & 1 & 1 \\ 0 & 0 & 0 & 0 & 0 & 1 \\ 0 & 0 & 0 & 0 & 0 & 1 \\ 1 & 0 & 0 & 0 & 0 & 0 \end{pmatrix}, D = \begin{pmatrix} 2 & 1 & 0 & 0 & 0 & 0 & 0 & 0 & 0 & 0 & 0 \\ 0 & 0 & 0 & 1 & 0 & 0 & 0 & 0 & 0 & 0 & 0 \\ 0 & 0 & 0 & 0 & 0 & 1 & 0 & 0 & 0 & 0 & 0 \\ 0 & 0 & 0 & 0 & 0 & 0 & 2 & 0 & 0 & 0 & 0 \\ 0 & 0 & 0 & 0 & 0 & 0 & 0 & 1 & 0 & 0 & 0 \\ 0 & 0 & 0 & 0 & 0 & 0 & 0 & 0 & 0 & 0 & 0 \end{pmatrix}^T$$

$$U = \begin{pmatrix} 4 & 2 & 1 & 0 & 0 & 0 & 0 & 0 & 0 & 0 & 0 \\ 0 & 0 & 0 & 1 & 1 & 0 & 0 & 0 & 0 & 0 & 0 \\ 0 & 0 & 0 & 0 & 0 & 1 & 0 & 0 & 0 & 0 & 0 \\ 0 & 0 & 0 & 0 & 0 & 0 & 1 & 0 & 0 & 0 & 0 \\ 0 & 0 & 0 & 0 & 0 & 0 & 0 & 1 & 0 & 0 & 0 \\ 0 & 0 & 0 & 0 & 0 & 0 & 0 & 0 & 1 & 2 & 3 \end{pmatrix}^T, V = \begin{pmatrix} 1 & 1 & 0 & 0 & 0 & 0 & 0 & 0 & 0 & 0 & 0 \\ 0 & 0 & 0 & 1 & 1 & 0 & 0 & 0 & 0 & 0 & 0 \\ 0 & 0 & 0 & 0 & 0 & 1 & 0 & 0 & 0 & 0 & 0 \\ 0 & 0 & 0 & 0 & 0 & 0 & 1 & 0 & 0 & 0 & 0 \\ 0 & 0 & 0 & 0 & 0 & 0 & 0 & 1 & 0 & 0 & 0 \\ 0 & 0 & 0 & 0 & 0 & 0 & 0 & 0 & 1 & 0 & 0 \end{pmatrix}^T$$

Table 2. The computing results of Π_1 in the first 15 steps

k	Z_k	T_k	W_k	X_k	Y_k	C_k
0	-	(0,0,0)	(0,0,0)	-	-	(2s-1,0,1)
1	(1,0,1)	(2,0,0)	(1,0,1)	(0,0,1)	(0,0,0)	(2s-2,0,0)
2	(0,0,0)	(1,0,0)	(1,0,0)	(0,0,0)	(0,0,0)	(2s-2,0,0)
3	(0,0,0)	(0,0,0)	(1,0,0)	(1,0,0)	(0,1,0)	(2s-2,1,0)
4	(1,0,0)	(2,0,0)	(1,0,0)	(0,0,0)	(0,0,0)	(2s-3,1,0)
5	(0,0,0)	(1,0,0)	(1,0,0)	(0,0,0)	(0,0,0)	(2s-3,1,0)
6	(0,0,0)	(0,0,0)	(1,0,0)	(1,0,0)	(0,1,0)	(2s-3,2,0)
7	(1,0,0)	(2,0,0)	(1,0,0)	(0,0,0)	(0,0,0)	(2s-4,2,0)
8	(0,0,0)	(1,0,0)	(1,0,0)	(0,0,0)	(0,0,0)	(2s-4,2,0)
9	(0,0,0)	(0,0,0)	(1,0,0)	(0,1,0)	(0,0,0)	(2s-4,3,0)
10	(1,0,0)	(2,0,0)	(1,0,0)	(0,0,0)	(0,0,0)	(2s-5,3,0)
11	(0,0,0)	(1,0,0)	(1,0,0)	(0,0,0)	(0,0,0)	(2s-5,3,0)
12	(0,0,0)	(0,0,0)	(1,0,0)	(1,0,0)	(0,1,0)	(2s-5,4,0)
13	(1,0,0)	(2,0,0)	(1,0,0)	(0,0,0)	(0,0,0)	(2s-6,4,0)
14	(0,0,0)	(1,0,0)	(1,0,0)	(0,0,0)	(0,0,0)	(2s-6,4,0)
15	(0,0,0)	(0,0,0)	(1,0,0)	(1,0,0)	(0,1,0)	(2s-6,5,0)

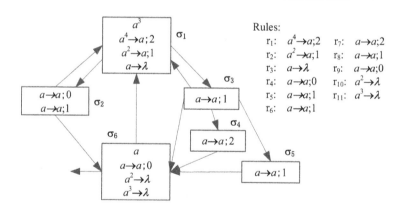

Fig. 3. SN P system Π_2 and its firing rules.

Initially, $C_0 = (3, 0, 0, 0, 0, 1)$, $W_0 = (0, 0, 0, 0, 0, 0)$, $T_0 = (0, 0, 0, 0, 0, 0)$. The parallel computation procedure of Π_2 is provided as follows.

Step (1) $Z_1 = (C_0, U, T_0^\downarrow) = (0, 0, 0, 0, 0, 0, 0, 0, 1, 0, 0)$,
$T_1 = T_0^\downarrow + Z_1 \cdot D = (0, 0, 0, 0, 0, 0)$, $W_1 = W_0 - W_0 \triangleright T_1 + Z_1 \cdot V = (0, 0, 0, 0, 0, 1)$,
$X_1 = W_1 \triangleright T_1 = (0, 0, 0, 0, 0, 1)$, $Y_1 = (X_1 \cdot L) \triangleright T_1 = (1, 0, 0, 0, 0, 0)$,
$C_1 = C_0 - Z_1 \cdot U + Y_1 = (4, 0, 0, 0, 0, 0)$.

Step (2) $Z_2 = \overbrace{(C_1, U, T_1^{\downarrow})}^{\cdots} = (1, 0, 0, 0, 0, 0, 0, 0, 0, 0, 0)$,
$T_2 = T_1^{\downarrow} + Z_2 \cdot D = (2, 0, 0, 0, 0, 0)$, $W_2 = W_1 - W_1 \triangleright T_2 + Z_2 \cdot V = (1, 0, 0, 0, 0, 0)$,
$X_2 = W_2 \triangleright T_2 = (0, 0, 0, 0, 0, 0)$, $Y_2 = (X_2 \cdot L) \triangleright T_2 = (0, 0, 0, 0, 0, 0)$,
$C_2 = C_1 - Z_2 \cdot U + Y_2 = (0, 0, 0, 0, 0, 0)$.

Step (3) $Z_3 = \overbrace{(C_2, U, T_2^{\downarrow})}^{\cdots} = (0, 0, 0, 0, 0, 0, 0, 0, 0, 0, 0)$,
$T_3 = T_2^{\downarrow} + Z_3 \cdot D = (1, 0, 0, 0, 0, 0)$, $W_3 = W_2 - W_2 \triangleright T_3 + Z_3 \cdot V = (1, 0, 0, 0, 0, 0)$,
$X_3 = W_3 \triangleright T_3 = (0, 0, 0, 0, 0, 0)$, $Y_3 = (X_3 \cdot L) \triangleright T_3 = (0, 0, 0, 0, 0, 0)$,
$C_3 = C_2 - Z_3 \cdot U + Y_3 = (0, 0, 0, 0, 0, 0)$.

Step (4) $Z_4 = \overbrace{(C_3, U, T_3^{\downarrow})}^{\cdots} = (0, 0, 0, 0, 0, 0, 0, 0, 0, 0, 0)$,
$T_4 = T_3^{\downarrow} + Z_4 \cdot D = (0, 0, 0, 0, 0, 0)$, $W_4 = W_3 - W_3 \triangleright T_4 + Z_4 \cdot V = (1, 0, 0, 0, 0, 0)$,
$X_4 = W_4 \triangleright T_3 = (1, 0, 0, 0, 0, 0)$, $Y_4 = (X_4 \cdot L) \triangleright T_4 = (0, 1, 1, 0, 0, 0)$,
$C_4 = C_3 - Z_4 \cdot U + Y_4 = (0, 1, 1, 0, 0, 0)$.

Step (5) $Z_5 = \overbrace{(C_4, U, T_4^{\downarrow})}^{\cdots} = (0, 0, 0, 1, 0, 1, 0, 0, 0, 0, 0)$,
$T_5 = T_4^{\downarrow} + Z_5 \cdot D = (0, 0, 1, 0, 0, 0)$, $W_5 = W_4 - W_4 \triangleright T_5 + Z_5 \cdot V = (0, 1, 1, 0, 0, 0)$,
$X_5 = W_5 \triangleright T_4 = (0, 1, 0, 0, 0, 0)$, $Y_5 = (X_5 \cdot L) \triangleright T_5 = (1, 0, 0, 0, 0, 1)$,
$C_5 = C_4 - Z_5 \cdot U + Y_5 = (1, 0, 0, 0, 0, 1)$.

Step (6) $Z_6 = \overbrace{(C_5, U, T_5^{\downarrow})}^{\cdots} = (0, 0, 1, 0, 0, 0, 0, 0, 1, 0, 0)$,
$T_6 = T_5^{\downarrow} + Z_6 \cdot D = (0, 0, 0, 0, 0, 0)$, $W_6 = W_5 - W_5 \triangleright T_6 + Z_6 \cdot V = (0, 0, 0, 0, 0, 0)$,
$X_6 = W_6 \triangleright T_5 = (0, 0, 1, 0, 0, 1)$, $Y_6 = (X_6 \cdot L) \triangleright T_6 = (2, 0, 0, 1, 1, 1)$,
$C_6 = C_5 - Z_6 \cdot U + Y_6 = (2, 0, 0, 1, 1, 1)$.

Table 3. The computing results of Π_2 in the first 15 steps

k	Z_k	T_k	W_k	X_k	Y_k	C_k
0	$\cdots$	(0,0,0,0,0,0)	(0,0,0,0,0,0)	$\cdots$	$\cdots$	(3,0,0,0,0,1)
1	(0,0,0,0,0,0,0,0,1,0,0)	(0,0,0,0,0,0)	(0,0,0,0,0,1)	(0,0,0,0,0,1)	(1,0,0,0,0,0)	(4,0,0,0,0,0)
2	(1,0,0,0,0,0,0,0,0,0,0)	(2,0,0,0,0,0)	(1,0,0,0,0,0)	(0,0,0,0,0,0)	(0,0,0,0,0,0)	(0,0,0,0,0,0)
3	(0,0,0,0,0,0,0,0,0,0,0)	(1,0,0,0,0,0)	(1,0,0,0,0,0)	(0,0,0,0,0,0)	(0,0,0,0,0,0)	(0,0,0,0,0,0)
4	(0,0,0,0,0,0,0,0,0,0,0)	(0,0,0,0,0,0)	(1,0,0,0,0,0)	(1,0,0,0,0,0)	(0,1,1,0,0,0)	(0,1,1,0,0,0)
5	(0,0,0,1,0,1,0,0,0,0,0)	(0,0,1,0,0,0)	(0,1,1,0,0,0)	(0,1,0,0,0,0)	(1,0,0,0,0,1)	(1,0,0,0,0,1)
6	(0,0,1,0,0,0,0,0,1,0,0)	(0,0,0,0,0,0)	(0,0,1,0,0,1)	(0,0,1,0,0,1)	(2,0,0,1,1,1)	(2,0,0,1,1,1)
7	(0,1,0,0,0,0,1,1,1,0,0)	(1,0,0,2,1,0)	(1,0,0,1,1,1)	(0,0,0,0,0,1)	(0,0,0,0,0,0)	(0,0,0,0,0,0)
8	(0,0,0,0,0,0,0,0,0,0,0)	(0,0,0,1,0,0)	(1,0,0,1,1,0)	(1,0,0,0,1,0)	(0,1,1,0,0,1)	(0,1,1,0,0,1)
9	(0,0,0,0,1,1,0,0,1,0,0)	(0,1,1,0,0,0)	(0,1,1,1,0,1)	(0,0,0,1,0,1)	(1,0,0,0,0,1)	(1,0,0,0,0,1)
10	(0,0,1,0,0,0,0,0,1,0,0)	(0,0,0,0,0,0)	(0,1,1,0,0,1)	(0,1,1,0,0,1)	(3,0,0,1,1,2)	(3,0,0,1,1,2)
11	(0,0,0,0,0,0,1,1,0,1,0)	(0,0,0,2,1,0)	(0,0,0,1,1,0)	(0,0,0,0,0,0)	(0,0,0,0,0,0)	(3,0,0,0,0,0)
12	(0,0,0,0,0,0,0,0,0,0,0)	(0,0,0,1,0,0)	(0,0,0,1,1,0)	(0,0,0,0,1,0)	(0,0,0,0,0,1)	(3,0,0,0,0,1)
13	(0,0,0,0,0,0,0,0,1,0,0)	(0,0,0,0,0,0)	(0,0,0,1,0,1)	(0,0,0,1,0,1)	(1,0,0,0,0,1)	(4,0,0,0,0,1)
14	(1,0,0,0,0,0,0,0,1,0,0)	(2,0,0,0,0,0)	(1,0,0,0,0,1)	(0,0,0,0,0,1)	(0,0,0,0,0,0)	(0,0,0,0,0,0)
15	(0,0,0,0,0,0,0,0,0,0,0)	(0,0,0,0,0,0)	(1,0,0,0,0,0)	(1,0,0,0,0,0)	(0,1,1,0,0,0)	(0,1,1,0,0,0)

Based on parallel computing algorithm described above, we can obtain the computing results in the subsequent steps. Table 3 gives the computing results of Π_2 in the first 15 steps.

5   Conclusions and Future Work

The distributed parallel computation is an attractive feature of SN P systems. However, parallel computation ability of SN P systems can not really be simulated on the current computer due to the restriction of serial architecture. Currently, some new computing devices such as GPU and FPGA, which support the parallel computation, provide an way to implement the parallel computation of SN P systems. This paper presented a matrix representation for SN P systems with delay, where several matrices, vectors and operations were introduced to express the parallel computation procedure of SN P systems. Since matrix operations are easily implemented on GPU and FPGA, the proposed representation method can help to achieve the parallel computation of SN P systems with delay on GPU or FPGA. Therefore, the future work is that based on the matrix representation, we will further discuss the implementation of SN P systems with delay and its variants on GPUs or FPGA.

Acknowledgements. This work was partially supported by the National Natural Science Foundation of China (No. 61472328), Research Fund of Sichuan Science and Technology Project (No. 2015HH0057) and the key equipment project of Sichuan Provincial Economic and Information Committee (No. [2014]128), China.

References

1. Păun, G.: Computing with membranes. J. Comput. Syst. Sci. **61**(1), 108–143 (2000)
2. Păun, G., Rozenberg, G., Salomaa, A.: The Oxford Handbook of Membrance Computing. Oxford Unversity Press, New York (2010)
3. Peng, H., Wang, J., Pérez-Jiménez, M.J., Riscos-Núñez, A.: An unsupervised learning algorithm for membrane computing. Inf. Sci. **304**, 80–91 (2015)
4. Peng, H., Wang, J., Shi, P., Riscos-Núñez, A., Pérez-Jiménez, M.J.: An automatic clustering algorithm inspired by membrane computing. Pattern Recognit. Lett. **68**, 34–40 (2015)
5. Peng, H., Wang, J., Shi, P., Pérez-Jiménez, M.J., Riscos-Núñez, A.: An extended membrane system with active membrane to solve automatic fuzzy clustering problems. Int. J. Neural Syst. **26**, 1–17 (2016)
6. Wang, J., Shi, P., Peng, H.: Membrane computing model for IIR filter design. Inf. Sci. **329**, 164–176 (2016)
7. Zhang, G., Gheorghe, M., Pan, L., Pérez-Jiménez, M.J.: Evolutionary membrane computing: a comprehensive survey and new results. Inf. Sci. **279**, 528–551 (2014)
8. Ionescu, M., Păun, G., Yokomori, T.: Spiking neural P systems. Fundam. Inform. **71**(2–3), 279–308 (2006)
9. Păun, G., Pérez-Jiménez, M.J., Rozenberg, G.: Spike train in spiking neural P systems. Int. J. Found. Comput. Sci. **17**(4), 975–1002 (2006)

10. Chen, H., Ishdorj, T.-O., Păun, G., Pérez-Jiménez, M.J.: Handling languages with spiking neural P systems with extended rules. Rom. J. Inf. Sci. Technol. **9**(3), 151–162 (2006)
11. Pan, L.Q., Wang, J., Hoogeboom, H.J.: Spiking neural P systems with astrocytes. Neural Comput. **24**, 805–825 (2012)
12. Song, T., Pan, L., Păun, G.: Asynchronous spiking neural P systems with local synchronization. Inf. Sci. **219**, 197–207 (2013)
13. Zhang, X.Y., Jiang, Y., Pan, L.Q.: A variant of P machine: splicing P machine. J. Comput. Theor. Nanosci. **10**, 1376–1384 (2013)
14. Zeng, X.X., Zhang, X.Y., Song, T., Pan, L.Q.: Spiking neural P systems with thresholds. Neural Comput. **26**, 1340–1361 (2014)
15. Zhang, G.X., Rong, H., Neri, F., Pérez-Jiménez, M.J.: An optimization spiking neural P system for approximately solving combinatorial optimization problems. Int. J. Neural Syst. **24**, 1–16 (2014)
16. Wang, J., Zhou, L., Peng, H., Zhang, G.: An extended spiking neural P system for fuzzy knowledge representation. Int. J. Innov. Comput. Inf. Control **7**(7A), 3709–3724 (2011)
17. Wang, J., Shi, P., Peng, H., Pérez-Jiménez, M.J., Wang, T.: Weighted fuzzy spiking neural P system. IEEE Trans. Fuzzy Syst. **21**, 209–220 (2013)
18. Peng, H., Wang, J., Pérez-Jiménez, M.J., Wang, H., Shao, J., Wang, T.: Fuzzy reasoning spiking neural P system for fault diagnosis. Inf. Sci. **235**, 106–116 (2013)
19. Wang, J., Peng, H.: Adaptive fuzzy spiking neural P systems for fuzzy inference and learning. Int. J. Comput. Math. **90**(4), 857–868 (2013)
20. Zeng, X., Adorna, H., Martínez-del-Amor, M.Á., Pan, L., Pérez-Jiménez, M.J.: Matrix representation of spiking neural P systems. In: Gheorghe, M., Hinze, T., Păun, G., Rozenberg, G., Salomaa, A. (eds.) CMC 2010. LNCS, vol. 6501, pp. 377–391. Springer, Heidelberg (2010). doi:10.1007/978-3-642-18123-8_29
21. Cabarle, F.G., Adorna, H., Martínez-del-Amor, M.A., Pérez-Jiménez, M.J.: Spiking neural P system simulations on a high performance GPU platform. In: Xiang, Y., Cuzzocrea, A., Hobbs, M., Zhou, W. (eds.) ICA3PP 2011. LNCS, vol. 7017, pp. 99–108. Springer, Heidelberg (2011). doi:10.1007/978-3-642-24669-2_10
22. Cabarle, F., Adorna, H., Martínez-del-Amor, M.A.: Simulating spiking neural P systems without delays using GPUs. Int. J. Nat. Comput. Res. **2**(2), 19–31 (2011)
23. Cabarle, F.G.C., Adorna, H., Martínez, M.A.: A spiking neural p system simulator based on CUDA. In: Gheorghe, M., Păun, G., Rozenberg, G., Salomaa, A., Verlan, S. (eds.) CMC 2011. LNCS, vol. 7184, pp. 87–103. Springer, Heidelberg (2012). doi:10.1007/978-3-642-28024-5_8

The Computational Power of Array P System with Mate Operation

P. Helen Chandra$^{(\boxtimes)}$, S.M. Saroja T. Kalavathy, and M. Nithya Kalyani

Jayaraj Annapackiam College for Women (Autonomous),
Periyakulam, Theni District, Tamilnadu, India
chandrajac@yahoo.com, kalaoliver@gmail.com, rnithraj@gmail.com

Abstract. In the field of DNA computing, splicing system was proposed by Tom Head in which the splicing operation is used. Various models have been studied with mate operation working on strings. The operations mate and drip considered in membrane computing resemble the operation cut and recombination well known from DNA computing. Here we introduce a new generative device called $AP_m(mate)$ system. A P system with mate operation working on array is focused. The power of P system with mate operation as a unique evolution rule is examined.

Keywords: P system · Splicing operation · Mate operation · Mate array operation

1 Introduction

DNA computing was introduced by Head in [1] more than twenty years ago, when he formalized the operation of splicing, well-known from biology as an operation on DNA stands. In [2], the range of Turing machines was encoded using iterated splicing on multisets. The splicing operation then mainly was used as a basic tool for building a generative mechanism called a splicing system or H system as formalized by Gheorghe Paun.

A new kind of generative mechanism was proposed in [3] with mate and drip operations working on strings. In P systems and tissue P systems the objects are placed inside the membranes. In the variant of membrane systems introduced by Cardelli [4], the objects are placed on the membranes. The computations in these models also called *brane calculus* are based on specific ways to divide and fuse membranes and to redistribute the objects on the membranes [5,6] the rules usually being applied in a sequential way in contrast to the (maximal) parallel way of applying rules in P systems. Various attempts have already been made to combine different models from the area of P systems and of brane calculi [7,8]. Following this research line by investigating tissue P systems with the brane operations mate and drip in [9] computational completeness results were obtained both for symbol objects as well as for string objects. It is of interest to note that systems using mate operation are Turing complete and they can compute all Turing computable sets of numbers.

© Springer Nature Singapore Pte Ltd. 2016
M. Gong et al. (Eds.): BIC-TA 2016, Part I, CCIS 681, pp. 200–214, 2016.
DOI: 10.1007/978-981-10-3611-8_19

In this paper we deal with the mate operation on arrays in terms of membrane computing formalism. We investigate the power of P systems with mate operation as a unique evolution rule.

2   Preliminaries

For an alphabet V, we denote the set of all strings over V, by V^*, the empty string λ included; the set of non-empty strings over V, that is $V^* - \lambda$ is denoted by V^+. The length of a string $x \in V^*$ is denoted by $\mid x \mid$ and $\mid x \mid_a$ for $a \in V$ is the number of occurrences of the symbol a in x. The set of all arrays over V is denoted by V^{**}.

2.1   Array P System [10]

The array-rewriting P system (of degree $m \geq 1$) is a construct

$$\Pi = (V, T, \#, \mu, F_1, \ldots, F_m, R_1, \ldots, R_m, i_o)$$

where V is the total alphabet, $T \subseteq V$ is the terminal alphabet, $\#$ is the blank symbol, μ is a membrane structure with m membranes labeled in a one-to-one way with $1, 2, \cdots, m$, $F_1, \cdots, F_m$ are finite sets of arrays over V associated with the m regions of μ, $R_1, \ldots, R_m$ are finite sets of array rewriting rules over V associated with the m regions of μ; the rules have attached targets *here, out, in* (in general, *here* is omitted), hence they are of the form $\mathcal{A} \to \mathcal{B}(tar)$; finally, i_o is the label of an elementary membrane of μ (the output membrane). The general case, when a set T is distinguished we speak about an *extended* P system, when $V = T$ we have a *non-extended* system. According to the form of its rules, an array P system can be monotonic, context-free (CF), $\#$ - context-free ($\#CF$) or regular (REG). In the extended case, a rule is called regular if it is of one of the following forms:

$$a \,\# \to b\,c, \quad \#\,a \to b\,c, \quad \begin{matrix} a & b \\ & \to \\ \# & c \end{matrix}, \quad \begin{matrix} \# & b \\ & \to \\ a & c \end{matrix}, \quad a \to b$$

where all a, b, c are non-blank symbols. In the non-extended case, we use the notion of a regular rule in the restricted sense; such a rule is of one of the forms:

$$a \,\# \to a\,b, \quad \#\,a \to b\,a, \quad \begin{matrix} a & a \\ & \to \\ \# & b \end{matrix}, \quad \begin{matrix} \# & b \\ & \to \\ a & a \end{matrix}$$

where all a, b are non-blank symbols.

The set of all arrays generated by a system Π is denoted by $AL(\Pi)$. The family of all array languages $AL(\Pi)$ generated by systems Π as above, with at most m membranes, with rules of type $\alpha \in \{REG, CF, \#CF\}$ is denoted by $EAP_m(\alpha)$. If non-extended systems are considered, then we write $AP_m(\alpha)$.

2.2 Mate Operation [3]

The operation mate is defined as Mate:$(u \mid a, b \mid v; x)$. This operation has the following meaning: $(u \mid a, b \mid v; x)$ fuses a membrane carrying the multiset sua and the membrane carrying the multiset bvw into one cell which then has the multiset $suxvw$, (i.e.) ab is replaced by x and the remaining multisets are taken as they are. A sequence of transitions constitutes a computation. A computation which starts from the initial configuration is successful if (i) it halts, that is, it reaches a configuration where no rule can be applied and (ii) in the halting configuration there are only two membranes, the skin (marked with λ) and an inner one. The result of a successful computation is given by the multiset which marks the inner membrane in the halting configuration. Here we consider as the result the vector describing the multiplicity of proteins in this multiset. Note that the computations which do not halt or halt with more than one inner membrane provide no output. The family of all sets of vectors $P(\Pi)$ computed by P systems Π using at any moment during halting computation with at most m membranes and mate rules is denoted by $POP_m(mate)$.

3 Array P System with Mate Operation

A P system with mate operation working on array is introduced here.

3.1 Definition

An Array P system with Mate operation is a construct

$$\Pi = (V, V_T, \#, \mu, A, R, i_0)$$

where V is a finite set of symbols, V_T is a set of terminal symbols; $V_T \subseteq V$, $\#$ is the blank symbol; $\# \notin V$, μ is a membrane structure with m membranes injectively labeled by $1, 2, \ldots, m$, $A = (A_1, A_2, \ldots, A_m)$ is a sequence of sets of axioms where $A_i \subseteq V^{**}, 1 \leq i \leq m$, describing the initial contents of the membranes, R is a finite set of tables $R_i, i = 1, 2, \ldots, m$ containing mate rules associated with the regions of μ and i_0 is the output membrane.

A computation in Π starts with the initial configuration described by A; a computation is performed by applying suitable mate rules from R in a non-deterministic, maximally parallel way, thereby passing from one configuration of the system to the next one. A sequence of transitions constitutes a computation.

The mate column operation on a membrane is defined on two arrays X, Y of order $m \times n$ and the rule R_i from the finite set of mate rules $R = (R_1, R_2, \ldots R_m)$ as follows:

$$\{\{(P \mid A, B \mid Q; Z), tar\}, \{p \quad \not\subset \quad a \quad \$_c \quad b \quad \not\subset \quad q; z\}\}$$

where $X = S\Phi P\Phi A$ and $Y = B\Phi Q\Phi W$; $X, Y, Z \subseteq V^{**}$. The mate column operation will be done to the elements of arrays X and Y, taking the sub arrays starting from the first row towards the end of the row. The sub arrays s, p, a, b, q, w and z of S, P, A, B, Q, W and Z respectively will be of order $p \times q, 1 \leq p \leq m$ and $1 \leq q \leq n$ such that the number of rows will be equal and the number of columns may differ. $\{p \not{L} a \; \$_c \; b \not{L} q \; ; z\}$ fuses the two arrays carrying $(s \; \Phi \; p \; \Phi \; a)$ and $(b \; \Phi \; q \; \Phi \; w)$ into an array which has the form $(s \; \Phi \; p \; \Phi \; z \; \Phi \; q \; \Phi \; w)$ where (a, b) is replaced by (z) and the remaining sub arrays are taken as they are.

The mate row operation on a membrane is defined on two arrays X, Y of order $m \times n$ and the rule R_i from the finite set of mate rules $R = (R_1, R_2, \ldots R_m)$ as follows:

$$\{\{(P \mid A, B \mid Q; Z), tar\}, \{p \quad \not{L} \quad a \quad \$_r \quad b \quad \not{L} \quad q; z\}\}$$

where $X = S \Theta P \Theta A$ and $Y = B \Theta Q \Theta W; X, Y, Z \subseteq V^{**}$. The mate row operation will be done to the elements of arrays X and Y, taking the sub arrays starting from the first column towards the end of the column. The sub arrays s, p, a, b, q, w and z of S, P, A, B, Q, W and Z respectively will be of order $p \times q, 1 \leq p \leq m$ and $1 \leq q \leq n$ such that the number of columns will be equal and the number of rows may differ. $\{p \not{L} a \; \$_r \; b \not{L} q \; ; z\}$ fuses the two arrays carrying $(s \; \Theta \; p \; \Theta \; a)$ and $(b \; \Theta \; q \; \Theta \; w)$ into an array which has the form $(s \; \Theta \; p \; \Theta \; z \; \Theta \; q \; \Theta \; w)$ where (a, b) is replaced by (z) and the remaining sub arrays are taken as they are.

The generated array in the form $S \Phi P \Phi Z \Phi Q \Phi W$ or $S \Theta P \Theta Z \Theta Q \Theta W$ is sent to the region indicated by tar. If $tar = here$, then the generated array remains in the same membrane where it is generated. If $tar = out$, then the generated array is moved to the region immediately outside the membrane. If $tar = in$, then the generated array is sent to the region immediately inside the membrane.

A computation is successful only if (i) it halts by reaching a configuration where no rule can be applied any more and (ii) the output array in the halting configuration is the required array. The set of all such arrays computed by a system Π is denoted by $MAL(\Pi)$. The family of all array languages generated by systems $MAL(\Pi)$, with at most m membranes with mate operation is denoted by $AP_m(mate)$.

3.2   Example

Consider the Array P system with mate operation

$$\Pi_1 = \left(\{x, b\}, \{x, b\}, \#, [_1[_2[_3]_3]_2]_1, \begin{Bmatrix} x \; x \; x \\ x \; b \; x \\ x \; x \; x \end{Bmatrix}, \phi, \phi, (R_1, R_2, R_3), 3 \right) \text{ where}$$

$$R_1 = \left\{ \begin{matrix} \left\{ \begin{array}{c|ccccc|cccc} x & x & \ldots & x & x & x & x & \ldots & x & x & x \\ x & b & \ldots & b & x & x & b & \ldots & b & x & b \\ \vdots & \vdots & \vdots & \vdots & \vdots & \vdots & \vdots & \vdots & \vdots & \vdots & \vdots \\ x & x & \ldots & x & x & x & x & \ldots & x & x & x \end{array} \right., (in) \right\}, \\ \left\{ \begin{array}{ccccccc} x & \not{L} & x & \$_c & x & \not{L} & x; (x \ldots x \, x \, x) \to (x), \\ x & \not{L} & b & \$_c & x & \not{L} & b; (b \ldots b \, x \, x) \to (b) \end{array} \right\} \end{matrix} \right\},
$$

$$R_2 = \left\{ \begin{array}{l} \left\{ \begin{array}{c} \left(\begin{array}{cc|cc} x\,x\,\ldots\,x\,x & x\,x\,\ldots\,x\,x \\ \overline{x\,b\,\ldots\,b\,x} & x\,b\,\ldots\,b\,x \\ \vdots\,\vdots \quad \vdots\,\vdots & \vdots\,\vdots \quad \vdots\,\vdots \\ x\,b\,\ldots\,b\,x & x\,b\,\ldots\,b\,x \\ x\,x\,\ldots\,x\,x & x\,x\,\ldots\,x\,x \end{array} \right), \begin{array}{c} x\,b\,\ldots\,x, (in, out) \end{array} \right\}, \\[3em] \left[\begin{array}{cccccc} x & \not{c} & x & \$_r & x & \not{c}\ x; \end{array} \left(\begin{array}{c} x \\ \vdots \\ x \\ x \\ x \end{array} \right) \to (x), \right] \\[3em] \left[\begin{array}{cccccc} x & \not{c} & b & \$_r & x & \not{c}\ b; \end{array} \left(\begin{array}{c} b \\ \vdots \\ b \\ x \\ x \end{array} \right) \to (b) \right] \end{array} \right\},$$

$R_3 = \{\phi\}.$

Intially, the axiom array $\begin{array}{c} x\,x\,x \\ x\,b\,x \\ x\,x\,x \end{array}$ is in the skin region and the other regions do not have objects. If the mate rule R_1 is applied with the object to itself in region 1, the generated array is moved to region 2. In region 2, the mate rule R_2 is applied and the generated array is sent to outer region 1 or inner region 3. When the generated array is sent to region 3, there is no rule to apply and hence the system halts. As a result, the array of solid square shape is obtained. The process is repeated, when the generated array in region 2 is sent out to region 1. The picture language generated by Π_1 consists of all solid squares of $b's$ surrounded by $x's$ as in Fig. 1.

$$\begin{array}{ccccc} x & x & x & x & x \\ x & b & b & b & x \\ x & b & b & b & x \\ x & b & b & b & x \\ x & x & x & x & x \end{array}$$

Fig. 1. Square of b' s surrounded by x' s

A vertical bar $'\,|\,'$ and a horizontal bar $'-'$ are used to indicate the place where cutting is done.

3.3   Theorem

The set of all chessboards with even side-length [11] is generated by $AP_3(mate)$.

Proof: Consider the Array P system with mate operation

$$\Pi_2 \;=\; \left(\{a,b\}, \{a,b\}, \#, [_1[_2[_3]_3]_2]_1, \left\{ \begin{matrix} \# \ \# \ \# \ \# \\ \# \ a \ b \ \# \\ \# \ b \ a \ \# \\ \# \ \# \ \# \ \# \end{matrix} \right\}, \phi, \phi, (R_1, R_2, R_3), 3 \right)$$

where

$$R_1 = \left\{ \begin{array}{l} \left\{ \begin{array}{ccc|ccc|ccc} \# \ \# \ \# \cdots \# \ \# & \# \ \# \ \# \ \# \cdots \# \ \# & \# \ \# \ \# \\ \# \ a \ b \cdots a \ b & \# \ \# \ a \ b \cdots a \ b & \# \ a \ b \\ \# \ b \ a \cdots b \ a & \# \ \# \ b \ a \cdots b \ a & \# \ b \ a \\ \vdots \ \vdots \ \vdots \ \ \vdots \ \vdots & \vdots \ \vdots \ \vdots \ \vdots \ \ \vdots \ \vdots & \vdots \ \vdots \ \vdots \\ \# \ a \ b \cdots a \ b & \# \ \# \ a \ b \cdots a \ b & \# \ a \ b \\ \# \ b \ a \cdots b \ a & \# \ \# \ b \ a \cdots b \ a & \# \ b \ a \\ \# \ \# \ \# \cdots \# \ \# & \# \ \# \ \# \ \# \cdots \# \ \# & \# \ \# \ \# \end{array} , (in) \right\}, \\[2em] \left\{ \# \ \not{c} \ \# \ \$_c \ \# \ \not{c} \ \#; (\# \ \# \# \# \cdots \# \#) \to (\# \ \#), \right. \\[1em] \left. \binom{b}{a} \not{c} \binom{\#}{\#} \$_c \binom{b}{a} \not{c} \binom{\#}{\#}; \binom{\# \ \# \ a \ b \ldots a \ b}{\# \ \# \ b \ a \ldots b \ a} \to \binom{a \ b}{b \ a} \right\} \end{array} \right\},$$

$$R_2 = \left\{ \begin{array}{l} \left\{ \begin{array}{ll} \# \ \# \ \# \cdots \# \ \# \ \# \ \# \cdots \# \\ \# \ a \ b \cdots \# \ \# \ a \ b \cdots \# \\ \# \ b \ a \cdots \# \ \# \ b \ a \cdots \# \\ \vdots \ \vdots \ \vdots \ \ \vdots \ \vdots , \vdots \ \vdots \ \vdots \ \ \vdots \ \vdots ; \ \dfrac{\# \ a \ b \ldots \#}{\# \ b \ a \ldots \#}, (in,out) \\ \# \ a \ b \cdots \# \ \# \ a \ b \cdots \# \\ \underline{\# \ b \ a \cdots \# \ \# \ b \ a \cdots \#} \\ \# \ \# \ \# \cdots \# \ \# \ \# \ \# \cdots \# \end{array} \right\}, \\[3em] \left\{ \# \ \not{c} \ \# \ \$_r \ \# \ \not{c} \ \#; \begin{pmatrix} \# \\ \# \\ \# \\ \# \\ \vdots \\ \# \\ \# \end{pmatrix} \to \binom{\#}{\#}, \right. \\[4em] \left. (b \, a) \not{c} (\# \, \#) \$_r (b \, a) \not{c} (\# \, \#); \begin{pmatrix} \# \ \# \\ \# \ \# \\ a \ b \\ b \ a \\ \vdots \ \vdots \\ a \ b \\ b \ a \end{pmatrix} \to \binom{a \ b}{b \ a} \right\} \end{array} \right\},$$

$R_3 = \{\phi\}$.

The picture language generated by Π_2 consisting of all $"chessboards"$ with even side-length as in Fig. 3 where $'a'$ stands for black and $'b'$ stands for white. The corresponding picture pattern is shown in Fig. 2.

Fig. 2. Chess board

$$
\begin{array}{cccccc}
a & b & a & b & a & b \\
b & a & b & a & b & a \\
a & b & a & b & a & b \\
b & a & b & a & b & a \\
a & b & a & b & a & b \\
b & a & b & a & b & a \\
\end{array}
$$

Fig. 3. Pattern of Chess board

4   Closure Properties

4.1   Theorem

The class $AP_m(mate)$ is not closed under union and concatenation.

Proof: Let L_1 be the set of solid squares of $b's$ surrounded by $x's$ [Example 3.2] and L_2 be the set of solid squares of $a's$ surrounded by $x's$ as in Fig. 4.

$$
\begin{array}{ccccc}
x & x & x & x & x \\
x & a & a & a & x \\
x & a & a & a & x \\
x & a & a & a & x \\
x & x & x & x & x \\
\end{array}
$$

Fig. 4. A member of L_2

Perform mate column operation on two initial arrays of the form

$$
\begin{array}{ccc}
x\,x\,x & x\,x\,x \\
x\,a\,x, & x\,b\,x \\
x\,x\,x & x\,x\,x
\end{array}
$$

by *'cutting'* inside the array and then *'fusing'* the resulting array according to the rules we will obtain arrays which will not be elements of $L_1 \cup L_2$.

Let L_1 be a language consisting of arrays with at least three rows and any number of columns with left border made of $x's$, right border of $y's$ and inner part of $a's$. A member of L_1 is shown in Fig. 5.

$$
\begin{array}{ccccc}
x & a & a & a & y \\
x & a & a & a & y \\
x & a & a & a & y
\end{array}
$$

Fig. 5. Member of L_1

Similarly, let L_2 be another language of arrays as in L_1 but left border made of $p's$, right border of $q's$ and inner part made of $a's$. A member of L_2 is shown in Fig. 6.

$$
\begin{array}{ccccc}
p & a & a & a & q \\
p & a & a & a & q \\
p & a & a & a & q
\end{array}
$$

Fig. 6. Member of L_2

In order to obtain arrays of $L_1 \Phi L_2$ (a member of which is shown in Fig. 7), the column mate operation of two arrays should maintain the inner part of $x's$ and $q's$ and two successive innermost column of $y's$ and $p's$. But this is not possible due to the mate rules. An analogous argument applies to row concatenation.

$$
\begin{array}{cccccc}
x & a & y & p & a & q \\
x & a & y & p & a & q \\
x & a & y & p & a & q
\end{array}
$$

Fig. 7. Member of $L_1 \Phi L_2$

4.2 Theorem

The class $AP_m(mate)$ is closed under reflections on the base and right leg and rotations by $90°$, $180°$ and $270°$.

Proof: Let $\Pi = (V, V_T, \#, \mu, A, R, i_0)$ be a system $AP_m(mate)$ generating a language L. Let P be a member array in L. Consider the mate column/row operation $(P \mid A, B \mid Q; Z)$.

Let the finite set of tables R_i containing mate column/row rules be given by

$(p \not\subset a \,\$_c\, b \not\subset q \,;\, z)$ and
$(p \not\subset a \,\$_r\, b \not\subset q \,;\, z)$

The language L_b consisting of reflections of pictures of L on the base are obtained by modifying mate rules:

$(p_\perp \not\subset a_\perp \,\$_c\, b_\perp \not\subset q_\perp \,;\, z_\perp)$ and
$(q_\perp \not\subset b_\perp \,\$_r\, a_\perp \not\subset p_\perp \,;\, z_\perp)$

$'\perp'$ represents the reflection on the base

Similarly, the language L_{rl} consisting of reflections of pictures of L on the right leg can be obtained by modifying mate rules:

$(q^R \not\subset b^R \,\$_c\, a^R \not\subset p^R \,;\, z^R)$ and
$(p^R \not\subset a^R \,\$_r\, b^R \not\subset q^R \,;\, z^R)$

where $'R'$ stands for the reversal.

The language L_1, by rotating the pictures of L by $90°$ is obtained by modifying mate rules:

$((p^T)^R \not\subset (a^T)^R \,\$_r\, (b^T)^R \not\subset (q^T)^R \,;\, (z^T)^R)$ and

$((q^T)^R \not\subset (b^T)^R \,\$_c\, (a^T)^R \not\subset (p^T)^R \,;\, (z^T)^R)$

where $'T'$ stands for the transpose.

The language L_2, by rotating the pictures of L by $180°$ is obtained by modifying mate rules:

$((q_\perp)^R \not\subset (b_\perp)^R \,\$_c\, (a_\perp)^R \not\subset (p_\perp)^R \,;\, (z_\perp)^R)$ and

$((q_\perp)^R \not\subset (b_\perp)^R \,\$_r\, (a_\perp)^R \not\subset (p_\perp)^R \,;\, (z_\perp)^R)$

The language L_3, by rotating the pictures of L by $270°$ is obtained by modifying mate rules:

$((q^T)^\perp \not\subset (b^T)^\perp \,\$_r\, (a^T)^\perp \not\subset (p^T)^\perp \,;\, (z^T)^\perp)$ and

$((p^T)^\perp \not\subset (a^T)^\perp \,\$_c\, (b^T)^\perp \not\subset (q^T)^\perp \,;\, (z^T)^\perp).$

5   Generative Power

We now compare the generative power of Array P system with mate operation with other description models.

5.1   Theorem

The family $AP_3(mate)$ intersects with the family HAP_3 [12].

Proof: Consider the Array P system with mate operation

$$\Pi_3 = \left(\{x,a\}, \{x,a\}, \#, [_1[_2[_3]_3]_2]_1, \left\{ \begin{matrix} a\ a\ a \\ x\ a\ x \\ x\ a\ x \end{matrix} \right\}, \phi, \phi, (R_1, R_2, R_3), 3 \right) \text{ where}$$

$$R_1 = \left\{ \begin{array}{l} \left\{ \begin{array}{ccccc} a \ldots a & a \ldots a & a \ldots a & a \ldots a & a\ a\ a \\ x \ldots x & a \ldots x & x \ldots a & x \ldots x & x\ a\ x \\ \vdots\ \vdots & \vdots\ \vdots\ \vdots & \vdots\ \vdots\ \vdots & \vdots\ \vdots\ \vdots & \vdots\ \vdots\ \vdots \\ x \ldots x & a \ldots x & x \ldots a & x \ldots x & x\ a\ x \end{array} ; (in) \right\}, \\ \left\{ \begin{array}{llllll} a & \not{c} & a & \$_c & a & \not{c} & a; (a\ a \ldots a \ldots a\ a) \rightarrow (a\ a\ a), \\ x & \not{c} & a & \$_c & a & \not{c} & x; (a\ x \ldots x \ldots x\ a) \rightarrow (x\ a\ x) \end{array} \right\} \end{array} \right\},$$

$$R_2 = \left\{ \begin{array}{l} \left\{ \begin{array}{l} a \ldots a\ a \ldots a \quad a \ldots a\ a \ldots a \\ x \ldots a\ x \ldots x \quad x \ldots a\ x \ldots x \quad x \ldots a\ x \ldots x \\ x \ldots a\ x \ldots x , x \ldots a\ x \ldots x ; x \ldots a\ x \ldots x, (in, out) \\ \vdots\ \vdots\ \vdots\ \vdots\ \vdots \quad \vdots\ \vdots\ \vdots\ \vdots\ \vdots \quad x \ldots a\ x \ldots x \\ x \ldots a\ x \ldots x \quad x \ldots a\ x \ldots x \end{array} \right\}, \\ \left\{ a \quad \not{c} \quad x \quad \$_r \quad a \quad \not{c} \quad x; \begin{pmatrix} x \\ \vdots \\ x \\ a \end{pmatrix} \rightarrow \begin{pmatrix} x \\ x \\ x \end{pmatrix}, \right. \\ \left. a \quad \not{c} \quad a \quad \$_r \quad a \quad \not{c} \quad a; \begin{pmatrix} a \\ \vdots \\ a \\ a \end{pmatrix} \rightarrow \begin{pmatrix} a \\ a \\ a \end{pmatrix} \right\} \end{array} \right\},$$

$R_3 = \{\phi\}.$

The picture language generated by Π_3 consists of T shapes as in Fig. 8. where $'x'$ stands for *empty*.

$$
\begin{array}{ccccc}
a & a & a & a & a \\
x & x & a & x & x \\
x & x & a & x & x \\
x & x & a & x & x \\
x & x & a & x & x
\end{array}
$$

Fig. 8. Array describing pattern T

This language also can be generated by HAP_3 [12].
Consider the Array P System Hybrid teams of degree 3.

$$\Pi = (\{S, A, B, a\}, \{a\}, \#, [_1[_2[_3]_3]_2]_1, S, \phi, \phi, R_1, R_2, R_3, 3) \text{ where}$$

$$R_1 = \{(Q_1, t)_{in}\}, \ R_2 = \{(Q_2, *)_{here}, (Q_2, *)_{in}\}, \ R_3 = \{(Q_3, t)_{here}\} ,$$

$$Q_1 = \{P_1\}, Q_2 = \{P_2, P_3, P_4\}, Q_3 = \{P_5, P_6\},$$

$$P_1 = \left\{ \begin{array}{ccc} \# \, S \, \# & & A \, a \, A \\ & \to & \\ \# & & B \end{array} \right\} , \ P_2 = \{\# A \to A\,a\}, \ P_3 = \{A\,\# \to a\,A\},$$

$$P_4 = \left\{ \begin{array}{c} B \\ \# \end{array} \to \begin{array}{c} a \\ B \end{array} \right\}, \ P_5 = \{A \to a\}, \ P_6 = \{B \to a\}.$$

This Array P systems with hybrid teams Π generates a language consisting of arrays in the shape of token T as shown in Fig. 8.

5.2   Theorem

The family $AP_3(mate)$ intersects with the family $EAP_5(REG)$ [13].

Proof: Let the Array P system $AP_3(mate)$ for all $m \geq 3$ be a construct

$$\Pi_4 = \left(\{x, y\}, \{x, y\}, \#, [_1[_2[_3]_3]_2]_1, \left\{ \begin{array}{ccc} y & x & y \\ x & x & x \\ y & x & y \end{array} \right\}, \phi, \phi, (R_1, R_2, R_3), 3 \right) \text{ where}$$

$$R_1 = \left\{ \begin{array}{l} \left\{ \begin{array}{c|c|c} \begin{array}{ccc} y & \cdots & y \\ \vdots & \vdots & \vdots \\ x & \cdots & x \\ y & \cdots & y \\ \vdots & \vdots & \vdots \\ y & \cdots & y \end{array} & \begin{array}{cccccc} x & y & \cdots & y & y & \cdots & y \, x \\ \vdots & \vdots & \vdots & \vdots & \vdots & \vdots & \vdots \\ x & x & \cdots & x & x & \cdots & x \, x \\ x & y & \cdots & y' & y & \cdots & y \, x \\ \vdots & \vdots & \vdots & \vdots & \vdots & \vdots & \vdots \\ x & y & \cdots & y & y & \cdots & y \, x \end{array} & \begin{array}{cccc} y & \cdots & y & y \, x \, y \\ \vdots & \vdots & \vdots & \vdots \vdots \vdots \\ x & \cdots & x & x \, x \, x \\ y & \cdots & y' & y \, x \, y \\ \vdots & \vdots & \vdots & \vdots \vdots \vdots \\ y & \cdots & y & y \, x \, y \end{array} \end{array} \, , (in) \right\}, \\[2em]
\left\{ \begin{array}{l} y \quad \not{c} \quad x \quad \$_r \quad x \quad \not{c} \quad y; (\, x\,y \cdots y \cdots y\,x \,) \to (\, y\,x\,y \,), \\ x \quad \not{c} \quad x \quad \$_r \quad x \quad \not{c} \quad x; (\, x\,x \cdots x \cdots x\,x \,) \to (\, x\,x\,x \,) \end{array} \right\} \end{array} \right\},$$

$$\left\{ \begin{array}{l} \left\{ \begin{array}{l} \begin{array}{ccccc} y \ldots x\, y \ldots y & y \ldots x\, y \ldots y \\ \vdots \;\; \vdots \;\; \vdots \;\; \vdots & \vdots \;\; \vdots \;\; \vdots \;\; \vdots & \vdots \;\; \vdots \;\; \vdots \\ y \ldots x\, y \ldots y & y \ldots x\, y \ldots y & y \ldots xy \ldots y \\ \overline{x \ldots x\, x \ldots x}, \, x \ldots x\, x \ldots x; \, x \ldots xx \ldots x, \, (in, out) \\ y \ldots x\, y \ldots y & y \ldots x\, y \ldots y & y \ldots xy \ldots y \\ \vdots \;\; \vdots \;\; \vdots \;\; \vdots & \vdots \;\; \vdots \;\; \vdots \;\; \vdots & \vdots \;\; \vdots \;\; \vdots \\ y \ldots x\, y \ldots y & y \ldots x\, y \ldots y \end{array} \end{array} \right\}, \right.$$

$$R_2 = \left\{ \begin{array}{l} \left\{ \begin{array}{l} y \;\; \not\!\!c \;\; x \;\; \$_r \;\; x \;\; \not\!\!c \;\; y; \; \begin{pmatrix} x \\ y \\ \vdots \\ y \\ \vdots \\ y \\ x \end{pmatrix} \rightarrow \begin{pmatrix} y \\ x \\ y \end{pmatrix}, \\[2em] x \;\; \not\!\!c \;\; x \;\; \$_r \;\; x \;\; \not\!\!c \;\; x; \; \begin{pmatrix} x \\ x \\ \vdots \\ x \\ \vdots \\ x \\ x \end{pmatrix} \rightarrow \begin{pmatrix} x \\ x \\ x \end{pmatrix} \end{array} \right. \end{array} \right\},$$

$R_3 = \{\phi\}.$

The picture language generated by Π_4 consists of *plus* shapes as in Fig. 9. where $'x'$ stands for $\diamond$ and $'y'$ stands for *empty*. The corresponding picture pattern is shown in Fig. 10.

Fig. 9. Array plus

$$y\ y\ y\ x\ y\ y\ y$$
$$y\ y\ y\ x\ y\ y\ y$$
$$y\ y\ y\ x\ y\ y\ y$$
$$x\ x\ x\ x\ x\ x\ x$$
$$y\ y\ y\ x\ y\ y\ y$$
$$y\ y\ y\ x\ y\ y\ y$$
$$y\ y\ y\ x\ y\ y\ y$$

Fig. 10. Array describing pattern plus

This language also can be generated by $EAP_5(REG)$ [13].

Consider the array P system generating the star-shaped arrays of L_{star}.

$$\Pi_s = \{V, \{\diamond\}, \#, \mu, F_1, F_2, F_3, F_4, F_5, R_1, R_2, R_3, R_4, R_5, 5\}, where$$

$V = \{A, B, C, D, B', C', D', X_1, X_2, X_3, X_4, a\}$, $\mu = [_1[_2[_3][_4]_4]_3]_2]_1$,

$$F_1 = \{M_1, M_2\}, M_1 = \begin{matrix} A \\ D \diamond B \\ C \end{matrix}, M_2 = \begin{matrix} X_1 \\ X_4 \diamond X_2 \\ X_3 \end{matrix}, F_2 = F_3 = F_4 = F_5 = \phi.$$

The sets of rules are given by

$$R_1 = \{r_{1,1} : \begin{matrix} \# \\ A \end{matrix} \to \begin{matrix} A \\ a \end{matrix} (in), r_{1,2} : X_1 \to \diamond (in)\},$$

$$R_2 = \{r_{2,1} : B \# \to \diamond B'(in), r_{2,2} : B' \to B(out), r_{2,3} : X_2 \to \diamond (in)\},$$

$$R_3 = \{r_{3,1} : \begin{matrix} C \\ \# \end{matrix} \to \begin{matrix} \diamond \\ C' \end{matrix} (in), r_{3,2} : C' \to C(out), r_{3,3} : X_3 \to \diamond (in)\},$$

$$R_4 = \{r_{4,1} : \# D \to D \diamond(out), r_{4,2} : \# D \to D' \diamond(in), r_{4,3} : X_4 \to \diamond (in)\},$$

$$R_5 = \{r_{5,1} : A \to \diamond, r_{5,2} : B' \to \diamond, r_{5,3} : C' \to \diamond, r_{5,4} : D' \to \diamond, \}$$

Intuitively a computation in Π_s, that starts with array A_1 moves the array from region 1 to region 4 through regions 2, 3 with each arm of the star-shaped array growing by the symbol $\{\diamond\}$ for each step. The array either comes back to region 1 from region 4 through regions 2, 3 or is sent to region 4. In the farmer case, the process repeats; while in the latter case, the desired array is formed over $\{\diamond\}$ and is collected in the language.

5.3   Theorem

(i) The class $AP_m(mate)$ of Array P system with mate operation and $L(2RLG)$ of picture languages generated by two-dimensional are incomparable but not disjoint.

(ii) The class LOC of local array languages and the class of $AP_m(mate)$ are incomparable but not disjoint.

5.4 Definition

Notations:

$| T |_c$ is the number of columns in array T.
$| T |_r$ is the number of rows in array T.

A language $L \subseteq V^{**}$ has the Bounded Step property if there is a constant k such that for each $T \in L$ with $| T |_c > k$ or $| T |_r > k$ either of the following properties (1), (2) holds:

1. There are $U, V \in L$ where $U = S\Phi P\Phi A$ and $V = B\Phi Q\Phi W$ such that $T = SPZQW$ and $| Z |_c \leq k$. (Column Bounded Step Property).
2. There are $U, V \in L$ where $U = S\Theta P\Theta A$ and $V = B\Theta Q\Theta W$ such that $T = SPZQW$ and $| Z |_r \leq k$. (Row Bounded Step Property).

5.5 Theorem

Every $AP_m(mate)$ language has the Bounded Step Property.

Proof: Let $L \in AP_m(mate)$ and $\Pi = (V, V_T, \#, \mu, A, R, i_0)$ be an Array P system with mate operation generating L.
Let $k_1 = max\{| T |_c : T \in A\}$,
$k_2 = max\{| T |_r : T \in A\}$,
$k_3 = max\{| z_i |_c\}$,
$k_4 = max\{| z_j |_r\}$.

Note that $| Z |_c = | z_i |_c$ if $Z = \begin{matrix} z_1 \\ z_2 \\ \vdots \\ z_l \end{matrix}$ for some l and $| Z |_r = | z_j |_r$ if $Z = z_1\, z_2 \ldots z_m$

for some m.
    Let $k = max \{k_1, k_2, k_3, k_4\}$. If $E \in L$ is such that either $| E |_c > k$ or $| E |_r > k$ then $E \notin A$. Hence either $E = S\Phi P\Phi Z\Phi Q\Phi W$ for some Z obtained by the mate column rule $(P \mid A, B \mid Q; Z)$, $F = S\Phi P\Phi A$, $G = B\Phi Q\Phi W$, $F, G \in L$ or $E = S\Theta P\Theta Z\Theta Q\Theta W$ for some Z obtained by the mate row rule, $(P \mid A, B \mid Q; Z)$, $F' = S\Theta P\Theta A$, $G' = B\Theta Q\Theta W$, $F', G' \in L$. Hence there is a constant k such that for each $E \in L$ either for $| E |_c > k$ there exist $F, G \in L$ such that $E = S\Phi P\Phi Z\Phi Q\Phi W$ and $0 < | Z |_c \leq k$ or for $| E |_r > k$ there exist $F', G' \in L$ such that $E = S\Theta P\Theta Z\Theta Q\Theta W$ and $0 < | Z |_r \leq k$. Hence L has the Bounded step property.

6 Conclusion

In this paper, we have introduced a new model called Array P system with mate operation. We have studied bounded step property and some closure properties such as union, concatenation and rotation on family of languages generated by

Array P system with mate operation. The generative power is compared with other models of picture description. It is worth examining further properties of the system.

References

1. Head, T.: Formal language theory and DNA: an analysis of the generative capacity of specific recombinant behaviours. Bull Math. Biol. **49**, 737–759 (1987)
2. Denninghoff, K.L., Pradalier, S.: On the undecidability of splicing systems. Int. J. Comput. Math. **27**, 133–145 (1989)
3. Rudolf, F., Marion, O.: Tissue P systems and (mem) brane systems with mate and drip operations working on strings. Electron. Notes Theor. Comput. Sci. **7**, 105–115 (2007)
4. Cardelli, L.: Brane calculi: interactions of biological membranes. In: Danos, V., Schachter, V. (eds.) CMSB 2004. LNCS, vol. 3082, pp. 257–278. Springer, Heidelberg (2005). doi:10.1007/978-3-540-25974-9_24
5. Busi, N.: On the computational power of the mate/bud/drip brane calculus: interleaving vs. maximal parallelism. In: Freund, R., Păun, G., Rozenberg, G., Salomaa, A. (eds.) WMC 2005. LNCS, vol. 3850, pp. 144–158. Springer, Heidelberg (2006). doi:10.1007/11603047_10
6. Busi, N., Gorrieri, R.: On the computational power of brane calculi. In: Priami, C., Plotkin, G. (eds.) Transactions on Computational Systems Biology VI. LNCS, vol. 4220, pp. 16–43. Springer, Heidelberg (2006). doi:10.1007/11880646_2
7. Cardelli, L., Paun, G.: An universality result for a membrane calculus based on mate/drip operations. Int. J. Found. Comput. Sci. **1**, 257–280 (2006)
8. Paun, G.: One more universality result for P system with objects on membranes. In: Proceedings of the Third Brainstorming Week on Membrane Computing, Sevilla (Spain), pp. 263–274 (2005)
9. Freund, R., Oswald, M.: Tissue p systems and mem (brane) systems with mate and drip operations working on strings. Electron. Notes Theor. Comput. Sci. **171**, 105–115 (2007)
10. Ceterchi, R., Mutyam, M., Paun, G., Subramanian, K.G.: Array rewriting P systems. Nat. Comput. **2**, 229–249 (2003)
11. Giammaresi, D., Restivo, A.: Two dimentional languages. In: Rozenberg, G., Salomaa, A. (eds.) Handbook of Formal Languages, vol. 3, pp. 215–267. Springer, Heidelberg (1997)
12. Chandra, P.H., Kalavathy, S.S.T.: Array P system with hybrid teams. In: Bansal, J., Singh, P., Deep, K., Pant, M., Nagar, A. (eds.) Proceedings of Seventh International Conference on Bio-Inspired Computing: Theories and Applications (BIC-TA 2012). AISC, vol. 201, pp. 239–249. Springer, Heidelberg (2013)
13. Subramanian, K.G., Isawasan, P., Venkat, I., Pan, L.: Parallel array rewriting P systems. Rom. J. Inf. Sci. Technol. **17**, 103–116 (2014)

The Computational Power of Watson-Crick Grammars: Revisited

Nurul Liyana Mohamad Zulkufli, Sherzod Turaev[(⊠)],
Mohd Izzuddin Mohd Tamrin, and Azeddine Messikh

Kulliyyah of Information and Communication Technology,
International Islamic University Malaysia, 53100 Kuala Lumpur, Malaysia
liyana.zulkufli@live.iium.edu.my, {sherzod,izzuddin,messikh}@iium.edu.my

Abstract. A Watson-Crick finite automaton is one of DNA computational models using the Watson-Crick complementarity feature of deoxyribonucleic acid (DNA). We are interested in investigating a grammar counterpart of Watson-Crick automata. In this paper, we present results concerning the generative power of Watson-Crick (regular, linear, context-free) grammars. We show that the family of Watson-Crick context-free languages is included in the family of matrix languages.

1 Introduction

Discoveries in bio-molecular science and related fields bring forth advancement in computing world, such as the birth of membrane computing and DNA computing. Both membrane computing and DNA computing stem from molecular biology although from different substances in living nature, where membrane computing get its insight from how membrane works in a cell, and DNA computing from how the deoxyribonucleic acid works.

In *membrane computing*, or *P systems*, introduced by Păun (see [1–3]), the most important part is the membrane structure which consists of several membranes or regions. The objects in the membranes can be interpreted as strings, which evolve according to the given rules. The computational properties of several variants of P systems such as tissue-like P systems in generating control languages [4], and neural-like or spiking neural P systems, with additional features such as weights and self-organization [5,6]. In this paper, we focus on the sister field of membrane computing - *DNA computing*. Paper [7] investigated the relationship between membrane computing and DNA computing, and how their results can be intertwined with each other.

Our focus lies on one of the DNA computing models, called a Watson-Crick finite automaton [8], which utilises a feature unique to DNA, namely the Watson-Crick complementarity. DNA can be recognized as a double-stranded string with four bases (symbols): adenine (A), guanine (G), thymine (T), and cytosine (C). The upper strand and lower strand can only be attached with the Watson-Crick complementarity, where base A can only be paired with base T, and base C with base G.

M. Gong et al. (Eds.): BIC-TA 2016, Part I, CCIS 681, pp. 215–225, 2016.
DOI: 10.1007/978-981-10-3611-8_20

A Watson-Crick finite automaton works on a double-stranded tape of symbols with two reading heads, instead of a single-stranded tape and one head in a finite automaton. The tapes are attached with relation similar to Watson-Crick complementarity in DNA. The symbols in each of the tapes are scanned separately usually from left to right, by their corresponding heads controlled by a common state. It is shown that a Watson-Crick automaton can recognize languages more powerful than what a finite automaton is able to. There are several types of Watson-Crick automata proposed, such as initial stateless Watson-Crick finite automata, Watson-Crick automata with a Watson-Crick memory, Watson-Crick transducers [9], and weighted Watson-Crick automata [10]. Compact information on Watson-Crick automata are given in the survey [11].

Interesting computational models do not materialise from automata part only, but also the formal grammars – their analytical counterparts. Earlier researches signify that the usage of context-free grammars also provide beneficial methods in analysing DNA strings [12,13]. The computational relations among context-free grammars and Watson-Crick automata are examined in [14,15]. Using Watson-Crick complementarity feature, (static) Watson-Crick regular grammars are introduced in [16]. Further variants of Watson-Crick grammars, i.e. Watson-Crick regular, linear, and context-free grammars, as well as their generative power and closure properties are investigated in [17–20].

In this paper, we present the latest results on the computational power of Watson-Crick grammars. Necessary notions and definitions from formal language theory are given in Sect. 2. Section 3 presents the results regarding the generative power, including the classifications between families of languages generated by Watson-Crick grammars, and also the upper bound of Watson-Crick context-free grammars. Finally, we conclude the paper with some open problems in Sect. 4.

2   Preliminaries

Let us recall necessary information on formal languages theory and automata. More details can be found in [9,11,21,22].

Let Σ be an *alphabet*, a finite set of symbols, then Σ^* denotes the set of all *strings*, finite sequences of symbols of Σ. The notion Σ^+ means $\Sigma^* - \{\lambda\}$, where λ is an empty string. For $x \in \Sigma^*$, $|x|$ is the *length* of a string x, and a set $L \subseteq \Sigma^*$ is a *language*.

A *Chomsky grammar* is defined by $G = (N, T, S, P)$ where N is a set of *nonterminal* symbols, T is a set of *terminal* symbols, $N \cap T = \emptyset$, $S \in N$ is the *start symbol*, and $P \subseteq (N \cup T)^* N (N \cup T)^* \times (N \cup T)^*$ is the set of *production rules*. A pair $(\alpha, \beta) \in P$ is also written as $\alpha \to \beta$. We say $x \in (N \cup T)^*$ *directly derives* $y \in (N \cup T)^*$, denoted by $x \Rightarrow y$, iff $x = a_1 \alpha a_2$ and $y = a_1 \beta a_2$ for some production rules $\alpha \to \beta \in P$. A *language* generated by a grammar G is defined by $L(G) = \{w \in T^* \mid S \Rightarrow^* w\}$.

A grammar $G = (N, T, S, P)$ is said to be

- *context-sensitive* if each production has the form $u_1 A u_2 \to u_1 u u_2$ where $A \in N$, $u_1, u_2, \in (N \cup T)^*$, and $u \in (N \cup T)^+$,

- *context-free* if each production has the form $A \to u$ where $A \in N$ and $u \in (N \cup T)^*$,
- *linear* if each production has the form $A \to u_1 B u_2$ or $A \to u$ where $A, B \in N$ and $u_1, u_2, u \in T^*$,
- *right-linear* if each production has the form $A \to uB$ or $A \to u$ where $A, B \in N$ and $u \in T^*$,
- *left-linear* if each production has the form $A \to Bu$ or $A \to u$ where $A, B \in N$ and $u \in T^*$,
- *regular* if it is either right-linear or left-linear.

Theorem 1 (Chomsky Hierarchy [22]).

$$\mathbf{FIN} \subset \mathbf{REG} \subset \mathbf{LIN} \subset \mathbf{CF} \subset \mathbf{CS} \subset \mathbf{RE}.$$

where **FIN, REG, LIN, CF, CS, RE** denote the families of finite, regular, linear, context-free, context-sensitive, and recursively enumerable languages, respectively.

A *finite automaton* (FA) is a quintuple $M = (Q, V, q_0, F, \delta)$, where Q is a set of *states*, V is an alphabet, $q_0 \in Q$ is the *initial state*, $F \subseteq Q$ is a set of *final states*, and $\delta : Q \times V \to 2^Q$ is the *transition function*. The language accepted by M is noted by $L(M)$, and the family of languages accepted by finite automata by **FA**. It is known that **FA = REG** [22].

Let for an alphabet V, $\rho \subseteq V \times V$ be a symmetric relation. Then $[V/V] = \{[a/b] \mid a, b \in V$ and $(a, b) \in \rho\}$. We denote an element of $V^* \times V^*$ by $\langle u/v \rangle$. We also use the form $\langle V^*/V^* \rangle$ instead of $V^* \times V^*$. The set $WK_\rho(V) = [V/V]^*_\rho$ of all well-formed double-stranded strings is called the *Watson-Crick domain*, while $WK^+_\rho(V) = WK_\rho(V) - \{[\lambda/\lambda]\}$. Let the *upper strand* be $u = a_1 a_2 \cdots a_n$ and the *lower strand* be $v = b_1 b_2 \cdots b_n$. Then, we denote $[a_1/b_1][a_2/b_2] \cdots [a_n/b_n] \in WK_\rho$ as $[u/v]$. Note that when the elements in the upper strand is complement and has the same length with the lower strand, $\langle u/v \rangle = [u/v]$.

A *Watson-Crick finite automaton* (WKFA) is a 6-tuple $M = (Q, V, q_0, F, \delta, \rho)$ where Q, V, q_0 and F are defined as for a FA, and $\delta : Q \times \langle V^*/V^* \rangle \to 2^Q$ is the transition function where $\delta(q, \langle u/v \rangle)$ is not an empty set only for finitely many triples $(q, u, v) \in Q \times V^* \times V^*$. The relation in transition function $q_2 \in \delta(q_1, \langle u/v \rangle)$ can be written as a rewriting rule in grammars, i.e., $q_1 \langle u/v \rangle \to \langle u/v \rangle q_2$. The reflexive and transitive closure of $\to$ is described as $\to^*$. The language accepted by a WKFA M is

$$L(M) = \{u : [u/v] \in WK_\rho(V) \text{ and } q_0[u/v] \to^* [u/v]q \text{ where } q \in F\}.$$

The family of languages accepted is denoted by **WKFA**. By [9,14], we have **REG** $\subset$ **WKFA** $\subset$ **CS**.

A *matrix grammar* is a quadruple $G = (V, \Sigma, S, M)$ where V, Σ, S are defined as for a context-free grammar, M is a finite set of *matrices* which are finite strings over a set of context-free rules (or finite sequences of context-free rules). The language generated by G is $L(G) = \{w \in \Sigma^* \mid S \xRightarrow{\pi} w$ and $\pi \in M^*\}$. The families of languages generated by matrix grammars without erasing

rules and by matrix grammars with erasing rules are denoted by **MAT** and
MAT$^\lambda$, respectively. By [23], **CF** $\subset$ **MAT** $\subset$ **CS** and **MAT** $\subseteq$ **MAT**$^\lambda$ $\subset$ **RE**.

We recall the definitions of Watson-Crick (regular, linear, context-free) grammars (for details, see [16–20])

Definition 1. *A Watson-Crick (WK) grammar* $G = (N, T, S, P, \rho)$ *is*

- *regular if each production has the form* $A \to \langle u/v \rangle B$ *or* $A \to \langle u/v \rangle$ *where* $A, B \in N$ *and* $\langle u/v \rangle \in \langle T^*/T^* \rangle$.
- *linear if each production has the form* $A \to \langle u_1/v_1 \rangle B \langle u_2/v_2 \rangle$ *or* $A \to \langle u/v \rangle$ *where* $A, B \in N$ *and* $\langle u_1/v_1 \rangle, \langle u_2/v_2 \rangle, \langle u/v \rangle \in \langle T^*/T^* \rangle$.
- *context-free if each production has the form* $A \to \alpha$ *where* $A \in N$ *and* $\alpha \in (N \cup (\langle T^*/T^* \rangle))^*$.

Definition 2. *Let* $G = (N, T, \rho, S, P)$ *be a WK context-free grammar. We say that* $x \in (N \cup \langle T^*/T^* \rangle)^*$ *directly derives* $y \in (N \cup \langle T^*/T^* \rangle)^*$, *denoted by* $x \Rightarrow y$, *if and only if* $x = \langle u_1/v_1 \rangle A \langle u_2/v_2 \rangle$ *and* $y = \langle u_1/v_1 \rangle \alpha \langle u_2/v_2 \rangle$ *where* $A, B \in N$, $u_i, v_i \in \langle T^*/T^* \rangle$, $i = 1, 2, 3, 4$, *and* $A \to \alpha \in P$. *The language generated by a WK grammar is a quintuple* G *is defined as*

$$L(G) = \{u : [u/v] \in WK_\rho(T) \text{ and } S \Rightarrow^* [u/v]\}.$$

3   The Computational Power

In this section, we would see interesting results on how the complementarity concept embedded in Chomsky grammars increases their computational power. Here, we mention several results regarding to the generative power of WK grammars. For further details on the omitted proofs, readers are referred to [17,20].

We first consider the relations of the families of WK languages. Then, we establish the upper bound for these families.

Theorem 2 [17,20].

> **WKREG** $\subseteq$ **WKLIN, LIN** $\subset$ **WKLIN,** *and* **CF** $\subset$ **WKCF**.

Theorem 3 [17,20].

> **LIN** − **WKREG** $\neq \emptyset$, **WKREG** − **CF** $\neq \emptyset$ *and* **WKLIN** − **CF** $\neq \emptyset$.

We further investigate the upper bound of the family of WK context-free languages. Since the family of matrix languages **MAT**$^\lambda$ is closed under homomorphism (see [23,24]), the next lemma holds.

Lemma 1. *Let* $L \in T^*$ *and* $L' = \{ww' \in T^* \mid w \in L, w' = h(w)\} \in$ **MAT**$^\lambda$ *where* $h : T^* \to T'^*$ *is a homomorphism. Then,* $L \in$ **MAT**$^\lambda$.

Theorem 4. **WKCF** $\subseteq$ **MAT**$^\lambda$.

Proof. Let $G = (N, T, S, P, \rho)$ be a WK context-free grammar. Define a matrix grammar $G' = (N'', T', S'', M)$ where $N' = N \cup \{A' \mid A \in N\} \cup \{S', S'', X\}$ and $T' = T \cup \{a' \mid a \in T\}$, and the matrices of M are defined as follows.

First, we define the start matrix $m_1 = (S'' \to SXS')$ where from S and S', we generate the upper and lower strands, respectively. Then, for every production of P in the form

$$A \to \langle u_1/v_1 \rangle B_1 \langle u_2/v_2 \rangle \cdots \langle u_s/v_s \rangle B_s \langle u_{s+1}/v_{s+1} \rangle,$$

where $\langle u_i/v_i \rangle \in \langle T^*/T^* \rangle$, $1 \leq i \leq s+1$, and $B_j \in N$, $1 \leq j \leq s$, we introduce a matrix:

$$(A \to u_1 B_1 u_2 B_2 \ldots B_s u_{s+1}, \ X \to Z_{u_1} Z_{u_2} \ldots Z_{u_{s+1}} X,$$

$$A' \to v_1' B_1' v_2' B_2' \ldots B_s v_{s+1}', \ Z_{v_1} \to \lambda, Z_{v_2} \to \lambda, \ldots, Z_{v_{s+1}} \to \lambda)$$

where Z_{u_i} and Z_{v_i}, $1 \leq i \leq s+1$, are new nonterminals introduced to count the numbers of the complements of u_i based on ρ which need to be generated in the lower strand of the derived string, and $v' = h(v)$, where $h : T^* \to T'^*$ is the homomorphism defined by for all $a \in T$, $h(a) = a'$, $a' \in T'$, and $h(\lambda) = \lambda$.

For each production of P in the form $A \to \langle x/y \rangle$ where $\langle x/y \rangle \in \langle T^*/T^* \rangle$, we introduce a matrix

$$(A \to x, A' \to y', X \to Z_x X, Z_y \to \lambda)$$

where Z_x and Z_y are new nonterminals. Thus, N'' consists of all nonterminals of N' and all "Z"-nonterminals defined above.

Lastly we introduce the erasing matrix $(X \to \lambda)$. Then, we can easily see that $L(G') = \{ww' \mid w \in L(G), w' = h(w)\}$. By Lemma 1, $L(G') = L(G)$. $\quad\square$

A construct of *balanced parentheses* is a string over opening and closing parentheses where each opening parenthesis has a corresponding closing symbol and the pairs of parentheses are properly nested. The ability to differentiate between parentheses that are correctly balanced and those that are unbalanced is an important part of recognising many programming language structures. The parsing algorithms of compilers and interpreters have to check the correctness of balanced parentheses in the blocks of codes including algebraic and arithmetic expressions.

In the following examples, we will show how different types of WK grammars generate strings with different levels of balanced parentheses. To avoid confusion, we denote "**(**" as the open bracket terminal symbol and "**)**" as the closed bracket terminal symbol, in bold font.

Example 1. Let $G_5 = (\{S, A, B\}, \{(,)\}, \{((,))\}\{((,))\}, S, P_5)$ be a WK regular grammar. P_5 consists of the rules:

$$S \to \langle (/\lambda \rangle S, \quad S \to \langle (/\lambda \rangle A,$$

$$A \to \langle)/(\rangle A, \quad A \to \langle)/(\rangle B,$$

$$B \to \langle \lambda/) \rangle B, \quad B \to \langle \lambda/\lambda \rangle | S.$$

From this, we obtain the derivation:

$$S \Rightarrow \langle (/\lambda \rangle S \Rightarrow^* \langle (^n /\lambda \rangle A$$
$$\Rightarrow \langle (^n)/(\rangle A \Rightarrow^* \langle (^n)^n /(^n \rangle B$$
$$\Rightarrow \langle (^n)^n /(^n) \rangle B \Rightarrow^* \langle (^n)^n /(^n)^n \rangle S$$
$$\Rightarrow \langle (^n)^n (/(^n)^n \rangle S \Rightarrow^* \langle (^n)^n (^m /(^n)^n \rangle A \Rightarrow \cdots .$$

Hence, the language obtained is:

$$L_5 = \{ \prod_{i=1}^{j} (^{n_i})^{n_i} \mid j \geq 1 \}.$$

WK regular grammar can store the information of how much the opening parentheses "(" it has produced while generating the same amount of the closing brackets ")". However, WK regular grammars can't store the additional information if the string in L_5 are to be accompanied by additional opening parentheses before the string and the same amount of additional closing parentheses in the end of the string.

Lemma 2. $L_6 = \{ (^k (^n)^n (^m)^m)^k : n, m, k \geq 1 \} \in \textbf{WKLIN} - \textbf{WKREG}.$

Proof. The language L_6 can be generated by the following WK linear grammar $G_6 = (\{S, A, B\}, \{(,)\}, \{((,))\}, S, P_6)$, built from G_5 where

$$P_6 = P_5 \cup \{ S \to \langle (/(\rangle S \langle)/) \rangle \}.$$

The derivation is:

$$S \Rightarrow \langle (/(\rangle S \langle)/) \rangle \Rightarrow^* \left\langle (^k /(^k \rangle S \langle)^k /)^k \right\rangle$$
$$\Rightarrow \left\langle (^k (/(^k \rangle S \langle)^k /)^k \right\rangle \Rightarrow^* \left\langle (^k (^n /(^k \rangle A \langle)^k /)^k \right\rangle$$
$$\Rightarrow \left\langle (^k (^n)/(^k (\rangle A \langle)^k /)^k \right\rangle \Rightarrow^* \left\langle (^k (^n)^n /(^k (^n \rangle B \langle)^k /)^k \right\rangle$$
$$\Rightarrow \left\langle (^k (^n)^n /(^k (^n) \rangle B \langle)^k /)^k \right\rangle \Rightarrow^* \left\langle (^k (^n)^n /(^k (^n)^n \rangle S \langle)^k /)^k \right\rangle$$

$$\Rightarrow \left\langle \binom{k}{(n)}^n (/ \binom{k}{(n)}^n \right\rangle S \left\langle \right)^k /)^k \right\rangle \Rightarrow^* \left\langle \binom{k}{(n)}^n \binom{m}{(n)} / \binom{k}{(n)}^n \right\rangle A \left\langle \right)^k /)^k \right\rangle$$

$$\Rightarrow \left\langle \binom{k}{(n)}^n \binom{m}{(n)} / \binom{k}{(n)}^n () \right\rangle A \left\langle \right)^k /)^k \right\rangle$$

$$\Rightarrow^* \left\langle \binom{k}{(n)}^n \binom{m}{(n)}^m / \binom{k}{(n)}^n \binom{m}{(n)} \right\rangle B \left\langle \right)^k /)^k \right\rangle$$

$$\Rightarrow \left\langle \binom{k}{(n)}^n \binom{m}{(n)}^m / \binom{k}{(n)}^n \binom{m}{(n)} \right\rangle B \left\langle \right)^k /)^k \right\rangle$$

$$\Rightarrow^* [\binom{k}{(n)}^n \binom{m}{(n)}^m)^k / \binom{k}{(n)}^n \binom{m}{(n)}^m)^k].$$

We show that $L_6 \notin$ **WKREG** by contradiction. Suppose that L_6 can be generated by the WK regular grammar G_5. The derivation is:

$$S \Rightarrow \langle(/\lambda)S \Rightarrow^* \left\langle \binom{k}{(}/\lambda \right\rangle S$$

$$\Rightarrow^* \left\langle \binom{k}{(}(/\lambda) S \Rightarrow^* \left\langle \binom{k}{(}\binom{n}{(}/\lambda \right\rangle A$$

$$\Rightarrow \left\langle \binom{k}{(}\binom{n}{(})/() \right\rangle A \Rightarrow^* \left\langle \binom{k}{(}\binom{n}{(})^k /\binom{k}{(} \right\rangle B.$$

In the above derivation, we can see that the generation of the first closing parentheses, ")", whose total numbers are supposed to be n, are affected by the opening parentheses "$\binom{k}{(}$". Thus, the string generated will be $\binom{k}{(}\binom{n}{(})^k)^n$, instead of $\binom{k}{(}\binom{n}{(})^n)^k$. Another example which show the same phenomenon is $L = \{a^n b^m c^n d^m \mid n, m \geq 1\}$ (see Example 2 in [17]).

This applies to any other WK regular grammars as well, because until all the amount of closing parentheses for the first opening parentheses, in this case "$\binom{k}{(}$", the closing parentheses for the second batch of opening parentheses "$\binom{n}{(}$" cannot be generated; we do not have any means to do the following by WK regular grammars:

- generate the n numbers of closing parentheses first for the n number second opening parentheses instead of the k number of the first opening parentheses,
- then generate m numbers of the next opening parentheses,
- closing parentheses them, and
- finally generate the k number of the closing parentheses for the first k number of the opening parentheses.

$\square$

Lemma 3.

$$L_7 = \{\binom{k_1}{(}\binom{n_1}{(})^{n_1}\binom{m_1}{(})^{m_1})^{k_1}\binom{k_2}{(}\binom{n_2}{(})^{n_2}\binom{m_2}{(})^{m_2})^{k_2}$$

$$\mid n_1, m_1, k_1, n_2, m_2, k_2 \geq 1\} \in \textbf{WKCF} - \textbf{WKLIN}.$$

Proof. The language L_7 can be generated by the WK context-free grammar $G_7 = (\{S, A, B\}, \{(,)\}, \{((,))\}, S, P_7)$ where $P_7 = P_6 \cup \{S \rightarrow SS\}$.

Then, we have the following derivation:

$$S \Rightarrow SS \Rightarrow \langle (/\langle\rangle S\langle\rangle/)\rangle S \Rightarrow^* \left\langle \binom{k_1}{/}\binom{k_1}{} \right\rangle S \left\langle \binom{k_1}{}/\right)^{k_1} \right\rangle S$$

$$\Rightarrow^* \left\langle \binom{k_1}{(}\binom{n_1}{}^{n_1}\binom{m_1}{})/\binom{k_1}{(}\binom{n_1}{}^{n_1}() \right\rangle A \left\langle \binom{k_1}{)}/\right)^{k_1} \right\rangle S$$

$$\Rightarrow^* \left\langle \binom{k_1}{(}\binom{n_1}{}^{n_1}\binom{m_1}{})^{m_1}/\binom{k_1}{(}\binom{n_1}{}^{n_1}\binom{m_1}{} \right\rangle B \left\langle \binom{k}{)}/\right)^{k_1} \right\rangle S$$

$$\Rightarrow \left\langle \binom{k_1}{(}\binom{n_1}{}^{n_1}\binom{m_1}{})^{m_1}/\binom{k_1}{(}\binom{n_1}{}^{n_1}\binom{m_1}{}) \right\rangle B \left\langle \binom{k_1}{)}/\right)^{k_1} \right\rangle S$$

$$\Rightarrow^* \left\langle \binom{k_1}{(}\binom{n_1}{}^{n_1}\binom{m_1}{})^{m_1})^{k_1}/\binom{k_1}{(}\binom{n_1}{}^{n_1}\binom{m_1}{})^{m_1})^{k_1} \right\rangle S$$

$$\Rightarrow \left\langle \binom{k_1}{(}\binom{n_1}{}^{n_1}\binom{m_1}{})^{m_1})^{k_1}(/\binom{k_1}{(}\binom{n_1}{}^{n_1}\binom{m_1}{})^{m_1})^{k_1} \right\rangle S$$

$$\Rightarrow^* \left\langle \binom{k_1}{(}\binom{n_1}{}^{n_1}\binom{m_1}{})^{m_1})^{k_1}\binom{k_2}{(}/\binom{k_1}{(}\binom{n_1}{}^{n_1}\binom{m_1}{})^{m_1})^{k_1} \right\rangle S$$

$$\Rightarrow^* [\binom{k_1}{(}\binom{n_1}{}^{n_1}\binom{m_1}{})^{m_1})^{k_1}\binom{k_2}{(}\binom{n_2}{}^{n_2}\binom{m_2}{})^{m_2})^{k_2}/$$
$$\binom{k_1}{(}\binom{n_1}{}^{n_1}\binom{m_1}{})^{m_1})^{k_1}\binom{k_2}{(}\binom{n_2}{}^{n_2}\binom{m_2}{})^{m_2})^{k_2}]$$

In the above derivation, we can see that the first non-terminal B is accompanied by non-terminal symbols on both left and right sides. Thus, there is no

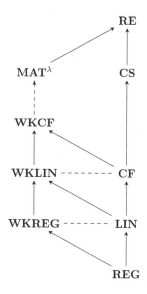

Fig. 1. The hierarchy of Watson-Crick, matrix, and Chomsky language families

way to generate the extra terminal symbols "$(^{k_2}(^{n_2})^{n_2}(^{m_2})^{m_2})^{k_2}$" from the said B, other than putting an extra non-terminal symbol besides B - in this case the second S in the rule $\{S \to SS\} \in P_7$. $\square$

Combining the results above, we obtain the following theorem.

Theorem 5. *The relations in Fig. 1 hold; the dotted lines denote incomparability of the language families and the arrows denote proper inclusions of the lower families into the upper families, while the dotted arrows denote inclusions.*

4 Conclusions

In this paper, we include further results on the generative power of Watson-Crick context-free grammars, classification between Watson-Crick languages, and closure properties, which are summarized below:

- WK linear grammars can generate some context-sensitive languages;
- the families of linear languages and WK regular languages are strictly included in the family of WK linear grammars;
- the family of WK linear languages is strictly included in the family of WK context-free languages;
- the families of WK regular languages and linear languages are not comparable;
- the family of WK regular languages is not comparable with the family of linear languages;
- the family of WK linear languages is not comparable with the family of context-free languages;
- the family of WK context free languages is included in the family of matrix languages (without appearance checking);
- WK regular grammars preserves the closure properties similar to the ones of regular languages;

The following problems related to the topic remain open:

1. Is the family of Watson-Crick context-free languages properly included in the family of matrix languages (without appearance checking)?
2. Is the family of Watson-Crick context-free languages (without erasing rules) included in the family of matrix languages (without appearance checking and without erasing rules)?
3. What are the remaining closure properties of Watson-Crick (regular, linear and context-free) grammars?

Acknowledgements. This work has been supported through International Islamic University Endowment B research grant **EDW B14-136-1021** and Fundamental Research Grant Scheme **FRGS13-066-0307**, Ministry of Education, Malaysia.

References

1. Paun, G.: Computing with membranes. J. Comput. Syst. Sci. **61**(1), 108–143 (2000)
2. Paun, G., Rozenberg, G.: A guide to membrane computing. Theor. Comput. Sci. **287**(1), 73–100 (2002)
3. Paun, G.: Introduction to membrane computing. In: Ciobanu, G., Paun, G., Pérez-Jiménez, M.J. (eds.) Applications of Membrane Computing, pp. 1–42. Springer, Heidelberg (2006)
4. Zhang, X., Liu, Y., Luo, B., Pan, L.: Computational power of tissue P systems for generating control languages. Inf. Sci. **278**, 285–297 (2014)
5. Zeng, X., Xu, L., Liu, X., Pan, L.: On languages generated by spiking neural P systems with weights. Inf. Sci. **278**, 423–433 (2014)
6. Wang, X., Song, T., Gong, F., Zheng, P.: On the computational power of spiking neural P systems with self-organization. Sci. Rep. **6**, 27624 (2016)
7. Freund, R.: An integrating view on DNA computing and membrane computing. In: Proceedings of the 9th WSEAS International Conference on Evolutionary Computing, Sofia, Bulgaria, pp. 15–20 (2008)
8. Freund, R., Paun, G., Rozernberg, G., Salomaa, A.: Watson-Crick finite automata. DIMACS Ser. Discret. Math. Theor. Comput. Sci. **48**, 297–327 (1999)
9. Păun, G., Rozenberg, G., Salomaa, A.: DNA Computing: New Computing Paradigms. Springer-Verlag, Heidelberg (1998)
10. Mohd Tamrin, M., Turaev, S., Tengku Sembok, T.M.: Weighted Watson-Crick automata. In: The 21st National Symposium on Mathematical Sciences (2013)
11. Czeizler, E., Czeizler, E.: A short survey on Watson-Crick automata. Bull. EATCS **88**, 104–119 (2006)
12. Lpez, V.F., Ramiro Aguilar, L.A., Moreno, M.N., Corchado, J.M.: Grammatical inference with bioinformatics criteria. Neurocomputing **75**(1), 88–97 (2012)
13. Sutapa, D., Mukhopadhyay, S.: A composite method based on formal grammar and DNA structural features in detecting human polymerase II promoter region. PLoS ONE **8**(2), e54843 (2013)
14. Okawa, S., Hirose, S.: The relations among Watson-Crick automata and their relations with context-free languages. IEICE Trans. Inf. Syst. E **89**(D(10)), 2591–2599 (2006)
15. Subramanian, K.G., Venkat, I., Mahalingam, K.: Context-free systems with a complementarity relation. In: Bio-Inspired Computing Theories and Applications (BIC-TA) (2011)
16. Subramanian, K., Hemalatha, S., Venkat, I.: On Watson-Crick automata. In: Proceedings of the Second International Conference on Computer Science, Engineering and Information Technology, CCSEIT 2012, Coimbatore, India, pp. 151–156 (2012)
17. Mohamad Zulkufli, N., Turaev, S., Mohd Tamrin, M., Messikh, A.: Watson-Crick linear grammars. In: The Second International Conference on Advanced Data and Information Engineering, DaEng 2015, Bali, Indonesia. Lecture Notes in Electrical Engineering (2015, to appear)
18. Mohamad Zulkufli, N., Turaev, S., Mohd Tamrin, M., Messikh, A.: Closure properties of Watson-Crick grammars. In: Proceedings of The 2nd Innovation and Analytics Conference and Exhibition (IACE), vol. 1691, p. 040032. AIP Publishing (2015)
19. Mohamad Zulkufli, N., Turaev, S., Mohd Tamrin, M., Messikh, A., Alshaikhli, I.F.T.: Computational properties of Watson-Crick context-free grammars. In: 2015 4th International Conference on Advanced Computer Science Applications and Technologies (ACSAT), pp. 186–191, December 2015

20. Mohamad Zulkufli, N.L., Turaev, S., Mohd Tamrin, M.I., Messikh, A.: Generative power and closure properties of Watson-Crick grammars. Appl. Comput. Intell. Soft Comput. **2016**, 12 p. (2016)
21. Linz, P.: An Introduction to Formal Languages and Automata. Jones and Bartlett Publishers Inc., Burlington (2006)
22. Rozenberg, G., Salomaa, A.: Handbook of Formal Languages, vol. 1-3. Springer-Verlag, Heidelberg (1997)
23. Dassow, J.: Grammars with regulated rewriting. In: Martín-Vide, C., Mitrana, V., Paun, G. (eds.) Formal Languages and Applications, vol. 148, pp. 249–273. Springer, Heidelberg (2004)
24. Dassow, J., Paun, G.: Regulated Rewriting in Formal Language Theory. Springer Publishing Company, Heidelberg (2012)

An Improvement of Small Universal Spiking Neural P Systems with Anti-Spikes

Shuo Liu[1], Kang Zhou[1(✉)], Shan Zeng[1], Huaqing Qi[2], and Xing Chen[2]

[1] Department of Math and Computer,
Wuhan Polytechnic University, Wuhan 430023, Hubei, China
zhoukang_wh@163.com

[2] Department of Economics and Management, Wuhan Polytechnic University,
Wuhan 430023, Hubei, China

Abstract. Spiking neural P systems are a class of distributed parallel computing devices inspired from the way neurons communicate by means of spikes. The necessary number of neurons to construct universal spiking neural P systems is a current research hotspot. In this work, we design the system by using the parallelism of the membrane system, and put all the instructions of the register machine in the same neuron. In this way, we can use less neurons to construct the system and make the simulation of instruction more concisely. With anti-spike, in instructions execution module, we only use standard rules. A universal systems without delay having 24 neurons is constructed.

Keywords: Spiking neural P systems · Anti-spike · Small universal

1 Introduction

Spiking neural P systems (SN P systems, for short) have been introduced in [1,2] as a new class of distributed and parallel computing devices. They were inspired by membrane systems (also known as P systems) [3–7] and are based on the neurophysiological behavior of neurons sending electrical impulses to other neurons. Since the model was put forward, for various SN P system, computation complete and the necessary number of neurons to construct universal P systems became a hotspot of research [8–10]. In this work, we investigate the necessary number of neurons to construct universal P systems with anti-spike. Păun put forward the problem for the first time in [11]. There is a universal computing SN P system with standard rules having 84 neurons and there is a universal number generating SN P system with standard rules having 76 neurons. Since then, Pan, see, e.g. [12–14] research separately the instruction of relationship, without delay rules, and weighted SN P system with rules on synapses. Small general research for SN P system, not only has the traditional computer science significance to require fewer resources, but also has its significance of life science to seek the minimum general "brain". Basic idea mainly comes from the [11], simulating the general register machine by SN P system, one neuron is associated

© Springer Nature Singapore Pte Ltd. 2016
M. Gong et al. (Eds.): BIC-TA 2016, Part I, CCIS 681, pp. 226–236, 2016.
DOI: 10.1007/978-981-10-3611-8_21

with each instruction of register machine. For the general register machine, each registry and each instruction have at least a corresponding neurons (It usually need auxiliary neurons to complete the corresponding instruction). Notice the membrane system parallelism, in the simulation, the advantage in parallel did not play completely. Because the instructions of register machine are serialized. For step t, the ith instruction is executed. At this point, only the neurons corresponding the ith instruction is fire, most other neurons are not fire. Considering the parallelism of membrane system, we can put all instructions in the same neuron, so the all instructions neurons and their corresponding auxiliary neurons was reduced to one. During the execution of the ith instruction, through the rules, only the neurons corresponding the ith instruction can take fire. In this way, we can greatly reduce the number of neurons. Compared with computer science, in the process of general simulation, registry is used to store data, corresponding hardware. And instruction is used to deal with the data according to certain rules, corresponding to the software. Pan and Zang put forward in literature [15], a neuron is used to store all of the instructions, and the corresponding small universal system is constructed. Through simulating the general register machine in literature [16,17], based on extended rules the small universal SN P system can be made up of 12 neurons without delay rule. In 2009 Pan proposes a SN P system with anti-spike and proves that under the pure rules, the system has the calculation completely. Readers can refer to [18] for more information. And then, in the literature [19] to study the ability to produce language. In the literature [20], the homogeneous SN P system with anti-spikes has proved its generality. There are many other works about anti-spikes you can refer to [21–23] and SN p you can refer to [24–30].

In this paper, based on the above work, according to [15], by constructing a neuron store all instructions, we construct a small general SN P system. The remainder of this paper is organized as follows: we first introduce related work in Sect. 2 and then elaborate the proposed small universal SN P Systems with anti-Spikes in Sect. 3. Comprehensive study and proof are discussed in Sect. 4. And finally, Sect. 5 give conclusion and acknowledgement.

2 Prerequisites

The reader must have some familiarity with language and automata theory, as well as with membrane computing, so that we recall here only a few important definitions. For more details you can refer to [13,14]. For an alphabet V, V^* is the free generated by V with respect to the concatenation operation and the identity λ (the empty string); the set of all nonempty strings over V, that is $V^* - \lambda$, is denoted by V^+.

A regular expression over an alphabet V is defined as follows:

(1) λ and each $a \in V$ are regular expressions over V;
(2) if E_1, E_2 are regular expressions, then $(E_1) \cup (E_2)$, $(E_1)(E_2)$ and $(E_1)^+$ are regular expressions over V;

(3) nothing else is a regular expressions over V.

In this work, the regular expression is mainly used as a judge in which neurons are fire.

Regular languages are defined by means of regular expressions, which will be essentially used also in our main definition in the next section. With each regular expression E there associate a language $L(E)$, defined as follow:

(1) $L(\lambda) = \lambda$ and $L(a) = a$, for all $a \in V$;
(2) $L((E_1) \cup (E_2)) = L(E_1) \cup L(E_2)$; $L((E_1)(E_2)) = L(E_1)L(E_2)$;
   $L((E_1)^+) = L(E_1)^+$ for all regular expressions $E_1, E_2 \in V$.

2.1   Universal Register Machine

The register machine has the form:

$$M = (m, H, l_0, l_h, I)$$

where m is the number of registers, H is the set of instruction labels, l_0 is the start label, l_h is the halt label, and I is the set of instructions (Table 1).

The instructions are of the following forms:

(1) $l_i : (ADD(r), l_j, l_k))$: add 1 to register r and then go to one the instructions with labels l_j and l_k, non-deterministically chosen.
(2) $l_i : (SUB(r), l_j, l_k))$: if register r is non-empty, then subtract 1 from it and go to the instruction with label l_j, otherwise go to the instruction with label l_k.
(3) HALT: the halt instruction.

A register machine is a construct $M_u = (8, H, l_0, l_h, I)$, which is of the following forms:

2.2   Spiking Neural P Systems with Anti-Spikes

A computing SN P system of degree $m \geq 1$, is a construct of the form:

$$\Pi = (O, \sigma_1, \sigma_2, \cdots, \sigma_m, syn, in, out)$$

where:

1. $O = \{a, \bar{a}\}$ is the alphabet, a is called spike, $\bar{a}$ is called anti-spike;
2. σ_i are neurons of the form: $\sigma_i = (n_i, R_i), 1 \leq i \leq m$, n_i is the initial number of spikes contained in σ_i; R_i is a finite set of rules, they have the two forms:
   (1) $E/a^c \to a^p; d$, where E is a regular expression over a, and $c \geq 1$, $d \geq 0$, $p \geq 1$, with the restriction $c \geq p$;
   (2) $a^s \to \lambda$, for $s \geq 1$, with the restriction that for each rule $E/a^c \to a^p; d$ of type(1) from R_i, we have $a^s \notin L(E)$;

Table 1. The universal register machine

$l_0 : (SUB(1), l_1, l_2)$	$l_1 : (ADD(7), l_0)$
$l_2 : (ADD(6), l_3)$	$l_3 : (SUB(5), l_2, l_4)$
$l_4 : (SUB(6), l_5, l_3)$	$l_5 : (ADD(5), l_6)$
$l_6 : (SUB(7), l_7, l_8)$	$l_7 : (ADD(1), l_4)$
$l_8 : (SUB(6), l_9, l_0)$	$l_9 : (ADD(6), l_{10})$
$l_{10} : (SUB(4), l_0, l_{11})$	$l_{11} : (SUB(5), l_{12}, l_{13})$
$l_{12} : (SUB(5), l_{14}, l_{15})$	$l_{13} : (SUB(2), l_{18}, l_{19})$
$l_{14} : (SUB(5), l_{16}, l_{17})$	$l_{15} : (SUB(3), l_{18}, l_{20})$
$l_{16} : (ADD(4), l_{11})$	$l_{17} : (ADD(2), l_{21})$
$l_{18} : (SUB(4), l_0, l_h)$	$l_{19} : (SUB(0), l_0, l_{18})$
$l_{20} : (ADD(0), l_0)$	$l_{21} : (ADD(3), l_{18})$
$l_h : HALT$	

3. $syn \subseteq \{1, 2, \cdots, m\} \times \{1, 2, \cdots, m\}, 1 \leq i \leq m, (i, i) \notin syn$.
4. $in, out \in \{1, 2, \cdots, m\}$ indicate the input and output neurons, respectively.

Note that the rules are used as in a usual SN P system, with the fact that $a, \bar{a}$ cannot stay together, a rule of the form: $a\bar{a} \to \lambda$ is applied immediately in a maximal manner, and it takes no time.

The initial configuration is described by the numbers $n_1, n_2, \cdots, n_m$ of spikes present in any neuron, with all being open. During the process, a configuration of the system is presented by both the number of spikes exit in any neuron and by the state of the neuron, that is, by the number of steps to count down until it becomes open. Thus, $\langle r_1/t_1, \cdots, r_m/t_m \rangle$ is the configuration where neuron σ_i contains $r_i \geq 0$ spikes and it will be open after $t_i \geq 0$ step, $i = 1, 2, \cdots, m$; with this notation, the initial configuration is $C_0 = \langle n_1/0, \cdots, n_m/0 \rangle$.

3   A Small Universal SN P System with Anti-Spike

We are still using the idea of simulated universal register machine to construct the small universal system in this work.

A SN P system with anti-spike consists of four modules: state instruction module, cycle trigger module, register module (simulation instruction in the registry operation) and output module (decoding output and an end to the system). Through to the corresponding part of the structure features and rules, the final system as shown in the figure below (Fig. 1):

Among them, the rounded part of the corresponding neurons for instruction selection module; the rectangular part of the corresponding neurons for instruction execution module. The dashed part is the registry neurons feedback signal, mainly is the instructions of subtraction and halt. In the instruction execution module, all rules are standard rules.

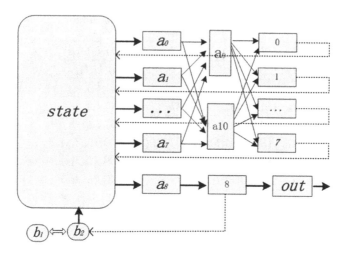

Fig. 1. The structure of system

First of all, there have a problem. The construction does not allow subtraction operation on the neuron where we place the result. Register 0 is subject of such operations, $l_{19} : (SUB(0), l_0, l_{18})$. So Păun deal with it in this way: add a register-label it with 8- and place the halt instruction with the following:

$$l_{22} : (SUB(0), l_{23}, l_{24})\ l_{23} : (ADD(8), l_{22})\ l_{24} : HALT$$

Considering the instruction of register machine are serialized, and parallel computing is one of the biggest advantage of the membrane system. For example, at time t, the ith instructions is executed. At this point, only the neurons corresponding the ith instruction is in the excited state, most other neurons are not excited state. Considering the parallelism of membrane system, we can put all instructions in the same neuron, so the all instructions neurons and their corresponding auxiliary neurons was reduced to one. During the execution of the ith instruction, through the rules, only the neurons corresponding the ith instruction can take fire. In this way, we can greatly reduce the number of neurons. We design the system is divided into two main modules. The first is instruction choice module, main task is to select the corresponding instruction, and go to next instruction; The second is the instruction execution module, main task is to do the calculation in the corresponding register (Table 2).

There are two tasks we must to solve: (1) for the neurons storing instruction, need to choose the next instruction and choose which register is operation at the same time. (2) for each neurons corresponding register, need to choose the type of instructions (addition or subtraction), and do the corresponding operation; For addition, the calculation results has no effect to choice the next instruction, easy to implement. But subtraction, we need to determine whether the number in the registry is 0, and need to return information to the neurons corresponding store instruction.

Table 2. The rules associated with neurons

neurons	The rules
$\sigma_{a_i}(0 \leq i \leq 8)$	$a \to \lambda, a^{2i+2} \to \bar{a}, a^{2i+3} \to a; a^{2j+3} \to \lambda, a^{2j+2} \to \lambda(j \neq i)$
σ_{a_9}	$\bar{a} \to \bar{a}, a \to a$
$\sigma_{a_{10}}$	$\bar{a} \to \lambda, a \to a$
$\sigma_i(0 \leq i \leq 7)$	$a(a^2)^+ / a \to a, \bar{a} \to \bar{a}$
σ_8	$a(a^2)^+ / a^2 \to a, a \to \bar{a}$
σ_{out}	$\bar{a} \to a, a^2 \to a, a \to \lambda$
$\sigma_{b_1}, \sigma_{b_2}$	$a^T \to a^T$
σ_{state}	$R_m = \left\{ a^{P(m)}(a^{20})^+ / a^{P(m)} \to a^{19} \right\}$
σ_{state}	$R_{l_i} = \left\{ a^{p(i)}(a^T)^+ / a^{p(i)+T-p(j)} \to a^{2r+3}, a^{p(i)}(a^T)^+ / a^{p(i)+T-p(k)} \to a^{2r+3} \right\}$
σ_{state}	$R_{l_i} = \left\{ \begin{array}{l} a^{p(i)}(a^T)^+ / a^{T+2} \to a^{2r+2} \\ a^{p(i)-1}(a^T)^+ / a^{p(i)-1+T-p(j)} \to a, a^{p(i)-3}(a^T)^+ / a^{p(i)-2+T-p(k)} \to a \end{array} \right\}$

3.1   The Structure of Neuron σ_{state}

As mentioned earlier, at time t, the ith instructions is executed. At this point, only the neurons corresponding the ith instruction is in the excited state, most other neurons are not excited state. Considering the parallelism of membrane system, we can put all instructions in the same neuron, so the all instruction neurons and their corresponding auxiliary neurons was reduced to one. During the execution of the ith instruction, through the rules, only the neurons corresponding the ith instruction can take fire. Now we put the 25 instructions in one neuron, refer to [8], called σ_{state}. The form as following:

$$R_{state} = l_0 \cup l_1 \cup \cdots \cup l_{25}$$

For neuron σ_{state}, need to solve at the same time: choose the next instruction and choose which register. We can use a forgetting rule to achieve it.

For add instruction, $l_i : (ADD(r), l_j, l_k)$, the forgetting rule as the following:

$$R_{l_i} = \left\{ a^{p(i)}(a^T)^+ / a^{p(i)+T-p(j)} \to a^{2r+3}, a^{p(i)}(a^T)^+ / a^{p(i)+T-p(k)} \to a^{2r+3} \right\}$$

For sub instruction, $l_i : (SUB(r), l_j, l_k)$, the forgetting rule as the following:

$$R_{l_i} = \left\{ \begin{array}{l} a^{p(i)}(a^T)^+ / a^{T+2} \to a^{2r+2} \\ a^{p(i)-1}(a^T)^+ / a^{p(i)-1+T-p(j)} \to a \\ a^{p(i)-3}(a^T)^+ / a^{p(i)-2+T-p(k)} \to a \end{array} \right\}$$

Among them, the first step is only selected the corresponding register; After the feedback of the corresponding register, if the corresponding information and regular expression match, and then select the next instruction.

Remark: We assume that $T = 20$; $P(i) = 4(i+1)$. The value of the T is difference from number corresponding instruction. As long as meet: $T > \max(P(i))$, and $P(i) = 4(i + 1)$ is mainly used in the subtraction instructions to different.

3.2   The Structure of Auxiliary Neurons σ_a

There are two kind auxiliary neurons. The first kind auxiliary neurons aim is to determine which neuron operate and do what kind operation (ADD or SUB) though accept the spikes from neuron σ_{state}. The spike from neuron must be identified by auxiliary neurons $\sigma_{a_i} (0 \le i \le 7)$, and need to differentiate instruction type. Based on coding theory, 19 kinds of signals can be used. There are rules corresponding auxiliary neurons:

Table 3. The rules of auxiliary neurons

Neurons	σ_{a_0}	σ_{a_1}	σ_{a_2}	σ_{a_3}	σ_{a_4}	σ_{a_5}	σ_{a_6}	σ_{a_7}	σ_{a_8}
SUB	2	4	6	8	10	12	14	16	18
ADD	3	5	7	9	11	13	15	17	19

Assume that at some moment, neurons $\sigma_{a_i} (0 \le i \le 7)$ receives 11 spikes, only neuron σ_4 can be fire by the rule: $a^{2i+3} \to a$, then we can see that this means register 4 should do ADD instruction, and the other registers do nothing (Table 3).

The second kind auxiliary neurons aim is to deal with the operation only use standard rule in the instruction execution module. Because the encoding of the value n of a register R is done by means of placing $2n$ spikes in the neuron associated with the register. If we want to add 1 in some register, we should send 2 spikes. When do ADD, neurons σ_9, σ_{10} accept one spike form $\sigma_{a_i} (0 \le i \le 7)$, then they send two spikes to the same neurons corresponding some register use rule $a \to a$. When do SUB, neurons σ_9, σ_{10} accept one anti-spike form $\sigma_{a_i} (0 \le i \le 7)$, then they send one anti-spikes to the same neurons corresponding some register by using rule $\bar{a} \to \bar{a}, \bar{a} \to \lambda$.

4   Proof and Conclusion

Theorem: There is a *universal* SN P *system* with anti-spike having 24 neurons, in the instruction execution module, all rules are *standard rules*.

4.1 Module ADD (Simulating $l_i : (ADD(r), l_j, l_k)$)

We start by activating neuron σ_{state} associated with the l_i label of M, when firing, neuron σ_{state} non-deterministically chose the rule

$$R_{l_i} = \left\{ a^{p(i)}(a^T)^+ \Big/ a^{p(i)+T-p(j)} \to a^{2r+3} \right\}$$

produces $2r+3$ spikes, which are sent to all neuron $\sigma_{ai}(0 \leq i \leq 7)$. The number of spikes in neuron σ_{state} is of the form $a^{p(j)}(a^T)^+$, it will activate neuron σ_{state} associated with the label l_j of M.

For the neuron $\sigma_{ai}(0 \leq i \leq 7, i \neq r)$, use the rule $a^{2i+3} \to \lambda$, and do nothing with others. But the number of spikes in neuron σ_{ar} is of the form $2i+3$, hence the rule can fire. Though the rule $a \to a$ of neuron $\sigma_{a9}, \sigma_{a10}$, neuron σ_r will accept 2 spikes, it means the number of associated register add 1. And then no rule can use. So in this way, we simulate $l_i : (ADD(r), l_j, l_k)$, the number of register is add 1, and non-deterministically chose next instruction.

Therefore, the system can simulated ADD instruction correctly. It add 1 to register r and then go to one instructions with labels l_j and l_k, non-deterministically chosen.

4.2 Module SUB (Simulating $l_i : (SUB(r), l_j, l_k)$)

We start by activating neuron σ_{state} associated with the l_i label of M, when firing, neuron σ_{state} use the rule:

$$a^{p(i)}(a^T)^+ \Big/ a^{T+2} \to a^{2r+2}$$

produces $2r+2$ spikes, which are sent to all neuron $\sigma_{ai}(0 \leq i \leq 7)$. The number of spikes in neuron σ_{state} is of the form $a^{p(i)-2}(a^T)^+$, it con not activate neuron σ_{state} next time.

For the neuron $\sigma_{ai}(0 \leq i \leq 7, i \neq r)$, use the rule $a^{2i+2} \to \lambda$, and then do nothing. But the number of spikes in neuron σ_{ar} is of the form $2i+2$, hence the rule $a^{2i+2} \to \bar{a}$ can fire, though the rule $\bar{a} \to \lambda, \bar{a} \to \bar{a}$ of neuron $\sigma_{a9}, \sigma_{a10}$, neuron σ_r will accept 1 anti-spike.

(1) If there have $2n$ spikes in neuron σ_r already, that means the number of spikes is not empty, now use the rule: $a\bar{a} \to \lambda$, then the number of spikes in neuron σ_r is of the form $a(a^2)^+$, and it can use the rule:

$$a(a^2)^+ \Big/ a \to a$$

it means the number of spikes in neuron σ_r reduce 2. And then the neuron σ_{state} accept the spike from neuron σ_r, the number of spikes in neuron σ_{state} is of the form $a^{p(i)-1}(a^T)^+$. Hence firstly the rule

$$a^{p(i)-1}(a^T)^+ \Big/ a^{p(i)-1+T-p(j)} \to a$$

can fire, it will activate neuron σ_{state} associated with the l_j label of M and secondly a spike sent to all neuron $\sigma_{ai}(0 \leq i \leq 7)$. By the rule: $a \rightarrow \lambda$, it con not activate any neuron next time.

(2) If there have no spike in neuron σ_r, then the number of spikes in neuron σ_r is only an anti-spike, it can use the rule: $\bar{a} \rightarrow \bar{a}$. It means the number of spikes in neuron σ_r is not change. And then the neuron σ_{state} accept the anti-spike from σ_r, the number of spikes in neuron σ_{state} is of the form $a^{p(i)-3}(a^T)^+$. Hence firstly the rule:

$$a^{p(i)-3}(a^T)^+ \Big/ a^{p(i)-3+T-p(k)} \rightarrow a$$

can fire, it will activate neuron σ_{state} associated with the l_k label of M and secondly a spike sent to all neuron $\sigma_{ai}(0 \leq i \leq 7)$. By the rule : $a \rightarrow \lambda$, it con not activate any neuron next time.

4.3   Module OUTPUT

We start by activating neuron σ_{state} associated with the halt label of M, when firing, neuron σ_{state} use the rule:

$$a^{P(m)}(a^{20})^+ \Big/ a^{P(m)} \rightarrow a^{19}$$

produces 19 spikes, which are sent to neuron σ_{a8}. The number of spikes from neuron σ_{a8} is of the form $2i + 3$, hence (1) the rule $a^{2i+3} \rightarrow a$ can fire, but (2) no rule used for neuron σ_{state} can fire.

Now register 8 has $2n$ spikes, add the spike from neuron σ_{a8}, the number of spikes in neuron σ_8 is of the form $2n + 1$, the rule $a(a^2)^+ \Big/ a^2 \rightarrow a$ fire, hence (1) the rule of neuron σ_{out}: $a^2 \rightarrow a$ can fire and send a spike to out, but (2) no rule used for neuron σ_{b2} can fire.

Then register 8 has $2n - 1$ spikes, the rule $a(a^2)^+ \Big/ a^2 \rightarrow a$ fire again, then the rule of neuron σ_{out}:$a \rightarrow \lambda$ can fire. It continue do until the neuron σ_8 only has one spike. The last time when neuron σ_8 fire, it use the rule $a \rightarrow \bar{a}$, hence neuron σ_{out} fire again, and then the system halts. In this way, we get the spike train 10^n1, encoding the number n as the result of the computation.

5   Conclusions and Remark

This paper mainly studied the small general of SN P system, based on the parallelism of P system, we put all the instructions on the same neurons, and reduces the number of necessary neuron greatly. In this way, we can use less neurons to construct the system and make the simulation of instruction more concise. In particular, using anti-spike, all instructions operation use standard rules. A universal systems without delay rules having 24 neurons is constructed.

But the choice of instruction must be implemented through rules, the difficulty of the rules greatly increased. Similar to computer science, through software programming to save hardware cost. How to find a way which can make not only the number of neurons decreased, but also the complexity of the rules moderate, This is a problem. At the same time, the anti-spikes is only used in the registry operation. How to use the two kind spikes to encode more information, such as 9 registry must have 18 spikes to differentiate, if we use the two kind spikes to reduce the number of spike for 9? this problem is to consider in the future. On the other hand, this idea can deal with other kind of SN P system? it is a quite interesting problem.

Acknowledgments. Zhou Kang is corresponding author. The work was supported by National Natural Science Foundation of China (Grant Nos. 61179032 and 61303116), the Special Scientific Research Fund of Food Public Welfare Profession of China (Grant No. 2015130043), the Research and Practice Project of Graduate Education Teaching Reform of Polytechnic University (YZ2015002), the Scientific research project of Wuhan Polytechnic University (2016Y01), the science and technology research project of the Hubei province (B201601).

References

1. Ionescu, M., Păun, G., Yokomori, T.: Spiking neural P systems. Fundam. Inform. **71**, 279–308 (2006)
2. Pan, L.Q., Paun, G.: Spiking neural P systems: an improved normal form. Theor. Comput. Sci. **411**, 906–918 (2010)
3. Păun, G.: Membrane Computing-An Introduction. Springer-Verlag, Berlin (2002)
4. Rozenberg, G., Salomaa, A.: Handbook of Formal Languages, 3 Volumes. Springer-Verlag, Berlin (1997)
5. Zhang, G.X., Cheng, J.X., Wang, T.: Membrane Computing: Theory and Applications. Science Press, Marrickville (2014)
6. Zhang, G.X., Pan, L.Q.: A survey of membrane computing as a new branch of natural computing. Chin. J. Comput. **33**(2), 208–214 (2010)
7. Zhang, X.Y., Liu, Y.J., Luo, B., Pan, L.Q.: Computational power of tissue P systems for generating control languages. Inf. Sci. **278**(10), 285–297 (2014)
8. Song, T., Gong, F., Liu, X.Y.: Spiking neural P systems with white hole neurons. IEEE Trans. Nanobiosci. (2016, in press). doi:10.1109/TNB.2016.2598879
9. Song, T., Pan, L.: Spiking neural P systems with request rules. Neurocomputing **193**, 193–200 (2016)
10. Wang, X., Song, T., Gong, F.: On the computational power of spiking neural P systems with self-organization. Sci. Rep. **6**, 27624 (2016)
11. Păun, A., Păun, G.: Small universal spiking neural P systems. BioSystems **90**(1), 48–60 (2007)
12. Zhang, X.Y., Zeng, X.X., Pan, L.Q.: Smaller universal spiking neural P systems. Fundam. Inform. **87**(1), 117–136 (2008)
13. Zhang, X.Y., Jiang, Y., Pan, L.Q.: Small universal spiking neural P systems with exhaustive use of rules. J. Comput. Theor. Nanosci. **7**(5), 890–899 (2010)
14. Pan, L.Q., Zeng, X.X., Zhang, X.Y., et al.: Spiking neural P systems with weighted synapses. Neural Process. Lett. **35**(1), 13–27 (2012)

15. Pan, L.Q., Zeng, X.X.: A Note on Small Universal Spiking Neural P Systems
16. Korec, I.: Small universal register machines. Theor. Comput. Sci. **168**(2), 267–301 (1996)
17. Minsky, M.: Computation-Finite and Infinite Machines. Prentice Hall, Upper Saddle River (1967)
18. Pan, L.O., Păun, G.: Spiking neural P systems with anti-spikes. Int. J. Comput. Commun. Control **4**(3), 273–282 (2009)
19. Krithivasan, K., Metta, V.P., Garg, D.: On string languages generated by spiking neural P systems with anti-spikes. Int. J. Found. Comput. Sci. **22**(1), 15–27 (2011)
20. Peng, X.W., Fan, X.: Homogeneous spiking neural P systems with anti-spikes. J. Chin. Comput. Syst. (2013)
21. Song, T., Pan, L., Wang, J., Venkat, I.: Normal forms of spiking neural P systems with anti-spikes. IEEE Trans. Nanobiosci. **11**(4), 273–282 (2012)
22. Song, T., Liu, X., Zeng, X.: Asynchronous spiking neural P systems with anti-spikes. Neural Process. Lett. **42**(3), 1–15 (2014)
23. Song, T., Jiang, Y., Shi, X.: Small universal spiking neural P systems with anti-spikes. J. Comput. Theor. Nanosci. **10**(4), 999–1006 (2013)
24. Zhang, X.Y., Pan, L.Q., Păun, A.: On universality of axon P systems. IEEE Trans. Neural Netw. Learn. Syst. **26**(11), 2816–2829 (2015)
25. Zeng, X.X., Xu, L., Liu, X.R., Pan, L.Q.: On languages generated by spiking neural P systems with weights. Inf. Sci. **278**, 423–433 (2014)
26. Wang, X., Song, T., Gong, F., Zheng, P.: On the computational power of spiking neural P systems with self-organization. Sci. Rep. (2016). doi:10.1038/srep27624
27. Zeng, X.X., Zhang, X.Y., Song, T., Pan, L.Q.: Spiking neural P systems with thresholds. Neural Comput. **26**(7), 1340–1361 (2014)
28. Zhang, X.Y., Wang, B.J., Pan, L.Q.: Spiking neural P systems with a generalized use of rules. Neural Comput. **26**(12), 2925–2943 (2014)
29. Zeng, X.X.: Research on computational property of spiking neural P systems. Hua Zhong University of Science Technology, Wuhan (2011)
30. Song, T.: Research on computational properties and applications of spiking neural P systems. Hua Zhong University of Science Technology, Wuhan (2013)

The Implementation of Membrane Clustering Algorithm Based on FPGA

Yunying Yang[1,2], Jun Ming[1,2], Jun Wang[1,2(✉)], Hong Peng[3], Zhang Sun[1,2], and Wenping Yu[1,2]

[1] Key Laboratory of Fluid and Power Machinery, Ministry of Education, Xihua University, Chengdu 610039, People's Republic of China
wj.xhu@foxmail.com
[2] School of Electrical Engineering and Electronic Information, Xihua University, Chengdu 610039, People's Republic of China
[3] School of Computer and Software Engineering, Xihua University, Chengdu 610039, People's Republic of China

Abstract. Compared with the theoretical research, the application research of membrane computing was started late. Firstly, cell-like P system is selected as a computational framework for data clustering based on studies of previous membrane clustering algorithm in this paper. Then, particle swarm optimization algorithm is used as the optimization algorithm to construct the membrane algorithm and the parallel computing characteristic of programmable logic device FPGA is used to realize data clustering. Finally, experimental results show that FPGA processor can realize the characteristics of parallel computing while the system operates the membrane clustering algorithm, which can improve the speed of operation at the same time. Besides, the proposed method can be used in practical engineering systems.

Keywords: Membrane computing · FPGA · Parallelism · Clustering algorithm

1 Introduction

As a branch of natural computing, membrane computing is designed to abstract computational models from the structure and function of life cells as well as the cell collaboration in organizations, which is firstly proposed by Păun in his research report presented in [1]. In past years, the studies of the membrane computing can be roughly divided into three aspects: (1) Modeling and theoretical analysis, namely, the establishment of a variety of membrane systems and the analysis of capacity and effectiveness of calculation; (2) Construction and application of membrane system for practical problems; (3) Development of simulation platform of membrane system in software and hardware. Nowadays, a large number of membrane systems have been constructed in the first aspect, and the fruitful results of the calculation ability and computational effectiveness have

© Springer Nature Singapore Pte Ltd. 2016
M. Gong et al. (Eds.): BIC-TA 2016, Part I, CCIS 681, pp. 237–248, 2016.
DOI: 10.1007/978-981-10-3611-8_22

been formed in [2–7]. At the same time, a number of membrane system software and hardware simulation platforms have been successfully developed in [8–10]. However, compared with the theoretical research, the application research of membrane computing was started late.

In recent years, some scholars have begun to pay attention on the study of membrane computing, including supervised learning (classification) and unsupervised learning (clustering), which has produced a number of meaningful research results in [11–15]. For example, the classical Hebbian learning law is used to develop a classification model through designing a simple spiking neural membrane system proposed by Gutierrez-Naranjo and Pérez-Jiménez in [11], and a model of membrane computing for fault diagnosis of power system has been studied in [12]. In addition, a learning model against the proposed fuzzy spiking neural membrane system is developed in [13]. For the unsupervised learning problem, a hierarchical clustering method has been discussed to be realized through the membrane computing by Cardona et al. in [14], which uses an evolutionary rule of the membrane system to realize the classical hierarchical clustering theory and verify the model. A modified clustering algorithm is proposed to realize the traditional k-medoids algorithm by using the rules of a cell membrane system in [15]. A clustering framework inspired by the membrane computing has been proposed in [16,17], and the test results on the benchmark data sets show that the clustering framework outperforms the classical clustering algorithm in clustering quality (accuracy), stability and convergence significantly. Therefore, it can be strongly predicted that the membrane computing has potential advantages and good prospects in dealing with data clustering problems.

A clustering algorithm in the framework of membrane computing has been proposed by Peng in [14–16], which is called membrane clustering algorithm (MC). The core of this method is to establish a tissue-like P system with degree of 3 and hybrid evolution mechanisms, and the final goal is to automatically search the optimal clustering centers for a data set to be clustered. In order to realize the distributed parallel clustering algorithm, how to implement the membrane clustering algorithm on the programmable logic device FPGA has been discussed in this paper. For this reason, a parallel implementation method of membrane clustering algorithm based on FPGA by using the particle swarm optimization algorithm is proposed. Then, the distributed parallel computing model is established, and the numerical calculation process with high density is described. Finally, the parallel simulation is performed on FPGA.

The rest of this paper is organized as follows. Section 2 states the structure and objection representation of membrane clustering algorithm and algorithm learning. Parallel implementation of the membrane clustering algorithm on FPGA is described in detail in Sect. 3. Experiment results and analysis are provided in Sect. 4. Finally, Sect. 5 draws the conclusion.

2   Membrane Clustering Algorithm

2.1   Structure of Membrane Clustering Algorithm

Inspired by the idea of membrane computing and combined with the evolutionary rule of particle swarm optimization algorithm, a membrane clustering algorithm is proposed. In this paper, a cell-like P system is constructed as computing framework, which is used for data clustering operations, and finally determines the optimal clustering centers. The cell-like P system of degree q can be formally described as follows:

$$\Pi = (O, \omega_1, \omega_2, \ldots, \omega_q, R_1, R_2, \ldots, R_q, R', i_0) \tag{1}$$

where

(1) O is a set of all objects.

(2) $\omega_i (1 \leq i \leq q)$ is initial multiset of objects in ith cell.

(3) $R_i (1 \leq i \leq q)$ is finite set of evolution rules in ith cell. The evolutionary rules are combined with the particle swarm algorithm and described by the following velocity-location model:

$$V_j^i = \omega \cdot V_j^i + c_1 r_1 (P_{best}^i - Z_j^i) + c_2 r_2 (G_{best} - Z_j^i) \tag{2}$$

$$Z_j^i = Z_j^i + V_j^i \tag{3}$$

where
(a) ω is the inertia weight, c_1 and c_2 are two constants, r_1 and r_2 are two random number in $[0,1]$.

(b) Z_j^i is jth object in ith cell and V_j^i is the corresponding velocity vector.

(c) P_{best}^i is the best object in ith cell, while G_{best} is the best object in the whole system.

(4) R_i' is finite set of communication rules of the form: $< i, Z/Z', 0 >$, where, Z and Z' are two objects, $i = 1, 2, ..., q$.

(5) i_0 indicates the output region.

In the above about the specific definition of P system, because the PSO has the advantages of fast speed, high calculation efficiency, simple algorithm logic and suitability for analysis and processing of real data, this paper chooses PSO as the evolution rules of the object. More importantly, PSO itself is a parallel computing processing operation and the algorithm won't produce competitive relationships between different particles in the process of running. Although it is easy to fall into local optimum, the object communication in the process of the calculation can be made continuously between the cellular nodes after the algorithm combined with the framework of cell-like P system, which can effectively overcome this disadvantage.

2.2   Object Representation in the Structure of the Membrane Clustering Algorithm

In this paper, the object of the data clustering in the structure of the membrane clustering algorithm is expressed as follows: suppose that in a d-dimensional space, the clustering problem is considered to partition data set $D = \{X_1, X_2, \ldots, X_n\}$ into k clusters, $C_1, C_2, \ldots, C_k$, where $Z_1, Z_2, \ldots, Z_k$ are the corresponding cluster centers. In order to process the clustering problem, the objects in the system are designed as a $k \times d$-dimensional vector, shown in Fig. 1.

$$Z = (Z_1, Z_2, \ldots, Z_k) = (Z_{11}, Z_{12}, \ldots, Z_{1d}, \ldots, Z_{k1}, Z_{k2}, \ldots, Z_{kd}) \qquad (4)$$

where $Z_i = (Z_{i1}, Z_{i2}, \ldots, Z_{id})$ is ith cluster center, namely the particle of PSO algorithm.

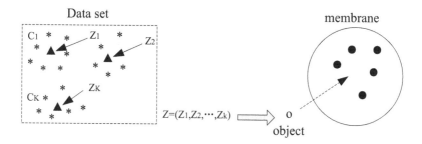

Fig. 1. Representation of the object in the clustering problem

As is well known for the theory of cluster problems, except choosing the appropriate classified measures, how to evaluate clustering centers of each iteration calculation is also an important question. The final clustering results make the same feature data compact, and loose conversely. Therefore, based on such a standard and combined with the characteristics of the data type, we choose the following way (5) as the evaluation function of the clustering centers, namely, the fitness function of the object in the cell.

$$f(Z) = M(C_1, C_2, \ldots, C_k) = \sum_{i=1}^{k} \sum_{X_j \in c_i} d(X_j, z_i) \qquad (5)$$

where, $d(X_j, z_i)$ represents the distance from the data point to the clustering centers. Generally, the value of particle is smaller, the object is better, and vice versa.

2.3 Learning Algorithm

PSO algorithm was put forward by Eberhart and Kennedy in 1995 at first, and its basic concept was derived from the study of the foraging behavior of birds in [17]. In this paper, PSO algorithm is used as the optimization algorithm of data clustering and the basic idea is to use the evolution mechanism of the PSO to make iterative optimization. The particles of PSO algorithm are the data points of data clustering. Firstly, the initial clustering centers can be determined after loading the data and initialization, and their fitness function can be calculated. Then, the clustering centers will be calculated by speed update function and location update function of PSO algorithm. Finally, the current local optimal particle and the global optimal particle are updated after completing fitness calculation and comparing with the initialized clustering centers. The iterative calculation can be completed following the steps, and the optimal clustering center can be obtained to realize data clustering. Through the implementation of evolution mechanisms of the PSO algorithm, the process of finding the local optimal particle and the global best particle is the process of finding the optimal cluster center.

3 Parallel Implementation of the Membrane Clustering Algorithm on FPGA

3.1 FPGA Parallel Computing Principle

Field Programmable Gate Array (FPGA for short) is a field programmable logic array in [18]. A typical FPGA internal structure is shown in Fig. 2, the FPGA chip mainly contains programming input and output unit, basic programming logic unit, clock management, embedded block ram, rich routing resources, embedded unit in the bottom function and embedded hardware module. As it can be seen from Fig. 2, the FPGA is composed of multiple internal programmable logic blocks (CLB), and there is an abundance of routing resources between logic programming blocks. In order to achieve different functions, the FPGA can be designed as different wiring to connect different circuits by the design of verilog. However, different functions within the FPGA are embodied in different arrays, and each array can be performed in parallel. It is generally known the circuit is a parallel process. In this paper, the use of connections inside the FPGA programmable logic blocks can be completed all the functions shown in Fig. 3, including the data loading, initialization, data processing and the final output, the whole process of data processing is done inside the FPGA without using any peripheral equipment.

3.2 Implementation Process of Membrane Clustering Algorithm on FPGA

In this paper, the object of single membrane cell will parallel execute the evolutionary mechanism in this environment by using cell-like P system as computing

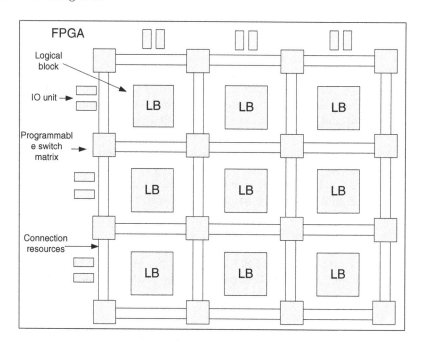

Fig. 2. A typical FPGA structure diagram

framework and regarding outer membrane as a public environment. Finally, the parallelism of membrane computing will be verified by implementing a minimum system.

The logic steps are shown in Fig. 3, and described as follows:

Step 1: Loading data: input parameters are given, q, m, k, $c1$, $c2$ as well as data set $D = \{X_1, X_2, \ldots, X_n\}$; here, only a minimum system is achieved temporarily. $q = 1$, $m = 2$.

Step 2: Initialization: m initial objects can be randomly generated for each of the q cells respectively.

Step 3: For each object in the q cells, the evolution and communication operations are performed as follows:

(1) Object evolution: the object is evolved by using Eqs. (2) and (3).
(2) Object evaluation: the fitness value of the object is computed by using Eq. (5).
(3) Object communication: the object is transported to update the global best object G_{best}.

Step 4: Halting judgment: if the preset stop condition is satisfied, the system halts and exports the global best object G_{best}; Otherwise, go to Step 3.

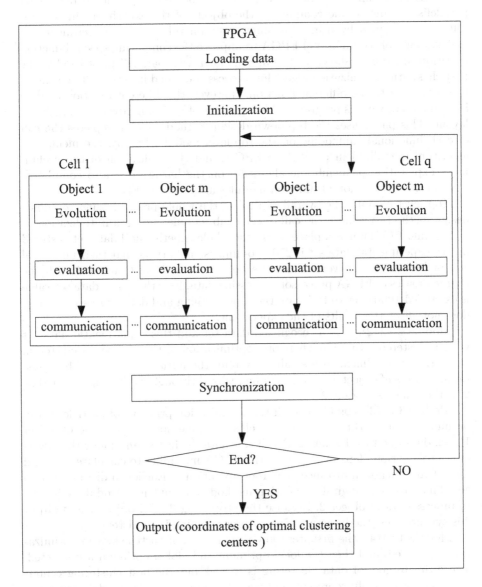

Fig. 3. The function of the membrane clustering algorithm on FPGA

3.3 Implementation Program Module Partitioning of Membrane Clustering Algorithm on FPGA

The PSO algorithm is operated on FPGA in the cell P system to performed parallelism of membrane computing, the objects of the experiment in the two cells are performed by using the same evolution rules, so the experiment can make full use of parallelism of FPGA to improve the computing speed. Function partition diagram is shown in Fig. 3, combined with parallelism of FPGA, the particle swarm optimization algorithm process is divided into the different modules according to the different function. However, the different function module is composed of various programmable logic unit of FPGA hardware structure by layout. This paper uses the top-down design method which completes the call of each functional submodule on the top-level module. Finally, the membrane algorithm is realized in parallel on FPGA, and the realization of the preliminary exploration of membrane algorithm on the hardware is also completed. The specific description of function modules are shown in Fig. 4:

Top level module: the overall control of the whole process, using top-down design method to achieve the call of each sub module and data initialization.

Module 1 ($M1$): it is a place where the whole experimental data set is stored in, the experimental data set is 250 two-dimensional arrays that their numerical size of horizontal and vertical axes is between 4 and 16. Combined with the characteristics of FPGA processor processing data, here the whole data set value is expanded 100 times to facilitate the programming and data processing, but it does not affect the results of the experiment.

Module 2 ($M2$): it is a recognized data set and this experimental data set is best clustered into k = 5, therefore, optimization of the number of clustering categories is simplified. In a smallest system, the initialization of the five clustering centers of object 1in a cell will be realized through module 2, and module 2' is the same as module 2.

Module 3 ($M3$): combined with the optimization principle of particle swarm optimization algorithm and the data clustering method, the particle of object 1(each data point of the data set) will calculate the fitness and judge the merits of the calculation. This module uses the FPGA multiplier to calculate Δx^2 and Δy^2 of the Euclidean distance. The root operation of Euclidean distance uses a coordinate rotation digital calculation method while judging. Module 3' is used to process data in object 2. Because the processing flow of object 1 and object 2 is synchronous, the basic principle of programming is consistent.

Module 4 ($M4$): the first iteration computation of particle swarm optimization is realized, and then the local optimum and global optimum are selected. The ultimate goal of data clustering is to pick out the best clustering center, which can accurately represent different characteristics of each data type and achieve the best classification data set. It needs to be explained that the global optimum after the iteration computation of the PSO algorithm is the best cluster center of data clustering.

Module 5 ($M5$): it will accomplish the velocity and position updating calculation of object 1. The experimental data is two-dimensional, so the method is used to complete the speed update and position update of abscissa and ordinate of data points respectively. Module 5' is to process particles of the object 2, and then the new local optimum particle and the global best particle are obtained after making comparison of the particle's fitness. Among them, the velocity update function of the PSO algorithm involves random number r_1 and r_2, then the programming way uses a LFSR (linear feedback shift register) principle to generate random numbers in this paper. Owing to the minimum system haven two objects, the clustering center of each object is two-dimensional, including x and y coordinates, and a velocity update requires two random numbers r_1 and r_2, the system contains eight random number generation modules. Note that the produce of r_1 and r_2 are changed along with the iteration, that is, the velocity updating formula is used while an iterative arithmetic is carried out. And the random numbers r_1 and r_2 will change in real-time following the whole system update.

4   Experiment Results and Analysis

The experimental parameters involved in this paper are set to $c1 = c2 = 1$, $q = 1, m = 2$. $AD.5$ is selected as the experimental data set for data clustering (combined with the characteristics of processing data on FPGA, this experiment will expand the size of all the data points 100 times, which does not impact on the analysis of experimental results). After writing and debugging stages of the entire program, the experimental data set is brought to the experiment. Then it can achieve programming control of data clustering inside the FPGA, observe the simulation results, and draw the conclusion of the experiment.

Table 1. Experimental results.

The number of iteration	f-1-para-old	f-2-para-old	f-1-para-new	f-2-para-new
1	70971	119406	70971	119406
2	64171	83403	64171	83403
10	63501	74514	59754	54748
50	95381	248791	49283	54748

Experiment results are shown in Table 1, f-1-para old and f-2-para old show the fitness values before iteration. f-1-para new and f-2-para new show the fitness values after iteration. The changes of the object's fitness values in the each cell reflect the implementation of membrane clustering algorithm based on FPGA. The experimental results show that fitness of particles decrease with the increasing of the number of iterations in the intracellular two objects. The convergence trend indicating that each particle is gradually closer to the best local, and the data clustering effect can be achieved. As long as it has been running to observe the results of the operation, the global optimal will be got to achieve the best

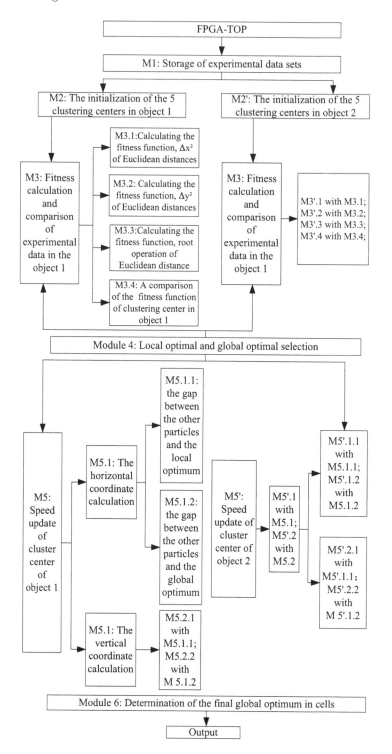

Fig. 4. Programs modular partition of membrane clustering algorithm on FPGA

division of the whole system data. In this section, the concept of parallel has been always adhered to the whole implementation process of programming, because the process of data clustering is parallel executed in the two objects of the system by using the PSO algorithm. Not only the better reflects the parallelism of membrane clustering algorithm, but also improves the efficiency of the clustering process, and obtains the ideal clustering effect.

5   Conclusions

In order to realize the parallelism of the membrane clustering algorithm, the PSO algorithm is presented based on FPGA hardware system in the cell-like P system. In this paper, the Euclidean distance is selected as the similarity measure. Thus, the smaller the f value, the closer to the clustering centers, which indicates the object is better. Finally, a preliminary realization is made by the application of the membrane computing in hardware, and it further expands the range of the membrane computing in practical engineering applications.

Acknowledgments. This work was partially supported by the National Natural Science Foundation of China (No. 61472328), Research Fund of Sichuan Science and Technology Project (No. 2015HH0057) and the key equipment project of Sichuan Provincial Economic and Information Committee (No. [2014]128), China.

References

1. Păun, G.: Computing with membranes. J. Comput. Syst. Sci. **61**(1), 108–143 (2000)
2. Ionescu, M., Păun, G., Pérez-Jiménez, M.J., Yokomori, T.: Spiking neural P systems. Fundam. Inf. **11**(4), 423–436 (2011)
3. Martin-Vide, C., Păun, A., Păun, G.: On the power of P systems with symport rules. J. Univers. Comput. Sci. **8**(2), 317–331 (2002)
4. Pan, L.Q., Păun, G.: Spiking neural P systems with anti-spikes. Int. J. Comput. Commun. Control **4**(3), 273–282 (2009)
5. Chen, H.M., Tseren-Onolt, I., Păun, G.: Computing along the axon. Prog. Nat. Sci. **17**(4), 417–423 (2007)
6. Wang, J., Shi, P., Peng, H.: Membrane computing model for IIR filter design. Inf. Sci. **329**, 164–176 (2016)
7. Wang, J., Shi, P., Peng, H., Pérez-Jiménez, M.J., Wang, T.: Weighted fuzzy spiking neural P systems. IEEE Trans. Fuzzy Syst. **21**(2), 209–220 (2013)
8. Cabarle, F., Adorna, H., Martínez-del-Amor, M.A.: Simulating spiking neural P systems without delays using GPUs. Int. J. Nat. Comput. Res. **2**(2), 19–31 (2011)
9. Peña-Cantillana, F., Díaz-Pernil, D., Christinal, H.A., Gutiírrez-Naranjo, M.A.: Implementation on CUDA of the smoothing problem with tissue-like P systems. Int. J. Nat. Comput. Res. **2**(3), 25–34 (2011)
10. Jin, J., Liu, H., Wang, F., Peng, H., Wang, J.: Parallel implementation of P systems for data clustering on GPU. In: Gong, M., Pan, L., Song, T., Tang, K., Zhang, X. (eds.) BIC-TA 2015. CCIS, vol. 562, pp. 200–211. Springer, Heidelberg (2015). doi:10.1007/978-3-662-49014-3_18

11. Gutierrez-Naranjo, M.A., Pérez-Jiménez, M.J.: A spiking neural P system based model for Hebbian learning. In: Ninth Workshop on Membrane Computing, pp. 189–208 (2008)

12. Peng, H., Wang, J., Pérez-Jiménez, M.J., Wang, H., Shao, J., Wang, T.: Fuzzy reasoning spiking neural P system for fault diagnosis. Inf. Sci. **235**, 106–116 (2013)

13. Wang, J., Peng, H.: Adaptive fuzzy spiking neural P systems for fuzzy inference and learning. Int. J. Comput. Math. **90**(4), 857–868 (2013)

14. Cardona, M., Colomer, M.A., Pérez-Jiménez, M.J., Zaragoza, A.: Hierarchical clustering with membrane computing. In: The 8th Workshop on Membrane Computing, pp. 185–204 (2007)

15. Zhao, Y., Liu, X., Qu, J.: The k-medoids clustering algorithm by a class of P system. J. Inf. Comput. Sci. **9**(18), 5777–5790 (2012)

16. Jiang, Y., Peng, H., Huang, X., Zhang, J., Shi, P.: A novel clustering algorithm based on P systems. Int. J. Innov. Comput. Inf. Control **10**(2), 753–765 (2014)

17. Huang, X., Peng, H., Jiang, Y., Zhang, J., Wang, J.: PSO-MC: a novel PSO-based membrane clustering algorithm. ICIC Exp. Lett. **8**(2), 497–503 (2014). (Selected from ICICIC2013) (EI)

18. Nwankpa, C., Johnson, J., Nagvajara, P., Chagnon, T., Vachranukunkiet, P.: FPGA hardware results for power system computation. In: Power Systems Conference and Exposition, pp. 1–3 (2009)

Tools and Simulators for Membrane Computing-A Literature Review

S. Raghavan$^{(\boxtimes)}$ and K. Chandrasekaran

National Institute of Technology Karnataka Surathkal, Mangalore, India
raghavan.sm2005@gmail.com, kch@nitk.ac.in

Abstract. Membrane Computing comes under the field of Natural Computing. This was introduced by Gheorghe Paun. This field has been there from a decade. To realize Membrane Computing it is important to have tools that can be used either to process or simulate membrane computing. There have been several attempts in this area. This paper is an attempt to provide the details of the tools that are available for membrane computing. Primarily the tools are classified into two components. On one hand we have tools that are being used for specific type of P Systems or the tools which have a specific application. On the other hand there are tools which are comparatively generic in nature. Further this paper lists the tools that have been designed and developed to be used for the biological applications of P Systems. After classification, a brief description of the tools is given in this paper. Finally a brief quantitative analysis of the tools is done. Though there have been few surveys of P System tools, this is a slightly different paper which tries to classify and tries to a give review of the tools.

Keywords: Membrane computing tools · P Systems · P System tools · P System simulators

1 Introduction

Membrane Computing was introduced by Paun in 1998 [39]. This is one of the few elegant works that aim at imitating the biological processes (based on cell). There are several applications of membrane Computing. Membrane Computing or P-Systems are characterized by high parallelizability. It is bio inspired computing paradigm which has a lot of applications because of its inherent structure. It was inspired by structure and functioning of a living cell. As the concept is based on the living cell, this is also being seen as a tool to be used to emulate or describe biological processes, which is one of the important applications of P Systems, which may even revolutionize the way biological processes are studied.

To realize the power of membrane computing it was necessary to develop the tools that will emulate/simulate biological processes. Not only this, there is also a need to have P System tools that will allow the simulation of P System to test/realize its computational properties and mathematical properties. Both

© Springer Nature Singapore Pte Ltd. 2016
M. Gong et al. (Eds.): BIC-TA 2016, Part I, CCIS 681, pp. 249–277, 2016.
DOI: 10.1007/978-981-10-3611-8_23

the types of the tools are necessary. The number of tools for the latter is more compared to the former. Initially, there were several tools developed with the sole purpose of demonstrating the power of P Systems for solving computational and Mathematical problem and then gradually tools started coming up for several applications of membrane computing.

These tools, apart from testing the P Systems also allowed the user to use P System to visualize and understand the way P Systems work, thereby giving more clarity to the user on certain fine issues of P Systems. Most of the systems are born out of research and are created for immediate necessities/requirement for the researchers.

As the membrane computing paradigm evolved theoretically, there were several methods and mechanism to experience the practical implication of membrane computing. Thus several simulation softwares and tools have been developed to experience or visualize the models of membrane computing. Though there have been several applications of each and every simulation model, the primary application is visualizing the actual membrane computing model.

The simulators or simulation tools can be primarily be classified into two, the simulators or simulation tools that concentrate more on biological aspects of membrane computing and help use the membrane computing paradigm for simulating biological processes; and, the set of tools/simulators that have been developed for using the membrane computing paradigm for solving problems related to Mathematics and Computer Science. All the simulators in these two areas have been discussed in this paper. There are several tools and softwares that have been developed by different researchers working on membrane computing. A list of these softwares has been given in the website that has been maintained for P-Systems [8]. There are also several initial studies made on tools for membrane computing. There are also a few surveys that have been done before [25,50,62]. Though the list also has been maintained [8], this paper is an attempt to classify all the available tools according to their topic, thus to have a systematic literature review of the tools that are available for P Systems. Apart from these, there is also some detail about all the simulators, thereby just giving a brief idea about the purpose, language and other properties of the simulator. The Fig. 1, lists the tools according to the timeline in the chronological order. There are further five sections in the paper, Sect. 2 talks about tools/simulators for membrane computing in general and classifications used in this paper. The next section gives the details about tools that are specific to a type of P System or specific to certain application of P System. The next section lists and briefly describes the tools that are a little generic in nature, i.e. the tool which allow more than two types of P Systems to be realized or which doesn't have any specific application. The next section lists the tools/simulation that are specific for biological application. The prefinal section analyses the survey and the final section concludes the paper.

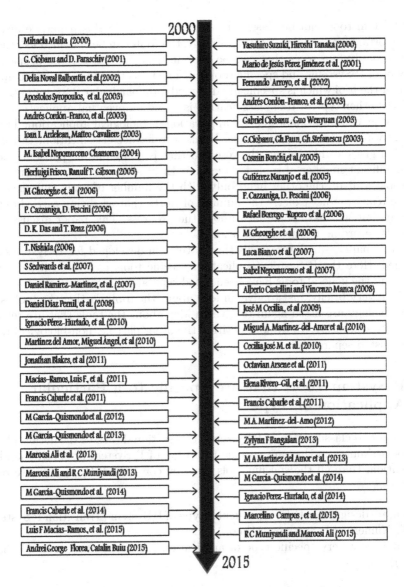

Fig. 1. Timeline of simulator and tools

2   Classification of Membrane Computing Tools

As discussed Membrane Computing is a vast topic. There are many researchers in this area working and expanding it from all the directions. As the research progresses and development progresses different type of tools are required for different areas. Thus keeping this view time to time several tools have been developed according to the need of the researchers.

P System tools can be classified in different ways, in this paper we discuss two important ways of classification. Firstly, the tools can be classified as generic tools i.e. P System tools that can be used in general to study the properties, behavior of P Systems and specific tools i.e. The tools that have a specific application or the tool which is specifically designed for a particular P System variant. Then the other type of tool classification is based on eventual application of P Systems i.e. computational/general application or biological application. This is another way of classifying the tools. Unlike the former classification, this classification gives an idea about the research that is going on one particular area and significant number of tools tells us that there are several works going over this topic. But on the other hand only with the number of tools, one may not be able really predict exactly the number of works that are being carried out in this area but will have some idea about the progress. This paper discusses all the tools according to the classification.

In this paper, simulators/tools that have been developed for P Systems are classified. Here the P System/application specific tools have been listed separately and the general tools have been listed separately. Mostly all the tools are explained very briefly, just to give an idea about the tool. Further the tools specific to biology are listed again to give an idea about the tools that are related to biology separately. To avoid repetition the other part i.e. non-biological tools are not listed separately.

3   P System Tools that are Specific to a Particular Application or Type

This is second classification of P Systems, this section discusses the details about the tools/simulators that are specific to a type of P System or specific kind of application. Here all the specific tools are only considered. By specific we refer the tools,

- That are designed only for a particular type of P System (Transition P Systems [39], Numerical P Systems [61] etc.)
- That have a very specific type of application (eg. Generating trees (J Plant [69]))

In this section all the tools that come under the above area are discussed.

From the time the P System simulator was being designed, it started from designing the specific type of P Systems. It all started from designing, first to come, the simplest transition P System. As it proceeded, there were several system which came for specific kinds of P Systems. On the whole if it is to be seen there are more number of simulator only for specific kinds of P Systems. This section describes in detail the specific kinds/type of P Systems. Out of total number of tools that have been listed in paper nearly Forty Five (Table 1) tools belongs to this category.

Table 1. List of tools for specific P Systems

Tool/software	Name of the developers	Base tool/framework/ language	Purpose
Membrane computing in prolog [47]	Mihaela Malita	Prolog	Transition P System
On a LISP implementation of a class of P Systems [71]	Yasuhiro Suzuki, Hiroshi Tanaka	LISP	Transition P System
Membrane software A P System simulator [24,35]	G. Ciobanu, D. Paraschiv	Visual C++	Two variants of P Systems
A CLIPS simulator for recognizer P Systems with active membranes [65]	Mario de Jesus Perez Jimenez and Francisco Jose Romero Campero	CLIPS	For recognizer P Systems with active membranes
A MzScheme implementation of transition P systems [58]	Delia Noval Balbontn, Mario J. Perez Jimenez, and Fernando Sancho Caparrini	MzScheme	Transition P System
A software simulation of transition P Systems in Haskell [10]	Fernando Arroyo et al.	Haskell	Transition P System
Distributed simulator for transition P-Systems [72]	Apostolos Syropoulos et al.	Java (with standard UDP protocol)	Distributed in nature, works for transition P-System
Sevilla carpets [26,60]	G. Ciobanu, Gh. Paun, Gh. Stefanescu	Python	Comparing solutions for subset sum problem
SubLP-Studio v0.1 [8]	Alexandros Georgiou	Java	For L-System and P-System
A prolog simulator for deterministic P Systems with active membranes [28]	Andres Cordon-Franco et al.	Prolog	Deterministic P
P Systems running on a cluster of computers [27]	Gabriel Ciobanu, Guo Wenyuan	C++, MPI	Generic
Modelling biological processes by using a probabilistic P system software [9]	Ioan I. Ardelean, Matteo Cavaliere	-	For biological processes

Table 1. *(Continued)*

Tool/software	Name of the developers	Base tool/framework/ language	Purpose
SimCM [55]	M. Isabel Nepomuceno Chamorro	Java	Transition P System
A simulator and an evolution program for conformon-P systems [34]	Pierluigi Frisco, Ranulf T. Gibson	Java	Conformon P System
A Simulator for confluent P systems [41]	Gutierrez Naranjo, Miguel Angel, Mario de Jesus Perez Jimenez, and Agustn Riscos Nunez	Prolog	For more than one type of P System
Simulation software for membrane approximation algorithm [57]	T. Nishida	-	Specifically designed for membrane approximation algorithm
Vibrio Fischeri [8]	P. Cazzaniga, D. Pescini	C	For biological process
Dynamical probabilistic P-Systems [66]	P. Cazzaniga, D. Pescini	MPI and C	Probabilistic P-System
Tissue simulator: a graphical tool for tissue P Systems [15]	Rafael BorregoCRopero, Daniel Díaz-Pernil, and Mario J. Perez-Jimenez	Java and C#	Specifically designed for tissue P-Systems
DasPsimulator [29]	D.K. Das and T. Renz	Java	P-System simulation with active membranes for transition P Systems
A tool for using the SBML format to represent P Systems which model biological reaction networks [56]	Isabel Nepomuceno, Juan Antonio Nepomuceno, Francisco Jose Romero Campero	CLIPS	To represent biological processes
A software tool for dealing with spiking neural P Systems [67]	Daniel Ramirez-Martinez, Miguel A. Gutierrez-Naranjo	Xbase++ and SWI C prolog	Spiking neural P System

Table 1. *(Continued)*

Tool/software	Name of the developers	Base tool/framework/ language	Purpose
MetaPlab: a virtual laboratory for modeling biological systems by MP systems [21]	Alberto Castellini and Vincenzo Manca	Java	For bio-systems
Simulation of P Systems with active membranes on CUDA [23]	Jose M. Cecilia et al.	C and C++ programing language along with CUDA extensions	P Systems with active membranes
A P-Lingua based simulator for tissue P systems [52]	Miguel A. Martinez-del-Amor et al.	P-Lingua	Specifically designed tissue P-Systems
Parallel simulation of probabilistic P Systems on multicore platforms [53]	Martnez del Amor, Miguel Angel et al.	OpenMp, P-lingua, MeCoSim	Probabilistic P Systems especially for modeling ecosystem
Simulating a P system based efficient solution to SAT by using GPUs [22]	Cecilia Jose M. et al.	CUDA	Solution for SAT
SNUPS [16]	Octavian Arsene, Catalin Buiu and Nirvana Popescu	Java	Numerical membrane computing
A PCLingua based simulator for spiking neural P Systems [45]	Macas-Ramos, Luis F. et al.	P-Lingua	Spiking neural networks
JPlant [69]	Elena Rivero-Gil et al.	Java	Generating graphics
A spiking neural P System simulator based on CUDA [18]	Francis Cabarle, Henry Adorna, and Miguel A. Martinez-del-Amor	CUDA C Python	Spiking neural P System
An improved GPU simulator for spiking neural P systems [19]	Francis Cabarle, Henry Adorna, and Miguel A. Martinez-del-Amor	CUDA C Python	Spiking neural P System
A Java-based P-Lingua simulator for Enzymatic Numerical P Systems (ENPS) [31]	M. Garca-Quismondo et al.	Java, P-Lingua	Biological process

Table 1. *(Continued)*

Tool/software	Name of the developers	Base tool/framework/ language	Purpose
DCBA: simulating population dynamics P Systems with proportional object distribution [51]	M.A. Martnez-del-Amo	CUDA, P-Lingua	Population dynamics P Systems environment ecology
A GPU simulator for Enzymatic Numerical P Systems (ENPS) models in CUDA [36]	M. Garca-Quismondo et al.	Java, P-Lingua	Biological process
A GPU simulation for evolution-communication P Systems with energy having no antiport rules [11]	Zylynn F. Bangalan	CUDA C, P-lingua	Evolution-communication P Systems
Simulating a family of tissue P Systems solving SAT on the GPU [54]	M.A. Martnez del Amor et al.	CUDA	Tissue P System
Accelerated simulation of membrane computing to solve the n-queens problem on multi-core [48]	Maroosi Ali and Ravie Chandren Muniyandi	Visual C++	N queens problem
A C++ simulator for PGSP systems [37]	M. Garca-Quismondo et al.	C++	PGSP, biological process
A P-lingua based for tissue P System with cell separation [63]	Ignacio Perez-Hurtado et al.	P-Lingua	Tissue P System
Simulating spiking neural P systems without delays using GPUs [17]	Francis Cabarle, Henry Adorna, and Miguel A. Martinez-del-Amor	CUDA, Pyhon	Spiking neural P System
Antibiotic Resistance Evolution Simulator (ARES) [20]	Marcelino Campos et al.	Java, P-Lingua	Biological processes
P-Lingua based simulator for P Systems with symport/antiport rules [46]	Luis F. Macas-Ramos et al.	P-Lingua	Generic
Lulu - a software simulator for P colonies [32,33]	Andrei George Florea, Catalin Buiu	Python	P Colonies
Enhancing the simulation of membrane system on the GPU for the N-Queens problem [68]	Ravie Chandren and Maroosi Ali	Visual C++	N queens problem

The tools are briefly explained here:

3.1 Membrane Computing in Prolog

This is the first working simulator that has been developed for membrane computing. This was developed by Malita [47]. This simulator was designed for Transition P System. This is one of the simplest simulators that was the first one to be developed to test the power of membrane computing. This simulator was developed in PROLOG, PROLOG then being one of the best languages known for its expressiveness.

3.2 On a LISP Implementation of a Class of P Systems

This simulator is also one of the earliest implementations of membrane computing. This simulator uses LISP language for implementation. This was developed by Suzuki and Tanaka [71]. This simulator was specifically developed for what ACS. This model was developed by same authors who have developed this simulator. This model is a variant of the existing model. This model allows dissolving and creating membranes.

3.3 Membrane Simulator

Membrane Simulator is a simulator designed by Ciobanu and Paraschiv [24,35]. It is a simulator which is specifically designed for two variants of P Systems namely for initial version of catalytic hierarchical cell system and for active membrane systems. It is one of the earliest simulator that was solely aimed at realizing P System (2002). It is developed using Microsofts Visual C++.

3.4 A CLIPS Simulator for Recognizer P Systems with Active Membranes

This is a simulator developed for simple recognizer P systems with active membranes. This simulator was developed by de Jesus Perez Jimenez and Campero [65]. This simulator is based on CLIPS (C Language Integrated Production System). Here the P Systems are represented using the production system techniques. This is a fairly simple simulator which allows the users to model recognizer P Systems with active membranes.

3.5 A MzScheme Implementation of Transition P Systems

This simulator allows the users to simulate transition P Systems using Mzscheme. This simulator was developed by Balbontn Noval et al. [58]. Mzscheme is a scheme language that was first introduced in 1975. This simulator is one of the only simulators in Mzscheme for simplest form of P Systems, i.e. transition P-Systems. This simulator in a sense is an implementation of transition P System in Mzscheme, albeit it was one of the earliest simulators for P Systems.

3.6 Simulation of Transition P System Using Haskell

This is a simulation algorithm developed by Arroyo et al. [10]. Here the developers have simulated a model of earlier proposed transition P-System. This is one of the few simulations that use Haskell as the programming language (The interpreter that has been used is hugs 98). This is one of the initial softwares simulations for transition P-Systems. This is a fairly simple simulation and primary simulation that was aimed to show a software model for transition P System.

3.7 Distributed Simulator for Transition P System

This was again developed by Syropoulos et al. [72]. This simulator is for transition P System. This tool is distributed in core. This is one of the old tool for Transition P Systems. The tool is developed using Java especially using of Remote Method Invocation (RMI), which gives the distributed nature to the simulator. This is a simple and preliminary tool that can be used for simulation and analysis of small, less complex problems. The main aim of development of this simulator was to a give a distributed implementation. Thus, the main drawback of the simulator is that it cannot be used for complex systems. Further this simulator can be extended to complex membrane systems.

3.8 SubLP-Studio

SubLP-Studio is a software simulator for the Sub LP-Systems model, a variant of L-Systems and P-Systems. This was developed by Alexandros Georgiou [8]. It optionally interfaces to cpfg, thus producing plant graphics using the turtle interpreter [8]. SubLP-Studio is an editor and simulator for the Sub LP-Systems computational model [8]. This model is based on a combination of L-Systems, originally proposed by Aristid Lindenmayer, and P-Systems, originally proposed by Gheorghe Paun. The model features membrane-delimited parallel string rewriting for parametric symbols, and has extensions for arithmetic using variables and user-defined functions.

3.9 A Prolog Simulator for Deterministic P Systems with Active Membranes

This simulator was developed by Cordon-Franco et al. [28]. Here the developers have used PROLOG for developing the simulator. PROLOG is one of the oldest languages that is used for logic programming. The main reason for choosing PROLOG is its expressiveness which is very useful in handling symbolic knowledge representation. This simulator which is specifically designed for deterministic P Systems with active membranes.

3.10 Modelling Biological Processes by Using a Probabilistic P System Software

This simulator allows the users to model simple biological processes. This was developed by Ardelean and Cavaliere [9]. This simulator is one of the earliest simulators for biological processes. This simulators use probabilistic P Systems. Probabilistic P Systems can be inherently used for modeling biological processes. The developers have shown the way the simulator works in their paper [9].

3.11 P Systems Running on a Cluster of Computers

This was developed by Ciobanu and Wenyuan [27]. This tool aims at simulating a simple P System. This is specifically designed on Cluster of Computers. This is one of the first simulators to use cluster of computers for deploying/simulating P Systems. This is used for simulating Transition P Systems. This simulator is simple in structure and can be used for simulating small problems and it can be extended for other special types of membranes. It has been implemented using C++ and uses message passing interface (MPI). This simulator is designed such that it can be easily extended.

3.12 SimCM

SimCM (Simulador de Computacion con Membranas) tool was developed by Ángeles Nepomuceno Chamorro et al. [55]. This tool is primarily designed for Transition P System. This tool allows dissolution of membrane and priority rules are also allowed. The program is written in Java, because of its properties such as scalability and distributed network. The authors have used Java as it will be helpful in capturing parallelism that is required for Membrane Computing. The simulator is designed in MVC (Model-View-Controller) model. There are two subsystem that have been created as part of this system, the subsystem I consist of the main simulator engine, that forms the core part of simulator. The subsystem II is used for Guide User Interface (GUI) that is used to interact with the user. The two subsystems interact with each other.

3.13 Conformon P System

This simulator is designed for Conformon P Systems. According to Frisco and Gibson [34]. Conformon P Systems have simple structure/definition that allows them to be used for modeling biological processes of any scale. The tool has been specifically designed for biologists, so as to allow them to use this tool for simulating simple known biological processes so that they study these processes. And further this can be extended to be used for unknown biological processes which can be a little complex or difficult to study. In short this tool could help the users to easily model part of the processes which are known. Thus this is a step towards biological application of Membrane computing (P Systems). The simulator uses Java for implementation. The aim of the simulator creators was to use any good object oriented programming language to create this simulator. The input format for the simulator is XML file. Because of XML formats simplicity and generality it has been used here as an input format. Thus the user has to give the input in a XML format, which can be easily understood.

3.14   Simulator for Confluent P Systems

This tool is developed by Naranjo et al. [41]. Earlier to this tool there have been several tools that have been developed for P Systems, specially the tools which allow simulating a P System. Most of the tools that have been developed are for specific type/class of P Systems. This tool that has been developed for P Systems is different from others as it is not created for a specific type of P Systems.

This tool is able to simulate more than one type of P System. According to the developers it is one of the first attempts to do so. This tool unlike the other tools, which need all predifined limited structures allows creativity to the user. It allows the user to mix up two or models to have a different model of P System. This is one of the features that has not been there in any of the softwares that have been proposed before.

The software is developed based on PROLOG. The decision to choose prolog has been attributed to the properties of the language, i.e. its vast expressiveness and also in this case, its ability of evolving through the different configurations. The important advantage of this tool is that it allows the users to use more than one type of P Systems, which has much better expressiveness than the other tools that have been developed before this tool and in addition to that it also allows verification of complex problems for P Systems. One of the main drawback of the simulator is that it may require more time for complex problems.

3.15   Simulator for Dynamical Probabilistic P System

Dynamic Probabilistic P System has been developed by Pescini et al. [66]. Dynamic Probabilistic P System are suitable for modelling complex biological and chemical processes. Thus aim here was to develop a simulator that can be used to simulate specific biological processes. The developers have used C Language for development of the simulator. The simulator here is used to define a simple biological model, here, in this case the predator prey model has been analysed.

3.16   Tissue Simulator: Tissue Based P System

It is another tool that is specifically designed for Tissue P-Systems. This simulator is designed by Borrego-Ropero et al. [15]. This is a graphical simulator that allows the users to simulate Tissue P-Systems with cell division. It is graph based tool specifically designed for tissue based system. The tool is developed using Java and C#. Java has been used to parse the grammar generated using

ANTLR. ANTLR is a commonly used parser, generator that is used to translate or parse structured text or binary file [7]. C# has been used to develop the kernel and the graphical interface which is widely used to build languages tools and frameworks. According to the developers, the interconnection between both the languages is transparent and a user can easily switch between the windows by clicking on buttons that have been developed [15]. The software follows Model-View-Controller model.

3.17   DasPSimulator

DasPSimuator is another simulator for specifically designed for Transition P System. This is similar to SimCM Simulator that has been created by Das and Renz [29]. There are several properties in this type of P System simulation in addition to that of SimCM. Some of the additional properties of the systems are that this system is able to perform membrane create, membrane division and membrane string replication operation in addition to membrane dissolution operation which was already a part of SimCM Simulator that has been developed.

The Simulator is based on Java. The Simulator uses Model View Controller architecture. The simulator has two subsystems. The first subsystem considers the core (program) part of the simulator. The second part of the simulator is mainly devoted to its GUI. The GUI portion is mainly done in Java. The two subsystems interact with each other. This software primarily allows the user to model Transition P Systems. The main drawback of this simulator is that it is designed only for transition P Systems. There can be several addition to the existing simulator so that it can be used for some other types of P Systems.

3.18   A Tool for Using the SBML Format to Represent P Systems Which Model Biological Reaction Networks

This tool was developed by Ángeles Nepomuceno Chamorro et al. [56]. The tool is basically used to represent P System, so that further this representation turns out to be useful in modelling the biological processes using this representation. Thus the main aim of the tool is to represent P-System in the most suitable format that is suitable to represent the biological processes. This tool uses System Biological Markup Language (SBML) [42]. Here CLIPS (C Language integrated production System) has been used [1]. The tool's main goal is to provide the user with the environment to write the description of processes using SBML, In addition to that the tool converts the SBML code written by the user is converted to CLIPS code automatically. This converted CLIPS code is used to for simulation. The tool is follows the MVC (Model View Controller) Architecture.

3.19   A Software Tool for Dealing with Spiking Neural P Systems

This software tool was developed by Martinez et al. [67]. This software tool is basically for spiking neural systems. This is one of the first attempts to create software for spiking neural systems. The developers have several tools/programming languages for simulation. There are three modules in the simulator. Each and every module has different purpose and thus accordingly more suitable language has been chosen for each module. The first module is used for graphical user interface (GUI) for this Xbase ++ has been used. Xbase ++ is an object oriented language that is specifically used for Database Oriented graphic implementation. The second module is developed using PROLOG-SWI. This acts as a inference engine. The main advantage of this tool is modularity which allows easy extension of the tool.

3.20   MetaPlab

MetaPlab is a simulator, designed for special class of P System called MetaPSystem. MP Systems are the systems that are used for modelling biological processes and biological system. MetaPlab is one of the softwares that is to be used for biological aspect of membrane computing. The Software is based on Java. This software is an extension of Psim Simulator. Psim Simulator is one of the generic simulators that have been used for biological aspects of membrane computing. This is a computationally intensive framework that is based on extensible set of plugins. MetaPlab software is specifically designed for biologists to understand the biological systems especially their internal mechanisms which specifically allows to reproduce and analyse the, in silico, phenomenon like response to external stimuli, structural changes and environmental condition alterations.

This is primarily plugin based (Plugin Framework) simulator. Thus each and every important task there is a plugin, For eg. There are plugins such as Flux Discovery, Simulation Plugin, Chart Plugin and HTML Plugin. This is one of the few systems that aim to find its applications to biological aspects of Membrane Computing and one of the tool with good graphical interface. There are several properties of this tool that are significant, these properties are better simulation and visualization. It also allows graphical and statistical analysis of curves, i.e. it allows the users to plot the graph. It also allows the users to import biological networks from online database.

3.21   Simulation of P Systems with Active Membranes on CUDA

This simulator was developed by Cecilia et al. [23]. This simulator is specially designed for P System with active membrane over CUDA. This is developed using C and C++ language with CUDA extension. This is one of the first attempts to simulate P Systems using CUDA. This is also a simple simulator which doesn't have a great GUI, as its main intention is to model P Systems using CUDA and to use the full power of GPU'S so that the membrane computing implementation can be efficiently parallelised to speed up the simulation processes.

3.22   P-Lingua Based Tissue Simulator

This is a simulator based on Tissue like P System developed by Martinez-del-Amor et al. [52]. This is one of the first few simulators for tissue like membrane computing. This simulator is an extension over the existing P-Lingua core library. Thus the previous versions of P-Lingua didn't have the provision for Tissue P Systems. The latest version of P-Lingua specifically has this feature. Here simulation of Tissue P System with cell division is presented. As told, this is not a separate tool and is an extension of P-Lingua.

3.23 Parallel Simulation of Probabilistic P Systems on Multicore Platforms

This tool is developed by Martnez del Amor et al. [53] The purpose of this tool is to allow the users to create a simulation for probabilistic P System. The tool is set to run on multicore platform. The main library that has been used for implementation is OpenMP, which is used for efficient parallelization of the algorithms. The simulator inherently uses P-Lingua Core and MeCoSim. These components would be used by the users to define the membrane structure of the P System. As this is a probabilistic P System model, the main aim here is to use this for defining biological processes. This was primarily designed for ecologists to model ecosystem.

3.24 SNUPS

SNUPS is a software tool for modeling simulations of numerical P System It was developed by Buiu et al. [16]. Numerical P Systems use numerical data and use numerical program, primarily in deterministic way. According to the developers, this is first simulator that has been designed specifically for Numerical P Systems. SNUPS is developed using Java. SNUPS is quite user friendly as it allows the user to use it using to modes, one way is to run it as a batch application and other way is to operate it using a GUI. The membrane structures here can be created using application. These membrane structures that are created are stored as XML file. These XML files can be given as input to the tool via command line. After processing the membranes the results are stored as CSV files. Further, the GUI is divided into three more components, membranes tree symbols assignment and rules definition. The advantage of using SNUPS is, that it is one of the best simulators for Numerical P System. The underlying architecture is parallel in nature, and thus the time taken for execution is less compared to other tools.

3.25 A P-Lingua Based Simulator for Spiking Neural P Systems

Spiking Neural P Systems were introduced in 2006 [43,44]. These kind of P Systems have been extensively popular because of its properties. Here Macas-Ramos et al. [45] have developed a simulator for spiking neural P System. Though there has been already an attempt in this direction but there are several improvements and differences here. Here the developers have used P-lingua for developing the simulator. As P-lingua has become a standard language to define a P System, this simulator serves as an extension of the framework, thereby allowing the framework to be used for SN-P Systems also.

3.26   JPlant

This tool was developed by Rivero-Gil et al. [69]. This tool has been written in Java. The primary aim of this tool is to create a membrane computing model, i.e. it is used for membrane creation. This tool computes the configuration of a restricted P System and then draws the respective graphical representation of the system. This is one of the kind of a tool which reduces the work of drawing P Systems. This tool has a good GUI (Graphical User Interface). Thus in simple terms this is the tool used for generating graphs using the P System Model.

3.27   A C++ Simulator for PGSP Systems

This software system is primarily developed is C++. This allows efficient simulation of Probabilistic Guarded Scripted P Systems. This simulator has been developed by Garca-Quismondo et al. [37]. PGSP Systems are special kind of P System that have been used to study the behaviour of Pieris napi olerace [59].

3.28   A P-Lingua Based Simulator for Tissue P Systems with Cell Separation

This was developed by Perez-Hurtado et al. [63]. This simulator is based on P-Lingua. This tool is also designed for Tissue P System. This tool is better than its predecessor, it is not an official successor of the tool but it also tries to solve the same problem of tissue P-Systems but with cell separation. Thus specifically this tool allows modelling tissue P System with cell separation. As this simulator is based on P-Lingua it has several advantages over other simulators. It would be easier for the users to define (give input) the P System file (model).

3.29   A Membrane Computing Simulator of Trans-Hierarchical Antibiotic Resistance Evolution Dynamics in Nested Ecological Compartments (ARES)

Antibiotic resistance evolution simulator was developed by Campos et al. [20]. This simulator based on membrane computing was specifically designed for Antibiotic resistance evolution. Antibiotic resistance is one of the important area in biomedical field. There is often a need for biologists to experiment on antibiotic resistance and thus this tool will be helpful to them as it allows antibiotic resistance evolution. Primarily this tool has five types of nested computing membranes which allow the users to create (emulate) hierarchy of ecobiological compartments. The tool has been implemented using Java. This tool specifically has been installed in a server.

3.30   Lulu - A Software Simulator for P Colonies

This is a first attempt to develop software for P colonies. This is a project which is at its initial stages. This is initiated by Florea and Buiu [32,33]. P Colonies are special types of P system variants that have a wide verity of real time applications. This tool has been developed in Python. This tool mainly is intended to be used for only P colony application. The tool consists of library which will allow the user to connect the P colony simulation to a robot and will in turn allow the user to control mobile robot through it.

4   P System Tools That Are Generic in Nature

There are a few tools which allow to simulate the P System and allow the users to understand the working of P System. These system are not designed for specific type of P System. This does not mean that all the P System types can be realized using these tools but it supports more than one basic simulation of membrane computing. This set of simulators not only includes the simulators used for computational purposes.

This list also includes the tools that are used for biological purposes. Thus, these tools are not too specific about the types of P system that they can be used for. Though there are a few in the list, the one which can really be called as generic tool is P-Lingua [30]. This is the one of the best framework that allows the users to create any kind of simulator according to their need. This simulator is based on Java. Using P-Lingua there has been a tool developed, which is called as MeCoSim. This tool gives a user a wide range option and allows the users to solve and simulate several kinds of computational problems as well as it also allows the users to use it for biological processes.

Based on Plingua there have been several simulators been designed. According to [5], there is PMCGPU project by Research Group in Natural Computing, University of Seville. This project uses primarily P-Lingua to design simulators using GPUs (Graphics Processing Unit), Primarily designed with CUDA these simulators use GPU for realizing different kinds of P Systems.

4.1   Web-PS: Web Based P-System Simulator with Query Facility

A Web based P-System simulator with Query Facility by Bonchis [14]. This is a web based tool for simulating P System. This tool is made up of several components developed in several languages. There are three level and accordingly different tools have been used for different levels. The first level is the internal level where CLIPS has been used. In the next level C language has been used. In the third level i.e. the outermost level which is accessed by the user is the web application, this is developed using PHP and Java Script. The tool processes the XML Files (i.e. it uses XML file for input and output).

Table 2. Generic tools for P Systems

Tool/software	Name of the developers	Base tool/framework/language	Purpose
Web-PS: web based simulator for membrane computing [14]	Cosmin Bonchi, Cornel Izba, Dana Petcu, Gabriel Ciobanu	Embedded C, CLIPS	Web based simulator
SL_P simulator [38]	M. Gheorghe et al.	Scilab	Biological processes
C_P simulator [38]	M. Gheorghe et al.	C	Biological processes
PSim [12]	Luca Bianco et al.	Java	Bio-Systems
Cyto-Sim: biological compartment simulator [70]	S. Sedwards et al.	J#	For bio-systems
P-Lingua 4.0: a programming language for membrane [30]	Daniel Daz Pernil et al.	P-Lingua Core	Generic P-System
MeCoSim: membrane computing simulator [64]	Ignacio Perez-Hurtado et al.	P-lingua	Generic
Infobiotics workbench [13]	Jonathan Blakes et al.	Jmcss-SBML, standalone software	Generic tool for biological aspects of membrane computing
Improved implementation of simulation for membrane computing on the graphic processing unit [49]	Maroosi Ali et al.	CUDA, C++	General
MeCoGUI: a simple, java-based graphic user interface for P-Lingua [2]	M. Garca-Quismondo et al.	Java, P-Lingua	Generic

4.2 SL_P Simulator

This simulator was developed by Gheorghe et al. [38]. This is a multicompartment P System simulator for biological processes that was developed using Scilab. This is a simple simulator devoid of several complexities which allows efficient multi-compartment simulation.

4.3 C_P Simulator

This simulator again was developed by Gheorghe et al. [38]. This has the same properties as SL_Psimulator but with a variance that is wholly developed using C.

4.4 Psim

Psim is a simulator developed by Bianco et al. [12]. This simulator is for bio molecular dynamics based on P Systems. The system is specifically made for Metabolic P System, which are deterministic P Systems. This tool is used to verify the biological aspect of the P System. This is probably the first tool for metabolic P System. Some of the important features of this software are: Its easy to use, Plugin based architecture, Flexibility, Portability (through XML) and cross platform acceptability. It allows the user to devise a system specification by using MP graphs and then further allows simulate its dynamics in a completely discrete way [12].

4.5 P-Lingua

P Lingua is one of the best accomplishments in the area of softwares/simulators for membrane computing. The Primary component of P-Lingua is the P-Lingua Core. It is a Java Library. As the developers say, the main aim behind creation of P-Lingua, was to have it as a standard for P Systems. Based on the tools that have been developed based on P Lingua, It has accomplished the task or aim for which this was created. Based on PLingua there have been several tools. This tool is developed by Pernil et al. [30]. The main aim here is to give platform for other users of membrane computing, to create simulators. As membrane computing is a vast area, it is always difficult to have simulator for each and every special type of cells/membrane. As it is a known fact that there are a several kinds of P Systems available. P Lingua is a standard for defining P Systems. This is tool is based on java. There are several reasons for creation of this language/framework but the main reason is to a have standard framework for describing all the types of P-Systems. Before having P-Lingua though there were not many attempts made to have a standard format, almost all tools were developed for specific purposes only.

P Lingua is an open tool (i.e. Open for contribution from people) and is especially designed in Java, so that users can easily contribute extensions to the existing framework. The framework facilitates addition of models. Specifically the framework allows the users to add several specific P Systems. Apart from provisions for input there are several provisions for output formats.

There are several simulators that have been developed using P-Lingua framework. This is kind of universal framework which is intended to become a standard for P System representation and for processing. Here the main aim of developers is to create Java (core) classes that will allow other developers working with P Systems to extend this core and use these files according to their needs. There are two main advantages: There will be single Java based tool which can be universally used by anybody who has knowledge of Java and P Systems and a user can use this tool to create a specific tool/simulator as required according to their need using P lingua i.e. usually as an extension P-lingua core. Thus, it would be a useful addition to the repository apart from having solved the intended problem.

P-lingua had an advantage that it can also add files in XML Format. P-lingua library has parsers and compilers that will parse XML Format. In addition to that it allows exporting the P System models that can be easily exported in XML and Binary Format.

4.6   Cyto-Sim

Cyto-Sim is simulator specifically developed for biochemical processes. It is a stochastic simulator for membrane enclosed hierarchy [70]. Here the membrane has three layers namely the inner layer, outer layer and the integral layer. Cyto-Sim was developed by Sedwards and Mazza [70]. It is developed using J#. Cyto-Sim allows the users to import as SBML format, it allows to export as SBML and m files (Matlab). Cyto-Sim is one of the few simulators that is specifically designed for biological processes.

4.7   MeCoSim: Membrane Computing Simulator

Membrane Computing Simulator is a software that is developed using P-lingua core. As per the developers, Perez-Hurtado et al. [64]. it is a general purpose software that is used to create specific P-Systems. The user has an advantage of customizing the configuration file given to the user.

MeCoSim was developed by Research Group on Natural Computing (RGNC), University of Seville, Spain [64]. The developers of MeCoSim have concetrated on its GUI (Graphical User Interface). This is one of first Softwares/Simulators that uses P-lingua Core. MeCoSim (Membrane Computing Simulator) is a software application that offers the users a General Purpose Application to generate their own specific simulators by simply customizing a configuration file for each case study.

MeCoSim is used to simulate P Systems for biological processes and also allows the users to solve computational or mathematical problems. As mentioned above there are two aspects of a P-Systems applications. One is to apply P-Systems for simulating biological processes and the other is for Mathematical and Computational Processes. Though there have been several attempts initially to have a simulator/tool for P-Systems that would be used for Mathematical and Computational purposes, they were not as successful as this.

This is one of the tools that has biological applications, for simulation of biological components, by using membrane computing (P-Systems). It is always not possible to have different customized software to simulate each type of biological process. The full form of MeCoSim is Membrane Computing Simulator. This is one of the first attempts to provide a customizable simulator that can simulate a range of biological processes using Membrane Computing Concept. A user can change the configuration file to customize it and create different type of simulator according to the need.

MeCoSim is developed using PLingua. Plingua is one of the Tool/Framework that has been extensively used for simulating with Membrane Computing. There are several important simulators that have been developed using Plingua.

PMCGPU Project

PMCGPU (Parallel simulators for Membrane Computing on the GPU) is a project by Research Group on Natural Computing, University of Seville, Spain [5]. This project aims at providing high performance tools for P Systems. This is one of the important projects that aim to use High Performance computing tools for membrane computing. These tools are based on CUDA. It also supports OpenCL, or Open MP.

There are several simulators being developed using GPUs under this. These simulators primarily aim of extracting as much parallelizability as possible. Majority of the GPU based tool mentioned here use CUDA [4], and majority of them use specifically CUDA with C. As mentioned, the main aim here is to increase computability and parallelizability as much as possible. The specific simulators that have been developed are

- A GPU Simulator for Enzymatic Numerical P Systems (ENPS) models in CUDA by Garca-Quismondo et al. [36]
- A GPU Simulation for Evolution-Communication P Systems with Energy Having no Antiport Rules Bangalan et al. [11]
- Simulating a Family of Tissue P Systems Solving SAT on the GPU by del Amor et al. [54]
- Accelerated simulation of membrane computing to solve the n-queens problem on multi-core by Maroosi and Muniyandi [48]. Simulating Spiking Neural P systems without delays using GPUs by Cabarle et al. [17].
- A Spiking Neural P system simulator based on CUDA by Cabarle et al. [18].
- An improved GPU simulator for spiking neural P systems by Cabarle et al. [19].

Though the simulators that have been mentioned here are not generic in nature, these are a part of project which is based on a generic tool called P-lingua. Thus to have a flow we have listed the tools here in this section.

4.8   The Infobiotics Workbench

A P System based tool for Systems and Synthetic Biology. The Infobiotics Workbench is a tool that has been developed by Blakes et al. [13]. It is one of the important applications for P Systems in Biology. As other P Systems, Infobiotics workbench allows the user to create/model biological processes and then allows the user to execute the models either using stochastic simulation or numerical methods. It also supports formal model analysis and model checking. Here two model representation languages have been used, mcss-SBML [3] (An extension of Systems Biology Markup Language) and a DSL (Domain Specific Language) which implements lattice population P Systems. This software can interface with two model checkers, PRISM [6] and MC2 [40]. The software is available under GPL3 for both Unix based systems, Windows and MacOS.

4.9   MeCoGUI: A Simple, Java-Based Graphic User Interface for P-Lingua

MeCoGUI is one of the additional package with P-lingua. It work has been initiated by Garca-Quismondo et al. [2]. It is a simple, java based graphic user interface for P-lingua. It is one of the best additional GUI packages for P-Systems that have been developed so far. This has been extensively used in all places, wherever P-lingua is used. This can be used with almost all types of simulating models in P-lingua. For Eg. This can be used with two simulators that have been developed for PGSP Systems (One in C++ and another in P-lingua).

5   P System Tools That Have Biological Application

This section lists out the tools that have been specifically designed for biological applications. This also includes the tools that can be used for biological applications in addition to other applications. Mostly every tool listed in this space is only for biological process. These biological processes might be specific or generic. But the exception is MeCoSim [64] which can be used for Computational/ Mathematical applications as well as for biological applications (Table 3).

Table 3. Tools and simulators with biological applications

Tool/software	Name of the developers	Base tool/framework/ language	Purpose
Modelling biological processes by using a probabilistic P system software [9]	Ioan I. Ardelean, Matteo Cavaliere	-	Biological processes
A simulator and an evolution program for Conformon P-Systems [34]	Pierluigi Frisco, Ranulf T. Gibson	Java	Conformon P System
Vibrio Fischeri [8]	P. Cazzaniga, D. Pescini	C	Biological process
Dynamical probabilistic P-Systems [66]	P. Cazzaniga, D. Pescini	MPI and C	Probabilistic P-System
SL_P simulator [38]	M. Gheorghe et al.	Scilab	Biological processes
C_P simulator [38]	M. Gheorghe et al.	C	Biological processes
Cyto-Sim: biological compartment simulator [70]	S. Sedwards et al.	J#	For Bio-Systems

Table 3. *(Continued)*

Tool/software	Name of the developers	Base tool/framework/ language	Purpose
A tool for using the SBML format to represent P Systems which model biological reaction networks [56]	Isabel Nepomuceno, Juan Antonio Nepomuceno, Francisco Jose Romero Campero	CLIPS	To represent biological processes
MetaPlab: a virtual laboratory for modeling biological systems by MP systems [21]	Alberto Castellini and Vincenzo Manca	Java	For bio-systems
MeCoSim: membrame computing simulator [64]	Ignacio Perez-Hurtado et al.	P-lingua	Generic
Parallel simulation of probabilistic P Systems on multicore platforms [53]	Martnez del Amor, Miguel Angel et al.	OpenMp, P-lingua, MeCoSim	Probabilistic P Systems especially for modeling ecosystem
Infobiotics workbench [13]	Jonathan Blakes et al.	Jmcss-SBML, Standalone software	Generic tool for biological aspects of membrane computing
A Java-based P-Lingua simulator for Enzymatic Numerical P Systems (ENPS) [31]	M. Garca-Quismondo et al.	Java, P-Lingua	Biological process
DCBA: simulating population dynamics P Systems with proportional object distribution [51]	M.A. Martinez-del-Amo	CUDA, P Lingua	Population dynamics P Systems environment ecology
A GPU simulator for Enzymatic Numerical P Systems (ENPS) models in CUDA [36]	M. Garca-Quismondo et al.	Java, P-Lingua	Biological process
A C++ simulator for PGSP systems [37]	M. Garca-Quismondo et al.	C++	PGSP, Biological process
Antibiotic Resistance Evolution Simulator (ARES) [20]	Marcelino Campos et al.	Java, P-Lingua	Biological processes

6   Analysis

This section quantitatively analyses the tools. The Fig. 2, depicts the year wise tools/simulator developed. This shows that there has been several simulators being developed for biological processes also. Though the number of tools developed for computational aspect of Membrane computing is more, but off late there have been considerable development for biological processes. Though the number of tools that have been developed for biological processes are less there has been a considerable amount of research going on in this area.

There is an increase in computational simulation in the later years because of the development in P Lingua. As a language/framework one of the most used language/framework is P Lingua. After its development there have been consistent work in this area and several tools have been created using this framework (Fig. 3). Though this framework is developed by using Java, for classification we have not included P-Lingua based tool under Java so as to know specifically the number of tools that exclusively use P Lingua and the tools which exclusive use only Java (Not Part of P-Lingua).

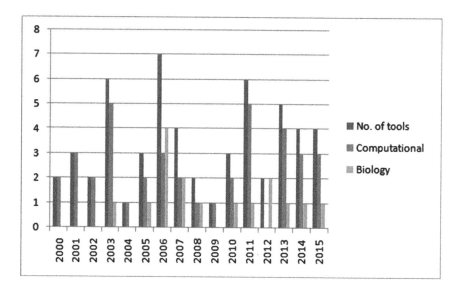

Fig. 2. Tools developed

From the tables in the previous sections (Tables 1 and 2) we can see that, as mentioned there is a rise in P Lingua in recent years such that not other language or framework is preferred, except that C++ for sequential simulation and Python [32]. Though many places CUDA with C is used but it is mainly being used with P Lingua.

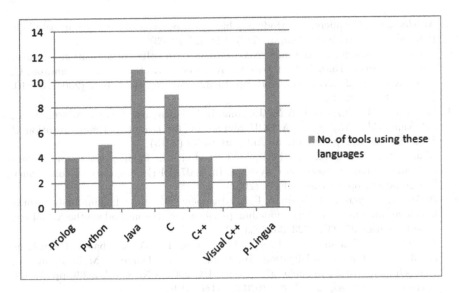

Fig. 3. Tools based on their language/framework

7 Conclusion

This paper is a survey of P System tools or simulators that have been developed till now from the inception of the concept called membrane computing. Here the tools have been classified according their generality. The tools that are specific in the type of P System and its application are considered as one part of the classification and the tools that are generic are considered as the other. There is also a list of P System tools/simulators that are specific to biological processes which is just to emphasize the use of P System for Biological Processes. The paper, briefly analyses the simulations/tools, specifically over the years from its inception.

References

1. CLIPS. www.ghg.net/clips/CLIPS.html
2. MeCoGUI. https://www.p-lingua.org/wiki/index.php/MeCoGUI
3. Multi-Compartmental Stoachastic Simulation. http://www.infobiotics.org/completeDocumentation/modelSimulation/modelSimulation.html
4. Parallel Programming and Computing Platform — CUDA. http://www.nvidia.com/object/cuda_home_new.html
5. PMCGPU. http://www.p-lingua.org/wiki/index.php/PMCGPU
6. PRISM Model Checker. http://www.prismmodelchecker.org/
7. What is ANTLR? http://www.antlr.org/
8. Software - The P Systems Page (2016). http://ppage.psystems.eu/index.php/Software

9. Ardelean, I.I., Cavaliere, M.: Modelling biological processes by using a probabilistic P system software. Nat. Comput. **2**(2), 173–197 (2003)
10. Arroyo, F., Luengo, C., Baranda, A.V., Mingo, L.: A software simulation of transition P systems in Haskell. In: Păun, G., Rozenberg, G., Salomaa, A., Zandron, C. (eds.) WMC 2002. LNCS, vol. 2597, pp. 19–32. Springer, Heidelberg (2003). doi:10. 1007/3-540-36490-0_2
11. Bangalan, Z.F., Soriano, K.A.N., Juayong, R.A.B., Cabarle, F.G.C., Adorna, H.N., del Amor, M.A.M., et al.: A GPU Simulation for Evolution-Communication P Systems with Energy Having no Antiport Rules (2013)
12. Bianco, L., Manca, V., Marchetti, L., Petterlini, M.: Psim: a simulator for biomolecular dynamics based on P systems. In: 2007 IEEE Congress on Evolutionary Computation, pp. 883–887. IEEE (2007)
13. Blakes, J., Twycross, J., Romero, F.J., Krasnogor, N., et al.: The infobiotics workbench: an integrated in silico modelling platform for systems and synthetic biology. Bioinformatics **27**(23), 3323–3324 (2011)
14. Bonchiş, C., Ciobanu, G., Izbaşa, C., Petcu, D.: A web-based P systems simulator and its parallelization. In: Calude, C.S., Dinneen, M.J., Păun, G., Pérez-Jímenez, M.J., Rozenberg, G. (eds.) UC 2005. LNCS, vol. 3699, pp. 58–69. Springer, Heidelberg (2005). doi:10.1007/11560319_7
15. Borrego-Ropero, R., Diaz-Pernil, D., Pérez-Jiménez, M.J.: Tissue simulator: a graphical tool for tissue P systems. In: Proceedings of the International Workshop Automata for Cellular and Molecular Computing. Satellite of the 16th International Symposium on Fundamentals of Computational Theory. MTA SZTAKI, Budapest, Hungary, pp. 23–34 (2007)
16. Buiu, C., Arsene, O., Cipu, C., Patrascu, M.: A software tool for modeling and simulation of numerical P systems. BioSystems **103**(3), 442–447 (2011)
17. Cabarle, F., Adorna, H., Martinez-del Amor, M.A.: Simulating Spiking Neural P systems without delays using GPUs (2014)
18. Cabarle, F.G.C., Adorna, H., Martínez, M.A.: A spiking neural P system simulator based on CUDA. In: Gheorghe, M., Păun, G., Rozenberg, G., Salomaa, A., Verlan, S. (eds.) CMC 2011. LNCS, vol. 7184, pp. 87–103. Springer, Heidelberg (2012). doi:10.1007/978-3-642-28024-5_8
19. Cabarle, F.G.C., Adorna, H., Martinez-del Amor, M.A.: An improved GPU simulator for spiking neural P systems. In: 2011 Sixth International Conference on Bio-Inspired Computing: Theories and Applications (BIC-TA), pp. 262–267. IEEE (2011)
20. Campos, M., Llorens, C., Sempere, J.M., Futami, R., Rodriguez, I., Carrasco, P., Capilla, R., Latorre, A., Coque, T.M., Moya, A., et al.: A membrane computing simulator of trans-hierarchical antibiotic resistance evolution dynamics in nested ecological compartments (ARES). Biol. Direct **10**(1), 1 (2015)
21. Castellini, A., Manca, V.: MetaPlab: a computational framework for metabolic P systems. In: Corne, D.W., Frisco, P., Păun, G., Rozenberg, G., Salomaa, A. (eds.) WMC 2008. LNCS, vol. 5391, pp. 157–168. Springer, Heidelberg (2009). doi:10. 1007/978-3-540-95885-7_12
22. Cecilia, J.M., García, J.M., Guerrero, G.D., Martínez-del Amor, M.A., Pérez-Hurtado, I., Pérez-Jiménez, M.J.: Simulating a P system based efficient solution to SAT by using GPUs. J. Logic Algebraic Program. **79**(6), 317–325 (2010)
23. Cecilia, J.M., García, J.M., Guerrero, G.D., Martínez-del Amor, M.A., Pérez-Hurtado, I., Pérez-Jiménez, M.J.: Simulation of P systems with active membranes on CUDA. Brief. Bioinform. **11**(3), 313–322 (2010)

24. Ciobanu, G., Paraschiv, D.: P system software simulator. Fundamenta Informaticae **49**(1–3), 61–66 (2002)
25. Ciobanu, G., Păun, G., Pérez-Jiménez, M.J.: Applications of Membrane Computing, vol. 17. Springer, Heidelberg (2006)
26. Ciobanu, G., Paun, G., Stefanescu, G.: Sevilla carpets associated with P systems. In: Proceedings of the Brainstorming Week on Membrane Computing, Tarragona, Spain, pp. 135–140 (2003)
27. Ciobanu, G., Wenyuan, G.: P systems running on a cluster of computers. In: Martín-Vide, C., Mauri, G., Păun, G., Rozenberg, G., Salomaa, A. (eds.) WMC 2003. LNCS, vol. 2933, pp. 123–139. Springer, Heidelberg (2004). doi:10.1007/978-3-540-24619-0_9
28. Cordón-Franco, A., Gutiérrez-Naranjo, M.A., Pérez-Jiménez, M.J., Sancho-Caparrini, F.: A prolog simulator for deterministic P systems with active membranes. New Gen. Comput. **22**(4), 349–363 (2004)
29. Das, D.K., Renz, T.: A simulation model for P systems with active membranes. In: 2006 IEEE Conference on Emerging Technologies-Nanoelectronics, pp. 338–340. IEEE (2006)
30. Díaz Pernil, D., de Mendoza, I.P.H., de Jesús Pérez Jiménez, M., Núñez, A.R., et al.: P-Lingua: A Programming Language for Membrane Computing (2008)
31. Manuel Garca-Quismondo Fernndez. A Java-Based P-Lingua Simulator for Enzymatic Numerical P Systems Available. http://www.cs.us.es/blogs/mgarcia/research/software_tools/java_simulator_enps/
32. Florea, A.G., Buiu, C.: Lulu-a software simulator for P colonies. Use case scenarios and demonstration videos (2015)
33. Florea, A.G., Buiu, C.: Development of a software simulator for P colonies-applications in robotics. Int. J. Unconv. Comput. **12**, 189–205 (2016)
34. Frisco, P., Gibson, R.T.: A simulator and an evolution program for conformon-P systems. In: SYNASC, vol. 7, pp. 26–27 (2005)
35. Ciobanu, G., Paraschiv, D.: Membrane software. A P system simulator. Technical report, Pre-Proceedings of Workshop on Membrane Computing, Curtea de Arges, Romania, August 2001, Technical report 17/01 of Research Group on Mathematical Linguistics, Rovira i Virgili University, Tarragona, Spain (2001)
36. Quismondo, M.G., Pavel, A.B., de Jesús Pérez Jiménez, M. et al.: Simulating Large-Scale ENPS Models by Means of GPU (2012)
37. García-Quismondo, M., Martínez-del-Amor, M.A., Pérez-Jiménez, M.J.: Probabilistic guarded P systems, a new formal modelling framework. In: Gheorghe, M., Rozenberg, G., Salomaa, A., Sosík, P., Zandron, C. (eds.) CMC 2014. LNCS, vol. 8961, pp. 194–214. Springer, Heidelberg (2014). doi:10.1007/978-3-319-14370-5_12
38. Gheorghe, M.: System Modeling Framework (2016). http://staffwww.dcs.shef.ac.uk/people/M.Gheorghe/PSimulatorWeb/Tools.htm
39. Paun, G., Rozenberg, G.: A guide to membrane computing. Theor. Comput. Sci. **287**(1), 73–100 (2002)
40. Grosu, R., Smolka, S.A.: Monte carlo model checking. In: Halbwachs, N., Zuck, L.D. (eds.) TACAS 2005. LNCS, vol. 3440, pp. 271–286. Springer, Heidelberg (2005). doi:10.1007/978-3-540-31980-1_18
41. Naranjo, M.A.G., de Jesús Pérez Jiménez, M., Núñez, A.R., et al.: A Simulator for Confluent P Systems (2005)
42. Hucka, M., Finney, A., Sauro, H.M., Bolouri, H., Doyle, J.C., Kitano, H., Arkin, A.P., Bornstein, B.J., Bray, D., Cornish-Bowden, A., et al.: The systems biology markup language (SBML): a medium for representation and exchange of biochemical network models. Bioinformatics **19**(4), 524–531 (2003)

43. Ionescu, M., Păun, A., Păun, G., Pérez-Jiménez, M.J.: Computing with spiking neural P systems: traces and small universal systems. In: Mao, C., Yokomori, T. (eds.) DNA 2006. LNCS, vol. 4287, pp. 1–16. Springer, Heidelberg (2006). doi:10.1007/11925903_1

44. Ionescu, M., Păun, G., Yokomori, T.: Spiking neural P systems. Fundamenta Informaticae **71**(2, 3), 279–308 (2006)

45. Macías–Ramos, L.F., Pérez–Hurtado, I., García–Quismondo, M., Valencia–Cabrera, L., Pérez–Jiménez, M.J., Riscos–Núñez, A.: A P–lingua based simulator for spiking neural P systems. In: Gheorghe, M., Păun, G., Rozenberg, G., Salomaa, A., Verlan, S. (eds.) CMC 2011. LNCS, vol. 7184, pp. 257–281. Springer, Heidelberg (2012). doi:10.1007/978-3-642-28024-5_18

46. Macías-Ramos, L.F., Valencia-Cabrera, L., Song, B., Song, T., Pan, L., Pérez-Jiménez, M.J.: A P_lingua based simulator for P systems with symport/antiport rules. Fundamenta Informaticae **139**(2), 211–227 (2015)

47. Malita, M.: Membrane computing in prolog. In: Pre-Proceedings of The Workshop on Multiset Processing (WMP-CdeA 2000), p. 8 (2000)

48. Maroosi, A., Muniyandi, R.C.: Accelerated simulation of membrane computing to solve the N-queens problem on multi-core. In: Panigrahi, B.K., Suganthan, P.N., Das, S., Dash, S.S. (eds.) SEMCCO 2013. LNCS, vol. 8298, pp. 257–267. Springer, Heidelberg (2013). doi:10.1007/978-3-319-03756-1_23

49. Maroosi, A., Muniyandi, R.C., Sundararajan, E.A., Zin, A.M.: Improved implementation of simulation for membrane computing on the graphic processing unit. Procedia Technol. **11**, 184–190 (2013)

50. Martínez-del-Amor, M.A., Macías-Ramos, L.F., Valencia-Cabrera, L., Riscos-Núñez, A., Pérez-Jiménez, M.J.: Accelerated simulation of P systems on the GPU: a survey. In: Pan, L., Păun, G., Pérez-Jiménez, M.J., Song, T. (eds.) BIC-TA 2014. CCIS, vol. 472, pp. 308–312. Springer, Heidelberg (2014). doi:10.1007/978-3-662-45049-9_50

51. Martínez-del-Amor, M.A., et al.: DCBA: simulating population dynamics P systems with proportional object distribution. In: Csuhaj-Varjú, E., Gheorghe, M., Rozenberg, G., Salomaa, A., Vaszil, G. (eds.) CMC 2012. LNCS, vol. 7762, pp. 257–276. Springer, Heidelberg (2013). doi:10.1007/978-3-642-36751-9_18

52. Martínez-del Amor, M.A., Pérez-Hurtado, I., Pérez-Jiménez, M.J., Riscos-Núñez, A.: A P-lingua based simulator for tissue P systems. J. Logic Algebraic Program. **79**(6), 374–382 (2010)

53. Martínez del Amor, M.A., Karlin, I., Jensen, R.E., de Jesús Pérez Jiménez, M., Elster, A.C., et al.: Parallel simulation of probabilistic P systems on multicore platforms. In: Proceedings of the Tenth Brainstorming Week on Membrane Computing, vol. 2, pp. 17–26. Sevilla, ETS de Ingeniería Informática, 30 de Enero-3 de Febrero (2012)

54. del Amor, M.A.M., Carrasco, J.P., de Jesús Pérez Jiménez, M., et al.: Simulating a Family of Tissue P Systems Solving SAT on the GPU (2013)

55. de los Ángeles Nepomuceno Chamorro, I., et al.: A Java Simulator for Basic Transition P Systems (2004)

56. de los Ángeles Nepomuceno Chamorro, I., Chamorro, J.A.N., Campero, F.J.R., et al.: A tool for using the SBML format to represent P systems which model biological reaction networks (2005)

57. Nishida, T.Y.: Membrane algorithms: approximate algorithms for NP-complete optimization problems. In: Ciobanu, G., Paun, G., Pérez-Jiménez, M.J. (eds.) Applications of Membrane Computing, pp. 303–314. Springer, Heidelberg (2006)

58. Balbontín Noval, D., Pérez Jiménez, M.J., Sancho Caparrini, F.: A MzScheme implementation of transition P systems. In: PĂun, G., Rozenberg, G., Salomaa, A., Zandron, C. (eds.) WMC 2002. LNCS, vol. 2597, pp. 58–73. Springer, Heidelberg (2003). doi:10.1007/3-540-36490-0_5

59. Pieris Oleracea. PGSP Systems. http://www.p-lingua.org/wiki/index.php/PGSP_systems:_Pieris_oleracea

60. Martín, D.O., Díaz, C.G., del Amor, M.Á.M., Núñez, A.R., Cabrera, L.V., et al.: Revisiting sevilla carpets: a new tool for the P-lingua era. In: Proceedings of the Twelfth Brainstorming Week on Membrane Computing, pp. 281–292. Sevilla, ETS de Ingeniería Informática, 3–7 de Febrero (2014)

61. Paun, G.: Membrane Computing: An Introduction. Springer Science & Business Media, Heidelberg (2012)

62. Paun, G., Rozenberg, G., Salomaa, A.: The Oxford Handbook of Membrane Computing. Oxford University Press Inc., Oxford (2010)

63. Perez-Hurtado, I., Valencia-Cabrera, L., Chacon, J.M., Riscos-Nunez, A., Perez-Jimenez, M.J.: A P-lingua based simulator for tissue P systems with cell separation. Sce. Technol. 17(1), 89–102 (2014)

64. Pérez-Hurtado, I., Valencia-Cabrera, L., Pérez-Jiménez, M.J., Colomer, M.A., Riscos-Núñez, A.: MeCoSim: a general purpose software tool for simulating biological phenomena by means of P systems. In: 2010 IEEE Fifth International Conference on Bio-Inspired Computing: Theories and Applications (BIC-TA), pp. 637–643. IEEE (2010)

65. de Jesús Pérez Jiménez, M., Campero, F.J.R., et al.: A CLIPS Simulator for Recognizer P Systems with Active Membranes (2004)

66. Pescini, D., Besozzi, D., Mauri, G., Zandron, C.: Dynamical probabilistic P systems. Int. J. Found. Comput. Sci. 17(01), 183–204 (2006)

67. Martínez, D.R., Naranjo, M.A.G., et al.: A Software Tool for Dealing with Spiking Neural P Systems (2007)

68. Ravie, C., Ali, M.: Enhancing the simulation of membrane system on the GPU for the N-queens problem. Chin. J. Electron. 24(4), 740–743 (2015)

69. Rivero-Gil, E., Gutiérrez-Naranjo, M.A., Romero-Jiménez, A., Riscos-Núñez, A.: A software tool for generating graphics by means of P systems. Nat. Comput. 10(2), 879–890 (2011)

70. Sedwards, S., Mazza, T.: Cyto-Sim: a formal language model and stochastic simulator of membrane-enclosed biochemical processes. Bioinformatics 23(20), 2800–2802 (2007)

71. Suzuki, Y., Tanaka, H.: On a LISP implementation of a class of P systems. Rom. J. Inf. Sci. Technol. 3(2), 173–186 (2000)

72. Syropoulos, A., Mamatas, E.G., Allilomes, P.C., Sotiriades, K.T.: A distributed simulation of transition P systems. In: Martín-Vide, C., Mauri, G., Păun, G., Rozenberg, G., Salomaa, A. (eds.) WMC 2003. LNCS, vol. 2933, pp. 357–368. Springer, Heidelberg (2004). doi:10.1007/978-3-540-24619-0_25

Parallel Contextual Hexagonal Array P Systems

James Immanuel Suseelan[1(✉)], D.G. Thomas[1], Robinson Thamburaj[1],
Atulya K. Nagar[2], and S. Jayasankar[3]

[1] Department of Mathematics, Madras Christian College,
Tambaram, Chennai 600 059, India
james_imch@yahoo.co.in, dgthomasmcc@yahoo.com, robin.mcc@gmail.com
[2] Department of Mathematics and Computer Science,
Liverpool Hope University, Liverpool, UK
nagara@hope.ac.uk
[3] Department of Mathematics, Ramakrishna Mission Vivekananda College,
Chennai 600 004, India
ksjayjay@gmail.com

Abstract. We introduce new P system models, called as external and internal parallel contextual hexagonal array P systems, based on the external and internal parallel contextual hexagonal array grammars. We can generate hexagonal arrays using these P system models with the help of Z-direction, X-direction and Y-direction external or internal parallel contextual hexagonal array rules. We discuss some basic properties of these P systems and give some comparison results in terms of their generative powers.

Keywords: P system · Hexagonal array · Parallel contextual array

1 Introduction

Two-dimensional languages are one of the extensions of string languages theory. To study the problem of picture generation and description, where pictures are considered as connected, digitized finite arrays in the two-dimensional plane, there has been a continued interest in adapting the techniques of formal string language theory for developing various new methods. Over the past several years there has been a steady growth in the literature on array grammars and array acceptors.

While investigating isometric array generation, Rosenfield [20,21] had pointed out the need for array rewriting rules for picture languages. The idea is to generalize the Chomsky string grammars to arrays by having rewriting rules that allow replacement of a sub-array of a picture with another sub-array. To describe digital pictures viewed as rectangular arrays of terminals, Siromoney et al. [22] proposed a simple generative model, called two-dimensional matrix grammar. And later motivated by the need to generate picture languages that cannot be generated by two-dimensional matrix grammars, Siromoney et al. [23]

© Springer Nature Singapore Pte Ltd. 2016
M. Gong et al. (Eds.): BIC-TA 2016, Part I, CCIS 681, pp. 278–298, 2016.
DOI: 10.1007/978-981-10-3611-8_24

introduced array models, generalizing the notion of rewriting rules in which the concatenation of strings is extended to row and column concatenation of arrays.

Hexagonal pictures occur in several application areas especially in picture processing and image analysis. Hexagonal kolam array grammars for generating hexagonal arrays and hexagonal patterns on triangular grids which can be treated as two-dimensional representation of three-dimensional blocks was constructed by Siromoney et al. [24]. We refer to [15,16] for the study of two-dimensional representations of three-dimensional blocks. Recently, the hexagons and the hexagonal tiling have been addressed by a symmetric coordinate frame in [7,14] and possible link of applications in [13].

Contextual grammars were introduced by Marcus [10] in 1969 as another model to describe natural languages. A contextual grammar produces a language by starting from a given finite set of strings and adding, iteratively, pairs of strings (called as contexts), associated to sets of words (called selectors) to the string already obtained. Many variants of contextual grammars have been considered in the literature and investigated from a mathematical point of view [5,11,12]. Two special cases of contextual grammars, called internal and external are very natural and have been extensively investigated. An external contextual grammar generates a language starting from a finite set of strings and iteratively adjoining to its contexts. In internal contextual grammars [5], the context are adjoined inside the current string.

In [26], Thomas et al. developed a new method of generating hexagonal arrays based on an extension of contextual grammars called parallel contextual hexagonal array grammars. Their systems yield languages of hexagons using parallel rewriting relations. They make use of 'window movement' on arrow heads to decide whether the languages are generated by array contexts of choice mappings by the applications of array contextual operations parallely. This concept was based on the contextual style of rectangular array generation using external and internal parallel contextual array grammars considered in [6].

The area of membrane computing, was initiated by Paun [17] introducing a new computability model, now called as P system, which is distributed highly parallel theoretical model based on the membrane structure and behavior of the living cells. A computation starts from an initial configuration of a system, defined by a membrane structure with objects and evolution rules in each membrane, and terminates when no further rule can be applied. One uses the Chomsky way of rewriting for computations, in a P system with string objects. In [9] the contextual way of handling string objects in P systems has been considered and that the contextual P systems are found to be more powerful than ordinary string contextual grammars and its variants. Ceterchi et al. [1] introduced array P systems of the isometric variety, extending the string rewriting P systems to arrays using context-free type of rules. Henceforth, several P system models for generating arrays, both isometric and non-isometric variety, have been considered in the literature (for example [2,8,25]). In [8] P system models namely, external and internal parallel contextual array P systems have been introduced based on the contextual style of array generation using external and internal parallel contextual array grammars.

In this paper we introduce new P system models, called as external and internal parallel contextual hexagonal array P systems, based on the contextual style of external and internal parallel contextual hexagonal array grammars considered in [26]. In Sect. 2, we list out some prerequisites. In Sect. 3, we define parallel internal contextual hexagonal array P system and give an example. In Sect. 4, we define parallel external contextual hexagonal array P system and give an example. In Sect. 5, some properties of both parallel internal and external contextual hexagonal array P systems are discussed. In Sect. 6, we give comparison results for the family of hexagonal array languages generated by the newly constructed P systems with other classes of hexagonal array languages. In Sect. 7, we conclude the article with a brief remark.

2 Preliminaries

In this section we recall some notions related to hexagonal array grammars and parallel contextual hexagonal array grammars. We can refer to [3, 26] for further details.

Definition 1. *We consider hexagons of the following type:*

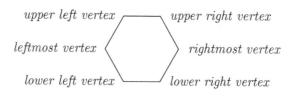

upper left vertex — *upper right vertex*

leftmost vertex — *rightmost vertex*

lower left vertex — *lower right vertex*

Let Σ be a finite alphabet of symbols. A hexagonal picture p over Σ is a hexagonal array of symbols over Σ. For example, a hexagonal picture over the alphabet $\{a, b, c\}$ is: $p = $. The set of all hexagonal arrays over Σ is denoted by Σ^{**H}. A hexagonal picture language L over Σ is a subset of Σ^{**H}. With respect to a triad $\overset{z}{{}_x\swarrow\searrow_y}$ of triangular axes x, y, z, the coordinates of each element of a hexagonal picture can be fixed.

Definition 2. *For $k \geq 2, a_j, b_j \in \Sigma, (j \geq 1)$, let*

1. *$xyTr$ be a trapezium array of type* $\begin{smallmatrix} a_1 a_2 \cdots a_k \\ b_1 b_2 \cdots b_k b_{k+1} \end{smallmatrix}$

2. *$yxTr$ be a trapezium array of type* $\begin{smallmatrix} a_1 a_2 \cdots a_k a_{k+1} \\ b_1 b_2 \cdots b_k \end{smallmatrix}$

3. *xxP_zA be a parallelogram array of type* $\begin{smallmatrix} a_1 a_2 \cdots a_k \\ b_1 b_2 \cdots b_k \end{smallmatrix}$

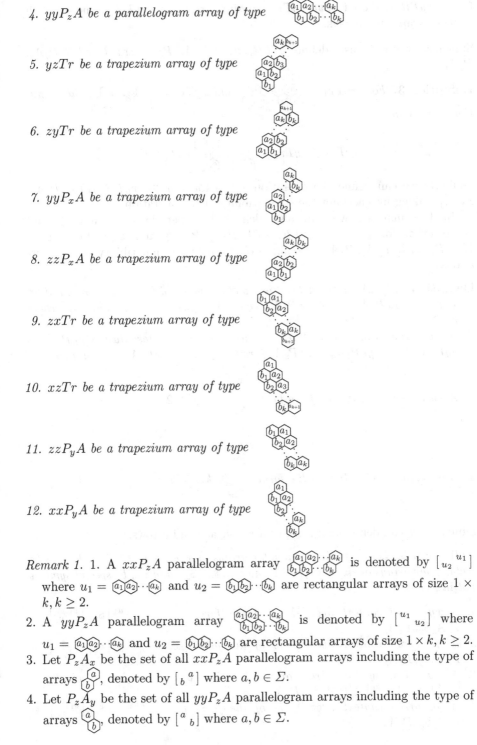

4. yyP_zA be a parallelogram array of type

5. $yzTr$ be a trapezium array of type

6. $zyTr$ be a trapezium array of type

7. yyP_xA be a trapezium array of type

8. zzP_xA be a trapezium array of type

9. $zxTr$ be a trapezium array of type

10. $xzTr$ be a trapezium array of type

11. zzP_yA be a trapezium array of type

12. xxP_yA be a trapezium array of type

Remark 1. 1. A xxP_zA parallelogram array $\begin{smallmatrix}a_1 a_2 \cdots a_k \\ b_1 b_2 \cdots b_k\end{smallmatrix}$ is denoted by $[_{u_2}{}^{u_1}]$ where $u_1 = a_1 a_2 \cdots a_k$ and $u_2 = b_1 b_2 \cdots b_k$ are rectangular arrays of size $1 \times k, k \geq 2$.

2. A yyP_zA parallelogram array $\begin{smallmatrix}a_1 a_2 \cdots a_k \\ b_1 b_2 \cdots b_k\end{smallmatrix}$ is denoted by $[^{u_1}{}_{u_2}]$ where $u_1 = a_1 a_2 \cdots a_k$ and $u_2 = b_1 b_2 \cdots b_k$ are rectangular arrays of size $1 \times k, k \geq 2$.

3. Let P_zA_x be the set of all xxP_zA parallelogram arrays including the type of arrays $\begin{smallmatrix}a\\b\end{smallmatrix}$, denoted by $[_b{}^a]$ where $a, b \in \Sigma$.

4. Let P_zA_y be the set of all yyP_zA parallelogram arrays including the type of arrays $\begin{smallmatrix}a\\b\end{smallmatrix}$, denoted by $[^a{}_b]$ where $a, b \in \Sigma$.

5. Let $xyTR$ be the set of all $xyTr$ trapezium arrays and $yxTR$ be the set of all $yxTr$ trapezium arrays.

Similarly, we can also define $yzTR, zyTR, P_xA_y, P_xA_z, zxTR, xzTR, P_yA_z, P_yA_x$.

Definition 3. For, $xyTr_1 = \begin{smallmatrix}\boxed{a_1}\boxed{a_2}\cdots\boxed{a_k}\\\boxed{b_1}\boxed{b_2}\cdots\boxed{b_k}\boxed{b_{k+1}}\end{smallmatrix}$ and $xyTr_2 = \begin{smallmatrix}\boxed{b_1}\boxed{b_2}\cdots\boxed{b_{k+1}}\\\boxed{c_1}\boxed{c_2}\cdots\boxed{c_{k+1}}\boxed{c_{k+2}}\end{smallmatrix}$, the operation $\ominus$ is defined as,

$$xyTr_1 \ominus xyTr_2 = \begin{smallmatrix}\boxed{a_1}\boxed{a_2}\cdots\boxed{a_k}\\\boxed{b_1}\boxed{b_2}\cdots\boxed{b_k}\boxed{b_{k+1}}\\\boxed{c_1}\boxed{c_1}\cdots\boxed{c_k}\boxed{c_{k+1}}\boxed{a_{k+2}}\end{smallmatrix}, k \geq 2.$$

Similarly we can define the operation $x \ominus y$ for $x, y \in \{xyTR, yxTR, P_zA_x, P_zA_y\}$, taking into account the compatibility of the operation.

In like manner, we can also define the operations $\oslash$ and $\odot$ and hence $y \oslash z$, for $y, z \in \{yzTR, zyTR, P_xA_y, P_xA_z\}$ and $z \odot x$ for $z, x \in \{zxTR, xzTR, P_yA_z, P_yA_x\}$, taking into account the compatibility of the operations.

Definition 4. 1. A xy arrow-head is a picture obtained from the representation $xxP_zA_1 \ominus xxP_zA_2 \ominus \ldots \ominus xxP_zA_r \ominus yyP_zA_1 \ominus yyP_zA_2 \ominus \ldots \ominus yyP_zA_s$, where $r, s \geq 1$.

2. A yx arrow-head is a picture obtained from the representation $yyP_zA_1 \ominus yyP_zA_2 \ominus \ldots \ominus yyP_zA_m \ominus xxP_zA_1 \ominus xxP_zA_2 \ominus \ldots \ominus xxP_zA_n$, where $m, n \geq 1$.

3. A xy arrow is a picture of the form $\begin{smallmatrix}\boxed{a_1}\\\boxed{a_2}\\\boxed{\frac{a_n}{b_1}}\\\boxed{b_2}\\\vdots\\\boxed{b_m}\\\vdots\\\boxed{c_1}\\\boxed{c_2}\end{smallmatrix}$, $n, m \geq 2$.

4. A yx arrow is a picture of the form $\begin{smallmatrix}\boxed{\frac{e}{d_1}}\\\boxed{d_2}\\\vdots\\\boxed{d_s}\end{smallmatrix}$, $k, s \geq 2$.

Similarly we can define yz, zy, zx, xz arrow-heads and arrows.

Definition 5. Let u_1, u_2 be rectangular arrays of size $1 \times k, k \geq 1$ and v_1, v_2 be rectangular arrays of size $1 \times r, r \geq 1$ and $\$_{xy}, \$_{yx}, \$_{xx}$ and $\$_{yy}$ be special symbols not in Σ.

1. A xy array context over Σ is of the form $xy = [_{u_2}{}^{u_1}]\$_{xy}[^{v_1}{}_{v_2}] \in P_zA_x\$_{xy}P_zA_y$

2. A yx array context over Σ is of the form $yx = [^{u_1}{}_{u_2}]\$_{yx}[_{v_2}{}^{v_1}] \in P_zA_y\$_{yx}P_zA_x$

3. A xx array context over Σ is of the form $xx = [_{u_2}{}^{u_1}]\$_{xx}[_{v_2}{}^{v_1}] \in P_zA_x\$_{xx}P_zA_x$

4. A yy array context over Σ is of the form $yy = [^{u_1}{}_{u_2}]\$_{yy}[^{v_1}{}_{v_2}] \in P_zA_y\$_{yy}P_zA_y$

Similarly we can define yz, zy, zx, xz, zz array contexts.

We now define Z-direction parallel internal xy, yx, xx, yy array contextual operations.

Definition 6. *Consider a hexagonal array $H = [a_{ijk}]$ of size (l, m, n). Suppose H can be written as $H = X_1 \bigotimes X_2 \bigotimes X_3$ where X_1 is a xy arrow-head or a xy arrow, X_3 is a yx arrow-head or yx arrow, $X_2 = [a_{i'j'k'}]$ is a hexagonal array of size (l, m, n') where $n' < n$. We write $H \Rightarrow H'$ if there exists,*

1. *a finite number of xy array contexts $xy_i \in XY'$ $(1 \le i \le m - 1$ if $l > m$ or $1 \le i \le l - 1$ if $m \ge l)$ not all need be distinct, where XY' is a finite subset of $P_z A_x \$_{xy} P_z A_y$.*
2. *a finite number of yx array contexts $yx_i \in YX'$ $(1 \le i \le m - 1$ if $l > m$ or $1 \le i \le l - 1$ if $m \ge l)$ not all need be distinct, where YX' is a finite subset of $P_z A_y \$_{yx} P_z A_x$.*
3. *a finite number of xx array contexts $xx_i \in XX'$ $(1 \le i \le l - m$ if $l > m)$ not all need be distinct or no xx array context in XX' if $m \ge l$, where XX' is a finite subset of $P_z A_x \$_{xx} P_z A_x$.*
4. *a finite number of yy array contexts $yy_i \in YY'$ $(1 \le i \le m - l$ if $m > l$ not all need be distinct or no yy array context in YY' if $l \ge m$, where YY' is a finite subset of $P_z A_y \$_{yy} P_z A_y$.*
5. *a choice mapping $\varphi_{xy} : xyTR \rightarrow 2^{XY'}$ such that*
   $$xy_i = [\,_{u_{i+1}}{}^{u_i}\,]\,\$_{xy}\,[\,^{v_i}\,_{v_{i+1}}]\in \varphi_{xy}(xyTr_i)$$
   $1 \le i \le m - 1$ if $l > m$ or $1 \le i \le l - 1$ if $m \ge l$
6. *a choice mapping $\varphi_{yx} : yxTR \rightarrow 2^{YX'}$ such that*
   $$yx_i = \begin{bmatrix} u'_i \\ u'_{i+1} \end{bmatrix}\$_{yx}\begin{bmatrix} v'_i \\ v'_{i+1} \end{bmatrix} \in \varphi_{yx}(yxTr_i)$$
   $1 \le i \le m - 1$ if $l > m$ or $1 \le i \le l - 1$ if $m \ge l$
7. *a choice mapping $\varphi_{xx} : P_z A_x \rightarrow 2^{XX'}$ such that*
   $$xx_i = [\,_{u_{i+1}}{}^{u_i}\,]\,\$_{xx}\,[\,_{v_{i+1}}{}^{v_i}\,]\in \varphi_{xx}(xxP_z A_i)$$
   $i = 1, 2, \ldots, l - m$ if $l > m$
8. *a choice mapping $\varphi_{yy} : P_z A_y \rightarrow 2^{YY'}$ such that*
   $$yy_i = [\,^{u_i}\,u_{i+1}]\,\$_{yy}\,[\,^{v_i}\,v_{i+1}]\in \varphi_{yy}(yyP_z A_i)$$
   $i = 1, 2, \ldots, m - l$ if $m > l$

$H = X_1 \bigotimes X_2 \bigotimes X_3$ and $H' = X_1 \bigotimes L \bigotimes X_2 \bigotimes R \bigotimes X_3$ where L is a xy arrow-head or xy arrow and R is a yx arrow-head or yx arrow.

Similarly we can define X-direction parallel internal yz, zy, yy, zz array contextual operations by considering the hexagonal array $H = [a_{ijk}]$ as $H = X_1 \bigoplus X_2 \bigoplus X_3$ where X_1 is a yz arrow-head or a yz arrow, X_3 is a zy arrow-head or a zy arrow, $X_2 = [a_{i'j'k'}]$ is a hexagonal array of size (l', m, n) where $l' > l$. We write $H \Rightarrow H'$ if $H' = X_1 \bigoplus L \bigoplus X_2 \bigoplus R \bigoplus X_3$ where L is a yz arrow-head or yz arrow and R is a zy arrow-head or zy arrow.

Similarly we can define Y-direction parallel internal zx, xz, zz, xx array contextual operations by considering the hexagonal array $H = [a_{ijk}]$ as $H = X_1 \bigotimes X_2 \bigotimes X_3$ where X_1 is a zx arrow-head or a zx arrow, X_3 is a xz arrow-head or a xz arrow, $X_2 = [a_{i'j'k'}]$ is a hexagonal array of size (l, m', n) where

$m' > m$. We write $H \Rightarrow H'$ if $H' = X_1 \bigotimes L \bigotimes X_2 \bigotimes R \bigotimes X_3$ where L is a zx arrow-head or zx arrow and R is a xz arrow-head or xz arrow.

Definition 7. *A Z-direction parallel internal contextual hexagonal array grammar with choice is an ordered system,*

$$G_{ZI} = (\Sigma, B, XY', YX', XX', YY', \varphi_{xy}, \varphi_{yx}, \varphi_{xx}, \varphi_{yy})$$

where

1. *Σ is a finite alphabet,*
2. *B is a finite subset of Σ^{**H} called the base of G_{ZI},*
3. *XY' is a finite subset of $P_z A_x \$_{xy} P_z A_y$ called the set of xy array contexts,*
4. *YX' is a finite subset of $P_z A_y \$_{yx} P_z A_x$ called the set of yx array contexts,*
5. *XX' is a finite subset of $P_z A_x \$_{xx} P_z A_x$ called the set of xx array contexts,*
6. *YY' is a finite subset of $P_z A_y \$_{yy} P_z A_y$ called the set of yy array contexts,*
7. *$\varphi_{xy} : xyTR \rightarrow 2^{XY'}$, $\varphi_{yx} : yxTR \rightarrow 2^{YX}$, $\varphi_{xx} : P_z A_x \rightarrow 2^{XX'}$, $\varphi_{yy} : P_z A_y \rightarrow 2^{YY'}$ are the choice mapping which perform the parallel internal xy, yx, xx, yy contextual operations respectively. When xy, yx, xx, yy are omitted we call G_{ZI} as a Z-direction parallel internal hexagonal array grammar without choice.*

The direct derivation with respect to G_{ZI} is a binary relation $\Rightarrow_{Z-in}$ on Σ^{**H}. It is defined as $H \Rightarrow_{Z-in} H'$ where $H, H' \in \Sigma^{**H}$ with $H = X_1 \bigotimes X_2 \bigotimes X_3$, $H' = X_1 \bigotimes L \bigotimes X_2 \bigotimes R \bigotimes X_3$, where X_1 is a xy arrow-head or a xy arrow, X_3 is a yx arrow-head or yx arrow, $X_2 \in \Sigma^{**H}$ is of size (l, m, n') where $n' < n$ and L is a xy arrow-head or xy arrow, R is a yx arrow-head or yx arrow are the contexts obtained by performing parallel internal xy, yx, xx, yy array contextual operations according to the choice mappings $\varphi_{xy}, \varphi_{yx}, \varphi_{xx}, \varphi_{yy}$.

Definition 8. *Let $G_{ZI} = (\Sigma, B, XY', YX', XX', YY', \varphi_{xy}, \varphi_{yx}, \varphi_{xx}, \varphi_{yy})$ be a Z-direction parallel internal contextual hexagonal array grammar. The language generated by G_{ZI}, is defined as*

$$L(G_{ZI}) = \{H' \in \Sigma^{**H} / there\ exists\ H \in B\ such\ that\ H \Rightarrow^*_{Z-in} H'\}$$

Similarly we can define X-direction and Y-direction parallel internal contextual hexagonal array grammars and also the language generated by them.

In the like manner, we can also define Z-direction, X-direction and Y-direction parallel external contextual hexagonal array grammars and also the language generated by them.

3   Parallel Internal Contextual Hexagonal Array P Systems

Definition 9. *An parallel internal contextual hexagonal array P system is a construct, $\prod = (V, T, \mu, XY, YZ, ZX, M_1, M_2, \ldots, M_h, (R_1, \varphi_1), (R_2, \varphi_2), \ldots, (R_h, \varphi_h), i_0)$*

where,

V is the finite nonempty set of symbols called total alphabet;
$T \subseteq V$ *is the set of terminal alphabet;*
μ *is the membrane structure with h membranes or regions;*
$XY = XY' \cup YX' \cup XX' \cup YY'$
$YZ = YZ' \cup ZY' \cup YY'' \cup ZZ'$
$ZX = ZX' \cup XZ' \cup ZZ'' \cup XX''$
XY' *is the finite subset of* $P_z A_x \$_{xy} P_z A_y$ *called xy array contexts;*
YX' *is the finite subset of* $P_z A_y \$_{yx} P_z A_x$ *called yx array contexts;*
YZ' *is the finite subset of* $P_x A_y \$_{yz} P_x A_z$ *called yz array contexts;*
ZY' *is the finite subset of* $P_x A_z \$_{zy} P_x A_y$ *called zy array contexts;*
ZX' *is the finite subset of* $P_y A_z \$_{zx} P_y A_x$ *called zx array contexts;*
XZ' *is the finite subset of* $P_y A_x \$_{xz} P_y A_z$ *called xz array contexts;*
XX' *is the finite subset of* $P_z A_x \$_{xx} P_z A_x$ *called xx array contexts;*
YY' *is the finite subset of* $P_z A_y \$_{yy} P_z A_y$ *called yy array contexts;*
ZZ' *is the finite subset of* $P_x A_z \$_{zz} P_x A_z$ *called zz array contexts;*
XX'' *is the finite subset of* $P_y A_x \$_{xx} P_y A_x$ *called xx array contexts;*
YY'' *is the finite subset of* $P_x A_y \$_{yy} P_x A_y$ *called yy array contexts;*
ZZ'' *is the finite subset of* $P_y A_z \$_{zz} P_y A_z$ *called zz array contexts;*
$M_i, 1 \leq i \leq n$ *is a finite set of hexagonal arrays over V called axioms, initially*
present in the region i.

$$\varphi_i \subseteq \{\varphi_{xy}, \varphi_{yx}, \varphi'_{xx}, \varphi'_{yy}\} \text{ or } \{\varphi_{yz}, \varphi_{zy}, \varphi''_{yy}, \varphi'_{zz}\} \text{ or } \{\varphi_{zx}, \varphi_{xz}, \varphi''_{zz}, \varphi''_{xx}\}$$

$\varphi_{xy} : xyTR \rightarrow 2^{XY'}$, $\varphi_{yx} : yxTR \rightarrow 2^{YX'}$, $\varphi'_{xx} : P_z A_x \rightarrow 2^{XX'}$, $\varphi'_{yy} : P_z A_y \rightarrow 2^{YY'}$ *are the choice mappings which perform the Z-direction parallel internal xy, yx, xx, yy contextual operations respectively.*

$\varphi_{yz} : yzTR \rightarrow 2^{YZ'}$, $\varphi_{zy} : zyTR \rightarrow 2^{ZY'}$, $\varphi''_{yy} : P_x A_y \rightarrow 2^{YY''}$, $\varphi'_{zz} : P_x A_z \rightarrow 2^{ZZ'}$ *are the choice mappings which perform the X-direction parallel internal yz, zy, yy, zz contextual operations respectively.*

$\varphi_{zx} : zxTR \rightarrow 2^{ZX'}$, $\varphi_{xz} : xzTR \rightarrow 2^{XZ'}$, $\varphi''_{zz} : P_y A_z \rightarrow 2^{ZZ''}$, $\varphi''_{xx} : P_y A_x \rightarrow 2^{XX''}$ *are the choice mappings which perform the Y-direction parallel internal zx, xz, zz, xx contextual operations respectively.*

$R_i = \phi$ *(or)*
$$\left\{ \left(\left\{ \varphi_{xy}(xyTr_i) = [\,_{u_{i+1}}{}^{u_i}\,] \$_{xy} [\,^{v_i}{}_{v_{i+1}}\,], \varphi_{yx}(yxTr_i) = \begin{bmatrix} u'_i \\ u'_{i+1} \end{bmatrix} \$_{yx} \begin{bmatrix} & v'_i \\ v'_{i+1} & \end{bmatrix}, \right.\right.\right.$$
$$\varphi'_{xx}(xxP_zA_j) = [\,_{u_{j+1}}{}^{u_j}\,] \$_{xx} [\,^{v_j}{}_{v_{j+1}}\,], \varphi'_{yy}(yyP_zA_k) = [\,^{u_k}{}_{u_{k+1}}\,] \$_{yy} [\,^{v_k}{}_{v_{k+1}}\,] \Big\}, \alpha \Big) \Big\}$$
$1 \leq i \leq m-1$ *if* $l > m$ *or* $1 \leq i \leq l-1$ *if* $m \geq l$, $j = 1, 2, \ldots, l-m$ *if* $l > m$
and $k = 1, 2, \ldots, m-l$ *if* $m > l$, $\alpha \in \{here, out, in_t\}$

Here, $xyTr_1 =$

where, $1 < p < q < n$

(or)

$$\left\{ \left(\left\{ \begin{array}{l} \varphi_{yz}(yzTr_i) = [\,{}^{u_i}\,{}_{u_{i+1}}\,]\,\$_{yz}\,[\,{}^{v_i}\,{}_{v_{i+1}}\,],\ \varphi_{zy}(zyTr_i) = [\,u_i'\,{}_{u_{i+1}'}\,]\,\$_{zy}\,\left[\,{}^{v_i'}_{v_{i+1}'}\,\right], \\ \varphi_{yy}''(yyP_xA_j) = [\,{}^{u_j}\,{}_{u_{j+1}}\,]\,\$_{yy}\,[\,{}^{v_j}\,{}_{v_{j+1}}\,],\ \varphi_{zz}'(zzP_xA_k) = [\,u_k\ u_{k+1}\,]\,\$_{zz}\,[\,v_k\ v_{k+1}\,] \end{array}\right\}, \alpha \right) \right\}$$

$1 \le i \le n-1$ if $m > n$ or $1 \le i \le m-1$ if $n \ge m$, $j = 1, 2, \ldots, m-n$ if $m > n$
and $k = 1, 2, \ldots, n-m$ if $n > m$. $\alpha \in \{here, out, in_t\}$

Here, $yzTr_1 =$

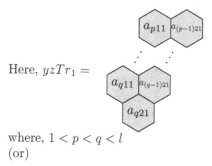

where, $1 < p < q < l$
(or)

$$\left\{ \left(\left\{ \begin{array}{l} \varphi_{zx}(zxTr_i) = [\,u_i\ u_{i+1}\,]\,\$_{zx}\,[\,v_{i+1}\ {}^{v_i}\,],\ \varphi_{xz}(xzTr_i) = \left[\,{}^{u_i'}_{u_{i+1}'}\,\right]\,\$_{xz}\,[\,v_i'\ v_{i+1}'\,], \\ \varphi_{zz}''(zzP_yA_j) = [\,u_j\ u_{j+1}\,]\,\$_{zz}\,[\,v_j\ v_{j+1}\,],\ \varphi_{xx}''(xxP_yA_k) = [\,u_{k+1}\ {}^{u_k}\,]\,\$_{xx}\,[\,v_{k+1}\ {}^{v_k}\,] \end{array}\right\}, \alpha \right) \right\}$$

$1 \le i \le l-1$ if $n > l$ or $1 \le i \le n-1$ if $l \ge n$, $j = 1, 2, \ldots, n-l$ if $n > l$ and
$k = 1, 2, \ldots, l-n$ if $l > n$. $\alpha \in \{here, out, in_t\}$

Here, $zxTr_1 =$

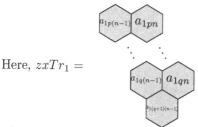

where, $1 < p < q < m$
i_0 is the output membrane

The direct derivation with respect to $\prod$ is a binary relation $\Rightarrow$ on V^{**H} and
is defined as $H \Rightarrow_{in} H'$, where $H, H' \in V^{**H}$ if and only if,

$H = X_1 \ominus X_2 \ominus X_3$, $H' = X_1 \ominus L \ominus X_2 \ominus R \ominus X_3$, where X_1 is a xy arrow-head
or a xy arrow, X_3 is a yx arrow-head or yx arrow, $X_2 \in V^{**H}$ is of size (l, m, n')
where $n' < n$ and L is a xy arrow-head or xy arrow, R is a yx arrow-head or
yx arrow are the contexts obtained by using the evolution rules R_i based on the
Z-direction parallel internal xy, yx, xx, yy array contextual operations according
to the choice mappings $\varphi_{xy}, \varphi_{yx}, \varphi_{xx}', \varphi_{yy}'$.

(or)

$H = X_1 \oslash X_2 \oslash X_3$, $H' = X_1 \oslash L \oslash X_2 \oslash R \oslash X_3$ where X_1 is a yz arrow-head or a yz arrow, X_3 is a zy arrow-head or a zy arrow, $X_2 \in V^{**H}$ is of size (l', m, n) where $l' > l$ and L is a yz arrow-head or yz arrow, R is a zy arrow-head or zy arrow are the contexts obtained by using the evolution rules R_i based on the X-direction parallel internal yz, zy, yy, zz array contextual operations according to the choice mappings $\varphi_{yz}, \varphi_{zy}, \varphi''_{yy}, \varphi'_{zz}$.

(or)

$H = X_1 \otimes X_2 \oslash X_3$, $H' = X_1 \otimes L \otimes X_2 \oslash R \otimes X_3$ where X_1 is a zx arrow-head or a zx arrow, X_3 is a xz arrow-head or a xz arrow, $X_2 \in V^{**H}$ is of size (l, m', n) where $m' > m$ and L is a zx arrow-head or zx arrow, R is a xz arrow-head or xz arrow are the contexts obtained by using the evolution rules R_i based on the Y-direction parallel internal zx, xz, zz, xx array contextual operations according to the choice mappings $\varphi_{zx}, \varphi_{xz}, \varphi''_{zz}, \varphi''_{xx}$.

Initially the P-system $\prod$ consists of the membrane structure μ with h membranes which are labeled as $1, 2, \ldots, h$. The outermost membrane being the skin membrane is labeled as 1, which also is our output membrane. We use the evolution rules R_i which is based on the choice mapping φ_i present in the membrane labeled i and carry out the step by step computation. The hexagonal array we obtain after each and every computation is considered to be of size (l, m, n). Thus obtained hexagonal array is placed in the membrane as indicated by α. If α is chosen as 'here', then the resulting hexagonal array remains in the same membrane. If α is chosen as 'in_t', then the resulting array is sent to the membrane with label t. If α is chosen as 'out', then the resulting hexagonal array is sent out from the present membrane and enters the immediate outer membrane. If that outer membrane is the skin membrane, then we say that the resulting hexagonal array is present in the language generated by this P-system. The computation is said to be successful, when there is no rule applicable to the hexagonal array obtained after the last computation and hence the system halts. A successful computation may result in a hexagonal array being sent out to the skin membrane depending on α. All the hexagonal arrays with symbols over T thus collected in the skin membrane is called the language generated by the parallel internal contextual hexagonal array P system and is denoted by PICHAL($\prod$).

The family of all hexagonal array languages PICHAL($\prod$) generated by the parallel internal contextual hexagonal array P systems with at most h membranes is denoted by PICHAP$_h$.

If a P system does not involve X-direction parallel internal yz, zy, yy, zz array contextual operations and Y-direction parallel internal zx, xz, zz, xx array contextual operations then we call that P system as Z-direction parallel internal contextual hexagonal array P system and denote it by ZPICHAL($\prod$). The family of all hexagonal array languages ZPICHAL($\prod$) generated by the Z-direction parallel internal contextual hexagonal array P systems with at most h membranes is denoted by ZPICHAP$_h$.

Similarly we can define XPICHAP$_h$ and YPICHAP$_h$, the family of all hexagonal array languages XPICHAL($\prod$) and YPICHAL($\prod$) generated by the

X-direction and Y-direction parallel internal contextual hexagonal array P systems with at most h membranes, respectively.

Example 1. Consider the parallel internal contextual hexagonal array P-system, $\prod = (V, T, \mu, XY, YZ, ZX, M_1, M_2, M_3, M_4, (R_1, \varphi_1), (R_2, \varphi_2), (R_4, \varphi_3), (R_4, \varphi_4), 1)$ where,

$V = \{a\}$

$T = \{a\}$

$\mu = [_1 [_2]_2 [_3]_3 [_4]_4]_1$

$XY = \left\{ [_a{}^a] \$_{xy} [{}^a{}_a], [{}^a{}_a] \$_{yx} [_a{}^a] \right\}$

$YZ = \left\{ [{}^a{}_a] \$_{yz} [a\ a], [a\ a] \$_{zy} [{}^a{}_a] \right\}$

$ZX = \left\{ [a\ a] \$_{zx} [_a{}^a], [_a{}^a] \$_{xz} [a\ a] \right\}$

$M_1 = \emptyset$

$M_2 = \left\{ \right.$ $\left. \right\}$

$M_3 = \emptyset$

$M_4 = \emptyset$

$R_1 = \emptyset$

$$R_2 = \left\{ \left(\left\{ \varphi_{xy} \left(\left[_{a^{i+1}} {}^{a^i} \right]_{2 \leq i \leq n} \right) = [_a{}^a] \$_{xy} [{}^a{}_a], \varphi_{yx} \left(\left[{}^{a^{i+1}}{}_{a^i} \right]_{2 \leq i \leq n} \right) = \right. \right. \right.$$
$$\left. \left. \left. [{}^a{}_a] \$_{yx} [_a{}^a] \right\}, in_3 \right) \right\}$$

$$R_3 = \left\{ \left(\left\{ \varphi_{yz} \left([a^j\ a^{j+1}]_{2 \leq j \leq l} \right) = [{}^a{}_a] \$_{yz} [a\ a], \varphi_{zy} \left(\left[{}^{'a^{j+1}}\ {}_{a^j} \right]_{2 \leq j \leq l} \right) = \right. \right. \right.$$
$$\left. \left. \left. [a\ a] \$_{zy} [{}^a{}_a], \varphi'_{zz} \left([a^j\ a^j]_{2 \leq j \leq l} \right) = [a\ a] \$_{zz} [a\ a] \right\}, in_4 \right) \right\}$$

$$R_4 = \left\{ \left(\left\{ \varphi_{zx} \left([a^{k+1}\ a^k]_{2 \leq k \leq m} \right) = [a\ a] \$_{zx} [_a{}^a], \varphi_{xz} \left(\left[_{a^k} {}^{a^{k+1}} \right]_{2 \leq k \leq m} \right) = \right. \right. \right.$$
$$\left. \left. \left. [_a{}^a] \$_{xz} [a\ a] \right\}, \alpha \right) \right\}, \alpha \in \{out, in_2\}$$

Membrane labeled 1 i.e., the skin membrane is the output membrane.

We consider the hexagonal array obtained after each computation to be of size (l, m, n).

The language generated by this P system is the set of hexagonal arrays over $\{a\}$ of sizes $(2l, 2m, 2n), l, m, n \geq 3$ with $l = m = n$.

4   Parallel External Contextual Hexagonal Array P Systems

Definition 10. *An parallel external contextual hexagonal array P system is a construct,* $\prod = (V, T, \mu, XY, YZ, ZX, M_1, M_2, \ldots, M_h, (R_1, \varphi_1), (R_2, \varphi_2), \ldots, (R_h, \varphi_h), i_0)$
where, $V, T, \mu, XY, YZ, ZX, M_i$ *are as defined in Definition 9,*

$\varphi_i \subseteq \{\varphi_{xy}, \varphi_{yx}, \varphi'_{xx}, \varphi'_{yy}\}$ *or* $\{\varphi_{yz}, \varphi_{zy}, \varphi''_{yy}, \varphi'_{zz}\}$ *or* $\{\varphi_{zx}, \varphi_{xz}, \varphi''_{zz}, \varphi''_{xx}\}$
$\varphi_{xy} : xyTR \to 2^{XY'}$, $\varphi_{yx} : yxTR \to 2^{YX'}$, $\varphi'_{xx} : P_zA_x \to 2^{XX'}$, $\varphi'_{yy} : P_zA_y \to 2^{YY'}$ *are the choice mappings which perform the Z-direction parallel external* xy, yx, xx, yy *contextual operations respectively.*

$\varphi_{yz} : yzTR \to 2^{YZ'}$, $\varphi_{zy} : zyTR \to 2^{ZY'}$, $\varphi''_{yy} : P_xA_y \to 2^{YY''}$, $\varphi'_{zz} : P_xA_z \to 2^{ZZ'}$ *are the choice mappings which perform the X-direction parallel external* yz, zy, yy, zz *contextual operations respectively.*

$\varphi_{zx} : zxTR \to 2^{ZX'}$, $\varphi_{xz} : xzTR \to 2^{XZ'}$, $\varphi''_{zz} : P_yA_z \to 2^{ZZ''}$, $\varphi''_{xx} : P_yA_x \to 2^{XX''}$ *are the choice mappings which perform the Y-direction parallel external* zx, xz, zz, xx *contextual operations respectively.*

$R_i = \phi$ *(or)*
$$\left\{ \left(\left\{ \varphi_{xy}(xyTr_i) = [_{u_{i+1}}{}^{u_i}] \$_{xy} [^{v_i}{}_{v_{i+1}}], \varphi_{yx}(yxTr_i) = [^{u'_i}_{u'_{i+1}}] \$_{yx} [_{v'_{i+1}}{}^{v'_i}], \right. \right. \right.$$
$$\left. \left. \left. \varphi'_{xx}(xxP_zA_j) = [_{u_{j+1}}{}^{u_j}] \$_{xx} [_{v_{j+1}}{}^{v_j}], \varphi'_{yy}(yyP_zA_k) = [^{u_k}_{u_{k+1}}] \$_{yy} [^{v_k}_{v_{k+1}}] \right\}, \alpha \right) \right\}$$
$1 \leq i \leq m - 1$ *if* $l > m$ *or* $1 \leq i \leq l - 1$ *if* $m \geq l$, $j = 1, 2, \ldots, l - m$ *if* $l > m$
and $k = 1, 2, \ldots, m - l$ *if* $m > l$, $\alpha \in \{here, out, in_t\}$

Here, $xyTr_1 = $

(or)

$$\left\{ \left(\left\{ \varphi_{yz}(yzTr_i) = [^{u_i}{}_{u_{i+1}}] \$_{yz} [^{v_i}{}_{v_{i+1}}], \varphi_{zy}(zyTr_i) = [^{u'_i}{}_{u'_{i+1}}] \$_{zy} [^{v'_i}_{v'_{i+1}}], \right. \right. \right.$$
$$\left. \left. \left. \varphi''_{yy}(yyP_zA_j) = [^{u_j}{}_{u_{j+1}}] \$_{yy} [^{v_j}{}_{v_{j+1}}], \varphi'_{zz}(zzP_zA_k) = [^{u_k}{}_{u_{k+1}}] \$_{zz} [^{v_k}{}_{v_{k+1}}] \right\}, \alpha \right) \right\}$$
$1 \leq i \leq n - 1$ *if* $m > n$ *or* $1 \leq i \leq m - 1$ *if* $n \geq m$, $j = 1, 2, \ldots, m - n$ *if* $m > n$
and $k = 1, 2, \ldots, n - m$ *if* $n > m$. $\alpha \in \{here, out, in_t\}$

Here, $yzTr_1 =$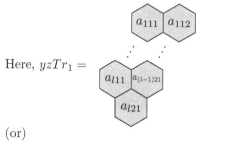

(or)

$$\left\{ \left(\left\{ \varphi_{zx}(zxTr_i) = [\,u_i \;\; u_{i+1}\,]\,\$_{zx}\left[\,v_{i+1} \;\;{}^{v_i}\,\right], \; \varphi_{xz}(xzTr_i) = \left[\,{}_{u'_{i+1}} \;\;{}^{u'_i}\,\right]\$_{xz}\left[\,v'_i \;\; v'_{i+1}\,\right], \right.\right.$$

$$\left.\left. \varphi''_{zz}(zzP_yA_j) = [\,u_j \;\; u_{j+1}\,]\,\$_{zz}\left[\,v_j \;\; v_{j+1}\,\right], \; \varphi''_{xx}(xxP_yA_k) = [\,u_{k+1} \;\;{}^{u_k}\,]\$_{xx}\left[\,v_{k+1} \;\;{}^{v_k}\,\right], \right\}, \alpha \right) \right\}$$

$1 \le i \le l - 1$ *if* $n > l$ *or* $1 \le i \le n - 1$ *if* $l \ge n$, $j = 1, 2, \ldots, n - l$ *if* $n > l$ *and*
$k = 1, 2, \ldots, l - n$ *if* $l > n$. $\alpha \in \{here, out, in_t\}$

Here, $zxTr_1 =$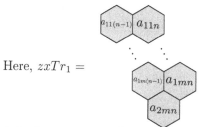

i_0 is the output membrane

The direct derivation with respect to $\prod$ is a binary relation $\Rightarrow$ on V^{**H} and is defined as $H \Rightarrow_{ex} H'$, where $H, H' \in V^{**H}$ if and only if,

$H' = L \bigcirc H \bigcirc R$, where L is a xy arrow-head or xy arrow, R is a yx arrow-head or yx arrow are the contexts obtained by using the evolution rules R_i based on the Z-direction parallel external xy, yx, xx, yy array contextual operations according to the choice mappings $\varphi_{xy}, \varphi_{yx}, \varphi'_{xx}, \varphi'_{yy}$.

(or)

$H' = L \bigcirc H \bigcirc R$ where L is a yz arrow-head or yz arrow, R is a zy arrow-head or zy arrow are the contexts obtained by using the evolution rules R_i based on the X-direction parallel external yz, zy, yy, zz array contextual operations according to the choice mappings $\varphi_{yz}, \varphi_{zy}, \varphi''_{yy}, \varphi'_{zz}$.

(or)

$H' = L \bigcirc X_2 \bigcirc R$ where L is a zx arrow-head or zx arrow, R is a xz arrow-head or xz arrow are the contexts obtained by using the evolution rules R_i based on the Y-direction parallel external zx, xz, zz, xx array contextual operations according to the choice mappings $\varphi_{zx}, \varphi_{xz}, \varphi''_{zz}, \varphi''_{xx}$.

The working of the parallel external contextual hexagonal array P system is the same as the parallel internal contextual hexagonal array P system except that the contexts are obtained externally using the evolution rules provided based on the Z-direction parallel external xy, yx, xx, yy array contextual operations according to the choice mappings $\varphi_{xy}, \varphi_{yx}, \varphi'_{xx}, \varphi'_{yy}$ or the X-direction parallel external yz, zy, yy, zz array contextual operations according to the choice mappings $\varphi_{yz}, \varphi_{zy}, \varphi''_{yy}, \varphi'_{zz}$ or the Y-direction parallel external zx, xz, zz, xx array contextual operations according to the choice mappings $\varphi_{zx}, \varphi_{xz}, \varphi''_{zz}, \varphi''_{xx}$. As like the parallel internal contextual hexagonal array P system every successful computation depending on α may result in an hexagonal array being sent out to the skin membrane. All the hexagonal arrays with symbols over T collected in the skin membrane is the language generated by the parallel external contextual hexagonal array P system and is denoted by PECHAL($\prod$).

The family of all hexagonal array languages PECHAL($\prod$) generated by the parallel external contextual hexagonal array P systems with atmost h membranes is denoted by PECHAP$_h$.

If a P system does not involve X-direction parallel external yz, zy, yy, zz array contextual operations and Y-direction parallel external zx, xz, zz, xx array contextual operations then we call that P system as Z-direction parallel external contextual hexagonal array P system and denote it by ZPECHAL($\prod$). The family of all hexagonal array languages ZPECHAL($\prod$) generated by the Z-direction parallel external contextual hexagonal array P systems with at most h membranes is denoted by ZPECHAP$_h$.

Similarly we can define XPECHAP$_h$ and YPECHAP$_h$, the family of all hexagonal array languages XPECHAL($\prod$) and YPECHAL($\prod$) generated by the X-direction and Y-direction parallel external contextual hexagonal array P systems with at most h membranes, respectively.

Example 2. Consider the parallel external contextual hexagonal array P-system, $\prod = (V, T, \mu, XY, YZ, ZX, M_1, M_2, M_3, M_4, (R_1, \varphi_1), (R_2, \varphi_2), (R_4, \varphi_3), (R_4, \varphi_4), 1)$

where,

$V = T = \{a\}$

$\mu = [_1[_2]_2[_3]_3[_4]_4]_1$

$XY = \left\{ \begin{bmatrix} & a \\ a & \end{bmatrix} \$_{xy} \begin{bmatrix} a & \\ & a \end{bmatrix}, \begin{bmatrix} a & \\ & a \end{bmatrix} \$_{yx} \begin{bmatrix} & a \\ a & \end{bmatrix} \right\}$

$YZ = \left\{ \begin{bmatrix} a & \\ & a \end{bmatrix} \$_{yz} \begin{bmatrix} a & a \end{bmatrix}, \begin{bmatrix} a & a \end{bmatrix} \$_{zy} \begin{bmatrix} a & \\ & a \end{bmatrix} \right\}$

$ZX = \left\{ \begin{bmatrix} a & a \end{bmatrix} \$_{zx} \begin{bmatrix} & a \\ a & \end{bmatrix}, \begin{bmatrix} & a \\ a & \end{bmatrix} \$_{xz} \begin{bmatrix} a & a \end{bmatrix} \right\}$

$M_1 = \emptyset$

$M_2 = \left\{ \begin{smallmatrix} & a & a & \\ a & a & a \\ & a & a & \end{smallmatrix} \right\}$

$M_3 = \emptyset$

$M_4 = \emptyset$

$R_1 = \emptyset$

$$R_2 = \left\{ \left(\left\{ \varphi_{xy} \left(\left[\begin{smallmatrix} & & a^i \\ a^{i+1} & & \end{smallmatrix} \right]_{i \geq n} \right) = \left[\begin{smallmatrix} & a \\ a & \end{smallmatrix} \right] \$_{xy} \left[\begin{smallmatrix} a & \\ & a \end{smallmatrix} \right], \varphi_{yx} \left(\left[\begin{smallmatrix} a^{i+1} & \\ & a^i \end{smallmatrix} \right]_{i \geq n} \right) = \right. \right.$$

$$\left. \left[\begin{smallmatrix} a & \\ & a \end{smallmatrix} \right] \$_{yx} \left[\begin{smallmatrix} & a \\ a & \end{smallmatrix} \right] \right\}, in_3 \right) \right\}$$

$$R_3 = \left\{ \left(\left\{ \varphi_{yz} \left(\left[a^j \ a^{j+1} \right]_{j \geq l} \right) = \left[\begin{smallmatrix} a & \\ & a \end{smallmatrix} \right] \$_{yz} \left[a \ a \right], \varphi_{zy} \left(\left[\begin{smallmatrix} a^{j+1} & \\ & a^j \end{smallmatrix} \right]_{i \geq l} \right) = \right. \right.$$

$$\left[a \ a \right] \$_{zy} \left[\begin{smallmatrix} a & \\ & a \end{smallmatrix} \right], \varphi'_{zz} \left(\left[a^j \ a^j \right]_{j = n-1} = \left[a \ a \right] \$_{zz} \left[a \ a \right] \right\}, in_4 \right) \right\}$$

$$R_4 = \left\{ \left(\left\{ \varphi_{zx} \left(\left[a^{k+1} \ a^k \right]_{k \geq m} \right) = \left[a \ a \right] \$_{zx} \left[\begin{smallmatrix} a & \\ & a \end{smallmatrix} \right], \varphi_{xz} \left(\left[\begin{smallmatrix} & a^{k+1} \\ a^k & \end{smallmatrix} \right]_{k \geq m} \right) = \right. \right.$$

$$\left[\begin{smallmatrix} a & \\ & a \end{smallmatrix} \right] \$_{xz} \left[a \ a \right] \right\}, \alpha \right) \right\}, \alpha \in \{out, in_2\}$$

Membrane labeled 1 i.e., the skin membrane is the output membrane.

Each hexagonal array obtained after each computation is of size (l, m, n).

The language generated by this P system is the set of hexagonal arrays over $\{a\}$ of sizes $(2l, 2m, 2n), l, m, n \geq 2$ with $l = m = n$.

5   Properties of Parallel Contextual Hexagonal Array P Systems

In this section we give some basic properties of parallel contextual hexagonal array P systems.

If H is a hexagonal array of size (l, m, n), then let $|H|_X = l, |H|_Y = m, |H|_Z = n$. If X is a xy arrow head, then $|X|_Z$ denotes the number of elements in the border of X in Z-direction. If X is a xy arrow, then $|X|_Z = 1$. We can give similar type of notions for yx, yz, zy, zx, xz arrow-heads or arrows.

Definition 11. *A language $M \subseteq \Sigma^{**H}$ has the Z-internal bounded step property (ZIBS) if there is a constant p such that for each $H \in M$, $|H|_Z > p$, there is a $H' \in M$ such that $H' = X_1 \oslash X_2 \oslash X_3$, $H = X_1 \oslash L \oslash X_2 \oslash R \oslash X_3$, and $|L|_Z + |R|_Z \leq p$.*

Similarly we can define X-internal bounded step property (XIBS) and Y-internal bounded step property(YIBS)

Definition 12. *A language $M \subseteq \Sigma^{**H}$ has the Z-external bounded step property (ZEBS) if there is a constant p such that for each $H \in M$, $|H|_Z > p$, there is a $H' \in M$ such that $H = L \oslash H' \oslash R$, and $|L|_Z + |R|_Z \leq p$.*

Similarly we can define X-external bounded step property (XEBS) and Y-external bounded step property (YEBS)

Note 1. For theorems 1 & 2 we consider, $R' = \Big\{ \varphi_{xy}(xyTr_i) = [\,u_{i+1}{}^{u_i}\,]\,\$_{xy}\,[\,^{v_i}{}_{v_{i+1}}\,],$

$\varphi_{yx}(yxTr_i) = \Big[\,^{u'_i}{}_{u'_{i+1}}\,\Big]\,\$_{yx}\,\Big[\,_{v'_{i+1}}{}^{v'_i}\,\Big],\ \varphi'_{xx}(xxP_zA_j) = \big[\,u_{j+1}{}^{u_j}\,\big]\,\$_{xx}\,\big[\,v_{j+1}{}^{v_j}\,\big],$

$\varphi'_{yy}(yyP_zA_k) = [\,^{u_k}{}_{u_{k+1}}\,]\,\$_{yy}\,[\,^{v_k}{}_{v_{k+1}}\,]\Big\}, 1 \le i \le m-1$ if $l > m$ or $1 \le i \le l-1$

if $m \ge l,\ j = 1,2,\ldots,l-m$ if $l > m$ and $k = 1,2,\ldots,m-l$ if $m > l$.

Theorem 1. *A language generated by a parallel internal contextual hexagonal array P system* $\prod$, *satisfies ZIBS property, if for every rule* $(R', here)$ *in* R_i, *there is a rule* (R', out) *in* R_i.

Here, $xyTr_1 = $, $1 < p < q < n$.

Proof. Let M be a language generated by a internal parallel contextual hexagonal array P system, $\prod = (V, T, \mu, XY, YZ, ZX, M_1, M_2, \ldots, M_h, (R_1, \varphi_1), (R_2, \varphi_2), \ldots, (R_h, \varphi_h), i_0)$

Let $p_1 = max\{|H|_Z / H \in M_i\}$ and

$$p_2 = max\Big\{|L|_Z + |R|_Z \Big| \Big(\Big\{ \varphi_{xy}(xyTr_i) = [\,u_{i+1}{}^{u_i}\,]\,\$_{xy}\,[\,^{v_i}{}_{v_{i+1}}\,], \varphi_{yx}(yxTr_i) =$$

$$\Big[\,^{u'_i}{}_{u'_{i+1}}\,\Big]\,\$_{yx}\,\Big[\,_{v'_{i+1}}{}^{v'_i}\,\Big], \varphi'_{xx}(xxP_zA_j) = \big[\,u_{j+1}{}^{u_j}\,\big]\,\$_{xx}\,\big[\,v_{j+1}{}^{v_j}\,\big], \varphi'_{yy}(yyP_zA_k) =$$

$$[\,^{u_k}{}_{u_{k+1}}\,]\,\$_{yy}\,[\,^{v_k}{}_{v_{k+1}}\,]\Big\}, here\Big), \Big(\Big\{ \varphi_{xy}(xyTr_i) = [\,u_{i+1}{}^{u_i}\,]\,\$_{xy}\,[\,^{v_i}{}_{v_{i+1}}\,], \varphi_{yx}(yxTr_i) =$$

$$\Big[\,^{u'_i}{}_{u'_{i+1}}\,\Big]\,\$_{yx}\,\Big[\,_{v'_{i+1}}{}^{v'_i}\,\Big], \varphi'_{xx}(xxP_zA_j) = \big[\,u_{j+1}{}^{u_j}\,\big]\,\$_{xx}\,\big[\,v_{j+1}{}^{v_j}\,\big], \varphi'_{yy}(yyP_zA_k) =$$

$$[\,^{u_k}{}_{u_{k+1}}\,]\,\$_{yy}\,[\,^{v_k}{}_{v_{k+1}}\,]\Big\}, out\Big) \in R_i\Big\}$$ where L is either a xy arrow-head or a xy arrow and R is either a yx arrow-head or a yx arrow obtained from some $H, H' \in M$ with $H' = X_1 \oslash X_2 \oslash X_3,\ H = X_1 \oslash L \oslash X_2 \oslash R \oslash X_3$ and $H' \Rightarrow_{in} H$.

Let $p = max\{p_1, p_2\}$. If $H \in M$ is such that $|H|_Z > p$ then $H \notin M_i$. Hence $H = X_1 \oslash L \oslash X_2 \oslash R \oslash X_3$, for some L and R and $H' = X_1 \oslash X_2 \oslash X_3$ with $H' \in M$.

Hence there is a constant p such that for each $H \in M$ with $|H|_Z > p$ there exists $H' \in M$ with $H' = X_1 \oslash X_2 \oslash X_3$ such that $H = X_1 \oslash L \oslash X_2 \oslash R \oslash X_3$ and $|L|_Z + |R|_Z \le p$. Hence M satisfies the ZIBS property.   □

Similar results can be shown for parallel internal contextual hexagonal array P systems with respect to the XIBS property and the YIBS property respectively.

Theorem 2. *A language generated by a parallel external contextual hexagonal array P system* $\prod$, *satisfies ZEBS property, if for every rule* $(R', here)$ *in* R_i, *there is a rule* (R', out) *in* R_i.

Here, $xyTr_1 =$

The proof is similar to Theorem 1, and hence omitted.

Similar results can be shown for parallel external contextual hexagonal array P systems with respect to the XEBS property and the YEBS property respectively.

Theorem 3. *If a language* $M \subseteq \Sigma^{**H}$ *satisfies XIBS, YIBS and ZIBS property, then that language* M *is generated by a parallel internal contextual hexagonal array P system.*

Theorem 4. *If a language* $M \subseteq \Sigma^{**H}$ *satisfies XEBS, YEBS and ZEBS property, then that language* M *is generated by a parallel external contextual hexagonal array P system.*

The proofs for Theorems 3 and 4 are straight forward.

Note 1. Hexagonal arrays produced in intermediate steps during computation while generating a hexagonal array belonging to the language are called as hexagonal array sentential form.

Definition 13. *A language* $M \subseteq \Sigma^{**H}$ *has the Weak Z-internal bounded step property (WZIBS) if there is a constant* p *such that for each* $H \in M$, $|H|_Z > p$, *there is a hexagonal array sentential form* H' *such that* $H = X_1 \bigotimes L \bigotimes X_2 \bigotimes R \bigotimes X_3$, $H' = X_1 \bigotimes X_2 \bigotimes X_3$ *and* $|L|_Z + |R|_Z \leq p$.

Similarly we can define Weak X-internal bounded step property(WXIBS) and Weak Y-internal bounded step property(WYIBS)

Definition 14. *A language* $M \subseteq \Sigma^{**H}$ *has the Weak Z-external bounded step property (WZEBS) if there is a constant* p *such that for each* $H \in M$, $|H|_Z > p$, *there is a hexagonal array sentential form* H' *such that* $H = L \bigotimes H' \bigotimes R$, *and* $|L|_Z + |R|_Z \leq p$.

Similarly we can define Weak X-external bounded step property(WXEBS) and Weak Y-external bounded step property(WYEBS)

Theorem 5. *A language generated by a parallel internal contextual hexagonal array P system, satisfies the WZIBS property.*

Proof. Let M be a language generated by a internal parallel contextual hexagonal array P system, $\prod = (V, T, \mu, XY, YZ, ZX, M_1, M_2, \ldots, M_h, (R_1, \varphi_1), (R_2, \varphi_2), \ldots, (R_h, \varphi_h), i_0)$

Let $p_1 = max\{|H|_Z / H \in M_i\}$ and

$$p_2 = max\Bigg\{|L|_Z + |R|_Z \Bigg| \Bigg(\Bigg\{ \varphi_{xy}(xyTr_i) = [\,_{u_{i+1}}{}^{u_i}\,]\,\$_{xy}\,[\,^{v_i}{}_{v_{i+1}}\,],\ \varphi_{yx}(yxTr_i) =$$

$$[\,^{u'_i}_{u'_{i+1}}\,]\,\$_{yx}\,[\,_{v'_{i+1}}{}^{v'_i}\,],\ \varphi'_{xx}(xxP_zA_j) = [\,_{u_{j+1}}{}^{u_j}\,]\,\$_{xx}\,[\,v_{j+1}{}^{v_j}\,],\ \varphi'_{yy}(yyP_zA_k) =$$

$$[\,^{u_k}{}_{u_{k+1}}\,]\,\$_{yy}\,[\,^{v_k}{}_{v_{k+1}}\,]\Bigg\},\alpha\Bigg) \in R_i\ \text{and}\ \alpha \in \{here, out, in_t\}\Bigg\}\ \text{where}\ L\ \text{is either a}\ xy$$

arrow-head or a xy arrow and R is either a yx arrow-head or a yx arrow obtained from some $H \in M$ with $H = X_1 \ominus L \ominus X_2 \ominus R \ominus X_3$ and $H' = X_1 \ominus X_2 \ominus X_3$ is a hexagonal array sentential form.

Let $p = max\{p_1, p_2\}$. If $H \in M$ is such that $|H|_Z > p$ then $H \notin M_i$. Hence $H = X_1 \ominus L \ominus X_2 \ominus R \ominus X_3$, for some L and R and $H' = X_1 \ominus X_2 \ominus X_3$ is a hexagonal array sentential form.

Hence there is a constant p such that for each $H \in M$ with $|H|_Z > p$ there is a hexagonal array sentential form H' with $H' = X_1 \ominus X_2 \ominus X_3$ such that $H = X_1 \ominus L \ominus X_2 \ominus R \ominus X_3$ and $|L|_Z + |R|_Z \le p$. Hence M satisfies the WZIBS property. □

Similar results can be shown for parallel internal contextual hexagonal array P systems with respect to the WXIBS property and the WYIBS property respectively.

Theorem 6. *A language generated by a parallel external contextual hexagonal array P system, satisfies the WZEBS property.*

The proof is similar to Theorem 5, and hence omitted.

Similar results can be shown for parallel external contextual hexagonal array P systems with respect to the WXEBS property and the WYEBS property respectively.

Theorem 7. *If a language $M \subseteq \Sigma^{**H}$ satisfies WXIBS, WYIBS and WZIBS property, then that language M is generated by a parallel internal contextual hexagonal array P system.*

Theorem 8. *If a language $M \subseteq \Sigma^{**H}$ satisfies WXEBS, WYEBS and WZEBS property, then that language M is generated by a parallel external contextual hexagonal array P system.*

The proofs for Theorems 7 and 8 are straight forward.

6 Comparison Results

In this section we give the comparison between the family of hexagonal array languages generated by the internal and external parallel contextual hexagonal array P system with families of local hexagonal array languages and other hexagonal array generating P systems [3]. For notions related to $HLOC$, we can refer to [4].

Theorem 9. *$PICHAP_h$ is incomparable with $HLOC$ but not disjoint.*

Proof. Consider the language L_1 to be a set of hexagonal arrays over $\{a\}$ of sizes $(2l, 2m, 2n), l, m, n \geq 2$ with $l = m = n$. This language is in $PICHAP_h$, as can be seen in example 1. But this language is not in $HLOC$ as can be seen in [4]. Consider the hexagonal local language given in example 4 of [4]. This language of hexagonal pictures of sizes (l, m, n) where $l = m = n$, a member of which

is, does not belong to $PICHAP_h$ because the xy, yx, yz, zy, zx, xz

trapezium arrays and also their respective parallelogram arrays cannot be fixed for performing the parallel internal contextual operations.

Consider the language L_2 to be a set of hexagonal arrays over $\{1, 2, 3\}$ of sizes $(2, 2, k), k \geq 2$. This language is in $PICHAP_2$ and is generated by the P system,

$\prod = (V, T, \mu, XY, YZ, ZX, M_1, M_2, (R_1, \varphi_1), (R_2, \varphi_2), 1)$ where,
$V = \{1, 2, 3\}$
$T = \{1, 2, 3\}$
$\mu = [_1[_2]_2]_1$

$XY = \left\{ \begin{array}{c} \text{(image)} \end{array} \$_{xy}\ , \ \$_{yx}\ \right\}$

$YZ = \emptyset$
$ZX = \emptyset$
$M_1 = \emptyset$

$M_2 = \left\{ \begin{array}{c} \text{(image)} \end{array} \right\}$

$R_1 = \emptyset$

$R_2 = \left\{ \left(\left\{ \varphi_{xy}\left(\begin{array}{c} \text{(image)} \end{array} \right) = \begin{array}{c} \text{(image)} \end{array} \$_{xy}\ , \varphi_{yx}\left(\begin{array}{c} \text{(image)} \end{array} \right) = \begin{array}{c} \text{(image)} \end{array} \$_{yx}\ \right\}, \alpha \right) \right\}, \alpha \in$
$\{here, out\}$

Clearly L_2 is in $HLOC$, as we have $\Delta = \left\{ \text{(images)} \right.$

$\left. \right\}$ and $L(\Delta) = L_2$.

$\square$

Theorem 10. 1. $PECHAP_h - EPHACP_h \neq \emptyset$
2. $PECHAP_h - IPHACP_h \neq \emptyset$

Proof. Consider the language L to be the set of all hexagonal arrays over $\{a, b, c\}$ of sizes (l, m, n) with $l = m = n > 2$, such that every member of L possesses the property that no two neighboring pixel letters are the same. For example, is a member of L. Based on the construction of external

and internal hexagonal array contextual P systems in [3], we can clearly see that the language L is not in $EPHACP_h$ and $IPHACP_h$. But the language can be generated by a parallel external contextual hexagonal array P system, $\prod$ and hence in $PECHAP_h$. The construction of $\prod$ for generating the language L is omitted.

7 Conclusion

In this paper, we have introduced parallel internal and external contextual hexagonal array P systems based on the contextual style of external and internal parallel contextual hexagonal array grammars. We have listed out some basic properties of these hexagonal array generating P systems. It is worth examining further properties of these P system models and also comparing these P systems models with certain other hexagonal array generating systems and finally studying their applications in some related areas.

References

1. Ceterchi, R., Mutyam, M., Păun, G., Subramanian, K.G.: Array - rewriting P systems. Nat. Comput. **2**, 229–249 (2003)
2. Dersanamibika, K.S., Krithivasan, K.: Contextual array P systems. Int. J. Comput. Math. **81**(8), 955–969 (2004)
3. Dersanambika, K.S., Krithivasan, K., Agarwal, H.K., Gupta, J.: Hexagonal contextual array P systems. In: Formal Models, Languages and Applications. Series in Machine Perception and Artificial Intelligence, vol. 66, pp. 79–96 (2006)
4. Dersanambika, K.S., Krithivasan, K., Martin-Vide, C., Subramanian, K.G.: Local and recognizable hexagonal picture languages. Int. J. Patt. Recogn. Artif. Intell. **19**, 853–871 (2005)
5. Ehrenfeucht, A., Păun, G., Rosenberg, G.: Contextual grammars and formal languages. In: Rozenberg, G., Salomaa, A. (eds.) Handbook of Formal Languages, vol. 2, pp. 237–293. Springer-Verlag, Heidelberg (1997)
6. Chandra, P.H., Subramanian, K.G., Thomas, D.G.: Parallel contextual array grammars and languages. Electron. Notes Discret. Math. **12**, 106–117 (2003)
7. Her, I.: Geometric transformations on the hexagonal grid. IEEE Trans. Image Process. **4**, 1213–1222 (2005)
8. Immanuel, S.J., Thomas, D.G., Thamburaj, R., Nagar, A.K.: Parallel contextual array P systems. In: Proceedings of ACMC 2014, Karunya University, Coimbatore
9. Madhu, M., Krithivasan, K.: Contextual P systems. Fund. Info. **49**, 179–189 (2002)
10. Marcus, S.: Contextual grammars. Rev. Roum. Math. Pures et Appl. **14**(10), 1525–1534 (1969)

11. Marcus, S., Martin-Vide, C., Păun, G.: On internal contextual grammarsa with maximal use of selectors. In: The Proceedings of the 8th Conference of Automata and Formal Languages, Salgotarjan (1996)
12. Martin-Vide, C., Mateescu, A., Miquel-Verges, J., Păun, G.: Contextual grammars with maximal, minimal and scattered use of contexts. In: Koppel, M., Shamir, E. (eds.) The Proceedings of the Fourth Bar-Ylan Symposium of Foundations of Al, BISFAI 1995, Jerusalem, pp. 132–142 (1995)
13. Middleton, L., Sivaswamy, J.: Hexagonal Image Processing: A Practical Approach. Springer-Verlag, Heidelberg (2005)
14. Nagy, B.: Shortest path in triangular grids with neighbourhood sequences. J. Comput. Inf. Technol. **11**, 111–122 (2003)
15. Nagy, B.: Generalized triangular grids in digital geometry. Acta Mathematica Academiae Paedagogicae Nyiregyhaziensis **20**, 63–78 (2004)
16. Nagy, B., Strand, R.: A connection between $\mathbb{Z}^n$ and generalized triangular grids. In: Bebis, G., Boyle, R., Parvin, B., Koracin, D., Remagnino, P., Porikli, F., Peters, J., Klosowski, J., Arns, L., Chun, Y.K., Rhyne, T.-M., Monroe, L. (eds.) ISVC 2008. LNCS, vol. 5359, pp. 1157–1166. Springer, Heidelberg (2008). doi:10.1007/978-3-540-89646-3_115
17. Păun, G.: Computing with membranes. J. Comput. Syst. Sci. **61**, 108–143 (2000)
18. Păun, G.: Marcus Contextual Grammars. Kluwer, Dordrecht (1997)
19. Păun, G., Rozenberg, G., Salomaa, A.: The Oxford Handbook of Membrane Computing. Oxford University Press, Oxford (2010)
20. Rosenfeld, A.: Isotonic grammars, parallel grammars and picture grammars. In: Michie, D., Meltzer, D. (eds.) Machine Intelligence, vol. 6, pp. 281–294. University of Edinburgh Press, Scotland (1971)
21. Rosenfeld, A.: Picture Languages: Formal Models for Picture Recognition. Acadamic Press, Cambridge (1979)
22. Siromoney, G., Siromoney, R., Krithivasan, K.: Abstract families of matrices and picture languages. Comput. Graph. Image Process. **1**, 234–307 (1972)
23. Siromoney, G., Siromoney, R., Krithivasan, K.: Picture languages with array rewriting rules. Inf. Control **22**, 447–470 (1973)
24. Siromoney, G., Siromoney, R.: Hexagonal arrays and rectangular blocks. Comput. Graph. Image Process. **5**, 353–381 (1976)
25. Subramanian, K.G., Venkat, I., Wiederhold, P.: A P system model for contextual array languages. In: Barneva, R.P., Brimkov, V.E., Aggarwal, J.K. (eds.) IWCIA 2012. LNCS, vol. 7655, pp. 154–165. Springer, Heidelberg (2012). doi:10.1007/978-3-642-34732-0_12
26. Thomas, D.G., Begam, M.H., David, N.G.: Parallel contextual hexagonal array grammars and languages. In: Wiederhold, P., Barneva, R.P. (eds.) IWCIA 2009. LNCS, vol. 5852, pp. 344–357. Springer, Heidelberg (2009). doi:10.1007/978-3-642-10210-3_27

Superadiabatic STIRAP: Population Transfer and Quantum Rotation Gates

Youssouf Hamidou Issoufa[✉] and Azeddine Messikh

Computer Science Department, International Islamic University Malaysia,
51000 Gombak, Kuala Lumpur, Malaysia
benyous005@yahoo.fr, messikh@iium.edu.my

Abstract. Stimulated Raman Adiabatic Passage is an important process for population transfer as well as for implementing quantum gates. This process requires large Rabi frequencies, which is an undesirable in many experimental applications. To overcome this problem transitionless (superadiabatic) STIRAP was proposed. In this paper we study the role of superadiabatic STIRAP in two examples, population transfer and quantum rotation gates. The effect of dephasing was also investigated by computing the fidelity. We have shown that the damping of the excited state has a little effect but the dephasing of the ground state leads to imperfect population transfer and imperfect rotation gates.

Keywords: Superadiabatic · Stirap · Tripod · Adiabatic theorem

1 Introduction

The adiabatic theorem describes the evolution of a system when the Hamiltonian is slow varying function of time [16]. It states that if a system starts in one of its eigenstates, it will follow adiabatically this initial eigenstate. The process of Stimulated Raman Adiabatic Passage (STIRAP) is based on this theorem. It is a simple and effective process used to transform population in three-level Λ system and to implement robust quantum gates [20]. This process requires large Rabi frequencies, which is an undesirable in many experimental applications. To overcome this problem a transitionless (superadiabatic) STIRAP was proposed [1,8]. It has been shown in [8] that transitionless quantum driving can produce a perfect transfer of the population in three-level Λ and cascade systems. Another alternative approach to transitionlessness was proposed in [6]. It is a technique based on parallel adiabatic passage, which leads to ultrafast population transfer.

It is well known that the interaction of a system with its surroundings leads to decoherence (dissipative effects). This decoherence has a negative impact on the manipulation of quantum systems. Recently, a design of fast and robust population transfer with dephasing and/or systematic frequency errors has been proposed in [15]. Moreover, different transitionless corrections were discussed recently in three-level Λ system [8]. Each correction leads to a different additional pulse which couples between the two lower states.

© Springer Nature Singapore Pte Ltd. 2016
M. Gong et al. (Eds.): BIC-TA 2016, Part I, CCIS 681, pp. 299–313, 2016.
DOI: 10.1007/978-981-10-3611-8_25

In this paper we will study the role of superadiabatic process in two examples, population transfer (in three level system) and quantum rotation gates (tripod system). The paper is organized as follows. In Sect. 2 we describe the equation of motion and reviewing briefly the superadiabatic Hamiltonian. In Sect. 3 we investigate the role of superadiabatic STIRAP in population transfer and the effect of dephasing. In Sect. 4 we explore the quantum rotation gates with Superadiabatic STIRAP and in the last section we give a conclusion.

2   Model and Equation of Motion

Our model in the first example is a three-level Λ system and a tripod in the second example. In both models and in the absence of decoherence (close system) the evolution of the system is governed by the Schrödinger equation

$$i\frac{d}{dt}|\Psi(t)\rangle = (H_0 + H_c)|\Psi(t)\rangle, \tag{1}$$

where H_0 is the Hamiltonian of the system, and H_c is the superadiabatic correction which is defined by [1,4,8]

$$H_c(t) = i\sum_n (|\partial_t n\rangle\langle n| - \langle n|\partial_t n\rangle|n\rangle\langle n|), \tag{2}$$

where the summation is over all the eigenstates of the Hamiltonian H_0. It is well know that close system is an ideal model since it is always interacting with the environment and it is subject to different types of decoherence. So, the Schrödinger equation (1) is replaced by the Lindblad master equation

$$\dot{\rho} = -i[H,\rho] + \frac{1}{2}\sum_i \left(2\,C_i\rho C_i^\dagger - C_i^\dagger C_i\rho - \rho C_i^\dagger C_i\right), \tag{3}$$

where ρ is the atomic density operator, $H = H_0 + H_c$ is the total Hamiltonian operator for the close system, and C_i are the collapse operators associated with the decoherence.

   In the next section we will focus on the role of Superadiabatic process in our first example, population transfer.

3   Example 1: Population Transfer

In our first example we use a three-level Λ system with two lower states $\{|0\rangle, |1\rangle\}$ and an excited state $|e\rangle$. The system is driven by two lasers, a pump beam Ω_p and a Stokes beam Ω_s. The pump beam acts on the transition $|0\rangle \leftrightarrow |e\rangle$, while the Stokes beam acts on $|1\rangle \leftrightarrow |e\rangle$. The dipole transition $|0\rangle \leftrightarrow |1\rangle$ is a forbidden transition. We assume that two-photon resonance condition is fulfilled. In the rotation wave approximation, the Hamiltonian of the system can be expressed in the atomic basis $\{|0\rangle, |1\rangle, |e\rangle\}$ in a matrix form

$$H_0 = \frac{1}{2} \begin{bmatrix} 0 & 0 & \Omega_p \\ 0 & 0 & \Omega_s \\ \Omega_p^* & \Omega_s^* & 2\Delta \end{bmatrix}, \tag{4}$$

where Δ is the common one-photon detuning of the two laser fields (see Fig. 1).

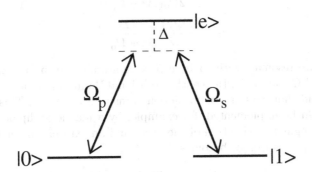

Fig. 1. Three-level Λ system driven by two coherent fields, a pump (Stokes) beam with Rabi frequency $\Omega_{p(s)}$. The two fields have the same detuning Δ.

The instantaneous adiabatic eigenvalues of the Hamiltonian H_0 are given by

$$\lambda_0 = 0, \quad \lambda_\pm = \frac{1}{2}\left[\Delta \pm \sqrt{\Delta^2 + \Omega_0^2}\right], \tag{5}$$

where $\Omega_0 = \sqrt{|\Omega_p|^2 + |\Omega_s|^2}$, and their corresponding eigenstates are given by the following states [13]

$$\begin{aligned}
|\Psi_0\rangle &= \cos\theta\,|0\rangle - e^{i\phi}\sin\theta|1\rangle, \\
|\Psi_+\rangle &= \sin\theta\cos\psi\,|0\rangle + e^{i\phi}\cos\theta\cos\psi\,|1\rangle + \sin\psi\,|e\rangle, \\
|\Psi_-\rangle &= \sin\theta\sin\psi\,|0\rangle + e^{i\phi}\cos\theta\sin\psi\,|1\rangle - \cos\psi\,|e\rangle,
\end{aligned} \tag{6}$$

where ϕ is the relative phase and

$$\tan\theta = \frac{|\Omega_p|}{|\Omega_s|}, \quad \tan\psi = \frac{\Delta + \sqrt{\Delta^2 + \Omega_0^2}}{\Omega_0}.$$

In our model, the states $|n\rangle$ used in Eq. (2) are members in $\{|\Psi_0\rangle, |\Psi_-\rangle, |\Psi_+\rangle\}$ which are given in Eq. (6). For simplicity we assume that the relative phase $\phi = 0$, that is, real Rabi frequencies. So, this additional Hamiltonian H_c can be written in a matrix form [8]

$$H_c = \begin{bmatrix} 0 & i\dot\theta(t) & i\Omega_{0e} \\ -i\dot\theta(t) & 0 & i\Omega_{1e} \\ -i\Omega_{0e} & -i\Omega_{1e} & 0 \end{bmatrix}, \tag{7}$$

where,

$$\dot{\theta} = \frac{\dot{\Omega}_p \Omega_s - \Omega_p \dot{\Omega}_s}{\Omega_0^2}, \tag{8}$$

$$\Omega_{0e} = \frac{\Omega_p(\dot{\Delta}\Omega_0 - \Delta\dot{\Omega}_0)}{2\Omega_0(\Delta^2 + \Omega_0^2)}, \tag{9}$$

$$\Omega_{1e} = \frac{\Omega_s(\dot{\Delta}\Omega_0 - \Delta\dot{\Omega}_0)}{2\Omega_0(\Delta^2 + \Omega_0^2)}. \tag{10}$$

If the fields are resonant with their respective atomic transitions, $\Delta = 0$, both terms Ω_{0e} and Ω_{1e} are zero. Hence, the additional Hamiltonian plays a role of an additional field that acts on the forbidden transition $|0\rangle \leftrightarrow |1\rangle$. This additional interaction can be implemented, for example, by a magnetic dipole interaction between the angular momentum of the atom and an external magnetic field [8]. For Gaussian pulses Eq. (8) becomes

$$\dot{\theta} = \frac{2\tau}{T^2 \cosh\left(4\tau\, t/T^2\right)}. \tag{11}$$

In our numerical results we always consider resonant fields ($\Delta = 0$), i.e., $\Omega_{0e} = \Omega_{1e} = 0$.

In the absence of decoherence, the evolution of the system is governed by Eq. (1). Using Einstein convention $|\Psi(t)\rangle = c_j|\Psi_j(t)\rangle$, we get

$$i\frac{d}{dt}\left[c_j|\Psi_j(t)\rangle\right] = i\left[\dot{c}_j|\Psi(t)\rangle + c_j|\dot{\Psi}_j(t)\rangle\right], \tag{12}$$

$$\text{with } j = 0, +, -.$$

Making use of

$$H_0|\Psi(t)\rangle = c_j\lambda_j|\Psi_j(t)\rangle, \tag{13}$$

$$H_c|\Psi(t)\rangle = ic_j\left[|\dot{\Psi}_j(t)\rangle - \langle\Psi_j(t)|\dot{\Psi}_j(t)\rangle|\Psi_j(t)\rangle\right], \tag{14}$$

and projecting the Schrödinger equation (1) on the eigenstate $|\Psi_k(t)\rangle$, we obtain

$$i\dot{c}_j\langle\Psi_k(t)|\Psi(t)\rangle = c_j\lambda_j\langle\Psi_k(t)|\Psi_j(t)\rangle - \langle\Psi_j(t)|\dot{\Psi}_j(t)\rangle\langle\Psi_k(t)|\Psi_j(t)\rangle, \tag{15}$$

which leads to

$$i\dot{c}_k = c_k\lambda_k. \tag{16}$$

Finally, we obtain three uncoupled differential equations

$$i\frac{d}{dt}\begin{bmatrix} c_0 \\ c_- \\ c_+ \end{bmatrix} = \begin{bmatrix} 0 & 0 & 0 \\ 0 & \lambda_- & 0 \\ 0 & 0 & \lambda_+ \end{bmatrix}\begin{bmatrix} c_0 \\ c_- \\ c_+ \end{bmatrix}. \tag{17}$$

Thus, if the system starts at time t_i in the dark state $|\psi(t_i)\rangle = |\Psi_0\rangle$ it remains in this dark state at later time

$$|\Psi(t)\rangle = |\Psi_0\rangle = \cos\theta(t)\,|0\rangle - \sin\theta(t)|1\rangle. \tag{18}$$

To transfer completely the population to the state $|1\rangle$ at time t_f, it is enough to have $|\sin\theta(t_f)| = 1$. In Fig. 2 we show the population transfer from the state $|0\rangle$ to the state $|1\rangle$.

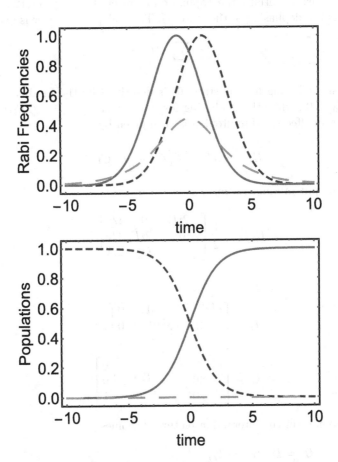

Fig. 2. Superadiabatic STIRAP, The upper figure represents the Rabi frequencies for Gaussian pulses. Ω_s (Solid line), Ω_p (Dashed line) and $\dot\theta$ (Long dashed line). The lower figure represents population transfer. The atom is initially in the state $|0\rangle$. The population of states $|0\rangle$ (dashed line), $|1\rangle$ (solid line) and $|e\rangle$ (long-dashed line). The parameter are $T = 3$, $\tau = 1$, and $\Omega = 1$.

3.1 Effect of Dephasing on Population Transfer

As we mention before, the close system is an ideal model. The Schrödinger equation (1) is replaced by the Lindblad master equation (3). Moreover, the population of the exited state $|e\rangle$ is barely populated during the evolution (see Fig. 2). Thus, the decay rate of this state has a little effect on the evolution of the system. However, dephasing caused by collisions or phase fluctuations of the fields produce important effects. It breaks the superposition of the states (coherence) and decreases exponentially the population transfer efficiency [11,12].

Let Γ_i is the dephasing of the state $|i\rangle$. The collapse operator is given by

$$C = \sum_i C_i^\dagger C_i.$$

The first dephasing for the state $|0\rangle$ is described by the Lindblad operator $C_0 = \sqrt{2\Gamma_0}|0\rangle\langle 0|$, while the dephasing for $|1\rangle$ is given by $C_1 = \sqrt{2\Gamma_1}|1\rangle\langle 1|$. The non Hermitian effective Hamiltonian is then given by

$$H_{eff} = H - \frac{i}{2}C_0^\dagger C_0 - \frac{i}{2}C_1^\dagger C_1, \tag{19}$$

which can be put in a matrix form as

$$H_{eff} = \frac{1}{2}\begin{bmatrix} -2i\Gamma_0 & 0 & \Omega_p \\ 0 & -2i\Gamma_1 & \Omega_s \\ \Omega_p^* & \Omega_s^* & 2\Delta \end{bmatrix}. \tag{20}$$

Using

$$T_l = \begin{bmatrix} e^{\Gamma_0(t-t_i)} & 0 & 0 \\ 0 & e^{\Gamma_1(t-t_i)} & 0 \\ 0 & 0 & 1 \end{bmatrix}, \tag{21}$$

$$T_r = \begin{bmatrix} e^{-\Gamma_0(t-t_i)} & 0 & 0 \\ 0 & e^{-\Gamma_1(t-t_i)} & 0 \\ 0 & 0 & 1 \end{bmatrix}, \tag{22}$$

our Hamiltonian (in the interaction picture) becomes

$$\begin{aligned} H_i &= T_l \cdot H_{eff} \cdot T_r, \\ &= \frac{1}{2}\begin{bmatrix} 0 & 0 & \Omega_p e^{\Gamma_0(t-t_i)} \\ 0 & 0 & \Omega_s e^{\Gamma_1(t-t_i)} \\ \Omega_p^* e^{-\Gamma_0(t-t_i)} & \Omega_s^* e^{-\Gamma_1(t-t_i)} & 2\Delta \end{bmatrix}. \end{aligned}$$

$$\tag{23}$$

Here we follow [5]. Since the effective Hamiltonian H_i is not Hermitian, it has right instantaneous adiabatic eigenstates

$$
\begin{aligned}
|\psi_0\rangle_r &= e^{\Gamma_0(t-t_i)}\cos\theta\,|0\rangle - e^{\Gamma_1(t-t_i)}e^{i\phi}\sin\theta\,|1\rangle, \\
|\psi_+\rangle_r &= e^{\Gamma_0(t-t_i)}\sin\theta\cos\psi\,|0\rangle + e^{\Gamma_1(t-t_i)}e^{i\phi}\cos\theta \\
&\quad \cos\psi\,|1\rangle + \sin\psi\,|e\rangle, \\
|\psi_-\rangle_r &= e^{\Gamma_0(t-t_i)}\sin\theta\sin\psi\,|0\rangle + e^{\Gamma_1(t-t_i)}e^{i\phi}\cos\theta \\
&\quad \sin\psi\,|1\rangle - \cos\psi\,|e\rangle, \tag{24}
\end{aligned}
$$

and left instantaneous adiabatic eigenstates

$$
\begin{aligned}
{}_l\langle\psi_0| &= e^{-\Gamma_0(t-t_i)}\cos\theta\,\langle 0| - e^{-\Gamma_1(t-t_i)}e^{-i\phi}\sin\theta\,\langle 1|, \\
{}_l\langle\psi_+| &= e^{-\Gamma_0(t-t_i)}\sin\theta\cos\psi\,\langle 0| + e^{-\Gamma_1(t-t_i)}e^{-i\phi}\cos\theta \\
&\quad \cos\psi\,\langle 1| + \sin\psi\,\langle e|, \\
{}_l\langle\psi_-| &= e^{-\Gamma_0(t-t_i)}\sin\theta\sin\psi\,\langle 0| + e^{-\Gamma_1(t-t_i)}e^{-i\phi}\cos\theta \\
&\quad \sin\psi\,\langle 1| - \cos\psi\,\langle e|. \tag{25}
\end{aligned}
$$

If we take $e^{\Gamma_1(t-t_i)}$ as a common factor, the right eigenstates can be written as

$$
\begin{aligned}
|\psi_0\rangle_r &= e^{(\Gamma_0-\Gamma_1)(t-t_i)}\cos\theta\,|0\rangle - e^{i\phi}\sin\theta\,|1\rangle, \\
|\psi_+\rangle_r &= e^{(\Gamma_0-\Gamma_1)(t-t_i)}\sin\theta\cos\psi\,|0\rangle + e^{i\phi}\cos\theta\cos\psi\,|1\rangle \\
&\quad +e^{-\Gamma_1(t-t_i)}\sin\psi\,|e\rangle, \\
|\psi_-\rangle_r &= e^{(\Gamma_0-\Gamma_1)(t-t_i)}\sin\theta\sin\psi\,|0\rangle + e^{i\phi}\cos\theta\sin\psi\,|1\rangle \\
&\quad -e^{-\Gamma_1(t-t_i)}\cos\psi\,|e\rangle. \tag{26}
\end{aligned}
$$

In similar way we can do for the left eigenstates. Since the population of the excited state is negligible, the last terms in Eq. (26) which are proportional to $e^{-\Gamma_1(t-t_i)}$ will not have a significant effect on the evolution of the system. So, we can neglect that exponent and keep the exponent which depends on $\Gamma_0 - \Gamma_1$. In this case, the right eigenstates depend only on $\Gamma_0 - \Gamma_1$. So, all the calculations based on two dephasing rates Γ_0 and Γ_1 can be obtained from the dephasing of the state $|0\rangle$ but with the effective rate $\Gamma_0 - \Gamma_1$. Then, without loss of generality we consider only the dephasing of the ground state $|0\rangle$. For small dephasing rates we can unravel the master equation by using quantum trajectory approach [2,3,5,17–19]. This approach was introduced by Carmichael and it is based on the master equation (3). It is composed of two evolutions. The continuous coherent evolution (nonjump evolution) and quantum jump. The nonjump evolution is based on an effective non-Hermitian Hamiltonian operator

$$
\begin{aligned}
i\frac{d|\psi(t)\rangle}{dt} &= H_{\text{eff}}(t)|\psi(t)\rangle, \\
&= [H - i\,\Gamma_0|0\rangle\langle 0|]\,|\psi(t)\rangle. \tag{27}
\end{aligned}
$$

Thus the uncoupled system of differential equations (17) becomes

$$
i\frac{d}{dt}\begin{bmatrix} c_0 \\ c_- \\ c_+ \end{bmatrix} = \begin{bmatrix} 0 & 0 & 0 \\ 0 & \lambda_- & 0 \\ 0 & 0 & \lambda_+ \end{bmatrix}\begin{bmatrix} c_0 \\ c_- \\ c_+ \end{bmatrix} - i\frac{\Gamma_0}{2}
$$
$$
\begin{bmatrix} 2\cos^2\theta & \sin 2\theta\cos\psi & \sin 2\theta\sin\psi \\ \sin 2\theta\cos\psi & 2\cos^2\theta\cos^2\psi & \sin^2\theta\sin 2\psi \\ \sin 2\theta\sin\psi & \sin^2\theta\sin 2\psi & 2\sin^2\theta\sin^2\psi \end{bmatrix}\begin{bmatrix} c_0 \\ c_- \\ c_+ \end{bmatrix}.
$$

(28)

Note that the solution of Eq. (28) should be normalized due to the fact that the effective Hamiltonian is not Hermitian. It is clear that there is coupling between all three instantaneous eigenstates. So if the system starts in the dark state, it will evolve at a later time to a state which is a superposition of all the three adiabatic eigenstates. In addition to the non-jump evolution, the system may randomly jump to the ground state $|0\rangle$ due to the collapse operator C_0. This is the so-called jump evolution. If a jump occurs at time t_j, the states of the system collapses to the state $|0\rangle$ which is given in term of instantaneous eigenstates by

$$
|0\rangle = \cos\theta(t_j)|\Psi_0(t_j)\rangle + \sin\psi(t_j)\sin\theta(t_j)|\Psi_-(t_j)\rangle
$$
$$
+ \cos\psi(t_j)\sin\theta(t_j)|\Psi_+(t_j)\rangle.
$$

(29)

According to the quantum trajectory theory, the average over all trajectories gives the same result as the master equation (3). If the dephasing rate is small, the probability for a system to have more than one jump is negligible. So, the non-jump evolution given by Eq. (28) is a good approximation to the master equation and gives a clear picture on the evolution of the system in terms of the adiabatic eigenstates.

In quantum computation what one is concerned with is how to reach the high fidelity target $F > 0.999$. Now we are ready to investigate the robustness to the dephasing of the ground state by computing the fidelity and compare it with the quantum computation target.

The fidelity is given by the probability to transfer the population at time t_f to the final state $|1\rangle$. It is given by $F = |\langle 1|\Psi(t_f)\rangle|^2$. It has been shown [8] that the condition to have high fidelity is verified for superadiabatic STIRAP even when the decay rate Γ of the exited state is much larger than the pulse width.

In Fig. 3, we plot the maximum fidelity as a function of dephasing in the presence of damping rate. The condition for obtaining high fidelity is $\Gamma_0 < 0.002$. Within this region the maximum fidelity does not depend on Γ, which indicates that the dephasing is more important factor than the damping rate [9]. This is why we did not consider the damping of the excited state in our Eq. (28).

Our calculations were based on Gaussian pulses. Furthermore, it is straightforward to generate them to different schemes of driving lasers. For more information on other pulses one can refer to [7,14].

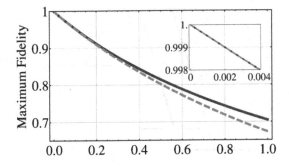

Fig. 3. Maximum fidelity as function of dephasing rate Γ_0 for $\tau = 0.5$. The damping rate of the excited state is $\Gamma = 0$ for solid line and $\Gamma = 10$ for dashed line. (Color figure online)

4   Example 2: Quantum Rotation Gates

The process of stimulated Raman adiabatic passage is one of the important techniques used to implement quantum gates. Lacour *et al.* [13] proposed an elegant experiment technique to implement generalized single-qubit rotation gates in three-level Λ system

$$R(a, \phi) = \begin{bmatrix} \cos a & e^{i\phi} \sin a \\ -e^{-i\phi} \sin a & \cos a \end{bmatrix}, \tag{30}$$

where a is the angle of rotation and ϕ is the phase of the gate. Their technique uses two STIRAPs. The first STIRAP is a reversed STIRAP, while the second STIRAP is a standard STIRAP. Each STIRAP has two pulses separated in time. For large detuning, the excited state $|e\rangle$ can be adiabatically eliminated. If the two f-STIRAP have the same pulse shapes with the same delay, the dynamical phases acquired by the bright states at the end of the two f-STIRAP are the same. Thus, a compensation of the dynamic phase is achieved. Therefore, a generalized rotation gate is obtained up to a global dynamical phase.

In what follows we use their idea and apply it to a tripod system rather than a three-level Λ system. The tripod consists of four-level systems driven by three resonant laser fields with Rabi frequencies Ω_0, Ω_1, Ω_2. These laser fields couple the three lower levels $|0\rangle$, $|1\rangle$, and $|2\rangle$ to the upper level $|e\rangle$ as depicted in Fig. 4. The laser fields are modulated by Gaussian pulses with width δ, amplitudes A_j, phase ϕ_j, and time delay t_j

$$\Omega_j(t - t_j) = A_j e^{i\phi_j} e^{-\dfrac{(t - t_j)^2}{\delta^2}}. \tag{31}$$

All parameters are scaled with respect to the width of the Gaussian pulses.

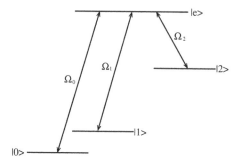

Fig. 4. Energy level for a four-level tripod. The three ground levels $|0\rangle$, $|1\rangle$ and $|2\rangle$ are coupled to the excited level $|e\rangle$ by three different lasers. The two ground states $|0\rangle$ and $|1\rangle$ are the states of the desired qubit.

We choose the two Rabi frequencies Ω_0 and Ω_1 as follows.

$$\Omega_0 = \Omega(t + T - \tau) + \Omega(t + T + \tau)\cos a,$$
$$\Omega_1 = \Omega(t + T + \tau)\sin a.$$

$$(32)$$

These fields represent two STIRAP processes separated by T in time, and each STIRAP has two pulses separated by τ in time. The first STIRAP is a reversed STIRAP starting with a constant ratio $\Omega_0/\Omega_1 \rightarrow \cot a$, while The second STIRAP process is a standard STIRAP where the pulses are switched on counter-intuitively and switched off in a given constant ratio $\Omega_0/\Omega_1 \rightarrow \tan a$. In addition to these STIRAP processes another STIRAP which consists of two pulses separated in time such that it starts before the two STIRAPs and ends after them (see Fig. 5).

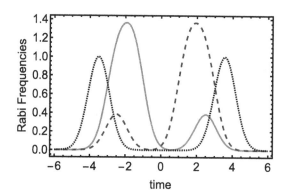

Fig. 5. The Rabi frequencies Ω_0 (solid line), Ω_1 (dashed line), and Ω_2 (dotted line), as a function of time. The parameters are: $A_0 = A_1 = A_2 = 1$, $\tau = 0.5$, $T = 2$, $a = \pi/8$. The time delay of the first(second) pulse of Ω_2 is $-3.5(3.57)$.

The Hamiltonian H_0 of the tripod is then given by

$$H_0 = \frac{1}{2} \begin{bmatrix} 0 & 0 & \Omega_0 & 0 \\ 0 & 0 & -\Omega_1 & 0 \\ \Omega_0 & -\Omega_1 & 0 & \Omega_2 e^{-i\phi_2} \\ 0 & 0 & \Omega_2 e^{i\phi_2} & 0 \end{bmatrix}, \tag{33}$$

where all the Rabi frequencies Ω_i are considered to be real numbers. This Hamiltonian was considered in [5]. It has four eigenvalues. They are called the instantaneous adiabatic eigenvalues [5]

$$\lambda_\pm = \pm \frac{1}{2} \sqrt{\Omega_0^2 + \Omega_1^2 + \Omega_2^2}, \qquad \lambda_i = 0 \ (i = 1, 2). \tag{34}$$

The eigenstate corresponds to zero energy is a degenerate state. It is composed of two dark states which can be written in the form

$$|D_1\rangle = -\cos\theta_1 \sin\theta_0 |0\rangle + \cos\theta_1 \cos\theta_0 |1\rangle$$
$$+ \sin\theta_1 e^{i\phi_2} |2\rangle,$$
$$|D_2\rangle = \cos\theta_0 |0\rangle + \sin\theta_0 |1\rangle, \tag{35}$$

where

$$\tan\theta_0 = \frac{\Omega_0}{\Omega_1}, \qquad \tan\theta_1 = \frac{\sqrt{\Omega_0^2 + \Omega_1^2}}{\Omega_2}. \tag{36}$$

The two other states are bright states which correspond to the non zero eigenvalues $\lambda_\pm$

$$|\pm\rangle = \frac{1}{\sqrt{2}} [-\sin\theta_1 \sin\theta_0 |0\rangle - \sin\theta_1 \cos\theta_0 |1\rangle$$
$$\pm |e\rangle + \cos\theta_1 e^{i\phi_2} |2\rangle]. \tag{37}$$

According the adiabatic theorem, if the tripod system starts in the superposition of the two dark states it remains in that superposition at later time.

To measure the performance of the rotation gate we use the fidelity which is given by

$$F = |\langle \psi(t_f)|R(a, \phi)|\psi(t_i)\rangle|, \tag{38}$$

where $|\psi(t_i)\rangle$ represents the initial state at time t_i and $|\psi(t_f)\rangle$ is the final state at time t_f. For numerical computations we focus on the generation of the rotation gate $R(\pi/4, 0)$ and we set $\phi_2 = 0$.

In Fig. 6 we plot the maximum, minimum and average fidelity as a function of the common amplitude A of the Gaussian pulses for the rotation gate with angle $a = \pi/4$ and phase $\phi = 0$. The fidelity are computed numerically for 1000 initial random states uniformly distributed on the Bloch Sphere

$$|\psi(t_i)\rangle = \cos(\pi u)|0\rangle + \sin(\pi u) e^{i\arccos(2v-1)}|1\rangle,$$

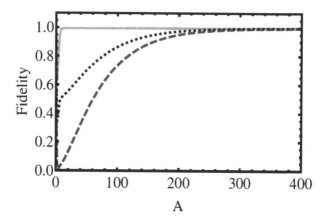

Fig. 6. Fidelity for rotation gate $R(\pi/4, 0)$. The Maximum (solid line), the average (dotted line) and the minimum (dashed line) fidelity as a function of A. The fidelity for the STIRAP process approaches 1 only for high Rabi frequencies. (Color figure online)

where u and v are two random numbers uniformly distributed on $[0, 1]$. It is clear that the fidelity is close to 1 only for large values of A. Large Rabi frequencies is a disadvantage in many experimental applications. Now, we study the role of superadiabatic process in implementing quantum rotation gates $R(\pi/4, 0)$.

The additional Hamiltonian can be written in a matrix form as

$$H_c = \begin{bmatrix} 0 & h_{0,1} & 0 & h_{0,2} \\ h_{0,1}^* & 0 & 0 & h_{1,2} \\ 0 & 0 & 0 & 0 \\ h_{0,2}^* & h_{1,2}^* & 0 & 0 \end{bmatrix}. \tag{39}$$

where

$$h_{0,1} = i\frac{\Omega_0 \dot{\Omega}_1 - \Omega_1 \dot{\Omega}_0}{\Omega_0^2 + \Omega_1^2},$$

$$h_{0,2} = i\Omega_0 \frac{(\Omega_0 \dot{\Omega}_0 + \Omega_1 \dot{\Omega}_1)\Omega_2 - (\Omega_0^2 + \Omega_1^2)\dot{\Omega}_2}{(\Omega_0^2 + \Omega_1^2)(\Omega_0^2 + \Omega_1^2 + \Omega_2^2)},$$

$$h_{1,2} = i\Omega_1 \frac{(\Omega_0 \dot{\Omega}_0 + \Omega_1 \dot{\Omega}_1)\Omega_2 - (\Omega_0^2 + \Omega_1^2)\dot{\Omega}_2}{(\Omega_0^2 + \Omega_1^2)(\Omega_0^2 + \Omega_1^2 + \Omega_2^2)}.$$

With our Gaussian pulses the term $h_{0,1} = 0$. That is, the Hamiltonian H_c is equivalent to additional driving fields which couple the two lower levels $|0\rangle$ and $|1\rangle$ to the level $|2\rangle$.

In Fig. 7 we plot the fidelity as function of the amplitude A. It shows that superadiabatic STIRAP leads to a perfect rotation gates for all Rabi frequencies. This is an important improvement over STIRAP which needs high Rabi frequencies.

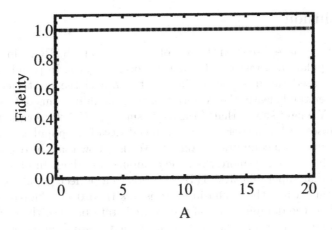

Fig. 7. Fidelity for rotation gate $R(\pi/4, 0)$ as a function of A. The fidelity is 1 for all Rabi frequencies.

4.1   Effect of Dephasing

It is interesting to check the robustness in the presence of dephasing caused by collisions or phase fluctuations of the fields [10]. Here we restrict ourselves to the dephasing of the ground state $|0\rangle$ which can be described by the Lindblad operators $C_0 = \sqrt{2\Gamma_0}|0\rangle\langle 0|$, where Γ_0 is the dephasing rate. Figure 8 shows the fidelity as a function of the dephasing rate Γ_0 for $A = 1$. One can see that the fidelity decrease linearly and the rotation gate becomes imperfect. So, the dephasing caused by collisions or phase fluctuations of the fields produces significant effect on the performance of the rotation gate.

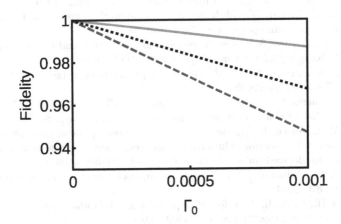

Fig. 8. Fidelity for rotation gate. The maximum, the average and the minimum fidelity as a function of Γ_0 for $A = 1$.

5   Conclusion

In this paper we have discussed the role of superadiabatic STIRAP in two examples, The population transfer and quantum rotation gates. In population transfer, we have used the quantum trajectory to unravel the master equation in order to understand clearly the evolution of the system in terms of the adiabatic eigenstates. We have shown that if the dephasing rate Γ_0 is larger than 0.002 for Gaussian pulses with time delay $\tau = 0.5$, the fidelity of the population transfer is far from the quantum computation target. We also show that the dephasing rate reduces the fidelity much more than the damping rate does. In other hand, we have shown that superadiabatic STIRAP leads to a perfect population transfer and it is robust when the dephasing rate is less than 0.002. Moreover, it does not depend on the damping rate of the excited state because the excited state is barely populated during the evolution. We have also focused on the quantum rotation gate with angle $a = \pi/4$ and phase $\phi = 0$. We have shown that the STIRAP requires high Rabi frequencies to implement the rotation gates. To overcome this disadvantage we use superadiabatic approach that leads to a perfect gate for small Rabi frequencies. Moreover, we have explored the effect of dephasing on the performance of the gate. The dephasing which cause by collisions or phase fluctuations of the field can leads to imperfect gate. Therefore, to get a perfect gate one must keep the dephasing as small as possible.

References

1. Berry, M.V.: Transitionless quantum driving. J. Phys. A: Math. Theor. **42**(36), 365303 (2009)
2. Carmichael, H.: Statistical Methods in Quantum Optics 2: Non Classical Fields, Theoretical and Mathematical Physics. Springer, New York (2009)
3. Dalibard, J., Castin, Y., Mølmer, K.: Wave-function approach to dissipative processes in quantum optics. Am. Phys. Soc. 68 (1992)
4. Demirplak, M., Rice, S.A.: On the consistency, extremal, and global properties of counterdiabatic fields. J. Chem. Phys. **129**, 154111 (2008)
5. Ditte, M., Lars, B.M., Klaus, M.: Geometric phases in open tripod systems. Phys. Rev. A **77**(6), 022306 (2008)
6. Dridi, G., Guérin, S., Hakobyan, V., Jauslin, H.R., Eleuch, H.: Ultrafast stimulated raman parallel adiabatic passage by shaped pulses. Am. Phys. Soc. 80 (2009)
7. Fewell, M.P., Shore, B.W., Bergmann, K.: Coherent population transfer among three states: full algebraic solutions and the relevance of non adiabatic processes to transfer by delayed pulses. Aust. J. Phys. **50**, 281–308 (1997)
8. Giannelli, L., Arimondo, E.: Three-level superadiabatic quantum driving. Am. Phys. Soc. **89** (2014)
9. Issoufa, Y.H., Messikh, A.: Effect of dephasing on superadiabatic three-level quantum driving. Phys. Rev. A **90**(5), 055402 (2014)
10. Issoufa, Y.H., Messikh, A.: Generation of single qubit rotation gates using superadiabatic approach. Quant. Inf. Rev. **3**(1), 17 (2015)
11. Ivanov, P.A., Vitanov, N.V., Bergmann, K.: Effect of dephasing on stimulated Raman adiabatic passage. Phys. Rev. A **70**(6), 063409 (2004)

12. Lacour, X., Guérin, S., Jauslin, H.R.: Optimized adiabatic passage with dephasing. Am. Phys. Soc. **78** (2008)
13. Lacour, X., Guerin, S., Vitanov, N., Yatsenko, L.: Implementation of single qubit quantum gates by adiabatic passage and static laser phases. Opt. commun. **5**(6) (2006)
14. Laine, T.A., Stenholm, S.: Adiabatic processes in three-level systems. Phys. Rev. A **53**, 2501–2512 (1996)
15. Lu, X.J., Chen, X., Ruschhaupt, A., Alonso, D., Guerin, S., Muga, J.G.: Fast and robust population transfer in two-level quantum systems with dephasing noise and/or systematic frequency errors. Am. Phys. Soc. **88** (2013)
16. Messiah, A.: Quantum Mechanics. North-Holland Publishing Company, Amsterdam (1962)
17. Molmer, K., Castin, Y.: Monte carlo wavefunctions in quantum optics. Quantum Semiclassical Opt.: J. Eur. Opt. Soc. Part B **8**(1), 49 (1996). http://stacks.iop.org/1355-5111/8/i=1/a=007
18. Mølmer, K., Castin, Y., Dalibard, J.: Monte carlo wave-function method in quantum optics. J. Opt. Soc. Am. B **10**, 524–538 (1993)
19. Plenio, M.B., Knight, P.L.: The quantum-jump approach to dissipative dynamics in quantum optics. Am. Phy. Soc. **70** (1998)
20. Xavier, L.: Information Quantique Par Passage Adiabatique: Portes Quantiques et Decoherence. Ph.D thesis (2007)

Image Segmentation Using Membrane Computing: A Literature Survey

Rafaa I. Yahya[1,2,3], Siti Mariyam Shamsuddin[1,3], Salah I. Yahya[3,4(✉)],
Shafatnnur Hasan[1,3], Bisan Al-Salibi[3,5], and Ghada Al-Khafaji[3,6]

[1] Faculty of Computing, Universiti Teknologi Malaysia,
81310 UTM Skudai, Johor, Malaysia
{iyrafaa2,mariyam,shafaatunnur}@utm.my
[2] Department of Computer, College of Science,
University of Al-Mustansiriyah, Baghdad, Iraq
[3] UTM Big Data Center, Ibnu Sina Institute for Scientific and Industrial Research,
Universiti Teknologi Malaysia, 81310 UTM Skudai, Johor, Malaysia
salah.ismaeel@koyauniversity.org, besansalipi@gmail.com,
hgkta2012@yahoo.com
[4] Department of Software Engineering, Koya University, Kurdistan Region, Iraq
[5] School of Computer Sciences, Universiti Sains Malaysia, USM,
11800 Gelugor, Penang, Malaysia
[6] Department of Computer Science, College of Science,
Baghdad University, Baghdad, Iraq

Abstract. Membrane computing, a recent branch of natural computing, has been gaining momentum attention in the last few decades due
to its massive parallelism and efficient computation. Many researchers in
the field of membrane computing have proposed sophisticated techniques
inspired by cell biology for computer science applications, especially when
they considered cell organization in tissues, organs, and most recently,
from the organization of neurons. The interdisciplinary applications of
membrane computing include, but not limited to computer science, biology, biomedicine, bioinformatics and several other fields such as mathematics, artificial intelligence, automation, economics, to name but a few.
Their applications are pertaining to computer graphics, approximate
optimization, cryptography, parallel computing and image processing.
Hence, in this paper we present an up to date comprehensive literature
review pertaining to the application of membrane computing in the area
of digital image analysis, especially image segmentation, comprehensively
and systematically. We thoroughly investigate the recent advancement
in the field of image segmentation using membrane system. Furthermore,
we highlight the merits and demerits of various software tools and methods. Finally, we suggest some intuitive future directions in light of the
current limitations.

Keywords: Membrane computing · Image segmentation · Tissue-like P
system · P-Lingua

© Springer Nature Singapore Pte Ltd. 2016
M. Gong et al. (Eds.): BIC-TA 2016, Part I, CCIS 681, pp. 314–335, 2016.
DOI: 10.1007/978-981-10-3611-8_26

1   Introduction

As a young branch of natural computing, membrane computing (MC) began in 1998 with its latest version that is related to the initial research studies published in 2000 by Păun [1]. The primary models for MC began with a single cell and its hierarchical structure of organized compartments called membranes, where localized biochemistry took place. The resulting computing device comprised a distributed parallel computing model with multi-sets of objects or chemicals that placed in regions (tree-like nodes) processed as reactions similar to those of natural biochemistry. Motivated by biological membranes, we obtain a computing device called a P system in honor of their initiator, Păun [1]. Coverage of the domain can be found in [2].

The conventional P system model was variously extended and enhanced, as per biological suggestion, to involve, for instance, the processing of objects by means of operations patterned after bio-symport/antiport functions, or as computational motivations extended from single cells to cell populations, or from tree-like membrane arrangements to arbitrary graph techniques as well as other biological processes such as neuro-pathways, etc.

The computing devices are verified to be quite powerful, equivalent with Turing machines even when using feature groups offering certain restrictions, and also computationally efficient (in certain cases, able to solve computationally hard problems, typically, nondeterministic polynomial time (NP)-complete problems, in a feasible/polynomial time) [3].

Interestingly, MC has been exploited in many real world applications including digital imaging analysis. To the best of our knowledge, this paper represents the first survey pertaining to the recent advancement of digital image analysis using MC.

In this paper, the recent literature works pertaining to image processing techniques using MC models are presented. In this regard, the presented works were classified into two main categories, membrane rules (which use the typical rules of P systems models) and membrane algorithms (which take inspiration from P system models without using their rules explicitly) as will be discussed in the following sections.

The remaining of the paper is organized as follows. In Sect. 2, an overview of MC is outlined. In Sect. 3, the various applications of MC are briefly explained. In Sect. 4, the different types of MC systems are explained. In Sect. 5, a presentation of MC in image processing is given. In Sect. 6, a comprehensive review of MC pertaining to image segmentation is presented. Section 7 concludes the paper and suggests some future directions.

2   Membrane Computing Overview

MC has emerged as a recent branch of molecular computing as shown in the taxonomy chart in Fig. 1. MC is mainly based on the assumption that the flow of metabolites within the compartmental architecture and functioning of biological cells can be interpreted as a flow of information for computations [4].

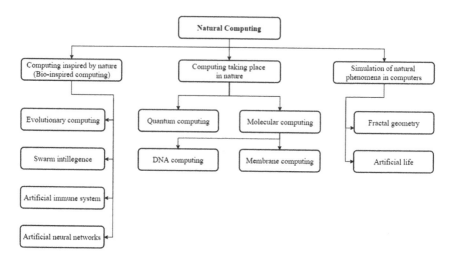

Fig. 1. Taxonomy of natural computing branches [5].

The main components of P system are inspired by the structure and functions of the biological cell that makes the P system computation devise consisting of; membrane structure, set of evolution rules and multisets of objects.

The design of MC is presented in a hierarchically structured manner similar to the structure of the cell. It is divided into many compartments (according to the cell) and the external membranes look like plasma membrane in the cell containing several sub-membranes called skin. Each membrane surrounding the compartment is called a region (see Fig. 2).

Membranes, which do not have a sub-membrane inside it, are called elementary membranes. Usually, every membrane has a label starting from number 1 and the skin membrane, labeled by 0 [6]. The structure of the membrane can be represented like a tree inspired from the vesicles where the root of the tree is the skin membrane and the leaves are the elementary membrane. This tree structure is represented by parentheses to explain the structure of membrane as shown in Fig. 2. The motorists are the set of objects placed in the region, according to the chemical objects in the cell compartment. These objects are described by the symbolic alphabet [6–8].

3   Membrane Computing Applications

Several features of MC are of great interest as they suit many real world applications. These include [6]:

– Distribution (with significant systempart interactions as well as emergent behaviors and non-linearity resulting from local behavioral composites).
– Discrete mathematics (continuous mathematics failed to prove adequate for linguistics, and cannot cover more than local processes in biology because of

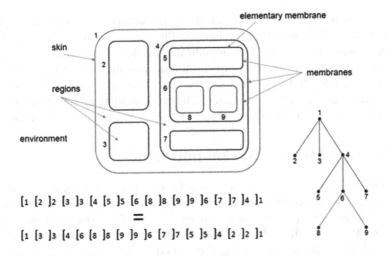

$$[_1 \ [_2 \ ]_2 \ [_3 \ ]_3 \ [_4 \ [_5 \ ]_5 \ [_6 \ [_8 \ ]_8 \ [_9 \ ]_9 \ ]_6 \ [_7 \ ]_7 \ ]_4 \ ]_1$$
$$=$$
$$[_1 \ [_3 \ ]_3 \ [_4 \ [_6 \ [_8 \ ]_8 \ [_9 \ ]_9 \ ]_6 \ [_7 \ ]_7 \ [_5 \ ]_5 \ ]_4 \ [_2 \ ]_2 \ ]_1$$

Fig. 2. Membrane structure and its associated tree [6]

the complexity of the processes and, in many cases, because of the imprecise character of the processes; The discrete nature of the biological reality is ruling out the usefulness of many tools from continuous mathematics).
– Algorithmicity (hence, easy programmability),
– Scalability and extensibility (major challenges when using differential equations in biological applications).
– Transparency (multi-set rewriting rules are little more than equations that mimic chemical reactions),
– Parallelism (a computer science dream, but commonly observed in biology).
– Nondeterminism (let us compare the program of a P system with the programs written in typical programming languages).
– Communication (marvelous way, and yet not perfectly understood, the life phenomenon that coordinates numerous processes within a cell. This stands in stark contrast to the costly way of coordinating computations in parallel electronic computing architectures, where the communication time becomes unaffordable with the increase in the number of processors).

Most P systems have proven to be both universal [1,9–11] and efficient [12–14]. Number of researches has been done on P systems with active membranes where almost researchers reduced time complexity from exponential to polynomial or linear time in an exponential workspace, by the so-called trading space by time. This improvement in time complexity involved P systems with 'division rules' showing that the NP-complete problem of Satisfiability (SAT) could be resolved in case of linear time [12].

Along similar lines, P systems have also solved other problems (mostly NP-complete) of linear or polynomial time complexity. These included, as instance, the SAT problem [15–17]; the Graph problem [18]; the subset sum problem [19]; the Three Coloring problem (3-COL) [20] and the Vertex Cover problem [21].

All researchers in this domain of study considered time units as steps of computation in a P system that implemented in parallel, using evolution rules, in all membranes of the system or its membrane divisions [22]. It has been claimed that executing the P system in a sequential hardware did not get suitable results unless it is implemented in parallel architecture. Therefore, the recent researches are performed on the implementation of MC on parallel architecture devices [23–27]. In all such studies, the speed of execution was impressively increased.

4   Types of Membrane Computing

Interestingly, researchers in the area of MC have been inspired by cell biology to design several applications in the area of computer science. As of the present writing, and according to membrane structure as so far introduced and investigated, the P systems have been classified into three main categories [28]. The first is called cell-like P system [1], the second is the tissue-like P system [29] and the third is the spiking neural-like P system [30].

In the first category, the P system emulates the (eukaryotic) cell. The main component of this type is the structure of membranes in a hierarchical arrangement which is viewed as three dimensional vesicles, i.e., when the multisets of objects are combined with other objects and the membranes are destructive by division and modeled on bio-like processes such as exocytosis, endocytosis, phagocytosis and others [1].

In the second category, tissue-like P systems, the membrane consists of several cells which can evolve in the same environment and include object multisets within an environment that also contains objects. The certain cell can be related directly by supplying channels between them and also these cells can communicate with the environment. These channels may be established in the beginning or may be established dynamically evolved with the latest case utilized in known as population P systems. Where in the case of simple cells and when the number of contained objects and the used rules are limited, then the idea of P colony is declared [29].

The third category of P systems is the neural-like P systems (see [30]). Variant types of neural-like P systems were newly presented, called spiking neural P systems, where this type uses just a single set of objects called the 'spike' in which the utilized basic data is the distance between successive spikes [31].

5   Membrane Computing in Image Processing

MC is a methodology that uses a number of rules inspired by the behavior and functioning of the biological cell to find the solution of popular problems related to graphics, approximate optimization, cryptography, to name but a few. MC has distinguishing characteristics such as the encapsulation of data and the simple representation of information as well as parallelism, all of which are most appropriate when dealing with digital images. Due to the fact that features in the segmentation of digital images that are parallel and/or local can be solved regardless of the actual image size, its implementation becomes more practical in parallel as they are independent. Furthermore, data can also be easily encoded according to efficient bio-inspired representations.

Hence, in light of the above, the aforementioned features make digital imaging more flexible and amenable for the implementation of techniques inspired by nature. In the last few decades, many studies in digital images have been developed in large scope. In the literature, one can find several attempts for solving problems from digital imagery with natural computing as presented in the work of Ceterchi, et al. [32] or the work of Chao and Nakayama [33] where natural computing and algebraic topology are linked together by the aid of Neural Networks [34]. The main goal of dealing the image in a digital form is to enhance the quality or to obtain artistic effect. MC is used in image processing operations in order to speed up and enhance the image operations such as smoothing which is often used in digital image processing to improve image quality by reducing the noise levels. For instance, a MC algorithm used to remove the noise was presented in [35] to smooth the 2D images with a framework of tissue-like P systems implemented by the novel architecture of Compute Unified Device Architecture (CUDA), obtaining homology groups of 2D images [36–38], counting cell [39], quantum-inspired sub-algorithms and its application to image processing [40] presents a membrane algorithm, called MAQIS, by appropriately combining concepts and principles of MC and quantum-inspired evolutionary method, skeletonizing images [41,42], thinning images based on MC [43], Corner Detection was presented in [44] in order to detect corners in digital images using MC framework and image segmentation. The related work pertaining to the use of MC on image segmentation operations will be illustrated in detail in the following sections.

6 Membrane Computing Pertaining to Image Segmentation

Image segmentation is an important field of digital image processing that is relevant to the area of computer vision. Several segmentation methods have been proposed based on the two main attributes of pixels in relative with local neighborhoods: the discontinuity and similarity methods. The former method was known as boundary-based methods that depend on pixel discontinuity, and the later method is called region-based which are based on similarity between pixel regions. However, it is claimed that these kind of segmentation methods that are based only on boundary or regional data, are usually tend to fail in achieving satisfactory results in a retail minute. Thus, the attention of the researchers moved in recent years towards that use of new techniques based on the complementary nature of such data [45]. The essential goal of image segmentation procedure is to divide the input image into multiple regions that are visually similar with respect to any property related to image such as gray level, image texture or associated color.

Segmentation process possesses several distinguishing features that enabled the digital image to be easy and suitable for implementation in any technique inspired by nature. Most importantly, it can be parallelized and locally resolved without affecting the size of the image, and it can be implemented in multifarious local areas. Furthermore, essential characteristic can easily encode the main information by bio-inspired representation [46]. According to these features, MC is used in image segmentation by an extensive number of researches as will be shown in the related work. Figure 3 presents a taxonomy of MC techniques based on published papers pertaining to MC-based image segmentation.

A comprehensive literature review pertaining to image segmentation using MC models has been presented with the aid of the taxonomy chart as shown in Fig. 3. According to the mechanism of how membrane systems employed, these methods have been classified into membrane rules-based methods and membrane algorithms-based methods. Those methods are further classified according to the sequential/parallel execution.

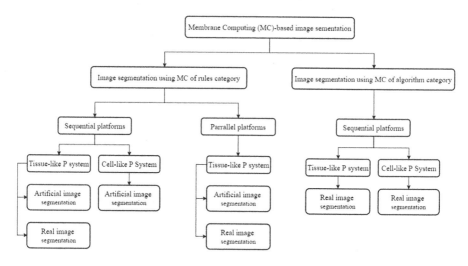

Fig. 3. Taxonomy of MC based on published papers related to MC-based segmentation

6.1   Rules-Based Membrane Computing for Image Segmentation

MC models depend on a set of rules which are inspired by the function and behavior of cell biology to solve many real world problems by employing important features of P systems concerning the way rules are used in a maximally parallel and non-deterministic manner [47]. In this section, related works pertaining to image segmentation using membrane rules are presented. The first part of this section presents the related works that have been done on sequential computing platforms, whereas, the second part presents the related works that have been done on parallel computing platforms.

Membrane Computing Based on Sequential Computing Platforms.
The execution of P systems on sequential computing platforms is not feasible
due to their built-in parallelism which will not be fully exploited in such a case.
However, application software which simulates implementation sequentially is
widely available [48].

*Tissue-like P System on Sequential Computing Platforms for Artificial Image
Segmentation.* In the work of [49], P systems have been linked to computational
topology with digital images where this development paved way for a new and
promising line of research. Christinal et al. [49] designed a collection of tissue-
like P systems that used the communication rules of MC to perform edge-based
segmentation. This communication entails the discovery of adequate different
region boundaries among the input images. The experiment was conducted such
that the artificial 2D and 3D images, using 4-adjacency and 26-adjacency, respectively, have been employed. Experiments show that results were obtained in a
fixed number of 9 and 26 steps pertaining to 2D and 3D images, respectively. It
is worth mentioning that the tissue simulator tool has been used in their work
for validation. The main shortcoming of such simulation is that the sequential
software used in edge-based segmentation could not utilize the full potential
parallelism of the model. Furthermore, this simulation restricted the use of the
input image to be manually codified, pixel by pixel, in the tissue simulator and
they did not comment on the time of segmentation in their experiments.

Christinal et al. [49] proposed that this strategy is not feasible when dealing
with large real images and only 4-adjacency relationship were considered when
using 2D images. It is worth mentioning that, in their work, no evaluation procedure has been considered to validate the quality of segmentation which prevented
a comparison with this work. Christinal et al. [50] calculated some algebraic-
topological information for two-dimensional (2D) and three-dimensional (3D)
images in a general and parallel manner with P systems. First, they presented
another method to achieve homologous groups of 2D digital images in logarithmic time with respect to input data. In addition, this work paved the way for
another area of study in which efficiency and power were used in topological
processes for the first time. They have considered 4-adjacency relationships for
2D, whereas a 6-adjacency has been used for 3D digital images. The obtained
results demonstrated edge-based segmentation, but they did not comment on
the time of segmentation in their experiments. However, the main limitation of
this work is the lack of automation where the input image has to be entered
manually to the system to manually visualize the output.

Along similar lines, Reina-Molina et al. [51] developed the work of Carnero
et al. [52] by proposing a new version of tissue-like P system to replace the concept of one cell with the concept of multiple auxiliary cells to deal with irrelevant
feature removal and homogenize colors with a general thresholding for color space
and segmentation problems. These processes are essentially applicable to use all
the available parallelization inherent in P systems models. Although the proposed method of Reina-Molina et al. [51] exploited the full parallelism of MC,
the input image has been manually codified in the system. Furthermore, Molina

et al. have not considered the same standard criteria to validate the accuracy of their segmentation method that makes a comparison with their work infeasible.

Moving on, in the work of Christinal et al. [53], a tissue-like P system was proposed with the use of MC rules for the design of a region-based segmentation algorithm in a constant number of steps. In their work [53], 4-adjacency relationships between neighboring pixels were adopted for 2D digital images. They proved that only 9 steps were sufficient to get a region-based segmentation for a 2D image. In addition, 26-adjacency relationships between voxel neighborhoods were implemented for 3D digital images. They also proved that 26 steps are required to get a region-based segmentation for a 3D image. Meanwhile, the main weakness of their method is the fact that the image has been manually codified in the tissue simulator as in their previous work. This leads to a lack of efficiency in favor of expressiveness. Hence, experiments performed using this software were very slow and at most could only use synthetic images of 30 x 30 pixels.

Recently, tissue-like P systems have been proposed for the parallel color segmentation of simple artificial images [54]. The images were segmented such that thresholding is employed to search for edge pixels. The tissue-like model for P systems uses fewer computation elements compared to conventional models, which is why it is the model of choice in this work. The work of Christinal et al. [54] depicts that, in theory, if a general color alphabet is taken into consideration, it is feasible to perform the parallel segmentation of an image. As such, if pixels do not have different colors than their neighboring pixels, then their edges are not selected. Therefore, a pixel is an edge if it is different from a neighboring pixel.

Most recently, Isawasan et al. [55] proposed the tissue-like model of P system to handle region-based segmentation based on the work in [53] of two-dimensional (2D) hexagonal artificial images using 6-adjaceny. The segmentation was executed using the official language of MC called P-Lingua. However, they used the language without illustrating the details that backup this usage, and did not consider the time of segmentation. Furthermore, no evaluation procedure has been performed to validate the segmentation results.

In the work of Yahya et al. [8], a region-based segmentation with tissue-like model of P system rules based on the work of Christinal et al. [53] was proposed. Yahya et al. [8] implemented an uncomplicated artificial image with a detailed illustration of how P system works which is more illustrative. In addition, varying color relationships have been explored to investigate the effect of color on the process outputs. Most recently, Yahya et al. [56] proposed a tissue-like P system with region-based and edge-based segmentations to segment two dimensional hexagonal images, wherein P-Lingua programming language has been used to implement and validate the proposed system. The achieved experimental results clearly demonstrated the effectiveness of using hexagonal connectivity to segment two dimensional images in a less number of rules and computational steps. The experimental results have shown that using the hexagonal connectivity is more efficient than the four connectivities, where the number of rules and computational steps can been reduced from 9 to 7 steps.

Tissue-like P System on Sequential Computing Platforms for Real Image Segmentation. Díaz-Pernil et al. [46] presented an application for the edge-based segmentation for 2D digital images based on a tissue-like P system. The C++ programming language was adopted in the execution of the software tool. However, the technicalities surrounding it were not clarified. The software tool used to segment the 2D digital image is based on Christinals work [49] using 4-adjacency connectivity. Díaz-Pernil et al. [46] concluded that the problem of edge-based segmentation in 2D images is solved in constant time with respect to the number of steps of any computation model. The application program input constitutes a digital 2D image format that can be of the most familiar raster image formats such as jpg, png, gif, etc. Real medical images and artificial color images were used in the work of Díaz-Pernil et al. [46], but they did not compute the accuracy of the segmentation to evaluate and validate their proposed method. Although the input images were automatically codified in the system, no standard medical dataset has been used for the experiments.

Along the same trend, Sheeba et al. [57] proposed tissue-like P systems for segmentation the nuclei of the White Blood Cells (WBCs) for peripheral blood smear images. The preparation process was such that the RGB image was converted to a Hue-saturation-Value (HSV) image. Sheeba et al. [57] followed three steps, namely: color-based, intensity-based and morphological-based step. In the color-based step, the segmentation uses color as a set of predefined criteria, whereas, in the intensity-based second step the partition image is based on a haphazard altering of the intensity with the use of the gray values of the pixel. However, there might be broken edges with a gulf after the use of intensity based approach in the second step. In so doing, the morphological approach, which is the third step, is employed to address this setback. MATLAB was used to run the experiments. The technique of Christinal et al. [49] was adopted by Sheeba et al. (see [57]), with the difference being that Christinal et al. [49] employed 4-adjacency, whereas, Sheeba et al. [57] employed 8-adjacency. However, the difference between both types of adjacency has not been illustrated in their work. The resulting HSV image forms a network of points of N2 that are sets of pixels. Findings from the experiments sample data show a percentage success rate of 75%. Conclusively, Sheeba et al. [57] suggested the need for advanced segmentation techniques for segmenting images, e.g., basophils and eosinophils, having granular complex structures. It is worth mentioning that a comparison with this method cannot be performed for two reasons; First, different medical datasets and different programming languages have been used in their method. Second, the evaluation procedure and the method to compute the success rate have not been mentioned.

Díaz-Pernil et al. [58] proposed a novel application program that simulates the behaviour of a tissue-like model for a MC device (P systems) as illustrated in [49]. This is done in order to address segmentation in digital imagery. This work adopted the work of Díaz-Pernil, et al. [46] by adding a new extra image for the experiment. However, the proposed application program is a good tool for the treatment of digital images since it was able to handle considerable image sizes. The input image data to process a 2D image can be jpg, png, gif, etc. and raster image formats. C++ programming language was the programing language chosen for implementation. Although the input image was automatically codified, their method lacks a proper evaluation procedure to make it comparable with other methods in the literature.

Yang et al. [59] proposed a region-growing based image segmentation method with a tissue-like P system. The MC model has a uniquely designed membrane structure and evolving objects. It employs evolution and communication rules in order to actualize regional growth. The membrane model was developed in such a way that it performs image segmentation automatically. The 8-adjcency relationship was utilized in their work. For experimental purposes and evaluation, it was restricted to gray-scale images. The results of the experiments revealed that the proposed image segmentation technique has a better effect and performance as compared with the conventional image segmentation techniques based on region growing. The weakness of this principle and method is that it only works for gray-scale images. Moreover, the programming language that has been used in their work was not mentioned. The evaluation method that has been adopted was the contrast across region.

Recently, Peng et al. [60] proposed a novel region-growing color image segmentation for P systems. The tissue-like model of P system is developed such that an adaptive selection of target regions is obtained. The method was evaluated on several real-life color images. In the experiment, the image segmentation was evaluated with several color images that were randomly collected from the international network. Experimental results of the method are closer to the results obtained in the artificial segmentation. However, the proposed segmentation technique has some irrelevant features or noise in the resulting image. Meanwhile, the proposed image segmentation has the advantage of fast segmentation based on tissue-like P systems. The experimental results also show improved segmentation performance. They have not explained the programming language that has been used in their work.

Carnero et al. [61] proposed a novel MC technique by using multiple membranes to solve segmentation issues in real images using multiple membranes and real images. The algorithm deals with cleaning, thresholding and edge-based segmentation. It is implemented in Python.

Christinal et al. [62] proposed a novel definition for the interior of a partially bounded region of an image. Christinal et al. [62] also proposed an algorithm for automatically searching bounded regions using a MC model. A definition and an algorithm are presented for determining whether a Black Connected Component (BCC) encircles a section of a white region in a binary image. The empirical implementation occurred at once, because BCC can be regarded as a closed curve that is not perfect and the enclosed region as an imperfect topological hole for the BCC. The definition of such partially bounded regions is a hard task even for human experts. A real case study of defining partially bounded regions that is a solid task for human experts/professionals in the field is a glomerulonephritis image (medical image).

Cell-like P System on Sequential computing Platforms for Artificial Image Segmentation. Christinal et al. [36] designed a MC application to solve the thresholding problem in linear time on a number of pixels. This is achieved using the rules for a cell-like model P system. Interestingly, the massive parallelism characteristics of MC aided the proposed work to be realized in linear time based on the size of the input image. Christinal et al. [36] presented a new cell-like model of the membrane system with two polarizations and dissolution. Artificial color images were employed in the implementation of the membrane computation system with the use of a tissue simulator. The work solved the traditional threshold by adopting a high degree of parallel processes and the likelihood of presenting the information in an uncomplicated way. However, the drawback of this work is in the execution of the tissue simulator that did not depict how long it takes to segment an image, and there was no evaluation procedure which makes their model unsuitable for comparison.

Membrane Computing Based on Parallel Computing Platforms. MC

investigates models of computation inspired by the structural and functional properties of biological cells. Because of their inherent large-scale parallelism, MC models can be fully exploited only through the use of parallel computing platforms [48].

The distinguishing feature of parallel computer architecture is that a number of processors have the ability to share information and communicate with each other in order to solve a relatively large problem as fast as possible. Here, parallel architectures in the internal structure of the parallel platforms have been utilized. However, parallel architectures and parallel platforms are used alternately. Note that parallel architectures consist of variant memories and processors which are connected to each other by the aid of interconnection networks [63,64].

Tissue-like P System on Parallel Computing Platforms for Artificial Image Segmentation. Carnero et al. [52] presented an implementation of a membrane solution for digital images for the removal of redundant and irrelevant features, edge-based segmentation and thresholding using hardware programming. Field Programmable Gate Array (FPGA) is incorporated into the hardware tool. It is made up of logic blocks. This component enables configuration and reconfiguration after fabrication. Base on image analysis, Carnero et al. [52] work is simple and the time taken to execute the segmentation process is uniform irrespective of image size. This confirms that it works specifically with high dimensional data images. The first stage, which deals with irrelevant feature removal, is achieved with the application of a fundamental irrelevant features filter. In so doing, the system discards some noise that could hinder the process. In the second stage, the system deals with the issue of degradation of colors for pixels with different colors in the adjacent region boundary. Finally, the approach of Christinal et al. [49] was employed for the segmentation execution process. As their system has been described by a hardware description language, a comparison with this approach is not straightforward.

Tissue-like P System on Parallel Computing Platforms for Real Image Segmentation. In addition, a report is presented in [65] on a stage by stage implementation of a hardware programming tool in FPGAs. This tool addresses the issue of segmentation in digital images using a tissue-like model of P systems. Stage of work deals with edge detection and focuses on particular image processing applications referred to as image segmentation [65]. Experiments were performed using a 2D digital image (2D-ES problem). It is defined that the 2D digital image is made up of different colors of pixels to obtain the boundaries of regions in the 2D digital image. The system first employs a fundamental irrelevant features filter so that pickle noise would not affect the segmentation process. Then, the system does a thresholding of the image in order to stop the occurrence of degradation of colors of pixels in the boundary of adjacent regions with varying color types. Carnero et al. [65] studied the advantages and limitations of working on a hardware implementation of tissue-like P systems for segmentation in FPGAs. The postulate work has been made via the language programming at the Very High-level Design Language (VHDL). Similarly, because their system had been described by a hardware description language, a comparison with this method is not feasible.

Peña-Cantillana et al. [35] implemented a bio-inspired parallel algorithm in a novel device architecture called CUDA. This algorithm addresses the issues in thresholding with the help of a membrane algorithm. P systems are computational device of MC. The model of P system that used in [35] is a tissue-like P system. This tissue-like model addresses the problem by adopting a 4-neighbourhood between pixels. This parallel application is a membrane algorithm tool for image binarization and quantization. Experimental findings as compared with time of traditional work in [66] indicated that the best option is to employ the novel parallel device architecture CUDA in MC processing instead of a single-processor device. By doing so, the full potential parallelism of MC can be efficiently exploited.

Along similar lines, Díaz-Pernil et al. [42] worked on digital images for the aspect of segmentation. They proposed an algorithm in this aspect in relation to gradient-based edge detection. This detection is achieved with the use of bio-inspired parallel computing. In addition, Díaz-Pernil et al. [42] followed the aspect of MC to depict classical algorithm. CUDA was used to implement the parallel algorithm. The execution was built on a MC device and P systems were designed as a tissue-like model. The A Graphical P (AGP) Segmentor was proposed. AGP segmentor is a new algorithm for edge detection. An experiment was setup in parallel with a 3×3 and 5×5 Sobel operator. The experiment results depict that the AGP segmentor enhances the classical version of the Sobel operator. Díaz-Pernil et al. [67] showed how to enhance conventional methods for handling digital images and compare the results with time of traditional methods [68]. This is done by giving an example of a parallel implementation of parallel naturally inspired computing algorithms.

6.2   Algorithms-Based Membrane Computing for Image Segmentation

In recent decades, the focus in research in practical usage of computer science entails optimization methods and effectiveness. This has been achieved by appropriately merging meta-heuristic search methods and membrane systems [2,69,70]. This new trend of optimization methods is referred to as MC algorithms, first introduced by Nishida [71], or membrane algorithms. Interestingly, Păun noted in several works [2,72,73] that MC algorithms are really powerful as they combine the advantages of both MC and evolutionary algorithms. They (MC algorithms) are regarded as a hybrid optimization method class that employs the principles and ideas of meta-heuristic search techniques. It also applies the principles and ideas of hierarchical or network structures and the rules of MC device (P systems) [70,74].

In order to address the traveling salesman (TSP) problem, the pioneer model of MC algorithms was first introduced by Nishida [71]. The algorithm merged a tabu search algorithm along with a Nested Membrane Structure (NMS) inspired by the cell-like P system [75]. In this section, the related work pertaining to image segmentation using membrane algorithm will be presented. The related work that has been done only on sequential platforms will be presented in the next sub-section.

Membrane Computing on Sequential Computing Platforms. *Tissue-like P System on Sequential Computing Platforms for Real Image Segmentation.* Peng et al. [76] proposed a novel work for a multi-level thresholding method based on tissue-like P systems for image segmentation. The work is evaluated using six standard test images to determine optimal segmentation thresholds. In this work, they can effectively search the optimal thresholds for multi-level thresholding based on fuzzy entropy. This is because of its parallel computing capability and the particular mechanisms of tissue-like P systems. The method has a fast convergence speed as compared with the Particle Swarm Optimization (PSO)-based and Genetic Algorithm (GA)-based methods. This indicates that membrane algorithms can achieve a good balance between exploration and exploitation, thus preventing the search process being stuck in local minima. Experiments also show that the method is more efficient and effective than other optimization methods for multi-level thresholding.

Cell-like P System on Sequential Computing Platforms for Real Image Segmentation. To enhance the computational efficiency of multi-level threshold, Peng et al. [77] presented a novel three-level thresholding method for image segmentation based on cell-like P systems. Essentially, the method can find optimal values effectively using total fuzzy entropy because of the cell-like P system and its parallel processing capability. The proposed method is evaluated based on applicability and efficiency on three standard test images. The proposed method has been tested on the aforementioned images and compared with the GA and PSO methods. The experimental results show that the method outperforms other methods in terms of applicability and computational efficiency. Another advantage of membrane algorithms is that they can maintain the diversity of the population during the course of evolution and thus provide fast convergence towards a global optimal. Peng et al. [77] did not illustrate the platform used in their work.

In another work, Zhang and Peng [78] presented a novel infrared object segmentation method using a MC model. The work is based on a uniquely designed cell-like model P system for calculating optimal parameters quickly. The experiential inspiration is to enhance the efficiency of thresholding methods based on the fuzzy entropy that is achieved by applying parallel computing capability as well as singularly designed structure and mechanisms of the systems. The performance of the method is compared with existing entropy-based object segmentation methods, GA and Ant Colony Optimization (ACO) methods on different infrared images. Apart from the visual comparisons of segmentation outputs, Zhang and Peng [78] also provided the accuracy of object segmentation. Meanwhile, absolute error ratio was utilized as the main comparison criterion. Experimental outputs indicated that the proposed method (thresholding) outperforms other existing methods in the aspect of efficiency for computation and its applicability. Although an evaluation procedure based on segmentation accuracy has been performed in their work, it is not comparable with our proposed work as it uses a membrane algorithm that is implemented in MATLAB, whereas, our work uses MC rules and P-Lingua programming language.

Along similar lines, most recently, Peng et al. [79] proposed a robust multilevel thresholding and an efficient technique in MC. The computing framework is a cell-like P system with a nested structure of three layers. However, from the communication mechanisms and membrane structure of objects, they developed an enhanced velocity-position model that is similar to the velocity-position model in the Particle Swarm Optimization (PSO) technique. Cell-like P systems efficiently utilizes the best multi-level magnitudes that must be exceeded for an image to be administered by the evolution-communication mechanism of objects. Experiments show that simulations on (9) standard images as compared with several state-of-the-art methods reveal its ascendancy. These experiments exhibited the influence of the proposed multi-level thresholding has enhanced computation efficiency, robustness and improved quality.

Tables 1 and 2 summarize the previous works of the MC-based image segmentation, for the two computation categories; rules and algorithms, respectively. Some notes and comments on each previous work are presented in the tables.

Table 1. Previous works of MC-based segmentation; MC rules category.

#	Study	Type of P system	Type of segmentation	Adjacent type	Image type	Platform	Notes
1	[49]	Tissue-like P system	Edge-based segmentation	4-adjacency in 2D image and 26-adjacency in 3D Image*	Artificial	Tissue simulator	No evaluation procedure has been considered
2	[50]	Tissue-like P system	Edge-based segmentation	4-adjacency in 2D image and 26-adjacency in 3D image	Artificial	Tissue simulator	No evaluation procedure has been considered
3	[36]	Cell-like P system	Threshold segmentation	-	Artificial	Simulation of cell-like P system	No evaluation procedure has been considered.
4	[52]	Tissue-like P system	Noise removal Edge-based and Threshold segmentation	4-adjacency	Real	FPGA unit in parallel	Design a new hardware tools. No evaluation procedure has been considered
5	[51]	Tissue-like P system	Threshold segmentation and homology	-	Artificial	Simulation	Multiple auxiliary cells. No evaluation procedure has been considered
6	[46]	Tissue-like P system	Edge-based segmentation	4-adjacency	Real	C++ Program language	No evaluation procedure has been considered
7	[53]	Tissue-like P system	Region-based segmentation	4-adjacency in 2D image and 26-adjacency in 3D Image	Artificial	Tissue simulator	No evaluation procedure has been considered
8	[65]	Tissue-like P system	Noise removal. Edge-detection Threshold seg.	-	Real	FPGA unit in parallel	No evaluation procedure has been considered
9	[35]	Tissue-like P system	Threshold segmentation	4-adjacency	Real	C++ with the plugging Parallel (CUDA)	Time-comparison with traditional work (see [66])
10	[57]	Tissue-like P system	Edge-based segmentation and morphology segmentation	4-adjacency and 8-adjacency	Real	MATLAB	They compute the rate of success the procedures carried out with the given samples was 75%
11	[37]	Tissue-like P system	Edge-based segmentation	4-adjacency	Real	C++ programming language	No evaluation procedure has been considered
12	[54]	Tissue-like P system	Threshold segmentation	-	Artificial	Tissue simulator	No evaluation procedure has been considered
13	[59]	Tissue-like P system	Region-grown based segmentation	-	Real-gray	MATLAB	Compared with the traditional image segmentation methods based on region growing
14	[67]	Tissue-like P system	Edge-based segmentation	-	Real	CUDA	Time comparison with traditional work (see [68])
15	[60]	Tissue-like P system	Region-grown based segmentation	-	Real	-	No evaluation procedure has been considered
16	[54]	Tissue-like P system	Region-based segmentation	6-adjacent	Artificial	P-Lingua	No evaluation procedure has been considered
17	[61]	Tissue-like P system	Cleaning noise. Thresholding. Edge-based segmentation	-	Real	Python	Using multi-membrane. No evaluation procedure has been considered
18	[62]	Tissue-like P system	Edge-based segmentation	-	Real	-	No evaluation procedure has been considered
19	[8]	Tissue-like P system	Region-based segmentation	4-adjacency	Artificial	Tissue simulator	No evaluation procedure has been considered
20	[56]	Tissue-like P system	Region-based and edge-based segmentation	6-adjacent	Artificial	P-Lingua	No evaluation procedure has been considered

* For more information about the comparison between the 4 and 6-adjacency, see [56].

Table 2. Previous works of MC-based segmentation; MC algorithm category.

#	Study	Type of P system	Type of segmentation	Adjacent type	Image type	Platform	Notes
1	[77]	Cell-like P system	Threshold segmentation	-	Real	-	**1.** Proposed three-level thresholding **2.** Compared with PSO-based and GA-based methods
2	[78]	Cell-like P system	Threshold segmentation	-	Real	-	**1.** A special membrane structure with three layers was designed **2.** Compared with those of the existing entropy-based object segmentation methods as well GA-based and ACO-based methods
3	[76]	Tissue-like P system	Threshold segmentation	-	Real	-	**1.** Multi-level thresholding method **2.** Compared with PSO-based and GA-based methods
4	[79]	Cell-like P system	Threshold segmentation	-	Real	-	**1.** Multi-level thresholding **2.** Compared with PSO-based and bacterial foraging (BF)-based multi-level thresholding methods

7   Conclusion and Future Directions

In this paper, a comprehensive and an up to date survey pertaining to image processing techniques using MC has been presented. The presented work has been classified into two main categories, membrane rules and membrane algorithms for the ease of presentation. Those categories have been further classified into sequential simulation and parallel simulation. According to the deep investigation of the related works, the research gaps have been identified. Based on the previously presented works, the main limitations with the current state-of-the-art methods pertaining to image segmentation using MC are the manual codification of the input image as long as the manual visualization of the output image after segmentaion. It is worthwhile to mention that, the use of tissue simulator affects the applicability of the proposed techniques as it is not flexible enough to deal with large images. From a different angle, only few works considered the region-based segmentation, whereas the majority of the surveyed works had focused on the edge-based segmentation. Furthermore, few related works had considered the 6-adjacency and the 8-adjacency, whereas the majority of the works had considered the 4-adjacency only. For the sake of further advancement in this field, we outline a number of future directions which could help in addressing the current state-of-the-art limitations as follows:

One of the major limitations of the majority of state-of-the-art methods is that only a sequential architecture simulation was used, which in turn does not exploit the massive parallelism inherited in P systems. To fully make use of the MC parallelism, a parallel architecture such as CUDA is recommended to gain higher performance speedups over the typical serial implantation.

There is clear evidence that MC has a potential to tackle real world problems like medical image segmentation and cancer detection. Hence, the use of the large standard medical dataset is recommended to help in advanced medical image segmentation domain.

Future works may find a way to automatic 2D hexagonal image segmentation. i.e., no need for manual entering of the hexagonal image to the segmentation system. This will definitely reduce the time and cost of segmentation.

Actually, segmentation of color images using P-Lingua requires large memory due to the large number of rules needed, relatively, to test all the possibilities of color relationships between the pixels. Consequently, this will increase the computational time to achieve the segmentation. Hence, some sort of fuzzy logic and artificial intelligence can be deployed to reduce the number of generated rules and consequently reduce the memory requirements and time of the segmentation.

Acknowledgments. This work is partially supported by The Malaysian Ministry of Higher Education under the fundamental research grant scheme (4F802 and 4F786). The authors would like to thank the Research Management Centre (RMC), Universiti Teknologi Malaysia (UTM) for their support in R&D.

References

1. Păun, G.: Computing with membranes. J. Comput. Syst. Sci. **61**(1), 108–143 (2000). doi:10.1006/jcss.1999.1693
2. Păun, G., Rozenberg, G., Salomaa, A.: The Oxford Handbook of Membrane Computing. Oxford University Press Inc., New York (2010)
3. Zandron, C., Ferretti, C., Mauri, G.: Solving NP-complete problems using P systems with active membranes. In: Antoniou, I., Calude, C.S., Dinneen, M.J. (eds.) Unconventional Moldels of Computation, pp. 289–301. Springer, Heidelberg (2012). doi:10.1007/978-1-4471-0313-4_21
4. Păun, G.: Introduction: membrane computing what it is and what it is not. In: Păun, G. (ed.) Membrane Computing, pp. 1–6. Springer, Heidelberg (2002). doi:10.1007/978-3-642-56196-2_1
5. Alsalibi, B., Venkat, I., Subramanian, K., Lutfi, S.L., Wilde, P.D.: The impact of bio-inspired approaches toward the advancement of face recognition. ACM Comput. Surv. (CSUR). **48**(1), 5 (2015). doi:10.1145/2791121
6. Păun, G.: Membrane computing: power, efficiency, applications. In: Cooper, S.B., Löwe, B., Torenvliet, L. (eds.) CiE 2005. LNCS, vol. 3526, pp. 396–407. Springer, Heidelberg (2005). doi:10.1007/11494645_49
7. Păun, G.: Membrane computing: an introduction. Springer, Heidelberg (2002). doi:10.1007/978-3-642-56196-2
8. Yahya, R.I., Hasan, S., George, L.E., Alsalibi, B.: Membrane computing for 2D image segmentation. Int. J. Adv. Soft Comput. Appl. **7**(1), 35–50 (2015)
9. Zhang, X., Jiang, Y., Pan, L.: Small universal spiking neural P systems with exhaustive use of rules. In: 3rd International Conference on Bio-Inspired Computing: Theories and Applications BICTA 2008, IEEE (2008). doi:10.1109/BICTA. 2008.4656713
10. Pan, L., Păun, G.: Spiking neural P systems: an improved normal form. Theor. Comput. Sci. **411**(6), 906–918 (2010). doi:10.1016/j.tcs.2009.11.010
11. Pan, L., Zeng, X.: Small universal spiking neural P systems working in exhaustive mode. IEEE Trans. Nanobiosci. **10**(2), 99–105 (2011). doi:10.1109/TNB.2011. 2160281

12. Păun, A.: On P systems with active membranes. In: Antoniou, I., Calude, C.S., Dinneen, M.J. (eds.) Unconventional Models of Computation, UMC'2K, pp. 187–201. Springer, Heidelberg (2011). doi:10.1007/978-1-4471-0313-4_15

13. Niu, Y., Pan, L., Pereez-Jimenez, M.J., Font, M.R.: A tissue P systems based uniform solution to tripartite matching problem. Fundamenta Informaticae 109(2), 179–188 (2011). doi:10.3233/FI-2011-503

14. Pan, L., Păun, G., Pereez-Jimenez, M.J.: Spiking neural P systems with neuron division and budding. Sci. China Inf. Sci. 54(8), 1596–1607 (2011). doi:10.1007/s11432-011-4303-y

15. Pan, L., Ishdorj, T.-O.: P systems with active membranes and separation rules. J. UCS. 10(5), 630–649 (2004). doi:10.3217/jucs-010-05-0630

16. Păun, G., Suzuki, Y., Tanaka, H., Yokomori, T.: On the power of membrane division in P systems. Theor. Comput. Sci. 324(1), 61–85 (2004). doi:10.1016/j.tcs.2004.03.053

17. Porreca, A.E., Leporati, A., Mauri, G., Zandron, C.: P systems with active membranes: trading time for space. Nat. Comput. 10(1), 167–182 (2011). doi:10.1007/s11047-010-9189-x. Springer

18. Alhazov, A., Mart-Vide, C., Pan, L.: Solving graph problems by P systems with restricted elementary active membranes. In: Jonoska, N., Păun, G., Rozenberg, G. (eds.) Aspects of Molecular Computing, pp. 1–22. Springer, Heidelberg (2004). doi:10.1007/978-3-540-24635-0_1

19. Díaz-Pernil, D., Gutiérrez-Naranjo, M.A., Pérez-Jiménez, M.J., Riscos-Núñez, A.: Solving subset sum in linear time by using tissue p systems with cell division. In: Mira, J., Álvarez, J.R. (eds.) IWINAC 2007. LNCS, vol. 4527, pp. 170–179. Springer, Heidelberg (2007). doi:10.1007/978-3-540-73053-8_17

20. Díaz-Pernil, D., Gutirez-Naranjo, M.A., Pez-Jimez, M.J., Riscos-Nez, A.: A uniform family of tissue P systems with cell division solving 3-COL in a linear time. Theor. Comput. Sci. 404(1–2), 76–87 (2008). doi:10.1016/j.tcs.2008.04.005

21. Díaz-Pernil, D., Pereez-Jimenez, M.J., Riscos-Nez, A., Romero-Jimez, A.: Computational efficiency of cellular division in tissue-like membrane systems. Rom. J. Inf. Sci. Technol. 11(3), 229–241 (2008)

22. Păun, G.: P systems with active membranes: attacking NP-complete problems. J. Automata Lang. Comb. 6(1), 75–90 (2001)

23. Guerrero, G.D., Cecilia, J.M., Garc, J., Martinez-del-Amor, M., Pérez-Hurtado, I., Pérez-Jimenez, M.J.: Analysis of P systems simulation on CUDA. XX Jornadas de Paralelismo 2009, 289–294 (2009)

24. Cecilia, J.M., Garc, J.M., Guerrero, G.D., Martinez-del-Amor, M.A., Pérez-Hurtado, I., Pérez-Jimenez, M.J.: Simulation of P systems with active membranes on CUDA. Briefings Bioinform. 11(3), 313–322 (2010). doi:10.1109/HiBi.2009.13

25. Cabarle, F.G., Adorna, H., Martínez-del-Amor, M.A., Pérez-Jiménez, M.J.: Spiking neural P system simulations on a high performance GPU platform. In: Xiang, Y., Cuzzocrea, A., Hobbs, M., Zhou, W. (eds.) ICA3PP 2011. LNCS, vol. 7017, pp. 99–108. Springer, Heidelberg (2011). doi:10.1007/978-3-642-24669-2_10

26. Cabarle, F.G.C., Adorna, H., Martínez, M.A.: A spiking neural P system simulator based on CUDA. In: Gheorghe, M., Păun, G., Rozenberg, G., Salomaa, A., Verlan, S. (eds.) CMC 2011. LNCS, vol. 7184, pp. 87–103. Springer, Heidelberg (2012). doi:10.1007/978-3-642-28024-5_8

27. Cecilia, J.M., Garca, J.M., Guerrero, G.D., Martez-del-Amor, M.A.: The GPU on the simulation of cellular computing models. Soft Comput. 16(2), 231–246 (2012). doi:10.1007/s00500-011-0716-1

28. Gelenbe, E.: Fundamental Concepts in Computer Science. Imperial College Press, London (2009)

29. Mart-Vide, C., Păun, G., Pazos, J., Rodruez-Pat, A.: Tissue P systems. Theor. Comput. Sci. **296**(2), 295–326 (2003). doi:10.1016/S0304-3975(02)00659-X

30. Ionescu, M., Păun, G., Yokomori, T.: Spiking neural P systems. Fundamenta Informaticae **71**(2), 279–308 (2006)

31. Ibarra, O.H., Păun, G.: Membrane computing: a general view. Ann. Eur. Acad. Sci., 83–101 (2006). EAS Publishing House, Liege

32. Ceterchi, R., Gramatovici, R., Jonoska, N., Subramanian, K.: Tissue-like P systems with active membranes for picture generation. Fundamenta Informaticae **56**(4), 311–328 (2002)

33. Chao, J., Nakayama, J.: Cubical singular simplex model for 3D objects and fast computation of homology groups. In: Proceedings of the 13th International Conference on Pattern Recognition. IEEE (1996). doi:10.1109/ICPR.1996.547259

34. Ceterchi, R., Mutyam, M., Păun, G., Subramanian, K.: Array-rewriting P systems. Nat. Comput. **2**(3), 229–249 (2003)

35. Peña-Cantillana, F., Díaz-Pernil, D., Berciano, A., Gutiérrez-Naranjo, M.A.: A parallel implementation of the thresholding problem by using tissue-like P systems. In: Real, P., Diaz-Pernil, D., Molina-Abril, H., Berciano, A., Kropatsch, W. (eds.) CAIP 2011. LNCS, vol. 6855, pp. 277–284. Springer, Heidelberg (2011). doi:10. 1007/978-3-642-23678-5_32

36. Christinal, H.A., Dz-Pernil, D., Gutirez-Naranjo, M.A., Pez-Jimez, M.J.: Thresholding of 2D images with cell-like P systems. Rom. J. Inf. Sci. Technol. (ROMJIST) **13**(2), 131–140 (2010)

37. Díaz-Pernil, D., Christinal, H.A., Gutirez-Naranjo, M.A., Real, P.: Using membrane computing for effective homology. Appl. Algebra Eng. Commun. Comput. **23**(5–6), 233–249 (2012). doi:10.1007/s00200-012-0176-6

38. Alsalibi, B., Venkat, I., Subramanian, K., Christinal, H.: A bio-inspired software for homology groups of 2D digital images. In: Asian Conference on Membrane Computing (ACMC), 2014 IEEE (2014). doi:10.1109/ACMC.2014.7065800

39. Ardelean, I., Díaz-Pernil, D., Gutirez-Naranjo, M.A., Pena-Cantillana, F., Reina-Molina, R., Sarchizian, I.: Counting cells with tissue-like P systems. In: Proceedings of the Tenth Brainstorming Week on Membrane Computing, vol. 1, p. 03 (2012)

40. Zhang, G., Gheorghe, M., Li, Y.: A membrane algorithm with quantum-inspired subalgorithms and its application to image processing. Nat. Comput. **11**(4), 701–717 (2012). doi:10.1007/s11047-012-9320-2

41. Peña-Cantillana, F., Berciano, A., Díaz-Pernil, D., Gutiérrez-Naranjo, M.A.: Parallel skeletonizing of digital images by using cellular automata. In: Ferri, M., Frosini, P., Landi, C., Cerri, A., Fabio, B. (eds.) CTIC 2012. LNCS, vol. 7309, pp. 39–48. Springer, Heidelberg (2012). doi:10.1007/978-3-642-30238-1_5

42. Díaz-Pernil, D., Pe-Cantillana, F., Gutirez-Naranjo, M.A.: A parallel algorithm for skeletonizing images by using spiking neural P systems. Neurocomputing **115**, 81–91 (2013). doi:10.1016/j.neucom.2012.12.032

43. Reina-Molina, R., Díaz-Pernil, D., Gutirez-Naranjo, M.A.: Cell complexes and membrane computing for thinning 2D and 3D images. In: Proceedings of the Tenth Brainstorming Week on Membrane Computing, vol. 2, p. 03 (2012)

44. Berciano, A., Christinal, H., Venkat, I., Subramanian, K.: First steps for a corner detection using membrane computing. In: Asian Conference on Membrane Computing (ACMC), 2014 IEEE (2014). doi:10.1109/ACMC.2014.7065805

45. Freixenet, J., Muñoz, X., Raba, D., Martí, J., Cufí, X.: Yet another survey on image segmentation: region and boundary information integration. In: Heyden, A., Sparr, G., Nielsen, M., Johansen, P. (eds.) ECCV 2002. LNCS, vol. 2352, pp. 408–422. Springer, Heidelberg (2002). doi:10.1007/3-540-47977-5_27

46. Díaz-Pernil, D., Molina-Abril., H., Real, P., Gutirez-Naranjo, M.A.: A bio-inspired software for segmenting digital images. In: Bio-Inspired Computing: Theories and Applications (BIC-TA), 2010. IEEE (2010). doi:10.1109/BICTA.2010.5645062

47. Păun, G.: Introduction to membrane computing. In: Ciobanu, G., Păun, G., Pérez-Jiménez, M.J. (eds.) Applications of Membrane Computting, pp. 1–42. Springer, Heidelberg (2006)

48. Nguyen, V., Kearney, D., Gioiosa, G.: An implementation of membrane computing using reconfigurable hardware. Comput. Inform. **27**(3+), 551–569 (2012)

49. Christinal, H.A., Díaz-Pernil, D., Jurado, P.R.: Segmentation in 2D and 3D image using tissue-like P system. In: Bayro-Corrochano, E., Eklundh, J.-O. (eds.) CIARP 2009. LNCS, vol. 5856, pp. 169–176. Springer, Heidelberg (2009). doi:10.1007/978-3-642-10268-4_20

50. Christinal, H.A., Díaz-Pernil, D., Real, P.: P systems and computational algebraic topology. Math. Comput. Modell. **52**(11), 1982–1996 (2010). doi:10.1016/j.mcm.2010.06.001

51. Reina-Molina, R., Carnero, J., Diaz-Pernil, D.: Image segmentation using tissue-like P systems with multiple auxiliary cells. Image-A **1**(3), 143–150 (2010)

52. Carnero, J., Díaz-Pernil, D., Molina-Abril, H., Real, P.: Image segmentation inspired by cellular models using hardware programming. In: 3rd International Workshop on Computational Topology in Image Context (2010)

53. Christinal, H.A., Díaz-Pernil, D., Real, P.: Region-based segmentation of 2D and 3D images with tissue-like P systems. Pattern Recogn. Lett. **32**(16), 2206–2212 (2011). doi:10.1016/j.patrec.2011.05.004

54. Christinal, H.A., Díaz-Pernil, D., Jurado, P.R., Selvan, S.E.: Color segmentation of 2D images with thresholding. In: Mathew, J., Patra, P., Pradhan, D.K., Kuttyamma, A.J. (eds.) ICECCS 2012. CCIS, vol. 305, pp. 162–169. Springer, Heidelberg (2012). doi:10.1007/978-3-642-32112-2_20

55. Isawasan, P., Venkat, I., Subramanian, K., Khader, A., Osman, O., Christinal, H.: Region-based segmentation of hexagonal digital images using membrane computing. In: 2014 Asian Conference on Membrane Computing (ACMC). IEEE (2014). doi:10.1109/ACMC.2014.7065806

56. Yahya, R.I., Shamsuddin, S.M., Hasan, S., Yahya, S.I.: Tissue-like P system for segmentation of 2D hexagonal images. ARO- Sci. J. Koya Univ. **4**(1), 35–42 (2016). doi:10.14500/aro.10135

57. Song, T., Pan, Z., Wong, D.M., Wang, X.: Design of logic gates using spiking neural P systems with homogeneous neurons and astrocytes-like control. Inf. Sci. **372**, 380–391 (2016)

58. Díaz-Pernil, D., Gutirez-Naranjo, M.A., Molina-Abril, H., Real, P.: Designing a new software tool for digital imagery based on P systems. Nat. Comput. **11**(3), 381–386 (2012). doi:10.1007/s11047-011-9287-4

59. Yang, Y., Peng, H., Jiang, Y., Huang, X., Zhang, J.: A region-based image segmentation method under P systems. J. Inf. Comput. Sci. **10**(10), 2943–2950 (2013)

60. Peng, H., Yang, Y., Zhang, J., Huang, X., Wang, J.: A region-based color image segmentation method based on P systems. Sci. Technol. **17**(1), 63–75 (2014)

61. Carnero, J., Christinal, H.A., Díaz-Pernil, D., Reina-Molina, R., Subathra, M.S.P.: Improved parallelization of an image segmentation bio-inspired algorithm. In: Babu, B.V., Nagar, A., Deep, K., Pant, M., Bansal, J.C., Ray, K., Gupta, U. (eds.) SocProS 2012. AISC, vol. 236, pp. 75–82. Springer, Heidelberg (2014). doi:10.1007/978-81-322-1602-5_9

62. Christinal, H.A., Berciano, A., Díaz-Pernil, D., Gutiérrez-Naranjo, M.A.: Searching partially bounded regions with P systems. In: Pant, M., Deep, K., Nagar, A., Bansal, J.C. (eds.) SocProS 2013, Volume 1. AISC, vol. 258, pp. 45–54. Springer, Heidelberg (2014). doi:10.1007/978-81-322-1771-8_5

63. El-Rewini, H., Abd-El-Barr, M.: Advanced Computer Architecture and Parallel Processing. Wiley, Hoboken (2005)

64. Kirk, D.B., Wen-mei, W.H.: Programming Massively Parallel Processors: A Hands-on Approach. Newnes, Oxford (2012)

65. Song, T., Liu, X., Zhao, Y., Zhang, X.: Spiking neural P systems with white hole neurons. IEEE Trans. Nanobiosci. (2016). doi:10.1109/TNB.2016.2598879

66. Hamadani, N.: Automatic target cueing in IR imagery. Master's thesis, WPAFB, Ohio (1981)

67. Wang, X., Song, T., Gong, F., Pan, Z.: On the computational power of spiking neural P systems with self-organization, Sci. Rep. doi:10.1038/srep.27624

68. Khalid, S., Tabędzki, M., Rybnik, M., Adamski, M.: K3M: a universal algorithm for image skeletonization and a review of thinning techniques. Int. J. Appl. Math. Comput. Sci. 20(2), 317–335 (2010)

69. Ciobanu, G., Păun, G., Pereez-Jimenez, M.J.: Applications of Membrane Computing. Springer, Heidelberg (2006). doi:10.1007/3-540-29937-8

70. Zhang, G.-X., Liu, C.-X., Rong, H.-N.: Analyzing radar emitter signals with membrane algorithms. Math. Comput. Model. 52(11), 1997–2010 (2010). doi:10.1016/j.mcm.2010.06.002

71. Nishida, T.Y.: An application of P system: a new algorithm for NP-complete optimization problems. In: Proceedings of the 8th World Multi-conference on Systems, Cybernetics and Informatics (2004)

72. Păun, G., Pereez-Jimenez, M.J.: Membrane computing: brief introduction, recent results and applications. Biosystems 85(1), 11–22 (2006). doi:10.1016/j.biosystems.2006.02.001

73. Păun, G.: Tracing some open problems in membrane computing. Rom. J. Inf. Sci. Technol. 10(4), 303–314 (2007)

74. Zhang, G., Liu, C., Gheorghe, M., Ipate, F.: Solving satisfiability problems with membrane algorithms. In: Fourth International Conference on Bio-Inspired Computing, BIC-TA 2009. IEEE (2009). doi:10.1109/BICTA.2009.5338159

75. Song, T., Pan, L.: Spiking neural P systems with request rules. Neurocomputing 193(12), 193–200 (2016)

76. Peng, H., Wang, J., Pereez-Jimenez, M.J., Shi, P.: A novel image thresholding method based on membrane computing and fuzzy entropy. J. Intell. Fuzzy Syst. 24(2), 229–237 (2013). doi:10.3233/IFS-2012-0549

77. Peng, H., Shao, J., Li, B., Wang, J., Pereez-Jimenez, M.J., Jiang, Y., Yang, Y.: Image thresholding with cell-like P systems. In: Proceedings of the Tenth Brainstorming Week on Membrane Computing, vol. 2, p. 03 (2012)

78. Zhang, Z., Peng, H.: Object segmentation with membrane computing. J. Inf. Comput. Sci. 9(17), 5417–5424 (2012)

79. Peng, H., Wang, J., Pereez-Jimenez, M.J.: Optimal multi-level thresholding with membrane computing. Digit. Sig. Process. 37, 53–64 (2015). doi:10.1016/j.dsp.2014.10.006

Integrated Membrane Computing Framework for Modeling Intrusion Detection Systems

Rufai Kazeem Idowu[1], Ravie Chandren Muniyandi[2(✉)],
and Zulaiha Ali Othman[3]

[1] Computer Science Department, College of Science and Information Technology,
Ijagun, Ogun-State, Nigeria
rufaiki@tasued.edu.ng
[2] Centre for Software Technology and Management,
Faculty of Information Science and Technology,
Universiti Kebangsaan Malaysia (UKM), Bangi, Malaysia
ravie@ukm.edu.my
[3] Centre for Artificial Intelligence Technology,
Faculty of Information Science and Technology,
Universiti Kebangsaan Malaysia (UKM), Bangi, Malaysia
zao@ukm.edu.my

Abstract. Several activities take place within a network environment which include (but not restricted to) movement of traffics (packets) among the nodes. An Intrusion Detection system (IDS) which is primarily concerned with the monitoring of an information system with the sole aim of reporting activities which are symptomatic of an attack, needs constant review and upgrade to enhance its operations. In this work, we argue that two of the variants of Membrane computing (MC); spiking neural P (SNP) system and tissue-like P system could best be used as tools to enhance the activities and security properties of any computer network system. Therefore, this paper proposes an alternative but dependable integrated modeling framework which applies membrane computing paradigms to intrusion detection systems. This framework combines the membrane systems model for rule-based intrusion detection systems as well as attack detection model implemented on GPU for high throughput and detection speedup for checkmating packet loss/drop. MC is a newly introduced but yet to be fully explored technology in the area of network/information system security. It is a versatile, non-deterministic and maximally parallel computing model.

1 Introduction

Membrane Computing (MC), otherwise called P systems was introduced by Gheorghe Păun over a decade ago Paun (2006), Paun and Rozenberg (2002). Since then, application of MC has cut across several fields because of its great parallelism which leads to reduction in computational time complexity. Basically, a MC is made up of three distinct features which mimic the structure and functionality of the biological living cell. These are; membrane structure, objects

© Springer Nature Singapore Pte Ltd. 2016
M. Gong et al. (Eds.): BIC-TA 2016, Part I, CCIS 681, pp. 336–346, 2016.
DOI: 10.1007/978-981-10-3611-8_27

found within the membranes and the operational rules which guide the activities within the membranes. Although presently, there are so many variants of P systems, but the well-known P systems types are; Cell-like P systems, Neural-like P systems and Tissue-like P systems. Whereas a cell-like P System has hierarchically arranged set of membranes which could be described by a tree, a tissue-like has its membranes placed in the nodes of arbitrary graph. A neural-like P system has neurons (cells) which are linked by a specific set of synapses Paun (2006). However, as part of this research work, we focus on the use of Tissue-like P system with the application of an embedded recognizer P system defined as having a total Boolean function over a halting computation $\prod$ Perez et al. (2003).

On the other hand, Intrusion or Attack Detection System (IDS, ADS) is a security measure usually deployed on a network or host based system to checkmate the activities symptomatic of attack. IDS may also be said to be a system which frequently oversees a networked environment for the sole purposes of flagging and reporting events which are capable of (i) compromising the systems integrity, (ii) denying its availability and (iii) rendering it inefficient in its performance Venter and Eloff (2003), Uma and Padmavathi (2013), Folorunso et al. (2010).

From literature, it has been observed that most of these detection systems were implemented using the conventional CPUs which were characterized by their inability to handle increasingly large data found within extremely high speed networks Giorgos et al. (2011), Bul'ajoul et al. (2014), Rietz et al. (2014). This main deficiency leads to the problem of packet dropping and eventual defective detection and false alarm rates.

However, with the myriad of detection methods available, while relatively very few have explored the parallelization offered by GPU, not a single one has delved into investigating how MCs inherent advantages coupled with that of GPU could be deployed in this regards. Consequently, this research work presents a novel approach in the use of MC for attack detection on GPU.

In the literature, many approaches abound as regards the provision of solutions to various intrusion detection systems concerns. These challenges which often result in poor quality (high false alarm and low detection rates) and inefficiency (low processing speed and throughput) are primarily caused by curse of dimensionality, boundary problem and huge real-time traffics. Constantly therefore, there is the need to improve these existing approaches with a view to fortifying them. So, in this paper we are proposing an integrated framework of Membrane computing (MC) approaches to further improve the existing Intrusion Detection systems (IDS).

Therefore, this integrated framework for modeling intrusion detection systems using membrane computing is considered highly desirable in order to assist researchers and especially other network security administrators who may wish to consider MCs paradigms as alternative tool.

The following sections of the paper are arranged thus: Sect. 2 presents the modeling framework of signature-based IDS with the application of trapezoidal Fuzzy Reasoning Spiking Neural P (tFRSN P) System to Denial of Service

Attack (DoS). While Sect. 3 gives a detailed overview of our attack detection
P systems model implemented on GPU, the fourth section evaluates the models.
Section five however presents the integrated framework for enhancing IDS using
MCs paradigms. Section 6 concludes the work.

2   Membrane Computing and Signature-Based IDS

A variant of MC called trapezoidal fuzzy reasoning spiking neural P (tFRSN
P) system proposed by Peng et al. (2013) was employed to model a denial-of-
service (DoS) attack. tFRSN P system is a decision fusion model between fuzzy
system and spiking neural P (SN P) system. With this combination, the system
is capable of overcoming the boundary problem of intrusion detection as well as
detecting attacks quickly. Also, because of the inherent parallelism advantage
in SN P system it could as well be well suited for real time detection. The
option of using trapezoidal fuzzy set in this model was to considerably reduce
the false positives by enhancing the computation scenario with large range of
fuzzy membership which is not possible with triangular fuzzy set and others
Terrence (2010).

2.1   tFRSN P System Model for Denial-of-Service Attack

In configuring tFRSN P system model for the detection of Denial-of-Service
(DoS) attack, it is important to identify significantly useful features (which Lee
& Salvatore 2000 called cheap but necessary conditions). However, from literature, there are no agreed features for detecting DoS attack. For example, while
Mukkamala and Andrew (2003) opined that eleven features {**1, 5, 6, 23, 24,
25, 26, 32, 36, 38, 39**} are those that are important for flagging a DoS attack,
Lee & Salvatore 2000 submitted that only three features; *count*, *srv_count* and
service are essential to determine a smurf (DoS) attack. So, as explained in
chapter three, four features of *duration*, *src_byte*, *dst_byte* and *count* were used
for defining the fuzzy production rules which were subsequently applied for the
modeling.

2.2   Defining the Fuzzy Production Rules for DoS

For adapting tFRSN P system to model DoS attack, rules of the type below
were generated using the four identified features and the nine trapezoidal fuzzy
membership set. Given that $c_i = 1$, these rules include:

(i) If duration = L, src_bytes = E, dst_bytes = M_s and count = E,
   $\Rightarrow$ Then DoS is highly likely (M_t).
(ii) If duration = M_l, src_bytes = M_e, dst_bytes = M and count = S,
   $\Rightarrow$ Then DoS is not suspected (L).
(iii) If duration = M, src_bytes = M_e, dst_bytes = M and count = M_e,
   $\Rightarrow$ Then DoS is probable (M).

(iv) If duration $= V_l$, src_bytes $= V_e$, dst_bytes $= S$ and count $= E$,
$\Rightarrow$ Then DoS is indisputably confirmed (A_t).

(v) If duration $= M_l$, src_bytes $= E$, dst_bytes $= M_s$ and count $= M_e$,
$\Rightarrow$ Then DoS is very unsuspected (V_l).

2.3 The Modeling of DoS Attack

As depicted in Fig. 1, the tFRSN P systems model for DoS attack is a construct:

$$\prod = (O, \sigma_1, \ldots, \sigma_{18}, \sigma_{19}, \ldots, \sigma_{23}, syn, in, out) \tag{1}$$

Where

(1) $O = \{a\}$

(2) $\sigma_1, \ldots, \sigma_{17}$ are proposition neurons having fuzzy truth values $p_1, \ldots, p_{17}$ respectively.

(3) $\sigma_{18}, \ldots, \sigma_{21}$ are "AND"–type rule neurons associated with production rules $R_1, \ldots, R_5$ respectively.

(4) $syn = \{(1,19), (2,20), (2,23), (3,21), (4,22), (5,19), (5,23), (6,20), (6,21),$
$(7,22), (8,19), (8,23), (9,20), (9,21), (10,22), (11,19), (11,22), (12,20), (13,21),$
$(13,23), (19,14), (20,15), (21,16), (22,17), (23,18)\}$.

(5) $in = \{\sigma_1, \sigma_2, \sigma_3, \sigma_4, \sigma_5, \sigma_6, \sigma_7, \sigma_8, \sigma_9, \sigma_{10}, \sigma_{11}, \sigma_{12}, \sigma_{13}\}$

(6) $out = \{\sigma_{14}, \sigma_{15}, \sigma_{16}, \sigma_{17}, \sigma_{18}\}$

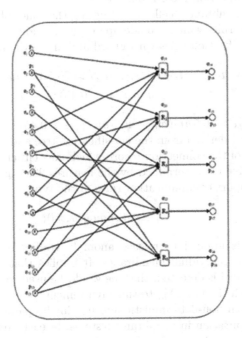

Fig. 1. tFRSN P model for DoS attack

3   Attack Detection P Systems Model on GPU

3.1   The $\prod_{AD\_P}$ Model

This computational model was configured along a recognizer tissue P systems because it is a decision making model (which distinguishes normal connection records from anomalous types) and has only the accepting computational halting modes of releasing anomalous traffics to the environment. In this work, network connection information was modeled as multiset of objects and the parameters of P system were defined in this respect. Objects were placed in different compartments using two types of rules namely communication and classification rules. While the execution of the communication rules were premised on symport rules application Prez–Hurtado et al. (2014), the classification rules which were generated using the 41 features of the KDD cup dataset, were conditioned by guards Ipate et al. (2012).

The Attack Detection P system ($\prod_{AD\_P}$) is formally defined as a system of degree $m \geq 1$ of the form:

$$\Pi_{AD\_P} = (O, Y_1 \cdots Y_m, r, \beta, l) \tag{2}$$

Where

- O is set of objects. An object represents a connection record in O, whereby $O| \in [0, 4898430]$. So, $\Rightarrow O_a \subseteq O$ where O_a denotes arbitrarily many copies of anomalous connection record found in β.
- $Y_1, \ldots, Y_m$ are membranes (cells) representing the zones of a network.
- r is a finite set of rules which is made up of types; r_1 and r_2 and defined thus:
  (i) r_1 are classification rules with guard and are of the type:

$$R_i = a_{i23}\, a_{i6}\, a_{i27} \rightarrow s_{i1}; (a_{i23} > 76.5\, and\, a_{i6} \geq 40.5$$
$$and\, a_{i27} > 0.45); 1 \leq i \leq MaxPac \tag{3}$$

  Where $(a_{i23} > 76.5\, and\, a_{i6} \geq 40.5\, and\, a_{i27} > 0.45)$ represents the conditional guard derived from the classification tree and $s_i = \{0, 1\}$ denotes the status of the connection record which may either be intrusive (0) or non-intrusive (1) determined by the features 23, 6 and 27.
  (ii) r_2 are symport communication rules of the type:

$$O_i \rightarrow (anomaly, \beta); \tag{4}$$

  This rule is applied to release anomaly traffics to the environment through the individual membranes. It implies that if anomalous connection record is detected, the rule would be used to transport affected object O within $Y_1 \ldots Y_m$ to the environment, β.

Rules were used in non-deterministic and maximally parallel manner as tradition with computation in membrane systems. In each step, all objects and all cells which can evolve must evolve.

- $\beta = O - \{Anomaly\}$; is the environment/zone. This external membrane environment is where the results of computation are obtained and so, it is called the output region. It does not hold any rule. Since the working packets are either *normal* or *anomaly*, hence the computation of $\prod_{\text{AD\_P}}$ system halts in the accepting mode if only anomalous packets O_a (and strictly excluding normal connection records (O_n)) are sent to the environment, otherwise, it is a rejecting computation. This stage signifies the end of computation (i.e. final configuration). Please note that $(O_n,\ O_a \subseteq O)$.
- $l \subseteq \{1, 2, \cdots, m\} x \{\beta\}$ which is a link (also known as channel or synapse) between the membranes and the environment, β.

3.2   Membrane Structure, Membrane/Object Representation in the $\prod_{\text{AD\_P}}$ Model

The structure of the membranes and how the objects are represented in the $\prod_{\text{AD\_P}}$ model are depicted in Fig. 2. Several one-membrane cells (ovals) are considered as evolving in a common external environment (β) where results are obtained. No direct communication exists in between the cells, but all the cells communicate with the environment since channels for transportation of such were specified in advance as $l \subseteq \{1, 2, \cdots, m\} x \{\beta\}$. These ovals were labelled with $1, 2, \ldots, m$ and objects with distinctive embedded 41 elements (features) and applicable set of rules were equally specified. However, the arrows indicate that the decided instances of '*anomaly*' obtained by the application of the classification rules, leave the cells in maximal mode through the channels $(1, \beta)$, $(2, \beta)$, $\ldots$, (m, β) to the external environment using symport rules. The dimension of the cells in the $\prod_{\text{AD\_P}}$ model is determined based on the number of thread blocks available on the GPU.

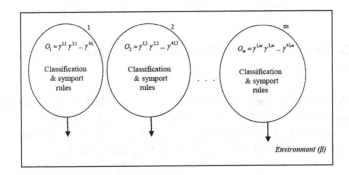

Fig. 2. Membrane/object representation in $\prod_{\text{AD\_P}}$ model

(a) The rules with guards for classification:
   Referred to as classification rules conditioned with guards are applied at the classification stage and they include:

$$R_1 = \gamma_{i23}\,\gamma_{i6}\,\gamma_{i27}\,\gamma_{i5} \rightarrow s_{i1}\,;\,(\gamma_{i23} > 76.5\,and\,\gamma_{i6} \geq\ 40.5\,and$$
$$\gamma_{i27} > 0.45\,and\,\gamma_{i5} > 0.495);\,1 \leq\ i\ \leq MaxPac \tag{5}$$

$$R_2 = \gamma_{i34}\,\gamma_{i37}\,\gamma_{i13}\,\gamma_{i40} \rightarrow s_{i0}\,;\,(\gamma_{i34} \geq\ 0.015\,and\,\gamma_{i37} < 0.495\,and$$
$$\gamma_{i13} < 0.5\,and\,\gamma_{i40} \geq\ 0.89)\,;\quad 1 \leq\ i\ \leq MaxPac \tag{6}$$

Where:

$$(\gamma_{i23} > 76.5\,and\,\gamma_{i6} \geq\ 40.5\,and\,\gamma_{i27} > 0.45\,and\,\gamma_{i5} > 0.495\,and$$
$$\gamma_{i34} \geq\ 0.015\,and\,\gamma_{i37} < 0.495\,and\,\gamma_{i13} < 0.5\,and\,\gamma_{i40} \geq\ 0.89)$$

represent some of the conditional guards derived from a classification tree and $s_i = \{1, 0\}$ denotes the status of the connection record O_i, which may either be intrusive (0) or non-intrusive (1) determined by the features 23, 6, 27, 5, 34, 37, 13 and 40.

(b) The symport (transportation) rule:

Basically, symport rules move objects across membranes together in one direction, and in this case, they move the objects toward the external environment. So, the rules are formulated in such a way that intrusive connections enjoy permeability through the membranes.

$$O_i \rightarrow (anomaly,\ \beta); \tag{7}$$

Where:

i denotes the membranes which release only anomalous connection record into the environment (β) after the invocation and execution of the classification rules.

Succinctly therefore, the rules were stated using the format:

$$Rule_{symp(i)} : [O^{anomaly}]_i \rightarrow []_i O^{anomaly} \tag{8}$$

4 Evaluation of the tFRSNP System and the $\prod_{AD\_P}$ Model

To establish the effectiveness of the two models, the KDD Cup dataset was used. While almost all the 5 million connection records in the dataset were used for evaluating the throughput of the $\prod_{AD\_P}$ model, 10 % of the dataset was used for evaluating the tFRSN P System in detecting DoS attacks.

4.1 Improving Throughput with $\prod_{AD\_P}$ Model

Since one of the key performance metrics for a network intrusion detection system is a sustainable throughput Subhan et al. (2010). The $\prod_{AD\_P}$ model achieved very good results in that regard.

As presented in Table 1, by initially using 314572 as tested packets, columns 1 shows all the randomly applied membranes. Similarly, columns 4 and 5 show

Table 1. Throughput of CPU and GPU using $\prod_{AD\_P}$ model

Membrane number used	Time(s) GPU	Time(s) CPU	Throughput (GPU) Pac/Sec	Throughput (CPU) Pac/Sec
128	9.3	34.7	33696.3	9039.7
256	7.5	34.7	41853.9	9039.7
512	6.6	34.7	47580.1	9039.7
1024	6.1	34.7	50944.9	9039.7
2048	5.9	34.7	53102.6	9039.7

the throughputs for both the GPU and CPU respectively which were obtained by dividing the packet size with the processing time.

It could be observed the highest throughput was recorded when membranes used were 2048. This is closely related to the increase in multiprocessor occupancy of the GPU which ultimately improves the systems efficiency by checkmating packet drop/loss.

4.2 Evaluating the tFRSN P System Model

The efficiency of trapezoidal fuzzy reasoning spiking neural P system model for detecting DoS attack was also evaluated using the KDD Cup dataset. The results obtained are here-under presented:

For the DoS attacks, the results obtained after implementation (as shown in the confusion matrix below), establish that the tFRSN P system performed well in the detection process. The 10% of the almost 5 million connection records in KDD cup dataset gives 494021 in which 97278 constitutes the non-intrusive event and 396743 are the attacks with DoS having the highest percentage.

Table 2. Confusion matrix

	Predicted normal	Predicted attack
Actual normal	TP (19.35%) 77400	FP (0.25%) 1000
Actual attack	FN (0.02%) 80	TN (80.38%) 321520

As shown in Table 2 above, while 0.02% and 0.25% were flagged as false negatives and positives respectively, 19.35% and 80.38% were returned as true positives and negatives respectively. Our experiments which were done by applying *decision fusion* of SN P systems combined with fuzzy logic, captured many real attacks in the dataset used (as TN returns the highest value). Furthermore, the percentage of most dangerous, i.e. FN, which managed to escape undetected by this system was just 0.02%.

5   The Integrated Framework for Enhancing IDS Using MC's Paradigms

From the literature, several issues may be responsible for the poor performance of an intrusion detection system depending on whether the detection technique is anomaly-based or signature-based. Researches have shown that majority of IDSs suffer from three main problems which are: (i) curse of dimensionality, (ii) blurriness of mid-point between intrusive and non-intrusive connection records and (iii) packet drop. These three identified problems usually lead to the challenges of low detection rate, high false positives/negatives, low classification accuracy rate, and above all, increase in computational cost.

The problem of curse of dimensionality has been recognized to be the bane of unsupervised learning in IDS because a linear increase in the number of dimensions leads to exponential increase in the number of training dataset (examples) Dash and Liu (2008), Lin et al. (2012). Therefore, in order to reduce the adverse impact of this problem on IDS, the thesis harnessed the communication benefit of membrane system (combined with Bee algorithm) in selecting relevant and effective features. So, when the features selected through this approach were evaluated in an anomaly-based IDS, it was discovered that high efficiency with remarkably low false alarm rate was achieved.

Another issue the thesis focused at is the boundary problem in IDS. Blurriness of the mid-point between normal and anomaly behaviours has been a source of major concern to network security experts over the years. This problem has been said to be responsible for high false positives/negatives in IDSs El-Hajj et al. (2008), Alheeti and Hamed (2012). This concern was handled through a means called decision fusion approach which enabled the synthesis of the method of *fuzzy* logic in the detection process with that of SN P system. In using this technique, a *fuzzy* space of nine sets was deployed. So, trapezoidal *fuzzy* reasoning spiking neural P (tFRSN P) system was applied in a signature-based IDS for the detection of denial-of-service and brute force attacks.

More importantly however, as network traffics grow heavy, IDSs are constantly faced with the challenge of loss of attack information because the peak processing throughput may be incapable to support it. This implies that with high volume of traffics, it becomes greatly expedient to design a detection system which would be able to cope with the capturing and processing of these large traffic volumes so as to prevent the problem of packet dropping Papadogiannakis et al. (2010), Schaelicke and Freeland (2005), Subhan et al. (2010). Also, Fig. 3 further depicts how membrane system was utilized through the introduction of the $\prod_{AD\_P}$ model and implemented on a GPU. With this approach, the parallelism architecture of P system and GPU were explored to achieve high throughput and speedup, and were ultimately utilized to remarkably decrease the computational cost.

Please note: The MS-B Algorithm which is one of the identified methods of using membrane system for intrusion detection is not discussed here because it is not within the scope of the paper.

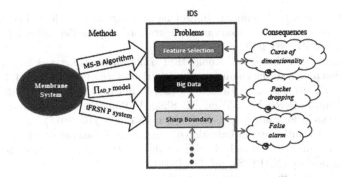

Fig. 3. Integrated framework architecture.

6 Conclusion and Future Works

This framework is a conglomerate of three distinct projects. Since each project within this framework implements a unique strategy and solves a particular problem then, a (modular) disjointed/peculiar method of evaluation is proposed. Consequent upon this, a testing framework which is project dependent is recommended which would be able to show a clear benefit of each project and how it could be achieved. However, two of the models were evaluated using KDD Cup dataset.

So, the future works would consider evaluating the other model of the framework using case studies and simulating it with the real-world problems. Also, it is envisioned for future research to investigate the application of the framework to other attacks in a rule-based environment.

References

Păun, G.: Introduction to membrane computing. In: Ciobanu, G., Păun, G., Pérez-Jiménez, M.J. (eds.) Applications of Membrane Computing, pp. 1–42. Springer, Heidelberg (2006)

Păun, G., Rozenberg, G.: A guide to membrane computing. Theoret. Comput. Sci. **287**, 73–100 (2002)

Jimenez M.J.P., Jimenez, A.R., Caparrini, F.S.: Complexity classes in models of cellular computing with membranes. Nat. Comput. **2**(3), 265–285 (2003)

Venter, H., Eloff, J.: A taxonomy for information security technologies. Comput. Secur. **22**(4), 299–307 (2003)

Uma, M., Padmavathi, G.: A survey on various cyber attacks and their classiffication. Int. J. Netw. Secur. **15**(6), 391–397 (2013)

Folorunso, O., Akande, O.O., Ogunde, A.O., Vincent, O.R.: ID-SOMGA: a self organising migrating genetic algorithm-based solution for intrusion detection. Comput. Inf. Sci. **3**(4), 80–92 (2010)

Giorgos, V., Michalis, P., Sotiris, I.: Midea: a multi-parallel intrusion detection architecture. In: ACM Conference on Computer and Communications Security, pp. 297–308 (2011)

Bulajoul, W., James, A., Pannu, M.: Improving network intrusion detection system performance through quality of service configuration and parallel technology. J. Comput. Syst. Sci. **81**, 981–999 (2014)

Rietz, R., Vogel, M., Schuster, F., König, H.: Parallelization of network intrusion detection systems under attack conditions. In: Dietrich, S. (ed.) DIMVA 2014. LNCS, vol. 8550, pp. 172–191. Springer, Heidelberg (2014). doi:10.1007/978-3-319-08509-8_10

Peng, H., Wang, J., Perez, M.J., Wang, H., Shao, J., Wang, T.: Fuzzy reasoning spiking neural P System for fault diagnosis. Inf. Sci. **235**, 106–116 (2013)

Terrence, F.P.: Evolutionary optimization of a fuzzy rule-based network intrusion detection system. In: 2010 Annual Meeting of the North American Fuzzy Information Processing Society (NAFIPS), pp. 1–6 (2010)

Mukkamala, S., Andrew, H.S.: Detecting denial of service attacks using support vector machines. In: The 12th IEEE International Conference on Fuzzy systems, vol. 2, pp. 1231–1236 (2003)

Perez-Hurtado, I., Valencia–Cabrera, L., Chacon, J.M., Riscos–Nunez, A., Perez–Jimenez, M.J.: AP–Lingua based simulator for tissue P systems with cell separation. Sci. Technol. **17**(1), 89–102 (2014)

Ipate, F., Dragomir, C., Lefticaru, R., Mierla, L., Perez-Jimenez, M.D.J.: Using a kernel P system to solve the 3-col problem. In: Proceedings of the 13th International Conference on Membrane Computing, Computer and Automation Research Institute, Hungarian Academy of Sciences, pp. 243–258 (2012)

Dash, M., Liu, H.: Dimensionality reduction. In: Wiley Encyclopedia of Computer Science and Engineering (2008)

Lin, S.W., Ying, K.C., Lee, C.Y., Lee, Z.J.: An intelligent algorithm with feature selection and decision rules applied to anomaly intrusion detection. Appl. Soft Comput. **12**(10), 3285–3290 (2012)

El-Hajj, W., Aloul, F., Trabelsi, Z., Zaki, N.: On detecting port scanning using fuzzy based intrusion detection system. In: Wireless Communications and Mobile Computing Conference, IWCMC 2008, International, pp. 105–110 (2008)

Alheeti, K.M.A., Hamed, R.I.: Application of a fuzzy neural network combined with an expert petri net system to intrusion detection system. In: The 13th International Arab Conference on Information Technology ACIT, pp. 10–13 (2012)

Papadogiannakis, A., Polychronakis, M., Markatos, E.P.: Improving the accuracy of network intrusion detection systems under load using selective packet discarding. In: Proceedings of the Third European Workshop on System Security, pp. 15–21 (2010)

Schaelicke, L., Freeland, J.C.: Characterizing sources and remedies for packet loss in network intrusion detection systems. In: 2005 Proceedings of the IEEE International Workload Characterization Symposium, pp. 188–196 (2005)

Subhan, A., Akhlaq, M., Alserhani, F., Awan, I.U., Mellor, J., Cullen, A.J., Mirchandani, P.: Smart Logic - preventing packet loss in high speed network intrusion detection systems. In: Weerasinghe, D. (ed.) ISDF 2009. LNCS (LNICSSITE), vol. 41, pp. 57–65. Springer, Heidelberg (2010). doi:10.1007/978-3-642-11530-1_7

Neural Computing

A Deep Learning Model of Automatic Detection of Pulmonary Nodules Based on Convolution Neural Networks (CNNs)

Xiaojiao Xiao, Yan Qiang, Juanjuan Zhao[✉], and Pengfei Zhao

College of Computer Science and Technology, Taiyuan University of Technology,
Taiyuan 030024, China
zhaojuanjuan@tyut.edu.cn

Abstract. Convolutional neural networks (CNNs), as one of the most classic representatives supervised deep learning, has been widely used for pedestrian tracking, voice recognition and image recognition. This paper innovatively proposes to apply CNNs to the detection of pulmonary nodules. For big data samples of thin slice scan CT images, we proposed model of pulmonary nodules detection based on user-defined convolutional neural networks (PndCnn-7). Our proposed method takes the CNNs advantages of the weights shared and automatic learning features. Firstly, the original CT images obtained lung parenchyma segmentation images through region growing and the images are stored into the sample library. Because CNNs can automatically learn image features, next, select the samples directly to train and test user-defined PndCnn-7 model, making it possible to detect pulmonary nodules accurately. Experimental results on sample library of this article indicates, the correct rate of identifying PndCnn-7 model can reach $99.66 \pm 0.3\%$, which is significantly better than traditional detection algorithm of pulmonary nodules.

Keywords: Convolutional neural networks · Detection · Pulmonary nodules

1 Introduction

Lung cancer, in the early stages, appears predominantly as pulmonary nodules. The pulmonary nodules, which are smaller than 3 cm diameter circular or existing oval opaque shadow, with moderate definite edge, may result in lung cancer [1]. With the rocketing development of medical imaging, computer tomography (CT), magnetic resonance (MR), B ultrasound, positron-emission tomography (PET) and other imaging tools play important roles for early lung cancer diagnosis. By contrast between many other chest imaging methods from chest X-rays to CT, we found that CT is a better imaging methods of detecting pulmonary nodules. In large hospitals, there are hundreds of patients everyday who need to diagnose diseases with CT scan. Because pulmonary nodules have complicated

© Springer Nature Singapore Pte Ltd. 2016
M. Gong et al. (Eds.): BIC-TA 2016, Part I, CCIS 681, pp. 349–361, 2016.
DOI: 10.1007/978-981-10-3611-8_28

shapes, and they are easy to adhere with other organizations, pulmonary nodules in visual always will be confused with protruding veins in CT. Distinguishing pulmonary nodules and artery need a doctors artificial analysis in a large number of multi-slice CT and volume. This long-term process will lead to eye fatigue or distractions, and there are other interferences, therefore, even experienced doctors may be difficult to make accurate judgments, inevitably results in cases of misdiagnosis and missed diagnosis.

With the continuous development of CT technology, especially the application of spiral technology, the detection accuracy is improved, scanned image of 1 mm thickness reached 400 to 500 layers, and 2 mm thickness of CT scan images reached 100 to 200 layers. Although thin slice scan CT can improve the detection rate of the nodule [2], and diminish missing small lesions, but, the large amount of heavy reading piece may cause radiologist subjective misdiagnosed, instead increasing the rate of misdiagnosis and missed diagnosis. Although most detected pulmonary nodules are benign, improving the detection rate of pulmonary nodules for improving the survival rate of early stage lung cancer patients lives is significant. Moreover, the false positive detection of nodules may result in increased costs, and bring serious anxiety for patients.

Artificial intelligence appears to solve the trouble to doctors caused by the thin slice scan CT, and reduce the workloads of doctors.

The remainder of this paper is organized as follows: Sect. 2 introduces previous work related to detection and diagnosis pulmonary nodules. Section 3 provides a detailed description of our method. The experimental results are presented with a detailed discussion in Sect. 4. And the conclusion is given in Sect. 5.

2   Related Works

With the rise of artificial intelligence in the computer field, the neural networks was once a hot point in field of machine learning. In 1980s, American scholar, Hinton et al. proposed completely a back-propagation algorithm (BP algorithm) [3] for artificial neural networks, injecting new blood to study machine learning. Carreira [4], who used two artificial neural networks to detect pulmonary nodules, with fewer features to determine pulmonary nodules, but detected effect is not ideal. Lin [5] defined the membership function with maximum gradient descent algorithm, and he proposed fuzzy system based on artificial neural networks in order to detect pulmonary nodules. There are some other people using artificial neural networks to analyze data pulmonary nodules on CT images, achieving matching good results, but it takes too long time. And BP algorithm while increasing the number of layers of neural networks is very easy to fall into local optimum or over-fitting. This phenomenon finally was broken in 2006. Hinton, Professor at the University of Toronto, Canada, the leader in the field of machine learning, with the help of his students, Salakhutdinov, published an article which presents the concept of the deep network and the deep learning in leading academic journal "Science", resulting in a research boom of deep learning.

With the propose of deep learning, convolutional neural networks (CNNs) [6], as one of the most classic representatives supervised deep learning, once again, become one of the hotspots of many subject areas. Le Net-5 model, proposed by Lecun et al. 1995, is a successful application of the earliest CNNs. With the reference of the theory of deep model, After CNNs was first proposed, it initially was applied in recognition of handwritten character. In recent years, it was gradually applied to various fields, such as pedestrian tracking, image recognition, voice recognition, natural language processing, etc. Though CNNs has broadly used, it is still not applied to pulmonary nodules detection.

This paper innovatively proposes to apply CNNs to the detection of pulmonary nodules. First of all, weight shared network structure, which makes CNNs more similar to biological neural networks, reduces the complexity of the network model and the number of weights. These advantages, which perform more obvious when the network operating multi-dimensional images, make images be used directly as input network, avoid the complex feature extraction and data reconstruction in traditional recognition algorithms. Secondly, in the field of image recognition, because CT images can be inputted directly as CNNs without the complex pre-operation, CT images are more suitable for detection of pulmonary nodules. In addition, there exists many CT image data, batch processing for dealing with big data uniquely can adapt to technological developments.

3   Method

3.1   Proposed Method of Detection

CNNs synthesize the advantages of previous detection algorithms, reducing the misdiagnosis rate effectively and improving learning efficiency. In addition, while adding a new learning sample, adjusting the weights of neuron only can significantly improve the diagnostic rate with the original study the results unchanged. We define this model as PndCnn-7 (Pulmonary nodules detection - Convolution neural network-7). The flowchart of the algorithm is shown in Fig. 1.

The process of applying the PndCnn-7 to detect pulmonary nodules follows: Firstly, the original CT images obtained lung parenchyma segmentation images through region growing and the images are stored into the sample library, we can apply the training samples to train forward propagation and error feedback propagation of PndCnn-7 model. Then adjust the parameters of PndCnn-7 model, when the error reaches the desired value, using testing samples to test PndCnn-7 model, and output the final classification results of the pulmonary nodules.

3.2   Pretreatment in CT

We can learn from the basic process of detection and identification of pulmonary nodules that the area of the lung parenchyma region just spans only about 15% of the total area of the lung CT images. Pulmonary nodules area is much smaller.

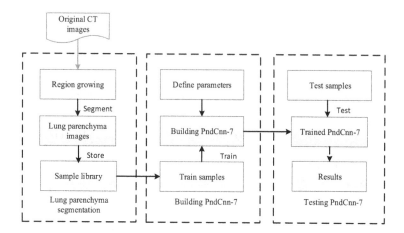

Fig. 1. The flowchart of the algorithm.

To accelerate the detection of pulmonary nodules and to prevent the impacts of extra pulmonary organs on testing, CT images requires lung segmentation before the detection of pulmonary nodule.

Firstly, segmenting lung parenchyma by the region growing. Region growing (RG), a classical image segmentation method, is to collect similar properties pixels into one region. The algorithm is shown in Algorithm 1.

Algorithm 1. Region Growing

1: Repeat
2: Select the seed region U and seed point x, computing region pixel grayscale average
   ?U and standard deviation σ, defined deviation factor f.
3: **for** Look seed point eight points in the neighborhood t, **do**
4:     Computing the absolute value m of pixel gray scale value difference between
       point t and seed point x.
5:     **if** $m \in [U - f\sigma, ?U + f\sigma]$ **then**
6:         Merge neighborhood point t to the region U
7:     **else**
8:         Abandon neighborhood point t from the region U
9:     **end if**
10:     The new merger t as the seed point x.
11: **end for**
12: Until no new pixel point added the divided region.

If directly output the lung parenchyma segmentation of CT images (512 × 512) to the input layer (64 × 64) of PndCnn-7 model, it will lose potential significant characteristics in CT images, leading to extra training time and low accuracy of the detection. So segment the images to the minimum circumscribed rectangle of lung parenchyma, ensuring pulmonary nodules features relatively more pronounced.

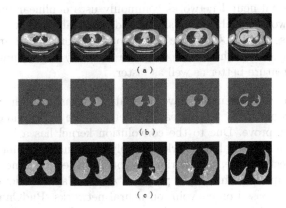

Fig. 2. Segmentation of region growing (a) The original CT images (b) segmentation images by region growing (c) Cropped images.

As shown in Fig. 2, (a) selected from the original CT image with 10 pictures interval, (b) lung parenchyma segmentation images by region growing (c) cropped images.

3.3   Build a Deep Belief Network

LeNet-5 – a classic CNNs – is used to identify number, which achieve a good detection results in handwriting digital databases Mnist sample set. The network consists of five layers, an input layer, an intermediate layer, which includes convolution layers and down-sampling layers, and an output layer. Each layer comprises training parameters, the size of convolution kernel is 5 × 5. Early experiments, directly put LeNet-5 to test pulmonary nodules sample set, the network can not find convergence, can not complete the detection of pulmonary nodules. After several tests analysis, the main reasons are as follows:

(1) In classic network model, the size of convolution kernel (5 × 5) can effectively extract the local features for the image of the sample set Mnist, but for CT sample set (64 × 64), convolution kernel is too small that the convolution results can not contain valid information of express local features. To solve this problem, by many experiments, we will define convolution kernel as 13 × 13 in PndCnn-7 model.

(2) Due to the nature of the last layer is a classifier, the size of the Mnist sample set image is 28 × 28, and the size of the pulmonary nodules sample set image is 64 × 64, the increasing image size leads to the output characteristic dimension of the hidden layer is too high, categorizer can not make the correct classification based on the high-dimensional features which its descriptive

power is limited. In order to avoid the loss of features and improve the classification accuracy, we will define convolution kernel as 13×13 in PndCnn-7 model.

(3) The traditional neural networks commonly uses nonlinear function, which enables network model to train slowly and easily falls into overfitting. In this paper we use the ReLU for the activation function. It can greatly shorten the learning curve while improving the accuracy of learning, and sparse extraction feature better as well as faster.

Network detection accuracy have a great relationship with constitute the number of neuronal, with the increase of neuron, the performance of the network will also improve. Due to the convolution kernel has a large amount of computation, if a large-scale network is simply constructed, it may increase the lung cancer detection rate, but sacrifices a lot of inspection time. After several experiments comparing, this paper proposes a seven-layer model of pulmonary nodules detection based on convolution neural networks (PndCnn-7). The hidden layer includes two convolution layers and two down-sampling layers, and each layer contains training parameters, the size of convolution kernel is 13×13, the basic structure is shown in Fig. 3.

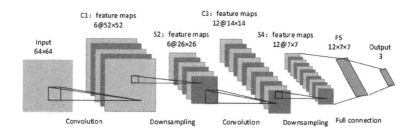

Fig. 3. The structure of PndCnn-7.

PndCnn-7 model is hierarchical model of automatic learning in a supervised manner. Input is the 64×64 image and output constituted by the three labels that represent normal nodules, benign nodules and malignant nodules. The PndCnn-7 model consists of two parts, the first part is a multi-level feature extraction, and the second part is a classifier.

The PndCnn-7 model can fully study the features, because its first party features are extracted from the low level to the high level [7], operated by convolution and down-sampling alternately. This process has a number of different with the traditional CNNs. First, through experience and comparison we use the convolution kernel which is 13×13. The purpose of this definition is to be able to extract the potential significant characteristics in CT image, as well as the effective local characteristics. As the deep increases, the extracted feature is more abstract and has a better expression ability. Secondly, the deep has great influence on the performance of the convolution neural networks, insufficient depth will weaken capability of the CNNs extraction feature. But too much network layer can lead to complicated network structure and the overfitting easily appears because of the increasing training time. Based on existing samples, we trained and finally adopted PndCnn-7 frame shown in Fig. 2.

3.4   The Training Process of PndDBN-5

Constructing PndCnn-7 model includes training that includes forward propagation and back propagation and testing process. First, the sample is taken 10000 from the sample library as training samples, leaving 8000 as the test samples. Samples by bilinear difference algorithm to scale the image to 64×64, constitute 64×64 one-dimensional array as input of PndCnn-7. At the same time define the parameters: learning rate (lr) $= 0.75$, batchsize $= 100$, the number of training epoch $= 50$, convolution kernel $= 13 \times 13$, down-sampling kernel $= 2 \times 2$.

Forward Propagation.   When calculation in the kth layer where $k = 1$, 2,3,4,5,6, suppose the input feature maps is $x^k = \{x_m^k | m = 1, ..., M\}$, output mapping feature have $y^k = \{y_n^k | n = 1, ..., N\}$ and $z^k = \{z_n^k | n = 1, ..., N\}$, where M and N respectively represent the maximum number of dimensions x^k and y^k or z^k. In convolution layer, each feature map y_n^k as

$$y_n^k = F(\sum_{m=1}^{M} Convn(x_m^k, fC_m^k, 1) + b_n^k$$

Where, Convn as convolution operation between feature maps x^k and convolution kernels fC_m^k, b_n^k as a bias and 1 represents the steps of 1. Nonlinear Rectified Linear Units (ReLU) function $F(x) = \max(0, x)$ as activation function. After convolution layer, each downsampling layer have adopted a fixed size kernels fS_{nm}^k downsampling y^k [8], getting feature mapping z_n^k

$$z_n^k = downsampling(y_n^k) = mapping(y_n^k, fS_{nm}^k, 2)$$

Where, downsampling on behalf of down-sampling operation, 2 for step 2. After down-sampling, through activating the function $Sigmoid(x) = \frac{1}{1+e^{-x}}$, getting output $net.o$.

$$net.o = Sigm(z_n^k \cdot w + b_n^k)$$

In the hidden layer, we choose ReLU activation function instead of the traditional nonlinear activation function.

$$ReLU \begin{cases} f(x) = \ln^{1+e^x} \\ f'(x) = \frac{1}{1+e^{-x}} \end{cases}$$

Firstly, ReLU function can better learn from the dimension of valid data to the relatively sparse features, plays automation dissociation effect. Secondly, in the deep network, because the illusion that the nonlinear activation function more advanced than of a linear activation function, we rely too much non-linear activation function. Based on the above, in PndCnn-7 model, use a simple and fast linear activation function may be more appropriate.

Back Propagation. Due to PndCnn-7 model using classical error back-propagation algorithm [4]. According to BP algorithm, as follows:

If it is the last layer, the input x should has a desired output Y, then the error and residuals are respectively define as:

$$net.e = net.o - Y, od = \varepsilon * (net.o * (1 - net.o))$$

The od pass back through a reverse gradient way to the level, lr as learning rate, updated output layer weights w and bias b as:

$$w = w - lr * od, b^k = b^k - lr * od^k$$

If it is the downsampling layer, od define as:

$$od^k = up(od^{k+1}, w^k)$$

where up as up-sampling function. Because this layer has no right weight w and bias b, it does not need to be updated.

If it is a convolution layer, od define as:

$$od^k = od^{k+1} * MaxGrad(Y))$$

where MaxGrad as derivative of the ReLU activation function. According to the formula, update the weights w and bias b.

A batchsize samples do once error back propagation. CNNs trained a large data sample, the error value tends to be stable and weights and bias are no longer updated, this model finally attained stabilize.

4   Experimental Result

4.1   Data Set

The data used in this paper are all selected from The Lung Image Database Consortium and Image Database Resource Initiative (LIDC-IDRI) [7] which is the world's largest database of pulmonary nodules. We selected 300 cases of LIDC-IDRI, including lung CT images 18000 pieces, of which 6000 include nodules, and 2183 with benign pulmonary nodules, 3217 with malignant pulmonary nodules.

4.2   Test Results

In this paper, assessing performance that detection of pulmonary nodules by PndCnn-7 model through each category recognition accuracy and overall accuracy. First, setting the basic parameter that indicates the performance, the benign pulmonary nodules as negative class, malignant pulmonary nodules as positive class. As shown in Table 1, TP, TN, FP, FN respectively are true positive, true negative, false positive and false negative [10].

Detection of pulmonary nodules algorithm mainly have four evaluation indicator: accuracy, sensitivity, specificity and false positive rate. According to the above performance parameters, the evaluation index can be defined as:

Table 1. The mixing matrix of predicated results and detection results

Mixing matrix (P, positive; N, negative)		Predicated results	
		P	N
Detection results	P	True Positive (TP)	False Positive (FP)
	N	False Negative (FN)	True Negative (TN)

1. **Accuracy:** In detection results, the percent of correctly detected samples in all detected samples, reflects the quality of detection.

$$Accuracy = \frac{TP + TN}{TP + TN + FP + FN}$$

2. **Sensitivity:** In detection results, the percent of correctly detected malignant nodules in all detected malignant nodule samples, reflects whether there are undetected.

$$Sensitivity = \frac{TP}{TP + FN}$$

3. **Specificity:** In detection results, the proportion of correctly detected benign nodules in all detected benign nodular samples, reflects whether there are wrong detected.

$$Specificity = \frac{TN}{TN + FP}$$

4. **FPF(False Positive Fraction):**

$$FPF = \frac{FP}{FP + TN} = 1 - Specificity$$

We select 8 sets of data as the test samples to test the PndCnn-7 model, each group randomly selected 1,000 CT images of test samples. Test results shown in Table 3.

According to Table 2, average accuracy of PocCnn-7 model can reach 0.997, indicating that this model can effectively detect and classify pulmonary nodules.

4.3 Experimental Discussion

In this paper, training process of the PndCnn-7 model uses four parameters:learning rate (lr), convolution kernel, $batchsize$ and epoch, the values of these four parameters will directly affect the accuracy of the detection of pulmonary nodules and training time of he PndCnn-7 model. Due to the limited number of training sample set, selecting same sample (train_x $= 10000$), finding the best value by adjusting the parameters, the following is a discussion of the different parameters. $epochs = \frac{train\_x}{batchsize} \times epoch$, where, pochs represents the total training batchsize.

Table 2. The detection results of pulmonary nodules

Number	TP	FP	TN	FN	Accuracy	Sensitivity	Specificity	FPF
1	998	2	996	4	0.997	0.996	0.998	0.002
2	995	5	998	2	0.9965	0.997	0.995	0.005
3	999	1	997	3	0.998	0.997	0.999	0.001
4	997	3	997	3	0.997	0.997	0.997	0.003
5	998	2	999	1	0.9985	0.999	0.998	0.002
6	999	1	993	7	0.996	0.993	0.998	0.002
7	997	3	996	4	0.9965	0.996	0.997	0.003
8	994	6	999	1	0.9965	0.999	0.994	0.006
Average	997	3	997	3	0.997	0.997	0.997	0.003

1. Analysis of Experimental Parameters.

(1) *Learning rate lr*. Learning rate lr is an important parameter affecting the performance and the convergence of the network. The lr value determines the size of the impact of the error on the weights. If lr too small, will makes slow convergence and easy falling into local optimum. If lr too large, it may lead to shock or divergence, affecting convergence stability. In conditions of train_x $= 10000$, $batchsize = 100$, convolution kernel $= 13 \times 13$. When the error rate to 0.02, the test is stopped. A contrast experimental results are shown in Fig. 4.

Through experiment results found when lr between in $[0.4, 1.05]$, minimum batch processing, shorter training time, the network will not occur shock. Therefore, we chose $= (0.4 + 1.05)/2 = 0.75$ in this paper.

(2) *Convolution kernel*. Due to the size of the sample for 64×64, the traditional 5×5 convolution kernel is too small, it can not extract effective local characteristics, but if the convolution kernel is too large, the complexity of extracted feature may far exceed the convolution kernel ability of express. Thus, the size of convolution kernel has a crucial impact on entire network performance. In conditions of train_x $= 10000$, $batchsize = 100$, $epoch = 50$ and $lr = 0.75$. A contrast experimental results are shown in Fig. 5.

Through experiment results found 13×13 convolution kernel makes the network quickly and smooth convergence, the shock does not occur. Therefore, we chose 13×13 as the size of convolution kernel.

(3) *Batch number: batchsize*. In PndCnn-7 model, back-propagation ways select batch processing mode, each pick batchsize size samples to train, then adjust the value of a weight, rather than read into a sample to calculate and adjust weights again. One hand, $batchsize$ set too large, it may weight adjustment is not complete and resulting in the error is too large. On the other hand, $batchsize$ set too small, the number of error propagation is more, long training time, waste of resources. In conditions of train_x $= 10000$ $lr = 0.75$,

$epoch$ = 50 and convolution kernel = 13 × 13, a contrast experimental results are shown in Fig. 6.

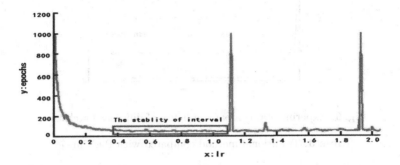

Fig. 4. Experimental comparison figure of different learning rate.

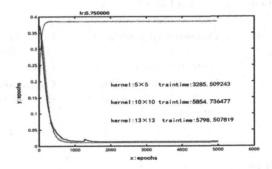

Fig. 5. Experimental comparison figure of different convolution kernel.

In image $A = \frac{1}{5} \times epochs$, $B = \frac{2}{5} \times epochs$, and so on. After the experimental comparison, in the sample of the same, when batchsize = 100, the traintime is almost same, and makes the network more rapid and smooth convergence.

4.4 Analysis of Technical

The basic idea of the traditional method of detection pulmonary nodules is to extract characteristic values of suspected pulmonary nodules, and selects the relative classifier, by analysis characteristic values to determine whether the target image pulmonary nodules. This paper proposed PndCnn-7 model has a different place that input is CT images but the output is the classfication, no required to calculate characteristic values of the target area. Table 3 shows the difference between compares traditional methods, such as CAD systems, and PndCnn-7 model on the recognition process and performance.

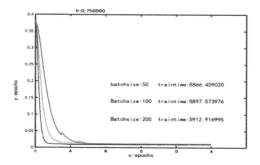

Fig. 6. Experimental comparison figure of different batchsize.

Table 3. Traditional method compared with PndCnn-7

	Traditional method of detection pulmonary nodules	PndCnn-7 model
Pulmonary nodules segmentation	Segmentation method based on a threshold, regional law, edge and a specific theory, etc.	Do not need to segment
Characteristic analysis	Geometry, edge feature, gray value characteristics, etc.	Pixel gray value of the local sub-region
Classifier	Linear classifiers, SVM, random forests, neural networks, etc.	Convolution neural networks

5   Conclusions

The basic idea of the traditional method of detection pulmonary nodules is to extract characteristic values of suspected pulmonary nodules, and selects the relative classifier, by analysis characteristic values to determine whether the target image pulmonary nodules. This paper proposed PndCnn-7 model has a different place that input is CT images but the output is the classfication, no required to calculate characteristic values of the target area. Table 3 shows the difference between compares traditional methods, such as CAD systems, and PndCnn-7 model on the recognition process and performance.

Acknowledgment. The work is supported by the found of National Natural Science Foundation of China (61540007, 61373100), the State Key Laboratory of Computer Science Open Foundation of China (BUAA-VR-15KF02, BUAA-VR-16KF13).

References

1. Austin, J.H., Müller, N.L., Friedman, P.J., et al.: Glossary of terms for CT of the lungs: recommendations of the nomenclature committee of the Fleischner Society. Radiology **200**(2), 327–331 (1996)
2. Brown, M.S., McNitt-Gray, M.F., Goldin, J.G., et al.: Patient-specific models for lung nodule detection and surveillance in CT images. IEEE Trans. Med. Imaging **20**(12), 1242–1250 (2001)
3. Hinton, G.E., Rumelhart, D.E., Williams, R.J.: Learning internal representations by back-propagating errors. In: Parallel Distributed Processing: Explorations in the Microstructure of Cognition, vol. 1 (1985)
4. Penedo, M.G., Carreira, M.J., Mosquera, A., et al.: Computer-aided diagnosis: a neural-network-based approach to lung nodule detection. IEEE Trans. Med. Imaging **17**(6), 872–880 (1998)
5. Lin, D.T., Yan, C.R., Chen, W.T.: Autonomous detection of pulmonary nodules on CT images with a neural network-based fuzzy system. Comput. Med. Imaging Graph. **29**(6), 447–458 (2005)
6. Lecun, Y., Jackel, L.D., Cortes, C., et al.: Learning algorithms for classification: a comparison on handwritten digit recognition. Neural Netw. Stat. Mech. Perspect. 261–276 (1995)
7. Jarrett, K., Kavukcuoglu, K., Ranzato, M.A., et al.: What is the best multi-stage architecture for object recognition. In: 2009 IEEE 12th International Conference on Computer Vision, pp. 2146–2153. IEEE (2009)
8. Krizhevsky, A., Sutskever, I., Hinton, G.E.: ImageNet classification with deep convolutional neural networks. In: Advances in Neural Information Processing Systems, vol. 25 (2012)
9. Lin, P.L., Huang, P.W., Lee, C.H., et al.: Automatic classification for solitary pulmonary nodule in CT image by fractal analysis based on fractional Brownian motion model. Pattern Recogn. **46**(12), 3279–3287 (2013)

A Study on the Recognition and Classification Method of High Resolution Remote Sensing Image Based on Deep Belief Network

Guanyu Chen[1,2], Xiang Li[1,2(✉)], and Ling Liu[3]

[1] School of Computer Science, China University of Geosciences,
Wuhan 430074, China
Lixiang@cug.edu.cn, 53222726@qq.com
[2] Hubei Key Laboratory of Intelligent Geo-Information Processing,
China University of Geosciences, Wuhan 430074, China
[3] China Trans Geomatics Co., Ltd., Beijing 100101, China

Abstract. High resolution remote sensing images can describe the geometric features, spatial features and texture features of objects more accurately, which are widely used in various fields. How to get more useful information from the remote sensing image, and then the recognition and classification of the image from the information has become one of the hot spots in the field of high resolution remote sensing image research. Deep learning is a learning algorithm based on the depth network structure, which can better fit the intrinsic structure of the sample, compared with the traditional shallow classifier. Depth of learning in a deep belief network model is based on single-layer Boltzmann machine learning algorithm, each layer is made up of the generation and cognition, and make the bidirectional weight updatin g come true, the net output of each layer can be reduced to the input signal, so that the model can be infinitely close to the global optimum in the pre training stage. The author propose an improved dropout strategy based on the study of deep belief network model, this strategy only chooses partial local area data to zero out the weight at each time. It not only maintains the local information of the image itself, but also enhances the generalization ability of the model. The experimental results show that the improved dropout strategy improves about 2.5% of the classification accuracy, and it has better classification performance.

Keywords: High resolution remote sensing image · Deep belief network · Dropout strategy · Classification

1 Introduction

Classification and recognition of remote sensing image is the basis of information extraction, which is helpful for the further understanding and analysis of remote sensing data. Through the identification of buildings, roads, vegetation and other

M. Gong et al. (Eds.): BIC-TA 2016, Part I, CCIS 681, pp. 362–370, 2016.
DOI: 10.1007/978-981-10-3611-8_29

targets, people can do something like urban planning, military reconnaissance, environmental monitoring, resource exploration, the detection of various natural disasters. At present, there are some common and effective methods, such as support vector machine classifier, random forest classifier, extreme learning machine and so on. In 2015, Xiang proposed the best band selection method for the high resolution remote sensing image [1], fusion technology multispectral image [4]. According to the recognition of bad geological body, Li compared several common classification methods, and analyzed the advantages and disadvantages of several methods in remote sensing classification [5,6]. Then a SVM classification algorithm based on feature fusion is proposed to explore the vegetation recognition in remote sensing images [7]. A set of perfect classification method for the classification of high resolution remote sensing images is then shaped based on the works introduced above.

Deep learning is a new direction of machine learning research in recent years, the main working principle of Go Alpha, which has been very concerned recently, is deep learning. Deep learning originates from the neural network which is imitating the basic structure of neurons of the brain, extracts feature of data from the lower layer to the top layer by exploring the characteristics of the data in time and space, it can improve the accuracy of recognition [10]. The deep belief network (DBN) was proposed by Hinton, a professor at University of Toronto, and his students in 2006, then they triggered a wave of deep learning [11]. DBN is a deep learning model which combined the advantages of supervised and unsupervised classification. It is made up of restricted Boltzmann machine. It can achieve data classification and dimensionality reduction, and also make maximize use of deep network to fit the linear and nonlinear classification problems, reducing the classification error. In 2010, Professor Hinton proposed to detect airborne remote sensing image in the road with the DBN model, it was the first time that Deep learning has been applied in the field of remote sensing [12]. In 2012, Professor Hinton put forward the theory of dropout. By join the dropout strategy in Deep learning, and introduce the concept of weight decay in the network, the network can prevent over fitting. This makes Deep Learning caused people's attention in image recognition [13]. Compared with shallow machine model, the Depth learning model can achieve the complex function approximation and learn the essential characteristic of the data with fewer parameters [3].

In this paper, the author proposes an improved stochastic Dropout strategy in the DBN model based on a classification method of remote sensing image of DBN model. The experimental results show that the improved DBN model can achieve better classification effect.

2   Stochastic Dropout Strategy

DBN is a deep layer modelwhich constituted by multiple restricted Boltzmann machine (RBM) [11]. Using layer by layer separated training, The network model accomplish the training process of the whole network, and make the system's ability of handling complex classification problems greatly ascend.

Dropout is randomly make some of the hidden layer nodes not working during the model training. Those nodes do not work temporarily, we can consider those nodes as not a part of the network structure, but its weight was retained (only temporarily not update it), because it may have to work when the next sample inputted. It will solve the problem of over fitting which is caused by too little training samples, and can also reduce the time complexity of the model. After each finished dropout, we get a thinner network from the original network. For a neural network with N nodes, with dropout, it can be seen as a collection of 2^n models, but the number of parameters needed to be trained is unchanged. So it solved the time consuming problem [2,8] (Fig. 1).

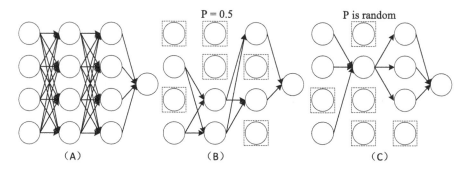

Fig. 1. DBN-network, DBN-network with dropout and DBN-network with stochastic dropout

Based on dropout, Author make some further improvement by adding a layer of randomization process which can further prevent over fitting problem. Training process in dropout have a fixed probability value P (such as 0.5) which will not change if it is defined. While the probability value of random dropout is not fixed, which makes the randomization more thoroughly.

3   Recognition and Classification of Remote Sensing Image

The experimental area is shown in Figure 2, combination of RGB432 was chosen by band. This picture is part of area sub-image of High-resolution II Satellite remote sensing image in Wuhan area, Wuhan city February, 2015. The selected area is 2520 * 2400 and contains 6048000 pixels. There abundant information in Image region.

According to Envi soft selecting the experimental sample from picture RGB, the author obtains the area of interest to define the training samples. In the Tool ROI dialog, the 6 sample names are defined as buildings, roads, vegetation, bare land, playground and other. Then these samples are assigned to different colors,

Fig. 2. Obtains the area of interest to define the training samples (Color figure online)

and respectively, in the main image window to draw the area of interest, ROI choose as shown in Fig. 2.

The author takes the training data and test data in accordance with the principle of 5/5, namely the pickup half, training data used for model training, and test data used for model evaluation. Spectral features for the image of R band and G band and the B band.

4   Remote Sensing Image Classification Based on Deep Belief Network

4.1   Parameter Sensitivity Test of Deep Belief Network

An important part of the DBN network is the RBM structure. Here is the first layer of the weight graph, the size of hidden layer of the first layer is 100, the dimension of the input signal is 3, the specific results are shown in Fig. 3. The horizontal coordinate is the size of the hidden layer, and the vertical coordinate

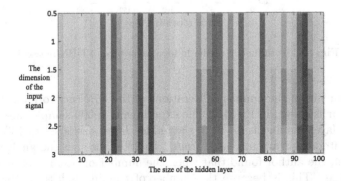

Fig. 3. The weight of single-layer network diagram

is the dimension of the input signal. Weight graph shows the weight of different dimensions of the signal size.

The main parameters of the DBN network are the number of iterations of the network, the size of the hidden layer, the layer number of the hidden layer. Then respectively verify what about the result of the classification when these parameters are changed.

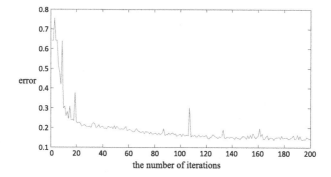

Fig. 4. The influence of the number of iterations of the DBN network

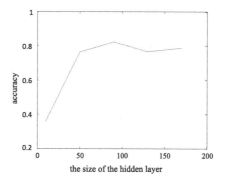

Fig. 5. The influence of the hidden layer size of DBN network

The influence of the number of iterations of the DBN network on the classification error is shown in Fig. 4, in the experiment, 10000 samples are selected, the hidden layer number is set to 3, the hidden layer size is set to 100, and the number of iterations are increased from 1 to 200. Through the analysis of the curve graph, the author found that when the number of training is smaller, the error is larger. This is because the number of training is less, at this time it did not fit into the real data characteristics. With the increase of the number of training, the network structure gradually learn the internal structure of the data, so the error is smaller and smaller, when the number reached 80, the change is not large. The number of iterations is set to 100 in the experiment.

The influence of the hidden layer size of DBN network on the classification accuracy is shown in Fig. 5. Through the analysis of the curve graph, the author found that when the size of the hidden layer is smaller, the error is larger. When the hidden layer of the size is on the 50 to 180, classification accuracy is little changed. The results show that the training results are stable at this time. The size of hidden layer is set to 100 in the experiment.

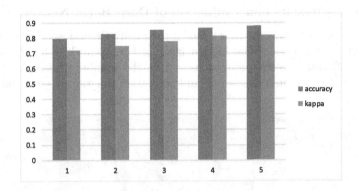

Fig. 6. The influence of the hidden layer number of DBN network

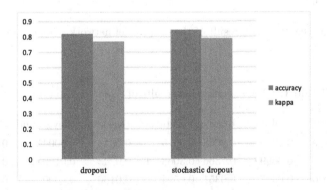

Fig. 7. Compared with the results before and after the improvement of dropout

The influence of the hidden layer number of DBN network on the classification accuracy is shown in Fig. 6. Through the analysis of the column chart, the author finds that when the hidden layer number is 1, 2, 3, 4, 5 layer, the recognition accuracy and kappa coefficient are increased layer by layer, with the increase number of layers of hidden layer, the network fitting ability is stronger, the more able to display the true characteristics of the target, so the classification ability of data is stronger, the accuracy of the data is higher. However, with the increase of the number of layers, the training time is greatly increased, so the Hidden layer number is set to 3 in the experiment.

Finally compared with the results before and after the improvement of Dropout, the results are shown in Fig. 7. By analyzing the column chart, the author found that the improved drop out strategy is more accurate than the original dropout strategy.

4.2 Sorting Results and Evaluation of Deep Belief Network

The author use deep belief network model to classify Remote sensing image, the parameters of the model: The hidden layer of the network is 3, the sizes are 100, 100, 100 respectively, *numepochs* is 100, the number of samples for each treatment is 400, *momentum* is 0.2, and activation function is sigma function.

(a)   (b)   (c)

Fig. 8. The segmentation result of the deep belief network (Color figure online)

Table 1. DBN classification results of remote sensing images

Category	Buildings	Roads	Vegetation	Bareland	Playground	Other
Buildings	0.8940	0.2068	0.0015	0.0043	0.0004	0.3071
Roads	0.0699	0.7306	0.3063	0.0243	0.0120	0.0010
Vegetation	0.0037	0.0351	0.6594	0.0160	0.0000	0.0000
Bareland	0.0062	0.0214	0.0328	0.9523	0.0684	0.0161
Playground	0.0042	0.0061	0.0000	0.0032	0.9193	0.0000
Other	0.0221	0.0000	0.0000	0.0000	0.0000	0.6758
Total classification accuracy = 0.8448			*Kappa coefficient* = 0.7911			

The segmentation result of the deep belief network is shown in Fig. 8. Among them (a) is the original remote sensing image. Different color markers in

(b) represent different samples. (c) is deep belief network segmentation result, in which the segmentation accuracy of building, bare land and playground in remote sensing image is the highest.

DBN classification results of remote sensing images are shown in Table 1.

5   Conclusion

Deep belief network overcomes so many problems such as the noise sensitivity of the traditional neural network classifier, easy to fall into the local minimum, error gradient dispersion. It improves the DBN model mainly according to the weight loss. In the output of the DBN model add drop out strategy, and improved drop out strategy: only select some data to clear the weight for each time, the improved drop out strategy is more accurate than the original dropout strategy, the degree which is about 2.5%. It also makes sensitivity experiments on the main parameters of the DBN network, such as the number of iterations, the hidden layer size, and the number of hidden layers. The results show when the number of iterations and the hidden layer of DBN network can reach a certain number, the results will remain stable, the accuracy of the change is not large, but the more number of network layers, the more complex of structure, and the higher of the accuracy form SN P systems [9,14].

References

1. Li, X., Wang, G.: Optimal band selection for hyper spectral data with improved differential evolution. J. Ambient Intell. Human. Comput. **6**(5), 675–688 (2015)
2. Song, T., Pan, L.: Spiking neural P systems with request rules. Neurocomputing **193**(12), 193–200 (2016)
3. Song T., Liu X., Zhao Y., Zhang X.: Spiking neural P systems with white hole neurons, IEEE Trans. Nanobiosci. (2016). doi:10.1109/TNB.2016.2598879
4. Li, X., Wang, L.: On the study of fusion techniques for bad geological remote sensing image. J. Ambient Intell. Human. Comput. **6**(1), 994–1004 (2015)
5. Wang, Q.Q., Li, X., Wang, L.L.: Research and analysis method based on the classification on the bad geological identification. Geol. Sci. Technol. Inf. **33**(6), 203–208 (2014)
6. Chen, G.Y., Li, X., An, K.: Identification and classification of adverse geological body based on convolution neural networks. Geol. Sci. Technol. Inf. **35**(1), 205–211 (2016)
7. Chen, G.Y., Li, X., Wang, L.L.: Identification and classification of remote sensing image of vegetation based on big data. Geol. Sci. Technol. Inf. **35**(3), 199–204 (2016)
8. Song, T., Pan, Z., Wong, D.M., Wang, X.: Design of logic gates using spiking neural P systems with homogeneous neurons and astrocytes-like control. Inf. Sci. **372**, 380–391 (2016)
9. Wang, X., Song, T., Gong, F., Pan, Z.: On the computational power of spiking neural P systems with self-organization. Sci. Rep. **6**, 27624 (2016). doi:10.1038/srep27624

10. Bengio, Y., Courville, A., Vincent, P.: Representation learning: a review and new perspectives. IEEE Trans. Pattern Anal. Mach. Intell. **35**(8), 1798–1828 (2013)
11. Hinton, G.E., Osindero, S., Teh, Y.W.: A fast learning algorithm for deep belief nets. Neural Comput. **18**(7), 1527–1554 (2006)
12. Hinton, G.E.: A practical guide to training restricted Boltzmann machines. Momentum **9**(1), 926 (2010)
13. Hinton, G.E., Srivastava, N., Krizhevsky, A.: Improving neural networks by preventing co-adaptation of feature detectors. Comput. Sci. **3**(4), 212–223 (2012)
14. Shi, X., Wu, X., Song, T., Li, X.: Construction of DNA nanotubes with controllable diameters and patterns by using hierarchical DNA sub-tiles. Nanoscale **8**, 14785–14792 (2016). doi:10.1039/C6NR02695H

Classification Based on Brain Storm Optimization Algorithm

Yu Xue[1]([✉]), Tao Tang[2], and Tinghuai Ma[2]

[1] Jiangsu Engineering Center of Network Monitoring,
Nanjing University of Information Science and Technology,
Nanjing 210044, People's Republic of China
xueyu@nuist.edu.cn
[2] School of Computer and Software,
Nanjing University of Information Science and Technology,
Nanjing 210044, People's Republic of China
taotang1993@163.com, thma@nuist.edu.cn

Abstract. As one of the important issues of data classification, classification has attracted the attention of many researchers in the field of data mining. Different from clustering research issues, in classification research issues, evolutionary clustering algorithms (EAs) were only used to improve the performance of classifiers either by optimizing the parameters or structure of the classifiers, or by pre-processing the inputs of the classifiers. Lots of evolutionary algorithms are employed to solve unsupervised classification, i.e., clustering. In this article, we will create a new mathematical model for supervised classification problem and use brain storm optimization algorithm (BSO) to search the global optimal solution, which resolved the problem of supervised classification with new ideas. The main objective is to find a better method. By using a new classification algorithm based on BSO, we are looking forward to optimizing the result.

Keywords: Data classification · Evolutionary classification algorithm · Evolutionary algorithm · Evolutionary training · Brain storm optimization algorithm (BSO)

1 Introduction

Optimization is a mathematical basic application of computer technology, which to find the optimal solution or satisfactory solution of many practical problems for the ultimate goal, usually used in scientific research and engineering. Data classification is a main research issue in machine learning and data mining. The purpose of classification is to correctly predict the classification labels of instances according to the properties of these instances. Classification can be classified into two categories, i.e. unsupervised classification and supervised classification. Unsupervised classification is often called clustering. The main methods are K-means [1], Fuzzy c-means (FCM) [2], and evolutionary algorithms (EAs) [3–5], with the goal of finding the optimal solution.

© Springer Nature Singapore Pte Ltd. 2016
M. Gong et al. (Eds.): BIC-TA 2016, Part I, CCIS 681, pp. 371–376, 2016.
DOI: 10.1007/978-981-10-3611-8_30

However, lots of them can easily fall into local optimum. Fortunately, EAs can be employed to search global optimization solution. To my surprise, almost no EA has been employed to solve supervised classification problem. Thus, we intend to use EAs to improve the performance of supervised classification. BSO [6] is an algorithm optimization. It has advantages like simple thought and clear. A simple algorithm gathers scattered thoughts from either a superior, by find local optimal clustering in local optimum on the basis of a new generation by individual variation.

In this paper, we introduce the feasibility of using BSO to solve some of the supervised classification problems. Besides, a new mathematical model framework for supervised classification was proposed and six data sets from UCI were applied.

2   Brain Storm Optimization Algorithm

BSO is simple to think, but with more implementation process parameters. And at different stages of optimization, it is difficult to determine the parameters. This algorithm uses clustering to find local optima. And produce new individuals by mutation and in the locally optimal basis. Therefore, clustering and variation played an important role in the algorithm process.

BSO mainly consists of clustering module learning modules and two modules. Clustering algorithm using clustering method module will gather information for the K classes. Each class cluster center is the optimal value of the class. Algorithm optimizing information amount through learning, for each category of information in parallel. This promotes local search. Algorithm makes itself out of mutual cooperation through local optimum between classes and mutation operations, to promote global search.

Optimization algorithm cluster centers to ensure its convergence. Variation of class information process Optimizing algorithm to ensure the diversity of the population.

The algorithm is shown in Algorithm 1.

Step 6 is a process to generate new information, the selected information is worth adding to a Gaussian random new information, Eq. (1) described below:

$$X_{new}^d = X_{selected}^d + \xi * n(\mu, \sigma) \tag{1}$$

Where $X_{selected}^d$ is the amount of information to select the first dimension d, X_{new}^d is newly generated information section dimension d, $n(\mu, \sigma)$ is the mean μ and variance σ Gaussian function; ξ is a weighting factor, ξ can be described by Eq. (2) Description:

$$\xi = \log sig((0.5 * \max\_iteration - current\_iteration) \div k) * rand() \tag{2}$$

Where $\log sig()$ is S-type logarithmic transfer function, $\max\_iterattion$ is the maximum number of iterations, $current\_iterattion$ is the current iteration number, k can change the function of the slope of the $\log sig()$, $rand()$ is a random value between $(0, 1)$.

Algorithm 1. Procedure of BSO

1.Randomly generate n potential solutions (individuals);
2. Cluster n individuals into m clusters;
3. Evaluate the n individuals;
4. Rank individuals in each cluster and record the best individual as cluster center in each cluster;
5. Randomly generate a value between 0 and 1;
  a) If the value is smaller than a pre-determined probability p_{5a},
    i. Randomly select a cluster center;
    ii. Randomly generate an individual to replace the selected cluster center;
6. Generate new individuals;
  a) Randomly generate a value between 0 and 1;
  b) If the value is less than a probability p_{6b},
    i. Randomly select a cluster with a probability p_{6bi};
    ii. Generate a random value between 0 and 1;
    iii. If the value is smaller than a pre-determined probability p_{6biii};
      1) Select the cluster center and add random values to it to generate new individual;
    iv. Otherwise randomly select an individual from this cluster and add random value to the individual to generate new individual;
  c) Otherwise randomly select two clusters to generate new individual
    i. Generate a random value;
    ii. If it is less than a pre-determined probability p6c, the two cluster centers are combined and then added with random values to generate new individual;
    iii. Otherwise, two individuals from each selected cluster are randomly selected to be combined and added with random values to generate new individual;
  d) The newly generated individual is compared with the existing individual with the same individual index, the better one is kept and recorded as the new individual;
7. If n new individuals have been generated, go to step 8; otherwise go to step 6;
8. Terminate if pre-determined maximum number of iterations has been reached; otherwise go to step 2;

3 Classification Method Based on EA

Given a data set $D = \{x_1, x_2, \ldots, x_m\}$ and a training set $T = \{(x_1, y_1), \cdots, (x_m, y_m)\}$, where (x_i, y_i) is the ith example, $x_i = x_{i1}, x_{i2}, \ldots, x_{id} \in X = R^d$ is the ith sample, $y_i \in Y = \{1, 2, \cdots, l\}$ $(i = 1, 2, \cdots, m)$ is the label of the ith sample. The object of classification is to learn a model $f(x) : X \to Y$ from the training set T.

The examples of training data can be written as

$$
\begin{bmatrix}
x_{11}, & x_{12}, & \ldots, & x_{1d}, & y_1 \\
x_{21}, & x_{22}, & \ldots, & x_{2d}, & y_2 \\
\ldots, & \ldots, & \ldots, & \ldots, & \ldots \\
x_{m1}, & x_{m2}, & \ldots, & x_{md}, & y_m
\end{bmatrix}
\tag{3}
$$

First, we introduce a weight vector $W = (w_1, w_2, \ldots, w_d)$, and let

$$\begin{cases} w_1 x_{11} + w_2 x_{12} + \ldots + w_d x_{1d} = y_1 \\ w_1 x_{21} + w_2 x_{22} + \ldots + w_d x_{2d} = y_2 \\ \ldots + \ldots + \ldots + \ldots = \ldots \\ w_1 x_{m1} + w_2 x_{m2} + \ldots + w_d x_{md} = y_m \end{cases} \tag{4}$$

We observed that if we can find a vector W which could satisfy Eq. (4), we could use this model to do classification. So we can transform the classification problem into solving a linear equation problem. Generally speaking, this kind of problems can be solved by EAs [7]. But, if these equations are uncorrelated and the number of the equations is more than the number of the weights, this problem will be a so called inconsistent equation. So there is no exact solution for these linear equations, and there is no exact method for solving such a problem. Fortunately, it is a classification problem in fact, so it is not necessary to find the exact solution. For classification problems, it is enough to find an approximate solution of the following equations:

$$\begin{cases} w_1 x_{11} + w_2 x_{12} + \ldots + w_d x_{1d} \approx y_1 \\ w_1 x_{21} + w_2 x_{22} + \ldots + w_d x_{2d} \approx y_2 \\ \ldots + \ldots + \ldots + \ldots \approx \ldots \\ w_1 x_{m1} + w_2 x_{m2} + \ldots + w_d x_{md} \approx y_m \end{cases} \tag{5}$$

Obviously, EAs can be employed to solve this kind of problems. The objective function can be defined as follow:

$$\min(f(W)) = \sqrt{\sum_{i=1}^{m} \sum_{j=1}^{d} (w_j \cdot x_{ij} - y_i)^2} \tag{6}$$

This is a continuous numerical optimization problem. There is a lot of methods to ensure lower boundary and upper boundary of $w_i, i = 1, 2, \ldots, d$.

In fact, this model is feasible when the following equations are satisfied. Because we can predict label of x_i belong to y_i when $y_i + \delta \le w_1 x_{i1} + w_2 x_{i2} + \ldots + w_d x_{id} < y_i + \delta$.

$$\begin{cases} y_1 + \delta \le w_1 x_{11} + w_2 x_{12} + \ldots + w_d x_{1d} < y_1 + \delta \\ y_2 + \delta \le w_1 x_{21} + w_2 x_{22} + \ldots + w_d x_{2d} < y_2 + \delta \\ \ldots \le + \ldots + \ldots + \ldots < \ldots \\ y_m + \delta \le w_1 x_{m1} + w_2 x_{m2} + \ldots + w_d x_{md} < y_m + \delta \end{cases} \tag{7}$$

In this paper, we estimate the lower boundary and upper boundary by following equations:

$$\pm \sigma \frac{\sum_{i=1}^{N} y_i}{\sum_{i=1}^{N} \sum_{j=1}^{d} x_{ij}} \tag{8}$$

4   Experiments and Comparisons

4.1   Data Sets Used in Classification

The classification data set is taken from the Machine learning repository [8]. The number of cluster k is 3, the objects of each data set n is 150 and the number of numeric attributes of each data set p is 4.

4.2   Setting for BSO

BSO was employed to find W to minimize $\sqrt{\sum_{i=1}^{m}(\sum_{j=1}^{d} w_j \cdot x_{ij} - y_i)^2}$ on each data.

For the BSO, run time is set to 20. The maximum number of iterations is set up to 2000. The other settings of BSO are in Table 1 which is applied in all the comparison experiments.

Table 1. Description of data

n	m	P_{5a}	P_{6b}	P_{6biii}	P_{6c}	Max_iteration
100	3	0.2	0.8	0.4	0.5	2000

4.3   Experimental Results and Analysis

The results of the experiment are listed as the following:

Table 2. Classification accuracy on iris and thyroid data set

Classification accuracy	Iris			
	Min	Max	Mean	Std
Test data	80%	96.67%	93.25%	0.0680

"min" and "max" means the minimum and maximum value of classification accuracy, mean and std denote the average and standard deviation of the corresponding classification accuracy obtained in 20 runs.

We use data collection to 70% of its solution to do training, and the remaining 30% of the data set do data classification test. From Table 2, we can see that the classification algorithm has a good performance in the experiment using data set iris.

5   Conclusion

Data classification is a classical problem in the field of machine learning and data mining research. Many researchers have proposed many great methods solving unsupervised and supervised classification problems. However, falling into local optimal solutions can easily occurred on traditional methods. Thus, we introduce EA to improve the performance of supervised classification. After a series of experiments, the data indicates that the EA make BSO play a significant role in optimization. It enables the BSO can generate more efficient, more acceptable results.

References

1. MacQueen, J.: Some methods for classification and analysis of multivariate observations. In: Proceedings of 5th Berkeley Symposium on Mathematical Statistics and Probability, vol. 1, pp. 281–297 (1967)
2. Bezdek, J.C., Ehrlich, R., Full, W.: FCM: the fuzzy C-means clustering algorithm. Comput. Geosci. **10**, 191–203 (1984)
3. Ma, A.L., Zhong, Y.F., Zhang, L.P.: Adaptive multiobjective memetic fuzzy clustering algorithm for remote sensing imagery. IEEE Trans. Geosci. Remote Sens. **53**, 4202–4217 (2015)
4. Mukhopadhyay, A., Maulik, U., Bandyopadhyay, S.: A survey of multiobjective evolutionary clustering. ACM Comput. Surv. **47**, 46 (2015)
5. Tvrdik, J., Krivy, I.: Hybrid differential evolution algorithm for optimal clustering. Comput. Geosci. **35**, 502–512 (2015)
6. Shi, Y.: Brain storm optimization algorithm. In: Tan, Y., Shi, Y., Chai, Y., Wang, G. (eds.) ICSI 2011. LNCS, vol. 6728, pp. 303–309. Springer, Heidelberg (2011). doi:10.1007/978-3-642-21515-5_36
7. Xue, Y., Zhuang, Y., Meng, X., Zhang, Y.Y.: Self-adaptive learning based ensemble algorithm for solving matrix eigenvalues. J. Comput. Res. Dev. **50**, 1435–1443 (2013)
8. Frank, A., Asuncion, A.: UCI machine learning repository (2010)

Stacked Auto-Encoders for Feature Extraction with Neural Networks

Shuanglong Liu[1], Chao Zhang[2], and Jinwen Ma[1(✉)]

[1] Department of Information Science, School of Mathematical Sciences and LMAM,
Peking University, Beijing 100871, China
jwma@math.pku.edu.cn

[2] Academy for Advanced Interdisciplinary Studies,
Peking University, Beijing 100871, China

Abstract. Auto-encoder plays an important role in the feature extraction of deep learning architecture. In this paper, we present several variants of stacked auto-encoders for feature extracting with neural networks. In fact, these stacked auto-encoders can serve as certain biologically plausible filters to extract effective features as the input to a particular neural network with a learning task. The experimental results on the real datasets demonstrate that the convolutional auto-encoders can help a supervised neural network to get the best performance of classification or recognition.

Keywords: Auto-encoder · Feature extraction · Deep learning · Neural networks · Classification

1 Introduction

Feature extracting or learning, especially in a deep learning architecture, has been playing an important role in pattern recognition and machine learning. The aim of unsupervised feature learning is to detect and remove input redundancies, to extract generally useful features from unlabelled data, and to preserve only essential aspects of the data in robust and discriminative representations [1].

In the neural network architectures, unsupervised layers could be stacked to build deep hierarchies on top of each other [2]. For all layers in the hierarchy system, input layer activations feeds the next which are fed to the first layer. Deep architectures with being fine-tuned later by back-propagation can be trained to become classifiers in an unsupervised layer-wise fashion [3]. Most methods are based on the encoder-decoder paradigm [4] to avoid local minima and increase the networks performance stability in unsupervised initializations [5]. The input is first transformed into a typically lower-dimensional space expressed as encoder, and then expanded to reproduce the initial data expressed as decoder. Once a layer is trained, its code is fed to the next, to better model highly non-linear dependencies in the input. The focus of this approach is to build high-level, class-specific feature detectors.

© Springer Nature Singapore Pte Ltd. 2016
M. Gong et al. (Eds.): BIC-TA 2016, Part I, CCIS 681, pp. 377–384, 2016.
DOI: 10.1007/978-981-10-3611-8_31

Much recent peering works in machine learning have focused on auto-encoders which have taken center stage again in the deep architecture approach [5–10]. Auto-encoders are simple learning circuits which aim to transform inputs into outputs with the least possible amount of distortion, which are stacked and trained bottom up in an unsupervised fashion, followed by a supervised learning phase to train the top layer and fine-tune the entire architecture [11]. In a great many challenging classification and regression problems, these deep architectures have been shown to lead to state-of-the-art results. In this paper, we present the possible variants of stacked auto-encoders in the deep learning architecture and compare their performances of feature learning on the deep learning system.

The rest of this paper is organized as follows. In Sect. 2, we describe three kinds of auto-encoders which can be stacked together for feature learning. Section 3 contains the comparative experiments of deep learning systems with different stacked auto encoders. Finally we conclude briefly in Sect. 4.

2 Auto-Encoders and Their Stacked Deep Hierarchy

2.1 Basic Auto-Encoder

An auto-encoder neural network [12] is essentially a supervised learning architecture of three forward layers that utilizes the back-propagation learning algorithm, setting the target values to be equal to the inputs. In fact, the auto-encoder takes an input $x \in R^d$ and first maps it to the latent representation $h \in R^d$ using a deterministic function of the type $h = f_\theta = \sigma_f(Wx + b)$ with parameters $\theta = \{W, b\}$ and $\sigma(z) = 1/(1 + exp(-z))$ which is the logistic sigmoid function. This representation or code is then used to reconstruct the input by a reverse mapping of g: $x' = g_{\theta'}(h) = \sigma_g(W'h + b')$ with $\theta' = \{W', b'\}$. The two sets of parameters are usually constrained to be of the form $W' = WT$, using the same weights for encoding the input and decoding the latent representation. Each training pattern x_i is then mapped onto its code h_i and its reconstruction x_i'. The parameters are optimized by minimizing an appropriate loss function as follows:

$$J_{AE+wd}(\theta) = \sum_{x \in R^d} L(x, g(f(x))) + \lambda \sum_{i,j} W_{i,j}^2. \tag{1}$$

2.2 Sparse Auto-Encoder (SAE)

The basic auto-encoders learn the identity mapping without any additional constraints. This problem can be circumvented by using a probabilistic RBM approach, or sparse coding, or denoising auto-encoders trying to reconstruct noisy inputs [13]. By imposing certain sparsity on the hidden units during the training, a Sparse Auto-Encoder (SAE) can learn useful structures in the input data which allows sparse representations of inputs. These are useful on the pretraining for classification tasks. The sparsity (Eq. 2) can be achieved by adding an additional relative entropy function $KL(\rho||\hat{\rho}_j)$ in the loss function during the training, or by manually zeroing all but the few strongest hidden unit activations.

$$J_{AE+wd+sp}(\theta) = \sum_{x \in R^d} L(x, g(f(x))) + \lambda \sum_{i,j} W_{i,j}^2 + \beta \sum_j KL(\rho||\hat{\rho}_j). \quad (2)$$

2.3 Convolutional Auto-Encoder (CAE)

For supervised image classification, Convolutional Neural Networks (CNNs) are among the most successful models and set the state-of-the-art result in many benchmarks [14]. The network architecture of Convolutional Auto-Encoder (CAE) consists of three basic building blocks which are respectively the convolutional layer, the max-pooling layer and the classification layer [14] to be stacked and composed as needed. CNNs are hierarchical models whose convolutional layers alternate with subsampling layers, reminiscent of simple and complex cells in the primary visual cortex [15].

CAE is a discriminative graphical model that takes feature maps as input and attempts to reconstruct them via minimizing an appropriate loss function over the training samples. Ignoring the 2D image structure in fully connected AEs could not only result in difficulty in dealing with realistically sized inputs, but also introduce redundancy in the parameters and force each feature to be global. However, CAEs differs from conventional AEs as their weights are shared among all locations in the input, preserving spatial locality. The detailed process, please refer to [1]. As for standard networks, the weights are then updated using stochastic gradient descent, while the back-propagation algorithm is applied to compute the gradient of the loss function.

For hierarchical networks in general and CNNs in particular, the input feature maps are convolved with the input kernels in the convolution layer and then pass through the max-pooling layer. The max-pooling layer is often introduced to obtain translation-invariant representations. Max-pooling down-samples the latent representation by a constant factor, usually taking the maximum value over non overlapping sub-regions. Especially over the hidden representation, Sparsity CAE (SCAE) can erase all non-maximal values in non overlapping subregions, which forces the feature detectors to become more broadly applicable and avoid trivial solutions. During the reconstruction phase, such a sparse latent code decreases the average number of filters contributing to the decoding of each pixel, forcing filters to be more general.

2.4 Stacked Deep Hierarchy

Several auto-encoders can be stacked (just as shown in Fig. 1) to form a deep hierarchy [13]. Each layer receives its input from the latent representation of the layer below. As for deep networks, unsupervised pre-training can be done in greedy, layer-wise, bottom-up fashion, and the top level activations can be used as feature vectors for SVMs or other classifiers. Afterwards the weights of the entire architecture can be trained and fine-tuned using back-propagation.

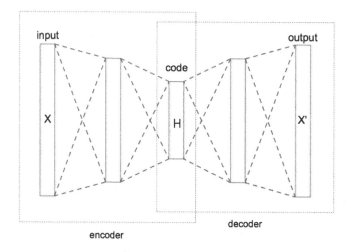

Fig. 1. Stacked auto-encoder structure

3   Experimental Results and Analysis

In this section, we conduct the experiments of deep learning systems with different stacked auto encoders on MNIST dataset to compare their performances of feature learning on the classification. Our experiments are implemented in the Linux system (Ubuntu 14.04.3) with gpu (device 0: GRID K520), and 16.00 GB RAM with running Python3.5 source codes.

3.1   Feature Extraction Using Stacked Auto-Encoders

We begin by visually inspecting the filters of various AEs, trained in various setups on MNIST dataset and vehicle images which are courtesy of German Aerospace Center (DLR). As shown in Figs. 2 and 3, we compare the source image with 5 different representations using the stacked CAEs of the same topology, but trained in different epochs. The structure of CAE is convolution layer (32 kernel of 3×3) → MaxPool (2×2) → Dense (10) → DePool (2×2) → DeConv layer (32 kernel of 3×3). The weights of the Convolution and Deconvolution layers are tied; MaxPool and DePool shares the activated neurons. The CAE without any additional constraints learns trivial solutions. Interesting and biologically plausible filters only emerge once the CAE is trained with a max-pooling layer which makes the filters become more localized. For this particular example, max-pooling yields the visually nicest filters which is an elegant way of enforcing a sparse code required to deal with the overcomplete representations of convolutional architectures.

3.2   Stacked Auto-Encoders in the Deep Learning System

We further use the stacked CAEs in the deep learning system for feature extraction with a MLP/CNN as the classifier. We investigate the benefits of

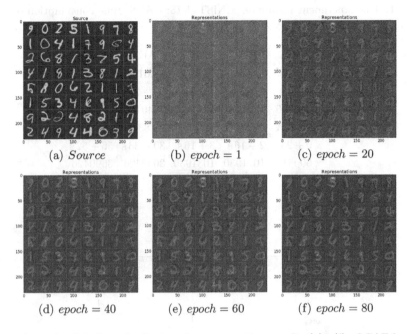

Fig. 2. A randomly selected subset and representation results (a)~(f) of CAE learned on MNIST dataset

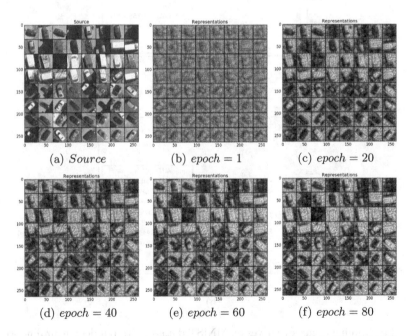

Fig. 3. A randomly selected subset and representation results (a)~(f) of CAE learned on CARs dataset.

Table 1. The experiment results on MNIST data: CARS, time consumption of each epoch, the total number of network parameters.

MNIST	Nan	AE	SAE	CAE	SCAE
MLP	98.53%	97.09%	97.69%	98.61%	98.66%
	$0+1\,\mathrm{s}$	$2+2\,\mathrm{s}$	$4+3\,\mathrm{s}$	$39+20\,\mathrm{s}$	$56+38\,\mathrm{s}$
	669706	1227146	1227146	3740106	3740106
CNN	99.26%	98.05%	97.87%	98.83%	98.79%
	$0+24\,\mathrm{s}$	$2+16\,\mathrm{s}$	$3+16\,\mathrm{s}$	$39+33\,\mathrm{s}$	$56+52\,\mathrm{s}$
	600810	1031930	1031930	3690426	3690426

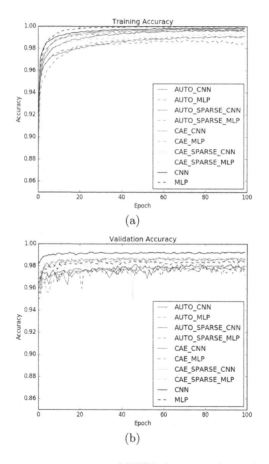

Fig. 4. (a) Training accuracy curves on MNIST dataset with ten deep neural networks algorithms; (b) validation accuracy curves on MNIST dataset with ten deep neural networks algorithms.

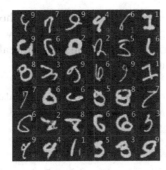

Fig. 5. Classification error digit on MNIST dataset. The top right corner digit is the correct class label; the lower right corner digit is the result of classification error.

unsupervised pre-training through comparisons with randomly initialized MLPs/CNNs. We begin with the well established MNIST benchmark [14] to show the effect of pre-training for the datasets. Classification results in Table 1 are based on the complete test set and the output layer has a softmax activation function with one neuron per class.

Table 1 shows the results of all the experiments which are combined different AEs and MLP/CNN, and the contents are the classification accuracy rates (CARS), the time consumption of each epoch (time consumption of auto-encoder training before "+" and time consumption of the whole neural network after "+") and the total number of neural network parameters.

From this table, we can see that (S)AE + MLP/CNN is not better than the original network on account of information loss by the basic AE. CAE and SCAE are better than the other algorithms except the basic CNN, because it uses all the pixels of the image. The time cost is proportional to the complexity of the network. Moreover, it can be seen from Fig. 4 that the convergence rates of CAE and SCAE are faster than other AEs on the training set, and their convergence behaviors are more stable. The performance improvement is so big on MNIST dataset because this classification problem is much harder and the network profits more from unsupervised pre-training. Figure 5 shows 36 samples of handwritten digits which are hard to recognize even with human eyes, not to mention machines. The top right corner digit is the correct class label, while the lower right corner digit is the result of classification error. It is shown by the experimental results that, contrary to the ordinary auto-encoders, the convolutional auto-encoders are able to learn edge detectors from natural image patches and larger stroke detectors from digit images effectively.

4 Conclusion

We have described different stacked auto-encoders and compared their performances of feature extraction in a deep learning system, which can be learned as certain biologically plausible filters for a learning task. While the convolutional auto-encoders' overcomplete hidden representation makes the learning even harder than that of standard auto-encoders, good filters emerge when we use a max-pooling layer. The experimental results show that the best performance of the deep learning system can be obtained with the stacked convolutional auto-encoders which actually establishes a tractable learning paradigm of useful higher level representations.

Acknowledgments. This work was supported by the Natural Science Foundation of China for Grant 61171138.

References

1. Masci, J., Meier, U., Cireşan, D., Schmidhuber, J.: Stacked convolutional auto-encoders for hierarchical feature extraction. In: Honkela, T., Duch, W., Girolami, M., Kaski, S. (eds.) ICANN 2011. LNCS, vol. 6791, pp. 52–59. Springer, Heidelberg (2011). doi:10.1007/978-3-642-21735-7_7
2. Fukushima, K.: Neocognitron: a self-organizing neural network for a mechanism of pattern recognition unaffected by shift in position. Biol. Cybern. **36**(4), 193–202 (1980)
3. Hinton, G.E., Osindero, S., Teh, Y.W.: A fast learning algorithm for deep belief nets. Neural Comput. **18**, 1527–1554 (2006)
4. Ranzato, M., Huang, F.J., Boureau, Y.L., LeCun, Y.: Unsupervised learning of invariant feature hierarchies with applications to object recognition. In: Proceedings of Computer Vision and Pattern Recognition Conference (2007)
5. Erhan, D., Bengio, Y., Courville, A., Manzagol, P.A., Vincent, P.: Why does unsupervised pre-training help deep learning? J. Mach. Learn. Res. **11**, 625–660 (2010)
6. Hinton, G.E., Salakhutdinov, R.R.: Reducing the dimensionality of data with neural networks. Science **313**(5786), 504 (2006)
7. Bengio, Y., LeCun, Y.: Scaling learning algorithms towards AI. In: Bottou, L., Chapelle, O., DeCoste, D., Weston, J. (eds.) Large-Scale Kernel Machines. MIT Press, Cambridge (2007)
8. Song, T., Liu, X., Zhao, Y., Zhang, X.: Spiking neural P systems with white hole neurons. IEEE Trans. Nanobiosci. (2016). doi:10.1109/TNB.2016.2598879
9. Song, T., Pan, Z., Wong, D.M., Wang, X.: Design of logic gates using spiking neural P systems with homogeneous neurons and astrocytes-like control. Inf. Sci. **372**, 380–391 (2016)
10. Wang, X., Song, T., Gong, F., Pan, Z.: On the computational power of spiking neural P systems with self-organization. Sci. Rep. **6**, 27624 (2016). doi:10.1038/srep27624
11. Baldi, P., Guyon, G., Dror, V., Lemaire, G., Taylor, D.: Autoencoders, unsupervised learning, and deep architectures. In: Guyon, I., Dror, G., Lemaire, V., Taylor, G., Silver, D. (eds.) JMLR: Workshop and Conference Proceedings (2012)
12. Bengio, Y., Lamblin, P., Popovici, D., Larochelle, H.: Greedy layer-wise training of deep networks. In: Neural Information Processing Systems, NIPS (2007)
13. Vincent, P., Larochelle, H., Bengio, Y., Manzagol, P.A.: Extracting and composing robust features with denoising autoencoders. In: Neural Information Processing Systems, NIPS (2008)
14. LeCun, Y., Bottou, L., Bengio, Y., Haffner, P.: Gradient-based learning applied to document recognition. Proc. IEEE **86**(11), 2278–2324 (1998)
15. Hubel, D.H., Wiesel, T.N.: Receptive fields and functional architecture of monkey striate cortex. J. Physiol. **195**(1), 215–243 (1968)

Fault Diagnosis of Power Systems Based on Triangular Fuzzy Spiking Neural P Systems

Chengyu Tao[1,2], Wenping Yu[1,2], Jun Wang[1,2(✉)], Hong Peng[3], Ke Chen[1,2], and Jun Ming[1,2]

[1] Sichuan Province Key Laboratory of Power Electronics Energy-saving Technologies and Equipment, Chengdu 610039, People's Republic of China
745257101@qq.com
[2] School of Electrical Engineering and Electronic Information, Xihua University, Chengdu 610039, People's Republic of China
[3] School of Computer and Software Engineering, Xihua University, Chengdu 610039, People's Republic of China

Abstract. Based on triangular fuzzy spiking neural P systems (TFSNP systems, in short), a fault diagnosis method for power system is presented in this paper. First, triangular fuzzy number (TFN) is integrated into spiking neural P systems (SNP systems, in short) to propose the TFSNP systems. Afterward, modeling and fuzzy reasoning methods based on TFSNP systems are developed. Finally, TFSNP systems are used for fault diagnosis in power system. A fault diagnosis example for ring network of the voltage level with 220 kV is used to demonstrate the availability and effectiveness of the proposed fault diagnosis model.

Keywords: Spiking neural P systems · Triangular fuzzy spiking neural P systems · Power systems · Fault diagnosis

1 Introduction

When a fault occurs in power systems, protective relays operate such that circuit breakers to isolate cause normal area and fault section and reduce the loss caused by the fault. Literatures [1–3] have discussed the fault diagnosis of power transmission networks with 35 kV and below. However, with the gradual development of economy and society, the voltage level continuously improves and users rely more and more on the power supply. Therefore, improving the reliability and the quality of power supply becomes more and more important. Obviously, current protection of this level has been unable to satisfy this demand. For power networks of the voltage level with 220 kV and above, longitudinal differential protection can quickly remove faulty high-voltage network, so it has been widely used.

In recent years, different methods have been developed for the fault diagnosis of power systems, for example, expert system (ES) [4], fuzzy logic (FL) [5], artificial neural network (ANN) [6], Petri nets (PN) [3], optimization algorithm [7] and

© Springer Nature Singapore Pte Ltd. 2016
M. Gong et al. (Eds.): BIC-TA 2016, Part I, CCIS 681, pp. 385–398, 2016.
DOI: 10.1007/978-981-10-3611-8_32

so on. However, each method has its own disadvantages: expert system is difficult to deal with the problem of multiple faults; artificial neural network is suitable for the fault diagnosis of small and medium power systems, but has a poor ability to get new data and is difficult to obtain the training samples; optimization algorithm has the characteristics of slow diagnosis and can not accurately diagnose in the case of inaccurate information and the loss of information.

Membrane computing is a class of distributed parallel computing models inspired by the structure and functioning of living cells as well as interaction of living cells in tissues and organs [8,9]. In past years, a various of P systems and variants have been proposed [10–15]. Spiking neural P system (SNP systems, in short) is one of main forms of P system. A SN P system can be viewed as a directed graph whose arcs represent the synaptic connections among the neurons [16–18]. In recent years, integrated different fuzzy logics into SNP systems, a class of extended SNP systems are developed, called the fuzzy spiking neural P system (FSNP systems, in short) [19–22]. There are a lot of uncertain and incomplete information in the fault diagnosis problem of differential protection technology. In order to deal with the uncertainty information of fault diagnosis, a triangular fuzzy spiking neural P system (TFSNP systems, in short) and the corresponding fault diagnosis model is proposed to deal with fault diagnosis of high voltage network in this paper.

The rest of paper is organized as follows. Section 2 describes the definition, the method of model-building and fuzzy reasoning algorithm based on triangular fuzzy spiking neural P system. In Sect. 3, we firstly state considerate problem, and then give examples and analysis of fault diagnosis. Finally, conclusions are drawn in Sect. 4.

2   Triangular Fuzzy Spiking Neural P Systems

In this section, the proposed triangular fuzzy spiking neural P systems (TFSNP Systems, in short), which are a kind variant of original SNP Systems, will be presented and used to deal with fault diagnosis of power systems in detail.

2.1   Definitions

Definition 1. *A TFSNP system of degree $m \geq 1$ is the following construct*

$$\Pi = (A, \sigma_1, \ldots, \sigma_m, syn, I, O) \tag{1}$$

where

(1) $A = \{a\}$ is a singleton alphabet (the object a is called the spike);
(2) $\sigma_1, \ldots, \sigma_m$ are neurons of the form $\sigma_i = (\alpha_i, \beta_i, r_i)$, $1 \leq i \leq m$, where
  (a) σ_i is a triangular fuzzy number representing the potential value of spikes contained in neuron σ_i.
  (b) β_i is a real number in [0, 1] corresponding to neuron σ_i.

(c) r_i represents a firing (spiking) rule associated with neuron σ_i, of the form $a^\alpha \rightarrow a^a$ or $a^\alpha \rightarrow a^{a'}$, where α and α' are two triangular fuzzy numbers.

(3) $syn \subseteq \{1,\ 2,\ \dots,\ m\} \times \{1,\ 2,\ \dots,\ m\}$ denotes the synapse connections between the neurons, and for all $1 \leq i \leq m$, $(i,i) \notin syn$;

(4) $I, O \subset \{1,\ 2,\ \dots,\ m\}$ represent the sets of input neurons and output neurons, respectively.

Different from original SNP systems, the pulse value of each neuron in the TFSNP system is represented by a triangular fuzzy number. The triangular fuzzy number (TFN) is usually expressed by a triple $A = (a_1, a_2, a_3)$. Figure 1 shows a triangular fuzzy number, where a_1, a_2 and a_3 are real number such that $0 < a_1 \leq a_2 \leq a_3$. The membership function $\mu_A(x)$ of the triangular fuzzy number is defined as follows.

$$\mu_A(x) = \begin{cases} 0, & x < a_1 \\ \frac{x-a_1}{a_2-a_1}, & a_1 \leq x \leq a_2 \\ \frac{x-a_3}{a_2-a_3}, & a_2 \leq x \leq a_3 \\ 0, & x > a_3 \end{cases} \tag{2}$$

where a_1, a_3 are the minimum and the maximum values of triangular fuzzy number A respectively, while a_2 represents the middle value.

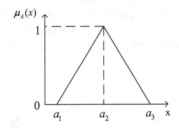

Fig. 1. A triangular fuzzy number

Definition 2. *Let A and B be two triangular fuzzy numbers, $A = (a_1, a_2, a_3)$ and $B = (b_1, b_2, b_3)$ and λ is a real number. Then five kinds of operations are defined as follows [23]:*

(1) $\lambda A = \lambda(a_1, a_2, a_3) = (\lambda a_1, \lambda a_2, \lambda a_3)$

(2) $A \oslash B = (a_1, a_2, a_3) \oslash (b_1, b_2, b_3) = (min(a_1, b_1), min(a_2, b_2), min(a_3, b_3))$

(3) $A \oslash B = (a_1, a_2, a_3) \oslash (b_1, b_2, b_3) = (max(a_1, b_1), max(a_2, b_2), max(a_3, b_3))$

In TFSNP systems, neurons are divided into proposition neurons and rule neurons. Proposition neurons are a kind of neurons, which correspond to the propositions in fuzzy knowledge base. Figure 2(a) shows a proposition neuron. There exist two class of rule neurons: "and"-type rule neurons and "or"-type rule neurons, which are labeled by $\oslash$ and $\oslash$ respectively. Figure 2(b) and (c) show an "and"-type rule neuron and an "or"-type rule neuron, respectively.

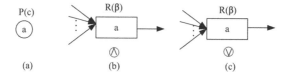

Fig. 2. (a) proposition neuron; (b) "and"-type rule neuron, and (c) "or"-type rule neuron.

2.2   Modeling Fuzzy Production Rules and Fuzzy Reasoning Based on TFSNP Systems

We use TFSNP systems to model the fuzzy production rules and consider the following fuzzy production rules of two types:

Type 1: IF p_1 AND p_2 AND ... AND p_{k-1} THEN p_k $(CF = \beta)$;
Type 2: IF p_1 OR p_2 OR ... OR p_{k-1} THEN p_k $(CF = \beta)$.

where p_1, p_2, ..., p_{k-1}, p_k are k propositions, and β is a real number in $[0, 1]$ representing the confidence factor (CF) of the fuzzy production rule.

Fuzzy production rule of type 1 can be represented by a TFSNP system, shown in Fig. 3(a). Initially, we provides a spike for each proposition neuron $\sigma_i(i = 1, 2, ..., k-1)$, with values $\sigma_1, \sigma_2, \sigma_3, ..., \sigma_{k-1}$ respectively. Secondly, the k-1 spikes of the initial proposition neurons are received by $\oslash$-type rule neuron σ_{k+1}. Then, the rule neuron fires and emits a spike into the successive proposition neuron σ_k. Finally, σ_k receives the spike with value $(\alpha_1 \oslash \cdots \oslash \alpha_k) \otimes \beta$.

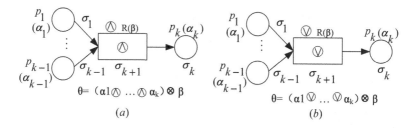

Fig. 3. (a) Fuzzy production rule of type 1; (b) Fuzzy production rule of type 2.

Fuzzy production rule of type 2 can be represented by a TFSNP system, shown in Fig. 3(b). Initially, we provides a spiking for each proposition neuron $\sigma_i(i = 1, 2, ..., k-1)$, with values $\sigma_1, \sigma_2, \sigma_3, ..., \sigma_{k-1}$ respectively. Secondly, the $k-1$ spikes of the initial proposition neuron are received by $\ovee$-type rule neuron σ_{k+1}. Then, the rule neuron fires and emits a spike into successive proposition neuron σ_k. Finally, σ_k receives the spike with value $(\alpha_1 \ovee \cdots \ovee \alpha_k) \otimes \beta$.

Usually, fuzzy truth values of propositions in fuzzy production rules can be expressed by linguistic values. The linguistic values and the corresponding triangular fuzzy numbers are provided in Table 1.

Table 1. Linguistic values and corresponding triangular fuzzy numbers.

Linguistic variables	Fuzzy numbers
Extremely poor (EP) s0	(0, 0, 0)
Very Very poor (VVP) s1	(0, 0, 0.125)
Very poor (VP) s2	(0, 0.125, 0.25)
Poor (P) s3	(0.125, 0.25, 0.375)
Slightly poor (SP) s4	(0.25, 0.375, 0.5)
Fair (F) s5	(0.375, 0.5, 0.625)
Slightly good (SG) s6	(0.5, 0.625, 0.75)
Good (G) s7	(0.625, 0.75, 0.875)
Very good (VG) s8	(0.75, 0.875, 1)
Very Very good (VVG) s9	(0.875, 1, 1)
Extremely good (EG) s10	(1, 1, 1)

In the following, fuzzy reasoning algorithm based on TFSNP systems will be discussed. For clarity, the following symbols are firstly introduced.

(1) $\alpha = (\alpha_1, \alpha_2, \ldots \alpha_s)^T$ is the fuzzy value vector of s proposition neurons, where α_i is a triangular fuzzy number representing the spike value contained in ith proposition neuron.

(2) $\delta = (\delta_1, \delta_2, \ldots \delta_t)^T$ is the fuzzy value vector of t rule neurons, where δ_j is a triangular fuzzy number representing the spike value contained in jth rule neuron.

(3) $\beta = diag(\beta_1, \beta_2, \ldots \beta_t)$ is a diagonal matrix, where β_j is a real number representing the confidence factor of the jth fuzzy production rule.

(4) $D_1 = (d_{ij})_{s \times t}$ is a two-dimensional matrix representing the directed connections from proposition neurons to $\oslash$-type rule neurons. If proposition neuron δ_i has a synaptic connection with $\oslash$-type rule neuron δ_j, $d_{ij} = 1$; otherwise, $d_{ij} = 0$.

(5) $D_2 = (d_{ij})_{s \times t}$ is a two-dimensional matrix representing the directed connections from proposition neuron to $\oslash$-type rule neuron. If proposition neuron δ_i has a synaptic connection with $\oslash$-type rule neuron δ_j, $d_{ij} = 1$; otherwise, $d_{ij} = 0$.

(6) $E = (e_{ij})_{t \times s}$ is a two-dimensional matrix representing the directed connections from rule neurons to proposition neurons. If rule neuron δ_j has a synaptic connection with proposition neuron δ_i, $e_{ij} = 1$; otherwise, $e_{ij} = 0$.

At the same time, the following three kinds of operations is introduced.

(1) $\beta \odot \delta = (\beta_1 \otimes \delta_1, \beta_2 \otimes \delta_2, \ldots, \beta_t \otimes \delta_t)^T$. Similarly, $D \odot \alpha = (d_1, d_2, \ldots, d_t)^T$, where $d_j = d_{1j}\alpha_1 \oplus d_{2j}\alpha_2 \oplus \cdots \oplus d_{sj}\alpha_s, j = 1, 2, \ldots, t$.

(2) $D^T \odot \alpha = (d_1, d_2, \dots, d_t)^T$, where $d_j = d_{1j}\alpha_1 \oslash d_{2j}\alpha_2 \oslash \cdots \oslash d_{sj}\alpha_s$, $j = 1, 2, \dots, t$.

(3) $E^T \circledast \delta = (e_1, e_2, \dots, e_t)^T$, where $e_j = e_{1j}\alpha_1 \oslash e_{2j}\alpha_2 \oslash \cdots \oslash e_{sj}\alpha_s$, $i = 1, 2, \dots, t$.

The main steps of the fuzzy reasoning algorithm based on TFSNP system can be described as follows. Note that the inputs are the triangular fuzzy numbers of propositions associated with the input proposition neurons, and reasoning output is the fuzzy value associated with the output proposition neuron.

(1) Set $g = 0$
(2) Assign C, D_1, D_2, E and the termination condition. Initial values of α and δ_g are separately set to be $\alpha_g = (\alpha_{1g}, \alpha_{2g}, \dots, \alpha_{sg})$ and $\delta_g = (\delta_{1g}, \delta_{2g}, \dots, \delta_{tg})$.
(3) $g = g + 1$.
(4) Evaluate firing states of input neurons and proposition neurons. If the states are satisfied, proposition neurons fire and simultaneously each emit a spike.
(5) Compute $\delta_g = (D_1^T \odot \alpha_{g-1}) \oplus (D_2^T \circledast \alpha_{g-1})$.
(6) If δ_g satisfies the termination condition, the system halts and the reasoning result is in output neuron; otherwise, go to step (7).
(7) Evaluate firing condition of each rule neuron. If the condition is satisfied, rule neuron fires and simultaneously emits a spike to its subsequent proposition neuron.
(8) Compute $\alpha_g = E^T \circledast (c \odot \delta_g)$, and go to step (3).

3 Fault Diagnosis of Power Systems Based on TFSNP Systems

3.1 Problem Description

Generally speaking, fault diagnosis has five steps: fault detection, fault section identification, fault type evaluation, fault isolation and recovery. Especially, fault section identification is extremely important in these steps. The data of relays and circuit breakers which are read from supervisor-control and data-acquisition (SCADA) system can be used to diagnose the fault of lines, buses and transformers in power systems. Usually, current protection is used to protect the fault area. However, the current protection is not fast to remove all faults in the faulty area and can only be used in power system below 35 kV. The faults of extra-high-voltage transmission line with 220 kV and above have to be quickly removed. Hence, current protection is no longer adapted to the power systems of the 220 kV and above. Therefore, longitudinal differential protection can quickly remove the high voltage fault. In the meantime, the relays of longitudinal differential protection contain the main protection relays and the backup protection relays. In other words, if the longitudinal differential protection is not operated, backup protection will operate around the fault area. Figure 4 shows a schematic of a ring network with sections and protection relays.

The power system in Guangdong Province is composed of 25 substations, 25 substations, 57 transformers, and 73 transmission lines with a voltage level

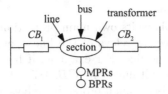

Fig. 4. Schematic illustration of a ring network with sections and a protection relays

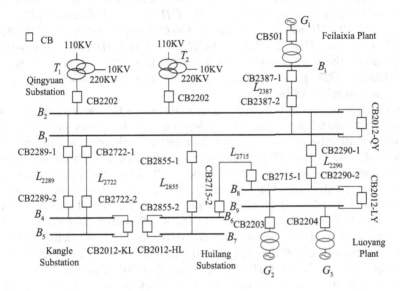

Fig. 5. Schematic illustration of ring network in power system

of 500 kV, and 511 substations, 511 transformers and 594 transmission lines with voltage level of 220 kV. And the operation rules of protective relays and circuit breakers are illustrated in [7,27,28]. For simply, some of the symbols are described as follows. A single bus, double bus, transformer, line, circuit breaker and generator are expressed by A, B, T, L, CB and G respectively, and main protection and backup protection are respectively represented by m and s. Figure 5 include circuit breakers $CB2201, CB2202, CB501, CB2387 - 1, CB2387 - 2, CB2012 - QY, CB2289 - 1, CB2289 - 2, CB2722 - 1, CB2722 - 2, CB2012 - KL, CB2855 - 1, CB2855 - 2, CB2012 - HL, CB2715 - 1, CB2715 - 2, CB2290 - 1, CB2290 - 2, CB2012 - LY$, buses $B_1, B_2, B_3, B_4, B_5, B_6, B_7, B_8, B_9$, lines $L_{2387}, L_{2289}, L_{2722}, L_{2855}, L_{2715}, L_{2715}, L_{2290}$, generators G_1, G_2, G_3 and transformers T_1, T_2.

In the following, we describe operational rules of the protection relays for lines, buses and transformers.

(1) Protection relays of line

Both ends of the line have its own main protection and backup protection. When the main protective relays of the line operate, the circuit breakers trip at both ends of the line. For example, if line L_{2387} faults, main protection relay of L_{2387} will make the $CB2387 - 1$ and $CB2387 - 2$ to trip simultaneously. Likewise, if main protective relays of the line fail to operate, its backup relays will operate and circuit breakers related to L_{2387} will trip. Similarly, if $CB2387 - 1$ trips and $CB2387 - 2$ fails to operate, the relay connected to B_3 will make $CB2012 - QY$, $CB2855 - 1$, $CB2202$, $CB2722 - 1$, $CB2722 - 2$, $CB2855 - 2$ trip. Also, if the $CB2387 - 2$ trips and $CB2387 - 1$ fails to operate, $CB501$ will trip. If $CB2387 - 1$ and $CB2387 - 2$ are both not operating, the relay connected to B_3 will make $CB2012 - QY$, $CB2855 - 1$, $CB2202$, $CB2722 - 1$, $CB2722 - 2$, $CB2855 - 2$ and $CB501$ trip.

(2) Protection relays of bus

Both ends of the bus have its own main protection and backup protection. Differential protection of bus depending on simultaneous operation of large/small differential protection is related to the connection and numbers of bus. Large differential protection is used to distinguish whether the fault is internal or external, while small differential protection is used to select faulted bus [24]. Normally, if B_8 faults, large differential protection is unbalanced at the area of B_8 and B_9. Small differential protection of B_8 is not balanced while small differential protection of B_9 is balanced. Therefore, the switches connected to B_8 trip, including bus tie switch, namely, $CB2715 - 1$, $CB2290 - 2$, $CB2012 - LY$, $CB2203$. Abnormally, when B_8 faults, $CB2012 - LY$ and $CB2203$ trip, while $CB2715 - 1$ and $CB2290 - 2$ are not operated. Thus, backup protection of bus makes $CB2290 - 1$ to trip. When B_8 faults, $CB2012 - LY$, $CB2203$ and $CB2290 - 2$ trip, while $CB2715 - 1$ is not operated. Hence, backup protection of bus makes $CB2715 - 2$ to trip.

(3) Protection relays of transformer

As the branch connected to the transformer is not fully displayed, the protection of the transformer in this paper is not introduced in detail. On the whole, operation of the differential protection of the transformer is roughly the same to that of the line and the bus.

In this paper, TFSNP systems are used to diagnose the fault of bus, line and transformer in the ring network when the protective relays and circuit breakers detect incomplete and uncertain signals. Main steps of fault diagnosis are described as follows. First of all, we read the operated information from the SCADA system. Secondly, the possible fault components are judged. Thirdly, fault diagnosis models are established for the most likely faulted position. Fourthly, fuzzy reasoning algorithm is used to calculate confidence level. Finally, faulted position is found by calculating confidence level.

3.2 Setting

Because the longitudinal differential protection can not be used as the backup protection of the adjacent elements (except for longitudinal differential protection of transformer). For example, the longitudinal differential protection of the line can not be used as backup protection for the line. Assume that the longitudinal differential protection of a device can not be used as the backup protection of the device. For example, backup protection of the faulted line is realized by the main protection of the bus. According to [25, 26], we use such a result that the average correct operating rate of lines, bus, transformers and circuit breakers with 220 kV and above are respectively 0.98902, 0.85128, 0.74855 and 0.98292 from 1999 to 2003. In this paper, data obtained from differential protection of the lines, bus, transformer and circuit breaker with 220 kV and above are used to ensure confidence levels of operated protection devices [2].

As stated above, the confidence levels of the operated and not operated circuit breakers as well as protective relay shown in Tables 2 and 3 are obtained from the reference [2]. There is only the main protection in differential protection of line and bus.

Table 2. Confidence value of the operated protective devices.

	Main		First backup		Second backup	
	Relay	CB	Relay	CB	Relay	CB
L	EG(0.98902)	EG(0.98902)	–	–	–	–
B	VG(0.85128)	EG(0.98902)	–	–	–	–
T	VG(0.85128)	EG(0.98902)	–	–	–	–

Table 3. Confidence value of the not operated protective devices.

	Main		First backup		Second backup	
	Relay	CB	Relay	CB	Relay	CB
L	SP(0.2)	SP(0.2)	–	–	–	–
B	F(0.4)	SP(0.2)	–	–	–	–
T	F(0.4)	SP(0.2)	–	–	–	–

According to the hypothesis in this paper, longitudinal differential protection for B, L, T are divided into two types. The fault fuzzy production rule set for B, L, T contains two rules, in which the meaning for each proposition is provided in Table 4.

R_1 ($c1 = 1$): (p1 operate) $\oslash$ (all or partial CB1 trips), B, L, T fails.
R_2 ($c2 = 0.875$): (p2 operate) $\oslash$ (CB2 trips), B, L, T fails.

Table 4. Meaning of each proposition in rule set of B, L, T.

P1	Main of B, L, T	CB1	CBs related to P1
P2	Backup protection of B, L, T	CB2	CBs related to P2

3.3   Case Studies

Two cases are proposed to verify the availability and effectiveness of the method presented in this paper. According to the experience, if confidence level α satisfies the condition $\alpha \geq (0.625, 0.75, 0.875)$, the section is faulty; If confidence level α satisfies the condition $\alpha \leq (0.25, 0.375, 0.5)$, the section is not faulty; otherwise, the section may be faulty. Two case studies are discussed as follows.

(1) Case I

Complete information is acquired from SCADA system: operated relays: L_{2387m}, B_{3S}, L_{2722S}, L_{2855S}, and tripped CBs: $CB2837 - 1$, $CB2012 - QY$, $CB2855 - 1$, $CB2202$, $CB2722 - 1$, $CB2722 - 2$, $CB2855 - 2$. According to operation of the circuit breaker and relay and the basic knowledge of the power system, it can be inferred that the fault section is most likely to be L_{2387}. In the following, we apply to the method mentioned in this paper to analyze L_{2387}. Based on TFSNP system, the fault diagnosis model of line L_{2387} that consists of 28 proposition neurons and 14 rule neurons is shown in Fig. 6. The fuzzy reasoning rules are described as follows.

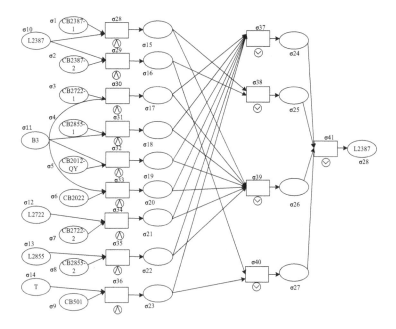

Fig. 6. The fault diagnosis model of L_{2387} based on TFSNP system

According to the alarm information of case I as well as Tables 1, 2 and 3, we can determine triangular fuzzy number α_0 and δ_0. In this case, δ is a vector of dimension 28, δ is a vector of dimension 14:

$$
\alpha_0 = \begin{pmatrix}
(0.875, 1, 1) \\
(0.25, 0.375, 0.5) \\
(0.875, 1, 1) \\
(0.875, 1, 1) \\
(0.875, 1, 1) \\
(0.875, 1, 1) \\
(0.875, 1, 1) \\
(0.875, 1, 1) \\
(0.25, 0.375, 0.5) \\
(0.875, 1, 1) \\
(0.75, 0.875, 1) \\
(0.875, 1, 1) \\
(0.875, 1, 1) \\
(0.375, 0.5, 0.625) \\
0
\end{pmatrix}, \delta_0 = \begin{pmatrix} 0 \end{pmatrix}
$$

When g = 1, we get the results

$$
\alpha_1 = \begin{pmatrix}
0 \\
(0.875, 1, 1) \\
(0.25, 0.375, 0.5) \\
(0.65625, 0.765625, 0.8575) \\
(0.65625, 0.765625, 0.8575) \\
(0.65625, 0.765625, 0.8575) \\
(0.65625, 0.765625, 0.8575) \\
(0.765625, 0.875, 0.875) \\
(0.765625, 0.875, 0.875) \\
(0.21875, 0.328125, 0.4375) \\
0
\end{pmatrix}, \delta_1 = \begin{pmatrix}
(0.875, 1, 1) \\
(0.25, 0.375, 0.5) \\
(0.75, 0.875, 1) \\
(0.75, 0.875, 1) \\
(0.75, 0.875, 1) \\
(0.75, 0.875, 1) \\
(0.875, 1, 1) \\
(0.875, 1, 1) \\
(0.25, 0.375, 0.5) \\
0
\end{pmatrix}
$$

When g = 2, we get the results

$$
\alpha_2 = \begin{pmatrix}
0 \\
(0.66992188, 0.765625, 0.765625) \\
(0.875, 1, 1) \\
(0.875, 1, 1) \\
(0.25, 0.375, 0.5) \\
(0, 0, 0) \\
0
\end{pmatrix}, \delta_2 = \begin{pmatrix}
0 \\
(0.765625, 0.875, 0.875) \\
(0.875, 1, 1) \\
(0.875, 1, 1) \\
(0.25, 0.375, 0.5) \\
(0, 0, 0) \\
0
\end{pmatrix}
$$

When g = 3, we get the results

$$\alpha_3 = \begin{pmatrix} 0 \\ (0.875, 1, 1) \end{pmatrix}, \delta_3 = \begin{pmatrix} 0 \\ (0.875, 1, 1) \end{pmatrix}$$

When g = 4, we get the results

$$\delta_4 = \begin{pmatrix} 0 \end{pmatrix}$$

Therefore, the termination condition is satisfied, the reasoning process stops. The fuzzy value of output neuron δ_{28} is (0.875, 1, 1). So, from confidence condition of fault judgement, confidence level of L_{2387} to be a fault is VVG.

(2) Case II

Incomplete information is acquired from SCADA system: operated relays are B_{3S}, L_{2722S}, L_{2855S}, and tripped CBs are $CB2837 - 1$, $CB2012 - QY$, $CB2855 - 1$, $CB2202$, $CB2722 - 1$, $CB2722 - 2$, $CB2855 - 2$. In addition, information of relay about L_{2387} is lost in this case. According to the alarm information of case II, Tables 2, 3 and 4, triangular fuzzy numbers α_0 and δ_0 can be determined as follows.

$$\alpha_0 = \begin{pmatrix} (0.875, 1, 1) \\ (0.25, 0.375, 0.5) \\ (0.875, 1, 1) \\ (0.875, 1, 1) \\ (0.875, 1, 1) \\ (0.875, 1, 1) \\ (0.875, 1, 1) \\ (0.875, 1, 1) \\ (0.25, 0.375, 0.5) \\ (0.25, 0.375, 0.5) \\ (0.75, 0.875, 1) \\ (0.875, 1, 1) \\ (0.875, 1, 1) \\ (0.375, 0.5, 0.625) \\ 0 \end{pmatrix}, \delta_0 = \begin{pmatrix} 0 \end{pmatrix}$$

According to reasoning algorithm discussed above, the final reasoning result is that the fuzzy value of output neuron δ_{28} is (0.765625, 0.875, 0.875). So, from confidence condition of fault judgement, confidence level of L_{2387} to be a fault is VG. In summary, the fault location can be accurately diagnosed based on TFSNP system, and the location of the fault can be also diagnosed correctly in the case of the missing information.

4   Conclusions

In this paper, a new fault diagnosis method based on TFSNP system is proposed, which is used to diagnose fault of the ring network. Comparing with the method proposed in [7], the proposed method not only can determine the location of the fault, but also can diagnose the confidence of the fault. Meanwhile, the method of this paper is simpler compared with the method proposed in the literature [7]. Besides, the method is able to deal with the incomplete and uncertain information which can not be processed in [7]. Moreover, for the fault diagnosis of ring network with 220 kV and above, compared with the literatures [1,2], the proposed algorithm for the longitudinal differential protection has faster speed and higher accuracy.

Acknowledgments. This work was partially supported by the National Natural Science Foundation of China (No. 61472328), Research Fund of Sichuan Science and Technology Project (No. 2015HH0057) and the key equipment project of Sichuan Provincial Economic and Information Committee (No. [2014]128), China.

References

1. Wang, T., Zhang, G.X., Zhao, J.B., He, Z.Y., Wang, J., Perez-Jimenez, M.J.: Fault diagnosis of electric power systems based on fuzzy reasoning spiking neural P systems. IEEE Trans. Power Syst. **30**, 1182–1194 (2015)
2. Tu, M., Wang, J., Peng, H., Shi, P.: Application of adaptive fuzzy spiking neural P systems in fault diagnosis of power systems. Chin. J. Electron. **23**, 87–92 (2014)
3. Sun, J., Qin, S.Y., Song, Y.H.: Fault diagnosis of electric power systems based on fuzzy Petri nets. IEEE Trans. Power Syst. **19**, 2053–2059 (2004)
4. Ferreira, V.H., Zanghi, R., Fortes, M.Z., Sotelo, G.G., Silva, R.B.M., Souza, J.C.S., Guimarães, C.H.C., Gomes, S.: A survey on intelligent system application to fault diagnosis in electric power system transmission lines. Electr. Power Syst. Res. **136**, 135–153 (2016)
5. Chin, H.C.: Fault section diagnosis of power system using fuzzy logic. IEEE Trans. Power Syst. **18**(1), 245–250 (2003)
6. Guo, X.C., Zhu, B.C., Cao, J.Y., Wu, X.: Research status and development trend of power system fault diagnosis. Autom. Electr. Power Syst. **30**, 98–103 (2006)
7. Guo, W.X., Wen, F.S., Ledwich, G., Liao, Z.W., He, X.Z., Liang, J.H.: An analytic model for fault diagnosis in power systems considering malfunctions of protective relays and circuit breakers. IEEE Trans. Power Syst. **25**, 1182–1194 (2010)
8. Păun, G.: Computing with membranes. J. Comput. Syst. Sci. **61**(1), 108–143 (2000)
9. Păun, G., Rozenberg, G., Salomaa, A.: The Oxford Handbook of Membrance Computing. Oxford University Press, New York (2010)
10. Wang, J., Shi, P., Peng, H.: Membrane computing model for IIR filter design. Inf. Sci. **329**, 164–176 (2016)
11. Zhang, X.Y., Jiang, Y., Pan, L.Q.: A variant of P machine: splicing P machine. J. Comput. Theoret. Nanosci. **10**, 1376–1384 (2013)
12. Zhang, G.X., Rong, H.N., Neri, F., Pérez-Jiménez, M.J.: An optimization spiking neural P system for approximately solving combinatorial optimization problems. Int. J. Neural Syst. **24**, 1–16 (2014)
13. Peng, H., Wang, J., Shi, P., Pérez-Jiménez, M.J., Riscos-Núñez, A.: An extended membrane system with active membrane to solve automatic fuzzy clustering problems. Int. J. Neural Syst. **26**, 1–17 (2006)
14. Peng, H., Wang, J., Pérez-Jiménez, M.J., Riscos-Núñez, A.: An unsupervised learning algorithm for membrane computing. Inf. Sci. **304**, 80–91 (2015)

15. Peng, H., Wang, J., Shi, P., Riscos-Núñez, A., Pérez-Jiménez, M.J.: An automatic clustering algorithm inspired by membrane computing. Pattern Recogn. Lett. **68**, 34–40 (2015)
16. Song, T., Pan, L.: Spiking neural P systems with request rules. Neurocomputing **193**(12), 193–200 (2016)
17. Song, T., Liu, X., Zhao, Y., Zhang, X.: Spiking neural P systems with white hole neurons. IEEE Trans. Nanobiosci. (2016). doi:10.1109/TNB.2016.2598879
18. Song, T., Pan, Z., Wong, D.M., Wang, X.: Design of logic gates using spiking neural P systems with homogeneous neurons and astrocytes-like control. Inf. Sci. **372**, 380–391 (2016)
19. Peng, H., Wang, J., Perez-Jimenez, M.J., Wang, H., Shao, J., Wang, T.: Fuzzy reasoning spiking neural P system for fault diagnosis. Inf. Sci. **235**, 106–116 (2013)
20. Wang, J., Shi, P., Peng, H., Perez-Jimenez, M.J., Wang, T.: Weighted fuzzy spiking neural P systems. IEEE Trans. Power Syst. **21**, 209–220 (2013)
21. Wang, J., Peng, H., Tu, M., Pérez-Jiménez, M.J., Shi, P.: A fault diagnosis method of power systems based on an improved adaptive fuzzy spiking neural P systems and PSO algorithms. Chin. J. Electron. **25**, 320–327 (2016)
22. Wang, J., Peng, H.: Adaptive fuzzy spiking neural P systems for fuzzy inference and learning. Int. J. Comput. Math. **90**(4), 857–868 (2013)
23. Wei, G.W., Zhao, X.F., Lin, R., Wang, H.J.: Generalized triangular fuzzy correlated averaging operator and their application to multiple attribute decision making. Appl. Math. Model. **36**, 2975–2982 (2012)
24. Wang, L., Huang, J.: Large differential protection and small differential protection in electrical protection. In: Proceedings of 4th Electric Power Safety Forum, vol. 4, pp. 269–271 (2010)
25. Zhou, L.Y., Wang, Y.J., Shu, H.Z., Cheng, X.: Operation of relay protection and safety automatic device in the national power system in 2002, vol. 27, pp. 55–60 (2003)
26. Zhou, L.Y., Zhan, R.R.: Operation of relay protection and safety automatic device in the national power system in 2003, vol. 5, pp. 74–79 (2004)
27. Wang, X., Song, T., Gong, F., Pan, Z.: On the computational power of spiking neural P systems with self-organization. Sci. Rep. (2016). doi:10.1038/srep27624
28. Song, T., Pan, L.Q., Păun, G.: Asynchronous spiking neural P systems with local synchronization. Inf. Sci. **219**, 197–207 (2013)

A Recognition Method of Hand Gesture
with CNN-SVM Model

Miao Ma[1,2], Zuxue Chen[1,2], and Jie Wu[1,2(✉)]

[1] Key Laboratory of Modern Teaching Technology,
Ministry of Education, Xi'an, China
`mmthp@snnu.edu.cn`, `607wujie2005@163.com`
[2] School of Computer Science, Shaanxi Normal University, Xi'an, China

Abstract. Given the popularity of hand gesture sign language, automatic interpretation of different gestures has received ever increasing interests. However, owing to the complex of background and similarity between different gestures, a more robust method is needed for effective gesture recognition. In this paper, given the robustness of depth image, a depth image based segmentation is designed to extract the gesture region, while Convolutional Neural Network (CNN) and support vector machine (SVM) are trained respectively for feature extraction and gesture recognition. Experiments on America Sign Language dataset demonstrate that our method is promising and more efficient than some existing methods like HSF + RDF, SIFT + PLS, MPC and classical CNN.

Keywords: Depth image · Convolutional neural networks · Support vector machine · Hand gesture recognition

1 Introduction

Sign languages are presented at the beginning of the human communication, which are usually used by both deaf and non-deaf people. Similar as the spoken language, sign language is also a rich and complex way in communication. As an important way to express the sign language, hand gesture can help people to understand each other very well. Thus, if human beings' hand gesture can be well recognized by computer, some more friendly automatic services will be provided to people, especially for the deaf mute. Recently, hand gesture recognition technology is getting more and more attentions and has been applied in our daily life. However, given the complex background and the large variations among the hand gestures that are of the same meaning, a more robust gesture recognition method is very necessary in our lives.

In the literature, to erase the influence of background on the gesture recognition, the gesture region is usually segmented in advance. Commonly, the region segmentation methods can be divided into four categories: (1) Pixel value based segmentation [1]. This kind of method treats every pixel in the picture as a classifiable object and divides all pixels into two categories: gesture region pixels and

© Springer Nature Singapore Pte Ltd. 2016
M. Gong et al. (Eds.): BIC-TA 2016, Part I, CCIS 681, pp. 399–404, 2016.
DOI: 10.1007/978-981-10-3611-8_33

non-gesture region pixels. (2) 2D shape based segmentation [2]. It is built on the fact that there are five fingers on one hand and each finger could bend. As the shape of fingers is used in the detection of gesture region, this kind of method is more robust on the influence of similar skin color and lightness. (3) Skin color based segmentation [3]. The assumption adopted in this kind of method is that the skin color of a hand is distributed in a certain range. So, the pixel whose color is distributed in this range would be treated as a gesture region pixel. It means that this kind of method is susceptible to lightness, ethnicity and similar background. (4) Depth information based segmentation [4]. These methods postulate the depth of each pixel in gesture region varies little. So, using a depth threshold and a reference point of the gesture region, the gesture region is properly determined.

After the extraction of gesture region, some features are computed on the regions for gesture recognition, such as local gradient features [7], SIFT point [8] and depth difference based features [1]. Recently, with the development of neural network, several deep neural network schemes have been proposed [4,10,12]. For the usage of data dependent feature learning scheme in CNN, CNN has shown good performance in various applications, such as character recognition [4], traffic sign recognition and gesture recognition [10–12].

However, by using a fix number of neural units in each layer, a deeper CNN is usually needed to obtained a satisfied result, which also causes a expensive time-cost. In our method, a simple depth image based pre-segmentation method is designed and combined with CNN for American Sign Language (ASL) dataset, with which the features of the gesture region are robustly extracted. And then, using the learned features, a support vector machine (SVM) is trained and adopted for gesture recognition.

The rest of this paper is unfolded as follows: in Sect. 2, the procedure of our method is given in detail. Using ASL dataset, the performance of our method is analyzed and compared with several well-known methods in Sect. 3. Finally, some conclusions are derived in Sect. 4.

2   Our Method

2.1   Gesture Segmentation

As the depth information implies the distance between the imaged object and the image acquisition device, a simple depth image based segmentation is designed in our method for the extraction of gesture region. The main steps are listed as:

1. Assuming the gesture region lies at the middle of the image, the center pixel (named as m) of the depth image is adopted as the reference pixel, whose value is modified as D_m which is the average of 8-neighbor pixels around m;
2. Using a threshold T, a binary map is formed via Eq. (1), where the region consisting of the pixels marked with 1 corresponds the gesture region.

$$IsHand(x,y) = \begin{cases} 0, if \, |D(x,y) - D_m| > T, \\ 1, if \, |D(x,y) - D_m| \leq T. \end{cases} \quad (1)$$

where $D(x, y)$ indicates the pixel value of the depth image.

3. To fill the small holes in the binary map, closed operation (defined as Eq. (2)) is used to obtain the final mask.

$$Mask(x, y) = (IsHand(x, y) \oplus SE) \odot SE \tag{2}$$

where SE is a structural element whose size is 9×9.

4. Using Eq. (3), corresponding gesture region is extracted from the luminance image (I) obtained from an original RGB image.

$$HandRegion(x, y) = \begin{cases} 0, if\ Mask(x, y) = 0, \\ I(x, y), if\ Mask(x, y) = 1. \end{cases} \tag{3}$$

In Fig. 1, a luminance image and the corresponding depth image are given. Using Eq. (3), the obtained binary map is also given as Fig. 1(c). Visually, the obtained binary map is reasonable for the extraction of gesture region.

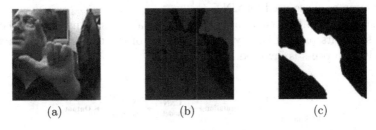

(a)   (b)   (c)

Fig. 1. Binary map obtained for a luminance image via its depth image. (a) Luminance image; (b) Depth image; (c) Obtained binary map.

2.2   CNN-SVM

In Fig. 2, the structure of CNN used in our method is given, which is composed of two convolution layers and two sampling layers. And, the convolution kernel is fixed as 5×5. Moreover, the number of neural units is set as 6 for the first convolution layer (C1) and sampling layer (S1), while it is 12 for the second convolution layer (C2) and sampling layer (S2).

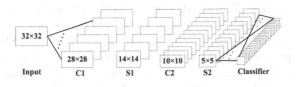

Fig. 2. Structure of CNN used in our method.

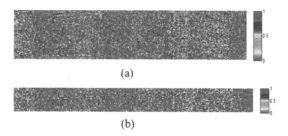

(a)

(b)

Fig. 3. Different maps of learned feature vectors. (a) Map of the same category; (b) Map of the different categories.

In Fig. 3, using the designed CNN, the features of some samples are given, form which we can find the extracted features (300 dimensions) are very similar at some dimensions for the different categories. This means a powerful classifier is very necessary for the designed CNN. In our method, the SVM is built with RBF kernel function and used for gesture recognition, whose training samples are the same as those used for CNN.

To sum up, the flow chart of the training stage is shown in Fig. 4. For the testing stage, its process is very similar to that of the training stage, in which no updating process is involved.

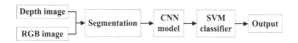

Fig. 4. Training process of CNN-SVM.

3 Experiments

In this section, ASL dataset is adopted to analyze the performance of our method, which contains about 60000 static gesture images indicating twenty-four English letters (except 'j' and 'z'). And, each gesture is recorded via Kinect and from five different persons under different light conditions and backgrounds. Thus, one RGB image and one depth image are provided for each record in ASL dataset. In the experiment, all RGB images are transformed into gray images, where 50,400 images are used as the training sample and 6000 images are used as the testing sample.

Besides, HSF-RDF [7], SIFT-PLS [8] and MPC [17] are chosen as comparison methods. For HSF-RDF, RGB images and depth images are both used, while Random Forest (RDF) is used for classification. In SIFT-PLS, SIFT feature is extracted and partial least squares (PLS) based classifier is adopted for gesture recognition. For MPC, Blob and Crop operators are used to extract the regions of interest, while Sobel operator is adopted subsequently to extract the gesture region whose centroid and area are used as features for gesture recognition.

Besides, the CNN model used in our method is also used as a comparison method whose classifier is Soft-Max. Among the comparison methods, the highest accuracy is achieved by our method (96.1%), the lowest is obtained by HSF-RDF (75%). For the rest, the second is CNN (92.55%) and the third is MPC, while the accuracy of SIFT-PLS is 71.51%.

To make a further analysis, the accuracy of our method on each category is given in Fig. 5(a). Moreover, the performance improvements of the usages of pre-segmentation and SVM are given in Fig. 5(b). Obviously, with the introduction of the pre-segmentation, the accuracy increases about 4%, while the performance is improved more than 3% by sequentially replacing Soft-Max classifier with SVM. Besides, by using SVM, our method becomes stable after 30-th iteration. So, the usages of pre-segmentation and SVM are very necessary and effective in our method.

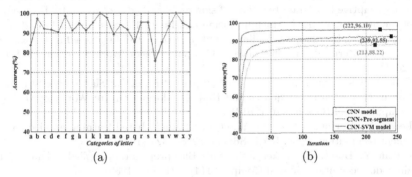

(a)   (b)

Fig. 5. Experiments on our method. (a) Accuracy of our method for different letters; (b) Effects of pre-segmentation and SVM.

4   Conclusion

In this paper, a CNN based method is proposed for the hand gesture recognition, where a depth image based segmentation is employed to extract the gesture region while CNN and SVM are trained respectively for feature extraction and gesture recognition. Experimental results imply that the usage of depth image based segmentation and SVM in the designed CNN model can significantly improve the recognition performance. Moreover, for the usage of SVM, our method can be stable quickly. This means the scheme of our method is reasonable and promising. Some more experiments and more complex CNN models will be studied in our further studies.

Acknowledgement. This work is supported by National Natural Science Foundation of China under grants 61601274, 61501286 and 61501287, Natural Science Basic Research Plan in Shaanxi Province of China under grants 2015JQ6208 and 2016NY-176, Coordinator Innovative Engineering Project of Shaanxi Province under grant 2015KTTSGY04-06 and the Fundamental Research Funds for the Central Universities under grants GK201503064 and GK201603083.

References

1. Radeva, P.: Graph cuts optimization for multi-limb human segmentation in depth maps. IEEE Conference on Computer Vision and Pattern Recognition, pp. 726–732 (2012)
2. Belongie, S.J., Malik, J., Puzicha, J.: Shape matching and object recognition using shape contexts. IEEE Trans. Pattern Anal. Mach. Intell. **24**(4), 509–522 (2002)
3. Stergiopoulou, E., Papamarkos, N.: Hand gesture recognition using a neural network shape fitting technique. Eng. Appl. Artif. Intell. **22**(8), 1141–1158 (2009)
4. Schmeing, M., Jiang, X.: Color segmentation based depth image filtering. In: Jiang, X., Bellon, O.R.P., Goldgof, D., Oishi, T. (eds.) WDIA 2012. LNCS, vol. 7854, pp. 68–77. Springer, Heidelberg (2013). doi:10.1007/978-3-642-40303-3_8
5. Tajbakhsh, N., Shin, J.Y., Gurudu, S.R.: Convolutional neural networks for medical image analysis. IEEE Trans. Med. Imaging **35**(5), 1299–1312 (2016)
6. Tofighi, G., Monadjemi, S.A., Ghasem-Aghaee, N.: Rapid hand posture recognition using adaptive histogram template of skin and hand edge contour. In: Proceedings of the 6th Iranian IEEE Machine Vision and Image Processing, pp. 1–5 (2010)
7. Pugeault, N., Bowden, N.: Spelling it out: real-time ASL fingerspelling recognition. In: IEEE International Conference on Computer Vision Workshops, pp. 1114–1119 (2011)
8. Estrela, B.N., Camara-Chavez, G., Campos, M.F., et al.: Sign language recognition using partial least squares and RGB-D information. In: Workshop de Visao Computacional (Congresso) (2013)
9. Lecun, Y., Bottou, L., Bengio, Y., et al.: Gradient-based learning applied to document recognition. Proc. IEEE **86**(11), 2278–2324 (1998)
10. LeCun, Y., Boser, B., Denker, J.S., et al.: Backpropagation applied to handwritten zip code recognition. Neural Comput. **1**(4), 541–551 (1989)
11. Hinton, G., Li, D., Dong, Y., et al.: Deep neural networks for acoustic modeling in speech recognition. IEEE Sig. Process. Mag. **29**(6), 82–97 (2012)
12. Radzi, S.A., Khalil-Hani, M.: Character recognition of license plate number using convolutional neural network. In: Badioze Zaman, H., Robinson, P., Petrou, M., Olivier, P., Shih, T.K., Velastin, S., Nyström, I. (eds.) IVIC 2011. LNCS, vol. 7066, pp. 45–55. Springer, Heidelberg (2011). doi:10.1007/978-3-642-25191-7_6
13. ChaLearnGestureData. http://gesture.chalearn.org/data/cgd
14. Singha, J., Das, K.: Recognition of Indian sign language in live video. Int. J. Comput. Appl. **70**(19), 17–22 (2013)
15. AuSL. http://www.datatang.com/data/45987
16. Thomas Moeslund. http://www.datatang.com/data/43703
17. Pansare, J.R., Gawande, S.H., Ingle, M.: Real-time static hand gesture recognition for American Sign Language (ASL) in complex background. J. Sig. Inf. Process. **3**, 364–367 (2012)

Cross-Media Information Retrieval with Deep Convolutional Neural Network

Liang Bai, Tianyuan Yu$^{(\boxtimes)}$, Jinlin Guo, Zheng Yang, and Yuxiang Xie

College of Information System and Management,
National University of Defense Technology, Changsha 410073, China
xabpz@163.com, yutianyuan92@163.com, gjlin99@gmail.com, yz_nudt@hotmail.com,
yxxie@nudt.edu.cn

Abstract. With the explosive growth of multimedia data, different types of media data often coexist in web repositories. Accordingly, it is more and more important to explore underlying intricate cross-media correlation so as to improve the retrieval results from cross-media data. However, how to effectively discover the correlations between multi-modal data has been a barrier to successful retrieval of cross-media information. To address the above problems, we propose a novel model projecting both the text modality and the visual modality into a common semantic feature space with the convolutional neural network feature. Unlike the existing approaches, the proposed model learns the high-level feature representation shared by multiple modalities for cross-media information retrieval. Experiments are conducted on public benchmark dataset, and results show the effectiveness of our approach.

Keywords: Cross-media retrieval · Two-stream network · CNN

1 Introduction

Nowadays, multimedia documents play a wide role in daily life applications by various forms of video, web pages, multimodal corpus, and even mobile document services. It is more and more difficult for users to obtain useful and valuable information from "information ocean". The phenomenon has attracted much attention from information retrieval (IR) research community. In this work, we consider this problem as cross-media IR, where for an image query we search for the relevant text, and vice versa.

Cross-media IR is a challenging research topic due to the so-called semantic gap, that is, the query and the result belong to different modalities, and they cannot be directly comparable. Therefore, the key problem in this task is how to measure distances or similarities between multiple modalities. The original works use the low-level feature space as they only use the simple visual descriptors and the individual keywords. However, the simple features cannot represent the semantic meaning in the visual and textual fields, leading the semantic gap between the modalities maximized. Therefore, the advanced visual and textual

© Springer Nature Singapore Pte Ltd. 2016
M. Gong et al. (Eds.): BIC-TA 2016, Part I, CCIS 681, pp. 405–410, 2016.
DOI: 10.1007/978-981-10-3611-8_34

features produced by multi-modal topic models [1] and latent Dirichlet allocation (LDA) [2] are extracted to construct the mid-level feature space so as to improve the effects. Recently, with deep learning methods having major breakthroughs in variety of fields in artificial intelligence, there has been a trend of developing a common feature space with deep learning features. A deep visual-semantic embedding model was introduced to identify visual objects using labeled image data as well as semantic information gleaned from unannotated text [3]. Similarly, Socher et al. proposed a Dependency Tree Recursive Neural Network (DT-RNN) to process textual information [4]. Recently, Karpathy et al. proposed a model which works on a finer level and embeds fragments of images and sentences into a common space [5].

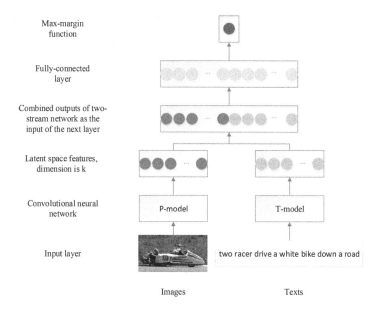

Fig. 1. Overview of the proposed model

In this work, we introduce a novel deep model, illustrated in Fig. 1, which learns mixed features in a common feature space from visual and textual representations respectively. Our contributions are three-fold. The primary one is that we introduce a deep convolutional neural network to map the cross-media data into a common feature space. Unlike the existing work, mixed features extracted here perform well in representing texts and images. Second, we use the CNN-like model to analyze the textual information and extract features. Furthermore, the approach proposed in this work is validated by extensive empirical evaluation. In particular, the deep network achieves convincing performance on Flickr30K dataset [6] for cross-media information retrieval.

2   Model

As shown in Fig. 1, our model can be divided into three parts. The first one is for training textual data with CNN and extracting the textual features. The second is to map the images into a common space where textual information has been embedded. The combination part includes a max-margin function with the purpose of making these relevant pairs to get a high inner product. Finally, we back propagate the whole network with SGD method. These three phases and optimization process are described respectively in the following sections.

2.1   Textual CNN

Deep semantic similarity model (DSSM) [7] has been proved to lead significant quality improvement on automatic highlighting and contextual entity search. This model can extract local and global features from a sentence. However, the convolutional layer sets a fixed number of words as a group of input, which limits its function in fact since these descriptions would possibly contain multiple adjective and a noun. Thus, we improve the model, especially in the step of extracting a more "localized" feature of a sentence. The overview of the textual model is showed in Fig. 2.

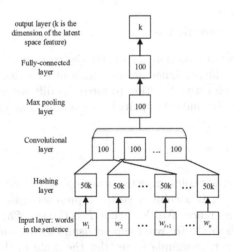

Fig. 2. The network architecture and information flow of the textual model

This model is based on a CNN. In the hashing layer, we build a vector of letter 3-grams (tri-letter vector) for each word so that all the words in the textual data are converted to tri-letter vectors. Then, the vectors are the input of the convolutional layer, in which the local features in the sentence are extracted. In this layer, we set a window to concatenate words in the window to generate a new vector as the input to a linear function and *tanh* activation. The size of window is varied from 1 to the number of words in the sentence. It is necessary to change the size of window rather than using a fixed-size window since the length of phrase is not certain. The followed layer is a max-pooling layer, and its aim is to globalize the local feature vector extracted from the convolutional layer. To reach the aim, we adopt the maximum operation to encourage the network to keep the most useful local features and form the mixed feature for each sentence. At the end of textual model, there are two fully-connected layers to reduce the dimension of the extracted mixed features. Finally, the initial description sentence is converted to a vector in a fixed-dimensional space.

2.2 Visual CNN

The visual model architecture used in this work is based on the network described in [8]. The network produced the best performance in ILSVRC in 2012. The deep neural network consists of several convolutional filters, local contrast normalization, and max-pooling layers, followed by several fully-connected layers and non-linear activation function trained using the dropout regularization technique to avoid overfitting. We remove the softmax prediction layer from this core visual model and add a linear layer that projects the 4096-D representation at the top of the model into the feature space where textual information has embedded. Finally, we fine-tune the entire CNN model with the experimental dataset.

2.3 Common Feature Space

The aim of the objective function is to make the corresponding pairs of images and sentences have a higher inner product than other pairs. We take the measure of max-margin objective function to force the difference between the inner products of correct pairs and other pairs to reach a fixed margin, which has been shown as follows:

$$loss = \sum_{(i,j) \in P} \sum_{(i,k) \notin P} \max(0, margin - v_i^T t_j + v_i^T t_k) + \sum_{(i,j) \in P} \sum_{(k,j) \notin P} \max(0, margin - v_i^T t_j + v_k^T t_j) \quad (1)$$

In the equation, v_i is a column vector denoting the output of our visual model for the given image, t_j is a column vector representing the output of textual model for the given sentence. We also define P is the set of all the corresponding image-sentence pairs (i,j). To avoid time-consuming, we randomly select nine false samples for one true sample to restrict the scale of the training dataset. The margin is empirically set to 0.5.

3 Experiments

Experiments are conducted on the dataset of Flickr30K [6] which consists of 30000 images, each with 5 sentences.

In the textual model, we directly use the existing tri-letters dictionary prepared by the open source demo "sent2vec". The dictionary includes about 50 thousand tri-letters. After removing the punctuation mark, the captions are mapped into the tri-letter vectors. If there are new tri-letters vector appearing, we add them in the dictionary. For images in Flickr30K, to separate luminance information from color information, we map them into YUV space. Then, color channels are normalized globally in the entire dataset so that each color component has 0-mean and 1-norm in the dataset. Furthermore, we set the dimension of the common feature space as 20 empirically.

3.1 Textual Feature

This part focuses on the mixed feature of textual model. First of all, all the sentences in the test dataset are mapped into the multi-modal space. Then, we can find which words or phrases are extracted by the network. A simple result is showed in Fig. 3. In the textual model, a 100-D mixed feature is extracted for each sentence through convolutional and max-pooling layers. Some words or phrases would keep more information in the global feature while others only keep a very low proportion of their own features. An example is illustrated in Fig. 3, the first underlined words (blue) are the main source of the global features, followed by the second underlined words (green), then the third lines (red). There are still other words existing in the final global feature, which only take up a low proportion. Therefore, we can find that the global feature repeat the keywords in order to keep the features, which satisfies our needs and demands.

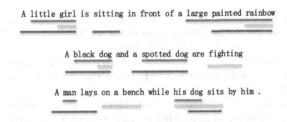

Fig. 3. Example of the textual feature. (Color figure online)

3.2 Image Annotation and Image Search

This experiment focuses on evaluating how well we can find textual or visual information that describes the content of the given image or sentence. Experimental results are showed in Table 1. From the table, we can find that our model outperform the state-of-the-art, especially in the index of R@10. The main reason we suggest is that the work [5] requires the fragments of images and sentences to be matched exactly to each other, which is hard to satisfy especially when the sentences may only focus on a part of contents in the images. So it would lead a wrong match in the test dataset. However, in our model, the mixed features are extracted according to the information in the sentence, and it is more likely to match the global feature of the corresponding image.

Table 1. Result comparison on Flickr30K data

Flickr30K								
Model	Image annotation				Image search			
	R@1	R@5	R@10	Med r	R@1	R@5	R@10	Med r
Random ranking	0.1	0.5	1.0	635	0.1	0.5	1.0	537
DeViSE [3]	4.5	18.1	29.2	26	6.7	21.9	32.7	25
SDT-RNN [4]	9.6	29.8	41.1	16	8.9	29.8	41.1	16
Karpathy et al. [5]	**16.4**	40.2	**54.7**	8	**10.3**	30.8	**44.2**	14
Our model	15.1	**41.3**	54.5	8	10.0	**31.1**	44.1	**13**

4   Conclusion

In this paper, we introduced a novel two-stream network model to solve the task of bidirectional cross-media information retrieval. Specifically, the textual and visual data is mapped into a common feature space and evaluate whether cross-media pair is relevant by the means of inner product. The new model outperforms baselines and other commonly used methods that carry out the same task. The mixed features extracted by the model are also proved to be robust to process different images and sentences.

References

1. Blei, D.M., Jordan, M.I.: Modeling annotated data. In: Proceedings of the 26th Annual International ACM SIGIR Conference on Research and Development in Informaion Retrieval. ACM, pp. 127-134 (2003)
2. Pereira, J.C., Coviello, E., Doyle, G., et al.: On the role of correlation and abstraction in cross-modal multimedia retrieval. IEEE Trans. Pattern Anal. Mach. Intell. **36**(3), 521–535 (2014)
3. Frome, A., Corrado, G.S., Shlens, J., et al.: Devise: a deep visual-semantic embedding model. In: Advances in Neural Information Processing Systems, pp. 2121–2129 (2013)
4. Socher, R., Karpathy, A., Le, Q.V., et al.: Grounded compositional semantics for finding and describing images with sentences. Trans. Assoc. Comput. Linguist. **2**, 207–218 (2014)
5. Karpathy, A., Joulin, A., Li, F.F.F.: Deep fragment embeddings for bidirectional image sentence mapping. Advances in Neural Information Processing Systems, pp. 1889–1897 (2014)
6. Young, P., Lai, A., Hodosh, M., et al.: From image descriptions to visual denotations: new simi-larity metrics for semantic inference over event descriptions. Trans. Assoc. Comput. Linguist. **2**, 67–78 (2014)
7. Huang, P.S., He, X., Gao, J., et al.: Learning deep structured semantic models for web search using clickthrough data. In: Proceedings of the 22nd ACM International Conference on Conference on Information and Knowledge Management. ACM, pp. 2333–2338 (2013)
8. Krizhevsky, A., Sutskever, I., Hinton, G.E.: Imagenet classification with deep convolutional neural networks. In: Advances in Neural Information Processing Systems, pp. 1097–1105 (2012)

Exploration of the Critical Diameter in Networks

Haifeng Du$^{(\boxtimes)}$, Jingjing Wang, Xiaochen He, and Wei Du

School of Public Policy and Administration, Center for Administration Complexity
Science, Xi'an Jiaotong University, Xi'an 710049, China
haifengdu@mail.xjtu.edu.cn, ericawjj@163.com, hexiaochen121vip@163.com,
duwei@mail.xjtu.edu.cn

Abstract. Diameter is an important index measuring the connectivity and the transfer efficiency of networks. In the process of minimizing APL (Average Path Length) by adding edges, we find that APL begins to decline linearly when the number of added edges increases to a turning point and the network diameter decreases to 2. We define this point as the critical state. Furthermore, we put forward the new concept of critical diameter and explore its properties. Memetic Algorithm combined with advantages of genetic algorithm and local search has shown good performance in solving combinational explosion problems. We propose an algorithm based on memetic algorithm in this paper to transform the network diameter into the critical diameter. The experiment results show that our proposed algorithm can efficiently transform the diameter into critical diameter.

Keywords: Networks · Optimization · Diameter · Memetic algorithm

1 Introduction

Network diameter and APL (Average Path Length) are both important indexes in network analysis. Based on the closeness between diameter and APL, the optimization of APL can be transferred to the optimization of network diameter to some extent [1–10]. As a result of the experiment in minimizing APL by adding edges, we find that there exists a turning point which relates to network diameter. As shown in Fig. 1, APL begin to decline linearly as the number of added edges increases when network reaches the turning point. In this paper we define the turning point as critical state. From the graph we can see that $D = 2$ when network diameter reaches critical state. When network has reached the critical state, but has not become full-connected yet, any new connection cannot make the network diameter decrease, under which circumstance diameter optimization does not make sense. Therefore, the optimization of APL can be transferred into the problem of network diameter optimization, and the optimization of diameter should focus on how to decrease diameter efficiently before network reaching the critical state.

© Springer Nature Singapore Pte Ltd. 2016
M. Gong et al. (Eds.): BIC-TA 2016, Part I, CCIS 681, pp. 411–416, 2016.
DOI: 10.1007/978-981-10-3611-8_35

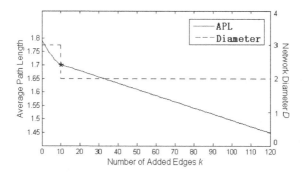

Fig. 1. The value of APL and network diameter D as the number of added edges increases.

2 Critical Diameter and Its Optimization

Based on the findings narrated above, we propose theorems about the critical state and define the critical diameter as follows.

Theorem 1. In the process of optimizing APL by adding edges, the network reaches the critical state only if the network diameter declines to 2 (i.e. $D = 2$).

Definition. For a network $G = (V, E)$, the network diameter declines to 2 only in the case of one more edge being added to G. The network diameter in this state is defined as Critical Diameter, denoted as D_c.

Theorem 2. For a network with the size of N, the biggest degree in the network is $k_{\max}$. If we are minimizing APL by adding edges, there must be a way of transforming the network diameter into critical diameter by adding $N - 1 - k_{\max}$ edges.

In this paper, we propose the method of connecting the Biggest-Degree Node to all the other nodes to transform the network diameter into the critical diameter, named as BDN. BDN is undoubtedly an effective way to reduce the network diameter, but it fails to create the global optimal solution. We hope to design a more effective method to cause the network to reach critical state compared to BDN. We focus on optimizing the process of bringing about critical state in the network and we call this the optimization of critical diameter. This problem can be formulated as:

$$\min k \tag{1}$$
$$s.t. \forall i \neq j, d_{ij} \leq 2$$

In Eq. (1), k is the number of the added edges, d_{ij} represents the path length between node i and j.

3 Algorithm

Memetic Algorithm (MA) combined with advantages of genetic algorithm and local search methods has shown good performance in both long-distance and short-distance search, so that we propose an algorithm based on memetic algorithm in this paper. And it has been proved to solve several combinatorial explosion problems effectively. Thus in this paper, we propose a Memetic Algorithm to optimize the Critical Diameter (MA-CD). Algorithm 1 shows the framework of MA-CD.

Algorithm 1. Framework of our algorithm

1: Input: maximum number of iterations: $I_{\max}$; size of population: S_{pop}; size of mating pool: S_{pool}; size of tournament: S_{tour}; probability of crossover: P_c; probability of mutation: P_m; the initial network adjacency matrix: A.
2: $P \leftarrow$ Initial_Population(S_{pop});
3: Repeat
4: $P_{parent} \leftarrow$ Tournament_Selection(P, S_{pool}, S_{tour});
5: $P_{offspring} \leftarrow$ Genetic_Operation(P_{parent}, P_c, P_m);
6: $P'_{offspring} \leftarrow$ Local_search($P_{offspring}$);
7: $P \leftarrow$ Update_Population(P, $P'_{offspring}$);
8: Until Termination($I_{\max}$)
9: Output: the number of added edges, the position of added edges.

---

4 Experiments and Results

In experiment section, we perform MA-CD on generated random networks and regular networks respectively to test its performance in different network structures. Specifically, we apply two methods to generate networks: (1) Generate random networks and regular networks with node size N ranging from 20 to 50 and the number of edges $\|E\| = N \cdot 4$ to examine the performance of MA-CD as the network density decreases. (2) Generate random networks and regular networks with node size N ranging from 20 to 50 and the number of edges $\|E\| = \frac{\rho \cdot N(N-1)}{2}$ (ρ is the network density). We record the number of added edges k as the optimal networks reach critical state, and compare the optimal solutions by strategies of MA-CD with Greedy Algorithm and BDN.

4.1 Experiments of Critical Diameter Optimization in Random Networks

As shown in Fig. 2(a), Greedy Algorithm could make network get critical state by less edge than MA-CD and BDN in small network sizes. But for bigger networks, MA-CD and BDN show better performance. Figure 2(b) shows that the number of added edges of the BDN optimal networks increase as the network size increases. However, the number of added edges of the MA-CD optimal networks fluctuates and is smaller than that of the BDN optimal networks. Though Greedy Algorithm performs better than BDN when the network size N is big, but it still does not exceed MA-CD. Overall, the experiment shows that MA-CD has excellent performance in optimizing critical diameter in random networks. Furthermore, we explore the difference in networks topologies between BDN and MA-CD. By computing the initial path length between the pairs of nodes connected by added edges, MA-CD prefers connecting long-distance pairs of nodes, which will reduce the network diameter effectively.

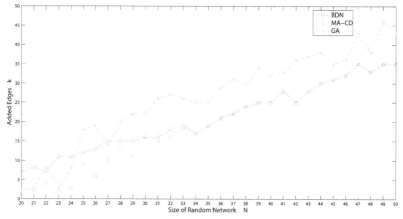

(a) Result of critical diameter optimization in random networks which are generated by method 1

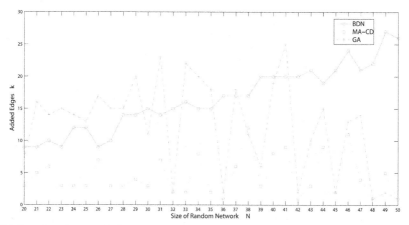

(b) Result of critical diameter optimization in random networks which are generated by method 2

Fig. 2. Result of critical diameter optimization in random networks

4.2 Experiments of Critical Diameter Optimization in Regular Networks

Figure 3(a) shows that Greedy Algorithm fails to show good performance in critical diameter optimization of regular networks, especially when network size N is large. MA-CD and BDN could use less edge to make network get critical state. As shown in Fig. 3(b), the number of added edges of BDN optimal networks shows step growth with the increasing network size N. Since the inefficiency of the Node-Learning, results of MA-CD in regular networks are worse than that in random networks. Greedy Algorithm still fails to show good performance. Generally Speaking, MA-CD still has higher efficiency of critical diameter optimization

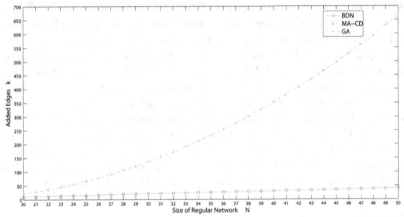

(a) Result of critical diameter optimization in regular networks which are generated by method 1

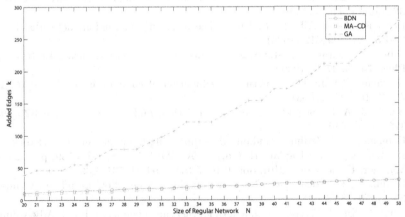

(b) Result of critical diameter optimization in regular networks which are generated by method 2

Fig. 3. Result of critical diameter optimization in regular networks

relatively. Furthermore, the network optimized by MA-CD has the small-world feature, in the sense that optimizing the critical diameter in regular networks by MA-CD will construct small-world networks.

To conclude, MA-CD is an efficient method to optimize critical diameter. Specifically, MA-CD is good at optimizing networks with different node degrees. MA-CD appears to be disassortative in the optimizing process of random networks, but appears to be assortative in regular networks. In addition, the network density may affect the performance of MA-CD.

5   Conclusion

Generally speaking, we focus on the network diameter in the process of optimizing APL by adding edges in this paper. We find a critical state when APL begins to decline linearly, in which case the network diameter is equal to 2. We propose several theorems based on this phenomenon and prove the existence of critical state in optimizing APL. To improve the connectivity and transfer efficiency of networks, the optimization of APL can be transformed to the optimization of the network. In this paper, we focus on the optimization of the network structure in terms of causing the network to reach the critical state at the lowest cost. A memetic algorithm is proposed to solve this problem, and the experimental results show the efficiency of our proposed algorithm. However our algorithm shows less efficiency in regular networks, the optimizing algorithm with better priori knowledge needs to be designed in our future work. And the application of our algorithm on the real world networks should also be explored.

References

1. Watts, D., Strogatz, S.H.: Collective dynamics of small-world networks. Nature **393**(June), 440–442 (1998)
2. Barabási, A.-L., Albert, R.: Emergence of scaling in random networks. Science **286**(5439), 509–512 (1999)
3. Albert, R., Barabási, A.-L.: Statistical mechanics of complex networks. Rev. Mod. Phys. **74**(1), 47–97 (2002)
4. Newman, M.E.J.: The structure and function of complex networks. SIAM Rev. **45**(2), 167–256 (2003)
5. Barabási, A.-L.: Scale-free networks: a decade and beyond. Science **325**(5939), 412–413 (2009)
6. Demaine, E.D., Zadimoghaddam, M.: Minimizing the diameter of a network using shortcut edges. In: Kaplan, H. (ed.) SWAT 2010. LNCS, vol. 6139, pp. 420–431. Springer, Heidelberg (2010). doi:10.1007/978-3-642-13731-0_39
7. Benini, L., De Micheli, G.: Networks on chips: a new SoC paradigm. Computer **35**(1), 70–78 (2002)
8. Peng, J., Xu, G.: Average path length for Sierpinski pentagon. Int. J. Adv. Comput. Technol. (2011)
9. Parhami, B., Yeh, C.H.: Why network diameter is still important (2000)
10. Imase, M., Itoh, M.: Design to minimize diameter on building-block network. IEEE Trans. Comput. **C–30**(6), 439–442 (1981)

Image Compression Based on Genetic Algorithm and Deep Neural Network

Haisheng Deng[1(✉)], Hongying Liu[2], Feixiang Wang[2], Zhi Wang[2], and Yikai Wang[3]

[1] Xijing University, Xi'an 710123, China
xaut0420@126.com
[2] Key Laboratory of Intelligent Perception and Image
Understanding of Ministry of Education, Xidian University, Xi'an 710071, China
hyliu@xidian.edu.cn
[3] Shaanxi Electrical Apparatus Research Institute, Xi'an 710025, China

Abstract. In conventional image compression algorithms, a high compression ratio can be obtained but at the cost of loss of details. In this paper, a new image compression algorithm is proposed. It is based on recently established deep learning model: deep auto encoder (DAE). We adopt the genetic algorithm to find optimal initial network weights to construct a DAE with multiple hidden layers for image compression. With the optimized network, the essential information from the input image can be extracted and represented. Experiments on typical images show that the proposed algorithm obtains higher Peak Signal to Noise Ratio (PSNR), and superior image quality is preserved at both low and high compression ratio compared with the existing algorithms.

Keywords: Image compression · Genetic algorithm (GA) · Deep neural network (DNN)

1 Introduction

As the advances of the computer networks and communication technologies, the demands on multimedia, such as texts, images and videos increase every day. Although images play important role in a variety of fields: politics, economics, military affairs and medical care, the large amount of information limits its storage, processing and transmission. Image compression becomes significant in this case. It is to develop different compression schemes that provide good visual quality with fewer bits to represent digital images.

Nowadays, there are a number of image compression [1] techniques. In general, they fall into two categories: the lossless and the lossy compression. The former always can not achieve high compression ratio. The latter although has flaws in completely recovering the original images, this is acceptable for human vision which is fault-tolerant. Therefore, the lossy compression is more popular.

Several methods were proposed, such as directionlets based [2], and hybrid methods that integrate Discrete Wavelet Transform (DWT), Fractal Coding [3]

© Springer Nature Singapore Pte Ltd. 2016
M. Gong et al. (Eds.): BIC-TA 2016, Part I, CCIS 681, pp. 417–424, 2016.
DOI: 10.1007/978-981-10-3611-8_36

and Discrete Cosine Transform (DCT) [4]. The DCT is well established encoding technique, and it is the core of the Joint Photographic Experts Group (JPEG) which is an international standard for static images. It is still being investigated to achieve high compression ratios without noticeable loss in the image quality. Delaunay et al. [5] suggested the use of an image compression scheme with a tunable complexity-rate-distortion trade-off and wavelet transform. Their technique was applied for the compression of satellite images. While Bita et al. [6] showed the criterion satisfied by an optimal transform of a JPEG2000 compatible compression scheme, using high resolution quantization hypothesis and without the Gaussian assumption.

Recently, the Artificial Neural Networks (ANNs) have also been used for image compression. They are a family of models inspired by biological neural networks which are used to approximate the functions of the central nervous systems in brain. As the development of the theory and techniques of ANN, it has been widely applied to damage identification, fault diagnosis, economy prediction, and image processing, etc. Similar to the human NN that has the extraction ability, ANN has provided a new way for image compression and reconstruction as shown by the studies [7–10]. The typical method is to use the error back propagation (short as BP) network [10] for image compression. The BP is a generalization of the learning rule to multi-layer feed forward networks ANNs, and by using the chain rule to iteratively compute gradients for each layer. The image data is input to the BP network, and through the non-linear transformation by the hidden layers and finally mapped to the output layer. These hidden layers always have less units and can represent the input image data, Its yielding is the compression, while the output layer designed with the identical number of units to that the input layer produces the recovered images. Although it achieves relative sound results, it is limited by inherent flaws: the conventional ANN easily falls into local minimum value and has low convergence.

Addressing the above flaws, we propose the genetic algorithm (GA) and the deep auto encoder (DAE) based image compression method, named as GAAE. As it is known that, a GA is a search heuristic which generate solutions to optimization problems using techniques inspired by natural evolution, such as inheritance, mutation, selection and crossover. The advantage is that it can obtain global optimal solution. We introduce it for the initial optimization of weight values in ANN. Moreover, as we know, deep learning [11,12] as one of the attracting nonlinear techniques which is implemented by a deep neural network (DNN), has multi-layers, and nonlinear transformation functions allowing it to compactly represent highly nonlinear and varying data. Considering the higher extraction ability on the data compared with the conventional NNs, we adopt the widely used DAE for image compression. In the proposed GAAE, original images are input to the network, the initial weights are optimized by GA, namely encoded as population, excellent individuals selected, crossover, mutated, and decoded. Then through the nonlinear transformation by the multiple hidden layers, the images are compressed. By utilizing the global optimization of GA, the DAE is expected to have powerful compression capability.

The remainder of this paper is organized as follows. Section 2 presents the proposed GAAE in details. Section 3 shows the experimental results in. Section 4 gives conclusions.

2   The Proposed Method

The key idea of the proposed GAAE is described in details in this section. Figure 1 shows the flowchart of GAAE. The GA is utilized to search the optimized weight values to initialize the DAE, which will overcome the flaws of the DAE and enhance the performance for compression and reconstruction. The details are explained as follows.

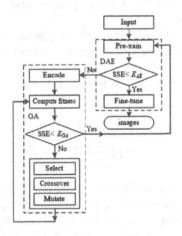

Fig. 1. The flow chart of the proposed GAAE.

Let x_j be the j-th input to the DAE, $W_j^{k-1,i}$ represent the weight associated with the connection between unit j in layer $k-1$ and unit i in layer $k(k \geq 2))$. b_i^{k-1} is the bias associated with unit i in layer $k-1$. $h_i^k(\cdot)$ is the output of unit i in layer k (namely hidden layer $k-1$), and s_k is the number of units in this layer. f represents the activation function. The common sigmoid function is used here: $f(z) = 1/1(1 + \exp(-z))$. z_i^k denote the total weighted sum of inputs to unit i in layer k, including the bias term (e.g., $z_i^2 = \sum_j W_j^{1,i}x_j + b_i^1(i = 1, 2, ..., s_1)$). Then the computations in each layer are as follows.

The input layer (layer 1/hidden layer 0) is

$$z_i^1 = x_i \, (i = 1, 2, ..., s_1). \tag{1}$$

The hidden layers (layer k/hidden layer k − 1) are

$$h_i^k(x_i) = f(z_i^k) = f(\sum_j W_j^{k-1,i}h^{k-1} + b_i^{k-1}) \, (i = 1, 2, ..., s_k). \tag{2}$$

The output layer n_k (layer 1/hidden layer $n_k - 1$) is

$$h_i^{n_k}(x_i) = f(z_i^{n_k}) = f(\sum_j W_j^{n_k-1,i} h_j^{n_k-1} + b_i^{n_k-1})\,(i = 1, 2, ..., s_{n_k}). \quad (3)$$

The layer-wise pre-training is conducted for DAE to better initialize the weight W and bias b. Thus the cost function $C(W, b)$ which should be minimized is given by

$$C(W, b) = \sum_{i=1}^{N} \frac{1}{2} \left\| h^k(x_i) - h^{k-1}(x_i) \right\|^2. \quad (4)$$

And we denote the training error of DAE as E_{AE}, and if $C(W, b)$ is not smaller than E_{AE}, we utilize the GA to optimize the weights, that is to start the following procedures.

Encode the weight W. Each individual corresponds to a weight in the DAE, and generally $3N$ individuals are necessary candidates to guarantee the final N sound individuals;

Compute the fitness. We use the following function to select N individuals which are with larger fitness:

$$Fit = \frac{1}{\exp(\sum_{i=1}^{N} (h_i^{n_k} - x_i)^2)}. \quad (5)$$

Conduct crossover on the weight at a probability of Pc;

Perform mutation on the weight at a probability of Pm;

Then the fitness is calculated again by Eq. (5), and if the square sum of error (SSE) is smaller than the predefined error E_{GA}, then superior weight values are obtained and send to DAE for the subsequent fine-tuning.

3   Experimental Results

To evaluate the performance of the proposed GAAE, we compare it with the conventional DCT and the DAE based compression.

All the experiments are performed under MATLAB 2012a environment on a PC with 2.6 GHz Intel Core i5 processor with 4 GB memory. Each experiment is repeated 10 times to reduce the randomness and bias in results, and the average result is reported. The quality of the reconstructed image is measured by the metrics of Peak Signal to Noise Ratio (PSNR) and normalized mean square of the error (NMSE) NMSE is the normalized mean square of the error between the original and the reconstructed images.

The data for test are several typical grayscale images: Cameraman, Lena, Circuit, Rice, Cell, and Eight. All of them are with size 256 * 256. In order to reduce the complexity of computation, the images are divided into 8 * 8 blocks, thus there are 1024 blocks for input to the network. The parameters for the methods are listed below. For GAAE: the learning rate is 0.01; the E_{AE} is

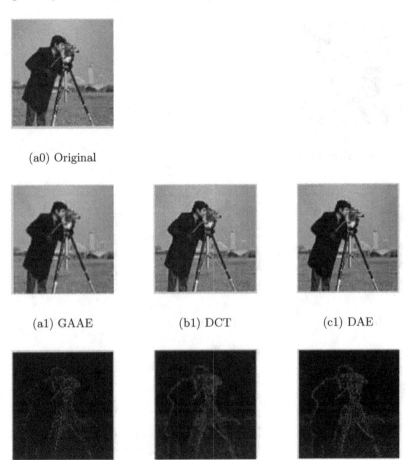

(a0) Original

(a1) GAAE   (b1) DCT   (c1) DAE

(a2) error image   (b2) error image   (c2) error image

Fig. 2. The compression results for Camera image at 8:1 ratio using different algorithms. (a0) The original image (a1) The compressed image using GAAE algorithm (a2) The error for reconstruction with GAAE (b1) The compressed image using DCT algorithm (b2) The error for reconstruction with DCT (c1) The compressed image using DAE algorithm (c2) The error for reconstruction with DAE.

0.001; E_{GA} is 0.001; The probability P_c is 0.3; The probability P_m is 0.01; The structure for AE in GAAE are the same for that DAE for fair comparison, and they are 1024-512-128-512-1024 (4 hidden layers) for 8:1 compression, and 1024-256-64-256-1024 for 16:1.

The visual results for compression of image Cameraman with ratio 8:1 are shown in Fig. 2. The reconstructed images and the error for reconstruction using GAAE are shown in Fig. 2(a1) and (a2), respectively. Among the three reconstructed images, the GAAE obtains superior results. It has much less

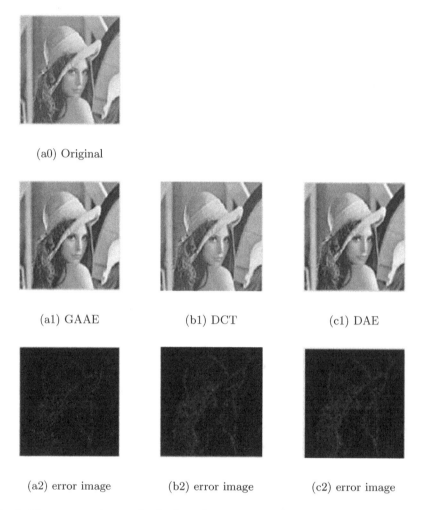

(a0) Original

(a1) GAAE   (b1) DCT   (c1) DAE

(a2) error image   (b2) error image   (c2) error image

Fig. 3. The compression results for Lena image at 8:1 ratio using different algorithms. (a0) The original image (a1) The compressed image using GAAE algorithm (a2) The error for reconstruction with GAAE (b1) The compressed image using DCT algorithm (b2) The error for reconstruction with DCT (c1) The compressed image using DAE algorithm (c2) The error for reconstruction with DAE.

reconstruction errors than the DCT and DAE. This can be explained by the optimization of the weights using GA which is better than the single application of DAE.

The visual results for compression of image Lena with ratio 8:1 are also shown in Fig. 3. It can be seen from the reconstructed images that GAAE obtains more clear results especially for the streaks on the hat. And this is verified by the reconstructed error image in Fig. 3(a2).

In addition, the PSNR and NMSE for the reconstructed Cameraman, Lena, and other four images at compression ratio 8:1 and 16:1 are shown in Tables 1 and 2 respectively. For the higher ratio, the proposed GAAE obtains highest PSNR and lowest NMSE for all the reconstructed images compared with DCT and DAE. These verify the effectiveness of the genetic algorithm optimized deep network.

Table 1. Comparison of the PSNR and NMSE for the reconstructed images (compression ratio 8:1) by different algorithms

Images	GAAE		DCT		DAE	
	PSNR	NMSE	PSNR	NMSE	PSNR	NMSE
Camera	46.5096	0.0721	42.281	0.0822	44.5992	0.0801
Lena	52.3128	0.1042	48.406	0.1184	49.774	0.1106
Circuit	50.2776	0.083	45.625	0.0682	47.0287	0.0985
Rice	47.8258	0.0031	41.5737	0.0952	43.7126	0.0267
Cell	60.0173	0.0125	52.4389	0.051	54.1529	0.0381
Eight	51.2801	0.0618	46.283	0.1134	48.1371	0.0698

Table 2. Comparison of the PSNR and NMSE for the reconstructed images (compression ratio 16:1) by different algorithms

Images	GAAE		DCT		DAE	
	PSNR	NMSE	PSNR	NMSE	PSNR	NMSE
Camera	45.9829	0.0798	40.3475	0.0978	42.9854	0.0899
Lena	50.3436	0.1154	47.8753	0.1321	48.4386	0.1294
Circuit	48.7916	0.0987	44.3092	0.079	46.3427	0.0703
Rice	46.2871	0.0098	40.0436	0.0998	44.7981	0.0384
Cell	58.0322	0.0246	50.9861	0.0687	52.853	0.0563
Eight	50.5799	0.0708	44.8217	0.1325	46.6512	0.0982

4   Conclusions

In this paper, a new image compression algorithm, named as GAAE is proposed. The implementation of deep auto encoder (DAE) combined with the optimal network weights using genetic algorithm constructs superior network structure which can extract the abstract information from the input images. The experiments on typical images indicated that higher PSNR and lower NMSE are obtained with the proposed GAAE. The details of the images are preserved at both low and high compression ratio compared with the conventional methods. In the future, the proposed algorithm will be evaluated on more images.

Acknowledgment. This work was supported by the Shaanxi collaborative innovation program (2015XT-61), Xijing University Research Foundation: (XJ150123), the National Natural Science Foundation of China (No. 61502369), the foundation from Ministry of Education of China (No. BK16015020001), the National Science Basic Research Plan in Shaanxi Province of China (No. 2016JQ6049), and the Fundamental Research Funds for the Central Universities (No. 7215598901).

References

1. Taubman, D., Marcellin, M.: JPEG2000 Image Compression Fundamentals, Standards and Practice: Image Compression Fundamentals, Standards and Practice. Springer Science & Business Media, New York (2012)
2. Velisavljevic, V., Beferull-Lozano, B., Vetterli, M.: Space-frequency quantization for image compression with directionlets. IEEE Trans. Image Process. **16**(7), 1761–1773 (2007)
3. Iano, Y., da Silva, F.S., Cru, A.L.M.: A fast and efficient hybrid fractal-wavelet image coder. IEEE Trans. Image Process. **15**(1), 98–105 (2006)
4. Elharar, E., Stern, A., Hadar, O., Javidi, B.: A hybrid compression method for integral images using discrete wavelet transform and discrete cosine transform. J. Disp. Technol. **3**(3), 321–325 (2007)
5. Delaunay, X., Chabert, M., Charvillat, V., Morin, G.: Satellite image compression by post transform in the wavelet domain. Signal Process. **90**(2), 599–610 (2010)
6. Bita, I., Barret, M., Pham, D.T.: On optimal transforms in lossy compression of multicomponent images with JPEG2000. Signal Process. **90**(3), 759–773 (2010)
7. Sicuranza, G.L., Ramponi, G., Marsi, S.: Artificial neural network for image compression. Electron. Lett. **26**(7), 477–479 (1990)
8. Abidi, M.A., Yasukiand, S., Crilly, P.B.: Image compression using hybrid neural networks combining the auto-associative multi-layer perceptron and the self-organizing feature map. IEEE Trans. Consum. Electron. **40**(4), 796–811 (1994)
9. Namphol, A., Chin, S.H.: Image compression with a hierarchical neural network. IEEE Trans. Aerosp. Electron. Syst. **32**(1), 326–338 (1996)
10. Tang, X., Liu, Y.: An image compressing algorithm based on classified blocks with BP neural networks. In: International Conference on computer Science and Software Engineering, pp. 819–822 (2008)
11. Hinton, G.E., Salakhutdinov, R.R.: Reducing the dimensionality of data with neural networks. Science **313**(5786), 504–507 (2006)
12. Bengio, Y.: Learning deep architectures for AI (Technical report 1312). Universit'e de Montr'eal, dept. IRO (2007)

DNN-Based Joint Classification for Multi-source Image Change Detection

Wenping Ma[✉], Zhizhou Li, Puzhao Zhang, and Tianyu Hu

Key Laboratory of Intelligent Perception and Image
Understanding of Ministry of Education, Xidian University,
Xi'an 710071, Shaanxi Province, China
wpma@mail.xidian.edu.cn

Abstract. In this paper, we propose a novel joint classification framework for multi-source image change detection, the multi-source image-pair is generated by different sensors, such as optical sensor and synthetic aperture radar, respectively. This framework is established for feature learning, which is based on deep neural networks. Firstly, in order to segment the optical image, deep neural networks are essential to extract deep features for clustering segmentation. Then the stacked denoising autoencoders is trained to learn capability of classification via choosing part of reliable segmentation results of optical image as labels. Next, the other image of the image-pair is entered in the trained stacked denoising autoencoders to classification automatically. Afterwards, two images passed joint classification are obtained. Finally, the difference image is produced by comparing the two images passed joint classification. Experimental results illustrate that the method can be applied to multi-source image and outperforms the state-of-the-art methods.

Keywords: Change detection · Multi-source image · Deep neural networks · Feature learning

1 Introduction

The technique of image change detection is used in same surface area covered by different historical periods. It combines corresponding characteristics and remote sensing imaging mechanism to identify and analyze the regional characteristics change, including changes in object location, scope changes and surface properties. Different sensors present multiple information of terrestrial globe for the ground, oceans, monitoring research [1].

In this paper, we propose a novel method to solve the issue of multi-source image change detection. The method described here is called deep neural networks (DNN)-based joint classification (DBJC) for multi-source image change detection. The method we proposed is joint classification based on DNN, which is taking results of one image clustering segmentation as labels to train DNN for the other image classification.

© Springer Nature Singapore Pte Ltd. 2016
M. Gong et al. (Eds.): BIC-TA 2016, Part I, CCIS 681, pp. 425–430, 2016.
DOI: 10.1007/978-981-10-3611-8_37

The rest of this article is divided into four parts as follows: Sect. 2 suggests the description of the problem and our motivations for multi-source image change detection. Section 3 exhibitions the application details of the proposed technique. Experimental results on real dataset and synthetic images are shown in the Sect. 4. Lastly, Sect. 5 summarizes the conclusion of our work.

2   Problem and Motivation

In this paper, the proposed of multi-source image change detection is to find out the changed areas of the given image-pair derived from different sensors. One co-registered multi-source image-pair is considered, one is SAR image denoted by: $I_S = \{I(x, y) | 1 \leq x \leq M, 1 \leq y \leq N\}$, and the other one is optical image denoted by: $I_O = \{I(x, y) | 1 \leq x \leq M, 1 \leq y \leq N\}$, SAR and optical images are of size $M \times N$ and are obtained in the same area at different times t_1 and t_2. The change detection results are presented in the form of binary image $DI = \{di(x, y) \in \{0, 1\} | 1 \leq x \leq M, 1 \leq y \leq N\}$, where $di(x, y) = 0$ represents that the pixel at location (x, y) is unchanged, while $di(x, y) = 1$ is changed.

The flowchart of the method in this article can be expressed in Fig. 1. We use clustering results of one image to guide the classification of another image, aimed at converting two images with different types of data into the same type of data.

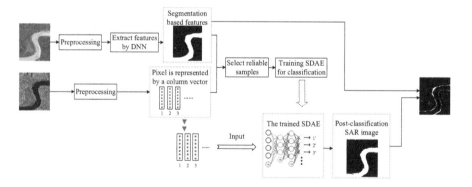

Fig. 1. Flowchart of our method

2.1   Unsupervised Feature Learning and Clustering

Artificial neural network has good performance in pattern recognition and machine learning [2], and has the capability of representing non-linear function. Stacked denoising autoencoders (SDAE) are deemed to have high-performance in learning edge features of image patches via training it unsupervised.

2.2 Joint Classification

As shown Yellow-River image in Fig. 2, the left SAR image is low resolution with ambiguous spatial details, however, the right optical image display its high resolution. Obviously, the two images are incommensurability directly. The model of SDAE contained a classifier shows lower classification error in classification problem via learning useful high-level representation in image patches [3].

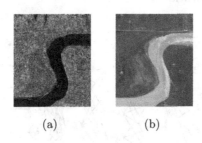

(a)   (b)

Fig. 2. Example of multisource image-pair obtained by different sensors, at different times. (a) The SAR image obtained by Radarsat. (b) The optical image acquired from Google Earth. (Color figure online)

3   Methodology

In this chapter, we will introduce the specific application of the proposed method in this paper. For two co-registered images obtained by different sensors, optical and SAR images are image-pair in this paper. First, image preprocessing should be taken in image-pair, and it mainly includes filtering and divides the image into patches. Second, learning deep level features is the key point for clustering optical image. The clustering algorithm used for the segmentation of optical image is features clustering, which based the extracted feature previously. Then we choose part of reliable pixels in the optical clustering results as labels, and the pixels in the SAR image corresponding position is the input of SDAE contained classifier, which is learning the capability of classification. After training SDAE, we input the SAR image patches to the trained SDAE for classifying SAR image. Finally, the difference image (DI) is produced by comparing the image-pair passed joint classification.

3.1   Stacked Denoising Autoencoders

SDAE, a fully connection multilayer networks, is built to learn the local representation of each pixel in our method. The features of two images are extracted at different stages. For optical image, features are extracted before clustering segmentation. The neighbor pixels of each central pixel are converted to raw vector, which is the input of SDAE, and the output is a feature vector.

In our method, the networks are fully connected multi-hidden layer SDAE, which is built for learning the local features. Multi-hidden layer SDAE includes multiple autoencoders. The training process is that each layer of the network is trained in layer-wise, and then whole deep neural network is trained. The 2-hidden-layer SDAE with structure 6-3-4 is presented in Fig. 3, where the deep neural networks with full structure 6-3-4-3-6. 6, 3 and 4 is the number of neurons in each layer. In our method, the second order representation is the useful features for joint classification.

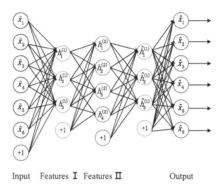

Input   Features **I**   Features **II**   Output

Fig. 3. 2-layer SDAE with structure 6-3-4-3-6

3.2   Classifier and Fine-Tuning

Fine-tuning is a common strategy in deep learning, it can significantly enhance the performance of stacked denoising autoencoders neural networks. Form a higher perspective, the process of fine-tuning treat all layers in stacked denoising autoencoders as a model, so the value of weight in networks can be optimized in each iteration. In this paper, we use softmax regression as the final classifier.

4   Experiments

In order to demonstrate the effectiveness of the proposed method, we experience two pairs of real dataset in multi-source image change detection problem in this article. The method of mapping-based feature change analysis (MBFCA) and the post-classification comparison (PCC) [4] are selected as the compared methods in this paper. In our method, the major parameters we set as the follow: the size of field window in the image block is 3×3, the number of hidden layer in multi-layer structure is 2, the structures which are 9-60-9 and 60-15-60, respectively. So, the 2-layer SDAE is fully connected with structure 9-60-15-60-9.

4.1 Evaluating Index

False negative (FN) represents the number of pixels which is sort out the unchanged areas but changed in the reference image. False positive (FP) represents the number of pixels which is classified into the change area but unchanged in the reference image. Then we calculate the overall errors (OE) and the correct classification rate (CCR), which is calculated by $OE = FN + FP$ and $CCR = \frac{TP+TN}{TP+TN+FP+FN}$, where TP represents the true positives, the number of pixels are correctly classified into the changed, TN represents the true negative, the number of pixels are correctly classified into the unchanged.

5 Results and Analysis

In our experiment, The first dataset is Sardinia region, the final change detection results shown in Fig. 4. In Fig. 4(a), the DI produced by PCC, which contained large amount of noise. While the change detection results in Fig. 4(b), which is produced by MBFCA, it have less noise. However, the change detection results generated by DBJC is shown in Fig. 4(c), and it demonstrated the performance of suppressing the noise significantly in our method. Table 1 shows the quantitative results for Sardinia dataset.

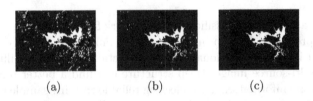

(a)   (b)   (c)

Fig. 4. Change detection results by using different method on the Mediterranean Sardinia dataset. (a) PCC. (b) MBFCA. (c) DBJC.

Table 1. Comparison of change detection results on Sardinia region dataset

Method	FN	FP	OE	CCR(%)	KAPPA
PCC	1249	8955	10204	91.74	0.516
MBFCA	1641	3411	5052	95.91	0.872
DBJC	**1641**	**2561**	**4202**	**96.60**	**0.717**

In the experiments of Yellow-River, the final change detection results shown in Fig. 5. The change detection results produced by DBJC is shown in Fig. 5(c), it have better performance compared with MBFCA, shown in Fig. 5(b), and PCC, shown in Fig. 5(a). Table 2 shows the quantitative results for Yellow-River dataset.

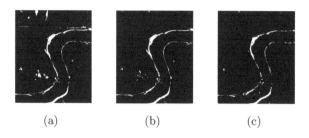

(a)   (b)   (c)

Fig. 5. Change detection results by using different method on the Yellow-River dataset. (a) PCC. (b) MBFCA. (c) DBJC.

Table 2. Comparison of change detection results on Yellow river dataset

Method	FN	FP	OE	CCR(%)	KAPPA
PCC	513	1537	2050	97.92	0.783
MBFCA	919	925	1844	98.13	0.943
DBJC	**500**	**720**	**1220**	**98.76**	**0.916**

6   Conclusions

In this paper, a novel joint classification framework for multi-source image change detection is proposed. Due to inconsistency of multi-source image in terms of spatial resolution, the traditional change detection method is difficult to use directly in multi-source image. Deep structure can find a better representation for image texture information, and selecting reliable training sample is key for the method. Experimental results on the real dataset illustrate that the method can be applied to multi-source image and outperforms the state-of-the-art methods in terms of detection accuracy.

References

1. Petit, C.C., Lambin, E.F.: Integration of multi-source remote sensing data for land cover change detection. Int. J. Geogr. Inf. Sci. **15**, 785–803 (2001)
2. Schmidhuber, J.: Deep learning in neural networks: an overview. Neural Netw. **61**, 85–117 (2014)
3. Vincent, P., Hugo, L., Isabelle, L., Yoshua, B., Pierre Antoine, M.: Extracting and composing robust features with denoising autoencoders. In: 25th International Conference on Machine learning, pp. 1096–1103. ACM Press, Helsinki (2008)
4. Colditz, R., Velázquez, J.A., Gallegos, D.J.R., Lule, A.D.V., Zúñiga, M.T.R., Maeda, P., López, M.I.C., Ressl, R.: Potential effects in multi-resolution post-classification change detection. Int. J. Remote Sens. **33**, 6426–6445 (2012)

Differencing Neural Network for Change Detection in Synthetic Aperture Radar Images

Feng Chen[1], Jiao Shi[1(✉)], and Maoguo Gong[2]

[1] School of Electronics and Information, Northwest Polytechnical University,
127 West Youyi Road, Xi'an 710072, Shaanxi, People's Republic of China
fernchen@mail.nwpu.edu.cn, jiaoshi@nwpu.edu.cn
[2] Key Laboratory of Intelligent Perception and Image
Understanding of Ministry of Education of China, Xidian University,
2 South TaiBai Road, Xi'an 710071, Shaanxi, China
gong@ieee.org

Abstract. This paper presents a completely unsupervised change detection approach for synthetic aperture radar (SAR) images based on stacked autoencoders (SAE). The proposed method innovatively implements the change detection task by establishing a differencing neural network with a novel cost function. Firstly, two SAR images are used to pre-train two stacked autoencoders, then these two stacked autoencoders are unrolled to initialize the parameters of differencing neural network. Next, a novel cost function, including the difference between bi-temporal features and an initial difference image, is designed to fine tune the networks for highlighting the changes. Finally, we can obtain the detection results by measuring the Euclidean distance between the outputs of the two neural networks. The experiments on real multitemporal SAR datasets prove the outstanding performance of the proposed method.

Keywords: Differencing neural network · Image change detection · Stacked autoencoder · Cost function · Synthetic aperture radar (SAR)

1 Introduction

Image change detection is to recognize the changes between two images which are taken over the same scene but at different times. Because of the independence of time and weather condition, synthetic aperture radar (SAR) image has received a lot of attention in recent years and is the main experimental object of the change detection algorithm. Nevertheless, due to the presence of the speckle noise, it is more difficult to achieve the change detection for SAR image [1].

In the last few decades, the common way to handle change detection for SAR images is post-comparison analysis according to the existed literature [2]. It is called difference image (DI) analysis [3]. However, the quality of DI will greatly affect result of change detection. In recent years, with the rise of neural

© Springer Nature Singapore Pte Ltd. 2016
M. Gong et al. (Eds.): BIC-TA 2016, Part I, CCIS 681, pp. 431–437, 2016.
DOI: 10.1007/978-981-10-3611-8_38

networks, researchers have tried to use the neural networks to solve change detection problems, such as a Hopfield-type neural network proposed for multispectral images [4].

This paper presents an unsupervised change detection approach for SAR images based on stacked autoencoder (SAE). To implement the aim of change detection, a novel cost function is designed to adjust the parameters of two coupled neural networks. Finally the trained deep neural networks are used for the classification of changed pixels by two original images directly. The whole framework is called differencing neural network by ourselves.

The rest of this paper is organized as follows. Section 2 will describe the proposed framework. In the next section, the proposed algorithm will be described in details. Section 4 will show the experimental results on real SAR images. Finally, conclusions are drawn in the last section.

2   Algorithm Framework

As mentioned in Sect. 1, this paper proposes an unsupervised change detection framework based on SAE. Change detection results are obtained from two original SAR images directly. In fact, there are two SAE networks included in the algorithm, and one network is associated with one original image separately. In order to get networks that have been trained, the process is divided into two steps: (1) Using layer-wise strategy to train each SAE networks; (2) Designing a novel cost function to fine tune the whole systems. After pre-training, each network can gain an output of raw data, which is a kind of characteristic representation of original image. The cost function is related to the two output of networks.

3   Methodology

3.1   Samples Generation

The samples for training differencing neural network are from the two original images. Let $P_{ij}^{I_1}$ represents the neighborhood with center (i, j) and of size $n \times n$ in images I_1. Then converting the neighborhood patch, either in row-major or column-major order, into a n^2-dimensional vector $V_{ij}^{I_1}$ to get a training example $X_{(i-1)\times col+j}^{I_1}$. Image I_1 is of size $row \times col$, which is equal to Image I_2. After visiting every pixel in Image I_1, we can get a sample matrix $X^{I_1} = \left(\left(X_1^{I_1}\right)^T, \left(X_2^{I_1}\right)^T, \ldots, \left(X_{(i-1)\times col+j}^{I_1}\right)^T, \ldots, \left(X_{row\times col}^{I_1}\right)^T \right)^T$, $i \in \{1, 2, \ldots, row\}$, $j \in \{1, 2, \ldots, col\}$, which is the final training samples. In the same way, we can obtain the samples X^{I_2} from image I_2. By the way, the values of features lie between 0 and 1.

We can train many autoencoders connected together one by one. The hidden layer of previous networks is connected to the input layer of next network.

In other words, all autoencoders without output layer are joined together. And the output of each layer is actually more abstract representation in the differencing neural network built.

3.2 Cost Function and Fine-Tune

We can pre-train two deep neural networks by two original images data separately. For the final detection result is related to raw images data, the outputs of two networks are taken account in fine-tune. As mentioned in Sect. 1, DI can express the two original images to some extent, so it can be used to optimize the network parameters. And with the optimization of network, DI will be also updated. In order to reduce the influence of speckle noise, the logarithmic ratio is widely used now [5, 6]. Therefore, log-ratio image is adopted initially [7]. Given that X^{I_1} and X^{I_2} represent the two original image, log-ratio image is defined by

$$X^L = \left| \log \frac{X^{I_1}}{X^{I_2}} \right| \tag{1}$$

In addition, in order to reduce the influence of speckle noise, the neighborhood information of each DI pixel should also be considered. It is measured by the distance of the center pixel and the mean of all pixels in neighborhood with the center. Finally, it is important to note that all values of DI will be updated to 1, when output of the two coupled networks is very close to each other. Therefore, a constraint term of DI should be included in cost function.

Summarizing the above content, the cost function is represented by

$$J_{tune}(W, b, X^L) = \frac{1}{m} \sum_{k=1}^{m} \left[\frac{1}{X_k^L} \cdot \frac{1}{2} DF_k + d_k + \left(X_k^L \right)^2 \right] + J_{re} \tag{2}$$

Where $DF_k = \left\| f_1 \left(X_k^{I_1} \right) - f_2 \left(X_k^{I_2} \right) \right\|^2$, $d_k = \left(X_k^L - \overline{X_k^L} \right)^2$. $f_1(X_k^{I_1})$ represents the output of the first deep neural network by the k-th sample with center (i, j) in Image I_1, and $f_2(X_k^{I_2})$ is similar to $f_1(X_k^{I_1})$. Therefore DF_k shows the output of the differencing neural network for k-th sample. $\overline{X_k^L}$ is the mean of all pixels in neighborhood with center (i, j). In order to prevent over fitting, the regularization term J_{re} is considered.

Considering that the majority of regions in the images are unchanged pixels, our aim is to optimize the network to minimize the cost function. Gradient descent algorithm is commonly used. Similar to BP algorithm, the parameters in proposed algorithm is updated by

$$\delta^{(l)} = \frac{1}{X_k^L} \cdot \left(\left(W^{(l)} \right)^T \delta^{(l+1)} \right) \cdot \left(\text{sigmoid} \left(W^{(l-1)} a^{(l-1)} + b^{(l-1)} \right) \right)' \tag{3}$$

$$X_k^L = X_k^L + \alpha \sum_{k=1}^{m} \frac{1}{m} \left[\frac{1}{(X_k^L)^2} \frac{1}{2} \left\| f_1(X_k^{I_1}) - f_2(X_k^{I_2}) \right\|^2 - 2X_k^L + \frac{X_k^L - \overline{X_k^L}}{N_k} + \overline{X_k^L} \right] \tag{4}$$

$W^{(l)}$ is a weight matrix between l-th layer and $(l+1)$-th layer and $b^{(l)}$ is the biase of l-th layer. $a^{(l)}$ represents the units in l-th layer of the deep neural network. Note that in Eq. (3) $X_k^L = (X_k^L, X_k^L, \ldots, X_k^L)^T$ is a vector whose length is equal to $\delta^{(l)}$. The error term in the last layer is different. The network trained by Image I_1 is defined by

$$\delta^{(n_l)} = \frac{1}{X_k^L} \cdot \left(f_1\left(X_k^{I_1}\right) - f_2\left(X_k^{I_2}\right) \right) \cdot \left(\mathrm{sigmoid}\left(W^{(n_l-1)}a^{(n_l-1)} + b^{(n_l-1)}\right) \right)' \quad (5)$$

However the network trained by Image I_2 is defined by

$$\delta^{(n_l)} = \frac{1}{X_k^L} \cdot \left(f_2\left(X_k^{I_1}\right) - f_1\left(X_k^{I_2}\right) \right) \cdot \left(\mathrm{sigmoid}\left(W^{(n_l-1)}a^{(n_l-1)} + b^{(n_l-1)}\right) \right)' \quad (6)$$

In fact, in (5) and (6) all symbols represent the different values, due to the different training samples.

The whole fine-tune has three key points: (1) designing a novel cost function which improves the efficiency of network optimization; (2) introducing initial DI to optimize the networks; (3) adjusting the parameters of the two coupled deep neural network each other.

After fine-tune has been completed, we can get change detection results by Euclidean distance between the output of two networks.

4 Experimental Study

The quantitative analysis of change detection results is set as follow: (1) the false negatives (FN); (2) the false positives (FP); (3) the true positives (TP); (4) the true negatives (TN); and (5) the percentage correct classification (PCC). For accuracy assessment, we introduce kappa statistic which is a measure of accuracy or agreement based on the difference between the error matrix and change agreement [8]. It indicates the degree of the change detection map and the reference image in agreement.

The results on the Ottawa dataset: This experiment aims to compare the proposed method with conventional algorithms, reformulated fuzzy local-information c-means algorithm (RFLICM) [3], and supervised deep neural networks, BP algorithm. The change detection results generated by the proposed method and the two comparative methods on Ottawa dataset are presented in Fig. 1. The final map generated by RFLICM is polluted by many noise spots on the black ground, because cluster methods are sensitive to noise. Deep neural network has strong learning ability for unknown distribution, therefore BP neural network can accomplish detection task very well. The PCC of the detection result runs up to 98.4%, which is more than the result yielded by RFLICM as shown in Table 1. However, many pixels, i.e. the region labeled by the red circle, are wrongly detected because of the gradient dispersion. The proposed method detects the changed region from the two original images entirely, and a new cost function improves the performance of training networks.

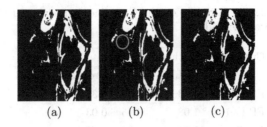

Fig. 1. Change detection results of the Ottawa dataset achieved by (a) RFLICM, (b) BP neural network, (c) proposed method

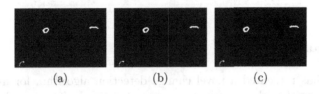

Fig. 2. Change detection results of the Ottawa dataset achieved by (a) RFLICM, (b) BP neural network, (c) proposed method

The results on the Coastline dataset: For the Coastline dataset, Fig. 2 shows the final maps of the three methods. RFLICM presents the worst performance. There are many noise spots on the black background, and the Kappa is just equal to 59.98% as shown in Table 2. BP neural network is trained by samples with labels, which is based on joint-classification and sample selection. As described in Table 2, the OE yielded by BP neural network is significantly reduced. Meanwhile, Fig. 2(b) also declares the point by the number of noise spots. The PCC yielded by the proposed method equals to 99.70% which is higher than 99.45% by BP and it is a big promotion at this level. In addition, the PCC and Kappa have the best performance in the overall context. Although FN of the proposed method is more than that of other methods, FP has lower values.

Table 1. Change detection results on the Ottawa dataset by RFLICM, BP neural network and proposed method

Criterion	Method		
	RFLICM	BP	Proposed method
FN (%)	1.20	1.10	0.75
FP (%)	0.52	0.50	0.20
OE (%)	1.72	1.60	0.95
PCC (%)	98.28	98.40	99.05
Kappa (%)	92.90	93.81	95.02

Table 2. Change detection results on the Coastline dataset by RFLICM, BP neural network and proposed method

Criterion	Method		
	RFLICM	BP	Proposed method
FN (%)	0.13	0.37	0.38
FP (%)	1.08	0.15	0.03
OE (%)	1.21	0.55	0.41
PCC (%)	98.79	98.45	99.70
Kappa (%)	59.98	78.90	81.27

5   Conclusion

This paper has presented a novel change detection algorithm for multitemporal SAR images based on differencing neural network. The samples obtained from the two original SAR images directly train two SAEs separately, then the two SAEs having been trained are unrolled into two deep neural networks that have the same parameters with corresponding layers. Next a novel cost function, including the difference between the outputs of the two neural networks and an initial DI, is designed to fine tune the networks. Meanwhile, the two networks affect each other. Finally, we can obtain the detection results by the Euclidean distance between the outputs of the two neural networks. The experiments on real multitemporal SAR datasets prove the high performance of the proposed method. Whether it is considered by the noise spots of result map or the evaluation criteria, the proposed method shows a great advantage on change detection compared with other methods.

Acknowledgments. This work was supported by the National Natural Science Foundation of China (Grant No. 61602385).

References

1. Kuruoglu, E.E., Zerubia, J.: Modeling SAR images with a generalization of the Rayleigh distribution. J. IEEE Trans. Image Process. **13**(4), 527–533 (2004)
2. Bruzzone, L., Prieto, D.F.: An adaptive semiparametric and context-based approach to unsupervised change detection in multitemporal remote-sensing images. J. IEEE Trans. Image Process. **11**(4), 452–466 (2002)
3. Gong, M., Zhou, Z., Ma, J.: Change detection in synthetic aperture radar images based on image fusion and fuzzy clustering. J. IEEE Trans. Image Process. **21**(4), 2141–2151 (2012)
4. Ghosh, S., Bruzzone, L., Patra, S., et al.: A context-sensitive technique for unsupervised change detection based on Hopfield-type neural networks. J. IEEE Trans. Geosci. Remote Sens. **45**(3), 778–789 (2007)

5. Bujor, F., et al.: Application of log-cumulants to the detection of spatiotemporal discontinuities in multitemporal SAR images. J. IEEE Trans. Geosci. Remote Sens. **42**(10), 2073–2084 (2004)
6. Inglada, J., Mercier, G.: A new statistical similarity measure for change detection in multitemporal SAR images and its extension to multiscale change analysis. J. IEEE Trans. Geosci. Remote Sens. **45**(5), 1432–1445 (2007)
7. Krinidis, S., Chatzis, V.: A robust fuzzy local information C-means clustering algorithm. J. IEEE Trans. Image Process. **19**(5), 1328–1337 (2010)
8. Rosenfield, G.H., Fitzpatrick-Lins, K.: A coefficient of agreement as a measure of thematic classification accuracy. J. Photogram. Eng. Remote Sens. **52**(2), 223–227 (1986)

Change Detection in Synthetic Aperture Radar Images Based on Fuzzy Restricted Boltzmann Machine

Na Li[1], Jiao Shi[1(✉)], and Maoguo Gong[2]

[1] School of Electronics and Information, Northwest Polytechnical University,
127 West Youyi Road, Xi'an 710072, Shaanxi, China
`linaflydream@163.com, jiaoshi@nwpu.edu.cn`
[2] Key Laboratory of Intelligent Perception and Image
Understanding of Ministry of Education of China, Xidian University,
2 South TaiBai Road, Xi'an 710071, Shaanxi, China
`gong@ieee.org`

Abstract. Image Change Detection is a process to identify the changes of two images of the same scene that were taken in different times. In this paper, we propose a novel change detection approach based on Fuzzy Restricted Boltzmann Machine. The approach applies Fuzzy Restricted Boltzmann Machine as unsupervised feature learning algorithm and Fuzzy Back Propagation as supervised fine-tuning algorithm. Fuzzy Restricted Boltzmann Machine applying to change detection can reduce the effect of speckle noise in Synthetic Aperture Radar Images, in which the parameters governing the model are replaced by fuzzy numbers. Experiments on real data sets and theoretical analysis show the proposed method can obtain promising results and outperforms some other methods.

Keywords: Fuzzy Restricted Boltzmann Machine (FRBM) · Image change detection · Synthetic Aperture Radar (SAR) image

1 Introduction

Image Change Detection is a technology to analyze and identify the change of surface qualitatively or quantitatively from multi-temporal image of the same scene but taken in different times. This technology is important and widely used in some field, such as for resources and environment monitoring, forest and vegetation coverage, the situation of urban expansion and agricultural survey. It also plays a great role in military field and the monitoring and evaluation of natural disaster [8].

Change detection in SAR images has classical three-step process including (1) pre-processing, (2) producing a difference image (DI) between the multi-temporal images, (3) analyzing the DI [8]. In respect of producing a DI, in order to reduce the impact of speckle noise, some classical methods have been proposed

© Springer Nature Singapore Pte Ltd. 2016
M. Gong et al. (Eds.): BIC-TA 2016, Part I, CCIS 681, pp. 438–444, 2016.
DOI: 10.1007/978-981-10-3611-8_39

such as Wavelet Fusion [2], etc. The methods to analyze the DI fall into four major categories including thresholding based methods such as Reformulated Fuzzy Local Information C-means (RFLICM) [5], and Markov Random Field FCM (MRFFCM) [3], graph-cut based methods such as Local Fit-search and Kernel-induced Graph Cut [6], level set methods such as CV model [7].

Neural network is used in image processing field as pattern recognition classifier and clustering technology originally. Along with the further research, neural network is fully applied to various fields. In addition, Gong et al. proposed a novel framework for image change detection based on deep neural network in [4], and the method of this paper is based on this framework.

This paper is organized into four section. In Sect. 2, the proposed method will be described in detail. Section 3 will present the experimental results on real multi-temporal SAR images to verify the feasibility of the method. Finally, the conclusion is drawn in Sect. 4.

2   Methodology

The two co-registered intensity SAR images $I_1 = \{I_1(i,j), 1 \le i \le A, 1 \le j \le B\}$ and $I_2 = \{I_2(i,j), 1 \le i \le A, 1 \le j \le B\}$ are applied to change detection, which have same size $A \times B$ and are acquired over the same scene at different times t_1 and t_2 respectively. Because of the contradiction between reducing the effect of speckle noise and retaining detail information it is quite difficult to estimate statistics item about changed and unchanged regions and carry out change detection accurately. The change detection problem is to design a method to find the change between the two images. The framework of the proposed method is described in [4].

In proposed method, data preprocessing is the first part. Firstly, a joint classifier of the two original images based on FCM (JFCM) is used as pre-classification [4]. Secondly, in order to reduce the effect of speckle noise, according to the result of pre-classification, selecting appropriate sample from two original image is necessary. The selection criteria is described in [4].

In the proposed method, the key is to train neural network. This part is made up of two steps, learning and fine-tuning. The learning step to learn the representation of the relationships between the two images is crucial and we use FRBM as the algorithm of the learning network. The FRBM model, in which the connection weighs and biases between visible and hidden units are fuzzy numbers, has rather powerful representation capability and robustness [1]. The fuzzy numbers of the FRBM can reduce the effect of speckle noise in change detection effectively. In addition, the FRBM belongs to unsupervised learning. These means the FRBM is a good choice.

In FRBM, placing "bar" over a capital letter, such as $\overline{W}_j$, is called a fuzzy number, which is defined as

$$\overline{W}_j(w) = \max\left\{1 - \frac{|w - w_j|}{\hat{w}_j}, 0\right\}. \tag{1}$$

The energy function for the FRBM is defined by $\overline{E}\left(\mathbf{x}, \mathbf{h}, \overline{\theta}\right) = -\overline{\mathbf{b}}^T \mathbf{x} - \overline{\mathbf{c}}^T \mathbf{h} - \mathbf{h}^T \overline{\mathbf{W}} \mathbf{x}$, where $\overline{E}\left(\mathbf{x}, \mathbf{h}, \overline{\theta}\right)$ is a fuzzified energy function, and $\overline{\theta} = \left\{\overline{\mathbf{b}}, \overline{\mathbf{c}}, \overline{\mathbf{W}}\right\}$ are fuzzy parameters. The fuzzy conditional probabilities of FRBM is defined by

$$
\begin{aligned}
P_L\left(h_i = 1|\mathbf{x}\right) &= P\left(h_i = 1|\mathbf{x}; \theta_L\right) = \sigma\left(c_i^L + W_i^L \mathbf{x}\right) \\
P_R\left(h_i = 1|\mathbf{x}\right) &= P\left(h_i = 1|\mathbf{x}; \theta_R\right) = \sigma\left(c_i^R + W_i^R \mathbf{x}\right) \\
P_L\left(x_j = 1|\mathbf{h}\right) &= P\left(x_j = 1|\mathbf{h}; \theta_L\right) = \sigma\left(b_j^L + W_j^L \mathbf{h}\right) \\
P_R\left(x_j = 1|\mathbf{h}\right) &= P\left(x_j = 1|\mathbf{h}; \theta_R\right) = \sigma\left(b_j^R + W_j^R \mathbf{h}\right)
\end{aligned}
\tag{2}
$$

where lower bound of connection W_{ij}^L, visible bias b_j^L, hidden bias c_i^L, and their upper bounds W_{ij}^R, b_j^R, c_i^R are six kinds of parameters for visible unit and hidden unit in the FRBM model. The change in the lower and upper bound of connection weight of FRBM is given by

$$
\begin{aligned}
\Delta \mathbf{W}^L &= \varepsilon(x^{(0)} \cdot P_L(h^{L(0)} = 1|x^{(0)}) - x^{L(1)} \cdot P_L(h^{L(1)} = 1|x^{L(1)})) \\
\Delta \mathbf{W}^R &= \varepsilon(x^{(0)} \cdot P_R(h^{R(0)} = 1|x^{(0)}) - x^{R(1)} \cdot P_R(h^{R(1)} = 1|x^{R(1)}))
\end{aligned}
\tag{3}
$$

Where ε is a learning rate.

After the learning of FRBM, in order to adjust weights further and adapt to the structure of FRBM, we put the idea of fuzzy number of FRBM into BP, which is called fuzzy BP (FBP). The change in the lower and upper bound of output layer weight of FBP is derived as follows

$$
\begin{aligned}
\Delta w_{jk}^L &= \tfrac{1}{2} \eta\left(d_k - o_k\right) o_k^L \left(1 - o_k^L\right) y_j \\
\Delta w_{jk}^R &= \tfrac{1}{2} \eta\left(d_k - o_k\right) o_k^R \left(1 - o_k^R\right) y_j
\end{aligned}
\tag{4}
$$

The change in the lower and upper bound of hidden layer weight of FBP is derived as follows

$$
\begin{aligned}
\Delta v_{ij}^L &= \tfrac{1}{2} \eta \sum_{k=1}^{l} \left(\delta_k^{oL} w_{jk}^L + \delta_k^{oR} w_{jk}^R\right) y_j^L \left(1 - y_j^L\right) x_i \\
\Delta v_{ij}^R &= \tfrac{1}{2} \eta \sum_{k=1}^{l} \left(\delta_k^{oL} w_{jk}^L + \delta_k^{oR} w_{jk}^R\right) y_j^R \left(1 - y_j^R\right) x_i
\end{aligned}
\tag{5}
$$

The major process of neural network training includes: (1) inputting neighborhood features of each position, (2) constructing a stack of FRBM network to learn the representation of the relationships between the two images, (3) fine-tuning neural network by fuzzy BP.

After data preprocessing and neural network training, the last part is to organize original data and feed that data into trained neural network. The network output is final change map of two images. The class label 0 represents that the pixel belongs to unchanged regions, showing black in change map, and the class label 1 represents the pixel belongs to changed regions, showing white in change map.

3   Experimental Study

The quantitative analysis of change detection results is set by calculating some values of criteria including: (1) the false negatives (2) the false positives (3) the percentage correct classification (PCC). For accuracy assessment, Kappa statistic is a measure of accuracy or agreement based on the difference between the error matrix and chance agreement.

In order to assess the effectiveness of the proposed approach, in this section, two data sets are considered in the experiments. We will also introduce the comparison experiments as well as some evaluation criteria of the experiment results. In this experiment, PCC and Kappa, as main criterion, are larger, which means the method is better.

Table 1. Values of the evaluation criteria of the Bern dataset

Method	FP	FN	OE	PCC	Kappa
FLICM	190	349	539	0.9911	0.7464
RFLICM	723	61	784	0.9913	0.8132
MRFEM	6390	**26**	6416	0.9292	0.2436
MRFSM	651	45	696	0.9923	0.7576
MRFN	1756	36	1792	0.9802	0.5471
MRFFCM	364	47	411	0.9955	0.8413
RBM_BP	124	156	280	0.9969	0.8755
The proposed method	**115**	155	**270**	**0.9970**	**0.8795**

Results on the Bern Data Set

The change detection results generated by the proposed method and the seven comparative methods on the Bern data set are presented in Fig. 1 and Table 1. The method called RBM_BP is proposed by Gong et al. in [4], and the method in this paper is based on that. As shown in Fig. 1, the final map generated by RBM_BP and the proposed method is better and have less white noise spots than other six method. That by MRFEM has most white noise spots among all present methods. From Table 1, the PCC and Kappa yield by the proposed method are both higher than that yield by RBM. Although the PCC of them approach each other, the Kappa of them, as accuracy assessment, are different significantly. That means the proposed method has a promotion comparing with RBM_BP. In addition, serving as an overall evaluation, PCC and Kappa of the proposed method exhibit best among all present methods, although FN of it is not best. That means the proposed method for image change detection on the Bern data set is best among.

Results on the Ottawa Data Set

The results of the experiment on the Ottawa Data set are shown and listed in Fig. 2 and Table 2. There are eight comparative methods to verify the superiority of the proposed method. In Fig. 2, the final map of the proposed method has little white noise spots. However, in Table 2, the FN yield by the proposed method is worse than that by seven method and is just lower than that by RBM_BP,

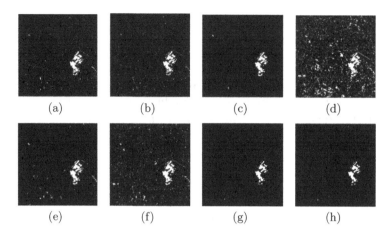

Fig. 1. Change detection results of Bern data set achieved by (a) FLICM; (b) RFLICM; (c) MRFFCM; (d) MRFEM; (e) MRFSM; (f) MRFN; (g) RBM_BP; (h) the proposed method.

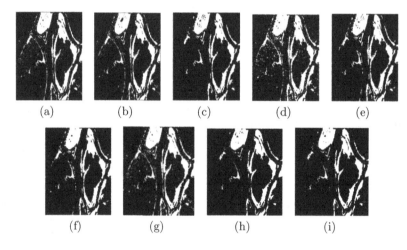

Fig. 2. Change detection results of Ottawa data set achieved by (a) FLICM; (b) RFLICM; (c) MRFFCM; (d) MRFEM; (e) MRFSM; (f) MRFN; (g) GKI; (h) RBM_BP; (i) the proposed method.

which means there are many change pixels undetected by the proposed method. The reason is the proposed method has a strong ability of reducing the effect of speckle noise so that many isolated and smallscale change area are regarded as noise. In spite of that, the OE is smallest among, because of the small FP. Moreover, the PCC and Kappa yield by the proposed method is highest among. That means not only the proposed method has promotion than RBM_BP, but also that is best. This experiment indicates the proposed method for image change detection on the Ottawa data set is best among.

Table 2. Values of the evaluation criteria of the Ottawa dataset

Method	FP	FN	OE	PCC	Kappa
FLICM	2608	369	2977	0.9707	0.9052
RFLICM	2381	469	2850	0.9719	0.9075
MRFEM	5397	298	5695	0.9439	0.8133
MRFSM	2855	487	3342	0.9671	0.8833
MRFN	2642	414	3056	0.9699	0.8929
MRFFCM	1636	712	2348	0.9769	0.9151
GKI	2801	**213**	3014	0.9702	0.8949
RBM_BP	**389**	1595	1984	0.9804	0.9239
The proposed method	557	1345	**1902**	**0.9813**	**0.9282**

4 Conclusion

This paper has presented a novel change detection method based on FRBM. Since the rather powerful representation capability and robustness, the FRBM can be applied to learn the representation of the relationships between the two images, which can reduce the effect the speckle noise effectively. In order to adapt to the structure of FRBM, we put the idea of fuzzy number of FRBM into BP, which is to adjust weights further. The experiments on the two data sets can demonstrate that the proposed method base on FRBM can achieve change detection well and is more exceptional than other present method in this paper.

Acknowledgments. This work was supported by the National Natural Science Foundation of China (Grant No. 61602385).

References

1. Chen, C.L.P., Zhang, C.Y., Chen, L., Gan, M.: Fuzzy restricted Boltzmann machine for the enhancement of deep learning. IEEE Trans. Fuzzy Syst. **23**(6), 2163–2173 (2015)
2. Gong, M., Cao, Y., Wu, Q.: A neighborhood-based ratio approach for change detection in SAR images. IEEE Geosci. Remote Sens. Lett. **9**(2), 307–311 (2012)
3. Gong, M., Su, L., Jia, M., Chen, W.: Fuzzy clustering with a modified MRF energy function for change detection in synthetic aperture radar images. IEEE Trans. Fuzzy Syst. **22**(1), 98–109 (2014)
4. Gong, M., Zhao, J., Liu, J., Miao, Q., Jiao, L.: Change detection in synthetic aperture radar images based on deep neural networks. IEEE Trans. Neural Netw. Learn. Syst. **27**(1), 125–138 (2016)
5. Gong, M., Zhou, Z., Ma, J.: Change detection in synthetic aperture radar images based on image fusion and fuzzy clustering. IEEE Trans. Image Process. **21**(4), 2141–2151 (2012)

6. Gong, M., Jia, M., Su, L., Wang, S., Jiao, L.: Detecting changes of the Yellow River Estuary via SAR images based on a local fit-search model and kernel-induced graph cuts. Int. J. Remote Sens. **35**(11–12), 4009–4030 (2014)
7. Gong, M., Li, Y., Jiao, L., Jia, M., Su, L.: SAR change detection based on intensity and texture changes. ISPRS J. Photogram. Remote Sens. **93**, 123–135 (2014)
8. Li, H., Liu, J., Gong, M., Su, L.: A survey on change detection in synthetic aperture radar imagery. J. Comput. Res. Dev. **53**(1), 123 (2016)

Machine Learning

Decision Variable Analysis Based on Distributed Computing

Zhao Wang, Maoguo Gong$^{(\boxtimes)}$, and Tian Xie

Key Laboratory of Intelligent Perception and Image Understanding,
Xidian University, Xi'an, China
gong@ieee.org

Abstract. For multiobjective optimization problems with large-scale decision variables, it is difficult to optimize all the decision variables at the same time. With the divide and conquer strategy, the decision variable analysis technique is applied to analyze the variables' property and divide the variables into subcomponents. However it takes too much time to analyze a large-scale set of decision variables. In this paper, we propose a distributed decision variable analysis algorithm. The proposed algorithm divides all the variables into subcomponents assigns each of them to a computation node. We test the proposed algorithm on some popular multiobjcetive optimization problems with large-scale decision variables and the results show that the proposed algorithm can boost the analysis process effectively.

Keywords: Multiobjective evolutionary algorithm · Distributed computing · Large-scale decision variables

1 Introduction

The multiobjective evolutionary algorithm (MOEA) has been widely used in solving complex multiobjective optimization problems (MOP) in the real world due to its various advantages [1]. The MOEAs are able to provide a series of solutions for decision makers to choose from in a specified number of iterations. Many MOEAs perform well on test suites with small-scale set of decision variables, however there are many MOPs that have a large-scale set of decision variables, which barricade the application of MOEAs. To address this issue, the MOPs with high dimensional decision variables attract much attention in these years [3–7]. With the divide and conquer strategy, the decision variables are analyzed and divided into subcomponents. And then the optimizers are applied on each of these subcomponents. However, with the increase of the number of decision variables, the decision variable analysis consumes more and more time. Ma *et al.* [2] proposed a multiobjective evolutionary algorithm based on decision variable analysis. However the sampling strategy inevitably consume too much time when dealing large-scale decision variable set. The distributed computing is an efficient way to deal with MOPs with large-scale set of decision variables [11–13].

© Springer Nature Singapore Pte Ltd. 2016
M. Gong et al. (Eds.): BIC-TA 2016, Part I, CCIS 681, pp. 447–455, 2016.
DOI: 10.1007/978-981-10-3611-8_40

In this paper, we investigate the parallel structure of the decision variable analysis and propose a distributed decision variable analysis algorithm (DDVA) based on Spark platform. The DDVA includes two parts. The first part is the distributed control variable analysis (DCVA), which classifies the decision variables into two sets: distance variable set and diverse variable set. The second part is the distributed variable dependency analysis (DVDA). The DDVA speeds the analysis by dividing the tasks into small subcomponents. DDVA is tested on some popular test problems compared with the sequential computation architecture using the same computation resource. The experimental results show that the proposed DDVA can effectively improve the efficiency with the same resource.

This paper is organized as follows. The multiobjective optimization problem and decision variable analysis are introduced in Sect. 2. We describe the distributed decision variable analysis in Sect. 3. In Sect. 4, the proposed DDVA is tested on some popular test problems and the experimental results are analyzed. We conclude this paper in Sect. 5.

2   Background

In this section, we introduce the multiobjective optimization problem and decision variable analysis.

2.1   Control Property

For a certain MOP, the decision variables control different aspects of the evolutionary process. We focus on a MOP described below:

$$\begin{cases} \min \ \boldsymbol{F}(\boldsymbol{X}) = (f_1(\boldsymbol{X}), f_2(\boldsymbol{X}) \dots, f_m(\boldsymbol{X})) \\ \text{subject to: } \boldsymbol{X} \in \boldsymbol{\Omega} \end{cases} \tag{1}$$

where m is the number of objectives and n is the number of decision variables.

For a given solution $\boldsymbol{X}$, if the change in a decision variable x_i only generates solutions that dominate or being dominated by $\boldsymbol{X}$, then x_i is a distance variable. If the change in x_i generates solutions that do not dominate or being dominated by solution $\boldsymbol{X}$, then x_i is a position variable. x_i is a mixed variable if the change in x_i can generate dominating, dominated or nondominated solutions. Examples of distance variables and position variables of test problem ZDT1 are shown in Fig. 1.

2.2   Variable Dependency

The large-scale set of decision variables makes it difficult to optimize the MOP. In [14], the authors indicate that the difficulty can be reduced rapidly if the functions can be transformed into a set of simpler functions. For an MOP with large-scale set of variables, the dependency need to be learned to perform the division as suggested in [15,16]. The dependency between two variables are defined as

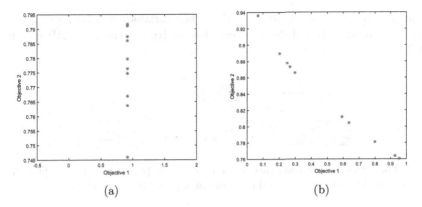

Fig. 1. The solutions obtained by changing decision variables. (a) Solutions obtained by changing distance variables. (b) Solutions obtained by changing position variables.

below. For a given objective function $f_j(\boldsymbol{X})$, decision variables x_{i_1} and x_{i_1} are interacted if there exists a_1, b_1, a_2, b_2 which satisfy:

$$\begin{cases} f(\boldsymbol{x})|_{x_{i_1}=a_2, x_{i_2}=b_1} < f(\boldsymbol{x})|_{x_{i_1}=a_1, x_{i_2}=b_1} \\ f(\boldsymbol{x})|_{x_{i_1}=a_2, x_{i_2}=b_2} > f(\boldsymbol{x})|_{x_{i_1}=a_1, x_{i_2}=b_2} \end{cases} \tag{2}$$

That is to say, there are two values of x_{i_2} where the monotonicity of the function of x_{i_1} is inversed.

There are many researches on the decision variable analysis. In [17], a predefined number of decision variables of different types can be set. Many definitions about the variables dependency is studied in [20]. The variable dependency and the separability of the objective function is discussed in [21,22]. For variable dependency detection, many methods like model building, interaction adaptation method, random method and perturbation method has been studied. In [2], the authors proposed a multiobjective evolutionary algorithm based on decision variable analysis which divides the large-scale set of decision variables into small subcomponents in a subsequential manner.

3   Distributed Decision Variable Analysis

In this section, we describe the detail of the distributed decision variable analysis. To distribute the computation to different computation nodes, we have to divide the whole computation task into small subtasks. Each of the subtask is computed in a resilient distributed data set (RDD), and the computation process is performed parallelly in each RDD.

The division of the distributed decision variable analysis is shown in Figs. 2 and 3. In Fig. 2, the decision variables are divided into a set of subtasks each contains only the variables to be analyzed. To analyze the dependency of the decision variables, each RDD contains all the variables, but only the dependency of the specified variable against all the other variables will be analyzed. The process of the distributed decision variable analysis is shown in Algorithms 1 and 2.

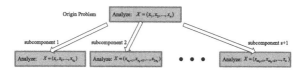

Fig. 2. The division of decision variables for control property analysis. All the decision variables are divided into $s + 1$ subtasks of size n_d, and $n = (s + 1)n_d$.

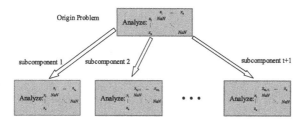

Fig. 3. The division of decision variables for dependency analysis. For a given objective, the decision variables is divided into $t + 1$ subtasks of size n_e, and $(t + 1)n_e = n$. The RDD includes all the decision variables so that the assigned decision variables can be analyzed with all the other variables.

4   Experimental Result and Discussion

In this section, we test our proposed algorithms on some test problems of popular test suit. The test problems are UF1, UF2, UF3, UF4, UF5, UF6, UF10 [18], ZDT1 and ZDT4 [19].

To demonstrate the efficiency of the distributed decision variable analysis, we compare the proposed algorithm with the sequential decision variable analysis. Each instance are repeated 30 times and the averaged CPU time is calculated. For each test problem, the number of decision variables is 100, 500, 1000, 10000 and 100000 respectively. For large-scale variable set, it takes too much time for the sequential decision variable analysis, and the CPU time is omitted. The experimental results is shown in Tables 1 and 2. The speed ratio is shown in Figs. 4 and 5.

From Table 1, we notice that the time to perform the sequential control prosperity analysis is bearable for low dimension decision variables like 100, 500, 1000

Algorithm 1. Distributed Control Property Analysis

1: **Input**: the size of decision variables: n, the number of sampling for each decision variable: NSC and the other parameters.
2: **Initialization**: Initialize the empty sets as below. $DistanceSet(s)$: records the indexes of the distance variables in the sth subcomponent. $DiverseSet(s)$: records the indexes of the position variables and mixed variables in the sth subcomponent. $CombinedDistanceSet$: combines the $DistanceSet$ of all the subcomponents. $CombinedDiverseSet$: combines the $DiverseSet$ of all the subcomponents.
3: Parallelly processing each subcomponent, which includes decision variables of $\{p, \ldots, q\}$ as below:
4: **for** $i=p$ to q **do**
5:     randomly generate a feasible solution: $(x_1, \ldots, x_p, \ldots, x_i, \ldots, x_q, \ldots, x_n)$.
6:     **for** $j=1$ to NSC **do**
7:         randomly sample a solution x_i' in an interval: $sample = (j-1) \times \frac{x_i^U - x_i^L}{NSC} + rand \times \frac{x_i^U - x_i^L}{NSC}$, $x_i' = x_i^L + sample$. the x_i^L and x_i^U are the lower and upper bounds of variable x_i
8:         calculate the objective values of the obtained solutions: $F(x_1, \ldots, x_p, \ldots, x_i', \ldots, x_q, \ldots, x_n)$ and add it to a sample set of variable x_i: S_i.
9:     **end for**
10:    Use the nondominated sort to obtain a series of nondominated fronts of S_i.
11:    **if** there are NSC nondominated fronts **then**
12:        Add i to the $DistanceSet(s)$
13:    **else**
14:        Add i to the $DiverseSet(s)$
15:    **end if**
16: **end for**
17: Combine all the $DistanceSet$ and $DiverseSet$ and get $CombinedDistanceSet$ and $CombinedDiverseSet$.
18: **Output**: $CombinedDistanceSet$, $CombinedDiverseSet$ and CPU time.

and 10000 decision variables. With the increase of dimension from 100 decision variables to 1000 decision variables, there are not distinct difference between CPU time for all the test problems. With respect to same number of decision variables, the time consumed is different. It takes more time to analyze the variable prosperity of UF3. UF4, UF5, UF6 and UF10 than ZDT1, ZDT4, UF1 and UF4. This means that the time for the evaluation is comparable to the overhead of the program. For different test problems, it also takes more time to evaluation a solution for a more complex problems. As for 10000 variables, it takes at least 4 times for the program to analyze the decision variables. This indicates that the sequential control prosperity analysis is faced with big time consumption when dealing with large-scale decision variable set. It is even impossible to analyze a test problem of 100000 decision variables. On the contrary, the distributed control prosperity analysis takes less time than the sequential counterpart, while showing similar time consumption pattern for the test problems.

Algorithm 2. Distributed Variable Dependency Analysis

1: **Input:** the size of decision variable set: n, the number of objectives: m, the set of distance variables: $CombinedDistanceSet$, and the number of sampling for each distance variable: NSD.

2: Parallelly processing each subcomponent including decision variables of $\{p, \ldots, q\}$ as below:

3: **for** $i=p$ to q **do**

4:   **for** $j=1$ to n **do**

5:     **for** $k=1$ to NSD **do**

6:       randomly generate a feasible solution $\mathbf{X} = (x_1, \ldots, x_p, \ldots, x_i, \ldots, x_q, \ldots, x_j, \ldots, x_n)$, where $x_i = a_1$ and $x_j = b_1$.

7:       randomly select a value a_2 in the feasible domain of x_i and a value b_2 in the feasible domain of x_j.

8:       calculate objective vectors of the four solutions: $\mathbf{F}(\mathbf{X}^1)|_{x_i=a_1, x_j=b_1}$, $\mathbf{F}(\mathbf{X}^2)|_{x_i=a_1, x_j=b_2}$, $\mathbf{F}(\mathbf{X}^3)|_{x_i=a_2, x_j=b_1}$, $\mathbf{F}(\mathbf{X}^4)|_{x_i=a_2, x_j=b_2}$.

9:       **for** $l=1$ to m **do**

10:         Calculate $\Delta f_{l1} = f_l(\mathbf{X}^3) - f_l(\mathbf{X}^1)$, $\Delta f_{l2} = f_l(\mathbf{X}^4) - f_l(\mathbf{X}^2)$.

11:         **if** $\Delta f_{l1} \times \Delta f_{l2} < 0$ **then**

12:           There exists dependency between x_i and x_j.

13:         **end if**

14:       **end for**

15:     **end for**

16:   **end for**

17: **end for**

18: Combine the dependency analysis result of each subcomponent.

19: **Output:** The dependency analysis result and CPU time.

From Table 2, we notice that the variable dependency is more sensitive to the number of decision variables. This is because the computation complexity is $O(n^2)$, on the contrary the computation complexity of control prosperity analysis is $O(n)$. For sequential variable dependency analysis, it takes more time than the distributed variable dependency analysis does. The difference is more distinct than the time difference of control variable analysis. The time consumed by 10000 and 100000 variables is unbearable.

In Fig. 4, we notice that the speed of DCPA is at least two times faster than the SCPA. The smallest speed-up ratio occurs on ZDT4 with 100 variables, and the biggest speed-up ratio occurs on UF10 with 100000 variables. With more variables, the speed-up ratio increases which means that the DCPA has bigger advantage over SCPA when dealing with large-scale decision variables. In Fig. 5, we notice that the smallest speed-up ratio is the test on ZDT1 with 1000 decision variables. The biggest speed-up ratio is 8, which is achieved on ZDT4 with 100 variables. The overall speed-up ratio of DVDA is smaller than that of DCPA, which results from the consumption of overhead.

Table 1. The averaged CPU time of sequential decision variable analysis and distributed decision variable analysis

Variables	Algorithms	ZDT1	ZDT4	UF1	UF2	UF3	UF4	UF5	UF6	UF10
100	SCPA (ms)	15387	14561	11361	11880	19854	20315	21358	24621	27856
	DCPA	3231	3429	5018	3021	5031	5246	6354	7652	8632
500	SCPA (ms)	16842	16215	13548	17892	20541	21502	22332	26482	29840
	DCPA	5631	3564	5194	5988	5732	5864	6584	7956	9251
1000	SCPA (ms)	17896	17863	15684	18975	25462	26784	28520	29898	33650
	DCPA	7219	3873	5378	6268	7428	6560	6915	8018	9820
10000	SCPA (ms)	60213	101548	153548	163251	201687	216803	223640	258870	298406
	DCPA	15212	29043	27470	29315	30518	30538	32168	37561	40351
100000	SCPA (ms)	NaN	NaN	NaN	NaN	NaN	NaN	NaN	NaN	NaN
	DCPA	648825	192881	2065685	2296183	2387710	2653034	2754631	2914524	3502136

Table 2. The averaged CPU time of sequential variable dependency analysis (SVDA) and distributed variable dependency analysis (DVDA)

Variables	Algorithms	ZDT1	ZDT4	UF1	UF2	UF3	UF4	UF5	UF6	UF10
100	SVDA	16845	18945	18742	19874	20154	23548	23481	24846	25680
	DVDA	3391	2412	6113	6845	7502	7684	7945	8015	8866
500	SVDA	178650	54213	65431	75153	77685	84502	102180	121540	143250
	DVDA	9991	12333	22573	24897	26458	24159	23648	26487	26982
1000	SVDA	189710	203154	124584	187865	235481	264810	302154	398100	456800
	DVDA	13485	44764	89904	98520	102236	105798	112357	120258	145690
10000	SVDA	60213	101548	153548	163251	201687	216803	223640	258870	298406
	DVDA	1357441	2031548	2354846	2459875	2543652	2758521	2987996	3021548	3535110
100000	SVDA	NaN	NaN	NaN	NaN	NaN	NaN	NaN	NaN	NaN
	DVDA	23054789	302154698	345132015	376894159	379965102	403154120	415689984	435687415	675484102

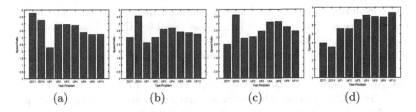

   (a)   (b)   (c)   (d)

Fig. 4. The speed ratio of DCPA over SCPA. (a). Problems with 100 variables. (b). Problems with 500 variables. (c). Problems with 1000 variables. (d). Problems with 10000 variables.

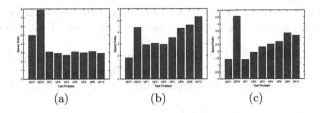

   (a)   (b)   (c)

Fig. 5. The speed ratio of DVDA over SVDA. (a). Problems with 100 variables. (b). Problems with 500 variables. (c). Problems with 1000 variables.

5   Conclusion

For a multiobjective optimization problem with a large-scale set of decision variables, it is necessary to analyze the control prosperity and the variable dependency to reduce the solving complexity. The present decision variable analysis methods deals with this problem in a sequential manner, which takes too much time for application in the real world. The inherent parallel structure of decision variable analysis is suitable for distributed computing.

In this paper, we proposed a distributed decision variable analysis method which based on Spark platform. The DDVA includes two main parts, the first part analyze the control prosperity parallelly and the second part detects the dependency between variables. The proposed algorithm is test on some popular test problems with a large-scale set of decision variables, and the results show that the proposed distributed variable analysis algorithm can effectively reduce the time consumption.

In the future, the proposed algorithm will apply on popular test problems with distributed evolution process. The distributed algorithm will be optimized to reduce the time consumption of the overhead. We will dive into the setting of the distributed program to study the influence of different parameters.

References

1. Deb, K.: Multi-Objective Optimization Using Evolutionary Algorithms. Wiley, New York (2001)
2. Ma, X., Liu, F., Qi, Y., Wang, X., Li, L., Jiao, L., Yin, M., Gong, M.: A multiobjective evolutionary algorithm based on decision variable analyses for multiobjective optimization problems with large-scale variables. IEEE Trans. Evol. Comput. **20**(2), 275–298 (2016)
3. Potter, M., Jong, K.: A cooperative coevolutionary approach to function optimization. In: Proceedings of the International Conference on Parallel Problem Solving from Nature, Jerusalem, Israel, vol. 2, pp. 249–257 (1994)
4. Li, X., Yao, X.: Cooperatively coevolving particle swarms for large scale optimization. IEEE Trans. Evol. Comput. **16**(2), 210–224 (2012)
5. Yang, Z., Tang, K., Yao, X.: Large scale evolutionary optimization using cooperative coevolution. Inf. Sci. **178**(15), 2985–2999 (2008)
6. Weise, T., Chiong, R., Tang, K.: Evolutionary optimization: pitfalls and booby traps. J. Comput. Sci. Technol. **27**(5), 907–936 (2012)
7. Mei, Y., Li, X., Yao, X.: Cooperative co-evolution with route distance grouping for large-scale capacitated arc routing problems. IEEE Trans. Evol. Comput. **18**(3), 435–449 (2014)
8. Danielis, P., Skodzik, J., Altmann, V., Kappel, B., Timmermann, D.: Extensive analysis of the Kad-based distributed computing system DuDE. In: IEEE Symposium on Computers and Communication, pp. 128–133. IEEE Press, Larnaca (2015)
9. Buyya, R., Ramamohanarao, K.: An innovative master's program in distributed computing. IEEE Distrib. Syst. Onli. **8**(1), 2 (2007)

10. Raghavan, N.R.S., Waghmare, T.: DPAC: an object-oriented distributed and parallel computing framework for manufacturing applications. IEEE Trans. Robot. Autom. **18**(4), 431–443 (2002)
11. Sinha, A., Saini, T., Srikanth, S.V.: Distributed computing approach to optimize road traffic simulation. In: International Conference on Parallel, Distributed and Grid Computing, pp. 360–364. IEEE Press, Solan (2014)
12. Hasan, M., Goraya, M.S.: A framework for priority based task execution in the distributed computing environment. In: International Conference on Signal Processing, Computing and Control, pp. 155–158. IEEE Press, Waknaghat (2015)
13. Hu, B., Gong, J.: A distributed geo-computing model of individual-based transmission simulation. In: 8th International Conference on Fuzzy Systems and Knowledge Discovery, pp. 2412–2416. IEEE Press, Shanghai (2011)
14. Thierens, D., Goldberg, D.: Mixing in genetic algorithms. In: 5th International Conference on Genetic Algorithms, pp. 38–45. IEEE Press, Urbana (1993)
15. Yu, T., Goldberg, D., Sastry, K., Lima, C., Pelikan, M.: Dependency structure matrix, genetic algorithms, and effective recombination. Evol. Comput. **17**(4), 595–626 (2009)
16. Omidvar, M., Li, X., Mei, Y., Yao, X.: Cooperative co-evolution with differential grouping for large scale optimization. IEEE Trans. Evol. Comput. **18**(3), 378–393 (2014)
17. Huband, S., Hingston, P., Barone, L., While, L.: A review of multiobjective test problems and a scalable test problem toolkit. IEEE Trans. Evol. Comput. **10**(5), 477–506 (2006)
18. Zhang, Q., Zhou, A., Zhao, S., Nagaratnam, P., Liu, W., Tiwari, S.: Multiobjective optimization test instances for the CEC 2009 special session and competition (2008)
19. Zitzler, E., Deb, K., Thiele, L.: Comparison of multiobjective evolutionary algorithms: empirical results. Evol. Comput. **8**(2), 173–195 (2000)
20. Chen, W., Weise, T., Yang, Z., Tang, K.: Large-scale global optimization using cooperative coevolution with variable interaction learning. In: Schaefer, R., Cotta, C., Kołodziej, J., Rudolph, G. (eds.) PPSN 2010. LNCS, vol. 6239, pp. 300–309. Springer, Heidelberg (2010). doi:10.1007/978-3-642-15871-1_31
21. Jiao, L., Li, Y., Gong, M., Zhang, X.: Quantum-inspired immune clonal algorithm for global optimization. IEEE Trans. Syst. Man Cybern. B Cybern. **38**(5), 1234–1253 (2008)
22. Tang, K., Li, X., Suganthan, P., Yang, Z., Weise, T.: Benchmark functions for the CEC 2010 special session and competition on large-scale global optimization. Nature Inspired Computation, Hefei (2010)

A Multi-task Learning Approach by Combining Derivative-Free and Gradient Methods

Yiqi Hu and Yang Yu$^{(\boxtimes)}$

National Key Laboratory for Novel Software Technology,
Nanjing University, Nanjing 210023, China
{huyq,yuy}@lamda.nju.edu.cn

Abstract. In multi-task learning, different but related tasks are solved simultaneously. Extracting and utilizing relationships between these tasks can be very helpful for learning predictors with strong generalization ability. Unfortunately, the optimization objectives of multi-task learning are commonly non-convex. Traditional optimization methods based on gradient are limited in those non-convex problems. Previous studies mainly focused on transforming the objective function to be convex. But those methods will distort the original intention. This paper tries to solve the original optimization objective by applying derivative-free methods, which is able to solve complex non-convex problems but usually suffer from slow convergence speed. In this paper, we investigate combining derivative-free and gradient optimization methods to inherit the advantages of the both. We apply this mixed method to solve multi-task learning problems with a low-rank constraint directly. Experiment results show that this method can achieve better optimization performance than the derivative-free and the gradient methods alone.

Keywords: Multi-task learning · Non-convex optimization · Derivative-free optimization · Gradient descent

1 Introduction

Multi-task learning, which solves multiple learning tasks simultaneously, is attracting researchers' attention as a sub-field of machine learning increasingly. In most cases, formalized objective function of multi-task learning is non-convex and hard to be solved directly by traditional optimization method based on gradient. Multi-task learners always relax original constraint and transform the non-convex objective function to convex one [1,2,4,14,16]. It sacrifices the precision of model for the efficiency of optimization. It will have a negative effect on the generalization performance of predictors.

Hence we want to solve the optimization problem under original constraint directly. However existing non-convex optimization algorithms are suffering from poor efficiency. Recently, a new algorithm RAndomized COordinate Shrinking (RACOS) [22] was proposed for solving non-convex optimization problems, and guarantees that it can get approximate global optima within finite querying

© Springer Nature Singapore Pte Ltd. 2016
M. Gong et al. (Eds.): BIC-TA 2016, Part I, CCIS 681, pp. 456–465, 2016.
DOI: 10.1007/978-981-10-3611-8_41

budget. In this paper, we propose an algorithm which combines RACOS and gradient method in a reasonable way (denoted as RACOSGD). RACOSGD can solve multi-task learning problem with low-rank constraint directly.

The rest of paper is organized in 4 sections. In multi-task learning, we introduce the background and formulate the objective function. In derivative-free optimization, we introduce algorithm RACOS and propose our algorithm according to the objective function. In experiments, we prove that our algorithm has better performance than other contrastive algorithms empirically. The last section is conclusion.

2 Multi-task Learning

Multi-task learning (MTL) is a machine learning approach that learns predictors for related problems simultaneously in shared feature space. Many applications can be regarded as multi-task learning problems, such as web image and video search [20], disease prediction [7] and therapy outcome [24]. In these cases, learning problem is composed of many sub-problems called tasks, and tasks are related with each other objectively. A simple approach to solve it is to consider every task is independent and solve them one by one. This approach is single-task learning (STL). In MTL, multiple tasks learn simultaneously by extracting and utilizing appropriate shared information across tasks. MTL makes full use of the relationship between tasks. Obviously the predictor learned by MTL has stronger generalization ability than the one obtained by STL.

2.1 Objective Function

In multi-task learning, previous works share same framework that objective function is combined with empirical loss and regularization term: $\min_W \mathcal{L}(W) + \Omega(W)$. Where W are the predictors of MTL that are estimated from the training data, $\mathcal{L}$ is loss function, and Ω is regularization term that defines specific relatedness between tasks. In fact, Ω is the assumptions on relatedness. The regularization terms are different in different applications. There are many prior works on modelling relationship among tasks using novel regularization [1–5,10,12,14,16].

In this work, we assume that tasks share same feature space and formalizing by low-rank constraint on W. Hence the objective function with specific regularization term can be expressed as:

$$\min_W \mathcal{L}(W) + \lambda \mathrm{rank}(W) \tag{1}$$

Where λ is a hyper-parameter to trade off empirical loss and regularization punishment. It has been proved that above optimization problem with low-rank constraint is NP-hard [19]. Before proposing our method, we will explain the symbols that appear in this paper.

2.2   Formulation

Assuming that multi-task learning problem contains T tasks. The dataset in t-th task can be denoted as $D_t = \{(x_{t,1}, y_{t,1}), (x_{t,2}, y_{t,2}), ..., (x_{t,m_t}, y_{t,m_t})\}$. Where $t \in \{1, 2, ..., T\}$, $x_{t,i} \in \mathbb{R}^d$ is the i-th instance in dataset corresponding to t-th task, $i \in \{1, 2, ..., m_t\}$, d is dimension size of instance, $y_{t,i} \in \{-1, +1\}$ is label, m_t is instance size in t-th task training dataset. In our work, we want to learn T different linear predictors $w_1, w_2, ..., w_T$ from T training datasets $D_1, D_2, ..., D_T$. For predictor w_t, the prediction can be given by $f_t(x_{t,i}) = \text{sign} \langle w_t, x_{t,i} \rangle$. Where sign $\langle \cdot \rangle$ is indicator function and $\langle \cdot, \cdot \rangle$ is inner product. Because predictors are learned simultaneous, our optimization objective is a orthogonal matrix $W = \{w_1, w_2, ..., w_T\}$, $W \in \mathbb{R}^{d \times T}$. Each column vector in W is a predictor. Considering low-rank assumption, W can be represented as the product of two low-rank matrices: $W = L \times R^T$. Where $L \in \mathbb{R}^{d \times r}$, $R \in \mathbb{R}^{T \times r}$ and $r \ll \min(d, T)$. Low-rank assumption is satisfied naturally because of the small integer r. The optimization objective is transformed from W into (L, R) by decomposition. We select logistic loss as empirical loss and low-rank assumption is constrained by decomposition. Hence learning problem in our work can be represented as:

$$\min_{(L,R)} f(L, R) = \min_{(L,R)} \sum_{t=1}^{T} \sum_{i=1}^{m_t} \log(1 + \exp(-Y_{t,i}(L \times R^T)_t^T x_{t,i})) \tag{2}$$

Where $f(L, R)$ is our objective function, $(L \times R^T)_t^T$ is the predictor of t-th task. If there is no other special instruction, (2) is the objective function which is solved by optimization methods mentioned later.

2.3   Traditional Multi-task Learning Methods

The optimization problem represented by (1) is NP-hard. In traditional methods trace norm [13] is introduced to (1) to simplify the complexity of optimization [1,2,4,14,16]:

$$\min_{W} \mathcal{L}(W) + \lambda ||W||_* \tag{3}$$

Where $||W||_*$ is the trace norm of W, $||W||_* = \sum_i \sigma_i(W)$, $\sigma_i(W)$ is a singular value of W. Trace norm is a convex relaxation for rank constraint. Gradient-based optimization methods can be applied to solving problem (3). The flaw of the relaxation has been mentioned above.

2.4   Alternative Gradient Descent (GDO)

Because of the product of L and R, the optimization problem represented by (2) is non-convex. But if we fix L as $\tilde{L}$, the optimization problem $\min_R f(\tilde{L}, R)$ is convex. Similarly, if we fix R as $\tilde{R}$, the optimization problem $\min_L f(L, \tilde{R})$ is convex too. We denote this kind of property alternative convex property. Then according to this property, the alternative gradient descent algorithm (GDO) is proposed to optimize problem (2). GDO fixes L and R alternatively and optimize another one using gradient descent method (GD) [8]. Repeating this step several times, we can get a pair solution $(\tilde{L}, \tilde{R})$ finally. But $(\tilde{L}, \tilde{R})$ is not the global optimal solution with high probability [11].

3   Derivative-Free Optimization

Because (2) is non-convex, it can not be solved by gradient-based methods and GDO can not get global optimal solution. Hence we want to introduce derivative-free optimization methods to solve this problem.

There exist some derivative-free optimization methods now such as evolutionary optimization algorithms and Bayesian optimization [9] etc. Evolutionary algorithms such as evolution strategy (ES) [6], particle swarm optimization (PSO) [15] are always used to solve kinds of complex non-convex optimization problems. Evolutionary algorithms are heuristic optimization algorithm. Compared with gradient-based methods, evolutionary algorithms suffer from weak theoretic foundation and poor efficiency. Recently a classification-based non-convex optimization algorithm RACOS was proposed to solve complex optimization problems with high efficiency and theoretic guarantee [22]. Focusing on multi-task learning problem represented by (2), we want to introduce RACOS to avoid falling into local optimum and utilize high convergence rate of gradient-based methods. In this work we propose a reasonable strategy (RACOSGD) of combining RACOS and gradient descent. Before giving details of RACOSGD, we will introduce RACOS briefly.

3.1   Classification-Based Optimization

RACOS [22] has be proposed for solving derivative-free optimization problem through classification. RACOS is an iterative algorithm, inspired from the statistical view of evolutionary algorithms [17,18,23] and is based on the sampling and learning framework [21]. The approach that RACOS generates offspring is based on classification. That is to say RACOS uses a classification learning model to classify sample space into two categories, positive or negative by regarding current population as training set. Then, sampling in the space with positive label with probability λ, and in original space with probability $1 - \lambda$ to avoid falling into local optimum.

Algorithm 1 is the pseudo-code of RACOS. Labeling and Sampling are subprocedures of RACOS. We use Labeling to label the samples in set P_i. For example, Labeling labels one or several samples in P_i with smallest evaluation values as $+1$ and labels others as -1 for minimization problem. If label is denoted as y, $B_i = \{(x_1, y_1), (x_2, y_2), \ldots, (x_m, y_m)\}$ is training data in i-th iteration. Sample(h, λ) is a sampling procedure. It samples from positive label space with probability λ or original space with probability $1 - \lambda$. RACOS initialize sample set P_0 by sampling from original space uniformly (step 1). Step 2 and 10 are used to update the best solution $\tilde{x}$ so far. In each iteration (step 3 to 11), RACOS

Algorithm 1. RACOS

Input:

    f: Objective function to be minimized; λ: Balancing parameter;

    $\mathcal{C}$: A binary classification algorithm; $N \in \mathbb{N}$: Number of iterations;

    B: A set with labeled samples; $m \in \mathbb{N}$: Sample size in each iteration.

Procedure:

  1: Collect $P_0 = \{x_1, x_2, \ldots x_m\}$ by i.i.d. sampling from $\mathcal{U}_X$

  2: Let $\tilde{x} = \operatorname{argmin}_{x \in P_0} f(x)$

  3: **for** $i = 1$ to N **do**

  4:    $B_i = \mathsf{Labeling}(P_{i-1})$ using f

  5:    Let $P_i = \varnothing$

  6:    **for** $j = 1$ to m **do**

  7:        $h = \mathcal{C}(B_i)$

  8:        $x_j = \mathsf{Sampling}(h, \lambda)$, query $f(x)$ and let $P_i = P_i \cup \{x_j\}$

  9:    **end for**

10:    $\tilde{x} = \operatorname{argmin}_{x \in P_i \cup \tilde{x}} f(x)$

11: **end for**

12: **return** $\tilde{x}$

---

need to generate offspring set P_i with m new samples: firstly, $\mathsf{Labeling}$ is used to evaluate each sample in P_{i-1} and generates B_i (step 4). During step 6 to 9, A unique sampling space is trained by $\mathcal{C}$ for each sample in P_i (step 7), and then $\mathsf{Sampling}$ sub-procedure is called to get a new sample (step 8). At the end of iterations, RACOS returns the best solution that is found so far (step 12).

Algorithm 2. Querying

Input:

    f: Objective function to be minimized;

    R': A fixed matrix of R.

Procedure:

  1: $\tilde{L} = \mathrm{GD}(L)$ for problem $\min_L f(L, R')$

  2: **return** $f(\tilde{L}, R')$

RACOS is based on sampling-querying framework and suitable for solving black-box optimization problem. But in multi-task learning it is not necessary to consider objective function as black-box. The gradient information in (2) can be used to improve convergence rate.

3.2 RacosGD

RACOSGD is not a simple combination of RACOS and GD, but embedding GD in RACOS. RACOS ensures that we can get approximate global optima with high probability and GD can accelerate convergence through making full use of gradient information in objective function. The main idea of RACOSGD is that we get a start point for GD from RACOS and then get precise solution by GD. Considering alternative convex property of (2), GD can also be used to simplify optimization problem that RACOS faces.

Algorithm 3. RACOSGD

Input:
    f: Objective function to be minimized;
    Querying: querying sub-procedure in RACOS.
Procedure:
1: R' =RACOS(R,f) with Querying
2: **repeat**
3:    L' =GD(L,f), fix R as R'
4:    R' =GD(R,f), fix L as L'
5: **until** stopping criterion is satisfied
6: **return** (L', R')

There are two objectives in (2), L and R. If R is fixed as R', we can get $\tilde{L}$ by applying GD to solve problem $\min_L f(L, R')$. Because GD can only get local optima for non-convex function. $f(\tilde{L}, R')$ is lower bound function value decided by R' and means the potential of R'. Hence in RACOS it is not necessary to optimize L and R simultaneously. The optimization objective of RACOS is only R, and then we embed GD in evaluating each R according to objective function. Algorithm 2 is the pseudo-code of querying sub-procedure. Algorithm 2 returns objective function value with best L as evaluation value for each R' generated by RACOS.

Overall, Algorithm 3 is pseudo-code of RACOSGD. In the first phase (step 1), we get start matrix R' by RACOS with Querying (Algorithm 2). The next phase is alternative gradient descent algorithm starting from R' (step 2 to 5). Finally we can get the best solution (L', R') and the predictors of multi-task learning can be recovered by $W' = L' \times R'^T$. There are some brief discussions about RACOSGD. R' is the starting point of GD. If R' does not fall into local optima, intuitively there is no local optima between R' and global optima, (L', R') generated by GD is global optima. GD is used for several times in RACOSGD, such as in Querying and in alternative gradient descent. In different cases, the hyper-parameter settings of GD are different. In Querying, GD is used to explore the potential of R', so the step size can be set slightly long and the stopping criterion can be slightly easy. But in alternative gradient descent, GD is used to get a exact solution, so step size and stopping criterion should be preciser than those in Querying.

4   Experiments

We selected four multi-label learning datasets from MULAN[1]. Table 1 shows the details of datasets. Multi-label learning is a special multi-task learning problem, because each label learning can be seen as a task.

Before presenting the details of our experiments, we will define the estimate criterion for each multi-task learning predictor (L, R) and denote it per-loss (PL, Definition 1). PL means loss for a solution in each task and each instance.

---

[1] http://mulan.sourceforge.net/.

Table 1. Datasets information

Data set	Task size	Dimension size	Instance size
Birds	19	260	322
CAL500	174	68	310
Emotions	6	72	391
Flags	7	19	129

Definition 1. *Per-Loss (PL). Given a solution* (L, R), f *is objective function of multi-task learning problem,* T *denotes the number of tasks and* m_t *denotes the number of instance in dataset corresponding to t-th task. PL can be expressed as:*

$$PL(L, R) = \frac{f(L, R)}{\sum_{t=1}^{T} m_t}$$

4.1 Settings

We want to validate following conclusions through experiments:

1. The low-rank assumption is satisfied by decomposition of W. The low-rank hyper-parameter r represents the relationships between tasks. Best settings of r are different in different datasets. We want to find best r setting for each dataset;
2. The solution obtained by RACOSGD is global optimum with high probability because of RACOS. The predictors generated by RACOSGD should be better than those generated by GDO;
3. RACOS performs stronger optimization ability than evolutionary optimization algorithms. This conclusion should establish in this problem;
4. Traditional multi-task learning methods optimize relaxed constraint (3) to get predictors. It will loss original assumption in this way. The predictors generated by RACOSGD will show stronger generalization ability than those generated by traditional way.

According to the targets, we choose compared approaches as follows: alternative gradient descent (GDO), evolution strategy combined with gradient descent (ESGD) and a traditional approach in multi-task learning (TNLL). GDO optimize L and R using GD alternatively with a stochastic starting point. ESGD is generated by replacing RACOS with evolution strategy (ES) in Algorithm 3. TNLL is implemented by a multi-task learning integration tool MALSAR[2] for problem (3). Then we design two groups of experiments to validate conclusions:

A For RACOSGD, GDO and ESGD, we set $r = 3, 5, 7, 9$ to study influence of r. For each r setting and dataset, each algorithm runs 5 times independently and the best PL of each algorithm will be chosen and compared.

---

[2] http://www.public.asu.edu/~jye02/Software/MALSAR/.

B For RACOSGD, GDO and TNLL, each algorithm runs 5 times in each dataset. We compare the best accuracy in test dataset for each algorithm.

Experiment A is used to validate conclusions 1, 2 and 3. Experiment B is used to validate conclusion 4.

4.2   Results

Figure 1 and Table 2 show the results of experiment A. From Fig. 1, in most cases RACOSGD can get the best solution (smallest PL) compared with other algorithms. In birds and CAL500, the best r setting maybe greater than 9 because PL has been reduced with increasing of r. In emotions and flags, the best setting of r maybe 7. Those results validate conclusion 1. Comparing RACOSGD with GDO, RACOSGD can get smaller PL than GDO in all datasets except emotions. This result validates conclusion 2. Comparing RACOSGD with ESGD, RACOSGD get smaller PL than ESGD in those four datasets. This result validates conclusion 3. Table 3 shows the results of experiment B. The accuracies obtained by RACOSGD and GDO are far greater than those obtained by TNLL. It means that relaxation of constraint has a negative effect on generalization ability of predictors. This result validates conclusion 4.

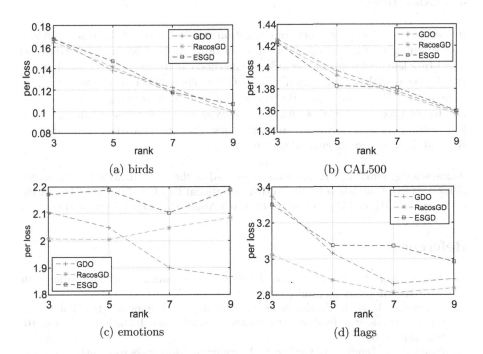

(a) birds   (b) CAL500

(c) emotions   (d) flags

Fig. 1. Illustrating the PL changes with rank hyper-parameter r in each dataset.

Table 2. The best PL value obtained by each algorithm in each dataset from experiment A. The PL value in bold means the best (smallest) value in each dataset.

Algorithm	Birds	CAL500	Emotions	Flags
RacosGD	**0.0986**	**1.3568**	2.0049	**2.8631**
GDO	0.1000	1.3586	**1.8663**	2.8813
ESGD	0.1065	1.3596	2.1029	2.8852
Racos	0.6398	2.9940	2.1146	2.8876
ES	0.7328	3.0757	2.6273	3.0917

Table 3. The testing accuracies for each algorithm in each dataset. The accuracy in bold represents the best (greatest) in each dataset.

Algorithm	Birds	CAL500	Emotions	Flags
RacosGD	**0.9202**	**0.8586**	0.7323	**0.7467**
GDO	0.8932	0.8467	**0.8246**	0.6976
TNLL	0.5232	0.5069	0.5140	0.6066

5   Conclusion

In this work, we propose a new optimization method RacosGD to solve multitask learning problem with low-rank constraint. It is different from tradition multi-task learning methods because our method can optimize the original objective function without relaxation. RacosGD embeds GD into Racos in a reasonable way. RacosGD uses Racos to find a suitable starting point and uses GD to get precise optimal solution. From experiments RacosGD shows excellent optimization performance in most cases, and the predictors generated by RacosGD shows great generalization ability.

Acknowledgment. This research was supported by the NSFC (61375061), JiangsuSF (BK20160066), Foundation for the Author of National Excellent Doctoral Dissertation of China (201451), and 2015 Microsoft Research Asia Collaborative Research Program.

References

1. Abernethy, J., Bach, F., Evgeniou, T., Vert, J.: Low-rank matrix factorization with attributes. In arXiv preprint (2006)
2. Abernethy, J., Bach, F., Evgeniou, T., Vert, J.: A new approach to collaborative filtering: operator estimation with spectral regularization. J. Mach. Learn. Res. **10**, 803–826 (2009)
3. Agarwal, A., Daume, H., Gerber, S.: Learning multiple tasks using manifold regularization, pp. 46–54 (2010)
4. Argyriou, A., Evgeniou, T., Pontil, M.: Convex multi-task feature learning. Mach. Learn. **73**, 243–272 (2008)

5. Argyriou, A., Micchelli, C., Pontil, M., Ying, Y.: A spectral regularization framework for multitask structure learning. In: Advances in Neural Information Processing Systems 20, pp. 25–32 (2008)
6. Beyer, H.-G., Schwefel, H.-P.: Evolution strategies: a comprehensive introduction. J. Natural Comput. **1**, 3–52 (2002)
7. Bickel, S., Bogojeska, J., Lengauer, T., Scheffer, T.: Multi-task learning for HIV therapy screening. In: Proceedings of the 25th International Conference on Machine Learning, pp. 56–63 (2008)
8. Boyd, S., Lieven, V.: Convex Optimization. Cambridge University Press, New York (2004)
9. Brochu, E., Cora, V.-M., Freitas, N.-D.: A tutorial on bayesian optimization of expensive cost functions, with application to active user modeling and hierarchical reinforcement learning. In arXiv preprint (2010)
10. Chen, J., Liu, J., Ye, J.: Learning incoherent sparse and low-rank patterns from multiple tasks. In: Proceedings of the 16th ACM SIGKDD International Conference on Knowledge Discovery and Data Mining, pp. 1179–1188 (2010)
11. Dai, Y.H., Yuan, Y.-X.: Alternate minimization gradient method. IMA J. Numer. Anal. **23**, 377–393 (2003)
12. Evgeniou, T., Pontil, M.: Regularized multiCtask learning. In: Proceedings of the Tenth ACM SIGKDD International Conference on Knowledge Discovery and Data Mining, pp. 109–117 (2004)
13. Fazel, M.: Matrix rank minimization with applications. Stanford University (2002)
14. Ji, S., Ye, J.: An accelerated gradient method for trace norm minimization. In: Proceedings of the 26th Annual International Conference on Machine Learning, pp. 457–464 (2009)
15. Kennedy, J., Eberhart, R.: Particle swarm optimization. In: IEEE International Conference on Neural Networks, pp. 1942–1948 (1995)
16. Obozinski, G., Taskar, B., Jordan, M.: Joint covariate selection, joint subspace selection for multiple classification problems. Stat. Comput. **20**, 231–252 (2010)
17. Qian, C., Yu, Y., Zhou, Z.-H.: Pareto ensemble pruning. In: Proceedings of the 29th AAAI Conference on Artificial Intelligence (AAAI15), pp. 2935–2941 (2015)
18. Qian, C., Yu, Y., Zhou, Z.-H.: Subset selection by pareto optimization. In: Advances in Neural Information Processing Systems 28 (NIPS15) (2015)
19. Vandenberghe, L., Boyd, S.: Semidefinite programming. In: SIAM Review, pp. 49–95 (1996)
20. Wang, X.-G., Zhang, C., Zhang, Z.-Y.: Boosted multi-task learning for face verification with applications to web image and video search. In: IEEE Conference on Computer Vision and Pattern Recognition, pp. 142–149 (2009)
21. Yu, Y., Qian, H.: The sampling-and-learning framework: a statistical view of evolutionary algorithm. In: Proceedings of the IEEE Congress on Evolutionary Computation, pp. 149–158 (2014)
22. Yu, Y., Qian, H., Hu, Y.-Q.: Derivative-free optimization via classification. In: Proceedings of the 30th AAAI Conference on Artificial Intelligence (2016)
23. Yu, Y., Yao, X., Zhou, Z.-H.: On the approximation ability of evolutionary optimization with application to minimum set cover. Artif. Intell. **180–181**, 20–33 (2012)
24. Zhou, J., Yuan, L., Liu, J., Ye, J.: A multi-task learning formulation for predicting disease progression. In: Proceedings of the 17th ACM SIGKDD International Conference on Knowledge Discovery and Data Mining, pp. 814–822 (2011)

A Collaborative Learning Model in Teaching-Learning-Based Optimization: Some Numerical Results

Bei Dong[1,2(✉)], Xiaojun Wu[1,2], and Yifei Sun[3]

[1] Key Laboratory of Modern Teaching Technology, Ministry of Education,
Shaanxi Normal University, Xi'an, People's Republic of China
dongbei@snnu.edu.cn
[2] School of Computer Science,
Shaanxi Normal University, Xi'an, People's Republic of China
[3] School of Physics and Information Technology,
Shaanxi Normal University, Xi'an, People's Republic of China

Abstract. By mimicking the learning process of human in real-life, teaching-learning-based optimization algorithm (TLBO) is proposed for global optimization. Since then, it has been widely and effectively used in kinds of fields. As a swarm intelligent optimization method, TLBO has the virtue of fewer algorithm-parameters adjusting, easy to implement, and good convergence. However, there exist no advising directions in the learning phase, which may result in a decrease of local search ability of the TLBO when solving complex problems. In this paper, a collaborative learning model (CLM) which modified learner phase and novel self-studying phase is proposed to enhance both the global and local searching ability. In CLM method, a collaborative pattern or competitive pattern is probability chosen by learners in the learner phase. To efficiently conduct learners, in the self-studying phase, teacher updates his/her position according to neighborhood information adaptively. We perform the CLM method on a series of real-world resource allocation problem in multi-cell networks. Experimental results indicate that the CLM method is able to achieve more satisfactory or at least comparable solutions on most real-world problems.

Keywords: Teaching-learning-based optimization · Collaborative learning · Neighborhood information · Resource allocation problem · Multi-cell network

1 Introduction

Global optimization problem which is defined as searching for the best solution to satisfy the given objective function among all possible feasible solutions arises frequently in every field of our real-world life [1]. Finding the global optima is often difficult especially in some complex problems since there may exist many

© Springer Nature Singapore Pte Ltd. 2016
M. Gong et al. (Eds.): BIC-TA 2016, Part I, CCIS 681, pp. 466–472, 2016.
DOI: 10.1007/978-981-10-3611-8_42

local optimal solutions. Furthermore, the derivative properties of some objective functions are hard or impossible to get when using analytic or numerical method. So plenty of intelligent algorithms which inspired by some natural situation or process are designed to overcome this shortage, such as genetic algorithm (GA) [2], simulated annealing (SA) [3], bat algorithm (BA) [4], particle swarm optimization (PSO) [5], harmony search (HS) [6] and so on.

Teaching-learning-based optimization (TLBO) is a population-based intelligent method which inspired by the learning process of a typical school studying scenario [7]. Recently, TLBO has been widely and effectively used for numerical functions and real-world optimization problems due to several appealing advantages (i.e., fewer and simple working parameters, easy to implement, fast convergence, etc.). Moreover, new learner or teacher phase and a set of other meta-heuristics have been incorporated into teaching-learning-based optimization to solve serials of discrete or mechanical problems [8–18]. In [9], a self-learning phase is involved to improve the weakly local search ability of classical TLBO.

In this paper, a collaborative learning model (CLM) that designed based on the TLBO framework is proposed for global optimization. In CLM method, there have three basic steps: the teacher phase, learner phase and self-studying phase. The teacher phase adopts the same operator as the original TBLO to undertake global searching mission. In learner phase, two learners are randomly chosen by the current learner, which learns through collaborative pattern or competitive pattern with a specified probability. In typical school teaching situation, teachers not only teach learners to improve their knowledge, but also upgrade own ability by self-studying or interaction simultaneously in order to give more effective guidance to the learners. So the self-studying concept is introduced in CLM, which utilize neighborhood information of the contemporary teacher to enhance the local search ability then conduct learners exploring more promising area. The performance of CLM is investigated on a series of resource allocation problems in multi-cell networks. The results indicate that the CLM can achieve more satisfactory or at least comparable solutions on most real-world problems [10–14].

The remainder of this paper is organized as follows: Sect. 2 presents a detailed description of the proposed CLM. Section 3 presents the experimental results and related analysis. Finally, Sect. 4 gives the concluding remarks.

2 The Collaborative Learning Model

In the classical TLBO, both the teacher phase and learner phase have good global searching ability. In the teacher phase, learners learn from the global optimal individual; and in the learner phase, the individual, which the current learner learns from is selected randomly. These may have the following drawbacks:

(1) Learning in the learner phase has no guiding direction;
(2) Too much emphasis in global performance causes weakly local searching ability.

To overcome these problems, novel learner phase and self-studying phase is proposed in CLM which are detailed as follows:

2.1   Learner Phase of CLM

As we all known, collaboration and competition are two typical models used in learning. Therefore, in the learner phase of CLM, two randomly selected individuals choose from the two modes with a certain probability for the learner to learn. In this work, a predefined probability P_L determines which learning mode will be adopted by a learner. The learning process is implemented as follows:

$$L_{i,new} = \begin{cases} L^1_{i,new}, & if \ rand \leq P_L \ (competition) \\ L^2_{i,new}, & otherwise(collaboration) \end{cases} \tag{1}$$

$$L^1_{i,new} = \begin{cases} L_{i,old} + r_1 * (L_{best} - L_{i,old}), & if \ L_{best} \ is \ better \ than \ L_i \\ L_{i,old} + r_1 * (L_{i.old} - L_{best}), & otherwise \end{cases} \tag{2}$$

$$L_{best} = \begin{cases} L_j, & if \ L_j \ is \ better \ than \ L_k \\ L_k, & otherwise \end{cases} \tag{3}$$

$$L^2_{i,new} = \begin{cases} L_{i,old} + r_2 * (L_j - L_k), & if \ L_j \ is \ better \ than \ L_k \\ L_{i,old} + r_2 * (L_k - L_j), & otherwise \end{cases} \tag{4}$$

Where L_j and L_k ($j \neq k \neq i$) are chosen by current ith learner randomly; r_1 and r_2 are randomly selected from range $[0, 1]$. Equations (2) and (3) is the competitive model, which indicates that the learner will learn from the better one between the two individuals. In the collaboration model shown as Eq. (4), the difference of the two individual is mainly considered when learning. Since this, by fully exploiting the information of the whole class, learning is always toward to a better direction.

2.2   Self-studying Phase of CLM

In general, in the process of the teacher teaching, they also interact with others or learn from themselves. The goal is to enhance their knowledge grade to give a better guide to learners in order to improve the overall performance of the class. In the proposed CLM method, to effectively enhance the local searching ability, position of the current teacher is updated by searching in the neighborhood area adaptively. The self-studying process is carried out as follows:

$$T_{new,j} = \begin{cases} T_{old,j}(g) + r_3 * TR, & if \ rand \ \leq P_{SL} \\ T_{old,j}(g), & otherwise \end{cases} \tag{5}$$

Where $T_{old,j}(g)$ and $T_{new,j}(g)$ are the jth component of the original and new teachers after local updating. g indicates the current iteration number, P_{SL} is a predefined mutation probability. r_3 is randomly selected from range $[0, 1]$ and TR is selected at random in the reasonable value range.

It is worth noticing that, in the later iteration of the algorithm, searching generally focus on the local area, so the random step r_3 used in Eq. (5) can ensure a certain probability jump out of local optima when searching in the neighborhood. In each iteration, the executing number of the self-studying process is equivalent to the current iteration number g.

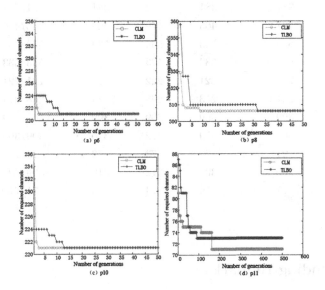

Fig. 1. Convergence curves of the CLM and TLBO on four benchmark problems.

3   Experimental Result

In this paper, we applied the CLM method to real-world resource allocation problem in multi-cell networks [19,20], and compared the results with TLBO and some related techniques [21,22]. The obtained comparison results indicate that the CLM method provides effective solutions when solving the optimal resource allocation problem. Detailed descriptions of the benchmark problem and resource allocation problem can be referred as [9,21,22]. A comparison results with TLBO and other two representative approaches [21,22] are presented in Table 1.

In this simulation, class size and maximum generations for TLBO and CLM are set to 100 and 500. In addition to demonstrating the coverage of the CLM, the comparison convergence curve of CLM and TLBO on two testing problems is illustrated (Fig. 1). From Fig. 1, it is clearly shown that the proposed CLM has fast convergent speed than TLBO. For the easy problem p6, p8 and p10, the CLM can reach the global optima within 10 generations. For the complex p10, TLBO converge faster than CLM within 160 generations. However, in the later generations, CLM can jump out to find global optimal solutions while TLBO is still trapped into local optima.

Table 1. The comparison results of the eleven problems

Problem index	Lower bound	[21] Best	[22] Best	TlBO Best	CLM Best/Mean
1	381	381	382	381	381/381
2	427	463	449	463	445/460
3	533	533	534	533	533/533
4	533	533	533	533	533/533
5	221	221	222	221	221/221
6	221	273	268	274	268/274
7	309	309	309	309	309/309
8	309	309	312	310	309/309
9	21	73	73	73	73/73
10	309	309	312	310	309/309
11	71	79	74	75	71/71.1

4   Concluding Remarks

In this paper, a collaborative learning model (CLM) is proposed for global optimization. Different from TLBO, the CLM consists of three mainly phases: teacher phase, learner phase and self-studying phase. To efficiently guide learners toward to a better direction, a competitive learning model and collaborative learning model is probably chosen when leaning [23,24]. In addition, in the self-studying phase, each teacher updates his position adaptively using the neighborhood information, which is intended to enhance local search ability of the algorithm. Through collaborative learning by teachers and learners, global search ability and local search ability of the algorithm have been improved.

Acknowledgment. This work was supported by the National Natural Science Foundation of China (Grant No. 11372167), the Fundamental Research Funds for the Central Universities of Shaanxi Normal University (Grant No. GK201603082) and the Key Science and Technology Innovation Team in Shaanxi Province, China (Grant No. 2014KTC-18).

References

1. Francisco, V.J., Efrn, M.M.: Adaptive evolution: an efficient heuristic for global optimization. In: Genetic and Evolutionary Computation Conference, Shanghai, pp. 12–14 (2009)
2. Yang, L., Shiu, Y.: Non-revisiting genetic algorithm with adaptive mutation using constant memory. Memetic Comput. 1–22 (2016)
3. Zhang, R., Wu, C.: A hybrid simulated annealing algorithm for the job shop scheduling problem. Appl. Soft Comput. 10, 79–89 (2010)
4. Wang, G.G., Chang, B., Zhang, Z.J.: A multi-swarm bat algorithm for global optimization. In: IEEE Congress on Evolutionary Computation, Sendai, pp. 480–485 (2015)
5. Coello, C.A.C., Pulido, G.T., Lechuga, M.S.: Handing multiple objectives with particle swarm optimization. IEEE Trans. Evol. Comput. 8, 256–279 (2004)
6. Wang, L., Yang, R.X., Xu, Y.: An improved adaptive binary harmony search algorithm. Inf. Sci. 232, 58–87 (2013)
7. Rao, R.V., Savasni, V.J.: Teaching-learning-based optimization: an optimization method for continuous non-linear large scale problems. Inf. Sci. 183, 1–15 (2012)
8. Wang, L., Zou, F.: A hybridization of teaching-learning-based optimization and differential evolution for chaotic time series prediction. Neural Comput. Appl. 25, 1407–1422 (2014)
9. Chen, D.B., Zou, F.: An improved teaching-learning-based optimization algorithm for solving global optimization problem. Inf. Sci. 297, 171–190 (2015)
10. Tuo, S.H., Yong, L.Q.: A novel harmony search algorithm based on teaching-learning strategies for 0–1 knapsack problems. Sci. World J. (2014)
11. Rao, R.V., Petel, V.: An elitist teaching-learning-based optimization algorithm for solving complex constrained optimization problems. Int. J. Ind. Eng. Comput. 3, 710–720 (2012)
12. Liu, X.C., Liu, Q.: A discrete teaching-learning-based optimization algorithm for the capacitated vehicle routing problem. Open J. Transp. Technol. 3, 16–21 (2014)
13. Suresh, C.S., Anima, N.: Modified teaching-learning-based algorithm for global numerical optimization-a comparative study. Swarm Evol. Comput. 16, 28–37 (2014)
14. Bouchekara, H.R.E.H., Abido, M.A.: Optimal power flow using teaching-learning-based optimization technique. Electr. Power Syst. Res. 114, 49–59 (2014)
15. Rao, R.V., Savsani, V.J.: Teaching-learning-based optimization: a novel method for constrained mechanical design optimization problems. Comput. Aided Des. 43, 303–315 (2011)
16. Zou, F., Wang, L.: Teaching-learning-based optimization with dynamic group strategy for global optimization. Inf. Sci. 273, 112–131 (2014)
17. Wang, L., Zou, F.: An improved teaching-learning-based optimization with neighborhood search for applications of ANN. Neurocomputing 143, 231–247 (2014)
18. Murty, M.R., Naik, A.: Automatic clustering using teaching-learning-based optimization. Appl. Math. 5, 1202–1211 (2011)
19. Zhang, G.P., Liu, P.: Energy efficient resource allocation in non-cooperative multi-cell OFDMA systems. J. Syst. Eng. Electron. 22, 175–182 (2011)
20. Zhu, H., Zhu, J.: Non-cooperative resource competition game by virtual referee in multi-cell OFDMA networks. IEEE J. Sel. Areas Commun. 25, 1079–1090 (2007)
21. Goutan, C.: An efficient heuristic algorithm for channel assignment problem in cellular radio networks. IEEE Trans. Veh. Technol. 50, 1528–1539 (2001)

22. Goutam, K.A., Koushik, S.: A new approach to fast near-optimal channel assignment in cellular mobile networks. IEEE Trans. Mob. Comput. **12**, 1814–1827 (2013)
23. Song, T., Pan, Z., Wong, D.M., Wang, X.: Design of logic gates using spiking neural P systems with homogeneous neurons and astrocytes-like control. Inf. Sci. **372**, 380–391 (2016)
24. Wang, X., Song, T., Gong, F., Pan, Z.: On the computational power of spiking neural P systems with self-organization, Scientific Reports. doi:10.1038/srep27624

Incremental Learning with Concept Drift: A Knowledge Transfer Perspective

Yu Sun and Ke Tang[✉]

USTC-Birmingham Joint Research Institute in Intelligent Computation and Its
Applications (UBRI), School of Computer Science and Technology,
University of Science and Technology of China, Hefei 230027, China
ketang@ustc.edu.cn

Abstract. Concept drift is one of the biggest challenges in applying incremental learning to real-world applications. A number of ensemble methods, especially the chunk-based ones, have been proposed for concept drift adaptation. To avoid the impact of the inconsistent information in historical chunks, a novel approach named TransferIL is proposed. A transfer method is used in TransferIL to extract the useful knowledge in historical models, which is then integrated for learning the new chunk of data. Empirical results, obtained from both synthetic data and real-world data, have confirmed the effectiveness of the learning strategy.

Keywords: Concept drift · Incremental learning · Transfer learning

1 Introduction

Incremental learning, which trains a model to generalize the data distribution in an incremental manner, has attracted growing attention in recent years. In real-world applications, the environment, from which the examples are generated, always changes. This phenomenon, caused by the change of the data distribution $p(\mathbf{x}, y)$, where $\mathbf{x}$ stands for the feature vector and y stands for the class label, is referred to as *concept drift*.

To deal with the challenge of concept drift, various works have been proposed, which can generally be divided into three categories, i.e., sliding window, drift detection method and ensemble method. Different from sliding window and drift detection method, in the ensemble methods [1,2], the historical knowledge is used to facilitate the learning of current data, instead of being dropped. To avoid the inconsistent information from the historical knowledge caused by concept drift, a novel approach, named as Transfer-based Incremental Learning (TransferIL), is proposed in this work. TransferIL employs a transfer operation to each historical models before using, to extract knowledge from historical models to facilitate the learning of the current data distribution.

© Springer Nature Singapore Pte Ltd. 2016
M. Gong et al. (Eds.): BIC-TA 2016, Part I, CCIS 681, pp. 473–479, 2016.
DOI: 10.1007/978-981-10-3611-8_43

2   Problem Description and Related Work

In incremental learning, at each time step t, a chunk of data is received, denoted as $D_t = \{(\mathbf{x}_t^1, y_t^1), (\mathbf{x}_t^2, y_t^2), \cdots, (\mathbf{x}_t^n, y_t^n)\}$. The i.i.d. assumption is assumed to be held inside each chunk and the data distribution is denoted as $p_t(\mathbf{x}, y)$ at step t. Since concept drift may happen at each time step, the underlying distribution may change at step t, i.e., $p_t(\mathbf{x}, y) \neq p_{t-1}(\mathbf{x}, y)$. The goal of incremental learning with concept drift is to obtain a model F_t to minimize the expected loss on distribution $p_t(\mathbf{x}, y)$ at each time step t, as follow

$$F_t = \arg\min_f \int \ell(f(\mathbf{x}), y) p_t(\mathbf{x}, y) \mathrm{d}\mathbf{x}\mathrm{d}y \tag{1}$$

where $\ell(\cdot, \cdot)$ is the loss function.

Sliding window, drift detection method and ensemble method are three typical strategies for concept drift adaptation. Both of sliding window and drift detection method intend to ensure that the model is trained with the examples from the current data distribution to fulfill the i.i.d. assumption. The potential valuable information in historical knowledge is dropped, which may be utilized to promote the learning performance. Ensemble model is another type of strategy that is widely studied in incremental learning with concept drift, which combines the historically trained models in current learning step.

To deal with concept drift, almost all the existing ensemble methods focus on how to assign an appropriate weight for each model in ensemble, and different weight assignment methods have been proposed. Uniform weight is a basic weighting method, which is used in SEA [1]. Most of the ensemble models utilize the weighting strategy that the highly performed model should be assigned a high weight, such as AUE2 [2]. In [5], a dynamic weight assignment method, in which the weight is determined by the local performance on the current data, is proposed. In addition to using the performance, the age of the model has also been considered to determine the weight as well (i.e., time-adjusted performance) in Learn^{++}.NSE [4].

In addition to assigning a proper weight to each model in ensemble, some other techniques are also applied. For example in AUE2, the new chunk of data is not only used to train a new model but also used to update the maintained historical models. To deal with the inconsistent knowledge, a feature representation transfer approach, named as TIX model [3], is presented to convey the useful historical knowledge.

3   The New Approach for Concept Drift Adaptation

Similar with the existing ensemble methods (e.g., [1]), TransferIL trains a model with each chunk of data and assembles them with weighted majority voting for classification. Different from these algorithms, TransferIL transfers the historical models with the current chunk of data first, instead of utilizing them directly in ensemble. The mining flow of TransferIL is shown in Fig. 1.

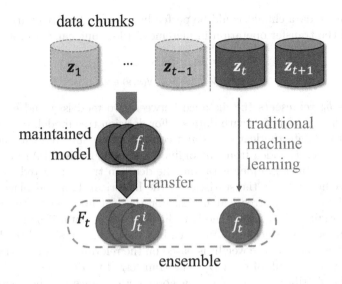

Fig. 1. Illustration of the mining flow of TransferIL.

Algorithm 1. TransferIL

Input: $D_1, D_2, \cdots, D_t, \cdots$: the data stream in incremental learning, S: the historical model set, m: the predefined archive size of S

Output: F_t: the predict model at learning step t

1 **while** *data chunk D_t is available* **do**
2      $f_t \leftarrow$ train a new model with D_t;
3      $f_i^t \leftarrow$ transfer all the maintained model f_i in S with D_t;
4      $w_i^t \leftarrow$ evaluate all the transferred model f_i^t;
5   **if** $|S| < m$ **then**
6          $S \leftarrow S \bigcup f_t$;
7   **else**
8          $f_w^t \leftarrow$ the transferred historical model with worst performance;
9   remove the worst performed model f_w^t;
10         $S \leftarrow$ replace f_w with f_t in S;
11     $F_t = (\sum_i w_i^t f_i^t + f_t)/(\sum_i w_i^t + 1)$

To extract the consistent knowledge in historical models, the proposed TransferIL adapts historical models to the current data distribution by a transfer-like update with fully respecting the current data distribution. Then, combine them with weighted majority voting into an ensemble model for prediction. TransferIL is described in Algorithm 1. The data stream can theoretically be infinitely long, but only a limited number of historical models can be preserved due to the limitation of memory size. Hence, a model selection is needed. In this framework, three main elements are involved, i.e., model transfer, model selection and model weighting.

In transfer operation in TransferIL, the inconsistent knowledge in historical models should be guaranteed not to be introduced, and the current chunk of data should be correctly expressed in the transferred models. For the case where all examples in data chunks could be perfectly classified by a regularized model, the goal of the transfer operation in incremental learning can be expressed as

$$
\begin{aligned}
&\underset{f_t^i}{\text{minimize}} \quad \|f_t^i - f_i\| \\
&\text{subject to } f_t^i(\mathbf{x}) = y, \ \forall (\mathbf{x}, y) \in \mathbf{z}_t
\end{aligned}
\tag{2}
$$

where $\|a - b\|$ represents the distance between two models a and b, and f_t^i is the transferred model of f_i with data $\mathbf{z}_t$. For decision tree model, it could be an operation to update the leaf nodes and construct new sub-tree with new data. For linear model, the idea from the online passive-aggressive (PA) model could be used herein. In the implementation, the decision tree is selected as the base model. Specifically, drop the statistics of the historical data and place the new chunk of data into the tree leaf nodes. For the leaf node with few examples, adjust the original labels of the node to fit the current data, if no split needed.

To combine the models into an ensemble, weights are assigned to them. For the transferred models, the weight is based on the relevance of a historical model f_i to the current chunk of data D_t. The transferred model from a relevant historical data distribution will obtain a good performance on the current data distribution. Therefore, the accuracy of the transferred historical model is evaluated and used as the weight in TransferIL. In incremental learning, the number of historical models can be infinite, and a model selection is needed. Similar with the existing algorithms, TransferIL selects the historical models by replacing the model with the lowest weight with the current model, if the model set is full.

4   Experiment

The proposed TransferIL is compared with four state-of-the-art algorithms, i.e., SEA [1], Learn[++].NSE [4], and AUE2 [2]. In order to comprehensively investigating the performance of TransferIL, two sets of synthetic data streams (i.e., SEA and rotate) and three sets of real-world data streams (i.e., covertype, Poker Hand, and CTR prediction) are tested. SEA data involve 3 features with value between 0 and 10, and uses $f_1 + f_2 \leq \theta$ to determine the class of a data point. Rotate concept drift (ROT) simulates the change of data distribution by rotating the decision boundary. Covertype (COV) and Poker Hand (POK) datasets are real-world datasets presented in the UCI Machine Learning Repository. CTR prediction data (CTR) is a data set obtained from a real-world application of Tencent company. The details of the datasets are described in Table 1.

To be fair, all of the compared algorithms use the model of decision tree as the learner. Since AUE2 needs to use an on-line model as the learner, Hoeffding tree model [6], an on-line version decision tree, is employed. For the other algorithms in the experiment, the traditional decision tree model CART is used. The archive model size, for the data of SEA, ROT, COV and POK, is set to 25 according to the suggestion in [1]. Considering the number of chunks in CTR data is limited, the archive size is set to 3 in the experiment on CTR data streams.

To investigate the ability of the algorithms in concept drift adaptation, the error rates in each chunk of data are evaluated, as shown in Fig. 2. Generally,

Table 1. Data streams in experiment. Size represents the chunk size.

Data	#Example	#Class	#Label	#Chunk	Size	Drift
SEA200A	24,000	3	2	120	200	$\theta : 10 \rightarrow 7 \rightarrow 3 \rightarrow 7 \rightarrow 10 \rightarrow 13 \rightarrow 16 \rightarrow 13$
SEA200G	24,000	3	2	120	200	$\theta : 10 \rightarrow 8 \rightarrow 6 \rightarrow 8 \rightarrow 10 \rightarrow 12 \rightarrow 14 \rightarrow 12$
SEA500G	60,000	3	2	120	500	$\theta : 10 \rightarrow 8 \rightarrow 6 \rightarrow 8 \rightarrow 10 \rightarrow 12 \rightarrow 14 \rightarrow 12$
ROT200A	24,000	2	6	120	200	rotate angle: $4 * \pi$
ROT200G	24,000	2	6	120	200	rotate angle: $2 * \pi$
ROT500G	60,000	2	6	120	500	rotate angle: $2 * \pi$
COV1000	581,000	51	7	581	1,000	real
COV2000	580,000	51	7	290	2,000	real
POK1000	1,000,000	10	10	1000	1,000	real
POK2000	1,000,000	10	10	500	2,000	real
CTR10000	600,000	100	2	60	10,000	real
CTR20000	600,000	100	2	30	20,000	real

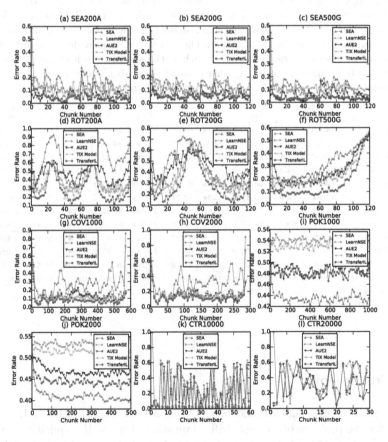

Fig. 2. Error rate of chunks for the compared algorithms.

TransferIL performs the best among the compared algorithms, with the lowest error rate on most of the data chunks on both the synthetic data streams and real-world data streams. The overall classification accuracy on each data stream are also evaluated for comparison, as shown in Table 2. Generally, TransferIL shows a big advantage compared with the compared algorithms, with obtaining the highest accuracy in most of the data streams. In addition, the standard deviation results of TransferIL are generally very low, which provides the evidence of the ability of TransferIL in concept drift adaptation. The Wilcoxon rank-sum test and the Friedman test are conducted on the accuracy results, as shown in the last two rows in Table 2. As shown in the last row of Table 2, TransferIL performed statistically significantly better than the other algorithms on the tested data streams in pairwise comparisons. Furthermore, the Friedman test gives a clear comparison of all the tested algorithms. The Friedman test result indicates that the proposed TransferIL ranks the highest among the compared algorithms.

Table 2. Average accuracy (%) of every chunk ($\pm$ the standard deviation of the accuracy for each chunk) for the tested algorithms. $\bullet$/$\circ$ indicates that TransferIL Is significantly better/worse than the corresponding algorithm. The values in boldface indicate the highest accuracy on the data stream. The last two rows provide the results of the Friedman test (Nemenyi test, CD = 1.76 with a 0.05 significance level) and Wilcoxon test (with a 0.05 significance level), where "w-d-l" indicates TransferIL is superior to, not significantly different from or inferior to the corresponding compared algorithms.

Data	TransferIL	SEA	Learn^{++}.NSE	AUE2	TIX Model
SEA200A	**94.80 $\pm$ 3.03**	86.31 $\pm$ 11.43$\bullet$	89.07 $\pm$ 5.13$\bullet$	94.66 $\pm$ 4.94	87.77 $\pm$ 3.97$\bullet$
SEA200G	94.15 $\pm$ 2.55	88.90 $\pm$ 10.02$\bullet$	90.02 $\pm$ 4.98$\bullet$	**94.58 $\pm$ 3.80**$\circ$	86.90 $\pm$ 4.26$\bullet$
SEA500G	**96.39 $\pm$ 1.66**	89.37 $\pm$ 10.17$\bullet$	91.10 $\pm$ 3.45$\bullet$	95.02 $\pm$ 4.05	88.85 $\pm$ 2.54$\bullet$
ROT200A	**71.59 $\pm$ 14.21**	37.88 $\pm$ 18.17$\bullet$	62.19 $\pm$ 11.49$\bullet$	52.72 $\pm$ 9.99$\bullet$	65.02 $\pm$ 11.45$\bullet$
ROT200G	**72.36 $\pm$ 14.48**	54.61 $\pm$ 17.45$\bullet$	63.41 $\pm$ 12.48$\bullet$	55.43 $\pm$ 9.76$\bullet$	64.97 $\pm$ 12.16$\bullet$
ROT500G	**83.92 $\pm$ 12.61**	69.81 $\pm$ 14.29$\bullet$	74.77 $\pm$ 11.57$\bullet$	74.34 $\pm$ 11.34$\bullet$	76.98 $\pm$ 10.44$\bullet$
COV1000	**91.44 $\pm$ 8.55**	71.46 $\pm$ 15.14$\bullet$	84.11 $\pm$ 12.45$\bullet$	87.09 $\pm$ 8.74$\bullet$	88.30 $\pm$ 9.19$\bullet$
COV2000	**87.91 $\pm$ 8.67**	68.27 $\pm$ 15.17$\bullet$	82.56 $\pm$ 11.22$\bullet$	85.34 $\pm$ 8.98$\bullet$	84.25 $\pm$ 8.82$\bullet$
POK1000	51.95 $\pm$ 1.79	**56.36 $\pm$ 2.54**$\circ$	45.93 $\pm$ 1.78$\bullet$	51.31 $\pm$ 1.79$\bullet$	46.93 $\pm$ 1.77$\bullet$
POK2000	55.59 $\pm$ 1.66	**58.97 $\pm$ 3.20**$\circ$	46.57 $\pm$ 1.40$\bullet$	53.21 $\pm$ 1.58$\bullet$	48.50 $\pm$ 1.28$\bullet$
CTR10000	**88.36 $\pm$ 19.67**	66.08 $\pm$ 19.36$\bullet$	77.13 $\pm$ 20.96$\bullet$	80.57 $\pm$ 21.34$\bullet$	80.57 $\pm$ 21.58$\bullet$
CTR20000	**69.05 $\pm$ 17.51**	59.80 $\pm$ 20.96	62.80 $\pm$ 17.40	67.42 $\pm$ 19.81	63.27 $\pm$ 18.93
Friedman-Test	1.25	4.04	3.79	2.71	3.21
Wilcoxon-Test	-	9/1/2	11/1/0	8/3/1	11/1/0

5   Conclusion

In this paper, a new chunk-based ensemble algorithm, named TransferIL, is proposed for the problem of concept drift adaptation. TransferIL explicitly extracts the useful knowledge in the historical models and then combines it with the currently trained model to facilitate the learning. TransferIL guarantees not to introduce the inconsistent knowledge in current learning and ensures the current chunk of data is correctly represented in the final model. The empirical studies verify the reliability of TransferIL and show that it outperforms the compared approaches in different kinds of concept drift scenarios.

References

1. Street, W.N., Kim, Y.: A streaming ensemble algorithm (SEA) for large-scale classification. In: KDD 2001, pp. 377–382. ACM, New York (2001)
2. Brzezinski, D., Stefanowski, J.: Reacting to different types of concept drift: the accuracy updated ensemble algorithm. IEEE Trans. Neural Netw. Learn. Syst. **25**(1), 81–94 (2014)
3. Forman, G.: Tackling concept drift by temporal inductive transfer. In: SIGIR 2006, pp. 252–259. ACM, New York (2006)
4. Elwell, R., Polikar, R.: Incremental learning of concept drift in nonstationary environments. IEEE Trans. Neural Netw. **22**(10), 1517–1531 (2011)
5. Tsymbal, A., Pechenizkiy, M., Cunningham, P., Puuronen, S.: Dynamic integration of classifiers for handling concept drift. Inf. Fusion **9**(1), 56–68 (2008). Special Issue on Applications of Ensemble Methods
6. Domingos, P., Hulten, G.: Mining high-speed data streams. In: KDD 2000, pp. 71–80. ACM, New York (2000)

Visual Tracking Based on Ensemble Learning with Logistic Regression

Xiaolin Tian$^{(\boxtimes)}$, Sujie Zhao, and Licheng Jiao

Key Laboratory of Intelligent Perception and Image Understanding of Ministry of
Education, International Research Center of Intelligent Perception and Computation,
International Collaboration Joint Lab in Intelligent Perception and Computation,
Xidian University, Xian 710071, Shaanxi, China
`xltian@mail.xidian.edu.cn`

Abstract. In this paper, we propose a novel visual tracking method
based on ensemble learning using logistic regression model. We adopt
logistic regression to achieve ensemble classifier to deal with object tracking problem. By using fast computable features, our approach learns the
appearance of the target during tracking. And thus, the proposed method
is able to adapt online to target appearance changes and its surrounding
background. Moreover, ensemble learning converts rough rules of thumb
into highly accurate prediction rule. Experimental results show that our
method outperforms relative trackers.

Keywords: Visual tracking · Logistic regression · Ensemble learning

1 Introduction

In computer vision field, visual tracking has been an important branch and has
wide applications including video surveillance, robotics, autonomous navigation
and human computer interaction [1]. Based on the discriminative model, the
tracking problem can be treated as a classification task [2]. Hough-based tracking
of non-rigid objects (HBT) [3] locates the support of the target through back
projection from a Hough Forest. Multiple instance learning (MIL) [4] learns a
discriminative classifier from positive and negative bags of samples. Struck [2]
applies a structured output (support vector machine) SVM to directly predict
the change in object location between frames, instead of using a labeler. Because
of the strong convexity and probabilistic underpinnings, logistic regression (LR)
is widely studied and used in many applications [5]. Compared with support
vector machine, the advantages of LR are its posterior model for model selection
and its probabilistic output for uncertainty prediction [5], which can be used for
comparing classifier outputs. Different from the previously proposed methods,
we introduce ensemble learning based on logistic regression model to deal with
the visual tracking problem. The remaining part of this paper is organized as
follows: Sect. 2 discusses the proposed method. Experiment results are described
in Sect. 3, and Sect. 4 concludes this paper.

© Springer Nature Singapore Pte Ltd. 2016
M. Gong et al. (Eds.): BIC-TA 2016, Part I, CCIS 681, pp. 480–486, 2016.
DOI: 10.1007/978-981-10-3611-8_44

2 The Proposed Method

2.1 Logistic Regression Classifier

Let $x \in R^N$ denote a vector of explanatory or feature variables, and $y \in \{-1, +1\}$ denotes the associated binary output. Logistic regression attempts to find a separating hyperplane in feature space, parameterized by normal vector $w \in R^N$, which separates the two classes [6]. The posterior label probability is modeled as:

$$P(y|x, w) = \frac{1}{1 + \exp(-yx^T w)} \tag{1}$$

Suppose we are given a set of training or observed examples $x = \{x_1, x_2, ..., x_M\}$ and their label $y = \{y_1, y_2, ..., y_M\}$, the model parameter w can be found by maximum likelihood estimation from the observed examples. The maximum likelihood estimate minimizes the average loss [7]:

$$l_{avg}(w) = \frac{1}{M} \sum_{i=1}^{M} \log\left(1 + \exp\left(-y_i w^T x_i\right)\right) \tag{2}$$

In many cases, the maximum-likelihood estimator may overfit to the training data [6]. To reduce overfitting, penalized likelihood methods based on l_2-regularization seek to minimize a version of:

$$J(w) = l_{avg}(w) + \lambda ||w||_2^2 \tag{3}$$

where $\lambda > 0$ is the regularization parameter. There are many methods for training logistic regression models. In fact, most unconstrained optimization techniques can be considered [8]. Quasi Newton [9, 10] is used to solve the weight W in our paper.

2.2 Weak Classifier

Haar-like feature is used in the proposed method. This feature is a simple rectangle features proposed by [11,12]. Each weak classifier h_k is composed of a haar-like feature f_k and four parameters $(\mu_+, \sigma_+, \mu_-, \sigma_-)$ that are estimated online [4]. The classifiers return the log odds ratio:

$$h_k(x) = log[\frac{P(y = +1|f_k(x))}{P(y = -1|f_k(x))}] = log[\frac{P(f_k(x)|y = +1)P(y = +1)}{P(f_k(x)|y = -1)P(y = -1)}] \tag{4}$$

where $P(f_k(x)|y = +1) \sim N(\mu_+, \sigma_+)$ and similarly for $y = -1$. We let $P(y = +1) = P(y = -1)$ and use Bayes rule to compute the above equation. When the weak classifier receives new data $\{(x_1, y_1), (x_2, y_2), ..., (x_M, y_M)\}$, we use the following update rules:

$$\mu_+ \longleftarrow \gamma\mu_+ + (1-\gamma)\frac{1}{M}\sum_{i|y_i=+1} f_k(x_i) \tag{5}$$

$$\sigma_+ \longleftarrow \gamma\sigma_+ + (1-\gamma)\sqrt{\frac{1}{M}\sum_{i|y_i=+1}(f_k(x_i)-\mu_+)^2} \tag{6}$$

where $0 < \gamma < 1$ is a learning rate parameter. The update rules for μ_- and σ_- are similarly defined.

2.3 Ensemble Learning Based on Logistic Regression Framework

The proposed ensemble learning method uses logistic regression to optimize their weighs of weak classifiers. Figure 1 shows the relevant steps. Ensemble learning refers to boosting the performance of a classifier by training many weak classifiers and combining them with weights [13]. When it is difficult to design a high performance classifier, boosting is particularly useful way for coping with the problem and providing simple decision rules to perform slightly better than random guessing. In general, the final strong classifier is a linear combination of the weak classifiers. The boosting algorithm is to find a way to boost a set of simple (weak) classifiers into a much stronger classifier through a certain learning method [13].

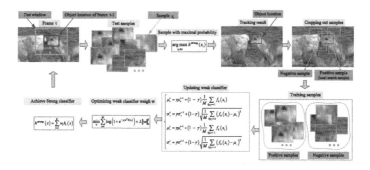

Fig. 1. Tracking model based on ensemble learning with logistic regression

Considering the simplicity and computational efficiency, we crop out a set of image patches within a test area based on the tracker location of previous frame when a new (current) frame arrives. The image patch with the highest posterior probability given by the boosting classifier is determined as object patch, and its location is defined as the objection location. The prediction function in the algorithm is

$$h^{strong}(x) = \sum_{i=1}^{K} w_i h_i(x) = w^T h(x) \tag{7}$$

where $h_i(x), i = 1, 2, ..., K$ is the 'better' weak classifiers.

Based on the objection location, we can acquire the positive and negative samples by cropping out several image patches. Each image patch is viewed as the training sample and corresponds to a feature vector in our case. The weak classifier parameter is updated according to Eqs. 5 and 6. We select some better weak classifiers and provide an appropriate weight for each of them by logistic regression.

$$min_w \sum_{i=1}^{M} \log \left(1 + \exp \left(-y_i w^T h(x_i)\right)\right) + \lambda ||w||_2^2 \qquad (8)$$

Equation 8 reduces entirely the error between the predicted label and the true label. Accordingly, the weights of weak classifiers are determined.

3 Experiments

We empirically set $\gamma = 0.95$, $N = 250$ and $K = 100$ in our experiments. To evaluate the effectiveness of the proposed approach, we compare our tracker against state-of-the-art algorithms (CT [2], CXT [14], DF [15], MIL [4], SCM [16], Struck [2], TLD [17] and VTD [18]) on several publicly available challenging image sequences. They cover various challenging situations (partial occlusion, illumination variation, pose change, motion blur, etc.) for object tracking.

Table 1 reports the average center location errors (in pixels), where a smaller value indicates a more accurate tracking result. Table 2 reports overlap success rate (%) with a threshold of 0.5, where the larger average scores indicate more accurate results. The provided qualitative comparison on seven challenging sequences are shown in Fig. 2. It confirms that our tracer handles the following situations:

Table 1. Average center location errors (in pixels). The red fonts and the blue fonts indicate the best and the second best performances respectively.

Sequence	CT	CXT	DF	MIL	SCM	Struck	TLD	VTD	Ours
Basketball	89	215	18	92	53	118	269	6	10
David3	89	222	51	30	73	107	281	67	13
Football	12	13	9	12	17	17	14	14	12
Jogging	92	6	31	96	132	62	7	83	5
Liquor	186	132	221	142	99	91	100	60	57

Occlusions and Deformation: Occlusion is one of the crucial problems in visual tracking. Figure 2(a), (d) and (e) show the performance of all trackers when the tracking object suffers partial and heavy occlusions. Only CXT, TLD and our method can keeps track of the target in the Jogging sequence. Our method even successfully deals with twice occlusion while other approaches

Table 2. Overlap success rate (%) with a threshold of 0.5. The red fonts and the blue fonts indicate the best and the second best performances respectively.

Sequence	CT	CXT	DF	MIL	SCM	Struck	TLD	VTD	Ours
Basketball	25.93	2.48	71.59	27.45	60.28	10.21	2.48	92.41	81.51
David3	34.92	13.89	74.21	68.25	48.02	33.73	10.32	48.41	84.52
Football	78.45	65.19	84.25	73.76	57.18	66.02	41.16	76.80	78.72
Jogging	22.48	95.44	21.50	22.48	21.17	22.48	96.74	21.50	95.11
Liquor	20.85	20.96	22.92	20.10	32.45	40.61	56.17	57.96	69.79

fail. Our local tracking model draws the visible part and keeps the track. The Basketball sequence has many deformations, but we still track accurately in the end.

Out of Plane Rotation: Tracking target rotation is also a big challenge in the field of visual tracking. In Fig. 2(e), the object rotates 1/4 turn. More

(a) Basketball

(b) David3

(c) Football

(d) Jogging

(e) Liquor

Fig. 2. Representative frames from ten sequences. The results obtained by those ten state-of-the-art algorithms and ours are shown in different colors: MIL in pink, VTD in purple, CT in green, DF in black, SCM in gray, CXT in blue, TLD in turquoise, Struck in orange, STC in dark red, ONNDL in cyan, and Ours in red. (Color figure online)

than half of trackers cannot handle with the situation, but our algorithm can implement accurate tracking.

Background Clutter: In the four background clutter sequences (Basketball, David3, Football and Liquor), our tracker performs more stable than other trackers. In the Basketball and Football sequences, there are many players wearing the same clothes. The background near the target has the similar color or texture as the target in the David3 and Liquor sequence. Background clutter can lead to drafting. However, our method achieves better tracking performance.

Both table and figures show that our method achieves favorable performance against other state of-the-art methods.

4   Conclusion

In this paper, we present a new visual tracking algorithm based on ensemble learning using logistic regression model. The sample is represented by haarlike features. The logistic regression model is adopted to obtain the weights of weak classifiers. The selection of weak classifier and weights of classifiers are implemented simultaneously. The experimental results show the effectiveness of the proposed method.

Acknowledgment. This work was supported by the National Natural Science Foundation of China under Grant 61571342, 61573267, 61473215; by the National Basic Research Program of China under Grant 2013CB329402.

References

1. Biederman, I., Subramaniam, S., Bar, M., et al.: Subordinate-level object classification reexamined. Psychol. Res. **62**(2–3), 131–153 (1999)
2. Branson, S., Wah, C., Schroff, F., Babenko, B., Welinder, P., Perona, P., Belongie, S.: Visual recognition with humans in the loop. In: Daniilidis, K., Maragos, P., Paragios, N. (eds.) ECCV 2010. LNCS, vol. 6314, pp. 438–451. Springer, Berlin (2010). doi:10.1007/978-3-642-15561-1_32
3. Hillel, A., Weinshall, D.: Subordinate class recognition using relational object models. In: NIPS, pp. 73–80 (2006)
4. Yang, J., Yu, K., Gong, Y., et al.: Linear spatial pyramid matching using sparse coding for image classification. In: CVPR, pp. 1794–1801 (2009)
5. Sivic, J., Zisserman, A.: Video google: a text retrieval approach to object matching in videos. In: CVPR, pp. 1470–1478 (2003)
6. Zheng, W., Gong, S., Xiang, T.: Associating groups of people. In: BMVC, pp. 23.1–23.11 (2009)
7. Yao, B.B., Bradski, G., Li, F.F.: A codebook-free and annotation-free approach for fine-grained image categorization. In: CVPR, pp. 3466–3473 (2012)
8. Lazebnik, S., Schmid, C., Ponce, J.: Beyond bags of features: spatial pyramid matching for recognizing natural scene categories. In: CVPR, pp. 2169–2178 (2006)
9. Sánchez, J., Perronnin, F., Mensink, T.: Image classification with the Fisher vector: theory and practice. Int. J. Comput. Vis. **105**(3), 222–245 (2013)

10. Perronnin, F., Sánchez, J., Mensink, T.: Improving the Fisher kernel for large-scale image classification. In: Daniilidis, K., Maragos, P., Paragios, N. (eds.) ECCV 2010. LNCS, vol. 6314, pp. 143–156. Springer, Berlin (2010). doi:10.1007/978-3-642-15561-1_11

11. Perronnin, F., Dance, C.: Fisher kernels on visual vocabularies for image categorization. In: CVPR, pp. 1–8 (2007)

12. Zhang, J., Marszalek, M., Lazebnik, S., et al.: Local features and kernels for classification of texture and object categories: a comprehensive study. Int. J. Comput. Vis. **73**(2), 213–238 (2005)

13. Liu, H., Su, Z.: Template-based multiple codebooks generation for fine-grained shopping classification, retrieval. In: ICDH, pp. 293–298 (2014)

14. Lowe, D.G.: Distinctive image features from scale-invariant keypoints. Int. J. Comput. Vis. **60**(2), 91–110 (2004)

15. Van de Sande, K., Gevers, T., Snoek, C.: Evaluating color descriptors for object and scene recognition. IEEE Trans. Pattern Anal. Mach. Intell. **32**(9), 1582–1596 (2010)

16. Hiremath, P.S., Pujari, J.: Content based image retrieval using color, texture, shape features. In: ADCOM, pp. 780–784 (2007)

17. Yu, J., Qin, Z., Wan, T., et al.: Feature integration analysis of bag-of-features model for image retrieval. Neurocomputing **120**, 355–364 (2013)

18. Li, L.J., Su, H., Xing, E., Li, F.F.: Object bank: a high-level image representation for scene classification and semantic feature sparsification. In: NIPS, vol. 26(6), pp. 719–729 (2010)

19. Maji, S., Bourdev, L., Malik, J.: Action recognition from a distributed representation of pose, appearance. In: CVPR, pp. 3177–3184 (2011)

20. Coates, A., Lee, H.: An analysis of single-layer networks in unsupervised feature learning. In: AISTATS, pp. 215–233 (2011)

21. Welinder, P., Branson, S., Mita, T., et al.: Caltech-UCSD birds 200. Technical report, Caltech (2010)

22. Farrell, R., Oza, O., Zhang, N., et al.: Birdlets: subordinate categorization using volumetric primitives and pose-normalized appearance. In: ICCV, pp. 809–818 (2011)

23. Lazebnik, S., Schmid, C., Ponce, J.: Beyond bags of features: spatial pyramid matching for recognizing natural scene categories. In: CVPR, pp. 2169–2178 (2006)

24. Yao, B.B., Khosla, A., Li, F.F.: Combining randomization, discrimination for fine-grained image categorization. In: CVPR, pp. 1577–1584 (2011)

A New Optimal Neuro-Fuzzy Inference System for MR Image Classification and Multiple Scleroses Detection

Hakima Zouaoui[1(✉)], Abdelouahab Moussaoui[1], Abdelmalik Taleb-Ahmed[2], and Mourad Oussalah[3]

[1] Computer Science Department, Ferhat Abbas University, Sétif, Algeria
Hak-soraya@yahoo.fr, Moussaoui.abdel@gmail.com
[2] LAMIH Laboratory, University of Valenciennes, Valenciennes, France
Abdelmalik.Taleb-Ahmed@univ-valenciennes.fr
[3] Centre for Ubiquitous Computing, University of Oulu, 91004 Oulu, Finland
Mourad.Oussalah@ee.oulu.fi

Abstract. In the present article, we propose a new approach for the segmentation of the MR images of the Multiple Sclerosis (MS) which is an autoimmune inflammatory disease affecting the central nervous system. Our algorithm of segmentation is composed of three stages: segmentation of the brain into regions using the algorithm FCM (Fuzzy C-Means) in order to obtain the characterization of the different healthy tissues (White matter, grey matter and cerebrospinal fluid (CSF)), the elimination of the atypical data (outliers) of the white matter by the optimization algorithm PSOBC (Particle Swarm Optimization-Based image Clustering), finally, the use of a Mamdani-type fuzzy model to extract the MS lesions among all the absurd data.

Keywords: Multiple sclerosis · Magnetic resonance imaging · Segmentation · Fuzzy C-means · Particle swarm optimization · Fuzzy controller

1 Introduction

Multiple sclerosis (MS) is a chronic inflammatory demyelinating disease of the central nervous system. Magnetic resonance imaging (MRI) detects lesions in MS patients with high sensitivity but low specificity, and is used for diagnosis, prognosis and as a surrogate marker in MS trials [1,2]. In this article, we are interested in the brain MRI analysis within the context of following up the patients suffering from Multiple Sclerosis (MS).

In this paper, we focus our studies to brain MR imaging where we propose a new automated segmentation method that detects the lesions of MS. Our algorithm of segmentation is composed of three stages: segmentation of the brain into regions using the algorithm FCM (Fuzzy C-Means) in order on obtain the characterization of the different healthy tissues (White Matter (WM), Grey Matter

© Springer Nature Singapore Pte Ltd. 2016
M. Gong et al. (Eds.): BIC-TA 2016, Part I, CCIS 681, pp. 487–493, 2016.
DOI: 10.1007/978-981-10-3611-8_45

(GM) and CerebroSpinal Fluid (CSF)). In the second stage, we use a particle swarm optimization-based image clustering algorithm to eliminate the atypical data of the white matter. Finally, in the third stage, a decision-making whether a given voxel is MS lesion is generated using a Mamdani-type fuzzy model.

The paper is organized as follows. First, related works are presented in Sect. 2. Next, our approach of automatic MS lesion detection and its various steps are highlighted in Sect. 3. Section 4 examines the results obtained on the MRI images. Finally, a conclusion is reported in Sect. 5.

2 Related Work

A variety of approaches to MS lesion segmentation have been proposed in the literature. Generally speaking, they can be classified into two groups: outlier-based and class-based methods.

In outlier-based methods [3–7], MS lesions are treated and detected as the outliers to the normal brain tissue distribution, which is usually modelled with a Finite Gaussian Mixture (FGM) of CSF, GM and WM classes. Van Leemput et al. [3] pioneered this approach where an (iterative) robustized expectation-maximization like method was promoted such that contextual information were incorporated.

Class-based methods [8–13] modeled the lesions as an independent class to be extracted. In [9], a combination of intensity-based k-nearest neighbor classification (k-NN) and a template-driven segmentation (TDS) was designed to segment different types of brain tissue. Lesions were modeled as one of the expected tissue types, and the class parameters were obtained through a supervised voxel sampling scheme on two randomly selected scans. A similar approach was proposed in [4] where the segmentation method determines for each voxel in the image the probability of being part of MS-lesion tissue, and the classification was conducted using K-NN algorithm.

3 Proposed Approach

In this study, we use information from T1-weighted, T2-weighted and proton density-weighted (PD) images. This is motivated by the fact that T1-w, T2-w and PD images contain information about white matter lesions [7]. Figure 1 summarizes the processing sequence proposed for the segmentation of MS lesions, while details of the different stages are provided in the subsequent subsections.

3.1 Segmentation of the Brain Tissues

The segmentation of the brain tissues into different compartments (white matter (WM), gray matter (GM) and cerebrospinal fluid (CSF)) is a key step in our study. Motivated by the lack of a fully comprehensive labeled database as reported in [15], a non-supervised like strategy based on fuzzy c-means algorithm

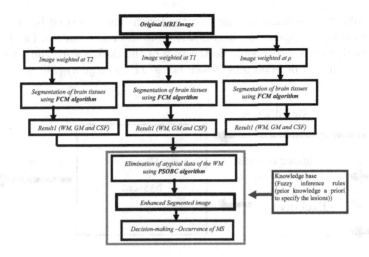

Fig. 1. General architecture of the steps of the automatic segmentation of MS lesions.

has been advocated. This is backed by its reported success in image analysis and medical diagnosis including magnetic imaging regardless of the modality and the type of acquisition (mono or multimodal) [14, 16–20], its reduced complexity, easy implementation [18]. The application of fuzzy c-means (FCM) approach for clustering in our case yields three distinct classes corresponding to (white matter (WM), gray matter (SG) and cerebrospinal fluid (CSF)).

3.2 Segmentation of the White Matter Using Particle Swarm Optimization Based Image-Clustering

The next stage in our methodology consists in eliminating the atypical data in previously identified WM voxels in order to highlight the different MS lesions. This is because the lesions of the multiple sclerosis are not well contrasted due to the partial volume in the surrounding tissues, which renders their segmentation rather a difficult task. For this purpose, an optimization based approach using particle swarm optimization based image-clustering algorithm (PSOBC) has been adopted in our approach. This is motivated by its simplicity, ability to deal with high dimension dataset, its proven efficiency in similar other segmentation tasks as pointed out in [21–23].

3.3 Decision-Making

The last step determines whether a given WM voxel is MS lesion or not. For this purpose, a Mamdani-type fuzzy inference system has been adopted. In the latter, (global) information about the image contrast and signals type are used as global variables. The outcome corresponds to the extent to which the MS attribute is persistent in the underlying WM voxel. Especially, the weighted images in T2 and

PD underline the myelin component in the lesions characterized by the edemas with hyper-intense appearance in comparison to the white matter. Furthermore, T1-w underlines the irreversible destruction of the tissues with the appearance in the white matter of persistent "black holes" (Hypo-signal) [24].

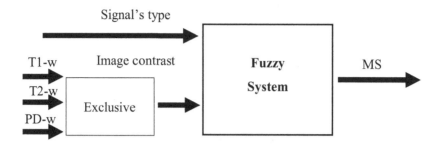

Fig. 2. Diagram of fuzzy system of the MS disease.

An instance of fuzzy rules is described below.

1. **If** [(the image contrast is T1-w active) AND (the signal is hyperintense)] **then** (MS is low).
2. **If** [(the image contrast is T1-w active) AND (the signal is hyperintense)] **then** (MS is normal).
3. **If** [(the image contrast is T2-w active) AND (the signal is hyperintense)] **then** (MS is high).
4. **If** [(the image contrast is PD -w active) AND (the signal is hyperintense)] **then** (MS is high).
5. **If** [(the image contrast is T1-w active) AND (the signal is hypointense)] **then** (MS is low).
6. **If** [(the image contrast is T2-w active) AND (the signal is hypointense)] **then** (MS is high).
7. **If** [(the image contrast is PD-w active) AND (the signal is hypointense)] **then** (MS is high).
8. **If** [(the image contrast is T1-w active) AND (the signal is hyperintense after injection of gadolinium)] **then** (MS is normal).
9. **If** [(the image contrast is T2-w active) AND (the signal is hyperintense after injection of gadolinium)] **then** (MS is high).
10. **If** [(the image contrast is PD-w active) AND (the signal is hyperintense after injection of gadolinium)] **then** (MS is high).

4   Results and Discussion

The Fig. 3 shows the results obtained after segmentation of the images (a) weighted T2 on axial plane. The images (b), (c), (d) and (e) are the results of segmentation realized by the expert, FCM, PSOBC and the approach successively proposed.

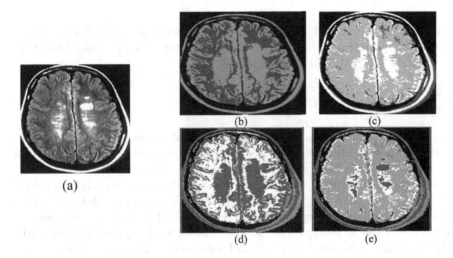

Fig. 3. Pathological image (a) and its segmentation gotten by (b) segmentation by the expert; (c) FCM; (d) PSOBC and (e) Proposed approach.

The interpretation of our results is done by an expert (hospital center of Ain Naadja Algiers) on simulated and real images. By analyzing the images of the Fig. 3, the expert has established the following statement:

- **Image (b):** The interpretation of the classes is totally improved in relation to (FCM, PSOBC), we notice the distinction between the 03 classes of the brain and the class of the pathology SEP.
- **Image (c):** The class CSF does not conform to the class of the original image. The lack of information about the small grooves (image (a)) and the poor discrimination CSF/GM make that the segmented CSF class does not well represent the fluid distribution. The detection of the pathology is indicated according to the expert but the details are not well expressed.
- **Image (d):** PSOBC is unsuitable in this segmentation in relation to the image (o).
- **Image (e):** the proposed approach brings a great performance to the segmenta-tion for the three classes and especially for the fourth one which is the pathology that specifies well the size and the details about this later.

Next, we compared in Table 1 the segmentation of T2-w RMI performed by the expert and that achieved using our automated approach for a given time of

Table 1. Comparison of the results gotten by different algorithms.

	GM (%)	CSF (%)	WM (%)	MS (%)
Segmentation by the expert	93	69	95	97
FCM	71	55.9	79.6	74
PSOBC	80.2	64	85	68
Proposed approach	88.7	66	90.5	95.8

acquisition. The results highlighted in Table 1 underline the advantages of the proposed approach in comparison to the segmentation by FCM and PSOBC for all tissues CSF, WM, GM and MS lesions.

5 Conclusion

In this article, we have proposed a new automatic approach of segmentation of the MS lesions' images. We have firstly split up the process of automatic segmentation of the MS lesions into three fundamental stages:

Firstly, we segmented the brain into regions by using the algorithm FCM (Fuzzy C-Means) in order to obtain the characterization of the different healthy tissues (White matter, Grey matter and cerebrospinal fluid (CSF)). Secondly, we eliminated of the atypical data of the white matter by the optimization algorithm PSOBC (Particle Swarm Optimization-Based image Clustering). Finally, in the framework of our application on the MS disease, we used a Mamdani-type fuzzy model to make decision of the MS disease. We presented the results of our work consisting in the use of an algorithm for the segmentation if medical images in order to improve the quality of the MS lesions' detection.

References

1. Miller, D.H.: Biomarkers and surrogate outcomes in neurodegenerative disease: lessons from multiple sclerosis. NeuroRX **1**(2), 284–294 (2004)
2. Daniel, G.-L., Sylvain, P., Douglas, A., Louis, C., Christian, B.: Trimmed-likelihood estimation for focal lesions and tissue segmentation in multisequence MRI for multiple sclerosis. In: IEEE Transactions on Medical Imaging, Institute of Electrical and Electronics Engineers (IEEE) Results and Discussion (2011)
3. Van Leemput, K., Maes, F., Vandermeulen, D., Colchester, D., Suetens, P.: Automated segmentation of multiple sclerosis lesions by model outlier detection. IEEE TMI **20**(8), 677–689 (2001)
4. Anbeek, P., Vinchen, K.L., van Osch, M.J.P., Bisschops, R.H.C., van der Grond, J.: Probabilistic segmentation of white matter lesions in MR imaging. NeuroImage **21**, 1037–1044 (2004)
5. Souplet, J.C., Lebrun, C., Anyche, N., Malandain, G.: An automatic segmentation of T2-FLAIR multiple sclerosis lesions. 3D segmentation in the clinic: a grand challenge II: MS lesion segmentation (2008)
6. Dugas-Phocion, G., Gonzalez, M.A., Lebrun, C., Chanalet, S., Bensa, C., Malandain, G., Ayache, N.: Hierarchical segmentation of multiple sclerosis lesions multi-sequence MRI. In: ISBI08 (2008)

7. Garcia-Lorenzo, D., Prima, S., Morrissey, S.P., Barillot, C.: A robust expectation-maximization algorithm for multiple sclerosis lesion segmentation. Segmentation in the clinic: a grand challenge II: lesion segmentation (2008)
8. Prastawa, M., Guido, G.: Automatic MS lesion segmentation by outlier detection and information theoretic region partitioning. 3D segmentation in the clinic: a grand challenge II: MS lesion segmentation (2008)
9. Wu, Y., Warfield, S.K., Tan, I.L., Wessl III, W.M., Meier, D.S., Van Schijndel, R.A., Barkhof, F., Guttmann, C.: Automated segmentation of multiple sclerosis lesion subtype with multichannel MRI. NeuroImage 32, 1025–1215 (2006)
10. Tu, Z., Narr, K., Dinov, I., Dollar, P., Thompson, P., Toga, A.: Brain anatomical structure parsing by hybrid discriminative/generative models. IEEE TMI 27(4), 495–508 (2008)
11. Morra, J., Tu, Z., Toga, A., Thompson, P.: Automatic segmentation of MS lesions using a contextual model for the MICCAI grand challenge. 3D segmentation in the clinic: a grand challenge II: MS lesion segmentation (2008)
12. Anbeek, P., Vinchen K.L., Viergever, M.A.: Antomated MS-lesion segmentation by K-nearest neighbor classification. 3D segmentation in the clinic: a grand challenge II: MS lesion segmentation (2008)
13. Bazin, P.-L., Pham, D.L.: Statistical and topological atlas based brain image segmentation. In: Ayache, N., Ourselin, S., Maeder, A. (eds.) MICCAI 2007. LNCS, vol. 4791, pp. 94–101. Springer, Heidelberg (2007). doi:10.1007/978-3-540-75757-3_12
14. Benaichouche, A.N., Oulhadj, H., Siarry, P.: Improved spatial fuzzy C-means clustering for image segmentation using PSO initialization, Mahalanobis distance and post-segmentation correction. Digit. Signal Proc. 23, 1390–1400 (2013)
15. Bezdek, J., Hall, I., Clarke, L.: Review of MR image segmentation techniques using pattern recognition. Med. Phys. 20, 1033–1048 (1993)
16. Ghosh, S., Kumar, S.: Comparative analysis of K-means and fuzzy C-means algorithms. Int. J. Adv. Comput. Sci. Appl. 4(4), 35–39 (2013)
17. Tejwant, S., Manish, M.: Performance comparison of fuzzy C means with respect to other clustering algorithm. Int. J. Adv. Res. Comput. Sci. Softw. Eng. 4(5), 89–93 (2014)
18. Bezdek, J.C.: Fuzzy mathematics in pattern classification. Ph.D. dissertation, Cornell University, Ithaca, NY (1973)
19. Zouaoui, H., Moussaoui, A.: Clustering par Fusion Floue de Donnes Appliqu la Segmentation dImages IRM Crbrales. CIIA, von CEUR Workshop Proceedings vol. 547. CEUR-WS.org (2009)
20. Premalatha, K., Natarajan, A.M.: A new approach for data clustering based on PSO with local search. Comput. Inform. Sci. 1(4), 139–145 (2008)
21. El Dor, A., Lepagnot, J., Nakib, A., Siarry, P.: PSO-2S optimization algorithm for brain MRI segmentation. In: Pan, J.S., Krömer, P., Snášel, V. (eds.) Genetic and Evolutionary Computing, pp. 13–22. Springer, Cham (2014)
22. Selvi, V., Umarani, R.: Comparative analysis of ant colony and particle swarm optimization techniques. Int. J. Comput. Appl. (0975–8887) 5(4), 1–6 (2010)
23. Shi, Y., Eberhart, R.C.: Empirical study of particle swarm optimization, vol. 3, pp. 1945–1950 (1999)
24. Aït-Ali, L.S., Prima, S., Edan, G., Barillot, C.: Longitudinal segmentation of MS lesions in multimodal brain MRI. In: 15ème Congrès Francophone AFRIF/AFIA de Reconnaissance des Formes et Intelligence Artificielle (RFIA), Tours, France, Janvier (2006)

The Influence of Diversification Strategy on Capital Structure

Xuefeng Li[⊠]

School of Economic and Management, Zhengzhou University of Light Industry,
Zhengzhou 450002, Henan, China
lxf@zzuli.edu.cn

Abstract. The paper aims to focus on a well-known topic in the financial literature: the relation between diversification strategy and capital structure. The investigation has been performed using panel data procedure for a sample of 320 Chinese companies listed on the Shanghai Stock Exchange during a three-year period. Using various measures of diversification, the regression results of this study reveal a significantly negative relation between diversification and capital structure. The result supports agency cost theory. The results also indicate that, firm size and growth opportunity have significantly positive effects on capital structure; profitability and liquidity have significantly negative relation with capital structure. Year and industry are also important impact factor of capital structure.v *abstract* environment.

Keywords: Diversification strategy · Capital structure · Agency cost theory

1 Introduction

The capital structure has a significant impact on the corporate operations. It can create opportunities to accelerate the company's development, but also limit and even hinder the company's growth. Starting from the provocative work of Modigliani and Miller (1958), capital structure became one of the main elements that following studies have shown as being essential in determining value. The capital structure of affirm is a specific mixture of debt and equity the firm uses to finance its operations. Capital structure decisions are crucial for any business organisation. The decision is important because of the need to maximize returns to various organisational constituencies an also because of the impact such a decision has on an organisation's ability to deal with its competitive environment (Abor and Biekpe 2005). In general, a firm can choose among many alternative capital structures. The firm can issue a large amount of debt or very little debt. It can issue dozens of distinct securities in countless combinations. A number of theories have been advanced in explaining the capital structure of firms. However, the impact of corporate strategies on capital structure is still unknown (Harris and Raviv 1991). Barton and Gordon (1987) pointed out that corporate strategies complement the traditional financial model, and enrich the

© Springer Nature Singapore Pte Ltd. 2016
M. Gong et al. (Eds.): BIC-TA 2016, Part I, CCIS 681, pp. 494–503, 2016.
DOI: 10.1007/978-981-10-3611-8_46

understanding of determinants of capital structure. Burgman (1996), Chen et al. (1997) and Chuang et al. (1999) find that diversification strategy is an important determinant of capital structure.

Until very recently, the studies of the diversification-capital structure relationship was rather scarce, so we know little about the strategic value of diversification in developing country such as China. The objective of this paper is the analysis of the effect of diversification strategy on capital structure form the Chinese perspective. To the end, the empirical results show statistically significant and negative associations between diversification and capital structure. The results also indicate that, firm size and growth opportunity have positive and significant effects on capital structure; profitability and liquidity have negative and significant relation with capital structure. Industry is also an important impact factor of capital structure.

The rest of the paper is organized as follows: the next session gives a review of the extant literature on the subject. Section 3 describes the methodology used for the study. Section 4 presents and discusses the results of the empirical analysis. Finally, Sect. 5 presents some conclusions.

2 Literature Review

In response to increasingly competitive business environment, diversification has become a major strategic initiative in the hospitality industry. This strategy has been widely applied in various business fields (Chang and Wang 2007). More than a tool for reducing business risks and uncertainties, diversification enables firms to gain, and more importantly, secure competitive advantages and market dominance that would otherwise be unattainable. In addition, from a resource-based perspective, diversification enables firms to exploit intangible resources (Andreu et al. 2009) and generates economies of scale and scope (George and Kabir 2012; Wang et al. 2014).

Diversification plays key roles in the strategic behavior of large corporate. Diversification strategy has also been shown to be an import determinant of capital structure. Dispersion risk theory argues that diversified firms can reduce the risk of operating risks, leading to enhance the debt capacity. Many strategic management scholars have studied the relationship between diversification strategies and capital structure. Chkir and Cosset (2001) think that the company's product diversification can reduce business risks, resulting in increased financial leverage. Barton and Gordon (1988) also confirm that the relationship between risk and diversification is a negative correlation, which leads to a positive correlation between diversification and debt levels. Studies have shown that diversification operations result in reduced risk. Diversification leads to a lower volatility of earnings as the diversified firms have cash flows in imperfectly correlated markets. This leads to reduction in bankruptcy risk and enables the diversified firms to utilize more leverage in their capital structure.

Berger and Ofek (1995) and Comment and Jarrell (1995) think that, with business across several product lines, the less than perfectly correlated income streams from different product lines reduce the volatility of returns, this coinsurance effect of debt gives diversified firms greater debt capacity than focused firms of similar size. Using United States data, Barton and Gordon (1988) provide evidence that diversification strategy is an important determinant of capital structure, the relationship between diversification strategy and capital structure is positive. Lowe et al. (1994) draw the same conclusion using Australian data. However, using small- and medium-sized firms (SMEs) data, Jordan et al. (1999) argue, contrary to the results found using large firms, that corporate strategy has no effect on the capital structure of SMEs.

However, agency cost theory suggests that, as owners and operators, owners and creditors, the general manager and manager exist agent problem, there will inevitably bring about the decrease in value. Due to agency cost, debt providers will require higher returns to finance diversified firms, which lead to an increase of the debt financing cost for these firms and therefore reduces their leverage. So, according to agency cost theory, the relationship between diversification and capital structure should be significantly negative.

3   Research Methodology

We investigate the relationship between diversification and capital structure of Chinese listed companies for the period from 2004 to 2006. All the companies included in the sample fulfill the following some criteria: they were all listed in the market before 2001; none of them was expelled from Shanghai Stock Exchange during the period 2004–2006; the sample companies only include the listed companies which issued A shares, not include financial listed companies and they also do not include ST or PT type of the listed companies.

We form our variables using data derived from China Center for Economic Research (CCER) database. The final samples, after considering abovementioned criteria, consist of 960 observations, 320 listed companies.

Table 1 summarizes the dependent, independent and control variables.

Table 1. Summarizes the dependent, independent and control variables

Variable	Sign	Definition
Capital structure	LEV	Total debt/total assets
	N	The number of segments
Diversification	DUM	Dum is 1 for firms reporting multiple segments; otherwise 0
	HI	Herfindahl index
	DT	Entropy index
Firm size	SIZE	LN (total assets)
Profitability	ROE	Net profit/equity
Growth opportunity	GROW	Sales growth rate
Liquidity	LIQU	Current assets/current liability
Year dummy	YEAR	Belonging to a certain year, equal to one; otherwise 0
Industry dummy	INDU	Belonging to a certain industry, equal to one; otherwise 0

3.1   Dependent Variables: Debt Ratio

The dependent variable is debt ratio. We use debt ratio as measure of capital structure. We define debt ratio as the ratio of total debt to total assets.

$$LEV = \frac{Total\ debt}{Total\ asset} \tag{1}$$

3.2   Independent Variables: Diversification

We measure a firm's diversification with four indices popular in the diversification literature: the number of segments (N), dummy of diversification (DUM), Herfindahl index (HI) and Entropy index (DT).

1. The number of segments (N): The more the number of segments of the corporation is, the higher the degree of the diversification.
2. Dummy of diversification (DUM): Dum is 1 for firms reporting multiple segments, otherwise 0.
3. Herfindahl index (HI): The Herfindahl index is calculated for all firms based on the distribution of the firm's sales across its various business segments. The Herfindahl index is calculated as:

$$HI = \sum P_i^2 \tag{2}$$

   where Pi represents the sales of a firm's operations in segment i, in proportion to the total sales of the firm. The Herfindahl index is inversely related to diversification. It takes one for firms specialized in a single industry and approach toward zero as a firm diversifies across many industries. Smaller levels of HI correspond to less industry focus and greater diversification.
4. Entropy index (DT): Entropy index has been widely used in measuring product diversification in the literature. One of the most important advantages of the entropy approach in measuring product diversification is that it allows for the decomposition of total diversification into the components of related and unrelated. The entropy measure takes the form of:

$$DT = \sum_{i=1}^{n} P_i \ln(1/P_i) \tag{3}$$

   where Pi is the ith business segment's sales divided by the firm's total sales, and n is number of the firm's business segments. Bigger levels of DT correspond to less industry focus and greater diversification.

3.3   Control Variables

There are other relevant variables which can affect capital structure: such as firm size, profitability, growth opportunities, liquidity and industry. These are briefly explained in turn.

(1) Firm size: We use the natural logarithm of total assets as a proxy for firm size.

(2) Profitability: According to pecking order theory, profitable firms tend to have less debt. In this study, profitability will be defined as net profit scaled by equity.

(3) Growth opportunity: According to the trade-off theory, firms holding future growth opportunity tend to borrow less than firms holding more tangible assets because growth opportunity cannot sever as collateral. In this paper, we proxy our growth opportunity measurement as sales growth rate.

(4) Liquidity: Pecking order theory thinks that firms with high liquidity will borrow less. In this paper, we proxy the liquidity of the firm considering its current ratio which is equal to current assets divided by current liabilities.

(5) Industry: This study pursues an investigation of the diversity-leverage relationship independent of industry effects. Firms in the data set were classified according to their sector of operations as listed on the Shanghai Stock Exchange.

3.4   Methodology

The model for the empirical investigation can be stated as follow:

$$
\begin{aligned}
LEV_{i,t} = \alpha_i &+ \beta_1 DIV_{i,t} + \beta_2 SIZE_{i,t} + \beta_3 ROE_{i,t} \\
&+ \beta_4 GROW_{i,t} + \beta_5 LIQU_{i,t} + \beta_6 YEAR \\
&+ \beta_7 INDU + \varepsilon_{i,t}.
\end{aligned}
\tag{4}
$$

where: $DIV_{i,t}$ = N, DUM, HI, and DT, respectively;
$SIZE_{i,t}$ = firm size (log of total assets) for firm i in time t;
$ROE_{i,t}$ = net profit///equity for firm i in time t;
$GROW_{i,t}$ = sales growth rate for firm i in time t;
$LIQU_{i,t}$ = current assets/current liabilities for firm i in time t.

4   Empirical Results

4.1   Descriptive Statistics

Table 2 shows the process of change on diversification for Chinese listed firms from 2004–2006.

Summary statistics of diversification for our sample are reported in Table 2. From Table 2, we can see that the number of segments is gradually increased, from 1.61 in 2004 to 1.64 in 2006, dummy of diversification and Entropy index are also gradually increased, form 0.46 to 0.49 and form 0.32 to 0.35 during the period from 2004 to 2006 respectively, while Herfindahl index is gradually decreased, from 0.75 in 2004 to 0.73 in 2006. Table 2 shows that, for Chinese listed companies in our sample, there is a discernible upward trend in diversification, despite the magnitude of change is not too great.

Table 2. The process of change on diversification

Year	N	DUM	HI	DT
2004	1.609	0.459	0.750	0.328
2005	1.634	0.478	0.739	0.345
2006	1.646	0.491	0.734	0.352

Table 3 provides a summary of the descriptive statistics of the dependent and independent variables for the sample of firms. This shows the average indicators of variables computed from the financial statements. Capital structure, given as the ratio of total debt to total assets, reveals an average of 47.5%. This suggests that about 47% of total assets are financed by debt capital. The average value of the number of segments, dummy of diversification, Herfindahl index, and Entropy index is 1.601, 0.467, 0.133, and 0.327 respectively.

Table 4 presents the correlation matrix of dependent and independent variables. Table 4 shows that leverage ratio and the degree of diversification are negatively correlated. The correlation between leverage ratio and the other variables is fairly low. The highest cross-correlation, between leverage ratio and firm size, is fairly moderate (Pearson: 0.29).

Table 3. Descriptive statistics of dependent and independent variables

Variable	Minimum	Maximum	Mean	Std. Dev.
LEV	0.028	1.685	0.475	0.174
N	1	5	1.601	0.745
DUM	0	1	0.467	0.493
HI	0.029	4.934	0.133	0.285
DT	0	1.538	0.327	0.359
SIZE	19.573	25.145	21.366	0.785
ROE	−1.173	1.627	0.058	0.147
GROW	−0.832	10.634	0.236	0.538
LIQU	0.075	36.762	1.467	1.712

To check whether independent variables are collinear, we perform a collinearity diagnostic. The values of our VIF tests are substantially lower than 5, so collinearity should not constitute a problem.

Table 4. The correlation matrix of dependent and independent variables

Variable	LEV	N	DUM	HI	DT	SIZE	ROE	GROW	LIQU
LEV	1								
N	−0.03	1							
DUM	−0.04*	0.85***	1						
HI	0.03*	−0.89***	−0.89***	1					
DT	−0.07*	0.95***	0.89***	−0.97***	1				
SIZE	0.29***	−0.05*	−0.06**	0.03	−0.04*	1			
ROE	−0.06***	−0.03	−0.02	0.03	−0.03	0.06***	1		
GROW	0.07***	−0.01	−0.02	0.03	−0.02	0.04	0.13***	1	
LIQU	−0.11***	−0.06**	−0.05**	0.05**	−0.06**	−0.12***	0.03	−0.01	1

4.2 Regression Results

(1) Univariate test

Table 5 presents univariate test statistics of all variable. The differences in mean tests (t-statistics) are reported. The average leverage ratio is 0.47 for diversified firms, and 0.48 for focused company. The mean difference is 1.4 moreover, Table 5 also indicates that diversified firms are less firm size and less liquidity than focused firms, but their average profitability and growth opportunity are not significantly different from that of focused firms. Yet, these results do not control other confounding effects to examine the pure diversification effect. Thus, we estimate the multivariate regression model with other control variables.

Table 5. The correlation matrix of dependent and independent variables

Variable	Diversified	Focused	Mean difference	t-value
LEV	0.477	0.489	−0.142*	−1.853
ROE	0.063	0.069	−0.008	−1.014
SIZE	21.432	21.593	−0.095**	−2.463
GROW	0.236	0.248	−0.024	−0.832
LIQU	1.473	1.662	−1.236**	−2.368

(2) Multivariate Regression result

Table 6 show the effects of the degree of diversification on capital structure after controlling for firm size, profitability, growth opportunity, liquidity, year and industry.

Regression analysis is used to investigate the relationship between diversification and capital structure. Generalized least square (GLS) regression results are presented in Table 6. The results denote that the independent variables explain

Table 6. The correlation matrix of dependent and independent variables

Variable	Coefficient	t-stat	Coefficient	t-stat	Coefficient	t-stat	Coefficient	t-stat
Intercept	−0.78**	−10.22	−0.77***	−9.61	−0.81***	−11.04	−0.78***	−10.58
N		−3.19						
DUM			−0.01***	−3.92				
HI					0.03***	3.53		
DT							−0.02***	−3.45
SIZE	0.07***	17.87	0.07***	17.96	0.068***	20.53	0.07***	19.46
ROE		−13.46	−0.15***	−13.17	−0.15***	−13.52	−0.15***	−13.81
GROW	0.03***	7.68	0.03***	8.25	0.029***	7.879	0.03***	7.53
LIQU	−0.06***	−24.96	−0.05***	−24.67	−0.05***	−26.19	−0.06***	−25.32
YEAR	Yes		Yes		Yes		Yes	
INDU	Yes		Yes		Yes		Yes	
R^2	0.704		0.698		0.703		0.701	
Adj. R^2	0.701		0.694		0.699		0.696	
F-statistic	187.01		182.15		186.81		184.78	
Prob. (F)	0.00		0.00		0.00		0.00	

diversification at 70.1, 69.4, 69.9, and 69.6%, respectively. The F-statistics prove the validity of the estimated models. Also, the coefficients are statistically significant in level of confidence of 99%.

The results as illustrated in Table 6 indicate that the number of segment, dummy of diversification, and Entropy index are significantly and negatively related to debt ratio. The regression results also show that Herfindahl index is significantly and positively related to leverage ratio, while higher levels of Herfindahl index correspond to less diversification. So the regression results indicate that diversification reduces the company's debt capacity, diversified firms have lower debt ratio than focused firms.

According to univariate test and multiple regression analysis results, we can be concluded that, for China's listed companies, diversification not only fails to reduce the company's business risk, but increases the company's business risk, reducing the company's debt capacity.

One possible explanation for this is that diversification exists the risk of economic of scope. Diversified firms enter into new business areas, and there are many uncertainties of new areas. New business areas may even pose a threat to the main industry. Diversification should disperse enterprise resources, while enterprises resources are always limited. New business expansion will compete with the core business for limited resources and even decline in growth of their core business, which weaken core competitiveness of companies.

Second possible explanation is that diversification exists the risk of management efficiency. Managers may be not familiar with market conditions and the technical characteristics of new industries. This increases the difficulty of the internal management of enterprises, which would bring about management inefficiency.

Third possible reason is that diversification has entrance risk. Diversified firms have more barriers and more cost to enter into new business, which damages the value of the enterprise.

5 Conclusion

One important financial decision firms are confronted with is the capital structure choice. This decision is particularly crucial given the effect it has on the value of the firm. This study has examined the relationship between diversification and capital structure of Chinese listed companies during a three-year period, 2004–2006.

The results obtained using Generalized Least Square (GLS) panel model. The characteristics of diversification used for this study include the number of segments, dummy of diversification, Herfindahl index, and Entropy index.

The empirical results indicate that diversification is significantly and negatively related to debt ratio, which shows for Chinese listed companies that the higher the degree of diversification, the lower its debt level. The result supports agency cost theory. For Chinese listed companies, we should adopt the specialized management and reduce the diversification management in order to reduce the financial risk. The results also indicate that, firm size and growth opportunity have significantly positive effects on capital structure; profitability and liquidity have significantly negative relation with capital structure. Year and industry are also important impact factor of capital structure.

References

Andreu, R., Claver, E., Quer, D.: Type of diversification and firm resources: new empirical evidence from the Spanish tourism industry. Int. J. Tourism Res. **11**(3), 229–239 (2009)

Barton, S.L., Gordon, P.J.: Corporate strategy: useful perspective for the study of capital structure? Acad. Manag. Rev. **12**, 67–75 (1987)

Barton, S.L., Gordon, P.J.: Corporate strategy and capital structure. Strateg. Manag. J. **9**, 623–632 (1988)

Berger, P.G., Ofek, E.: Diversification's effect on firm value. J. Financ. Econ. **37**, 39–65 (1995)

Burgman, T.A.: An empirical examination of multinational corporate capital structure. J. Int. Bus. Stud. **3**, 553–570 (1996)

Chang, S.C., Wang, C.F.: The effect of product diversification strategies on the relationship between international diversification and firm performance. J. World Bus. **42**(1), 61–79 (2007)

Chen, J.P., Cheng, S.A., He, J., Kim, J.: An investigation of the relationship between international activities and capital structure. J. Int. Bus. Stud. **3**, 563–577 (1997)

Chkir, I.E., Cosset, J.: Diversification strategy and capital structure of multinational corporations. J. Multinational Financ. Manag. **2**, 17–37 (2001)

Chuang, C.T., Li, P.P.: The internationalization and capital structure of taiwanese multinationals. Am. Asian Rev. **17**, 51–75 (1999)

Comment, R., Jarrell, G.A.: Corporate focus and stock returns. J. Financ. Econ. **37**, 67–87 (1995)

George, R., Kabir, R.: Heterogeneity in business groups and the corporate diversificationfirm performance relationship. J. Bus. Res. **65**(3), 412–420 (2012)

Harris, M., Raviv, A.: Corporate control contests and capital structure. J. Financ. Econ. **20**, 55–86 (1998)

Harris, M., Raviv, A.: The theory of capital structure. J. Financ. **46**, 297–355 (1991)

Jordan, J., Lowe, J., Taylor, P.: Strategy and financial policy in UK small firms. J. Bus. Financ. Acc. **25**, 1–27 (1999)

Lowe, J., Naughton, A., Taylor, P.: The impact of corporate strategy on the capital structure of Australian companies. Manag. Decis. Econ. **15**, 245–257 (1994)

Wang, Y., Ning, L., Chen, J.: Product diversification through licensing: empirical evidence from Chinese firms. Eur. Manag. J. **32**(4), 577–586 (2014)

An Improved Hybrid Bat Algorithm for Traveling Salesman Problem

Wedad Al-sorori$^{(\boxtimes)}$, Abdulqader Mohsen, and Walid Aljoby ßer

University of Science and Technology, Sana'a, Taiz, Yemen
{w.alsrori,a.alabadi,waljoby}@ust.edu

Abstract. A new metaheuristic, bat algorithm, inspired by echolocation characteristics of micro-bats has been extensively applied to solve various continuous optimization problems. Numerous intelligent techniques are hybridized with bat algorithm to optimize its performance. However, there are only two discrete variants have been proposed to tune the basic bat algorithm to handle combinatorial optimization problems. However, both of them suffer from the inherited drawbacks of the bat algorithm such as slow speed convergence and easy stuck at local optimal. Motivated by this, an improved hybrid variant of discrete bat algorithm, called IHDBA is proposed and applied to solve traveling salesman problem. IHDBA achieves a good balance between intensification and diversification by adding the evolutionary operators, crossover and mutation, which allow performance of both local and global search. In addition, 2-opt and 3-opt local search techniques are introduced to improve searching performance and speed up the convergence. Using extensive evaluations based on TSP benchmark instances taken from TSPLIB, the results show that IHDBA outperforms state-of-the-art discrete bat algorithm i.e. IBA in the most of instances with respect to average and best solutions.

Keywords: Hybrid Bat Algorithm · Crossover operator · Mutation operator · Discrete bat algorithm · TSP · Intensification and diversification

1 Introduction

Many computational optimization problems remain difficult to solve in a polynomial time and, therefore, they are classified as non-polynomial hard problems (NP-hard problems) [1]. In this context, traveling salesman problem, or TSP for short, is one of the most famous cases of NP-hard problems [2]. Given a set of cities, TSP aims to minimize the overall trip cost that a salesperson may need for traveling from one city to visit each city in the set only once and return back to the start one. TSP is often used for testing optimization algorithms as a benchmark to measure their abilities to solve other NP-hard problems [3,4].

Recently, a new meta-heuristic method, bat algorithm, has been successfully applied to solve several optimization problems including TSP [5]. In addition to

© Springer Nature Singapore Pte Ltd. 2016
M. Gong et al. (Eds.): BIC-TA 2016, Part I, CCIS 681, pp. 504–511, 2016.
DOI: 10.1007/978-981-10-3611-8_47

its advantages of simplicity, easy implementation and its higher stability mechanism, BA has the ability of dealing with non-linear, multi-modal and large scale optimization problems. However, BA still has some limitations. (i) It may suffer from stagnation in the early stages when A_i and r_i vary too quickly. (ii) BA also loses its exploration as the iterations flow since r_i exponentially increased; hence, its condition becomes less probable to be satisfied. (iii) BA may not be able to perform global search because it suffers from premature convergence in some cases and may be trapped into local optima.

To enhance the performance of basic BA [6], several hybrid variants were proposed to solve both continuous and combinatorial optimization problems such as in [7–18]. It is worthy to note that the enhancement of BA by hybridization to solve combinatorial problems has not been explored enough. To address TSP, two papers were introduced. Yassine Saji et al. [19] proposed a discrete version of BA. Then, Eneko Osaba et al. also introduced an improved discrete bat algorithm for both symmetric and asymmetric TSP called IBA [20].

In this paper, we proposed an improved hybrid discrete BA variant to solve TSP problem to solve the premature convergence, stagnation problem and speed up the convergence.

2 Background

In the following subsections, we briefly review the bat algorithm and its IBA discrete variant.

2.1 Bat Algorithm

Bat algorithm was initiated by Yang 2010 [6] as a relatively new meta-heuristic to solve hard optimization problems. An overview of BA, its inspiration idea, its variants and application domains is shown in [5]. BA was inspired by micro-bats behavior when they search for prey. The three idealization rules of bat-inspired algorithm can be summarized as follows: (i) all bats sense their direction and the distance of obstacles/prey using echolocation; (ii) each bat i flies randomly with velocity v_i at position (solution) x_i with a fixed frequency f_{min}, varying wavelength λ and loudness A_0. Bats can adjust the frequency of their emitted pulses rate in the range of $r \in [0, 1]$ when searching for prey depending on the proximity of their target; and (iii) the loudness can vary in many ways; it was assumed that it varies from a large positive A_0 to a minimum constant value A_{min}. The main steps of BA are illustrated as follows:

Step1 (Initialization): an initial population $X = [x_1, x_2, \ldots, x_n]$ of n bats is generated randomly. Each bat i in the population represents a potential location (solution of the problem under consideration) with random rate of pulse r_i, random loudness A_i and initial frequency f_i; each of which is evaluated using fitness function.

Step2 (Generation of new solutions): During each iteration, every bat i updates its frequency f_i, velocity v_i and position (solution) x_i at iteration t according to Eqs. 1, 2 and 3 respectively.

$$f_i = f_{min} + (f_{max} - f_{min})\beta \tag{1}$$

$$v_i^t = v_i^{t-1} + (x_i^{t-1} - x_*), \tag{2}$$

$$x_i^t = x_i^{t-1} + v_i^t, \tag{3}$$

where β is a random vector in the range of [0,1] drawn from a uniform distribution; and x^* is the current global best location (solution) among all solutions in the population.

Step3 (Local Search): After that, with some probability of pulse rate r_i, a solution is selected among the best solutions and random walk is applied to generate a local solution around the selected one according to Eq. 4:

$$x_{new} = x_{old} + \varepsilon A_i^t, \tag{4}$$

where the random number ε is a scale factor drawn from $[-1, 1]$ and A_i^t is the average loudness of all bats. Then, the new solutions will be accepted if they are improved or by flying randomly with some probability depending on A_i.

Step4 (Loudness and Pulse Emission): If the solution is accepted, the pulse emission rate r_i increases and the loudness A_i decreases like what happen when natural bat finds its prey. Mathematically, this is defined using Eqs. 5 and 6:

$$A_i^{t+1} = \alpha A_i^t, \tag{5}$$

$$r_i^{t+1} = r_i^0[1 - \exp(-\gamma t)], \tag{6}$$

Step5 (Finding the global best solution): Finally, rank the solutions and find the current global best solution(s). Steps 2–5 continue until the termination condition is satisfied.

2.2 An Improved Bat Algorithm (IBA) for TSP

Eneko Osaba et al. presented an improved discrete version for bat algorithm called IBA [20]. It was used to solve TSP but it failed to reach the optimal solution in the most of instances. IBA used the same philosophy for the basic BA parameters r_i and A_i. Velocity parameter v_i is calculated according to Eq. 7:

$$v_i^t = random[1; hammingDistance(x_i^t, x^*)], \tag{7}$$

where v_i of a bat i at iteration t is a random number between 1 and the difference between the current bat position x_i and the best bat position x^* in the population calculated by hamming distance. The modification in IBA was based on the movement behavior of bats in which all bats were given some kind of intelligence so that each bat moves differently depending on how far away it is from the best bat of the population. In this way, when one bat moves, it will first examines its velocity v_i^t. If the velocity value is less than the half of cities, the bat i performs short move using 2-opt local search; otherwise, it performs long move using 3-opt.

3 Improved Hybrid Bat Algorithm (IHDBA)

In this section, we will present an improved hybrid discrete BA, called IHDBA, to overcome the shortcomings of bat algorithms mentioned above. Combining crossover and mutation operators of EA has achieved the purpose of improved BA. Furthermore, two local search strategies (2-opt and 3-opt) are employed to speed up the convergence. IHDBA can increase the diversity of BA and alleviates the effect of premature convergence. The following are the steps of IHDBA:

Step 1 Initialization: Generate the initial population of BA with n bats. Each bat consists of m cities from TSP instance. Assign the initial values of pulse rate r_i, loudness A_i and velocity v_i for each bat. Then, evaluate the length of the routes completed by the bats. After that, calculate the velocity of each bat i by calculating its hamming distance from the current global best solution and choosing the velocity as a random number between 1 and the hamming distance.

Step 2 Crossover: Perform the crossover operation between the current bat position x_i and the current global best bat position x^*. After the crossover, the fitness of current bat position x_i is compared with the two offspring produced after crossing. And then, we choose the best one as the new bat position x_i.

Step 3 Local Search: If the velocity is small ($v_i \leq number\_of\_cities/2$), perform 2-opt move for current bat position x_i; otherwise, do 3-opt move.

Step 4 Random Walk: With probability of pulse r_i, solution is selected among the ten best solutions in its neighborhood and random walk is applied to generate a local solution around the selected one. And then, it is improved using 2-opt or 3-opt according to the velocity v_i.

Step 5 (Loudness and Pulse Emission): If the solution is accepted, the pulse emission rate r_i increases and the loudness A_i decreases according to Eqs. 5 and 6.

Step 6 (Mutation): If the diversity is less than 0.5, it means that the algorithm will loose the diversity and may get stuck in the local minima. Therefore, BA needs to increase the diversity by applying the mutation operation with predefined probability.

Step 7 Finding the global best solution: Sort out solutions and assign the current global best solution. Steps 2–7 continue until the termination condition is satisfied, either the optimal solution is found or the maximum number of iteration is reached.

4 Experimental Results

In order to test the performance of IHDBA, it was initialized with a population of 50 bats with initial random values in the range 0.7–0.1 and 0.0–0.4 for the loudness and pulse parameters respectively. Alpha and gamma were set to 0.98 and the maximum number of iterations was 1000.

IHDBA implemented in Java with different data structures using an Intel Core-i5 PC. The experiments were conducted using twenty symmetric TSP standard benchmark problems, with different lengths obtained from TSPLIB (http:// comopt.ifi.uni-heidelberg.de/software/TSPLIB95/).

To evaluate the proposed hybrid bat algorithm, three bat variants with different strategies are implemented. The first one is a standard discrete bat algorithm with the 2-opt and 3opt strategies (denoted by BA-opt); the second is BA-opt with crossover operation (denoted by BA-xover); and the third is BA-opt-xover with the mutation operation (denoted by IHDBA). Table 1 shows the improvement of the computational results over the evolution of algorithm.

Table 1. Computational results using BA-opt, BA-xover and IHDBA. All of the results are taken from 10 runs. The best results are given in bold.

Instances	Optimal	BA-opt		BA-xover		IHDBA	
		Average	best	Average	best	Average	best
Oliver30	420	420	**420**	420	**420**	420	**420**
berlin52	7542	7542	**7542**	7542	**7542**	7542	**7542**
St70	675	676.8	**675**	678.3	**675**	675	675
Eil51	426	427.1	**426**	427.1	**426**	426.4	426
Eil76	538	544.6	**538**	542	**538**	538	538
Eil101	629	636.2	631	636.4	631	629	629
KroA100	21282	21335.3	**21282**	21311.2	**21282**	21282	21282
Krob100	22141	22245.4	**22141**	22200.2	22193	22141	22141
Kroc100	20749	20769.3	**20749**	20778	**20749**	20749	20749
Krod100	21294	21428.6	21309	21348.6	**21294**	21309.3	21294
Kroe100	22068	22143.4	**22068**	22121.7	**22068**	22094.5	22068
Pr107	44303	44432.4	**44303**	44401.6	**44303**	44316.5	44303
Pr124	59030	59065.7	**59030**	59139.1	**59030**	59030	59030
Pr136	96772	97654.8	97007	97603.3	96861	96850.8	96785
Pr144	58537	58676.4	**58537**	58631.5	**58537**	58537	58537
Pr152	73682	74354.2	73818	74151.8	73840	**73822.8**	73682
Pr264	49135	49410	**49135**	49401.1	49235	49135	49135
Pr299	48191	48903.5	48609	48687.6	48372	48273.5	48197
Pr439	107217	109232.5	108524	109058.6	108387	**107815.1**	107408
Pr1002	259047	267616.1	266302	266719.8	265459	**266433.0**	264288

Table 2 shows the comparison results between IBA and IHDBA with respect to best solution, average solution, percentage deviations of the average solution PD_{avg} to the best known solution shown in the TSPLIB web site and the percentage deviations of best solution PD_{best} to the best known solution shown in the TSPLIB.

In summary, numerical results show that IHDBA is able to solve small and large size problems better than IBA. It is worthy to mention that incorporation of the evolutionary operators, crossover and mutation, and the local search techniques, 2-opt and 3-opt, to BA improves the results significantly which means that combining these operators into BA is effective, feasible and promising.

Table 2. Computational results of IHDBA in comparison with IBA. All of the results for IHDBA are taken from 10 runs. The best results are given in bold.

Instances	Optimal	IHDBA				IBA			
		average	best	PD_{avg}	PD_{best}	average	best	PD_{avg}	PD_{best}
Oliver30	420	**420**	**420**	0	0	**420**	**420**	0	0
berlin52	7542	**7542**	**7542**	0	0	**7542**	**7542**	0	0
St70	675	**675**	**675**	0.0000	0	679.1	**675**	0.0061	0
Eil51	426	**426.4**	**426**	0.0009	0	428.1	**426**	0.0049	0
Eil76	538	**538**	**538**	0.0000	0	548.1	539	0.0188	0.1859
Eil101	629	**629**	**629**	0.0000	0	646.4	634	0.0277	0.7949
KroA100	21282	**21282**	**21282**	0	0	21445.3	**21282**	0.0077	0
Krob100	22141	**22141**	**22141**	0.0000	0.0000	22506.4	22140	0.0165	−0.0045
Kroc100	20749	**20749**	**20749**	0.0000	0	21050	**20749**	0.0145	0
Krod100	21294	**21309.3**	**21294**	0.0007	0	21593.4	**21294**	0.0141	0
Kroe100	22068	**22094.5**	**22068**	0.0012	0	22349.6	**22068**	0.0128	0
Pr107	44303	**44316.5**	**44303**	0.0003	0	44793.8	**44303**	0.0111	0
Pr124	59030	**59030**	**59030**	0.0000	0	59412.1	**59030**	0.0065	0
Pr136	96772	**96850.8**	96785	0.0008	0.0134	99351.2	97547	0.0267	0.8009
Pr144	58537	**58537**	**58537**	0	0	58876.2	**58537**	0.0058	0
Pr152	73682	**73822.8**	**73682**	0.0019	0	74676.9	73921	0.0135	0.3244
Pr264	49135	**49135**	**49135**	0.0000	0	50908.3	49756	0.0361	1.2639
Pr299	48191	**48273.5**	48197	0.0017	0.0125	49674.1	48310	0.0308	0.2469
Pr439	107217	**107815.1**	107408	0.0056	0.1781	115256	111538	0.0750	4.0301
Pr1002	259047	**266433.0**	264288	0.0285	2.0232	274420	270016	0.0593	4.2344

5 Conclusion

In this paper, we have introduced a hybrid variant of bat algorithm combined with two evolutionary operators (crossover and mutation) and two local search strategies (2-opt and 3-opt). The evolutionary operators strike a balance between diversification and intensification and enable algorithm to escape from local optima. The local search strategies (2-opt and 3-opt) speed up the BA convergence. IHDBA is applied to solve the traveling salesman problem. Experiments conducted using twenty instances obtained from the TSPLIB The results show that IHDBA outperformed the recent BA variant i.e. IBA with respect to average and best solution and is able to obtain the optimal solution for most instances.

References

1. Stutzle, T., Hoos, H.: Stochastic Local Search: Foundations and Applications (2005)
2. Laporte, G.: The traveling salesman problem: an overview of exact and approximate algorithms. Eur. J. Oper. Res. **59**(2), 231–247 (1992)
3. Lenstra, J.K., Kan, A.R.: Some simple applications of the travelling salesman problem. Oper. Res. Q. (1970–1977) 26(4), 717–733 (1975). http://www.jstor.org/stable/3008306
4. Reinelt, G.: The Traveling Salesman: Computational Solutions for TSP Applications. Springer, Heidelberg (1994)
5. Yang, X.-S., He, X.: Bat algorithm: literature review and applications. Int. J. Bio-Inspired Comput. **5**(3), 141–149 (2013)
6. Yang, X.-S.: A new metaheuristic bat-inspired algorithm. In: González, J.R., Pelta, D.A., Cruz, C., Terrazas, G., Krasnogor, N. (eds.) Nature inspired cooperative strategies for optimization (NICSO 2010). Studies in Computational Intelligence, vol. 284, pp. 65–74. Springer, Heidelberg (2010)
7. Wang, G., Guo, L.: A novel hybrid bat algorithm with harmony search for global numerical optimization. J. Appl. Math. **2013**, 21 (2013)
8. Pan, J-S., Dao, T.-K., Kuo, M.-Y., Horng, M.-F., et al.: Hybrid bat algorithm with artificial bee colony. In: Pan, J.-S., Snasel, V., Corchado, E.S., Abraham, A., Wang, S.-L. (eds.) Intelligent Data analysis and its Applications, Volume II, vol. 298, pp. 45–55. Springer, Heidelberg (2014)
9. Pan, T.S., Dao, T.-K., Chu, S.-C., et al.: Hybrid particle swarm optimization with bat algorithm. In: Sun, H., Yang, C.-Y., Lin, C.-W., Pan, J.-S., Snasel, V., Abraham, A. (eds.) Genetic and Evolutionary Computing. Advances in Intelligent Systems and Computing, vol. 329. Springer, Heidelberg (2015)
10. Meng, X., Gao, X., Liu, Y.: A novel hybrid bat algorithm with differential evolution strategy for constrained optimization. Int. J. Hybrid Inf. Technol. **8**(1), 383–396 (2015)
11. Wang, G., Guo, L., Duan, H., Liu, L., Wang, H.: A bat algorithm with mutation for UCAV path planning. Sci. World J. **2012**, 15 (2012)
12. Zhang, J.W., Wang, G.G.: Image matching using a bat algorithm with mutation. In: Applied Mechanics and Materials, vol. 203, pp. 88–93. Trans Tech Publications (2012)
13. Fister Jr., I., Fister, D., Yang, X.-S.: A hybrid bat algorithm, ArXiv e-prints, March 2013
14. Perez, J., Valdez, F., Castillo, O.: Modification of the bat algorithm using fuzzy logic for dynamical parameter adaptation. In: 2015 IEEE Congress on Evolutionary Computation (CEC), pp. 464–471, May 2015
15. Lin, J.-H., Chou, C.-W., Yang, C.-H., Tsai, H.-L., et al.: A chaotic levy flight bat algorithm for parameter estimation in nonlinear dynamic biological systems. Comput. Inf. Technol. **2**(2), 56–63 (2012)
16. Abdel-Raouf, O., Abdel-Baset, M., El-Henawy, I.: An improved chaotic bat algorithm for solving integer programming problems. Int. J. Mod. Educ. Comput. Sci. (IJMECS) **6**(8), 18 (2014)

17. Gandomi, A.H., Yang, X.-S.: Chaotic bat algorithm. J. Comput. Sci. **5**(2), 224–232 (2014)
18. Khan, K., Nikov, A., Sahai, A.: A fuzzy bat clustering method for ergonomic screening of office workplaces. Third International Conference on Software, Services and Semantic Technologies S3T. Advances in Intelligent and Soft Computing, vol. 101, pp. 59–66. Springer, Heidelberg (2011)
19. Saji, Y., Riffi, M.E., Ahiod, B.: Discrete bat-inspired algorithm for travelling salesman problem. In: Second World Conference on Complex Systems (WCCS), pp. 28–31. IEEE (2014)
20. Osaba, E., Yang, X.-S., Diaz, F., Lopez-Garcia, P., Carballedo, R.: An improved discrete bat algorithm for symmetric and asymmetric traveling salesman problems. Engineering Applications of Artificial Intelligence **48**, 59–71 (2016)

Design of Selecting Security Solution Using Multi-objective Genetic Algorithm

Yunghee Lee, Jaehun Jung, and Chang Wook Ahn[✉]

Department of Computer Engineering, Sungkyunkwan University (SKKU),
Seoul, South Korea
{llit,a12gjang,cwan}@skku.edu

Abstract. In any corporation and organizations, the owner wants to introduce a best and efficient security solution with low cost and wants to get the high efficiency. In this paper, we suggest a method to select the best security solution among various security solutions using multi-objective genetic algorithm that considers the trade-off between cost and security. The designed system can support the best security solution from various aspects of security concerns. We use NSGA-II algorithm that is verified in various fields, and provide comparison results with the existing genetic algorithm.

Keywords: Information security · Machine learning · Evolutionary algorithm · Genetic algorithm · AI

1 Introduction

Information technology system and Internet get interconnectivity so that productivity of corporation and market value are very increased. But it also causes negative effects like cyber attack that hampers the corporations development [1]. To prevent it, each corporation and organization makes security solutions on the sidelines of their common business. Security solution generally means physical or logical action against the trouble of the information system [2]. But in most cases, companies do not want to invest a lot of money for the security solution. Because security solution cannot show tangible achievement in short time. Furthermore, to increase the security of the company, they should sure that how much cost will they invest for it and decide that which security solution will be selected.

In this paper, we design a selecting security solution system by using multi-objective genetic algorithm. It will help to select the best security solution among the candidates for any organization.

The remainder of this paper is organized as follows: in Sect. 2, we explain the genetic algorithm (GA) and Pareto-optimization. And in Sect. 3, we explain the multi-objective genetic algorithm. We will design a creating security solutions and weakness decrease point and explain the program code in Sect. 3. Our proposed system is presented in Sect. 4 by using the multi-objective genetic algorithm to select security solution. Section 5 concludes the paper.

M. Gong et al. (Eds.): BIC-TA 2016, Part I, CCIS 681, pp. 512–517, 2016.
DOI: 10.1007/978-981-10-3611-8_48

2   Related Works

This section will describe Pareto-optimality after the simple description on genetic algorithm and knapsack problem.

2.1   Genetic Algorithm and Pareto-optimality

A genetic algorithm is a heuristic search that mimics the process of natural selection [3].

Table 1. The list of solution sets that generated randomly

Name	250 - cost	Value
A	104	84
B	206	72
C	94	112
D	213	16
E	208	18
F	15	190
G	146	200
H	157	114
I	181	80
J	176	16
K	201	12

Generally, we use the concept of "Pareto-optimality" for solving the problem when there are multi-objectives to achieve the best result. For example, the list of solutions for the security plan for an organization is shown in Table 1. We can make a chart for the solutions as shown in Fig. 1. In the chart, the x-axis means (250 - cost) and the y-axis means a decrease of danger in security.

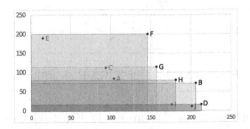

Fig. 1. Chart to select best solution from various candidates.

From the chart in Fig. 1, we can say the solution positioning right side and upper is good and efficient. The optimal solution is a solution that locates at uppermost and most right side, but generally, the cost is proportional to value so it is so hard to find an optimal solution like that. Instead, it is possible to find Pareto-optimal set that has the upper hand than the other solutions [4]. Quadrangles in the chart show the relationship about Pareto-dominance. For example, the solution E has a very high value, but there is a solution that has a higher value and a less cost than the solution E, that is named the solution F. In other word, the solution F is perfectly superior to the solution E. We can say this situation as Pareto-dominated. When we make a chart like Fig. 1, we call the set of solutions that does not dominated by any other solutions Pareto-optimal set, and the line that connects the elements of Pareto-optimal set is called by Pareto-frontier. In conclusion, the thing we finally have to find is Pareto-optimal set.

3   NSGA-II Multi-objective Genetic Algorithm

There are many kinds of multi-objective genetic algorithms (MOGA) to solve the problem. NPGA, NSGA and SPEA are the most popular MOGA, and in this paper, we use the NSGA-II algorithm for solving the problem. NSGA-II is the algorithm that is upgraded from the existing multi-objective algorithm NSGA, which has less complexity metric for non-dominated solutions sorting method. NSGA-II introduced the new method that named Crowding Distance so it can distribute each resource much efficiently than the existing algorithm. Furthermore, NSGA-II introduced elitism, which is the method that helps to maintain best solutions to next generation so high fitness solutions cannot be eliminated easily [5]. NSGA-II algorithm is easy to use and efficient way to find high fitness solution. It also shows high performance and so this algorithm is very widely and generally used [6].

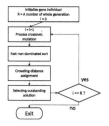

Fig. 2. Flowchart for NSGA-II algorithm.

NSGA-II algorithm follows the process in Fig. 2 [7]. Non-dominated rank means the rank that how many other solutions are dominating than a solution. In other word, if any solution is dominating one solution, the solutions non-dominated rank is zero. So in some generation, Pareto-optimal solution has most high order of priority, and the solution that located far from the other solutions has more and more low order of priority. Like this, non-dominated rank sorting process induces the set of solution to convergence to Pareto-optimal set. And Crowding-distance means how many solutions are located in the same area. It is the index for evaluating the diversity of solution set which one has same non-dominated rank. Each solution gets high crowding-distance if it has less similarity with near solutions. This is the method for selecting the solution that has a different attribute in the set of gene individual that belongs to same non-dominated rank group [5]. The process of crossover and mutation is the same as in the existing simple genetic algorithm [6].

We also have to create some samples of the best security solution for experiments and each security solution should have a cost for introducing and weakness decrease point. But weakness decrease point cannot be digitized easily. Therefore, in this paper, we will use the meaningful random number to weakness decrease point for creating the sample of security solutions. We can make the meaningful random weakness decrease points with our made program. Weakness decrease point will almost be proportional to security solutions cost. But there can be rarely too high weakness decrease point than security solutions cost or the opposite case.

4   Selecting Security Solution Using Multi-objective Genetic Algorithm

In this section, we will suggest a scheme to select the best security solution among candidates using NSGA-II MOGA mentioned in the previous sections. Park et al. proposed a solution for this with simple genetic algorithm [8]. They tried to solve this problem with a simple genetic algorithm and used a list of ten virtual solutions. For the comparison with the solution, we materialized the program as the same with the simple genetic algorithm used in Park et al.'s solution. And we compare the result with the case of using newly created solution sets. From the results, we can find a set with 3 optimal solutions. The first solution set has 55,036 weakness decrease points and needs 36,217 cost. And the second one has 51,048 decrease points and needs 33,137. The last set has 56,637 decrease points and needs 37,237 cost.

And in the simple genetic algorithm, we use the single fitness function for evaluating solutions fitness or value, but in MOGA, we can use multiple fitness functions for evaluating solutions fitness or value.

$$f_1 = \sum_{i=1}^{n} (100000 - vc_i.c \times vc_i.s) \tag{1}$$

$$f_2 = \sum_{i=1}^{n} vc_i.d \times vc_i.s \tag{2}$$

In this paper, we use two fitness functions like in Eqs. 1 and 2. The Eq. 1 uses the value (100,000 - solutions whole cost) for evaluation measure. The Eq. 2 uses the value about whole solutions security weakness decrease points for evaluation measure. n is the number the of whole chromosomes, in other word, n means the number of solutions. vc means each chromosome structure. $vc.d$ includes the decrease point of security weakness, and $vc.c$ includes the cost for selecting that solution. $vc.s$ includes the binary number for check whether each solution was selected or not selected. So if $vc.s$'s value is 0, that means the solution was not selected.

And the things that make a difference of performance are the type of mutation and crossover. This is an important element of the genetic algorithm. There are many types of mutation and crossover like Uniform Mutation, Parent-Centric Crossover, Bit Flip Mutation, Half-Uniform Crossover and etc. In this paper, we will use the Simulated Binary Crossover (SBX) for crossover process and Polynomial Mutation (PM) for mutation process in NSGA-II. SBX is the operator that has search ability similar to that of a single-point binary-coded crossover operator [9]. And the PM is the operator that is widely used in evolutionary optimization algorithms as a variation operator [10]. It attempts to simulate the offspring distribution of binary-encoded bit-flip mutation on real-valued decision variables. Of course, the variable type that is used in our process is binary but PM shows better performance than Bit Flip Mutation so we used it for the test. PM is similar to SBX, it favors offspring nearer to the parent [11].

Finally, we set the population size for the genetic algorithm to 5,000 and fixed generation number to 150.

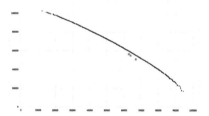

Fig. 3. The graph about selecting security solution using NSGA-II

Figure 3 shows a graph of result values on selecting security solutions found by an experiment using NSGA-II algorithm. Horizontal axis is f_1 value, and vertical axis is for f_2 value. In a case of existing researchs result, we reversed the cost value for easy comparison. So the cost value of original researchs result was replaced to (100,000 - original cost) value. And for dividing, we drew the original researchs result with quadrangle, and this papers result with dots. We can find the fact that Pareto-optimal sets found by NSGA-II algorithm are perfectly dominating the result of original research that used a simple genetic algorithm in the graph. The result of this paper provides various solution sets from the solution set that use low cost to the solution set that uses high cost and gets high weakness decrease points.

5 Conclusion

In this paper, we suggested a new method of selecting the best security solution among candidates, which is necessary in corporations and organizations. It used NSGA-II MOGA. The proposed method considered more objectives than the existing schemes that use the simple genetic algorithm for evaluating fitness. It could provide more various solution sets in a short time than the original scheme.

Acknowledgement. Following are results of a study on the "Leaders in INdustry-university Cooperation" Project, supported by the Ministry of Education, Science & Technology (MEST).

References

1. Chai, S.W.: Economic effects of personal information protection. Korea Consum. Agency **33**, 43–64 (2008)
2. Kwon, Y.O., Kim, B.D.: The effect of information security breach and security investment announcement on the market value of Korean firms. Inf. Syst. Rev. **9**(1), 105–120 (2007)
3. Mitchell, M.: An Introduction to Genetic Algorithms. MIT Press, Cambridge (1998)
4. Horn, J., Nafpliotis, N., Golberg, D.: A niched Pareto genetic algorithm for multiobjective optimization. In: Proceedings of 1st IEEE Conference on Evolutionary Computation, vol. 1, pp. 82–87 (1994)
5. Yoon, J., Lee, J., Kim, D.: Feature selection in multi-label classification using NSGA-II algorithm. J. KIISE Softw. Appl. **40**(3), 133–140 (2013)
6. Deb, K., Pratap, A., Agarwal, S., Meyarivan, T.: A fast and elitist multiobjective genetic algorithm: NSGA-II. IEEE Trans. Evol. Comput. **6**(2), 182–197 (2002)
7. Khu, S.T., Madsen, H.: Multi-objective calibration with Pareto preference ordering: an application to rainfall-runoff model calibration. Water Resour. Res. **41**(3) (2005). http://onlinelibrary.wiley.com/doi/10.1029/2004WR003041/full
8. Park, J., Bang, Y., Lee, G., Nam, K.: Generation of security measure by using simple genetic algorithm. Proc. KIISE Conf. **30**(21), 769–771 (2003)
9. Kalyanmoy, D., Amarendra, K.: Real-coded genetic algorithms with simulated binary crossover: studies on multimodel and multiobjective problems. Complex Syst. **9**(6), 431–454 (1995)
10. Hamdan, M.: A dynamic polynomial mutation for eolutionary multi-objective optimization algorithms. Int. J. Artif. Intell. Tools **20**(01), 209–219 (2011)
11. Deb, K., Deb, D.: Analysing mutation schemes for real-parameter genetic algorithms. Int. J. Artif. Intell. Soft Comput. **4**(1), 1–28 (2014)

A Multi-agent System for Creating Art Based on Boids with Evolutionary and Neural Networks

Tae Jong Choi, Jaehun Jeong, and Chang Wook Ahn$^{(\boxtimes)}$

Department of Computer Engineering, Sungkyunkwan University,
2066, Seobu-ro, Jangan-gu, Suwon-si, Gyeonggi-do, Republic of Korea
{gry17,a12gjang,cwan}@skku.edu

Abstract. In this paper, we proposed a multi-agent system for creating art that can produce a set of abstract and complex style images given an input image. The proposed system consists of Boids, and each Boid object contains the genetic programming trees and neural networks. The role of genetic programming is to create unique color patterns, which will be embellished to the input image. And neural networks in each agent adjust its Boids properties, to perform more emergent group behavior in the progress of art creating. The results of the proposed system can show abstractly and complexly embellished images given an input image in each run.

Keywords: A-Life Art · Multi-agent systems · Boids · Evolutionary algorithms · Neural networks

1 Introduction

Artificial life (A-Life) is a research area to study life-as-it-might-be [1,2]. One of the key aspects within A-Life is emergent properties that can present complex and unpredictable behaviors from their interactions. Artists and scientists combined A-Life with art and design fields that resulted in the birth of Artificial Life Art (A-Life Art) [3–5]. The composition of A-Life and art might be considered as living artworks, which can make users immersed in an artwork and provide amusement.

In this paper, we proposed a new A-Life Art based on multi-agent systems [6–8]. The proposed system receives an input image and gives back to an image that modified with abstract and complex styles. Also, the proposed system can exhibit the progress of creating art, which shows an emergent group behavior of Boids [9]. In the proposed system, each Boid object has a neural network and three genetic programming trees. The neural network is used to adjust the behavior properties of Boids such as the maximum force, the maximum speed, and the ranges of three steering rules. The three genetic programming trees are used to create color patterns, which will be embellished to the input image. Therefore, each Boid object contains its unique behavior properties and color

© Springer Nature Singapore Pte Ltd. 2016
M. Gong et al. (Eds.): BIC-TA 2016, Part I, CCIS 681, pp. 518–523, 2016.
DOI: 10.1007/978-981-10-3611-8_49

patterns, which make it possible to embellish the input image with different styles in each run.

As a result, by combining the Boids model with genetic programming and multilayer perceptron, the proposed system can possess more improved emergent properties. To the best of our knowledge, the proposed system is the first attempt to incorporate the Boids model with both evolutionary algorithms and neural networks to create and provide abstractly and complexly embellished artworks.

2   Boids

Craig Reynolds proposed a computer model that can emulate the behavior of bird flocks or fish schools called Boids [9]. The simulation model contains the population of Boid objects and each Boid object maneuvers through three basic steering rules (Fig. 1) based on its neighbors positions and velocities. Although these steering rules are fairly simple and straightforward, the Boids model can present complex and unpredictable the group behavior.

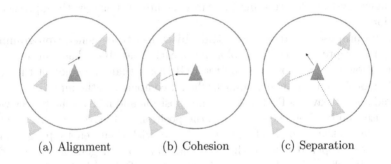

(a) Alignment   (b) Cohesion   (c) Separation

Fig. 1. The basic steering rules of Boids

3   The Proposed System

In this paper, we proposed a new A-Life Art based on multi-agent systems. The proposed system receives an input image and gives back to an image that modified with abstract and complex styles. Also, the proposed system can exhibit the progress of creating art, which shows an emergent group behavior of Boids. We designed the proposed system to use the Boids model with genetic programming [10] and multilayer perceptron. By combining the Boids model with genetic programming and neural networks, each Boid object can perform not only evolution but also learning. The combined Boid object moves around the white canvas image that has the same size with the input image based on its behavior properties and leaves its unique color that provided by its genetic programming trees. The Boids model can exhibit emergent group behavior based

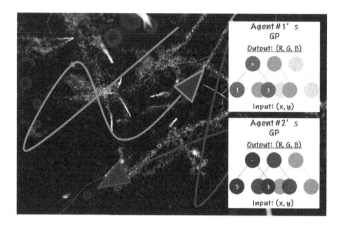

Fig. 2. Genetic programming embedded Boid agents (Color figure online)

on basic steering rules. Therefore, by applying the Boids model, the proposed multi-agent systems for creating art can generate an image with unpredictable behavior.

In the proposed system, each Boid object has three genetic programming trees, which represents an RGB color. Also, each Boid object has a fitness value. When a Boids object possessed better RGB color than the color of the corresponding position in the canvas image when it compared to the input image, then the Boid object leave its RGB color in that position and increase its fitness value. Otherwise, the Boid object just passes the position and moves another position. Figure 2 shows the example of two Boid objects with their genetic programming trees. In the proposed system, the terminal nodes of our genetic programming are X, Y, R, where X and Y are the locations of a Boid object and R, is a real value. The non-terminal nodes of our genetic programming are as follows:

1. Bit-wise AND: $X \& Y$ (or R)

2. Bit-wise OR: $X \| Y$ (or R)

3. Bit-wise XOR: $X \oplus Y$ (or R)

4. NOT: $!X$

5. Left-shift: $X \ll 2$ (multiplied by 2)

6. Right-shift: $X \gg 2$ (divided by 2)

7. ADD: $X + Y$ (or R)

8. SUB: $X - Y$ (or R)

9. MUL: $X \cdot Y$ (or R)

10. DIV: X/Y (or R) if $Y > 0.0001$

11. SIN: $sin(X) \cdot 255$

12. COS: $cos(X) \cdot 255$

13. TAN: $tan(X) \cdot 255$

The proposed system evaluates our Boid objects every predetermined period and finds the best Boid object. After that the population of the Boid objects undergoes the crossover and mutation operators with the best Boid object in the manner of genetic programming [5].

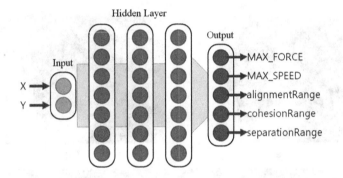

Fig. 3. Multilayer perceptron for the unique behavior properties of Boid agents

Neural networks are considered as a non-linear processing system that can be applied to many practical problems. Especially, when there is only a little information about a problem, neural networks are suitable for the situation. The strength of neural networks is that they perform well on many problems because it does not require any pieces of knowledge such as continuity or differentiability, similar to EA.

In the proposed system, each Boid object contains multilayer perceptron to hold its unique behavior of Boids properties (Fig. 3). Therefore, each Boid object has not a unique color but also unique behavior, which can promote more emergent properties. The neural networks are also undergoing to evolve every predetermined period. The population of the Boid objects evolves based on the best objects network weights. In detail, the network weights of the best object are extracted and are used to the extended line crossover [11] with other objects network weights.

As a result, by using genetic programming and multilayer perceptron with the Boids model, the proposed system can embellish a received input image to provide abstract and complex images.

4   Results

In this section, we present the several outcomes of the proposed system. Figure 4 is the input image (a) and the set of results (b), (c), (d) of the proposed system. The outcomes of the proposed system embellished the original input image in each run. As we can see from these results, the proposed system can embellish the given input image as abstract and complex images and every time it provides a different image. Each Boid object contains its unique behavior properties and color patterns, which make it possible to embellish the input image with different styles in each run. As a result, by combining the Boids model with genetic programming and multilayer perceptron, the proposed system can possess more improved emergent properties.

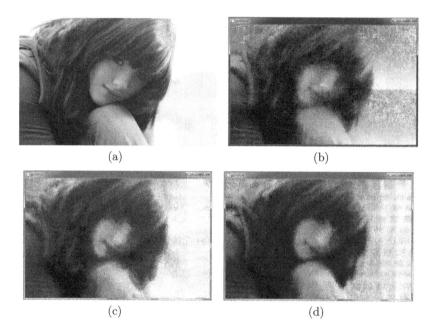

(a)   (b)

(c)   (d)

Fig. 4. The outcome images

5   Conclusion

In this paper, we proposed a multi-agent system for creating abstract and complex art given an input image. The proposed system can embellish the given input image with abstract and complex styles. Also, the creating progress of the proposed system can exhibit emergent properties, which different and diverse in each run. We combined the Boids model with evolutionary algorithms and neural networks. The proposed system is designed to boost the emergent properties by incorporating the Boids model with genetic programming and multilayer perceptron, and hence, can take advantage of these approaches to create abstract and complex artworks. We believe that the proposed system can be used for not only creating art but also in a variety of creating digital contents.

Acknowledgments. This research was supported by Basic Science Research Program through the National Research Foundation of Korea (NRF) funded by the Ministry of Education (NRF-2015R1D1A1A02062017).

References

1. Langton, C.G.: Artificial Life. Addison-Wesley Publishing Company, Redwood City (1989)
2. Langton, C.G.: Artificial Life: An overview. MIT Press, Cambridge (1997)
3. Eldridge, A.: You pretty little flocker: exploring the aesthetic state space of creative ecosystems. Artif. Life **21**, 289–292 (2015)
4. Greenfield, G., Machado, P.: Ant-and ant-colony-inspired alife visual art. Artif. Life **21**, 293–306 (2015)
5. Boden, M.A.: Creativity and alife. Artif. Life **21**, 354–365 (2015)
6. Wooldridge, M.: An Introduction to Multiagent Systems. Wiley, Chichester (2009)
7. Weiss, G.: Multiagent Systems: A Modern Approach to Distributed Artificial Intelligence. MIT Press, Cambridge (1999)
8. Sycara, K.P.: Multiagent systems. AI Mag. **19**(2), 79 (1998)
9. Reynolds, C.W.: Flocks, herds and schools: a distributed behavioral model. ACM SIGGRAPH Comput. Graph. **21**(4), 25–34 (1987)
10. Koza, J.R.: Genetic Programming: On the Programming of Computers by Means of Natural Selection, vol. 1. MIT Press, Cambridge (1992)
11. Yoon, Y., Kim, Y.-H.: The Roles of Crossover and Mutation in Real-Coded Genetic Algorithms. INTECH Open Access Publisher (2012)

Author Index

Yahya, Rafaa I.   I-314
Yahya, Salah I.   I-314
Yan, Jianan   II-41
Yan, Xuesong   II-80, II-107
Yang, Dandan   II-114
Yang, Guangming   II-271
Yang, Hua   II-454
Yang, Jing   I-47
Yang, Shuling   II-179
Yang, Tianxiong   II-497
Yang, Xing   II-185
Yang, Yunying   I-237
Yang, Zheng   I-405
Yao, Lina   I-64
Ye, Lian   I-133
Yin, Jian   II-185
Yin, Zhixiang   I-47
Yu, Jing   II-191
Yu, Pan   II-497
Yu, Tianyuan   I-405
Yu, Wenping   I-237, I-385
Yu, Yang   I-456
Yuan, Fayou   II-420
Yunyun, Niu   II-441

Zeng, Dong   II-513
Zeng, Rongqiang   II-10
Zeng, Shan   I-85, I-226, II-489
Zhang, Chao   I-377
Zhang, Chunjiong   II-513
Zhang, Cong   II-127
Zhang, Dongbo   II-407, II-448
Zhang, Gexiang   I-109
Zhang, Guixu   II-163
Zhang, Jun   II-285

Zhang, Kai   II-278
Zhang, Kun   II-54, II-310
Zhang, Puzhao   I-425
Zhang, Shanqiang   II-420
Zhang, Wei   II-379
Zhang, Xuncai   I-39, II-141
Zhang, Zhiqiang   I-118
Zhang, Zhongshan   II-265
Zhao, Binping   II-35
Zhao, Chunxia   II-394
Zhao, Jing   II-80
Zhao, Juanjuan   I-349
Zhao, Pengfei   I-349
Zhao, Sujie   I-480
Zhao, Wei   II-41, II-328
Zhao, Xinchao   II-219
Zhao, Yan   II-420
Zhao, Ying   II-524
Zhao, Yong   II-343
Zhao, Yuzhen   I-95, I-168
Zheng, Xiaolong   II-47
Zheng, Xuedong   I-3
Zhou, Aimin   II-163
Zhou, Changjun   I-3
Zhou, Kang   I-85, I-118, I-226, II-204, II-285, II-475, II-489
Zhou, Qinglei   I-12
Zhou, Shihua   I-3
Zhou, Yalan   II-185
Zhu, Weijun   I-12
Zhu, Xinjie   II-420
Zhu, Zhibin   II-127
Zou, Jie   II-54
Zouaoui, Hakima   I-487
Zuo, Xingquan   II-219

Printed in the United States
By Bookmasters